BOOKS I and II *of*
The Faerie Queene,
THE MUTABILITY CANTOS
AND SELECTIONS *from*
The Minor Poetry

PLATE 1. *St. George Slaying the Dragon*, by Vittore Carpaccio [c.1465—c.1522]

PLATE 2. *Mars and Venus United by Love,* by Paolo Veronese [1528—1588]

EDMUND SPENSER

BOOKS I and II *of*
The Faerie Queene

THE MUTABILITY CANTOS
AND SELECTIONS *from*
The Minor Poetry

Newly Edited by
ROBERT KELLOGG *and* OLIVER STEELE

THE ODYSSEY PRESS
A Division of Bobbs-Merrill Educational Publishing
Indianapolis

ACKNOWLEDGMENTS

Appleton-Century-Crofts. For excerpts from *The Rhetoric of Aristotle*, trans. and ed. Lane Cooper, copyright © 1932.

The Bobbs-Merrill Company, Inc. For excerpts from *The Consolation of Philosophy*, Boethius, trans. Richard Green, copyright © 1962; from *Odi et Amo*, Catullus, trans. Roy Arthur Swanson, copyright © 1959; and from *Theogony*, Hesiod, trans. Norman O. Brown, copyright © 1953.

Burns & Oates Ltd. For excerpt from *From Shadows to Reality*, Jean Daniélou, trans. Walston Hibberd, copyright © 1960.

Doubleday & Company, Inc. For excerpt from *The Stoic Philosophy of Seneca*, trans., Moses Hadas, Doubleday Anchor Books, copyright © 1958.

E. P. Dutton & Co. Inc. For excerpt from *The Romance of the Rose*, Guillaume de Lorris and Jean de Meun, trans. Harry W. Robbins, copyright © 1962.

The Folger Shakespeare Library. For excerpt from *An Apology of the Church of England*, John Jewell, ed. J. E. Booty, copyright © 1963.

Panofsky, Erwin. For excerpt from *Meaning in the Visual Arts*, Doubleday Anchor Books, copyright © 1955. By permission of the author.

Penguin Books Ltd. For excerpts from the following: *Aeneid*, Virgil, trans. W. F. Jackson Knight, copyright © 1958; *Ethics*, Aristotle, trans. J. A. K. Thompson, copyright © 1953; *Iliad*, Homer, trans. E. V. Rieu, copyright © 1963; *Metamorphoses*, Ovid, trans. Mary M. Innes, copyright © 1961; *Pastoral Poems*, Virgil, trans. E. V. Rieu, copyright © 1954; *Penguin Book of Italian Verse*, ed. George Kay, copyright © 1958; *Penguin Book of French Verse*, Vol. I, ed. Brian Woledge, copyright © 1961; *Odyssey*, Homer, trans. E. V. Rieu, copyright © 1960.

The Macmillan Company. For excerpt from "After Long Silence," William Butler Yeats, *Collected Poems*, copyright © 1956.

S. F. Vanni. For excerpts from *Orlando Furioso*, Ariosto, trans. Allan Gilbert, copyright © 1954. 2 vols.

The University of Chicago Press. For excerpts from *The Triumphs of Petrarch*, trans. Ernest Hatch Wilkins, copyright © 1962; and from *The Odes of Pindar*, trans. Richard Lattimore, copyright © 1947.

A. Watkins, Inc., agents. For permission to quote from the *Inferno*, Dante, trans. Dorothy L. Sayers, Penguin Books Ltd., copyright © 1955 by Dorothy L. Sayers.

The Bobbs-Merrill Company, Inc.
4300 West 62nd Street
Indianapolis, Indiana 46268

Library of Congress Catalog Card Number 65-22702
ISBN 0-672-63034-6 (pbk)

Eleventh Printing—1981

Preface

In this edition, the texts for Books I and II of *The Faerie Queene* and for the "Mutability Cantos" are based on copies of the first editions in the Alderman Library at the University of Virginia. Those for the minor poems are based on microfilm copies of first editions in the Folger Shakespeare Library and the Huntington Library. In the case of the first two books of *The Faerie Queene* we have in rare instances preferred a second edition reading to that of the first. In each case our divergence from the earliest text has been noted. In almost all cases, however, the substantive differences between the two editions are no more than could be expected in an Elizabethan reprint, and we have judged them to be insignificant.

Spelling has been modernized except in the few cases where Spenser's original does not have a modern analogue reflecting simply normal sound changes. Spenser is the only major poet of his age whose works have hitherto been unavailable in modern spelling. Since it is the custom to read the Elizabethan poets with a modern pronunciation, and since, even if it were not the custom to do so, modern spelling is still the only feasible "normalization" of the inconsistent and idiosyncratic orthography of individual sixteenth-century typesetters, little of literary value is to be gained by perpetuating the spelling of the early editions.

It is, on the other hand, neither possible nor desirable to impose a consistently modern system of punctuation on Spenser's text. In a number of important cases, Spenser's syntax appears to be sufficiently different from that of modern English to make a strict application of modern punctuation irrelevant and misleading. We have, for example, not attempted to differentiate consistently between what modern readers might feel are restrictive and nonrestrictive modifiers. We know too little about Spenser's syntax and the intonation used to signal syntactic constructions in Elizabethan English to depart radically from the punctuation of the early editions with an easy conscience.

Elizabethan words that may be unfamiliar to the modern reader, even though they appear in most desk dictionaries, have been glossed in the margin. Spenser consciously repeats set phrases and epithets as a feature of his epic diction. Of these and other words of high frequency, we have glossed only the first few occurrences. We hope that those readers who prefer to let Spenser's words define themselves in context will not find the glosses distracting.

vii

It is the nature of things that we cannot read Spenser's poetry through Elizabethan eyes, even with many volumes of commentary. Spenser's contemporaries immediately understood the romantic quests of the Red Cross Knight and Sir Guyon as reflections of moral and theological values. If we are to enjoy *The Faerie Queene*, we must, like the Elizabethans, proceed to its allegorical implications only from a careful reading of the story. The introductions and notes in this edition are intended to make the story as clear as possible, but they can merely suggest the ideal allegorical commentary.

The notes are very largely citations of classical, medieval, and renaissance texts. In many cases Spenser's knowledge of these texts was direct and his dependence upon them clear. However, we are not primarily interested in demonstrating the *sources* of Spenser's ideas, language, and imagery. We have argued in a part of the Introduction that Spenser was a poet intensely aware of writing within a long-established tradition. Much of the power of his poetry derives from his conscious and skillful articulation of the conventions of thought and language of the traditions he felt himself a part of. Our notes attempt to illustrate in brief the literary *tradition* from which Spenser's poetry arises and which it enriches.

We could not have attempted the kind of commentary which accompanies these poems without the help of a number of distinguished studies of Spenser's poetry:

1. *The Works of Edmund Spenser, A Variorum Edition*, ed. Greenlaw, Osgood, and Padelford, Johns Hopkins University Press, 1932–1949.

2. Harry Berger, Jr. *The Allegorical Temper*, Yale University Press, 1957.

3. Robert Ellrodt, *Neoplatonism in the Poetry of Spenser*, Geneva: Librarie E. Droz, 1960.

4. A. C. Hamilton, *The Structure of Allegory in "The Faerie Queene,"* Oxford University Press, 1961.

5. A. Kent Hieatt, *Short Time's Endless Monument: The Symbolism of the Numbers in Edmund Spenser's Epithalamion*, Columbia University Press, 1960.

6. Graham Hough, *A Preface to "The Faerie Queene,"* W. W. Norton, 1963.

7. William Nelson, *The Poetry of Edmund Spenser*, Columbia University Press, 1963.

A bibliographical description of each work cited in our commentary will be found in two places: in the first citation and in the Bibliography, pp. 539–542. Wherever possible we have included with citations of classical texts the appropriate page number of an easily accessible translation. The particular translation used is also specified in both the first citation and the Bibliography.

Our debt to previous Spenser scholarship is great, and we regret that the form of this edition does not permit thorough documentation of our dependence, for both ideas and facts, upon many important scholarly works. We owe thanks to Professors Herschel Baker, Sears Jayne, and Ernest Sirluck for their encouragement, and to our University of Virginia colleagues, Professors Lester Beaurline and David Bevington. Our work was made easier by a grant from the Research Committee of the University of Virginia.

R. K.

O. S.

Outline of Spenser's Life

Edmund Spenser (1552–1599) was born in London and educated at the Merchant Taylors' School and Cambridge University (M.A. 1576). Before the appearance of Books I–III of *The Faerie Queene* in 1590, he had published only a few schoolboy exercises in 1569 and the somewhat startling and virtuoso *Shepherd's Calendar* in 1579. Spenser's poetry was written during an active public life in the administration of Ireland. From 1580 until the year before his death he was far from the geographical center of the brilliant Elizabethan culture his poetry has done so much to perpetuate. The first installment of *The Faerie Queene* was an immediate success. The demand for more of his poetry was met by the publication of a number of early and inferior poems in the volumes *Muiopotmos* (1590), *Complaints* (1591), and *Daphnaïda* (1591). Between these and Books IV–VI of *The Faerie Queene* were *Colin Clout's Come Home Again* (1595) and *Amoretti and Epithalamion* (1595). The next year saw the publication of Books IV–VI, *Prothalamion* and *Four Hymns*. Of his unpublished works, only two cantos from an unfinished book of *The Faerie Queene* survived his death. Known as the "Mutability Cantos," this interesting fragment was published in the 1609 edition of *The Faerie Queene*. Spenser is buried in Westminster Abbey.

Contents

BOOKS I and II *of*

The Faerie Queene,

THE MUTABILITY CANTOS
AND SELECTIONS *from*

The Minor Poetry

The Faerie Queene

INTRODUCTION

From Spenser's *Letter of the Author's* to his friend Sir Walter Raleigh which accompanied the first edition of *The Faerie Queene*, we learn much about the poet's general intention in writing his masterpiece. First, we learn that the whole poem, of which only the first three books were published in 1590, was to have been a long allegorical epic in twelve books—an ambitious plan the poet did not live to complete. In 1596, Books I–III were reprinted, and in the same volume Books IV–VI appeared for the first time. Of the second half of his projected epic, however, only a fragment from Book VII survives. Secondly, we learn from the *Letter* that he was conscious of writing in an epic tradition running from Homer to the contemporary Italian poet Torquato Tasso (1544–1595), and that one of the main purposes of this tradition was to set forth examples of virtuous behavior in the characters of the epic heroes. And finally, we learn that the subject of *The Faerie Queene* is the fashioning of "a gentleman or noble person in virtuous and gentle discipline." The renaissance English conception of the gentleman, synthesized from the ethics of classical Greece and Rome and the chivalric ideal of the late Middle Ages, is still relevant today; and of Spenser's twelve virtues, those of holiness (Book I) and temperance (Book II) are the ones that accord best with our own ethical and religious notions. Even so, much of Spenser's thought and art seems strange upon first meeting. Before a detailed discussion of the allegory of Books I and II, it may be helpful to sketch in a little of the background which Spenser's *Letter* so clearly indicates he was drawing upon.

RENAISSANCE HUMANISM AND THE EPIC TRADITION

The Faerie Queene, although many of its features may be called medieval, is a product of "renaissance humanism"—a term complicated by wide disagreement among scholars about the meaning of both of its parts. In the last hundred years or so, the term "humanism" has become associated more and more with scientific discovery and liberal movements in politics. But the humanism of the Renaissance (1300–1600) was concerned very little with either of these subjects. It was primarily a literary movement, though it included philosophical elements and was in fact responsible for the rediscovery and publication of many ancient scientific texts. As a movement, it was characterized by an enthusiastic revival in classical studies, particularly the study of Roman literature. Although there had been no lack of interest in classical literature in the Middle Ages, still in the fourteenth century the literature of Rome—and later the literature and philosophy of Greece—began to acquire a greater importance in European culture than it had had for a thousand years. Partly the change was a matter of approach. Classical learning in the Middle Ages was, by and large, in the service of the church and theology, the queen of the sciences. In the Renaissance, study of the classics became, if not an end in itself, a servant to secular concerns. At the same time, renaissance scholars very greatly increased the availability of classical texts, not only rediscovering many texts which had hardly been known in the Middle Ages, but also reproducing the available texts, first in manuscript copies and later in printed editions, to give them wide circulation. Poets and scholars like Petrarch (1304-1374) and Boccaccio (1313-1375) began to collect manuscripts of the chief Latin authors, to analyze their diction and style, and to imitate their themes and manner in Latin and in the vernacular. Other scholars, mainly Italian at first, prepared critical editions of almost every Latin author whose works had survived, with translations and editions of Greek authors following later.

The most immediate result of this fervor of activity was a revolution in the educational program of Western Europe. Many of the early humanists were teachers in the schools and universities, and they began to call for changes in the teaching of Latin, which had for centuries been the language of theology, of medicine, and of government. Medieval Latin and medieval rhetoric were condemned as barbaric, and it was proposed to teach a pure Latin based on the prose styles of Cicero and Seneca and on the diction of Virgil, Horace, and Ovid. The program which developed from this revolution was, of course, largely a literary education, though moral philosophy and history were not neglected. Sir Thomas Elyot, an English humanist of the mid-sixteenth century, recommended the following classical works in his proposals for the education of young men: Aesop's fables, Lucian's *Dialogues*, Ovid's *Metamorphoses*, Homer's *Iliad* and *Odyssey*, Virgil's *Aeneid*, Horace's poetry, Cicero's *Topics* and *De Officiis*, Quintilian's *Rhetoric*, orations of Isocrates, Xenophon's *Anabasis*, Caesar's *Commentaries*, Aristotle's *Ethics*, and the works of Plato.[1] Elyot's program is ambitious, containing about as many Greek authors as Latin, but it is safe to say that the graduate of a good Elizabethan grammar school such as the Merchant Taylors' School, which Spenser attended, would have known intimately the *Aeneid*, the *Eclogues*, and the *Georgics* of Virgil; the *Metamorphoses* and the *Amores* of Ovid; *The Art of Poetry* and some of the odes of Horace; the *Topics* and *De Officiis* of Cicero; the *Commentaries* of Caesar; some of the comedies of Terence; and the rhetorics of Quintilian and the pseudo-Cicero. At the same time he would have received a grounding in French and Italian and in Greek as far as Xenophon and Plato, while his knowledge of Greek literature would have been further

[1] See Stanford E. Lehmberg, *Sir Thomas Elyot: Tudor Humanist*, University of Texas Press, 1960, pp. 57-62.

enlarged by the study of Latin translations and commentaries. He would have spent hour upon hour polishing his Latin style to the model of Cicero's prose and composing Latin imitations of passages from Virgil and the other poets.

The great poets of the Renaissance, who were the products of the educational program just described and who wrote for a similarly educated audience, were intensely conscious of the fact that they wrote within a tradition which began with Homer and Pindar and included Virgil, Ovid, Lucan, and Statius; their aim was to rival the great works of antiquity. Although the period is full of turgid imitations of Latin poetry, the best poets attempted to modify the tradition in works appropriate to the languages and the times in which they wrote. They were not bound by the ancient epic tradition as they understood it; they used it to achieve a richness of allusion that could not have been produced outside of it.

But the renaissance epic tradition, in which Ariosto (*Orlando Furioso*, 1532), Ronsard (*Franciade*, 1572), Tasso (*Rinaldo*, 1562, and *Jerusalem Delivered*, 1574), and Spenser wrote, was not the tradition of Homer and Virgil as we think of it. The ancient epics had been filtered through many centuries of scholarly commentaries, glosses, and scholia, and their influence had been combined with that of the romance tradition of the Middle Ages. In classical times, early and late, and all during the medieval period, the Homeric epics and the *Aeneid* were subjected to a thoroughgoing allegorical interpretation (*allegoresis*), as were the Greek and Roman myths. Ancient philosophers had found it impossible to accept the Homeric gods literally, but they found plenty in the stories of Achilles, Odysseus, and Aeneas to illustrate their own ethical and cosmological doctrines. Their philosophical commentaries were written to show that Homer too was a philosopher and that his works could be interpreted to support physical, metaphysical, and cosmological speculation.

Somewhat later the *allegoresis* of myths and epic poetry became a fixed feature of the continuing debate between apologists for poetry, on the one hand, and philosophers, historians, and (later still) Christian theologians, on the other. Both the growing rationalism of classical antiquity (which had at first used Homer to support its discoveries) and the doctrines of Christian theology tended to regard imaginative literature as untruthful and destructive of morality. The apology for poetry in ancient Greece as in medieval Europe depended upon the defensive argument that the truth and morality of poetry were disguised beneath a fictional surface that was, in the words of Spenser's *Letter*, "delightful and pleasing to common sense." Thus, from the pre-Socratic Greek philosophers of the sixth century B.C. to the anxious booksellers of Ariosto's *Orlando Furioso* in the sixteenth, an allegorizing commentary accumulated about the works of the epic poets, first as a support for philosophical inquiry, and then as a defensive wall against the two-pronged attack of the moralists and the rationalists.

Central to the tradition of the allegorical epic as it was inherited by Tasso and Spenser was the *Aeneid* and the commentary accompanying it. Such commentaries as those of Servius (late fourth century), Fulgentius (early sixth century), and Bernard Silvestris (twelfth century) were elaborated upon by Italian humanists like Petrarch and Landino (*Questiones Camaldulenses*, 1480) to provide a large body of commonplace interpretations of the moral and intellectual development of Virgil's hero as he passed from the Old Troy of the senses to the New Troy (Rome) of the spirit. Troynovant, as Spenser calls London in *The Faerie Queene,* had its origin in the commentary on the moral and spiritual significance of Virgil's idealized Rome, and it carries with it all the meaning that centuries had bestowed upon an ancient image.[2]

The great force and intelligibility of the two Troys of Virgilian commentary as images depend not so much upon the Greek commentary on Homer as upon the far more powerful and ultimately more influential allegorizing tradition that begins in the Epistles of St. Paul and the introduction of Platonic thought into the traditional Hebrew concept of the Bible as a literal account of historical events. Whereas Greek *allegoresis* destroyed the literal meaning of the Homeric text in the explanation of its underlying meaning, Hebrew exegesis of the Bible affirmed the literal truth of the historical events recorded, while at the same time discovering spiritual significance in those events. The powerful new Pauline system of scriptural "typology" culminated in the works of St. Augustine (354–430). More will be said below of Augustine's concept of the two cities and of the general method of Christian typology. For the moment it is convenient merely to note that Spenser was a characteristically renaissance poet in his ability to synthesize so completely the heroic and mythological writers of pagan antiquity and the truths of Christian doctrine. It was the merging of two traditions of *allegoresis* in late antiquity and the Middle Ages that made this synthesis possible.

The medieval romances, also an influence on the renaissance epic tradition, differed most radically from the epics of Homer and Virgil in the construction of their plots. Whereas Aristotle had described the Homeric epic as a narrative of one man and one action, the medieval romance is most characteristically a narrative of many men and many, often only loosely connected, actions. The Homeric singers whose tradition produced the *Iliad* and the *Odyssey* were no doubt quite unaware that, within a few generations of the composition of the Homeric epics, the Greeks were going to demand either a much greater fidelity to historical and literal fact from their narrative writers or else, in the presence of superhuman actors and actions, an allegorizing commentary designed to make clear the poet's "meaning" in discursive language. The Homeric singers combined in their epics all of the mythical elements of their poetic tradition with the plausibility in cause and effect of an otherwise historical narrative. The completeness and the plausibility of the actions in the Homeric epics do not suggest that any sort of philosophical meaning, requiring an interpretive commentary, lies beneath the surface. Homer's epics, in other words, appear to have been composed primarily as "fiction" and only secondarily as meaning or "theme." The medieval romances, however, admit far more implausibility of cause and effect, the actions and characters seem far less complete in themselves, and the reader is often led to inquire about the poet's probable meaning. Occasionally, such an inquiry can be productive, and we discover that a unity of theme compensates for the disunity and improbability of plot. Although it is late and

---

[2] For an introduction to the vast subject of pagan and Christian *allegoresis* of ancient mythological art and literature, see Jean Seznec, *The Survival of the Pagan Gods,* trans. Barbara F. Sessions, Harper Torchbooks, 1961.

in prose, and therefore perhaps not typical, the *Morte d'Arthur* of Sir Thomas Malory (*ca.* 1400–1471) exemplifies the tendency of medieval romance to organize itself thematically rather than "fictionally."

Another respect in which medieval romance differs from the classical epic is in its treatment of love. Apollonius of Rhodes (*ca.* 200 B.C.) in his *Argonautica*, Ovid (43 B.C.–A.D. 17) in his *Amores*, *Heroides*, and *Metamorphoses*, and even Virgil in the Dido episode of the *Aeneid* had written about women who were irrationally driven by an overpowering passion. But these classical students of psychological instability imply that only women, because of their supposed intellectual inferiority, can serve as sympathetic characters overcome by emotion. Medieval attitudes toward women changed all of this.

The Provençal poets of the eleventh and twelfth centuries sang the praises of the gentle aristocratic lady, a paragon of grace, beauty, and virtue. She became the chief character in the courtly love poetry of the Middle Ages. Beautiful but unattainable, she was both the object of the knight's impassioned adoration and the cause of his bitter suffering. It is not surprising that the lady, thus exalted, sometimes became in medieval poetry the symbol of a high spiritual goal, through the attainment of which the knight could find his salvation. The best known example of the exaltation of the aristocratic lady is Dante's Beatrice, who in the *Divine Comedy* (1319) symbolizes divine revelation. Parallel to the exaltation of the lady in medieval literature, and perhaps related to it, was the elevation in theology of the Virgin Mary to the position of merciful intercessor with a just Christ on behalf of the sinner too miserable to approach him directly. Thus the sensibilities of literate Europe were centered upon the gracious lady as a symbol of the highest values of the age. As a result, the medieval romances are crowded with beautiful virgins who may represent not just the goal at the end of the knight's ordeal but perhaps honor, truth, or the soul.

On the other hand, the classical concept of woman as irrational and as a temptress of man to irrationality was immeasurably strengthened by the Christian interpretation of Eve's temptation of Adam. The most common interpretation treats Adam as man's reason and Eve as his passionate nature tempting reason to renounce its sovereignty and follow instead the promptings of Satan to give in to the blind urgings of the flesh. Thus woman becomes a symbol of corrupting sensuality and sin. The knight who is delayed in his rescue of the lovely virgin by falling into the soft clutch of the irresistably voluptuous enchantress of medieval romance may be experiencing the fall of his father Adam. He is at least testing his virtue against the strongest possible temptation to vice.

The treatment of love in medieval literature does not only elevate the theme of love to a much greater importance than it had had in classical times. It tends naturally to treat the theme symbolically. We can generalize to the extent of saying that when a modern reader attributes to a medieval writer the portrayal of a feminine character as an end in itself, merely for the sake of creating a memorable individual, the reader has made the mistake of interpreting medieval art with modern expectations.

The medieval romance, the allegorizing commentary on classical epics, the humanistic devotion to learning as an end in itself—all of these forces in the renaissance epic tradition influenced Spenser to a greater degree than they did any of his contemporary epic poets. Ariosto was more comic and episodic, but less allegorical than Spenser. Tasso and Camoëns were allegorical, but approached the unity and high seriousness of the *Aeneid* far more closely than did Spenser. Ronsard was the least influenced by medieval tradition—and the least successful.

ALLEGORY

The habit of *allegoresis* was so ingrained in the Renaissance, and the methods so traditional and ingenious, that almost no poem of classical antiquity could resist the allegorizer's effort to find beneath the surface fiction a structure of meaning that would accord with the general tenets of Christian belief and the more specific tenets of various metaphysical and ethical systems. From Boccaccio (1313-1375) to Bacon (1561-1626) writers compiled collections of ancient myths to illustrate what Bacon called the "wisdom of the ancients," an inspired wisdom in the light of which the ancient authors were supposed to have constructed poetic fictions containing the truths made directly available to Christians through divine revelation. In his *Defense of Poesy*, Spenser's friend Sir Philip Sidney (1554-1586) continues the tradition of Greek *allegoresis* by arguing that, because it veils a profound truth beneath a pleasing surface, poetry is superior to the intellectual prose of philosophers and historians. It becomes quite clear, then, that if the critics and scholars of the Renaissance could think of such works as the epics of Homer and Virgil, the impassioned love letters of Ovid's *Heroides*, and the Greek tragedies as being allegorical, they meant something different by the term than do the authors of our contemporary handbooks when they include only such explicitly allegorical works as *Piers Plowman* and *Pilgrim's Progress* under the heading of "allegory."

Since the eighteenth century the term *allegorical* has been used only for those literary works which tend to become discursive in the sense that each element of the fiction bears an unmistakable reference to some element in a continuous argument. A better term for symbolism of this sort is "naive allegory" or "allegory of ideas." Naive allegory in a pure form is rare in literature. Only with difficulty can poets manage to create a fiction in which the characters and actions represent nothing other than elements in a coherent argument. When the characters begin to take on lives of their own, when they and the actions they engage in are understood as imitations of real people and events, naive allegory gives place to something else.

Northrop Frye has reminded us that when we construct an interpretive commentary on a play of Shakespeare's, or even on a naturalistic novel, we are engaging in *allegoresis*.[3] We imply by such an activity that a structure of meaning exists within or beneath the fiction we are commenting on and that our commentary lays such a structure bare. In this sense all literature is allegorical.

---

[3] *Anatomy of Criticism*, Princeton University Press, 1957, p. 89. A new theory of literary symbolism, somewhat like Frye's, upon which we have in part based our subsequent discussion, is to be found in Graham Hough, *A Preface to "The Faerie Queene,"* W. W. Norton, 1962, pp. 100-137.

A pure naive allegory, however, would require only a minimum of commentary. When each element in the fiction had been identified, the fictional action would immediately be understood as the metaphorical statement of an idea easily paraphrased in non-metaphorical language. If a character named Free Trade should be strangled by a character named Tariff Barrier we are quite rightly not tempted to inquire very deeply into the motives and personality of the villain. Any commentary is directed instead toward the ideas represented by the fiction.

At the opposite end of an imaginary axis from naive allegory lie such narrative genres as history and reporting. Here a commentary is similarly restricted. If we should read in the newspaper of a character named Henrietta Forbes, 24, who was strangled by a character named Clyde Robinson, 42, all commentary will direct itself to the actual events represented by the narrative rather than to deeper levels of the author's meaning. In naive allegory the commentary tends to focus upon the idea; in history and reporting it tends to focus upon the event. In all the forms of narrative fiction which lie between these two poles there is a tripartite relationship among idea, fiction, and the actual world that is subject to a more or less legitimate *allegoresis*.

In a literary fiction located at a midpoint on the axis between naive allegory and reporting, the representation of actuality and idea are in balance. As we move towards reporting the fiction becomes more realistic, representing actuality with a greater degree of fidelity. As we move in the opposite direction, away from the midpoint toward naive allegory, the fiction represents ideas more powerfully than it does the actual world. If we should provisionally locate Shakespeare's plays at roughly the midpoint of this axis, we should probably agree that *The Faerie Queene* belongs in the general area between Shakespeare and naive allegory. We should likewise agree that most of classical literature and modern realistic fiction lies in the area between Shakespeare and reporting. This does not rule out all symbolism from realistic fiction nor all imitation of actuality from *The Faerie Queene;* it is merely a method of distinguishing the main tendencies of the two types of fiction.

Realistic fictions, of which Aristotle is the chief theoretician, locate the merging of actuality and idea in the typical. The characters and actions of the Homeric epics and of the Greek tragedies, for example, are similar to people and events in real life; but as Aristotle pointed out, the poet is superior to the historian and reporter in that he does not restrict himself to observed facts but only to the laws of probability. Poetry for Aristotle expresses the universal; history the particular. By the universal Aristotle meant "how a person of a certain type will on occasion speak or act, according to the law of probability or necessity" (*Poetics*, IX.4). For Aristotle fiction was the imitation of an action. Insofar as he was concerned with the agents performing the actions, he wanted them to be consistent, universal, ethical types.

Allegorical fictions do not imitate actual people and events to produce ethically typical characters and probable actions. Even when they are most mimetic, allegorical fictions illustrate some further metaphysical, theological, ethical, or social doctrine through the manipulation of images that have stipulated meanings *other than* their meanings as imitations of the actual world. The writer of an allegorical fiction looks back to literary tradition for images that have acquired some meaning other than mere representation of the actual world, and he looks to his intellectual and religious tradition for the ideas his fiction is to illustrate. It would be a mistake to imagine that the allegorical poet writes solely in order to purvey his doctrine. He simply conceives of his art dualistically, with fiction and idea in more or less continuous symbolic interdependence. Through their speeches and actions, the characters in an allegorical fiction occasionally establish their similarity to types of humanity. At the same time, they establish their similarity to traditional images which have taken on some additional meaning. Chaucer's Wife of Bath, for example, is clearly reminiscent of La Vieille in *The Romance of the Rose*, of the Samaritan woman in John 4:7–36, and of innumerable wives in a long tradition of antifeminist moralizing. As an allegorical image she should be located nearer the midpoint of our axis than any of Spenser's characters. But she has an important essential similarity to the allegorical characters of *The Faerie Queene*, for her full significance is dependent upon the reader's familiarity with a conventional literary image and with the doctrine, attached to that image, of man's fall through permitting his passions to gain sovereignty over his reason.

Much of Spenser's allegory is of this sort. For Spenser, Hercules was the hero *par excellence*, and we see occasions on which Prince Arthur, the Red Cross Knight, and Sir Guyon each identify themselves as types of Hercules. Other classical heroes, such as Aeneas, Odysseus, Jason, Perseus, and Theseus (more as they existed in commentaries than in poetry) were evoked by Spenser not as mannerist rhetorical ornamentation but as a method of establishing the allegorical identity of his heroes.

While Spenser does not go so far as does Chaucer in clothing allegorical characters in realistic dress, he does frequently follow the practice of such masters of the allegory of ideas as Jean de Meun in *The Romance of the Rose* and William Langland in *Piers Plowman* in combining the personification of abstract ideas with mimetic detail. In such characters as Despair in Book I and Mammon in Book II, the method of revealing idea indirectly through traditional ethical types is abandoned in favor of a direct identification of the character with an abstract concept and then developing the character as if he were an ethical type. Despair becomes a despairing man, Mammon an avaricious one. Langland carried the process even further by locating his personifications in fourteenth-century England. Spenser never moves nearer the actual than a highly generalized representation of the ethically typical. He calls the Red Cross Knight and Arthur Englishmen, but he does not locate them in England. His setting remains Faeryland.

Spenser not only drew upon the ethical types of allegorized classical literature for his characters; he also alluded to characters and events of the Bible in the spirit in which these were interpreted by the commentators. At its most elaborate, medieval and renaissance biblical exegesis conceived of four "levels" of scriptural symbolism. On the first level, the "literal" or "historical" level, the language of the Bible was understood to be an accurate report of actuality. The Bible was a literally and historically true account composed by the Holy Spirit. The exegete's duty on this level of interpretation was to understand the meanings of the letters, words, and rhetorical figures, so that he would have an accurate idea of the objective reality to which they referred. When he had understood the literal meaning of the scriptures he could then move on to other levels of interpretation.[4]

The "things" to which the literal meaning of the Bible referred were themselves the symbols of God's meaning. In other words, God revealed his meaning to man in actual happenings, recorded these happenings in a literally true account, and then gave man the task of interpreting his "spiritual" meaning as it was revealed in the literal text of his writings. God was an allegorist in his creation and its historical unfolding, but an historian in his scriptural record of events. The allegorical meaning of reality was not restricted, of course, to those characters and events recorded in the Bible. God remained an allegorist. Actuality as medieval men experienced it was held to be precisely as symbolical of God's meaning as the actuality recorded in scripture.

The great advantage of Christian *allegoresis* over that of the pagans was that it interpreted the sacred texts of scripture with a method which was in harmony with the Christian analysis of physical nature and human history. For St. Augustine, the world of visible forms and of history was a vast and often baffling collection of outward husks beneath which lay the kernel of divine truth, but the truth that lay hidden there to be discovered by the expert interpreter was a marvelously coherent and simple truth. As the Old Testament is in one sense a physical book with a literal story, it is in another sense a spiritual book with a spiritual story, whose characters and events can be understood as "types," or foreshadowings, of the salvation of man through the incarnation and crucifixion of Christ.

In traditional scriptural exegesis three kinds of spiritual meaning were thought to be signified by the personages, utterances, and events recorded in the literal text of the Old Testament. First, an Old Testament personage (type) could in his actions and in the nature of his own personal development foreshadow Christ (antitype). This foreshadowing of Christ is a "typological" meaning. Second, if a type foreshadows some element in the life of Christ with a specific doctrinal meaning, such as baptism, which applies to the life of the individual Christian, it has a "moral," or "tropological" meaning. And finally, an Old Testament type can foreshadow the union at the end of time of the resurrected membership of the church and God. This is an "anagogical" meaning.

The life of Christ is central to scriptural interpretation as it is to Christian doctrine in general. Everything in the Old Testament that can be typologically related to Christ is doctrinally significant. The plot line of the Bible and of the history of mankind as Augustine formulated it in *The City of God* can be imagined as a sharp downward line that represents the fall of Adam and mankind,

---

[4] A clear and authoritative account of the interpretation of the Bible in the Middle Ages is to be found in Charles Donahue, "Summation," *Critical Approaches to Medieval Literature: Selected Papers from the English Institute, 1958–1959*, ed. Dorothy Bethurum, Columbia University Press, 1960, pp. 61–82. The other essays in the same volume should be consulted for their views of the uses to which a study of the images significant in exegetical tradition may legitimately be put in literary criticism.

followed by both a horizontal line, representing the temporal history of the earthly kingdoms, and a gradually rising line representing the history of the spiritual kingdom on earth—that is, the church. Both the lives of Christ and of the Christian who takes up membership in the spiritual kingdom on earth follow the sharp descent and gradual rise: Christ because he had descended to assume the guilt of man and his suffering in the world, after which he was resurrected and reunited with God the Father; the Christian because he attempts to imitate the perfection of Christ in order to redeem himself from the consequences of his own sin, in which he had imitated Adam. The life of Christ, therefore, comprehends mystically all of human history and is a pattern for the salvation of the individual. It is the antitype according to which the lives of Old Testament heroes and of ordinary humans at all periods of history (types) become spiritually significant.

The tradition of Greek *allegoresis* thus took on an unmistakable Christian character during the Middle Ages when such heroes of pagan literature as Aeneas and Hercules came to be understood as types of Christ. Corresponding to the renaissance synthesis of Christian and pagan philosophy, and intimately related to it, the renaissance synthesis of traditions by which significance was attached to poetic images produced in Spenser's allegorical poetry an extraordinary richness of meaning. In both Books I and II of *The Faerie Queene* Prince Arthur is at times a recognizable type of Christ. The hero of Book I, the Red Cross Knight, is also represented as a human being who must conform himself to the image of Christ and whose career, therefore, follows roughly the spiritual plot line of the Bible. Sir Guyon, however, the hero of Book II, is not a type of Christ, his career does not follow the same line as Red Cross's, and he is not represented as a human being. He can probably best be understood as the representation of a classical ideal, of man as he was conceived in classical ethics. He may at one point represent temperance and at another point the temperate man, but he does not represent the Christian for whom temperance is only a means toward the ultimate end of spiritual perfection. For his two heroes, Red Cross and Sir Guyon, Spenser draws in Book I upon the modes of thought represented in Christian typology and in Book II upon the modes of thought represented in Greek *allegoresis*.

ST. GEORGE AND THE DRAGON: THE MAKING OF A SAINT

Spenser could hardly have chosen a more popular hero for the first book of *The Faerie Queene* than the soldier-saint, St. George. Although the church had rejected the legendary figure as early as the fifth century, the crusaders of the late Middle Ages adopted him as their patron and made his veneration prominent throughout Europe. Then, in the thirteenth century Jacobus de Voraigne composed the tremendously popular and influential *Legenda Aurea*, a collection of saints' lives in which the Perseus myth was incorporated into the older and less romantic legend of St. George. Jacobus' version of the legend was undoubtedly responsible for fixing the mind of Europe upon the combat between St. George and the dragon as the most striking and important episode in the life of the hero. In England the popularity of the St. George legend and, particularly, of the combat with the dragon was enhanced by the institution in 1344 of the Order of the Garter by Edward III. St. George was made the patron of the new order and the combat was adopted as its insignia. It was, however, around the beginning of the fifteenth century that the *Legenda Aurea* became widely known in England, and it is from this time that the St. George legend in English translations, St. George pageants, and, especially, paintings of the saint's combat proliferate. A recent investigation lists ninety-four murals depicting episodes from the life of St. George.[5] Most of these were on the walls of churches, the majority of them were painted in the fifteenth century, and the subject of most of them is the dragon combat. There were undoubtedly many more. Add to these murals, which were on view to a very large public, large numbers of tapestries and paintings in both private and public places, and it can be seen that the famous victory of St. George of England over the dragon and his deliverance of the virgin princess from a horrible death was as familiar to Englishmen of the fifteenth and sixteenth centuries as the clothes they wore and the food they ate.

The pictorial tradition has been emphasized not only to show how familiar Spenser's subject was to his audience. It might also be argued that Book I of *The Faerie Queene* was based primarily upon the pictorial tradition rather than upon the literary tradition established by the *Legenda Aurea*. Spenser's treatment of the St. George legend has little but a general similarity to the literary versions which depend on the *Legenda Aurea*, and he made use only of the combat episode in his story—precisely the episode which was most popular in art. Whether or not Spenser's inspiration came from the pictures which were everywhere around him, an analysis of one of the famous renaissance paintings of St. George and the dragon is an enlightening introduction to the structure and meaning of the first book of *The Faerie Queene*. The well-known picture of the combat by Raphael, commissioned by the Duke of Urbino and presented by him to Henry VII, is less typical of the tradition than the version by Vittore Carpaccio in the Scuola San Giorgio Degli Schiavoni, Venice. Carpaccio's fresco is detailed and very much in the spirit of Spenser's story, and so the analysis will be centered upon it (Plate I).

In the foreground of Carpaccio's picture are the central figures of the combat. On the right is St. George mounted and fully armed as a medieval knight. His lance has just pierced the dragon through the throat and has broken. On the left the great winged dragon is poised to strike. The ground on which the combat takes place is littered with the mutilated bodies and the dried bones of the dragon's victims, and the dragon's tiny offspring run about. Behind St. George at the extreme right is the princess standing in prayer, and behind her is a rocky hill whose narrow winding paths lead to a domed church at the top. At the extreme left behind the dragon is a marsh full of skulls and a skeleton. Behind this is a great walled city lying on a plain. Its most prominent structure is a three-tiered tower upon whose balconies crowds stand watching the combat. In the background between the two central figures is a tree. The limbs growing to the left are withered while those that grow to the right are green with leaves.

[5] Ethel Carleton Williams, "Mural Paintings of St. George in England," *Journal of the British Archaeological Association*, 3rd series, XI (1948), 19–36.

Although Carpaccio's St. George is generally faithful to the legend of literary tradition, still the background is richly allegorical. And it is this quality which makes the picture so close in intention to Book I of *The Faerie Queene.*

The art historian Erwin Panofsky has noted that the division "of landscape background into two halves of symbolically contrasting character" is common in late-medieval and renaissance religious painting.[6] The low plain at the left in Carpaccio's picture represents what Panofsky calls the *aera sub lege*, mankind bound to the old law of Moses and thus subject to sin, death, and hell. The high rocky ground on the right represents the *aera sub gratia*, man under the new dispensation, redeemed from sin and death by Christ's sacrifice and his grace. The tree behind the central figures is a symbol of the same opposition between grace and damnation. The barren and withered limbs on the left represent not only the sterility of life under the old law; they are also symbolic of the origin of man's bondage to sin and death, for they represent that tree in paradise whose fruit condemned Adam and, in Adam, all mankind to death. The living branches on the right represent the death-dealing tree of knowledge transformed into the tree of life by Christ, the new Adam. By his death on the cross, man is rescued from death and offered eternal life.

Carpaccio's background is more than an allegorical landscape. The great city on the left and the small church at the top of the hill certainly represent in a general way the *aera sub lege* and the *aera sub gratia* suggested by the landscape generally, but they represent these contrasting concepts more specifically as the City of Man and the City of God. This opposition, made famous by St. Augustine's *The City of God*, is another contrast between the life of sin, destined to eternal death in hell, and the Christian life of faith, destined to eternal bliss in heaven. The nature and history of the two cities is fully developed in Books XI–XXII of *The City of God*. The two cities "have been formed by two loves: the earthly by the love of self, even to the contempt of God; the heavenly by the love of God, even to the contempt of self. The former, in a word, glories in itself, the latter in the Lord. For the one seeks glory from men; but the greatest glory of the other is God, the witness of conscience."[7] The citizens of the City of Man live according to the flesh, loving the things created by God, whether these be wealth, pleasure, power, or knowledge, rather than the creator himself. Its origin is in Satan and the other fallen angels who loved themselves rather than God and were cast into hell. The City of God has its origin in the angels who remained firm in their love of God.

In human society the two cities are inextricably mixed and will remain so until the last day when Christ will come to divide the two cities forever. But there are in human history archetypes of both cities. The first type of the City of Man is Babylon, whose citizens attempted to build a tower which reached to the sky (Genesis 11:2–4). The other great type of the City of Man was Rome, "like another Babylon, and as it were the daughter of the former Babylon" (*City of God*, XVIII.22). In these earthly and sinful cities the City of God and its citizens lived like aliens, as the Jews lived in Egypt and Babylon, and as the early Christians lived in Rome, persecuted and in hiding. For Augustine, both

---

[6] *Studies in Iconology,* Harper Torchbooks, 1962, p. 64.
[7] *The City of God,* XIV.28, trans. Marcus Dods, Modern Library, 1950, p. 477.

Eden before the fall of Adam and the church are types of the City of God. Its members in human society, those who through God's grace and Christ's sacrifice are able to live not according to man but according to God, will in time inherit eternal life.

Carpaccio's background implies all of this. The great open gate on the left and the narrow winding paths of the mountain on the right illustrate the biblical text: "Enter yet in at the strait gate: for wide is the gate, and broad is the way, that leadeth to destruction, and many there be which go in thereat: because strait is the gate, and narrow is the way, which leadeth unto life, and few there be that find it" (Matthew 7:13–14).[8] This text also explains the crowds of spectators in the city as opposed to the few travelers on the mountain path to the church.

Although the allegorical richness of Carpaccio's great fresco has by no means been exhausted by this discussion, enough has been said to show that the central figures, St. George and the dragon, are engaged in a cosmic struggle— the new law of Christ triumphant over the old law of Moses, grace over sin and death, the church over the world, Christ over Satan. All of these are present in the saint's victory over the great beast.

The heart of Spenser's story of the Red Cross Knight takes place within the context of Carpaccio's picture, but it begins and in part develops outside, for Spenser's hero begins as a young knight, brave but inexperienced. Guided by the princess, Una, he starts his quest with a sincere but untested faith. The accomplishment of his quest is to have the same significance as the victory of Carpaccio's St. George, but before the Red Cross Knight can defeat the dragon which holds the princess's parents captive, he must in St. Paul's words, "be conformed to the image of his [God's] Son" (Romans 8:29). If his victory over the dragon is to be a type of Christ's victory over sin and death, and of his deliverance of mankind from damnation, then the Red Cross Knight must become St. George, a type of Christ. And so, for the most part, Book I of *The Faerie Queene* is the story of how the hero, a beginning Christian, becomes "conformed" to the image of God's son.

But if it is the Red Cross Knight's destiny to become a type of Christ, he is unaware of and, in fact, unequal to that destiny. After an initial victory over the dragon Error, he is rather easily tricked by Archimago, clearly a type of Satan, into deserting his guide, Una, who in Spenser's story is much more than the conventional damsel in distress. Una is truth, true religion, and the true church, and having deserted her, Red Cross has no alternative but to ally himself with falsehood, false religion, and the false church, Spenser's Duessa.

From this point on, the Red Cross Knight's progress can be plotted on Carpaccio's fresco as on a spiritual map. Led by Duessa and his own weakness he journeys to Babylon, the City of Man—in Spenser's poem, the House of Pride. There he succumbs to the vanity and corruption of fleshly life, and finally, in an act symbolic of total depravity, he commits adultery with the false Duessa. In St. Paul's terms he has completely given over the life of the spirit for the life of the flesh, and punishment comes immediately. In Canto vii,

[8] All quotations from the Bible, including those from the Apocrypha, are taken from the King James version.

the Red Cross Knight, weak and unable to defend himself, is taken captive by the giant Orgoglio, another type of Satan, and thrown into the hell of the giant's dungeon. When, in Canto viii, Prince Arthur rescues the hero, he resembles nothing so much as the shrunken cadaver at the left of Carpaccio's painting.

It may seem strange that a story about a hero destined to become a Christian saint should give a detailed account of his gradual descent into total depravity and damnation. But the road taken by the Red Cross Knight is the Pauline pattern so well put by St. Augustine: "The fact is that every individual springs from a condemned stock and, because of Adam, must be first cankered and carnal, only later to become sound and spiritual by the process of rebirth in Christ" (*City of God*, XV.1). As the son of Adam, the Red Cross Knight must recapitulate the sins of his father. He cannot save himself, for only the grace and the sacrifice of Christ, the new Adam, can do that. Prince Arthur, who in Canto viii defeats Orgoglio, Duessa, and her many-headed beast and rescues the hero from his dungeon, represents Christ's entry into the Pauline pattern. His actions are the beginning of the Red Cross Knight's rebirth in Christ. Reunited, by the grace of Christ, with true religion (Una), the hero makes his way painfully up the mountain to the right in Carpaccio's painting until he reaches the church at the top, the House of Holiness in Spenser's story. There he repents in great suffering, the corruption of sin is destroyed in his body and soul, and he is taught faith, hope, and charity. Finally he learns his destiny and his true identity, for he is granted a vision of the New Jerusalem, the heavenly city, and he finds out that he is St. George. Leaving the House of Holiness he descends the mountain with Una and in a ferocious three-day battle destroys the great beast. In his victory, which is analogous to Arthur's earlier victory, the Red Cross Knight has become conformed to the image of Christ. St. George's betrothal to Una in Canto xii is but another symbol of his sainthood. It is clearly a type of Christ's marriage to the church.

As has already been mentioned, Spenser announced in his letter to Sir Walter Raleigh that the intention of his poem was "to fashion a gentleman or noble person in virtuous and gentle discipline." In Book I, he has fashioned a saint, showing not so much what a Christian should do to be saved, but rather what his destiny will be—what failure, what suffering, and finally what glory he will experience. The pattern of sin and redemption which Spenser's St. George follows applies to all men, according to St. Augustine. Thus, as the detailed commentary which follows will suggest, the Red Cross Knight represents not only the individual Christian, but human history generally. In his desertion of Una in Canto ii is the fall of Adam. His progressive degeneration is the history of the City of Man unconformed to the image of the City of God. His rescue by Arthur is the new law of grace entering human history with the life, death, and resurrection of Christ. His rehabilitation, the victory over the dragon, and his betrothal to Una represent the history and ultimate destiny of the City of God.

For Spenser's readers the Red Cross Knight's quest was also a pattern of the history of the Christian church. It is this aspect of Book I that modern readers, especially Christians, are likely to find distasteful. Spenser's century saw in life the same oppositions which St. Augustine wrote about in *The City of God*—

Christ and Satan, the church and worldly society, truth and falsehood, the old law and the new. But in the bitter religious strife of the Reformation, men saw these oppositions in a special light. For Protestants like Spenser and his readers, the opposition between the City of God and the City of Man was likely to be seen as the struggle of the true church, the Protestant churches, against the worldly and corrupt Roman Catholic church. The firm establishment of the Church of England under Elizabeth I was likely to be compared with the foundation of the church under the apostles and the early fathers. This aspect of Book I was important in Spenser's time and for hundreds of years afterward, and the commentary which follows attempts to do justice to it. However, readers should remember that the more important theme of Book I is the universal one, the making of a saint.

A SUMMARY OF THE PLOT AND ALLEGORY OF BOOK I

i.1–28: The Red Cross Knight at Error's Den

The origin and motive of the Red Cross Knight's quest are mentioned in the poet's letter to Sir Walter Raleigh. As the Red Cross Knight and his beautiful companion, Una, ride over the plain toward the adventure which the Faery Queen has given Red Cross, a terrible storm breaks and they are forced to take cover in a dark forest. They walk slowly down some of the well-traveled paths that lead into the heart of the forest, delighting as they go in the song of the birds and in the variety of the giant trees. When the storm blows over, however, and the knight and his lady attempt to return to the open plain, they find themselves lost in the maze of paths. Resolving to find their way out, they choose the path which seems most worn and follow it until they come to a cave in the heart of the forest. Red Cross immediately dismounts to investigate and walks boldly up to the cave's entrance, in spite of Una's warning that the cave is the den of Error, a hideous monster, half woman, half serpent. Error, suckling her monstrous young in the darkness of the cave, sees the glimmering light from Red Cross's armor and rushes out; but when she meets the full glare of the armor she tries to turn back. The knight, however, engages her with his sword and strikes her a heavy blow, which glances down her shoulder. Enraged, Error attacks Red Cross and twists her tail about him. Una advises him to "add faith unto" his strength, to strangle the monster before she can destroy him; but when the knight grips Error's throat a disgusting black vomit of poison, full of half-digested lumps of flesh, books, and papers, pours out. Sickening at the stench, Red Cross loosens his grip and Error releases from her stomach an army of her repulsive little offspring, who crawl about the knight's feet. In desperation, Red Cross strikes at the monster and cuts off her head. Her brood then devour their mother and, as the amazed knight stands watching, gorge themselves until they burst. Una, who has been watching from afar, comes to congratulate her champion, and the two mount and finally find their way out onto the open plain again.

As Spenser says in the letter to Raleigh, the Red Cross Knight's armor is that of the Christian prepared to withstand and combat evil (Ephesians 6:10–22):

"Put on the whole armor of God, that ye may be able to stand against the wiles of the devil. . . . Stand, therefore, having your loins girt about with truth, and having on the breast-plate of righteousness. . . . Above all, taking the shield of faith, wherewith ye shall be able to quench all the fiery darts of the wicked." The cross on Red Cross's breast appropriately represents Christ crucified, a satisfaction of divine justice, and man crucified or dead to sin. The cross on the shield represents Christ resurrected and the human hope of salvation. The armor is dented because it has been worn by every Christian and, indeed, by Christ himself, whose wounds on the cross were the first and deepest dents. Clearly, in putting on the armor which Una has brought to the court of the Faery Queen, Red Cross has become an aspiring imitator of Christ, as is every Christian.

Una represents truth, true religion, and the true church. Her name, reminiscent of Unitas in *Piers Plowman* (B XIX–XX), implies the qualities of truth and of the true church. Truth is one and eternal; it admits of no contradiction and no relativity. Her name also suggests the Platonic unity of truth and beauty, applicable to the true church, which is the bride of Christ. Una's parents are Adam and Eve and all men, who were given dominion over all the earth (Genesis 2:28) but, tempted by Satan, fell from grace and truth and were driven from Paradise. The fall of Adam and Eve, and of all men as a result, accounts both for Una's sadness and for her veiled face. Because of the fall of man, Una or truth has lost her home among men. Originally, man was perfect in his obedience to and love of God, but with the fall he became sinful and incapable of understanding God's law. He could no longer see truth. In his impure state, even if he had been able to see truth, its pure light would have blinded him. Una's veil is, then, a symbol of man's imperfection since the fall of Adam. Undoubtedly too it is the veil of the synagogue, which was torn apart with the coming of Christ, as well as the bridal veil of the church, Christ's betrothed. The white ass which Una rides represents the Christian clergy, instruments of the word of God and, thus, bearers of truth. The lamb is a sign that Una is Christian truth, whose law is mercy and self-sacrifice, rather than the truth of the philosophers. The dwarf who follows Una is probably human reason. He is at best a humble servant of truth.

Una represents the ideal of true religion, best exemplified by the perfect understanding, love, and obedience between Adam and Eve in Paradise before the fall. The mission of Christ, and of every Christian following him, is to reestablish through his sacrifice, love, and grace the ideal of true religion on earth. For sixteenth-century Protestants the ideal of true religion was most closely approached by the church of primitive Christian times, the church described in the *Acts of the Apostles* and in St. Paul's letters. All of the reformed churches were attempting to recreate what they considered the original purity of the early church and to remove what they considered the corruption in doctrine, liturgy, and morals which had infiltrated the Roman Catholic church over the centuries. Thus Una may be considered a symbol of the early Christian church and of the reformed English church, which was attempting to reestablish the purity of the primitive church, and thus to approximate the perfection of life before the fall of Adam.

The monster Error is theological error generally, including the error which was responsible for the fall of man in Eden. The serpent who tempted Eve in the garden is one symbol of this error, and in late medieval art the serpent sometimes has the same form as Spenser's Error.[9] Error's monstrous brood are the false doctrines which have developed during the life of the church. She lives in a dark cave because false doctrine cannot survive exposure to the light of reason and faith. In attacking Red Cross, Error throws herself upon his shield and winds her tail about his body. Allegorically, false doctrine attacks faith (the shield) and tries to replace the truth which should gird the loins of the Christian (Ephesians 6:14) with falsehood (her tail). Red Cross correctly opposes the sword of the word of God (Ephesians 6:17) to Error, for the Bible is a sufficient refutation of heresy. But Una's advice to add faith to his force indicates that Red Cross depends too much on his own virtue, perhaps his own reason, to combat Error. On the most general level, Red Cross's struggle with Error simply represents the situation that all men since the fall of Adam live in. All men having fallen with the fall of Adam, falsehood becomes one of man's chief enemies in his attempt to recreate himself in the image of Christ, the new Adam (Romans 5:14). With the fall, man's reason was weakened and his will inclined toward evil. Thus every man who attempts to imitate Christ and to establish true religion on earth must do battle with Error. On a less general level, the battle with Error represents the doctrinal strife which characterized the early centuries of the church's growth. Spenser's readers undoubtedly saw in the battle a reference also to the theological battle which the reformed churches, especially the English church, waged against what they considered to be the errors of the Roman Catholic church. The weapons which Red Cross uses in defeating Error, the sword of the word of God and the shield of faith, are those of the Reformation, which emphasized both the authority of the Bible and the doctrine of salvation by faith, whereas Roman Catholic doctrine of the time placed a greater emphasis on the authority of theological tradition and on the doctrine of works.

On the allegorical level, Red Cross's battle with Error serves as an epitome or miniature of the action of Book I. The ultimate trial in the quest will be the knight's struggle with the dragon Satan, who holds Una's parents captive. Error is in a sense a type of all of the monstrous enemies to true religion and the true church that Red Cross and Arthur encounter on the quest. In Red Cross's final battle with the dragon, for instance, Una will again be watching from afar and will congratulate him on his victory. The first battle is, then, a prophecy of final victory. At the same time, the battle with Error suggests some of the weaknesses in the Red Cross Knight, in all men, which will make his quest a story of successive failures before the final triumph. Chief of these faults is a weak faith and a corresponding excessive confidence in his own virtue. Because of this weakness he ignores Una's warning about Error. And though he is advised to add faith unto his force, he defeats Error not by the strength of his faith but by a desperate fear of shame. Later his lack of faith will lead him to a self-righteous rejection of Una herself.

[9] See plate 89, D. W. Robertson, Jr., *A Preface to Chaucer*, Princeton University Press, 1962.

i.29–ii.11: Archimago, the False Una, and the Disloyalty of the Red Cross Knight

Continuing their travels, Red Cross and Una meet a humble old hermit. The holy man kindly invites the two travelers to rest the night in his hut in the valley, and they accept. After some pleasant conversation, night draws on and the tired travelers retire. Then the hermit throws off his disguise and becomes Archimago, the evil magician whose driving compulsion is his hatred of Una. With the help of horrible spells he raises demons to serve him in his plot against his hated guests. One spirit he sends to Hades, into the realm of Morpheus, the god of sleep, to get from the god an evil dream to delude and tempt Red Cross. Another of the demons he fashions into a likeness of Una. He instructs the evil dream to inflame the sleeping knight's imagination with erotic visions of a wanton and seductive Una. When Red Cross, shocked out of his sleep, awakes he finds the demonic imitation of his lady offering to kiss him and declaring her desire shamelessly. Grieved by what he takes to be Una's looseness, Red Cross tactfully comforts the lady and returns to his sleep. The false Una and the evil dream report their failure to seduce Red Cross to Archimago. The magician, in a rage, then tries a more desperate plot. He fashions the evil dream into the image of a wanton young squire and lays him and the false Una together in a secret bed. He then awakens Red Cross and shows him what appears to be his lady in the arms of a stranger. Burning in jealous anger, Red Cross attempts to kill the adulterers but is restrained by the old hermit. As soon as it is morning, the knight and Una's dwarf leave the hermit's hut, deserting the true Una, who is ignorant of the night's terrible work. When she awakens to find Red Cross and her dwarf gone, she rides after them as fast as her slow beast will go. Archimago, not satisfied with the injury he has done his enemy, plots more cruelty and, to further his scheme, disguises himself as the Red Cross Knight.

Archimago (arch magician), introduced here as a holy hermit, represents hypocrisy. Posing as Contemplation, the highest end of Christian life (see Canto x.46), he is in fact Satan, the arch enemy of God, man, and true religion. As the father of lies, he is responsible for the fall of Adam and for man's bondage to sin and death. The idea that evil typically assumes the appearance of virtue, innocence, and beauty in order to deceive and destroy men is basic in Christian thought. Archimago, as Satan, is behind all of the deceit and suffering that Red Cross falls victim to, and he is less directly responsible for the trials of Una. Unable to attack truth and true religion directly, Satan attempts instead to divide men from truth and bind them to falsehood. In the historical allegory, Archimago remains simply a type of Satan, but his manifestations and alliances show him to be working primarily through the sixteenth-century Roman Catholic church.

In the most general allegory, Red Cross's desertion of Una represents the fall of Adam, which was brought about by the malice and deception of Satan. In Book IV of *Paradise Lost* Milton imitated the false dream which Spenser here uses to explain Red Cross's desertion of Una. Milton's Gabriel finds Satan

> Squat like a toad, close at the ear of Eve;
> Assaying by his devilish art to reach

> The organs of her fancy, and with them forge
> Illusions as he list. . . .

Red Cross, like Eve, is attacked when he is most vulnerable. It is the function of reason in man to distinguish between the false and the true appearances presented to the senses and to the imagination or fancy, to reject the false and accept the true. In sleep, reason ceases to function and the false is accepted along with the true, at least temporarily. Thus the image of Una as a lustful and trivial woman—of truth as falsehood and evil—is planted in Red Cross's mind at a time when he cannot refute it by reason. The effect of the false dream is to arouse a conflict in Red Cross between desire and indignation. He feels lust for the seductive false Una at the same time that he feels indignation at her wantonness. This conflict finally clouds his reason so that he is unable to distinguish between the false Una and the true. The false Una's speeches are composed of the clichés of the erotic courtly love tradition, and Red Cross should have seen through her and rejected her on that ground alone. His failure to do so is a measure of the weakening of his faith in Una which the false dream has caused. Finally, the conflict between lust and indignation, triggered by the false dream, breaks out overtly when Archimago shows Red Cross the false Una in the arms of the squire. Satan has accomplished his purpose. Man is divided from truth. The fall of Adam is repeated in the life of every man. Historically, Red Cross's desertion represents what the Protestant churches considered the defeat of true religion by Roman Catholicism in the early centuries of Christianity. It could also represent England's temporary desertion of the reformed church of Henry VIII and Edward VI during the reign of Mary Tudor.

Archimago, in taking on the appearance of the Red Cross Knight, plays a role similar to that of the false Una and, later, Duessa. As a mere man Red Cross is, like other men, a type of Adam, but as a Christian he is a type of the new Adam, Christ. As the false Una represents false religion posing as truth, so Archimago in the costume of the Red Cross Knight represents the antichrist. Since the pope was considered the chief manifestation of the antichrist in Protestant polemics of the time, the historical meaning of Archimago's disguise is probably that, with the beginning of Mary Tudor's reign, the pope falsely pretended to be the protector of the true church. Possibly the rise of the Bishop of Rome to power in the early history of the church is also referred to.

ii.12–27: Duessa and Sansfoy

Red Cross and the dwarf, after leaving the hermit's house, wander aimlessly until they meet the fierce Saracen Sansfoy and his lady, Duessa. The knights prepare for battle, and after a terrible struggle during which Red Cross is saved from death only by his shield, the Saracen is killed. His lady, terrified by the death of her champion, turns and flees, but Red Cross pursues, assuring her that he intends no harm to her. The lady—in reality Duessa, the ally of Archimago—tells Red Cross that she is Fidessa, daughter of an emperor of the west. Her father betrothed her to the son of a great king, but the prince was killed by his enemies and his body stolen away. Fidessa tells Red Cross that she had been all over the world looking for his body when the Saracen captured her. She declares that she had kept her virginity in spite of Sansfoy's entreaties and begs Red Cross not to do her any harm. Red Cross, full of sympathy for her trials, vows to protect her, and the two ride away together.

Sansfoy's companion Duessa is the opposite of Una. As one (Una) represents truth, goodness, beauty, order, and whatever is perfect and eternal in Platonic thought (*Timaeus*); so two (Duessa) represents all that is imperfect, chaotic, earthly, and evil. Spenser's description of Duessa shows that she is the Whore of Babylon of Revelation 17:3–4: "... and I saw a woman sit upon a scarlet coloured beast, full of names of blasphemy, having seven heads and ten horns. And the woman was arrayed in purple and scarlet colour, and decked with gold and precious stones and pearls, having a golden cup in her hand full of abominations and filthiness of her fornication. ...." She was from early Christian times understood to represent false religion. For Protestants she was the false church, Roman Catholicism. Her gaudy dress represents the lascivious splendor of Roman Catholic ceremony, especially her Persian headdress, since Persia stood for all that was luxuriously immoral. The headdress represents also the pope's mitre. Duessa's role is essentially the same as Archimago's. False religion and Roman Catholicism destroy men by appearing as Fidessa, true faith. Duessa's story illustrates both her attempt to pose as true religion and the true church and also the falseness which lies behind that pose. On one level, the history is true. God (the emperor) did betroth his daughter, the true church, to the son (heir) of a mighty king (God). The son was killed by his enemies and his body taken and hidden in a tomb. But Duessa betrays her falseness on another level. She says that the pope (emperor of the West) had betrothed her to Christ (heir), Son of God (mighty king), who was killed by his enemies. Spenser's readers would have seen through this level of the story immediately. Duessa blasphemously gives higher status to the pope than to God, she speaks of Christ's death on the cross as a fall from honor, and, most telling, she does not know that Christ has risen from the dead. Another indication that Duessa is not Fidessa is that, whereas Una can claim to be the universal church because her parents held dominion over the entire earth, Duessa can claim dominion over the west alone because the eastern churches had broken away from Rome.

Duessa's companion and lover, Sansfoy, is simply another and more direct representation of the essential falseness of his mistress. He is atheism. Having been persuaded by Archimago that Una is false, that the true church is impure, Red Cross is naturally tempted or attacked by faithlessness (Sansfoy). When faithlessness appears overtly as atheism, the Christian is proof against it. Red Cross has not rejected true religion knowingly; he has been tricked by Satan into believing that truth is falsehood. With Sansfoy it is a different matter, for he advertises upon his shield what he stands for. Red Cross's victory over Sansfoy makes the same point as his earlier victory over Error. For the Christian, the problem is not with the kinds of evil which show themselves as evil. The real problem, the stumbling block that stands in the way of faith and salvation, is the evil that wears the mask of truth and goodness. The irony and the tragedy of Red Cross's, of man's, situation is that he runs into the arms of the false religion (Duessa) he thought he was escaping when he deserted Una, true religion; in championing Duessa he falls into the faithlessness he thought he had conquered in his triumph over Sansfoy. Allegorically, this episode is a clarification of the meaning of Red Cross's desertion of Una. On the historical level it represents both the rise to power of the church at Rome and, more narrowly, the return of England to Roman Catholicism under Mary Tudor.

ii.28–45: Fradubio and Fraelissa

The Red Cross Knight and the false Fidessa travel for a long time together. Finally weary and hot, they stop under the shade of two large trees where they rest and entertain each other in pleasant conversation. Red Cross tears from one of the trees a bough to make a garland for his new lady, and is amazed to see blood dropping from the broken bough and to hear a voice from the tree pleading to be spared further injury. The voice urges Red Cross to fly immediately. The knight stands horrified and then listens as the voice identifies itself and tells its strange story. In his youth, the voice says, he was Fradubio, a courageous and adventurous knight. He and his lady, Fraelissa, were riding together when they met another knight and his lady. The stranger brags that his lady, who is in fact Duessa, is the most beautiful of all women, and Fradubio stands up for Fraelissa. The two knights battle furiously for the honor of their ladies, the stranger knight is killed, and Fradubio wins the apparently beautiful Duessa as his prize. By means of black magic, Duessa makes Fraelissa appear ugly and deformed to Fradubio. Thus deceived, the knight rejects Fraelissa, deserts her, and takes Duessa as his new love. The two travel together for a long time, Fradubio perfectly happy with his new mistress, until by chance he sees Duessa bathing herself in secret. He then sees, instead of the beautiful woman for whom he had deserted Fraelissa, a repulsive old witch. Frightened, the knight resolves to slip away from the old hag at the first opportunity, but Duessa senses the change in her former lover and casts a spell on him. Then she brings him to the desolate spot where Red Cross and his lady have found him and changes him and Fraelissa into trees. Red Cross, all sympathy, asks how long the two lovers must remain imprisoned in the trees and is told that they will escape only when they are bathed in a "living well." The false Fidessa faints as if in terror during Fradubio's tale, and is revived by the kisses of her knight.

This episode is a masterpiece of irony. It is a measure of the success of Archimago's scheme to separate Red Cross from truth, a measure of the depth of the knight's bondage to false religion, for in Fradubio's story, Red Cross hears a summary of his own situation. A victim of a diabolical piece of witchcraft, Fradubio (doubt) was made to reject the beautiful Fraelissa as ugly, only to accept as beautiful a repulsive old hag. Similarly, by means of Archimago's black magic, Red Cross has been made to reject true religion, Una, as false and immoral, only to run into the arms of the Whore of Babylon, the essence of worldly corruption. He listens to Fradubio's tale, but he is too far gone in faithlessness to hear himself being described. The fate of Fradubio should have been a warning and a prophecy to him. As Fradubio and Fraelissa are imprisoned in the trees and as Una's parents are held prisoner by the dragon, so Red Cross, having fallen away from true religion, will be imprisoned in the castle of Orgoglio. Because Red Cross represents man, he will experience the fall and the subsequent bondage to falsehood and sin that are the legacy of the first man, Adam. But Red Cross is more than fallen man, the old Adam. He is also a Christian, and the "living well" of grace which will release Fradubio and his beloved will also free him (Canto xi). As a type of Christ, the new Adam, the Red Cross Knight in releasing Una's parents will free all men. Thus Fradubio's tale is not only an ironic commentary on fallen man's tragic situation, but also a prophecy of his salvation through the grace of Christ.

iii: The Trials of Una—the Lion, Kirkrapine, Sansloy

In the meantime, Una, totally ignorant of the successful deceptions of her demonic host, awakens to find herself deserted by Red Cross. Desperately she searches through desert and wilderness for her champion, until one day, weary and despondent, she lies down in the grassy shade of the forest to rest, putting aside her veil and revealing the heavenly brightness of her face. Suddenly a raging lion comes crashing through the forest looking for prey and sees the helpless virgin; but as he draws nearer, his hungry rage changes to worship and he lovingly licks Una's hands and feet. Frightened at first, Una soon recognizes the great beast's gentleness, and she leaves the forest followed by her new protector. Continuing her search, Una meets a maiden carrying a pot of water on her shoulder and asks her if there is a dwelling nearby. The girl, Abessa, struck dumb by Una's beauty and terrified by the fierce lion, throws down her burden and runs home, where her blind mother, Corceca, sits in eternal darkness. The two frightened women bar the door and withdraw shivering into the darkest corner of the cottage. Soon afterward, Una and the lion arrive. When they are refused shelter, the lion bursts through the door. After some time the gentle Una is able to convince Corceca that she means no harm, and as the night draws on, they all lie down to sleep. But in the middle of the night there is a loud banging at the door, and a voice outside curses and demands immediate entrance. The voice belongs to Kirkrapine, the lover of Abessa, a thief who robs churches and brings all of the stolen wealth to his mistress. Enraged not to find his usual ready welcome, he bursts open the door only to be met by the lion, who quickly tears him to pieces. When Una leaves the next morning to resume her search, Abessa and Corceca, who have been afraid to say anything, bemoan the death of their only support and run after Una cursing her vilely and praying that she may suffer forever. At this point a knight appears dressed in armor bearing red crosses on the breast and shield. He asks Corceca whether she has seen Una. After listening to the blind old hag's grievances, the knight, really the disguised Archimago, rides off after his hated enemy but keeps his distance when he sees the lion. Una, however, sees the knight and rides to greet him, thinking of course that she has found her champion. Archimago makes plausible excuses for having left his lady and there is a joyous reunion, interrupted almost immediately by a fierce knight bearing the name "Sansloy" on his shield. The cruel Sansloy immediately attacks the false Red Cross, who, he thinks, is the slayer of his brother, Sansfoy. He quickly wounds Archimago and knocks him off his horse. Deaf to Una's plea for mercy, Sansloy unlaces his enemy's helmet in order to kill him, only to discover that his supposed enemy is in fact Archimago, his friend and ally. Leaving Archimago unconscious on the ground, Sansloy turns in fierce lust to Una and pulls her off her mount. The lion then attacks Sansloy, who kills the beast and rides away with Una.

This canto is the first of three episodes in an allegory of the fate of the true church on earth when it is deserted by Christians of weak faith. Una's story since the captivity of her parents, Adam and Eve, has been a tale of wandering and sorrow. As the Elizabethan bishop John Jewel puts it,

> It hath been an old complaint, even from the first time of the patriarchs and prophets, and confirmed by the writings and testimonies of every age, that the truth wandereth here and there as a stranger in the world and doth readily find enemies and slanderers amongst those that know her not.[10]

In her wandering Una is a type of the woman of the book of Revelation who fled into the wilderness from the great dragon (12:1–6, 13–16). Renaissance and earlier commentators identified the woman as the true church; Protestants identified her as the reformed church. This first episode deals primarily with the dangers the church and true religion are subject to; later episodes deal more with the support which true religion finds in a fallen and unchristian world. In this canto the only support for true religion is the lion. He represents nature generally. The point seems to be that truth, even though obscured by evil and deserted by men, manifests itself clearly in nature (the lion), which conforms of necessity to its law. To Spenser's readers the fact that Una is befriended by the lion was a demonstration that the truths of the Christian religion are inherent in all of creation. The lion, king of beasts, was one of a number of conventional symbols or types of God, the ultimate protector of truth and the church. Thus, when the human imitators of Christ (Red Cross) desert true religion, it is only right that nature come to her aid. The lion's protection of Una is also a variant of the traditional indictment of man (Red Cross), who falls away from the truth of reason and revelation, whereas the lower creatures conform exactly to the same truth, as it is manifested in nature.

Abessa, as her name (abbess) suggests, represents the monastic orders. All of the Protestant churches of the sixteenth century were violently opposed to the monastic ideal of Roman Catholicism, and two of the charges most often made against the monastic orders by the reformers were that they were havens of ignorance and of irregular sexual practices. Abessa's name (Latin *ab esse*) also suggests spiritual poverty and perversion. Abessa's mother is Corceca—blind heart. The name probably comes from Ephesians 4:17–19:

> Henceforth walk not as Gentiles walk, in the vanity of their mind, having the understanding darkened, being alienated from the life of God through the ignorance that is in them, because of the blindness of their heart: who being past feeling have given themselves over unto lasciviousness, to work all uncleanness with greediness.

[10] *An Apology of the Church of England*, ed. J. E. Booty, Cornell University Press, for the Folger Shakespeare Library 1963, p. 7.

Corceca, the blind substitution of superstition for true religion, is motivated by fear rather than faith. She is the natural cause of the ignorance and immorality of the monastic orders. Kirkrapine, Abessa's lover, is a type of greediness (see the quotation from Ephesians above). His name means literally, "church robbery." Through such greediness the wealth of the true church, which should go to charity and to the maintenance of a vigorous preaching clergy, is taken to support the ignorance and immorality of the monastic orders. Criticism of the abuses of monasticism, particularly of the mendicant orders, was prevalent all through the late medieval period, as witness *The Romance of the Rose* (twelfth century) and *Piers Plowman* (fourteenth century). It was naturally accelerated during the Reformation. The allegorical import of the Abessa, Corceca, Kirkrapine episode is that, deserted by faithful Christians, true religion can find shelter only among her enemies, superstition and greed; or, to put the same point another way, that when the true church is deserted by Christians it is corrupted by ignorance and greed. On the historical level, Kirkrapine probably represents the Roman Catholic hierarchy of the sixteenth and earlier centuries, especially the popes, who supported the monastic orders, often against the opposition of the regular clergy. Kirkrapine's death in the claws of the lion represents Henry VIII's break with Rome and the subsequent dissolution of the monastic orders in England. The lion was, of course, a conventional symbol of royalty. The lion's defeat of greed (Kirkrapine) is, on the most general level of allegory, a type of Christ's casting the money changers out of the temple (Matthew 21:12).

In the general allegory, the false Red Cross, Archimago, continues to represent hypocrisy. When the true Christians withdraw their support from true religion, only hypocrites are left. Thus Archimago in the disguise of Red Cross is a natural result of the true Red Cross's defection to Duessa, false religion. But the attack by Sansloy is even more naturally and necessarily a result of Red Cross's faithless desertion. Sansloy, lawlessness, represents a demonic opposition to law in all aspects of the creation. Spenser and his readers saw the whole creation as an ordered world, a world established by divine law and upheld by that law. This law was manifest in the hierarchal structure of the universe, each element of the hierarchy occupying a position assigned to it by divine law. The most general hierarchy was: mineral, vegetable, animal, human, angelic, divine (God, the creator of the hierarchy). Within this general structure there were many lesser hierarchies. Among men there were the political hierarchy of king, noble, knight, citizen, peasant; and the family hierarchy of husband, wife, child. The elements within each hierarchy were ordered according to a principle of inherent superiority both of function and power. All the hierarchies were analogous to each other and to the great hierarchy of the creator; thus the diamond, the lion, the father, the king, the bishop, and God were analogous. All spheres of creation except man and the angels were absolutely subservient to the divine law; it bound them to their proper places within the great hierarchy. But men and angels, created with free will, are able to revolt against the divine law inherent in the hierarchies, and thus against truth and the will of God. Satan and his angelic supporters fell from heaven because they did revolt, and as one result, Adam turned in rebellion against divine law and fell. Insofar as Red Cross represents Adam, and Una true religion, Sansloy is the natural result of Red Cross's fall, his desertion of Una. Sansloy is the enemy of all law, but particularly of the new law of love and mercy revealed by the New Testament, for it transcends all other forms of law. This explains his particular hatred of the cross on the false Red Cross's armor, for he is Red Cross's natural enemy as well as Una's. Indeed, he is the overtly hostile manifestation of Red Cross's self-deceived allegiance to sin, Duessa. The irony of Sansloy's attack on and defeat of Archimago is delightful and just. The cunning of evil ends in self-defeat; the devil is an ass; and since lawlessness arises from ignorance of truth it is aroused to hatred by the mere appearance of true faith. The false Red Cross is absolutely helpless against lawlessness because Satan's hypocrisy is the ally of all rebellion against divine law: hypocrites can only pose as protectors of true religion, they cannot really protect her. On the other hand, neither is the law of nature alone sufficient to protect true religion, for the truth of Christianity is not based solely upon the law of nature. It is based also upon revealed law, the word of God. And the protection of true religion requires men whose faith in the revealed law is strong. Ultimately it will require Christ, whose faith is so strong that he will die for his church and for the law of the New Testament. Sansloy's defeat of the lion looks forward to the time when Red Cross, having lost his desire for truth, will become like an animal, unable to defend himself against lawlessness (Canto vii). It is possible that in the death of the lion Spenser means to suggest that the English church of the reigns of Henry VIII and Edward VI was protected primarily by the temporal power of the crown (the lion) and was adhered to primarily by hypocritical Roman Catholics (the false Red Cross). The criticism is that the early English reformed church was unsuccessful because it was based on temporal power rather than on faith and was undermined from within by Roman Catholics, who returned to the Roman church (Duessa) during the reign of Mary Tudor.

iv–v: The House of Pride and Sansjoy

Red Cross and Duessa continue their travels until they come to a beautiful palace topped by many lofty towers and surrounded by a wall of golden foil. Duessa instructs Red Cross to take the broad highway leading to the palace, and they soon arrive at the ostentatiously sumptuous reception hall of the castle, where they are welcomed by Lucifera, the proud queen of the palace, and her crowd of vain, primping courtiers. Lucifera, the daughter of Pluto and Proserpina, is not really a legitimate ruler; she and her six counselors rule by schemes and force rather than by law. But she is so proud that she rejects her true parents and claims instead to be the daughter of Jove. Duessa is received warmly by the court, for she is well known there. But Red Cross feels slighted by the proud Lucifera. Suddenly the queen calls for her glittering carriage, and she and her six counselors, all riding beasts appropriate to their characters, lead out a fantastic pageant, with Satan riding the shaft of Lucifera's coach. The court moves out into the open fields beyond the palace, followed by a shouting holiday mob. Duessa joins the procession, but Red Cross, feeling that such conduct is not fitting for a brave knight, stays behind. Almost immediately after Lucifera and her court return to the palace from their outing, a strange knight, bearing the name *Sansjoy*, appears. Sansjoy sees the shield of his dead brother, Sansfoy, in the hands of Red Cross's companion, the dwarf. In a fury, he snatches the shield away. At once, Red Cross attacks and retrieves his trophy, and then a savage battle between the two knights begins. Lucifera, outraged by the uncourtly behavior of the knights, commands them to stop. She then arranges for them to settle their differences the next day in a formal tournament. During the night Duessa, Sansfoy's former mistress, goes secretly to Sansjoy's apartment and offers her love to him. Morning comes and the tournament begins. The fighting is furious on both sides until Sansjoy, enraged by the sight of his dead brother's shield, strikes Red Cross a blow on the helmet which sends him reeling almost to his knees. At that point Duessa shouts words of encouragement to Sansjoy. Red Cross, thinking the false Fidessa's encouragement is meant for him, regains the faith and strength that he had nearly lost and strikes Sansjoy such a terrible blow that he is forced to his knees. However, just as Red Cross is preparing to dispatch his enemy with a second stroke, a magical cloud covers Sansjoy, leaving Red Cross bewildered. Duessa rushes up to Red Cross and congratulates him on his victory. Then the procession starts back to the palace, where the victorious knight is placed in the care of skillful doctors who dress his wounds, as Duessa watches tearfully by his bedside. But as night falls, the false Fidessa slips away to find the wounded Sansjoy, still unconscious and now almost dead. Quickly she hurries off to find Night, the mother of all evil and grandmother of Sansjoy. When finally she does find the terrible goddess, she pleads with her to help her dying grandson, and the two of them ride off in Night's iron chariot to find the wounded Sansjoy. They lift him into the chariot, and then Night begins a journey which ends in the depths of hell at the cave of the famous physician, Aesculapius, who has been cast into hell by Jove because of his miraculous cure of the torn body of Hippolytus. Night threatens the great doctor with eternal tortures when at first he refuses to treat Sansjoy, and he finally agrees to cure the pagan knight. Then Night and Duessa return to the world and Duessa goes back to the castle and to the recuperating Red Cross. But when she arrives, she learns that her knight, his wounds still unhealed, has suddenly and secretly left the palace.

While Red Cross was recovering and Duessa was on her infernal mission, the dwarf had begun scouting the palace and had found a huge dungeon packed to overflowing with miserable people. Inquiring of some of the prisoners the cause of their captivity, he learned that it was the law of Lucifera's realm that all who lived the life of her court, a life of pride, greed, and luxury, were eventually condemned eternally to her dungeon. When the dwarf reported his horrible discovery to Red Cross, the knight got up from his bed and, with the dwarf, left by a secret back passage.

Lucifera's palace, the House of Pride, is St. Augustine's City of Man as opposed to the City of God. It is the world of fallen man, where everything is vanity, and it can be identified with other cities of this world, primarily Babylon, but also Egypt and Rome, all havens of human pride and corruption and all punished by the wrath of God. The hidden dungeon in the palace is a type of damnation, the necessary result of the life of sin which Lucifera's subjects lead. Lucifera herself represents the chief of the seven deadly sins, pride. She is perhaps the daughter of Lucifer, the angel who led the revolt against God in heaven, was cast into hell, and became Satan. (Pluto, the classical king of Hades, was commonly treated as a type of Satan in medieval and renaissance mythography.) Lucifera's counselors are the deadly sins. She is their queen because, as Chaucer writes, "At the root of these seven sins is pride, the general root of all evils; for from this root spring certain branches, such as ire, envy, . . . sloth, avarice, . . . gluttony, lechery. . . ." [11] The fact that Lucifera and her counselors rule the palace by force and fraud rather than by law shows that they and the palace, the life they represent, are another aspect of the same lawlessness which attacks Una in the person of Sansloy.

Having deserted true religion and, self-deceived, fallen into the hands of false religion, Red Cross naturally falls into a life of vanity and pride, the inevitable end of which is damnation. His reaction to Lucifera and her court is complex. He sees the empty vanity all about him and, in part, rejects it. But at the same time he feels hurt by the cool reception of Lucifera. He is himself guilty of pride and vanity. Later, Red Cross falls in with Lucifera's plan to turn his bitter fight with Sansjoy into an entertainment for her court, and, after defeating his enemy, he kneels and offers his service to her. He thus becomes a willing participant in the empty pride of Lucifera's court, falling into the lawlessness of the sins represented by Lucifera's beastly counselors. Having espoused false religion mistakenly, Red Cross is bound to end in the House of Pride, for Duessa is simply returning to her home. In the general allegory, Sansjoy's attack on Red Cross is also a natural result of his desertion of Una and his new alliance with Duessa. Sansjoy represents a state akin to despair. The meaningless pride and vanity of Lucifera and her court, which Red Cross perceives perfectly well, leads the knight to question the meaning of his own life. Thus Red Cross's rejection of the vain show of the City of Man ironically lays him open to the attack of Sansjoy, much as his rejection of the false Una made him vulnerable to the attack of Sansfoy. For the man who is separated from the true church, false religion and the vain pomp and pleasure of the world lead ultimately to despair. Ironically too, Red Cross is saved by his faith in the false Fidessa. His faith is real, but its object is not. Finally he is saved from the utter damnation which awaits him by common sense (the dwarf), which simply as the result of experience and observation can see the inevitable tragedy of life in the cities of men. For, like the hideous tail of the monster Error and the disgusting nether parts of Duessa, the House of Pride is a hell underneath.

The allegorical point of the descent of Duessa and Night into hell to save Sansjoy is obscure. Certainly the episode emphasizes the demonic origin of Duessa, Sansjoy, and Red Cross's other enemies. More important, the entire episode is meant to contrast in detail with the ascent of Una and Red Cross into the House of Holiness, where the nearly dead Red Cross is brought back to health by skilled physicians (Canto x).

[11] *Parson's Tale,* I.386.

vi: Una and the Satyrs

After Sansloy has defeated the false Red Cross, he rides away with Una into a wild forest. Full of lustful desire, he attempts to seduce his captive. But when Una resists his advances firmly, the pagan knight tears her veil away roughly, revealing the shining beauty of Una's face. Enflamed with even greater lust at the sight of such beauty, Sansloy then tries to rape the helpless maiden, who cries out desperately. Deep in the forest, a group of dancing fauns and satyrs hear her shrieks and run to find out what the trouble is. When Sansloy sees the strange creatures approaching, he leaves Una behind and rides swiftly away. But if Una is relieved by her deliverance from Sansloy, she is terrified by the savage creatures who stand around her amazed by her beauty. The stayrs see her terror and by smiles and humble behavior manage to convey their friendliness and admiration. Eventually Una's fears are calmed and the satyrs crown her with an olive garland and lead her into the forest, singing and shouting as they go. Arriving in the heart of the forest, Una is met by old Sylvanus, who is reminded by her dazzling beauty of former loves and welcomes her cordially. Thus surrounded by worshipping crowds, Una decides to stay with the savage nation to rest herself awhile. She spends her time trying to teach the rough satyrs the truth, but instead of learning, they make an idol of Una and worship that instead of truth. And when Una tries to restrain their idolatry of her, they turn instead to the worship of her ass. While Una is with the satyrs, a knight arrives in the forest. Famous in many lands for his warlike deeds, he is the noble Satyrane, son of a human mother and a satyr. Brought up in the forest by his father, even as a child Satyrane was absolutely fearless and could conquer the boldest beast with his bare hands. When he reached manhood and had conquered every beast in the forest, the heroic youth desired to make himself known in the outside world, where he had accomplished many noble feats. But periodically, Satyrane returned to the forest and to his satyr kinsmen, and it is on one of these visits that he meets Una. He is immediately conquered by her sweetness and wisdom and, at the same time, disturbed by her sadness. After some time Una secretly tells the satyr knight her history and reveals her desire to leave the satyrs and continue her search for the Red Cross Knight. And so on a day when all of the satyrs are offering feudal service to old Sylvanus, Una and her new champion steal out of the forest together. They soon meet a poor pilgrim, and when Una asks whether he has seen Red Cross, he reports that he has just that day seen him killed in a furious battle with another knight. While Una stands crushed and incredulous, Satyrane asks the poor pilgrim where Red Cross's killer can be found and is told that he is at a nearby fountain washing his wounds. Satyrane spurs off to find the stranger knight, Una following slowly and sadly. He arrives at the fountain to find Sansloy resting. The two knights then join battle furiously, while Una, recognizing Sansloy, rides terrified away from the scene. The pilgrim, who is in fact Archimago, watches the battle in secret, sees Una flee, and pursues her.

First, it should be said that this episode, one of the most attractive in *The Faerie Queene*, requires a great deal more scholarly research. Its allgeorical meanings are presently obscure. In the most general allegory perhaps some such meaning as the following is intended: With the fall of Adam (Red Cross) true religion is left without any support or witness except the manifestation of divine law in nature itself (the lion); then she finds the enthusiastic but idolatrous support of savage peoples. Perhaps the satyrs represent the ancient cultures of Egypt, Greece, and Rome, which in their myths and religions approached the truths of religion darkly. It was a commonplace among renaissance thinkers that the myths of Greece and Rome concealed philosophical and theological truths, a commonplace indeed of late medieval thought also. (The idea that the hieroglyphs and mythological images of ancient Egypt were symbols of religious truths was a more esoteric notion of the Renaissance.) The fact that the satyrs turn from idolatry of Una to worship of the ass suggests the animal worship of ancient Hebrew, Egyptian, and Babylonian cultures. If the satyrs represent the mythological and idolatrous stages of ancient pre-Christian cultures, Satyrane, heroic man, most probably represents the philosophical era, the age of Plato and Aristotle in Greece, of Cicero and Seneca in Rome. The philosophers, like Satyrane, come out of the ancient cultures dominated by myths and idols (the satyrs), but they got even nearer the truths of Christianity. It is relevant to remember the heavy debt which Christian theology owed to Plato, Aristotle, and the Neoplatonists. The entire episode then is part of the general religious allegory, which might be called the "progress of true religion." In this allegory history is seen to be moving closer and closer to religious truth, from the original break with truth in the fall of Adam to the coming of Christ, an event which will be represented in Canto vii by the entrance of Prince Arthur into the story. The idea that history since the fall of man was a progress toward the spiritual perfection of Christ is an ancient idea in Christian theology. The first and one of the greatest proponents of this reading of pre-Christian history was St. Irenaeus.[12] In terms of the hierarchy of creation Spenser represents the progress of true religion by making each of Una's protectors after the desertion of Red Cross superior to the previous one. The lion is nonhuman nature, the satyrs are natural man, and Satyrane is heroic man, made more humane by his human mother and his wide travels. All of these harbor some religious truth, and each is therefore capable of offering some protection against lawlessness, sin, and crime. But since none of them is capable of more than a partial expression of true religion, it will take someone more perfect to reunite man (Red Cross) and the true church (Una)—to redeem Una's parents (Adam and Eve).

vii.1–18: Orgoglio and the Fall of the Red Cross Knight

When Duessa returns from Hades to the House of Pride, she finds that Red Cross has left. Setting out immediately in pursuit, she soon discovers him wearily resting beside a shady spring, his armor and weapons laid aside. Half-seriously Duessa accuses the knight of desertion, but the conversation turns to more pleasant subjects as the knight and his lady enjoy the coolness of the shady grove. Unknown to Red Cross, the spring he rests beside has been enchanted by Diana. All who drink from it lose their strength. When the knight drinks, his

---

[12] Jean Daniélou, *From Shadows to Reality*, trans. Walston Hibberd, Burns and Oates, 1960, pp. 30–47.

powers begin to fail imperceptibly and he becomes faint. However, his loss of strength does not prevent him from making love to Duessa, and presently the two are locked in adulterous embrace. Almost immediately a horrible crashing is heard; and as Red Cross leaps up with his sword, before he has time to put on his armor, a terrible giant, Orgoglio, strides toward him, his arm brandishing a huge oak snatched by force out of the earth. Red Cross, frightened by the giant and miserably weakened by the enchantment of the spring, advances on his new enemy with only his sword. Orgoglio aims a crushing blow at the knight, which he barely avoids by leaping aside. But the blow is so powerful that its mere proximity knocks Red Cross to the ground and stuns him. Seeing Red Cross helpless, the giant prepares to crush him with another blow, but Duessa intervenes. She suggests that Orgoglio take the knight captive and make a slave of him. At the same time, she offers herself to the giant as mistress. The giant gladly accepts Duessa's suggestion and takes Red Cross to his castle, where he flings him into a dark dungeon. Duessa is then installed officially as Orgoglio's mistress. Dressed in a royal robe and crowned with a triple crown, she rides upon a hideous seven-headed monster to strike dread into the hearts of men.

Red Cross's fornication with Duessa and his subsequent defeat and imprisonment at the hands of Orgoglio are the nadir of his quest. In these episodes he fulfills completely the tragic destiny implicit in his mistaken desertion of Una in Canto ii. The irony is profound, for in the lustful embrace of Duessa, Red Cross acts out the dreams and apparitions of the false Una which led him to reject true religion as false. He has, in fact, become the wanton young squire whom Archimago placed in the arms of the false Una in order to deceive the knight. Self-deceived, Red Cross in the embrace of the false Fidessa has now almost become, like the wanton squire, an instrument of the devil (Archimago). He is now completely alienated from truth. As champion of the true church (Una) and as imitator of Christ, Red Cross's purpose is to rescue mankind (Una's parents) from the devil (the dragon) and reconcile them with true religion (Una). But success in this quest depends upon Red Cross's ability to defeat the very enemies who are responsible for the captivity of Una's parents. In imitating Christ, the new Adam, he must defeat the enemies of the old Adam. In Christian tradition these enemies are the world, the flesh, and the devil. Red Cross's desertion of Una and his alliance with Duessa have led him to the House of Pride, where he barely escapes destruction by the vanity of the world. Rejecting the temptations of the world, the knight immediately falls prey to the temptations of the flesh. His idleness at the enchanted spring, his loss of strength on drinking from it, and above all, his fornication with Duessa, these are the temptations of the flesh: sloth, gluttony, and lust. Ironically Red Cross escapes the vain pride of the world, Lucifera, only to be made the victim of the animal pride of the flesh, Orgoglio. Orgoglio (Italian, "pride") represents the grossest carnality of human nature, man fallen to the state of the animal and in revolt against God and reason. Spenser's description of Orgoglio and of his parentage, Earth and Aeolus, identifies him as one of the Titans, a race of giants who revolted against the Olympian gods. In medieval mythography the Titans, as rebels, are types of Satan, who revolted against God. They are also identified with earthquakes, volcanic eruptions, and other natural disorders—violations of the law of nature. Red Cross falls into the hands of Satan through the natural disorder of lust. His feeble opposition to Orgoglio inevitably suggests David's heroic victory over Goliath, which is a conventional type of Christ's victory over Satan. The contrast between David and Red Cross at this point is the measure of Red Cross's failure as a follower of Christ and protector of true religion. The knight's imprisonment in Orgoglio's dungeon represents fallen man's damnation and the dungeon itself, a kind of hell. Here again, considering the purpose of Red Cross's quest—to release Una's parents from captivity to the dragon—Red Cross's imprisonment is heavy with irony. With the victory of fleshly pride over mankind, false religion, Duessa, gains dominion over the world. The source of Spenser's description of Duessa upon the seven-headed monster, cited in introductory notes to Canto ii, is worth quoting again:

> I saw a woman sitting upon a scarlet beast, full of names of blasphemy, having seven heads and ten horns. And the woman was arrayed in purple and scarlet color, and decked with gold and precious stones and pearls, having a golden cup in her hand full of abominations and filthiness of her fornication: And upon her forehead was a name written, MYSTERY, BABYLON THE GREAT, THE MOTHER OF HARLOTS, AND ABOMINATIONS OF THE EARTH. (Revelation 17:3–5)

Spenser's references to the monster's tail, which reached "to the house of heavenly gods" and brought down "the ever-burning lamps from thence," is a clear reference to Revelation 12:3–4:

> And there appeared another wonder in heaven; and behold a great red dragon, having seven heads and ten horns, and seven crowns upon his heads. And his tail drew the third part of the stars of heaven, and did cast them to the earth. . . .

This passage was generally interpreted as a reference to Satan, who, as Lucifer, revolted against God, and with a third of the angels of heaven, was cast into hell. Thus the monster, like Orgoglio, is a type of Satan. Spenser's comparison of Duessa's beast with the Lernian Hydra is a suggestive one. The Hydra was a nine-headed monster that Hercules killed as one of his twelve labors. In late medieval and renaissance mythography, Hercules was often treated as a type of Christ and his labors as types of Christ's victory over sin and the devil. Thus the reference to Hercules' victory over the Hydra brings to mind Christ's victory over Satan, just at the point when Red Cross's (mankind's) plight seems most hopeless. It foreshadows Arthur's rescue of Red Cross and Red Cross's final victory over the dragon.

vii.19–viii: Prince Arthur and the Rescue of the Red Cross Knight

When the dwarf sees Red Cross made captive by Orgoglio, he takes up the knight's armor and weapons sadly and goes in search of help. Shortly he meets Una, who is fleeing while Sansloy is held at bay by Satyrane. Seeing the sadness of her dwarf and recognizing the armor of Red Cross, Una falls to the ground in a faint, and when the dwarf revives her and tells her of the knight's captivity, she complains bitterly against her fate. Then, her outburst of grief over, she resolves to find her champion dead or alive, and sets out again with her dwarf. After long travels she meets a splendid knight, all dressed in glittering armor. The knight, who is in fact Prince Arthur, carries a marvelous shield of solid diamond fashioned for him by Merlin, the great wizard. No weapon can pierce this shield, nor can it be affected by magic of any kind. Its dazzling light has the power to destroy illusions and false appearances; it can turn men to stone and terrify huge monsters. Because of its terrible powers, Arthur keeps it covered with a veil. When he first sees Una, Arthur immediately senses that she is concealing some deep sorrow, and he gently and courteously coaxes her to pour out her grief to him. Finally, Una tells the prince the story of Red Cross— the beginning of the quest, Archimago's treachery, Duessa's subtle betrayal, and Orgoglio's easy victory. Arthur hears the sad history to the end and then promises Una that he will rescue her imprisoned knight.

The dwarf leads Arthur, his squire, and Una to Orgoglio's castle. Arthur's squire takes from his side a marvelous horn, proof against any enchantment and able to burst open the strongest locks, and with a thunderous blast the doors of Orgoglio's castle fly open. The giant, followed by Duessa upon the many-headed beast, rushes out to see who has challenged him with such a terrifying sound. When he sees Prince Arthur standing armed and ready for combat, he charges furiously, his huge knotty club raised to strike. But Arthur is too quick. He lightly dodges Orgoglio's murderous club, which plows deep into the earth. Then, while the giant tries to retrieve his weapon, the prince strikes off his left arm. At this point Duessa and her monstrous beast move to help the giant, but Arthur's squire keeps them at bay. Finally Duessa sprinkles the contents of her poisonous cup upon the squire, who immediately becomes weak and afraid and finally faints, whereupon the beast fastens its claws about the squire's neck and begins to crush out his life. But Arthur, seeing his brave squire's plight, turns from Orgoglio and attacks the beast. He strikes so furiously that he splits one of the beast's heads. In the meantime, Orgoglio has recovered his club and, en-raged by his terrible wound, aims a blow at Arthur so powerful that it strikes his shield and knocks him to the ground. As Arthur falls, however, the veil which covers his shield is parted and Orgoglio, who is poised for the death stroke, is made helpless by the dazzling brightness of the shield. At the same time, the many-headed beast upon which Duessa rides is struck blind by the light and falls to the ground as if dead. Duessa desperately calls to Orgoglio for help, but he has not even the strength to lift his weapon. Arthur leaps up and strikes off Orgoglio's leg so that he falls to the earth; then he beheads the giant. As soon as the breath has left the giant, his huge body dwindles away until only an empty bladder is left. When Duessa sees the fall of her protector she throws her cup and her crown away and attempts to escape, but Arthur's squire captures her. Una, who has been looking on from a distance, rushes to thank the prince for his victory over her enemies.

Leaving the captive Duessa with his squire, Arthur enters the castle to find and release Red Cross. At first the castle seems to be completely empty, but finally a blind old man comes creeping slowly toward Arthur, supporting his feeble steps with a staff. The old man carries a rusty bunch of keys on his arm and as he walks toward the prince his head is turned away in the opposite direction. Arthur asks the old man, Ignaro, where the people of the castle are and where Red Cross can be found, but Ignaro answers all questions with "I don't know." After several futile attempts to get information from the senile keeper, Arthur takes the bunch of keys from his arm and begins to open all the doors of the castle. In the richly furnished chamber there is an altar of stone on which the blood of holy martyrs has been often spilt, and the spirits of these saints cry out continually for God's vengeance on their cruel enemy. Arthur searches all of the rooms for Red Cross, but finds no trace until he comes to an iron door with a small grate in it. Calling through the grate, the prince hears in return a low mournful voice welcoming death and despairing of life. He quickly breaks open the door and finds in the deep dungeon below the emaciated body of the Red Cross Knight. Gently he lifts Red Cross from his filthy prison and brings him to Una, who greets him joyously, though saddened by his decayed condition. Arthur then turns to the captive Duessa and asks Red Cross to pass sentence on her. Una advises that she be stripped of her scarlet robe and released. When her finery is taken from her, Duessa appears in her true character, a filthy, toothless, bald, diseased hag. As the knights stand amazed at the horrible transformation of Duessa, she runs off into the wilderness to hide her repulsive nakedness in rocks and caves. The knights and Una then enter the deserted castle to rest themselves for a while.

This episode, the center of the narrative structure of Book I, is the climax of the allegorical structure as well. For with the entrance of Arthur into the story both Red Cross's tragedy of error and Una's anxious wandering come to an end. The two are reunited and proceed to the successful accomplishment of the quest which Red Cross originally set out upon. Whether Red Cross's adventures are considered an allegory of human history, of the Christian church, of the reformed Church of England, or of the salvation of the individual Christian, Arthur's exploits in this episode are types of Christ and his redemption of man. Just when mankind's plight seems most helpless, when he appears forever doomed to the eternal bondage of Satan and his own pride, Christ enters history and, through his death on the cross, defeats Satan, destroys man's bondage to the rebellious pride of Adam (Orgoglio), rescues him from eternal damnation, and reunites him with true religion.

Just as history is redeemed by Christ, so the individual Christian, a little world to himself, rehearses the history of the world in his quest for salvation. As a child of Adam, the Christian, seeking to deliver himself from captivity to Satan and the sins of the world, falls away from the true church, loses his faith and becomes a lover of the false religion of the world. The Elizabethan bishop John Jewell, speaking for the Church of England, wrote:

> We say . . . that every person is born in sin, and leadeth his life in sin; that nobody is able truly to say his heart is clean . . . that the law of God is perfect and requireth of us perfect . . . obedience; that we are able by no means to fulfill that law in this worldly life; and therefore that our only succor and refuge is to fly to the mercy of our Father by Jesus Christ, and

assuredly to persuade our minds that he is the obtainer of forgiveness for
our sins, and that by his blood all our spots of sin be washed clean. . . .
(*Apology*, p. 38)

The Christian is saved, not by his own efforts, but by the love of Christ, who in
his death on the cross defeats man's enemies and takes upon himself the punish-
ment for sin, and thus frees the sinner from damnation to new life.

Both of these interpretations of this episode would have been apparent to
Spenser's Elizabethan readers. But as Protestants in a largely Roman Catholic
and hostile world; as Englishmen at war with Spain, the great Roman Catholic
power of Europe; and as men who had only recently passed through the per-
secutions of the Roman Catholic reign of Mary Tudor (1553–1558), they would
have seen Arthur's rescue of Red Cross as an allegory of the Reformation, the
salvation of England from the worldly corruption of the Roman church, and
its restoration of the true church of primitive Christianity.

As Arthur approaches Orgoglio's castle his squire blows a blast on his horn
which bursts open the doors of the building. Very likely the horn represents the
preaching of the gospel, which delivered mankind from the false religion of the
synagogue, and the squire a type of John the Baptist, who announced the
coming of Christ. In the allegory of the Reformation the blast on Arthur's horn
probably represents the great emphasis placed on reading and preaching from
the Bible in all of the reformed churches. Bishop Jewell is typical in the following
accusation against the Roman Catholic church:

> I wot not how, whether it be for fear, or for conscience, or despairing of
> victory . . . these men always abhor and fly the word of God, even as the
> thief fleeth the gallows. . . . Therefore the holy scriptures, which our
> Saviour Jesus Christ did not only use for authority in all his speech, but
> did also at last seal up the same with his own blood, these men, to the
> intent they might with less business drive the people from the same . . .
> have used to call them a bare letter, uncertain. . . . (*Apology*, pp. 76–77)

Protestants believed that "the same word which was opened by Christ, and
spread abroad by the apostles, is sufficient, both our salvation and all truth to
uphold" (*Apology*, p. 42). To them the Roman church's unwillingness to make
the Bible generally available and its emphasis on theological tradition amounted
to a denial of the means of salvation to men. It kept man locked in Orgoglio's
castle.

In his battle with Orgoglio, before he finally destroys the giant, Arthur is
knocked to the ground by a blow from the giant's club; at the same time the
veil which covers Arthur's shield opens and the dazzling light paralyzes
Orgoglio and casts the seven-headed beast to the ground. Arthur's fall to the
ground undoubtedly is an allegory of the crucifixion of Christ, and the blinding
light of his shield represents the effects of the crucifixion, the outpouring of
grace into the world. In his death Christ not only saves man from damnation
but also triumphs over man's enemies. Arthur's shield should be compared
both to Red Cross's shield and to the unveiled face of Una. Its brightness is the
source of whatever light they possess. Arthur's wounding one of the heads of
Duessa's beast, taken from Revelation 13:3, is probably another type of the

crucifixion. The wounded beast of Revelation fulfills God's curse placed upon Satan when he tempted Eve in the shape of the serpent: "I will put enmity between thee and the woman, and between thy seed and her seed; it shall bruise thy head . . ." (*Genesis* 3:15). Christ is the seed of Eve who in his death wounds the head of the serpent. Commentators in all ages generally identified the beast of Revelation as Satan or the antichrist, but they often added more narrow contemporary interpretations to the chief one. Thus the Elizabethan bishop John Bale identifies this beast as antichrist, the visible manifestation of Satan's power in the world "comprehending in him all the wickedness, fury, falsehood, frowardness, deceit, lies, crafts, slights, subtilties, hypocrisy, tyranny, mischiefs, pride, and all other devilishness, of all his malicious members which have been since the beginning." [13] To this traditional interpretation he adds the identification of the beast with the pope, and writes of the wounded head,

> What should ail this wounded head here, not to signify his supremacy suppressed, his usurped authority and power diminished, and his whole prodigious occupying condemned in this latter age of the church . . . ? Are not now in many parts of Germany, and in England also, the pope's pardons laid aside; his power put down, his name abolished, his purgatory, pilgrimages . . . utterly exiled. . . . (*Select Works*, p. 426)

Bale's allegory of the triumph of Protestantism over the corruption of the pope and the Roman church is a common one in Elizabethan commentaries on Revelation. The bloody mouths of Duessa's beast are taken from Revelation 17:6, where the Whore of Babylon is described as "drunken with the blood of the saints, and with the blood of the martyrs." Spenser probably transfers the blood-thirstiness of the woman to the seven-headed beast in order to avoid destroying Duessa's mask of the beautiful voluptuous woman, though, when the time comes, that mask is stripped completely off. At any rate, the verse from Revelation makes clear how the bloody mouths of the beast are to be interpreted. Protestant commentators often identified the blood of the saints and martyrs of this verse as the persecution of the reformers by the Roman church and the Inquisition. Spenser's readers were likely to associate the bloody mouths of the beast with the persecution of Protestants in Mary Tudor's reign.

Duessa's magic cup is taken from Revelation 17:4, where the Whore of Babylon is described as "having a golden cup in her hand full of abominations and filthiness of her fornications." Again Bishop Bale interprets:

> This cup is the false religion that she [the Roman church] daily ministereth, besides the chalice [communion cup] whom her merchants most damnably abuse; and it containeth all doctrine of devils, all beastly errors and lies, all deceitful power . . . all prodigious kinds of idolatry, fornication. . . . Outwardly it seemeth gold, pretending the glory of God, the holy name of Christ, the sacred scriptures of the Bible . . . and all are but counterfeit colors and shadows of hypocrisy. (*Select Works*, p. 497)

All of the reformed churches attacked the Roman Catholic theology of Holy Communion, in particular the doctrine of transubstantiation and the doctrine

[13] *Select Works of John Bale, D.D.*, ed. Rev. Henry Christmas, Parker Society, 1848, p. 420.

of the reservation of the Communion wine to the clergy. The effect of Duessa's cup on Arthur's squire illustrates what Protestants considered the destructive effect of the Roman Catholic Communion.

Arthur's entrance into the castle of Orgoglio and his rescue of Red Cross from the dungeon probably represents Christ's harrowing of hell and his deliverance of the seed of Adam from Satan. Ignaro, the old keeper of Orgoglio's castle, is obviously related to Corceca (Canto iii), who is also blind. He seems from certain details to represent a particular kind of ignorance, ignorance of the new law, the law of redemption and mercy. His backward turned face is a common medieval representation of bondage to the old law and the Old Testament. He is the proper keeper of the prison of hell because, under the old law, all men are sinful and thus condemned to death and hell. Without knowing it, he carries the means of releasing the prisoners of hell, for the old law prophesies the coming of Christ and the deliverance of man. But Ignaro, ignorant of the new law, cannot use the keys. It takes Christ himself (Arthur) to open the dungeon. Perhaps also for Spenser's readers, Arthur's taking the keys from Ignaro represented the reformed churches' emphasis on the Bible and preaching, which rescued man from ignorance of the new law. Bishop Jewel writes of the keys of the kingdom of heaven: "We with Chrysostom say they be 'the knowledge of the Scriptures'; with Tertullian we say they be 'the interpretation of the Law'; and with Eusebius we call them 'the word of God' " (*Apology*, p. 27). Arthur's use of the keys to unlock the prison cells of Orgoglio's castle and his rescue of Red Cross suggest Christ's descent into hell after his crucifixion to rescue Adam and his seed.

The rich chamber stained by the blood of children recalls both Pharaoh's order that the new born sons of the Jews be killed, from which Moses is saved (Exodus 1:16–22), and Herod's slaughter of the children in Bethlehem in an attempt to kill Christ (Matthew 2:16). Since both Pharaoh and Herod are conventionally types of Satan, the scene emphasizes Arthur's victory over Orgoglio as a type of Christ's victory over Satan. The altar upon which the martyrs were killed and from which they cry out for vengeance is taken from Revelation 6:9–11. It also establishes Arthur as a type of Christ. To an Elizabethan audience the scene generally would have suggested the Inquisition and the persecution of Protestants under Mary Tudor.

The feeble, wasted Red Cross, rescued by Arthur, is related closely to the great bulk and strength of Orgoglio. Orthodox Christian theology does not consider evil to have any real existence or being. Evil is instead simply the privation of good. The greatest evil is the least good. As St. Augustine puts it, "Even those natures [beings] which are vitiated by an evil will, so far indeed as they are vitiated, are evil, but in so far as they are natures [have existence] they are good" (*City of God*, XII.3, p. 383). Red Cross's shrunken body is his being, deprived by sin. As his body represents the original goodness of his being — "integrity, beauty, welfare, virtue"—diminished by sin, so the brute power of Orgoglio represents the greatness of that depriving sin. Orgoglio is Red Cross's sin at the same time that he is Satan, the least possible good because he is farthest from the absolute being and goodness of God (*City of God*, XII.2, p. 382). It is for this reason that the giant withers to an empty bladder when Arthur kills him. His greatness is the greatness of nonbeing, the absence of goodness.

The stripping of Duessa, which finally reveals the hideousness which she hides under the disguise of Fidessa, is a sign of the restoration of Red Cross's reason. As his reason was clouded through the trickery of Archimago and he became incapable of recognizing truth (Una), so now through the heroism of Arthur he becomes capable of recognizing falsehood (Duessa). False religion is deposed from its place of power and forced to go into hiding.

ix.2–19: Prince Arthur and the Faery Queen

Prince Arthur, Una, and Red Cross rest for a while at the deserted castle of Orgoglio and then begin their journey again. But before Una and Red Cross part from their deliverer, she asks the prince who he is and what land he comes from. Arthur tells her that he is unable to answer her questions. He knows only that when he was an infant he was taken from his mother and placed in the care of Timon, a wise old man who had been a great warrior in his youth. Often Merlin the magician came to oversee the young prince's education, but when Arthur asked Merlin about his parents and his country the wizard would only tell him that he was the son of a king and that all would be made clear in time. Then, after some coaxing, Arthur tells Una about his own quest. Having been brought up by the wise Timon to distrust and condemn love, Arthur had always laughed at lovers and their sorrows. But one day while riding in the fields he had become tired and had lain down to rest. While he slept, a beautiful princess came to him in a vision and lay down beside him. She pleaded with him to love her and promised to show proof of her love at the appropriate time. Before she left she told him she was the Faery Queen. Arthur awoke ravished by his vision, and vowed to search until he found the unknown lady. He tells Una that he has been searching nine months already. After many compliments Una and Red Cross, on the one hand, and Prince Arthur, on the other, prepare to go separate ways. Red Cross and Arthur exchange gifts and Arthur leaves. Una decides that Red Cross is still too weak to travel and they wait awhile before resuming the quest.

This episode is less important to the allegory of Book I than it is to the structure of *The Faerie Queene* generally. Spenser's intention was to have Prince Arthur enter each of the projected twelve books of the poem at a crucial point and to demonstrate the perfection of the virtue which was the subject of that book. Arthur's vision of the Faery Queen provides him with a motive for carrying out Spenser's intention. Arthur's search will be a long one, and he will find his lady only after he has demonstrated his perfection in all of the virtues. The mystery of Prince Arthur's "name and nation" is revealed to him in Book II, Canto x.

ix.21–54: Red Cross in the Cave of Despair

As Una and Red Cross continue their travels they suddenly see a knight riding towards them. The knight appears to be terrified of something. Seeing his blanched face, his hair standing on end, and a rope about his neck, Red Cross rides to the knight to find out who he is and what he is frightened of. The knight, Trevisan, after being assured of his safety by Red Cross, begins to explain his terror. Trevisan had been the companion in arms of another knight, Sir Terwin, who loved a noble lady. The lady, however, did not return his love and, indeed, took pleasure in causing him sorrow and pain. One day Trevisan and the disconsolate Terwin, returning from a visit to the lady, met a villain called Despair, who immediately began to play upon the grief of the two knights. By cunning arguments he persuaded Terwin that his plight was hopeless and that suicide was the only solution. Trevisan, horrified by his friend's desperate act, luckily escaped Despair and was fleeing when Red Cross stopped him. Red Cross, indignant, asks Trevisan to guide him to Despair so that he can confront the criminal. Trevisan agrees to take him but refuses to stay. Before long they come to the dreary cave of Despair, a place scattered with corpses and peopled by wailing ghosts. Entering the cave they find Despair, a melancholy old man whose disordered gray locks cover his face and hide his dull, shrunken eyes. Beside the villain lies the dead body of Terwin, a rusty knife still in his chest. Red Cross, full of angry zeal, resolves to avenge the knight's death and prepares to kill Despair. But the old man stops him, and in a masterful piece of rhetoric, composed of commonplaces from the Old Testament and classical philosophy, persuades Red Cross that death is the only way out of the suffering he has experienced and that his sins are so great that he cannot hope to escape damnation. He argues that longer life would merely increase Red Cross's sin and, thus, his punishment in hell. His resistance sapped by the brilliance of Despair's argument and by his awareness of the sins of his past, the knight is preparing to kill himself when Una enters and stops him. She accuses him bitterly of weakness and sinfulness, and charges him with forgetting his responsibility. Finally she reminds him that God's grace is greater than the knight's sin, that he is chosen by God, and that he has no cause for despair. Then she leads him away from the dismal cave. When Despair sees that he has lost Red Cross, he tries to hang himself, but he cannot die.

The Red Cross Knight's confrontation with Despair represents a false start on the path to repentance and justification. Repentance, and thus rebirth in the image of Christ, begins with the consciousness of sin. For this reason, the beginning of the sinner's conversion is viewed by Christian theology as an especially crucial period. The consciousness of sin may lead either to what the theologian John Calvin calls "legal repentance" or to true repentance. In the first,

> The sinner, wounded by the envenomed dart of sin, and harassed by the fear of divine wrath, is involved in deep distress, without the power of extricating himself. From a knowledge of the greatness of their sins [such men] dreaded the divine wrath, but that considering God only as an avenger and a judge, they perished under that apprehension. Their repentance, therefore, was only, as it were, the ante-chamber of hell. . . .[14]

Calvin advises that

> Some limit must be observed, that we may not be overwhelmed in sorrow [for sin]; for to nothing are terrified consciences more liable than

---

[14] *The Institutes of the Christian Religion*, III.3, trans. John Allen, Wm. B. Eerdmans, 1949, p. 652.

to fall into despair. And with this artifice, also, whomsoever Satan perceives to be dejected by a fear of God, he plunges them further and further into the deep gulf of sorrow, that they may never rise again. (*Institutes,* III.3, p. 666–667)

"Which damnable sin," says Chaucer's Parson about despair, "if that it continue unto his end, it is cleped sinning in the Holy Ghost" (I. 694).

Despair's easy victory over Red Cross shows that the knight's faith is as yet extremely weak. He does not truly repent his sins, but thinks only of God's hatred of sin and of the pains of hell. He demonstrates again that man, without divine grace, is incapable of saving himself. Without grace he merely falls into despair. It takes Una, the true church, to remind man that if his sins are great, God's loving mercy is greater. Having saved the knight from the hell of despair, Una can now bring him into the path of true repentance.

The whole episode is designed to show the terrible weakness of Red Cross's will. Sir Terwin's tragic tale is conventional and even trite—the rejected lover, the cold-hearted lady, despair, and suicide. It is one of the favorite themes of courtly poets in both the Middle Ages and the Renaissance. Red Cross's situation is quite different from Terwin's. Not only is his mistress not cold; she has indeed proved her steadfast love, in spite of his own disloyalty, and it is through her that he lives at all. Thus he does not even have the conventional lover's small reason for despair and self-destruction.

x: Red Cross in the House of Holiness

Una, seeing that Red Cross is too weak to continue his quest, brings the knight to an ancient castle to rest and be cured of his wounds. When they arrive they are courteously received and brought to Caelia, the mistress of the house. Caelia greets Una joyously, recognizing her heavenly origin, and asks why she and the knight are visiting her house. As they converse, two of Caelia's virgin daughters appear arm in arm. Fidelia, the eldest, carries a cup of wine and water with a snake inside and a mysterious book. The other, Speranza, holds a silver anchor on her arm. They greet Una and Red Cross warmly, and when Una asks about the youngest sister, Charissa, they reply that she is recovering from the birth of her latest child and cannot be present. Caelia notices that the two travelers are weary and advises them to go to their rooms and rest. Having rested sufficiently, Una and Red Cross return to Fidelia, whom Una asks to undertake to educate the knight in her divine wisdom. She agrees, and teaches him heavenly doctrines from her sacred book. The knight learns so quickly that soon he feels only contempt for wordly life and deep sorrow for his sins. So much does he hate his wicked life that he wishes to end it. But, at this point, Speranza offers him comfort. Patience, a wise doctor, offers the knight medicines and advice which enable him to endure his agony. But to treat the symptoms of the Red Cross Knight's illness is not enough, and so Patience begins to attack the cause, the inner corruption of sin. He prescribes first a regimen of strict abstinence and continual prayer, and soon the bloated flesh begins to rot away from the patient's body. With the aid of his assistants, Penance, Remorse, and Repentance, every spot of filth is removed from the knight and he is restored to health. Red Cross is then returned to Una, who takes him to see the young matron Charissa, now sufficiently recovered to receive the guests. They find a beautiful young woman, bare to the waist and surrounded by a crowd of infants. Una asks Charissa to instruct Red Cross in her laws, which the matron joyously agrees to do. She teaches him love, righteousness, and good works. Finally she shows him the way to heaven, and appoints an old woman, Mercy, to guide him there. Mercy takes her charge by the hand and guides him up a narrow path to the house of seven holy men, each of whom practices one of the seven works of corporal mercy. Red Cross stays in their house until he becomes expert in each of these acts of charity; then he and his guide continue their journey up a steep mountain, on the top of which is a chapel with a hermit's hut nearby. As they approach the top of the mountain, the old hermit, Contemplation, reluctantly interrupts his religious meditation to inquire of Mercy what she and the knight have made their painful journey for. Mercy tells the old man that Fidelia commands him to show Red Cross the way to heaven. Contemplation agrees and, after Red Cross has spent some time in fasting and praying, takes his guest to the highest point of the mountain. From there he shows a long, narrow path leading to a marvelously beautiful walled city. As Red Cross gazes at the city he can see angels descending into the city from heaven. When the knight asks about the wonderful city, the hermit tells him that it is the New Jerusalem, heavenly dwelling place of the saints. Contemplation then tells Red Cross that after he has finished his obligation to the Faery Queen he will take the path to the heavenly city, where he will live as St. George of England. Full of wonder at this vision of heaven, Red Cross asks to be allowed to stay on the mountain peak or to begin the journey to the New Jerusalem immediately, but Contemplation reminds him of his obligation to Una. The knight then asks the old man why he called him an Englishman when he was known to be a faery knight. Contemplation then tells Red Cross that he is, in fact, the son of English kings, stolen from his crib by faeries and brought up by a plowman. Finally the knight takes his leave of Contemplation and returns to Una. After a short rest the two travelers leave the House of Holiness and continue their quest.

The general allegory of the House of Holiness and the Red Cross Knight's progress through it has already been touched upon (p. 14). There is an elaborate parallel between the House of Holiness and the House of Pride. Roughly the same parallel as that between Una and Duessa, this comparison emphasizes the contrast between the life of the flesh and the life of the spirit, appearance and reality, sickness and health, love and lust, heaven and hell—all of those oppositions inherent in the contrast between the City of God and the City of Man.

The extremely rich allegory of this episode is primarily an exposition of the conversion of the sinner. It also emphasizes the operation of the three theological virtues, faith, hope, and charity, in conversion. Spenser's treatment of the theological virtues is traditional. Faith (Fidelia) and Hope (Speranza) appear arm in arm because they are so linked by St. Paul. "Now faith is the substance of things hoped for, the evidence of things not seen" (Hebrews 11:1).

As Calvin puts it, "faith exists not without hope . . ." (*Institutes*, III.3, p. 653). St. Paul's statement also explains why Fidelia and Speranza, though espoused, are not married. For faith and hope find their consummation only in heaven after earthly life where "we see through a glass darkly" (I Corinthians 13:12). Fidelia's cup is the chalice of St. John. According to legend, St. John was ordered to drink a cup of poisoned wine. He blessed the cup and drank its contents without harm. It is a traditional symbol of redemption from sin. (See the famous painting of this cup by Hans Memling in the National Gallery, Washington.) The serpent in Fidelia's cup is especially a symbol of redemption. It is associated with healing not only in biblical but also in classical literature, where it is associated with the physician Aesculapius. Most important of all, the serpent is a type of Christ the Physician, who cured the sin of the world in his death on the cross. Specifically, this serpent is to be associated with the brazen serpent which Moses held aloft in the wilderness to cure the plague of the fiery serpents (Numbers 21:8–9). St. John points out the relation between this serpent and Christ: "And as Moses lifted up the serpent in the wilderness, even so must the Son of man be lifted up" (John 3:14). Fidelia's cup is most clearly the sacrament of Communion, and the serpent simply emphasizes the redemptive power of the sacrament. The cup contains both water and wine because the wound in Christ's side, the mystical source of the sacrament, flowed both blood and water (John 19:34), and because wine and water were mixed in the Communion cup in the primitive church. It is probably correct, also, to interpret the wine and water of Fidelia's cup as a symbol of both the sacraments felt by Protestants to be necessary to salvation. The water represents baptism and the wine Communion. ("This is he that came by water and blood, even Jesus Christ; not by water only, but by water and blood," I John 5:6.) Fidelia's book is the New Testament. Faith has charge of the sacraments and the New Testament because both of these, necessary to salvation, are made efficatious by faith.

Fidelia's sister, Speranza, holds a silver anchor upon her arm because, as St. Paul says of the Christian's hope of salvation, we should "lay hold upon the hope set before us: which hope we have as an anchor of the soul, both sure and steadfast . . ." (Hebrews 6:18–19). Spenser's Charissa, unlike her two sisters, is married because charity, the subject of the final two commandments, bears fruit in life. In the soul of the converted sinner it issues in good works continually. The details of Charissa's description are traditional in medieval and renaissance art.

The relation between the three theological virtues is allegorized in the ages of the three sisters and the fact that Charissa does not appear until the Red Cross Knight has been thoroughly instructed by Fidelia and Speranza. St. Thomas Aquinas, considering the question of whether faith precedes charity, concludes that this question may be answered yes or no, depending upon whether one is speaking of the "order of generation" or "the order of perfection." According to Aquinas,

> The movement of the appetite cannot tend to anything, either by hoping or loving, unless that thing be apprehended by the sense or by the

intellect. Now it is by faith that the intellect apprehends what it hopes for and loves. Hence, in the order of generation, faith must precede hope and charity.[15]

In the same discussion St. Thomas argues, "Hence, for the very reason that a man bases his hopes in someone, he proceeds to love him; so that in the order of generation, hope precedes charity." This discussion explains why in Spenser's allegory Fidelia is the eldest and Charissa the youngest. It also explains why Red Cross is instructed and ministered to first by Fidelia, then by Speranza, and finally by Charissa. On the other hand, St. Thomas continues, "in the order of perfection, charity precedes faith and hope, because both faith and hope are quickened by charity, and receive from charity their full complement as virtues. For thus charity is the mother and the root of all the virtues." This passage does much to explain Spenser's treatment of Charissa. Although Charissa is the youngest of the sisters, she is in another sense the oldest, the most mature, since only she is married and bears children. Even more significant is the fact that when Red Cross first enters the House of Holiness, Charissa has just given birth to a child and is not able to greet the knight. In the "order of generation" this simply means that Red Cross must be perfected in faith and hope before he can learn charity. But the baby that Charissa has just given birth to represents undoubtedly the birth of charity in Red Cross's soul, and in a sense the rebirth of the knight in Christ, who is love. Thus charity is the root and mother of Red Cross's faith and hope.

The first step in Red Cross's conversion begins in faith, under the tutelage of Fidelia, for as Calvin argues, "repentance not only immediately follows faith, but is produced by it" (*Institutes*, III.3, p. 649). And, as he further points out, "conversion commences with a dread and hatred of sin . . . when we not only dread punishment, but hate and abhor sin itself, from a knowledge that it is displeasing to God" (*Institutes*, p. 656). Red Cross's first reaction to Fidelia's teaching, then, is to hate his sin and the world and to desire to die. This time, however, Red Cross's repentance is real, not the hopeless fear of punishment which he fell victim to in the cave of Despair. Calvin calls such repentance evangelical repentance, which "we discover in all who have been distressed by a sense of sin in themselves, but have been raised from their depression, and reinvigorated by a confidence in the Divine mercy" (*Institutes*, p. 652). Thus Speranza offers comfort and help to Red Cross after Fidelia's teaching. The agonies which Red Cross suffers under the care of Patience and his assistants are simply the natural effects of his conversion. Again, Calvin says, "I apprehend repentance to be regeneration, the end of which is the restoration of the Divine image within us." In this restoration "the Lord destroys the carnal corruptions of his chosen, purifies them from all pollution, and consecrates them as temples to himself" (*Institutes*, pp. 657–658).

So far Red Cross has completed that stage of conversion or repentance which theologians call "mortification," the process of pain through which the sinner passes on the way to health. The rest of his stay in the House of Holiness is his

---

[15] *Summa Theologica*, II, Q. 62, Art. 4, trans. Fathers of the English Dominican Province, 21 vols., Burns, Oates, and Washburn, 1912–1925.

vivification, the second stage of his conversion. Vivification is the acquisition of

> a disposition of righteousness, judgment, and mercy. This takes place
> when the Spirit of God has tinctured our souls with his holiness, and given
> them such new thoughts and affections, that they may be justly consid-
> ered as new. (*Institutes*, p. 657)

Vivification bears the fruit of good works. These stages are not, of course, exclusive of each other. They are rather two continuous movements in the process of conversion. Mortification never ends for the Christian; nor is vivification ever absent. It is a question of which is dominant in the various stages of the Christian's life.

Fidelia and Speranza having accomplished the work of mortification, it is now time for Charissa to instruct Red Cross in the new life. From her, or under her sponsorship, he will learn Christian love, the greatest of all virtues (I Corinthians 13:13). His experiences in the house of the seven beadsmen and later on the Mount of Contemplation amount to the Christian's conforming of his heart to the first two commandments, on which "hang all the law and the prophets" (Matthew 22:40). The knight's stay in the hospital of the seven beadsmen represents his instruction in the seven corporal works of mercy, those actions of love which pertain to the Christian's relations with his neighbors. They are subsumed in the second commandment. The vision of the New Jerusalem on the Mount of Contemplation represents the love of God, the subject of the first and greatest commandment. According to Aquinas, man's greatest happiness and his true end is in the contemplation of God (*Summa Contra Gentiles*, III.37). And Red Cross's vision of the New Jerusalem, whose light is God, brings eternal life (*Summa Contra Gentiles*, III.61). It is thus understandable that he should condemn earthly life and wish to stay forever with Contemplation, for "if the terrestrial life be compared with the celestial, it should undoubtedly be despised and accounted of no value" (*Institutes*, III.9, p. 781). Contemplation's insistence that Red Cross remember his obligation to Una is an emphasis shared by Protestantism and reforming elements of the medieval church on action as opposed to contemplation.

> First, a man travail and give him to good exercise in prayer and in
> study of holy scriptures and other good workings in common conversa-
> tion, amending his life and withdrawing fro vices and profiting in getting
> of virtues; and after then, secondly, resting in contemplation, that is to say
> in solitude at the list of heart, forsaking all world's business, with all his
> might being about continually to think on God and heavenly things,
> only attempting to please God; and then hereafter, when he is perfectly
> in those two forcsaid exercises taught and stabled in very wisdom and
> virtues and lightened through grace, desiring the ghostly profit of other
> men, then may he sickerly take upon him the cure and governail of
> others.[16]

[16] Nicholas Love, *The Mirror of the Blessed Life of Christ* (1410), quoted from William Matthews, ed., *Later Medieval English Prose*, Appleton-Century-Crofts, 1963, pp. 145–146.

Red Cross learns of his true destiny as St. George from Contemplation because, as St. Thomas argues, his vision has given him eternal life. It remains for him to learn that he is not a faery knight, but a human. This is important knowledge, mainly for the reader. Spenser's faery knights represent virtues, and they have some of the incompleteness of abstractions. But his representation of holiness, man conformed to the image of Christ, cannot be less than human.

xi: The Triumph of Red Cross

Leaving the House of Holiness, Una leads the Red Cross Knight to her native land, there to combat the terrible dragon who keeps her parents imprisoned in a brazen tower. As they approach the tower, they hear the terrible roar of the great beast and see his vast bulk stretched over the side of a nearby hill. When the dragon sees them, Red Cross tells Una to withdraw, and he prepares to meet the monster, who charges fiercely, half flying with his great wings. The knight meets the charge just as fiercely, but when he strikes the beast with his lance the point simply glances off the thick, scaly back. Angered by his foe's attack, the beast turns and charges again, knocking both horse and rider to the ground with his long tail. Red Cross and his mount, however, leap up immediately and go to the attack. The angry dragon then grasps horse and man in his claws and sails into the air, but is forced by the knight's struggles to bring them back to earth. Striking with his spear again, Red Cross slashes a deep wound in the monster's wing. The wounded beast roars in rage, snorts flames from his nostrils, and thrashes his dangerous tail about wildly, knocking the knight to the ground again. Red Cross attacks with his sword so furiously that the beast retires. Finally, however, he spits out a huge flame which envelops the knight and nearly bakes him alive in his armor. Then while his enemy is still in great pain, the dragon strikes him down with his tail. Fortunately for the stricken hero, there is a marvelous healing spring, the Well of Life, right behind him, and he falls into its pure waters. As the sun sinks and darkness falls, the knight lies as though dead in the miraculous spring and the dragon exults in his apparent victory. The anxious Una, watching from afar, prays all night for her champion. With the new day, Red Cross arises from the Well of Life refreshed and stronger than ever. Bravely attacking, with one huge stroke of his sword he hews a great gash in the dragon's skull. Amazed, the beast thrashes about in a frenzy of wrath and then strikes with his treacherous tail. The venomous sting pierces the hero's shield and lodges in his shoulder. Red Cross tries in vain to remove the sting; then in great anger he strikes off a long section of the monster's tail. The maimed beast belches forth flames and smoke and, in desperation, charges down on his foe and grasps his shield in his monstrous talons. The knight rains blows fiercely on his attacker and forces him to release one paw, but with the other he grips more tightly. Finally Red Cross strikes at the beast's claw and hews it off at the joint. Again smoke and flame pour from the dragon's throat and Red Cross retreats to save himself from the heat and stench; but as he backs away he slips in the mud and falls exhausted to the ground. Again the Red Cross Knight is saved from death. Behind him grows an ancient and marvelous tree, the Tree of Life, from which flows continually a stream of healing balm, able to heal the wounded and revive the dead. It is into this stream that the knight falls. The raging dragon, unable to invade the powerful stream, waits beside the Tree of Life as darkness draws to a close the second day of battle. Una again spends the night in anxious prayer. With the dawn of the third day, Red Cross leaps up healed and renewed in strength. The waiting dragon in desperation rushes to battle, his great jaws open to devour his enemy. But the knight first repels the charge and then, taking advantage of the beast's open jaws, thrusts his bright weapon into the cavernous mouth and, in that stroke, finally kills the fiend. Like a huge mountain the dragon falls. Una, beholding the triumph of her hero, hastens to congratulate the knight.

The Red Cross Knight's battle with the great dragon is in broadest outline a type of Christ's conquest of hell during the three days between the crucifixion and the resurrection (Good Friday to Easter). Christ's harrowing of hell, his victory over the great beast Satan, and his rescue of Adam and Eve and their children were great themes of medieval and renaissance art. The story is told in the apocryphal Gospel of Nicodemus. In each of the first two days of combat Red Cross suffers a kind of death, a type of the crucifixion; but on the third day he prevails over the dragon and releases Una's parents from captivity, a type of Christ's victory and the resurrection. But Red Cross is only a type of Christ, a saint conforming to the image of God, and his victory over Satan is won only by means of Christ's victory, his death on the cross and his resurrection. Therefore, throughout the three day combat Christ's grace is present to revive the merely human saint. The saint, through his strong faith, may defeat Satan and sin in many ways, as Red Cross wounds the great dragon. But in this battle he is taxed to his limit, and without Christ's loving grace he cannot ultimately win the battle. At the end of the first day's fighting, Red Cross falls burned and exhausted into the Well of Life and is revived. This well is both the river of Paradise which "went out of Eden to water the garden" (Genesis 2:10) and the Well of Life in the New Jerusalem: "And he showed me a pure river of water of life, clear as crystal, proceeding out of the throne of God and of the Lamb" (Revelation 22:1). Both these rivers are symbols of Christ's grace, indeed types of Christ, his death and resurrection. As representations of the sacrament of baptism they imply both grace and its cause. The baptismal prayer in the second Prayer Book of Edward VI (1552) indicates the significance of the sacrament:

> Grant that the Old Adam in these children may be so buried that the new man may be raised up in them . . . grant that all carnal affections may die in them . . . grant that they may have power and strength to have victory and to triumph against the devil, the world, and the flesh.[17]

Thus baptism implies death of the old Adam (crucifixion) and rebirth as a "new man" (resurrection). Through Christ's grace in baptism, Red Cross is enabled to conform himself to the life of Christ.

Similarly the Tree of Life, in whose miraculous balm the Red Cross Knight is revived, represents Christ, his crucifixion and victory over sin and Satan, and his grace. St. Augustine points out that "Christ Himself is prophetically

[17] *First and Second Prayer Books of Edward VI*, Everyman, 1952, p. 397.

called the Tree of Life" (*City of God*, XX.26, p. 755), and both the Tree of Life
in Paradise (Genesis 2:9) and the other in the New Jerusalem, the second
Paradise, are types of Christ (Revelation 22:2). In his death upon the cross,
Christ is the true Tree of Life because in the crucifixion Satan is defeated and
the old Adam is revived to new life. Christ's death on the cross also establishes
the sacrament of Holy Communion, through which, as in baptism, sinful man
is made new and conformed to the image of Christ. The balm into which Red
Cross falls is, thus, the life-giving blood of the crucified Christ and the wine
of Communion. Again, through the grace of Christ, Red Cross is able to live
the pattern of death and resurrection of his Savior.

If the Christian saint's victory over sin is a type of Christ's victory over
Satan, death, and sin on the cross, it is also a type of Christ's ultimate victory
over Satan, his deliverance of all the saints from death and the City of Man in
the last days (Revelation 15:2 and 20:10). Thus the life of the saint, Red Cross,
is placed in the context of world history and gains its significance only in that
context. Red Cross's battle with the dragon is made necessary by the fall of
Una's parents, Adam and Eve, at the beginning of history. His victory is made
possible by grace of Christ's conquest of sin and death upon the cross. Finally,
the saint's triumph prefigures the triumph of Christ and the church at the end
of time.

For the most part, Spenser's allegory in this canto is profoundly traditional.
There are, at the same time, elements which are probably Protestant. In the
Well of Life and the Tree of Life episodes, Spenser's treatment of the sacraments
of baptism and Holy Communion is richly typological in the medieval tradi-
tion, but his concentration on those two sacraments alone represents the
Protestant view that only those two sacraments have scriptural authority and
are necessary to salvation. Red Cross's victory perhaps represents also the
defeat of Roman Catholicism in England by Protestantism and the freeing of
the nation (Una's parents) from a false religion.

xii: The Betrothal of the Red Cross Knight and Una

As the morning of the fourth day breaks, the watchman on the brazen tower
sees the body of the great dragon stretched dead over the plain. He calls loudly
to inform Una's parents of their deliverance from the beast, and after he has
seen the miracle for himself, Una's father, the king, commands the gates of the
brazen walls to be thrown open and proclaims the joyous news throughout the
land. The jubilant citizens flock to the gate, from which the king and his court
lead out a festive procession. Coming to a stop before Red Cross, they kneel in
praise of their deliverer, and afterward a band of dancing maidens crown their
returned princess Una with green garlands. While the wondering crowd stands
in admiration and fear around the great bulk of the dead dragon, the king
showers Red Cross with costly gifts and then escorts him to his palace where
there is a stately banquet for the triumphant hero. After the guests have mod-
erately satisfied their hunger, Una's parents ask Red Cross to recount his
adventures and the court listens with great sympathy to his tale of past trials.
The king then invites the champion to stay and rest after his battle conquest,
but the knight calls Una to witness to the fact that he must return to Faeryland

to serve the Faery Queen for six years. The king expresses sorrow and disappointment at the knight's having to leave, for he had vowed to give Una in marriage to the champion who should conquer the dragon. He is determined to celebrate at least the formal betrothal of his daughter and her knight before he leaves, and so he sends for Una. She comes, but not as Red Cross had ever seen her before, for now her black mantle and her veil have been removed and she appears radiant in spotless white. Just as she bows humbly before her father, a breathless messenger arrives to read to the king a letter from Duessa. The enchantress writes that Red Cross can not be married to Una, that he is already betrothed to her, that he is dishonest and unfaithful. The amazed king asks the knight to explain, and Red Cross tells of the treacherous schemes of Duessa. Una interrupts to advise her father that Duessa's letter is just one more evil turn in Archimago's plot to destroy her, and that the messenger is, indeed, the wicked sorcerer himself. The angry king orders his servants to seize Archimago, bind him in chains, and cast him into the deepest dungeon. Then the king celebrates the betrothal of his daughter and the Red Cross Knight with great ceremony and amidst general rejoicing throughout the land. After many pleasant days spent with his beloved, Red Cross takes his leave and begins his journey back to the Faery Queen.

The crucial episodes of this canto are the betrothal of Red Cross and the unmasking and imprisonment of Archimago. The first of these represents the mystical marriage of Christ and the church at the end of time, the final triumph of the City of God. The radiant appearance of Una, her dark clothes of mourning now discarded for a spotless robe of lily white, is clearly a type of the triumphant church: "The marriage of the Lamb is come, and his wife hath made herself ready. And to her was granted that she should be arrayed in fine linen, clean and white: for the fine linen is the righteousness of saints" (Revelation 19:7–8). Una's garment is "without spot" because Christ, in his praise of the church, his bride, says, "Thou art all fair, my love; there is no spot in thee" (The Song of Solomon 4:7). Her radiant appearance

> As bright as doth the morning star appear
> Out of the east with flaming locks bedight
> To tell that dawning day is drawing near,
> And to the world does bring long wishèd light,

suggests the brightness of the New Jerusalem: "And her light was like unto a stone most precious, even like a jasper stone, clear as crystal," which is described as "a bride adorned for her husband" (Revelation 21:11 and 2). The Red Cross Knight is then a type of Christ the Triumphant Bridegroom.

But Red Cross, the triumphant St. George, is only a type of Christ. He is only betrothed to Una, the true church, and his marriage must wait until, as a resurrected saint and a member of the body and bride of Christ, he participates in the marriage of Christ and the church in the New Jerusalem. As a saint, his betrothal to Una signifies his conformity to the image of his Maker, Christ, and his union with true religion; at the same time it is a prophecy of his salvation and of the ultimate triumph of Christ and the City of God over Satan and the City of Man.

As the patron saint of England, Red Cross's betrothal represents, no doubt, the triumph of Protestantism over the Roman church; and it represents this triumph as, again, the marriage of Christ and the church at the end of time. It is thus an apocalyptic prophecy of the salvation of England, of the conformity of the whole nation to the image of Christ. But for both the individual Christian saint and the true Church of England the final union with Christ must wait, and in the meantime there are more battles against evil and falsehood to be fought. The promise of salvation is sure. Neither the true saint nor the Christian nation, however, can forsake the world and the evils which beset it. Thus, the import of Red Cross's betrothal to Una is much the same as that of his vision of the New Jerusalem in Canto x. The Christian saint rises, with the constant help of Christ's grace, to a perfection which assures his eventual union with truth and Christ, and which enables him to defeat Satan in his own flesh and in the world; but the final triumph is not in time nor in this world.

Archimago's capture and imprisonment is a type of Christ's victory over Satan:

> And I saw an angel come down from heaven, having the key of the bottomless pit and a great chain in his hand. And he laid hold on the dragon, that old serpent, which is the Devil, and Satan, and bound him a thousand years, and cast him into the bottomless pit, and shut him up, and set a seal upon him, that he should deceive the nations no more, till the thousand years should be fulfilled: and after that he must be loosed a little season. (Revelation 20:1-2)

Significantly this passage does not represent the *final* triumph over Satan (Revelation 20:10), though it does clearly imply it. Archimago's imprisonment is not his final defeat, nor is it man's or England's final deliverance from evil, though it implies and prophesies it. Bishop Bale's commentary on this passage relates it first to Christ's victory over Satan in his death and resurrection, then to the pure life and doctrine of the primitive church, and finally to the triumph of the Protestant churches over a corrupt anti-Christian Roman church (*Works*, pp. 558–564).

One aspect of Canto xii does not need a great deal of comment, but should be noticed. As in the House of Holiness episodes, there is here a detailed parallel, for the sake of contrast, between the scenes and events in the land of Una's parents, Eden, and those at the House of Pride. The most obvious of these parallels is the betrothal of Red Cross to Una as contrasted with his adultery with Duessa. But the manners and actions and feelings of the king's court and the common throng are also part of this comparison between the City of God and the City of Man.

TEMPERANCE AND THE DOCTRINE OF RIGHT REASON

Book II of *The Faerie Queene* was created from a world view which had its origin in Platonic philosophy and was further developed and modified by

Aristotle and the Stoic philosophers. Early Christian theologians, above all St. Augustine, borrowed much of this world view from Neoplatonic and Stoic writers, while later theologians, gaining access to writings of Aristotle through Arabic texts, produced a synthesis of the early theologians and Aristotle which purported to explain every aspect of nature and existence in their relations to the truths of Christianity as revealed in the Bible. The chief philosophical expression of this synthesis is St. Thomas Aquinas' *Summa Theologica;* the chief artistic expression, Dante's *Divine Comedy.* Spenser was heir to this world view. His understanding of his own culture was based on the medieval synthesis as it found expression in Elizabethan theology, in the sermons officially appointed to be read in all the churches of England periodically, and in theological treatises, the best of which is *Of the Laws of Ecclesiastical Polity* by Richard Hooker, a contemporary of Spenser.

Whereas modern thought is broken into separate fields having little relation to each other, the thought of the Renaissance was bound together in unity. Natural science, psychology, ethics, political science, metaphysics were all considered partially analogous to each other and all were interpretable in light of the great events of Christian history—the creation, the fall of Adam, the life and death of Christ, and the judgment to come. The universe created by God was characterized by order, by a hierarchal principle which placed each created thing in an ascending scale from the lowest stone to the highest angel according to its possession of a nature more or less near the perfection of God. There was, then, a sort of chain of command of creation. There was such a hierarchy in the mineral world, from common clay to the ruby and the diamond; there were others among the plants, the animals, men, and angels. The hierarchies were themselves part of the larger system since the highest, or most precious, mineral was slightly less perfect than the most imperfect plant. The stability of the created universe depended upon such a hierarchal organization, which was indeed an expression of the mind of God, in fact of God's love for his creation. The universe of minerals, plants, and animals was bound by God's love in such a way that the proper relation within and between the hierarchies could not degenerate or become confused. God's sustaining love was natural law. But the higher creatures, man and the angels, were not so bound; instead they were endowed with the gifts of reason and will. With the one, men could understand the law of creation intuitively from nature; with the other, they could obediently follow it in their political, social, and religious lives.

The divine love as it manifested itself in human affairs was called right reason. Right reason, since it was analogous to natural law and was indeed the law of man's nature, sanctioned a hierarchal structuring of society. Thus Queen Elizabeth was seen by many Englishmen, including Spenser and Shakespeare, as a sovereign whose position in the social hierarchy was a metaphor of God's rule over the universe. In principle every man had his proper place in society; every man had his superiors and his inferiors and he had responsibilities to both. In such a political theory the great crime was revolution, amounting to the revolt of Satan against God, which led not only to the creation of man but to his fall as well. Ambition in all ranks was condemned because it threatened chaos in the hierarchies of society—as the ambition of Satan brought chaos into the order of creation.

If there are natural hierarchies in creation and divinely sanctioned but not necessary hierarchies in human society and in heaven, man as the center of creation is the reflection of all of this ordered structure. At the head of this little world of man is the "rational soul," containing the will and reason. Reason apprehends the laws of right reason; will, under the advice of reason, acts in accord with right reason. The rational soul commands and is served by the "sensible soul," which comprises the emotions. Most Renaissance authorities recognized two "powers" of the sensible soul—basically classes into which all emotions may be placed—the "irascible" power and the "concupiscible." The concupiscible power includes all of those emotions related to desire, pleasure, and displeasure. The irascible, on the other hand, is made up of the emotions related to anger and fear. When a man is healthy and virtuous these powers of the sensible soul are servants to the will, moving it to resist evil and persevere in the attainment of the good, but when the man is vicious or unhealthy these emotions, like devils or a revolutionary rabble, corrupt reason and the will, sometimes going completely out of control and destroying the rational man. Inferior to the sensible soul and serving both it and the rational soul is what was called the "vegetable soul." It contained the forces of procreation and the functions which sustain the physical, and thus the emotional and moral, life of man. The most important products of the vegetable soul were four substances called the "humors." Each of these substances—blood, phlegm, black bile or melancholy, and yellow bile or choler—had important physiological functions, but they also were related to emotional and, therefore, moral life. When the humors were in perfect balance, the powers of the sensible soul were likely to be in harmony with themselves and with reason. Any serious imbalance among the humors caused a corresponding imbalance in the emotions, making man particularly vulnerable to the temptations of the world and the devil. The healthy man was likely to desire sex in a reasonable measure for the virtuous purpose of reproducing his kind; the man in whom the harmony of the humors had become broken was likely either to be obsessed with sexual desire or to be completely indifferent to sex. Anger is necessary to the virtuous life under some conditions; the will must be moved to resist and even to conquer evil. But the man in whom the choleric humor predominates becomes the slave of anger, unable to distinguish good and evil; his obsessive anger is directed indiscriminately to all. On the other hand, when choler is deficient, the man is unlikely to be able to resist evil strongly enough.

Book II of *The Faerie Queene* is very much concerned with the emotional life of man, specifically with a virtue which was said by Aristotle and his Roman and medieval followers to characterize the man whose emotional life was in harmony with his reason. As has been said, the emotions are good in themselves. Men could not act at all without them. But as renaissance authorities insist, they are good only if they are "tempered" by reason, and only if reason tempers them in accordance with the general principles of right reason. Right reason teaches that everything has its proper function and place. The emotions have the function of directing the will toward ends which the reason approves;

their place is to move the will only as strongly as is necessary to achieve the end. Fear is good under some conditions; excessive fear or insufficient fear is evil under any circumstances. Aristotle in the *Nicomachean Ethics* and St. Thomas Aquinas in the "Treatise on Temperance" in *Summa Theologica* agree that reason dictates that the emotions should follow "the mean" between too much and too little in all matters, for both the excess and the defect endanger man's moral life and ultimately his reason. Honor itself could be loved too much or for the wrong reasons.

The healthy functioning and harmonious balancing of the concupiscible and irascible powers were represented for the Renaissance by the union of Venus and Mars. Plutarch writes of their love, "In the fables of the Greeks, Harmony was born from the union of Venus and Mars: of whom the latter is fierce and contentious, the former generous and pleasing."[18] The *Mars and Venus* of Paolo Veronese (Plate 2) represents allegorically the chastening effect of the harmony between the irascible and the concupiscible. Mars hides the lower part of Venus's body and thus chastens concupiscence; Venus puts one arm on the shoulder of the kneeling Mars, restraining irascibility. And the restraint of irascibility is playfully restated by the Cupid who uses Mars's sword to restrain his war-horse. It is such an image of harmony that Spenser evokes in the Proem to Book I while announcing that love and war shall be his themes:

> And thou most dreaded imp of highest Jove,
> Fair Venus' son . . . .
> Lay now thy deadly ebon bow apart,
> And with thy mother mild come to mine aid.
> Come both, and with you bring triumphant Mart,
> In loves and gentle jollities arrayed,
> After his murderous spoils and bloody rage allayed.

And it is the destruction of such an image of harmony that starts Sir Guyon on his quest in Book II. On one level at least, Mordant and Amavia, the couple whose death Guyon seeks to avenge through the destruction of Acrasia's Bower of Bliss, are types of the Mars and Venus of Veronese's painting. Married and fruitful, Mordant and Amavia are a symbol of the temperance Aquinas describes in *Summa Theologica*: "The passions of the irascible appetite counteract the passions of the concupiscible appetite: since concupiscence, on being roused, diminishes anger; and anger, being roused, diminishes concupiscence in many cases" (I.81.2). In the specific context of the sexual appetite, their harmonious union is an emblem of chastity, one of the virtues of temperance. By chastity, the Renaissance did not mean virginity. The proper end of sexual desire is procreation, and in the temperate man reason and the will direct sexual desire to its proper end and moderate it so that it does not become an end in itself. Rationally directed and moderated desire and the pleasure which results is chastity. It is important for understanding the whole allegory of Book II to see that Spenser's symbol of temperance is fruitful sexual union.

[18] *De Iside et Osiride*, quoted from Edgar Wind, *Pagan Mysteries of the Renaissance*, Yale University Press, 1958, p. 82.

As we shall see, Sir Guyon undertakes to destroy the forces which tempt men to excessive desire or, as medieval and renaissance writers would have put it, excessive concupiscence. In the course of his adventure he has to conquer all of the chief temptations to emotional excess. And in the process he has to conquer himself, for the man who cannot control himself cannot defeat his enemies— indeed, cannot always recognize his enemies. For a part of his quest he is guided and controlled by right reason, the palmer, but at other times he must depend upon his own reason, his experience, and his habits of self-control and virtue. That Guyon does not always find his quest easy, that occasionally he falters, shows that Spenser's temperance is not quite that of Plato and Aristotle. The temperate man of the Greek philosophers was one whose emotions were in perfect harmony with his reason. Such a man never experienced emotional upheavals, for he never was tempted to emotional excess under any circumstance. He always experienced the appropriate degree of emotion, never more and never less—in feeling as in action he always followed the golden mean. As a Christian, Spenser could not accept this picture as a reality, for Adam had fallen and man was imperfect.

The inevitability of the emotional disorders occasioned by Adam's fall, the hereditary intemperance that leaves the harmonious union of Mars and Venus at best only a temporarily realizable ideal, is also symbolized by the story of Mordant and Amavia. Their son Ruddymane, whose bloodstained hands can never be cleansed, bears a token that paradoxically proclaims both the innocence of his mother and the crime that drove her to suicide. As an emblem of original sin, Mordant, Amavia, and Ruddymane are types of Adam, Eve, and fallen mankind. On this level, Mordant is the rational soul, Amavia the sensitive soul, and Ruddymane the product of their union in man, who must at the same time bear witness to their destructive disharmony. As a consequence of the fall all men are subject to the temptations of the world, the flesh, and the devil; and hence they experience "perturbations" in the form of excessive emotional reactions. Guyon, as the temperate man in a fallen world, does feel tempted and must struggle against his own tendencies to emotional excess. Spenser, therefore, treats Guyon as a symbol of what the Greeks called the "continent man," man striving for the harmony of temperance and opposing the enemies of that harmony. Aristotle's continent man does feel temptation and the emotional perturbations which result, but he imposes a reasonable control over his emotions through the will.

Yet Guyon's struggles against the enemies of temperance must impress the reader as mild compared with the life and death clashes of Arthur, who enters Book II in Canto viii. The explanation of Guyon's comparatively easy victories lies in the fact that in Arthur and Guyon, Spenser dramatizes two different answers to the question: what are the enemies of temperance? Guyon's adventures, for the most part, develop the answer that Aristotle and Cicero would have given to the question: excessive anger, excessive desire for pleasure, money, and power. All of these are destructive of that inner harmony which makes a man temperate and virtuous; all tend to subordinate reason to emotion. Arthur's struggles, on the other hand, show that the classical (and pagan) answer is limited, for they pose another question: what lies behind these enemies of temperance? The answer is that excessive anger and misdirected desire are not simply human tendencies capable of being controlled by reason; behind these tendencies lies a demonic mover, an evil principle devoted to the destruction of temperance and the men who attempt to practice that virtue. Arthur's struggles, like those of Red Cross in Book I, are with Satan, and his victories are final. Guyon's victories are less profoundly significant and only partial. This is not to say that Guyon is to be considered a failure. He is, with the help of Arthur, a huge success. But Spenser gives him the limitations of the classical virtue he represents.

A SUMMARY OF THE PLOT AND ALLEGORY OF BOOK II

i.1–34: The Meeting of Guyon and Red Cross

At the beginning of Book II, Guyon, the Knight of Temperance, guided by right reason, the palmer, so that he does not stray into irrational behavior, is met by an old squire, Archimago in disguise, who complains that his mistress has been raped by a knight. Full of indignation, Guyon leaves the palmer and rushes off to hear the lady, really Duessa, accuse St. George, the Red Cross Knight, of the crime. Guyon, who knows of Red Cross's fame, is shocked, but vows to avenge the lady's injury and follows Archimago, who shows him Red Cross resting beside a stream. He attacks zealously and Red Cross prepares himself for battle. However, just before the two knights clash, Guyon sees the cross on Red Cross's shield, lowers his lance, and reins in his charger. Red Cross is not able to stop his horse immediately, but lowers his lance when he recognizes his supposed enemy. The palmer arrives as Guyon and Red Cross apologize to each other. The palmer praises Red Cross for the victory over the evil captor of Una's parents he had accomplished in Book I, reminds Guyon that he has "a like race to run," and prays for God's guidance.

The episode makes two very important points in the allegory. The first point is that the virtue which Guyon represents has limitations as well as strengths. Temperance, the classical virtue, has the strength which makes it possible for a man to control his emotions, and thus his actions. Guyon is able to bring his horse to a stop when he perceives the cross on St. George's shield because, as the Knight of Temperance, he can deal with the kind of irrational behavior that can result from excessive emotion. In this respect, Guyon appears to be superior to Red Cross, the Knight of Holiness or Faith. On the other hand, Guyon is easily aroused to a high pitch of anger by Archimago and Duessa. Not that his anger is in itself bad, for it is what the theologians called "zealous anger," anger directed against vice. But Guyon's zeal does violate the warning that "we must beware lest, when we use anger as an instrument of virtue, it overrule the mind, and go before it as its mistress . . ." (quoted from Pope Gregory by Thomas Aquinas, *Summa Theologica*, II.158.1). Guyon is no proof against the deception of Archimago and allows his zeal to be misdirected. This is not to be taken as a condemnation of Guyon; it rather shows a limitation in the virtue of temperance. The triumphant Red Cross would not have been taken in by the disguises of Archimago and Duessa, for holiness has the function of defeating the demonic evil which attacks the theological virtues of faith, hope, and love. Learning to recognize Archimago beneath any disguise was one of the lessons Red Cross learned in Book I. But temperance deals with the emotional enemies of rationality, not with the spiritual enemies of the soul. Thus Guyon is deceived.

The second point made is that reason and faith are complementary to each other and in essential agreement. In the meeting of Guyon and Red Cross, Spenser dramatizes an intellectual conflict which rocked Europe all during the sixteenth century and which remained a live issue into the nineteenth century. The terms around which the conflict developed were "free will and predestination," "good works and faith," "nature and grace," "reason and faith." One group of Protestant theologians, led by Martin Luther and later by John Calvin, argued on the authority of the Bible and early fathers of the church, especially St. Augustine, that man was saved by faith alone and by the freely given and undeserved grace of God. They argued that when Adam fell, he corrupted the nature of all men so that their reason was darkened to such a degree that they could neither know or desire the good. Men rather tended toward evil. Therefore, all men were doomed to sin and eventual damnation except that God freely granted grace to the elect, those predestined to salvation. Man's "nature," his reason and will, were of no account—only his faith, the gift of grace, saved him. However, this position was opposed by the Roman Catholic church and by many Protestant thinkers as well. Spenser's contemporary, Richard Hooker, was one of the theologians who argued that man's reason was not so darkened nor his will so weakened by the fall of Adam as to make him completely helpless. Hooker believed that reason might still apprehend right reason in the law of nature and that the will might still have the strength to follow the direction of reason in virtuous action. Neither he nor any other influential theologian of the time believed that human reason and right reason were sufficient for salvation, but he did believe that man had two means of salvation—on the one hand, faith and grace, on the other, reason and nature—and that both of them were necessary for salvation. In narrating the meeting of his two heroes, Spenser showed that he was of Hooker's party, not the party of Luther and Calvin. Faith and grace may appear to be opposed to reason; the devil can make it seem so. But, in truth, reason and faith, nature and grace, Guyon and Red Cross are in accord. The temperance of reason is a necessary complement of the fully committed zeal of faith, just as faith is necessary to combat the spiritual enemies which attack and deceive that temperance.

i.35–ii.12: Mordant, Amavia, and the Bloody-handed Babe

After winning many hard victories and gaining wide fame, Guyon chances to pass beside a dense forest from which he and the palmer hear the screams of Amavia. As Guyon rushes in to aid her, he sees the corpse of her husband, the handsome young knight Mordant, lying near the bleeding body of the fainting Amavia, who still holds their tiny son Ruddymane to her breast. Guyon and the palmer had overheard her complaining against the hostility of heaven and commending her baby to a kinder fate, saying that his bloody hands will be a reminder of his mother's innocence. Guyon succeeds in reviving her tempo-rarily, long enough for her to tell them her story. Mordant had left her pregnant when he went off on his last knightly adventure. After he had been away some time, she learned that he had fallen into the power of the evil enchantress Acrasia, who with drugs and spells had bound him in servitude to lust. Dressed in the clothing of a palmer she set out to rescue him, but before she found him she gave birth to Ruddymane in the wilderness. Eventually, she came to Acrasia's Bower of Bliss, and after long effort succeeded in convincing Mordant to free himself and come away with her. As they were leaving, Acrasia gave Mordant a drink from a cup charmed with the lines,

> Sad verse give death to him that death does give,
> And loss of love to her that loves to live
> So soon as Bacchus with the nymph does link.

They departed, but soon come to the well where Guyon has found them. Mor-dant stooped to drink, the curse was fulfilled, and he sank dead to the ground. Thereupon Amavia plunged a knife into her heart, and as her blood streamed down into the well beside which she and Mordant were lying, the baby bathed his little hands in it. As she finishes telling them of Mordant's death, Amavia dies too. In commenting to the palmer upon the story and the tragic scene before them, Guyon generalizes about the weakness of mortal nature and the fatal results of allowing raging passion to rob "reason of her due regality." The palmer replies that temperance can "measure out a mean" between succumb-ing to pleasure as Mordant had done or to pain as Amavia had done. Deciding to let judgment of the couple be postponed until the final judgment, Guyon and the palmer bury them, and Guyon swears to avenge their deaths. This vow is the major spring of the plot of Book II. After attempting unsuccessfully to wash Ruddymane's hands in the well Mordant had drunk from and then hear-ing an explanation of the well's inviolable purity from the palmer, Guyon gives the bloody-handed baby to his ancient guide and picks up the armor of Mordant. The two then start out on foot for the Castle of Medina, where Guyon will entrust Ruddymane's education in temperance to Medina while he goes off on a series of adventures leading ultimately to the captivity of Acrasia.

The episode of Mordant, Amavia, and Ruddymane is not only a device to motivate the plot of Book II. It serves as an image for the whole book, an image of the fall of man through intemperance, of the stain man bears in his flesh as the result of his parents' fall, and of the inability ever to remove that stain. Allegorically, it is one of the most important and certainly the most complex episodes in Book II. On the fictional level, Mordant's chivalric adventures suggest a strong irascible power, while Amavia's love and fidelity suggest a strong concupiscent power. Guyon's remark that passion weakens the strong and "arms the weakest heart" (i.57) would seem to bear this out. Also, Aquinas in the *Summa Theologica* says of the irascible power that it "is, as it were, the champion and defender of the concupiscible, when it rises up against what hinders the acquisition of the suitable things which the concupiscible desires, or against what inflicts harm, from which the concupiscible flies" (I.81.2). If then we read the Mordant and Amavia episode as a moral allegory, we might say that excessive pleasure destroys the irascible power and that destruction of the irascible power results in a fatal inability to withstand pain and deprivation. This idea is perfectly classical and will be repeated in other forms throughout Book II. On this level, the episode relates the two powers of the sensible soul and analyzes at least one of the effects of incontinence. Mordant as the irascible power and Amavia as the concupiscible power may justify the epithets "who death does give" and "who loves to live." But the epithets are appropriate for other reasons as well.

If we pursue the suggestion that in the manner of biblical typology Mordant and Amavia represent Adam and Eve, we confront what at first appears to be a confusing reversal in roles. In the Bible, Adam falls as a result of being tempted by Eve; but Mordant does not fall through temptation by Amavia. Indeed she nearly rescues him. Spenser makes every effort to establish Amavia's innocence and to emphasize that the concupiscible power itself is not evil. The fictional Amavia is destroyed through the curse brought on by Mordant's failure rather than through her own inherent weakness. The biblical story was itself allegorized, however, by the Middle Ages and the Renaissance, with Adam representing man's reason and Eve his sensitive and vegetable souls. Man was thus tempted through his lower faculties but did not fall until his reason concurred. The lower faculties were themselves not responsible, though they did share in the effects of the fall. Of Adam's sin St. Paul wrote, "Sin came into the world through one man and death through sin, and so death spread to all men because all men sinned. . . . Death reigned from Adam to Moses, even over those whose sins were not like the transgression of Adam, who was a type of the one who was to come" (Romans 5:12–14). Both Adam as a type of Christ and the reign of death before the law was given to Moses are topics to which we will return, but the point here is that as Adam gave us death through his sin, so Mordant gave death through Acrasia's curse. That Mordant is he "who death does give" is then reinforced on the typological level of allegory. On this level, Amavia would seem to answer to the conventional exegesis of Eve. She represents man's nature as distinguished from his intellective soul or, in the words of the character Nature in *The Romance of the Rose*, she represents the gifts of Nature to the whole man:

> He has from me in body and in soul
> Three energies—existence, feeling, life. . . .
> Being he owns in common with the stones;
> Life he enjoys in common with the herbs;
> Feeling he has in common with the beasts.[19]

Thus Amavia represents man's body, his generative, and his emotional elements. In his generative as well as in his appetitive faculties, man may be said to love life. Amavia rightly calls Mordant her lord and love, for in the first man the higher powers of the soul ruled the lower nature.

---

[19] Guillaume de Lorris and Jean de Meun, *The Romance of the Rose*, trans. Harry W. Robbins, Dutton, 1962, pp. 403–404.

The nymph's well from which Mordant drinks to fulfill Acrasia's curse and in which it is impossible to cleanse the bloody hands of Ruddymane is reminiscent of several Ovidian springs into which nymphs were transformed. But the particular myth the palmer tells Guyon to explain the well's purity was evidently invented by Spenser. The well appears in both Cantos i and ii, and Spenser seems to have revised the poem at this point. In the *Letter to Raleigh* Guyon's introduction to Ruddymane and his parents is given in a version that is difficult to reconcile with the poem as we have it. There, Spenser says that the palmer brought the bloody-handed babe to Gloriana's court, where Guyon was granted the adventure of avenging the dead parents. This trip of the palmer's to Gloriana's court would almost have to come (in terms of the plot of the story as it stands) between Cantos i and ii, after the burial of Mordant and Amavia and before the washing episode. In that case, the two wells, that of Mordant's death and that of the washing episode, may not originally have been the same well. Our analysis, however, will have to proceed as if they were the same well, as they are in the completed poem. Another inconsistency in the story at this point comes with the putrefaction of the bodies mentioned in Canto ii but not in Canto i. A third inconsistency is Guyon's reference in ii.2 to Ruddymane as having been "in dead parents' baleful ashes bred." Everything in Canto i points to Ruddymane's having been bred and born in a state of prelapsarian innocence. The innocent child is the third and most important element in Spenser's emblem of chastity.

The effects of original sin and the fall of man were believed to have remained in Adam's descendents. Ruddymane's bloodstained hands are then best interpreted as the effects of original sin. Nor can the effects of original sin be washed away in baptism, for they include the darkening of reason, the weakening of the will, and the resultant tendency to sin. Baptism cleanses of guilt but not of the effects of original sin. The pure well receives the blood of Amavia but not the stains on Ruddymane's hands. This is, of course, precisely the crux at which the Greek and Christian views of temperance diverged. Spenser's story of the washing of Ruddymane's hands is therefore a mythical statement of this difference, of the impossibility in the Christian world view of perfect temperance. Acrasia's prompting Mordant to sin becomes a type of Satan's tempting Adam. From the very first, Book II, by an extraordinarily complex set of images and correspondences, is intelligible in terms of Christian doctrine.

In developing his thesis of the parallelism between Adam and Christ, St. Paul says that because of sin they both died. He continues, showing how we must imitate them both. "Do you not know that all of us who have been baptized into Christ Jesus were baptized into his death? We were buried therefore with him by baptism into death, so that as Christ was raised from the dead by the glory of the Father, we too might walk in newness of life" (Romans 6:3–4). This may explain Guyon's characterizing the new baby as "in dead parents' baleful ashes bred." Paul goes on to examine the role of the law, that is the Mosaic law of the Old Testament, in saving man. His main thesis is that the law teaches us what sin is.

Nay, I had not known sin, but by the law: for I had not known lust, except the law had said, "Thou shalt not covet." But sin, taking occasion by the commandment, wrought in me all manner of concupiscence. . . . Was then that which is good made death unto me? God forbid. But sin, that it might appear sin, working death in me by that which is good; then sin by the commandment might become exceeding sinful. For we know that the law is spiritual: but I am carnal, sold under sin. For that which I do I allow not: for what I would, that do I not; but what I hate, that do I. If then I do that which I would not, I consent unto the law that it is good. Now then it is no more I that do it, but sin that dwelleth in me. (Romans 7:7-17)

Paul seems to say that Adam's sin is repeated in us when sin takes advantage of the law and kills us. Without the law we would not know what sin is; when we discover through the law, sin kills us. He also says that baptism kills us to sin. Here he is using another metaphor to show our similarity to Christ, the second Adam. Two quite different deaths are involved. The first is a spiritual death through sin, the second is a spiritual rebirth through killing sin. The first is the death of Adam, the second, the death of Christ, the second Adam. Spenser's myth of Mordant's death is more like the first than the second of Paul's metaphoric deaths, but it includes them both. In the washing episode the nymph's spring strongly suggests the Old Law. But even Mordant must die to sin (in baptism) that he may conquer the weakness of his mortal flesh and live forever.

As Sir Guyon and the palmer leave on their journey from the nymph's well to the Castle of Medina, two small incidents occur. First, Guyon takes up the bloodstained armor of Mordant; second, he finds that his own horse is missing. He must therefore make his way on foot with a double burden. A possible but not completely satisfying interpretation is that Guyon here begins the fulfillment of his vows by taking himself the burden of Mordant's guilt. He, like Ruddymane, is heir to the fall from temperance. Not only does he have to take up the extra load of Mordant's armor; he must do so without the strength provided by his own horse.

ii.12–46: The Castle of Medina

After Guyon and the palmer bury Mordant and Amavia, they take up Ruddymane and begin their journey to find Acrasia. Soon they come to a castle set upon a rock in the sea inhabited by three sisters. The oldest sister, Elissa, is sullen and hostile to all pleasure; the youngest, Perissa, is wildly devoted to every form of sensuality. Medina, the second sister, is a gracious and chaste virgin who is resented by her sisters, who also hate each other. As Guyon and the palmer enter the castle they are received by Medina, who then leaves them to prepare for their entertainment. Soon Guyon hears the clash of arms in another apartment and goes to investigate. He finds two knights fighting furiously. The first is Huddibras, the stern lover of Elissa; the other is Sansloy, Perissa's lustful lover, who had attempted to rape Una. Guyon tries to part the knights, but immediately they turn their wrath on him and he is forced to defend himself. Guyon strikes out so strongly that the two knights retire and begin fighting each other again, though each time Guyon tries to calm them they again turn against him. In the meantime Medina hears the disturbance below and hurries to calm it. Elissa and Perissa urge Huddibras and Sansloy not to listen to Medina but to continue the attack on Guyon, but Medina's pleading is so sweet and so reasonable that the two knights grudgingly agree to a peace. Medina ushers them all into a banquet, which Elissa refuses to enjoy, while Perissa indulges in every lustful excess. Guyon is persuaded to tell of his adventures, and his tale consumes most of the night. The next morning Guyon and the palmer continue their quest, leaving Ruddymane with Medina for his education.

The Castle of Medina episode is in the main a dramatization of Aristotle's doctrine of the mean. For Aristotle, virtue or "goodness of moral character" exists in following a mean between extremes. "If we feel . . . too much or too little, we are wrong. But to have these feelings at the right times on the right occasions towards the right people for the right motive and in the right way is to have them in the right measure, that is, somewhere between the extremes; and this is what characterizes goodness. The same may be said of the mean and extremes in actions." [20] The hatred of Elissa and Perissa for each other and for Medina, like the hostility of their lovers, is an exact allegory of Aristotle's notion that ". . . there are three dispositions, two of them taking a vicious form (one in the direction of excess, the other of defect) and one a good form, namely, the observance of the mean. They are all opposed to one another, though not all in the same way. The extreme states are opposed both to the mean and one another, and the mean is opposed to both extremes" (*Ethics*, II.8, p. 72). The Castle of Medina is an allegory of virtue, but not of a cloistered virtue. Medina is an embattled virtue continually exerting the strength of her reason to calm the opposition between the extreme elements in her house. Spenser complicates Aristotle's notion of the mean by combining with it the Platonic and Aristotelian division of the sensible soul into irascible and concupiscible powers. Huddibras and Sansloy represent the tendency of these powers since the fall of man, shadowed in the death of Mordant and Amavia. The irascible is prone to harsh cruelty, the concupiscible to lawless lust. The dramatization of the doctrine of the mean is largely in terms of pleasure. Spenser allies Huddibras, the corruption of the irascible, to a defect in the desire for pleasure, Elissa; the excess of pleasure is allied to the corruption of the concupiscible. Medina's castle is then an emblem of the precarious virtue that is possible in a fallen world; it is also an emblem of Guyon's nature.

iii: Braggadochio and Belphoebe

While Guyon and the palmer are busy with Amavia and Ruddymane, a foolish peasant, Braggadochio, sees Guyon's horse and lance beside the road and steals them, intending now to make his way in the world as a knight. Soon he meets an unarmed rascal, Trompart, and attacks him furiously. Trompart cowers and begs for mercy and Braggadochio spares his life and takes him as his squire. After some travel the paper knight and his squire meet Archimago, who complains bitterly against Guyon and Red Cross, accusing them of killing

[20] *Ethics*, II.6, trans. J. A. K. Thompson, Penguin Books, 1953, pp. 65–66.

Mordant and Amavia. Braggadochio breaks out into a frenzy of rage against
the two knights, and Archimago, fooled by the wrath of Braggadochio, believes
he has found a champion to defeat Red Cross and Guyon. However, noticing
that Braggadochio lacks his sword, the enchanter offers to get Arthur's en-
chanted sword. When he spreads his wings and disappears, Braggadochio and
Trompart flee in terror. Soon they find themselves at the edge of a forest, where
they are surprised by the appearance of Belphoebe, a beautiful virgin huntress.
Braggadochio is so frightened that he hides himself in some bushes while
Trompart, the more courageous of the two, speaks to the huntress. When
Belphoebe, seeing Braggadochio's shivering body in the bushes, takes aim at
what she thinks is her quarry, the braggart is persuaded to show himself. After
making absurd excuses for his conduct, Braggadochio tries to persuade Bel-
phoebe to leave the rough forest and try her fortune at court, where honor and
pleasure are found, but Belphoebe answers with an attack on the vices of court
life and argues that virtue and bravery are rather to be found in the hard paths
of the wilderness. Braggadochio, as he listens to the beautiful maiden, is stirred
to lust and attempts to attack her, but she threatens him with her spear and
runs off into the forest. Too frightened to follow, Braggadochio and Trompart
assure each other of the inadvisability of pursuit.

The episode of Braggadochio and Belphoebe is essentially a comic interlude,
and the fact that it is comic suggests its place in the allegorical structure of the
poem. In Braggodochio's burlesque character are combined several vices
opposed to the virtue of fortitude or courage, the proper virtue of the irascible
power of the soul. He is an example of Aristotle's "rash man," who "would like
people to believe that he is animated by the same feelings as the brave man when
danger threatens. . . . For this reason most rash men are of the forcible feeble
type. They swagger a good deal when things look bright, but make themselves
scarce in the presence of actual danger" (*Ethics*, III.7, p. 96). He also illus-
trates the "defect" of bravery, "a man so constituted that he is scared by any-
thing, even the squeak of a mouse . . ." (*Ethics*, VII.5, p. 206). He is primarily
a figure of vainglory, of which his boasting is merely a symptom. Thomas
Aquinas writes that "glory may be called vain in three ways. First on the part
of the thing for which one seeks glory: as when a man seeks glory for that which
is unworthy of glory . . . ; secondly, on the part of him from whom he seeks
glory . . . ; thirdly, on the part of the man himself who seeks glory, for that he
does not refer the desire of his own glory to a due end, such as God's honor, or
the spiritual welfare of his neighbor" (*Summa Theologica*, II.132.1). Bragga-
dochio desires praise for his "gay portance" and "gallant show," not for any
brave or honorable actions; he desires glory out of self-love, not for any due
end. In his desire to win easy glory at court, and in Belphoebe's attack on court
life and her defense of the hard way of deserted places, Spenser dramatizes
some conventional symbols of vice and virtue. The court represents vanity,
sloth, luxury, envy, and other vices opposed to temperance or fortitude; the
difficult ways of isolated nature represent the obstacles and temptations which
must be overcome before virtue can be achieved. These two opposed ways of
life are described in such a way as to show Spenser's familiarity with one of the

most popular renaissance allegories of virtue and vice, "Hercules at the Cross-roads," an important element in the allegorical structure of Book I, though less important in this book. For the court as a conventional symbol of vice in renaissance satire see John Skelton's *The Bouge of Court;* Sir Thomas Wyatt's *Letter to Sir John Poins;* and John Donne's *Satire IV*.

Braggadochio is appropriately treated comically because he represents essentially various emotional "defects," not excesses. Spenser felt, with great artistic justification, that, although the excesses could be characterized as dangerous to his hero, the notion of deficiency in courage could not be treated as a serious enemy to Guyon. Belphoebe represents an opposite to the defective Braggadochio, a kind of absolute temperance, perhaps transcending the ideal of the mean. Thomas Aquinas treats virginity as one of the virtues of temper-ance, denying, however, that it departs from the mean (*Summa Theologica,* II.152.2). Guyon, by implication, is related to Belphoebe as Aeneas was related to the disguised Venus, whom he at first mistook for Diana. The continued parallel between Aeneas and Braggadochio not only deepens the comedy by making Braggadochio a ludicrously inadequate imitator; it also indicates that Guyon, the British Aeneas, in the same circumstance would have shown the wonder and worship with which Virgil's hero reacts to Venus.

iv: Occasion, Furor, and Phedon

Having left the Castle of Medina, the palmer and Guyon journey on their quest until, in the distance, they see what appears to be a madman dragging a handsome young man along the ground at the urging of an old hag who follows behind. Guyon, rushing in to rescue the youth, grapples with the madman, Furor, who throws the knight to the ground and beats him furiously. The palmer warns Guyon that he cannot hope to defeat Furor until he has silenced the old hag, Occasion. Guyon breaks Furor's hold and then puts a lock on Occasion's tongue, finally binding her hand and foot. His conquest of Furor is then relatively easy. After binding Furor, he turns to the young man, Phedon, and asks how he came into Furor's hands. Phedon tells how a series of events caused him to become so enraged that Furor caught up with him. As Phedon finishes his story, a messenger is seen approaching in a cloud of dust. He is Atin, servant to Pyrochles, who has been sent ahead by his master to seek Occasion. Atin loudly insults Guyon for his cowardly victory over a helpless old woman, throws a dart which is warded off by Guyon's shield, and departs as swiftly as he had arrived.

For the next two cantos, and for part of a third, Guyon's enemies are chiefly representatives of excessive anger, vices of the irascible power. Undoubtedly Spenser throws these enemies of temperance in Guyon's way before he faces the temptations to excessive pleasure and desire because, as Aristotle writes, "it is hard to fight against anger, but it is harder still to fight against pleasure" (*Ethics*, II.3, p. 60). Guyon must conquer the less difficult vices and temptations to vice first. Spenser's Occasion is a variant of the most usual figure of Occasion in renaissance emblems. She is usually a beautiful nude figure standing on a wheel in the sea or on a globe. A long lock of hair streams out in front and the back of her head is bald. The usual figure represents the opportunity which fortune brings; it must be grasped immediately or it cannot be caught at all. Spenser's Occasion differs because she is Occasion to Wrath—the kinds of situations fortune throws in the paths of men to tempt them to uncontrolled anger and irrational behavior. She has some of the features of conventional emblems of envy and discord—her ugliness, her age and her staff. Perhaps her lameness represents the impotence of wrath, illustrated by Furor's wild lashing out at Guyon during their combat. Furor represents what might be called the essence of anger, anger raised to the highest power. His flashing eyes and grinding teeth are conventional signs of wrath, as in Robert Burton's characterization: "Anger . . . is a cruel tempest of the mind, making his eyes sparkle fire, and stare, teeth gnash in his head. . . ." [21] And the blindness of anger is a common notion, as in Aquinas: ". . . of all passions, anger is the most manifest obstacle to the judgment of reason, according to Ps. XXX. 10: *My eye is troubled with wrath*" (*Summa Theologica*, II. 48.3).

At first Guyon makes the mistake of fighting Furor on the madman's terms. He lets his anger do the work of his reason and temporarily becomes himself the victim of Occasion. Guyon should not have allowed the occasion of Furor's mistreatment of Phedon to arouse him to irrational behavior. The palmer's advice that Occasion must be removed first is the standard advice in renaissance medical works (*Anatomy of Melancholy*, p. 473). Burton specifically advises the withstanding of the occasions to wrath (p. 553). What Guyon must do is remove the occasions to wrath, which Aquinas, following Aristotle's *Rhetoric*, helps define: "All the causes of anger are reduced to slight. For slight is of three kinds . . . ; *contempt, despiteful treatment . . . and insolence:* and all the motives of anger are reduced to these three" (*Summa Theologica*, II.47.2). Thus the violent, insulting language of Occasion is appropriate to the allegory. In a way, she comprises all of Aquinas's "causes of anger." After Occasion is silenced. Furor weakens and is defeated because anger is by nature a short-lived aberration without external support (*Ethics*, IV.5, p. 128).

Phedon's story is a concrete example of how fortune gives occasion for wrath. Phedon believed that his beloved Claribell had been disloyal, and he naturally desires revenge. Aquinas points out that the desire for revenge is necessary for the arousing of anger (*Summa Theologica*, II.46.1). His anger becomes uncontrollable when he learns that his best friend, Philemon, has trapped him into believing in Claribell's disloyalty and that she has instead been entirely faithful. Aristotle writes, "Our anger is more readily excited by our friends than by those who are not; for men think they are entitled to good treatment from their friends. . . ." [22] After Phedon killed Philemon, he became obsessed with revenge and attempted to kill Claribell's maid, Pryene, who had been an innocent dupe of Philemon. Phedon has been driven to the brink of insane wrath by a series of events over which, at first, he had no control, and his justifiable desire for revenge on the apparently guilty becomes irrational: ". . . if one desire . . . vengeance in any way whatever contrary to the order of reason, for instance if

[21] *Anatomy of Melancholy*, ed. Floyd Dell and Paul Jordan-Smith, Tudor Publishing Company, 1948, p. 234.

[22] *Rhetoric*, II.2, trans. and ed. Lane Cooper, Appleton-Century-Crofts, 1932, p. 97.

he desire the punishment of one who has not deserved it, or beyond his deserts
. . . then the desire of anger will be called sinful. . . . Secondly . . . the movement
of anger should not be immoderately fierce, neither internally nor exter-
nally . . ." (*Summa Theologica*, II.158.2). Phedon allows the occasion for anger
to develop both internally and in action into rampant wrath, at which time
he is attacked by Furor.

iv.39–vi.51: Pyrochles, Cymochles, and Phaedria

As Phedon ends his story, Atin appears to warn Guyon that his master, the
bloody Pyrochles, is approaching to seek occasion to wrath. He threatens and
insults Guyon and leaves. Soon afterward Guyon sees a knight rushing toward
him. Without a word, the stranger charges Guyon furiously and strikes him
with his sword. Guyon, enraged, draws his sword and the battle is on. Pyrochles,
like Furor, soon loses control of himself. Blinded by rage and, thus, ineffective,
he is easily beaten by Guyon, who keeps his head. Still full of inner wrath,
Pyrochles accepts Guyon's offer to spare his life, then asks Guyon to release
Furor and Occasion. Though reluctant, Guyon allows Pyrochles to unbind the
captives, who immediately attack their rescuer. Furor grapples with Pyrochles
and soon is dragging him through the mud. Guyon, on the advice of the palmer,
does not intervene. Full of chagrin at his master's defeat, Atin rushes away to
find Pyrochles' brother Cymochles, who is idly basking in the pleasures of the
Bower of Bliss, surrounded by a bevy of un-and-half-clothed girls. Atin quickly
stirs Cymochles to anger by insult and exhortation, and the two set out to
avenge Pyrochles' defeat. Soon they come to a lake, where they see a small boat
occupied by a gay young lady. Cymochles asks the lady, Phaedria, to ferry him
to the other side, and she agrees but will not allow Atin in the boat. Instead of
taking Cymochles to the opposite shore, however, Phaedria takes him to a float-
ing island paradise of idleness and sensual delight, and Cymochles quickly
forgets his revenging wrath. After some amorous play, Phaedria lulls Cymochles
to sleep, enters her boat, and sails out onto the lake again. In the meantime,
Guyon and the palmer have reached the shore of Phaedria's lake. Phaedria
offers to take Guyon to the other shore but refuses to allow the palmer on board.
After she and Guyon reach the island, Cymochles awakes and, remembering
his vow to avenge his brother's defeat, he strides toward the shore of the island,
where he sees Guyon and Phaedria. Filled with jealousy, he challenges Guyon
and they fight until Phaedria calms them. Then she takes Guyon back to the
shore of the Lake of Idleness, while Cymochles forgets his purpose again and
sinks back into idle pleasure. As Guyon steps ashore he sees Atin, who curses
him roundly. After Guyon has left, Atin sees a madman approaching in desper-
ate haste. Without pause, the madman throws himself into the lake, thrashing
and crying out in anguish, and the shocked Atin recognizes his master, Pyroch-
les. When Pyrochles cries out for help, Atin jumps in to rescue his master.

Atin represents discord both in the inner man and in the external world.
He disposes men to anger, a kind of inner discord of the soul when it is not
under the control of reason. Pyrochles suffers a pathological form of anger,
caused by an imbalance among the four bodily humors. As the legend on his

shield (Burnt I do Burn) shows, his disease is an excess of "choler." Renaissance authorities would have called Pyrochles' condition "choler adust," adustion occurring when a humor becomes burnt through excessive heat. Pyrochles seeks occasion to wrath because he is one of those who is "choleric, so-called because they lose their tempers at anything and on any occasion" (Aristotle, *Ethics*, IV.5, p. 128). His strength in battle is not true courage, for according to Burton, men who have choler adust are "bold and impudent . . . apt to quarrel, and think of such things, battles, combats, and their manhood, furious . . ." (*Anatomy of Melancholy*, p. 341). And Aristotle writes that "the most one can say of those who fight from no higher motive than anger is that they are good fighters; one cannot call them brave. For they are not moved by honor or guided by principle; simply they are swayed by their feelings" (*Ethics*, III.8, p. 100). Thus Guyon's battle with Pyrochles represents the temptation to intemperate anger which must be conquered in the course of the quest for temperance. His defeat of Pyrochles confirms Guyon in true courage, as opposed to the false courage of the choleric man.

Pyrochles' sullen taciturnity is characteristic of the angry man: "Consequently anger may cause such a disturbance, that the tongue is altogether deprived of speech; and taciturnity is the result" (*Summa Theologica*, II.48.4). Although Pyrochles is defeated by Guyon, he does not accept defeat because he is constitutionally incapable of accepting it. His defeat is merely another "occasion to wrath" and leads him to unbind Furor. His battle with Furor illustrates the madness which unchecked anger leads to, for all renaissance authorities agreed that choler in excess leads to frenzy and eventually to death. (See the portrait of the choleric man in Christopher Marlowe's *Tamburlaine*, II.) When he jumps into the Lake of Idleness, Pyrochles illustrates the end of the choleric man. His burning rage has ended in the adustion of choler, and the diseased humor is literally burning him up. In Galenic medicine the principle of treatment was "opposites by opposites," the dry heat of choler by the cool moisture of "phlegm." Pyrochles tries to cure himself by jumping into the lake, but he is beyond natural remedy, and, besides, one moral disease (wrath) is not cured by another (idleness). Pyrochles' jumping into the lake gains its most profound significance from the fact that Atin's attempt to rescue his master is parallel to Guyon's attempt to wash the hands of Ruddymane. Spenser emphasizes the parallel by describing the two acts in almost the same language (Canto ii.3 and Canto vi.46). A contrast between the Lake of Idleness and the nymph's well is thus implied. The lake washes the blood from Pyrochles' armor but does nothing for the fire within; the well does nothing to the blood on Ruddymane's hands but purifies him internally.

Pyrochles' brother, Cymochles, is a more complicated character. His greatest tendency is toward excessive sensual pleasure. He represents essentially, then, an excess of the concupiscible power, like Sansloy. He comes closest to Aristotle's naturally incontinent man. He is a slave to his own desires, changeable like a wave. His wrath is not the result of any unusual tendency toward excessive anger; it springs rather from his love of sensual pleasure and indolence and is quickly overcome by pleasure (*Ethics*, VII.10, p. 217). His impulsive changes from idle lust to fierce anger are characteristic of the incontinent man (*Summa*

Theologica, II.156.1). Aquinas calls such changeableness "weakness": ". . . when a man does not stand to what he has been counselled; wherefore this kind of incontinuence is called weakness" (*Summa Theologica*, II.156.1). Cymochles' easy neglect of his vowed revenge is, therefore, an act of incontinence. In defeating Cymochles, Guyon defeats both the idle lust and the anger which spring from excessive sensuality. Unlike Cymochles, Guyon does not forget his purpose—to avenge the deaths of Mordant and Amavia.

The pleasure Phaedria offers Guyon is mainly an absence of pain, or at least the pleasure of satisfying nature's desires without exercising the virtues of the irascible power. Her parody of the Sermon on the Mount invites Cymochles—and presumably all who come to her island—to give up needless pain, fruitless labor, care for the world. In this respect, her appeal is much like that of the traditional sin of sloth. Her parody of Medina's calming speech to Guyon and the champions of excess and defect again reminds us of the prelapsarian harmony of Mordant and Amavia, for Phaedria cites the example of the sub-dued Mars. The context makes clear, however, that she does not have in mind the chastened Venus. Her Venus is that of fruitful Nature, who seems to preside over the whole island and in whose embrace the wayward warrior could easily forget his responsibilities. Unlike Medina, whose intention is to maintain the mean, and hence the continence of both the irascible and concupiscible powers, Phaedria wishes to subdue the irascible power by convincing Guyon of its uselessness. She misrepresents it as seeking harms and pains rather than com-batting them. Aristotelian fortitude, the virtue of the irascible power, is as necessary for the pursuit of good (generally in Book II called "honor") as is temperance, in Aristotle the virtue of the concupiscible power. Idleness, ease, frivolity, empty mirth are the pastimes of the slothful, those who attempt to satisfy the demands of the concupiscible power without exercising the virtues of the irascible power, that is, without actively engaging in the pursuit of honor, which is the reward of virtue.

From Homer to the popular tales of the Renaissance, wandering islands and magical boats are fairly common features of fictional travel narratives. The rootless wandering and rudderless motion must certainly have been for Spenser an appropriate symbol for sloth and insufficient fortitude. The wandering island is in the sharpest contrast with the castle of Medina, which was built on a rock, while Phaedria's boat is the opposite of the ferryboat steered by the palmer and rowed by Alma's tireless boatman that will take Guyon across perilous seas to the Bower of Bliss.

vii: The Cave of Mammon

Guyon, still without the palmer from whom he was separated in the Phaedria episode, wanders for a long time in a wilderness before coming upon a dark, ill-looking man in a shady glade sitting surrounded by piles of gold. The man is Mammon, who proposes to show Guyon the source of the world's wealth. Guyon consents more out of curiosity than covetousness, and the pair descend past forboding shapes that line the way to the gate of Hades. Entering a little door to one side of the main gate, they begin their journey through the realm of Mammon. A monster walks behind Guyon, ready to strike the moment he falls asleep or touches anything with covetous hand, lustful eye, or lips. That Guyon never does so is evidence of his never being tempted. After viewing a huge room full of chests of gold, they pass on into another treasure-laden room where a fiendish spirit has been set as guard of the wealth of the world. From here they pass on to a furnace room where sweating fiends work at purifying gold and thence into a rich room guarded by the monster Disdain, where Mammon's daughter Philotime holds court over a pushing, climbing, flattering crew. Guyon courteously refuses Mammon's offer of his daughter in marriage, and the angry money god takes him on to the next sight, the Garden of Proserpina. Here Guyon sees a black, poisonous garden, in the midst of which is a silver seat beside a tree of golden apples, the apples that Hercules took from the Hesperides. Surrounding the garden is the black river Cocytus, into which the golden apples hang down. Guyon discovers countless people tormented in the river, one of whom is Tantalus, who keeps grasping at the golden fruit, and another of whom is Pilate, who vainly tries to wash his filthy hands. Unwilling to have him witness more, Mammon makes one last unsuccessful, insulting attempt to lure Guyon into touching something with covetous hand, lustful eye, or lips. He then conducts him back to the upper world, where with his first breath of fresh air the weakened Guyon, not having eaten or slept for three days, faints.

The rich and suggestive allegory of the Mammon episode is on the whole more accessible than that of the Mordant and Amavia episode—its chief rival in complexity. In addition to the rather obvious moral allegory of the temptation to incontinence through avarice, the episode abounds with types of the temptation of Christ, the fall of man, and the harrowing of hell. Mammon, according to the Sermon on the Mount, is the antithesis of God. The "fatal Stygian law" by which Guyon will be destroyed if he yields to temptation is like the law by which Adam was punished. In the Garden of Proserpina is a type of Eden especially appropriate to Mammon because the apples—of which Proserpina had eaten when she doomed herself to die—are golden. At the farthest reaches of the underworld, where Tantalus and Pilate are punished, is the deserted garden of death. The garden is not only an antitype of Gloriana's court; it is in a sense an antitype even of the idle fruitfulness of Phaedria's island. The Boethian distinction of which Guyon makes so much in his debate with Mammon, the distinction between the little that is necessary to sustain life and a superfluity of wealth, is one between fruitfulness and sterility. If the fruits of the earth are used to sustain man in health that he may be fruitful in his actions, they are good. If they are accumulated and hoarded and made the objects of pride, they are evil. Even Phaedria scoffs at the image of Tantalus' fruitless pursuit of the means of satisfying his boundless avarice. Phaedria argues that fortitude ought to be lulled to sleep, for its ends are pointless. Mammon argues that the ends of fortitude are fine but that they can be purchased with money.

The honor that can be purchased with money is the honor Braggadochio seeks, not the honor that rewards Aristotle's magnanimous man (*Ethics*, IV.3, p. 121). Braggadochio would be the ideal courtier in the court of Philotime, whose golden chain of ambition reverses the hierarchies of the renaissance world view. A natural peasant, Braggadochio might suitably exist on the island of Phaedria. A natural aristocrat and follower of Belphoebe's ideal of magnanimity, Guyon must not only avoid the idle ease of animal nature represented in Phaedria's isle; he must even more forcefully resist the unnatural reversal of Belphoebe's vital ideal which is represented in the descending orders of Mammon's realm. Pilate, who freed a murderer and allowed the Lord of Life to die, is the ultimate symbol of the misuse of worldly power, the ultimate corruption of the concupiscible power "that loves to live."

Guyon's faint is difficult. On the fictional level, the narrator tells us that he faints from lack of food and sleep. There is no evidence that he found Mammon's temptations difficult to resist or that doing so cost him any expense of energy. In seeking an allegorical meaning, we are forced to look for correspondences between this episode and others in Book II. Guyon's fainting from a breath of pure air is analogous to Mordant's dying from a draught of pure water. Both episodes suggest death to sin and the world and an analogy with the crucifixion. Also analogous to baptism and crucifixion is the ideal of death to the world expounded by Socrates in the *Phaedrus*. The so-called "philosopher's death" is probably best known from Plato's use of it in the myth of the cave in the *Republic*. On the fictional level, Guyon has been forced through his intense, but self-inflicted, duel with Mammon to neglect his body and the satisfaction of nature's legitimate demands. On the moral level, this neglect leads to the extreme condition of the philosopher's death, an ideal of the contemplative man in the dualistic tradition of Greek and Christian thought but an unsatisfactory condition for the renaissance man of action whose responsibilities keep him in this world and whose ethics make ample allowance for the control rather than the total subjection and death of the lower faculties of human nature. The allegory of the Castle of Alma develops fully Spenser's idea of the relationship between the well-regulated and cared for body and the governing soul.

vi.47–51 and viii.10–32: Pyrochles and Cymochles Again

As Atin and Pyrochles flounder in the Lake of Idleness, Archimago comes to the shore and Atin cries out for help. Archimago examines Pyrochles' wounds and cures them with herbs and with magic so that he is quickly restored to health. Later, after Guyon has successfully withstood the temptations of Mammon's Cave, only to faint the moment he reaches fresh air, Pyrochles and Cymochles, now in the service of Archimago, attack the unconscious knight, who they believe is dead. Since they cannot avenge themselves in battle, they propose to strip Guyon of his armor and leave his body for the vultures. The palmer pleads with them not to commit such a shameful act, but they insult him and prepare to strip Guyon. At this point Prince Arthur appears in the distance and Archimago warns Pyrochles and his brother to prepare for battle. Pyrochles, who lacks his sword, seizes the sword which Archimago carries; this weapon is, in fact, Arthur's enchanted sword, which Archimago had stolen for Braggadochio. Archimago warns Pyrochles that the marvelous weapon will not harm its true master, but the enraged knight refuses to listen. Arthur arrives and asks the palmer what the trouble is. When he learns what Pyrochles and Cymochles intend he attempts first to dissuade them by reason, but in the end they attack him without warning. Beset on two sides Arthur is knocked from his horse and forced to defend himself with only his lance, which is quickly hacked in two. Eventually Pyrochles wounds Arthur in the right side and the attack becomes more furious. The palmer, seeing Arthur's desperate situation, gives him Guyon's sword and the tide turns. Arthur kills Cymochles and wards off the wild blows of the insane Pyrochles. In desperation, Pyrochles throws away the enchanted sword of Arthur and grapples with the prince, but Arthur is stronger and throws Pyrochles to the ground. Arthur offers life to his enemy if he will renounce his crimes and promise to serve the prince, but Pyrochles refuses and Arthur regretfully kills his enemy.

The association of Pyrochles and Cymochles with Archimago is the signal for a change in their significance. Guyon had fought these two and had had little trouble holding his own with them, but when Arthur fights them they wound him and very nearly kill him before he defeats them. As opponents of Guyon, the continent man of classical ethics, the two brothers represented natural internal enemies to temperance, tendencies of the sensible soul which are potentially destructive. As natural tendencies they are capable of being controlled, though not defeated completely. Guyon was able to get the better of Pyrochles and to hold his own with Cymochles. But is the classical concept of continence sufficient? Can it lead to true temperance, free from emotional perturbation and from temptation to excess? Are wrath and incontinence merely natural defects which can be controlled and ultimately eradicated by self-control and by reason? Doesn't something more sinister than the Greeks imagined lie behind these natural tendencies to emotional excess? In fact Guyon is helpless against Pyrochles and Cymochles when they are allied with Archimago, that is, when they are seen in their most profound dimension, the realm of the Satanic. For perturbations came into life to threaten and destroy the inner perfection of man only with Satan's temptation of Adam and Eve and the fall of our first parents, an event hidden in the story of Mordant and Amavia just as demonic power is hidden in the tendencies against which Guyon fights. Against the Satanic, something more than Greek continence is required, for although continence may hold its own against anger and intemperance for a time, only Christ and Christian faith can destroy them. Arthur's victory over the two brothers represents not only Christ's victory over the temptations of the devil in the wilderness, but also Christ's final victory on the cross over sin and Satan, as the wound in Arthur's right side clearly indicates. In Arthur's victory, Spenser again touches on the limitations of the Greek notion of continence and virtue, and again Guyon is not condemned for his limitation. It is Guyon's sword with which Arthur wins his victory, just as Christ's victory was won in his humanity.

ix: The Castle of Alma

Guyon regains consciousness after Arthur has defeated Pyrochles and Cymochles, and the palmer explains how Arthur has saved the knight's life.

After Guyon thanks the prince, the two knights set out together, Guyon to fulfill his vow to avenge the death of Mordant and Amavia, Arthur to find Gloriana, whom he had seen in a vision and worshipped immediately. After some traveling the knights come to a castle and decide to stay there the night, but they are denied entrance because the castle is under attack by a disordered but fierce mob. Almost at once, Guyon and Arthur are attacked by the mob, but charging in fiercely the knights put the ragged attackers to flight. The gate of the castle is then opened to them and they are welcomed by the lady of the castle, the virgin Alma. Alma entertains Guyon and Arthur graciously and takes them on an inspection of her marvelously furnished and perfectly organized castle. After viewing the walls of the castle, the knights visit the kitchen, a presence chamber, and finally the castle turret, where three of Alma's counselors live. In the chamber of the oldest counselor, Eumnestes, Arthur finds an old book called *Briton Monuments* and Guyon another called *Antiquity of Faery-land*. They ask Alma to allow them to read these chronicles and she consents.

Alma is the rational soul and her castle is the body and the inferior powers in perfect harmony with the rational soul. The castle of Alma is best understood by comparison with the Castle of Medina in Canto ii. Medina's castle is attacked from within; the balance which Medina is able to achieve is temporary and precarious and demands her attention and intervention continually. The Castle of Alma, on the other hand, is perfectly ordered internally. Alma's presence is enough to preserve calm. But the castle is attacked by fierce enemies from without, who will eventually destroy the castle if they are not defeated. The Castle of Medina represents man's psychological condition since the fall. The harmony which existed between all of the elements of man's nature was broken, and the rational part found itself in a perpetual conflict with the body and the emotions. Medina's castle is an emblem of self-control or continence; thus it is an appropriate symbol of Guyon's nature. Alma's castle is a more perfect state than Medina's. It symbolizes Plato's and Aristotle's temperance—the state in which all elements of man's nature are in harmony and under the authority of reason. It is a symbol of the ideal toward which Guyon is questing, and it represents the nature of Arthur. At the same time it is made clear that Guyon could never have attained the condition of Alma's castle without Arthur, though he can approach it. For without Arthur, as Canto xi makes clear, the harmony in Alma's castle—Alma herself—is doomed. Guyon's classical ideal is an impossible one. If man's enemies were only the tendencies of his own nature, perhaps the harmony of temperance could be attained, but there is a fierce mob on the outside battering at the gates. Guyon's visit to Alma's castle shows him an ideal he has fought to attain; and he has deserved, because of his victories, to see the inner perfection which he desires. But it will require Arthur to establish that perfection as a possibility for Guyon and all men.

x: *The British and Elfin Chronicles*

The chronicle that Arthur reads in Eumnestes' study high in the turret of Alma's castle is a legendary history with, by modern standards, almost no basis in fact whatsoever. Geoffrey of Monmouth's account in the *Historia Regum Britanniae* of the generations from Brutus, the founder of Britain, to the coming of the Anglo-Saxons had been incorporated into at least a dozen later chronicles from which Spenser also borrowed. Even though this legendary history is not literally true, it served Spenser's purposes beautifully as a poetic equivalent of history. In fact, it provided the English poet with a much fuller and richer legendary past than his great Roman master Virgil could draw upon. This poetic equivalent of history is important to an understanding of the overall mythic structure of *The Faerie Queene*, not just of Book II alone. The three ideal kingdoms in Spenser's conception—Britain, Faeryland, and the New Jerusalem (Book I, Canto x)—suggest the world as it is, the world as philosophers have imagined it might be, and the world that is to come with the spiritual perfection of man. The first answers to Augustine's City of Man, and the last to his City of God; but Faeryland has no place in the Augustinian conception. While the City of God is a spiritual ideal, Faeryland is a philosophical ideal. As a type of Christ, Arthur unites the Cities of Man and of God, Britain and the New Jerusalem. As a type of ethical perfection (magnanimity) he will unite Britain and Faeryland.

Both Britain and Faeryland are types of Spenser's England. Historically, the Chronicle of Briton Kings foreshadows contemporary political instability and military conquest. The tranquil and untroubled succession of elfin emperors becomes manifestly an idealization of the Tudor succession preceeding Elizabeth. In terms of Book II, one of this canto's most important functions is to illustrate through their kingdoms' histories the difference between Arthur, the historical human being, and Guyon, the idealized elf. In the psychological allegory of Alma's castle we are told that the two chronicles are products of the human mind. But since the Chronicle of Briton Kings is a record of the historical past as well, the two chronicles are vastly different from each other. Spenser's meaning seems to be that human history and human ideals will merge only with the union of Arthur and Gloriana. As types of contemporary England, the wide disparity is more significant than the promise of eventual reconciliation. Allegorically, Spenser has already demonstrated in Books I and II that the reconciliation of Faeryland and Britain can come only with the achievement of the New Jerusalem.

xi.5–49: Arthur and Maleger

After Guyon and the palmer have left Alma's castle, the mob outside renews its fierce assault. The captain of the mob, Maleger, sends out troops against the main gate and against the five bulwarks of the castle. Alma's guards defend the castle valiantly but the situation is desperate. Arthur, seeing Alma's distress, puts on his armor and sallies out to fight Maleger. The hideous Maleger, riding a tiger, shoots his bolts at Arthur, who wards them off with his shield. When Arthur draws near, Maleger retreats; when Arthur stops, Maleger waits. As Maleger shoots his arrows at Arthur, one of two old hags accompanying him retrieves them. Arthur decides to stop the hag first so that Maleger will not have a continual supply of arrows, but when he does so both hags attack him and throw him to the ground. Maleger, seeing his advantage, charges in also, and Arthur is in great danger. But Timias, Arthur's squire, attacks the two hags and leaves his master to fight Maleger. Arthur first strikes Maleger a fierce blow with his mace so that he falls to the ground as though dead, but soon he is up again stronger than ever. Arthur then hacks Maleger nearly in half and is amazed and terrified to see his enemy apparently unhurt. He throws his weapons away and grapples with Maleger, crushing the life out of his foe and throwing him to the ground. To his horror Maleger rises vigorously again. Then Arthur remembers that Maleger is the son of Earth and gains strength in contact with his mother. He grasps Maleger, breaks his body, and holds him aloft until there is no life, then runs with him to a lake into which he casts Alma's hideous foe. As he makes his way back to the castle, he faints from his ordeal. His squire helps him to the castle, where he is cared for tenderly.

In one sense, this is the most crucial episode in the allegorical structure of Book II. The notes explain the detailed allegory of the fight with Maleger, and it remains only to indicate the significance of the canto in the structure of the poem. Arthur has already defeated and destroyed the inner enemies of temperance in his victory over Pyrochles and Cymochles. Now he defeats the outward destroyers of temperance. In both cases the enemy is something more than natural, something in the service of Satan. Here Arthur destroys sin and Satan himself, and his victory is a type of Christ's victory over sin and the devil. As a type of Christ, Arthur represents something which alone makes the ideal of temperance a possibility. Reason and self-control may hold its own against temptation to excess, but Christ alone can destroy sin. Arthur's victory over Maleger makes possible Guyon's victory over Acrasia.

xii: The Bower of Bliss

After reading the history of his elfin ancestors, Guyon enjoys dinner and a night's rest at the Castle of Alma before setting out on his final adventure. Steered by the palmer and rowed by Alma's boatman, he sails for three days to the island where, with the destruction of Acrasia's Bower of Bliss, he may fulfill the vow he made at the funeral of Mordant and Amavia. On the third day, the three voyagers see many strange and perilous sights, but the palmer's wisdom and the boatman's fortitude keep them from going amiss. The boatman remains behind when Guyon and the palmer at last set out across land for the Bower. They encounter a pack of wild animals which the palmer subdues with his magical wand, a porter called Genius, a lady named Excess, two enticing nude girls bathing in a fountain, and a singer whose beautiful music invites them to take their pleasure. At last they come upon the enchantress herself, still perspiring from her recent amorous toil. Dressed in transparent gauze, which conceals only that it may reveal, she leans over the senseless body of Verdant, her current lover, drinking his swooning spirit. She does not see Guyon and the palmer until the old man has firmly thrown a well-made net over her lover and her. With Acrasia and Verdant strongly bound, Guyon utterly destroys the beautiful Bower. The palmer then releases the shamefaced Verdant, restores the wild animals, transformed by Acrasia, to their human forms, and sets off with Guyon and the captive enchantress.

The perils Guyon encounters on his sea voyage constitute a gallery of emblems of incontinence. Canto xii is in one sense an allegorical anticlimax to Arthur's defeat of Maleger. We are told in xi.9.9, for example, that two of the most powerful machines in Maleger's army, wealth and beauty, were brought to the siege of the eyes of Alma's castle. Insofar as the assault upon the senses is represented in images, the besieging forces are hideous. The allegorical meanings of the images are stipulated rather than inferable from appearances. Spenser's use of naive allegory in Canto xi results in the representation of the spiritual reality that underlies the mere external appearance of things. With the X-ray vision of the experienced Christian, Arthur can perceive directly the spiritual threat implicit in the body's surrender to the appeal of the besieged senses. Arthur's allegorical struggle with Maleger is narrated from the hero's *spiritually realistic* point of view. Guyon's encounter with the sensuous appeal of the Bower of Bliss in Canto xii is an equivalent in concrete natural imagery of Arthur's encounter with Maleger and is narrated from the elfin hero's *naturally realistic* point of view. Yeats called the method of Canto xi *allegorical* and that of Canto xii *symbolic*.

Throughout Book II Guyon remains significant on the "Faeryland-level" of Spenser's meaning. His adventures represent an idealization of human experience, informed by the best insights of classical and medieval philosophy, set forth in poetic images made philosophically significant by generations of medieval and renaissance mythographers, but essentially independent of a mystical Christian significance. Arthur, in contrast, moves from the City of Man to the City of God, levels of existence lower and higher, respectively, than Faeryland. Because of the difference between Cantos xi and xii in the poetic representation of what in actuality would be a single experience, the conflict between appearance and reality becomes an explicit theme with the introduction of the evil Genius in Canto xii. He is the philosophical equivalent of Satan, the principle of false-seeming in the universe that misleads men into pursuing apparent good instead of true good. It is the operation of this principle that makes beauty such a powerful instrument for evil in the allegory of Alma's castle. The evil Genius of false-seeming is to Acrasia as the palmer is to Guyon. Right reason is universal order and man's perception of this order through his own reason. Temperance is both the harmonious balance between emotional excesses and emotional deficiencies and the will's direction of the emotions in pursuit of ends approved of by reason.

The beautiful enchantress Acrasia represents both the disharmonious imbalance of emotional excesses and deficiencies and the rational soul's incapability of controlling the emotions. In particular, she is represented as weakening the irascible emotions and strengthening the concupiscible, but the various transformations she works on her victims are understood to result from all forms of *akrasia*, "incontinence." It is impossible to deny that the Bower of Bliss is beautiful. Its description is one of the most sensuously appealing passages in English literature. Nor is the appeal of the Bower all to the eye, as Verdant must have discovered shortly before Guyon and the Palmer arrived. The beauty of nature is combined with that of art, and Acrasia is an epitome of the whole. The inescapable conclusion to be drawn from Spenser's allegory is that physical beauty is not always truth. As an artist, Spenser is not likely to have preferred the beauty of nature to that of art. Both kinds of beauty are included in the indictment. Indeed the combination of the two produces the greatest beauty of all. Through the power of the porter Genius, physical beauty of any kind is capable of masking the greatest enemy to temperance and therefore to heroic action. Had Arthur or Red Cross been the wrecker of the Bower of Bliss he might have stripped Acrasia to find the foul Duessa beneath. But Guyon's triumph resides in the fact that for him, the elfin idealization of natural man, Acrasia was the most beautiful of enchantresses.

A LETTER OF THE AUTHOR'S
EXPOUNDING HIS WHOLE INTENTION
IN
THE COURSE OF THIS WORK

Which, for that it giveth great light
to the reader, for the better understanding
is hereunto annexed.

To the right noble and valorous Sir Walter Raleigh, Knight, Lord Warden of the Stannaries and her Majesty's Lieutenant of the County of Cornwall.

Sir, knowing how doubtfully all allegories may be construed, and this book of mine which I have entitled *The Faerie Queene* being a continued allegory or dark conceit, I have thought good—as well for avoiding of jealous opinions and misconstructions as also for your better light in reading thereof—being so by you commanded, to discover unto you the general intention and meaning which in the whole course thereof I have fashioned, without expressing of any particular purposes or by-accidents therein occasioned.[1] The general end therefore of all the book is to fashion a gentleman or noble person in virtuous and gentle discipline. Which for that I conceived should be most plausible and pleasing being colored with an historical fiction—the which the most part of men delight to read, rather for variety of matter than for profit of the example— I chose the history of King Arthur, as most fit for the excellency of his person, being made famous by many men's former works and also furthest from the danger of envy and suspicion of present time.[2] In which I have followed all the antique poets historical. First Homer, who in the persons of Agamemnon and Ulysses hath ensampled a good governor and a virtuous man, the one in his *Ilias*, the other in his *Odysseis*.[3] Then Virgil, whose like intention was to do in

---

[1] Raleigh had apparently requested that Spenser clarify only the general intention and meaning of *The Faerie Queene*. Although this *Letter of the Author's* is a valuable guide to the interpretation of the poem, it is not here Spenser's purpose to explicate every detail of his thought and method.

[2] Spenser had to choose a hero equally acceptable to all contemporary political factions.

[3] *Iliad* and *Odyssey*.

the person of Aeneas. After him Ariosto comprised them both in his Orlando.[4] And lately Tasso dissevered them again and formed both parts in two persons, namely that part which they in philosophy call ethics, or virtues of a private man, colored in his Rinaldo; the other named politics in his Godfredo. By ensample of which excellent poets, I labor to portray in Arthur before he was king the image of a brave knight perfected in the twelve private moral virtues as Aristotle hath devised,[5] the which is the purpose of these first twelve books. Which if I find to be well accepted, I may be perhaps encouraged to frame the other part of politic virtues in his person after that he came to be king.

To some I know this method will seem displeasant, which had rather have good discipline delivered plainly in way of precepts or sermoned at large, as they use, than thus cloudily enwrapped in allegorical devices. But such, me seem, should be satisfied with the use of these days, seeing all things accounted by their shows and nothing esteemed of that is not delightful and pleasing to common sense. For this cause is Xenophon preferred before Plato, for that the one in the exquisite depth of his judgment formed a commonwealth such as it should be, but the other in the person of Cyrus and the Persians fashioned a government such as might best be. So much more profitable and gracious is doctrine by ensample than by rule.

So have I labored to do in the person of Arthur. Whom I conceive, after his long education by Timon to whom he was by Merlin delivered to be brought up so soon as he was born of the Lady Igrayne, to have seen in a dream or vision the Faery Queen, with whose excellent beauty ravished, he awaking resolved to seek her out, and so being by Merlin armed and by Timon thoroughly instructed, he went to seek her forth in Faeryland. In that Faery Queen I mean glory in my general intention, but in my particular I conceive the most excellent and glorious person of our sovereign the Queen, and her kingdom in Faeryland.[6] And yet in some places else I do otherwise shadow her. For considering she beareth two persons, the one of a most royal queen or empress, the other of a most virtuous and beautiful lady, this latter part in some places I do express in Belphoebe, fashioning the name according to your own excellent conceit of Cynthia (Phoebe and Cynthia being both names of Diana).[7] So in the person of Prince Arthur I set forth magnificence in particular, which virtue, for that—according to Aristotle and the rest—it is the perfection of all the rest and containeth in it them all, therefore in the whole course I mention the deeds of Arthur appliable to that virtue which I write of in that book.

But of the twelve other virtues, I make twelve other knights the patrons for the more variety of the history, of which these three books contain three. The first, of the Knight of the Red Cross, in whom I express holiness; the second, of

[4] Lodovico Ariosto (1474–1533), an Italian poet whose *Orlando Furioso* was a major source for Spenser's conception of the epic. Torquato Tasso (1544–1595), a contemporary Italian poet, the author of *Rinaldo* and *Jerusalem Delivered*.

[5] Medieval commentaries on Aristotle's *Nicomachean Ethics* specified twelve moral virtues.

[6] In the Faery Queene he represents Queen Elizabeth I, and in Faeryland he represents England.

[7] Raleigh had complimented Queen Elizabeth in a poem called *Cynthia* which survives only in manuscript fragments. The queen's presumed virginity made her identification with Diana, the chaste goddess of the hunt, appropriate in the minds of renaissance court poets.

Sir Guyon, in whom I set forth temperance; the third, of Britomartis, a lady knight, in whom I picture chastity. But, because the beginning of the whole work seemeth abrupt and as depending upon other antecedents, it needs that ye know the occasion of these three knights' several adventures; for the method of a poet historical is not such as of an historiographer. For an historiographer discourseth of affairs orderly as they were done, accounting as well the times as the actions, but a poet thrusteth into the midst, even where it most concerneth him, and there recoursing to the things forepassed and divining of things to come, maketh a pleasing analysis of all.

The beginning therefore of my history if it were to be told by an historiographer should be the twelfth book, which is the last, where I devise that the Faery Queen kept her annual feast twelve days, upon which twelve several days the occasions of the twelve several adventures happened, which being undertaken by twelve several knights are in these twelve books severally handled and discoursed. The first was this. In the beginning of the feast there presented himself a tall clownish young man [8] who, falling before the queen of faeries, desired a boon (as the manner then was) which during the feast she might not refuse: which was that he might have the achievement of any adventure which during that feast should happen. That being granted, he rested him on the floor, unfit through his rusticity for a better place. Soon after, entered a fair lady in mourning weeds, riding on a white ass with a dwarf behind her leading a warlike steed that bore the arms of a knight, and his spear in the dwarf's hand. She, falling before the queen of faeries, complained that her father and mother, an ancient king and queen, had been by an huge dragon many years shut up in a brazen castle, who thence suffered them not to issue; and therefore besought the Faery Queen to assign her some one of her knights to take on him that exploit. Presently, that clownish person upstarting desired that adventure; whereat the queen much wondering and the lady much gainsaying, yet he earnestly importuned his desire. In the end, the lady told him that unless that armor which she brought would serve him (that is the armor of a Christian man specified by St. Paul, Ephesians 6:10-22) that he could not succeed in that enterprise, which being forthwith put upon him with due furnitures thereunto, he seemed the goodliest man in all that company and was well liked of the lady. And eftsoons taking on him knighthood and mounting on that strange courser, he went forth with her on that adventure. Where beginneth the first book, *viz.*

A gentle knight was pricking on the plain. . . .

The second day, there came in a palmer bearing an infant with bloody hands, whose parents he complained to have been slain by an enchantress called Acrasia, and therefore craved of the Faery Queen to appoint him some knight to perform that adventure, which being assigned to Sir Guyon, he presently went forth with that same palmer. Which is the beginning of the second book and the whole subject thereof.

[8] The "tall clownish young man" is a common type in myth, epic, and romance. This is St. George, who is raised as a plowman, a fact that Spenser probably intended to be allegorically significant. Percival and Beowulf are the best known examples of the "unpromising hero" in medieval narrative.

The third day, there came in a groom who complained before the Faery Queen that a vile enchanter called Busirane had in hand a most fair lady called Amoretta, whom he kept in most grievous torment because she would not yield him the pleasure of her body. Whereupon, Sir Scudamour, the lover of that lady, presently took on him that adventure. But being unable to perform it by reason of the hard enchantments, after long sorrow, in the end met with Britomartis, who succored him and rescued his love. But by occasion hereof, many other adventures are intermeddled, but rather as accidents than intendments: as the love of Britomart, the overthrow of Marinell, the misery of Florimell, the virtuousness of Belphoebe, the lasciviousness of Hellenora, and many the like.

Thus much, Sir, I have briefly over-run to direct your understanding to the well-head of the history, that from thence gathering the whole intention of the conceit ye may as in a handful grip all the discourse, which otherwise may haply seem tedious and confused. So humbly craving the continuance of your honorable favor towards me and the eternal establishment of your happiness, I humbly take leave.

23 January 1589
Yours most humbly affectionate
ED. SPENSER

THE FIRST BOOK OF
THE FAERIE QUEENE

Containing

The Legend of the Knight of the Red Cross, or of Holiness

i	Lo I, the man whose muse whilom° did mask,	*formerly*
	As time her taught, in lowly shepherd's weeds,°	*clothes*
	Am now enforced° a far unfitter task:	*assigned*
	For trumpets stern to change mine oaten reeds,	
	And sing of knights' and ladies' gentle° deeds;	*noble*
	Whose praises having slept in silence long,	
	Me, all too mean, the sacred muse areads°	*advises*
	To blazon broad amongst her learnèd throng.	
	Fierce wars and faithful loves shall moralize my song.	
ii	Help then, O holy virgin, chief of nine,	
	Thy weaker° novice to perform thy will;	*too weak*
	Lay forth out of thine everlasting scrine°	*chest for records*
	The antique rolls,° which there lie hidden still,	*records*
	Of faery knights and fairest Tanaquill,	
	Whom that most noble Briton prince so long	
	Sought through the world and suffered so much ill	

i.1–9 an imitation of Virgil's *Aeneid* in which Spenser establishes himself and his poem within the tradition of Virgil. "I am thát poet who in times past made the light melody of pastoral poetry. In my next poem I left the woods for the adjacent farmlands, teaching them to obey even the most exacting tillers of the soil; and the farmers liked my work. But now I turn to the terrible strife of Mars" (Proem, trans. W. F. Jackson Knight, Penguin Books, p. 27, to which all subsequent citations of the *Aeneid* will refer). Spenser's pastoral poetry was *The Shepherd's Calendar*, a cycle of pastoral eclogues published in 1579.

i.5 "The ladies, the knights, the arms, the loves, the courtesies, the bold exploits I sing . . ." (Lodovico Ariosto, *Orlando Furioso*, I.1, trans. Allan Gilbert, 2 vols., S. F. Vanni, to which subsequent citations of *Orlando Furioso* will refer).

ii.1 *O holy virgin:* Calliope, the muse of epic poetry.

ii.5 *Tanaquill:* Gloriana, or the Faery Queen.

ii.6 *most noble Briton prince:* Arthur.

That I must rue his undeservèd wrong.
O help thou my weak wit, and sharpen my dull tongue.

iii And thou most dreaded imp° of highest Jove,   *child*
Fair Venus' son, that with thy cruel dart
At that good knight so cunningly didst rove°   *shoot*
That glorious fire it kindled in his heart,
Lay now thy deadly ebon° bow apart,   *ebony*
And with thy mother mild come to mine aid.
Come both, and with you bring triumphant Mart°   *Mars*
In loves and gentle jollities arrayed,
After his murderous spoils and bloody rage allayed.°   *calmed*

iv And with them eke,° O goddess heavenly bright,   *also*
Mirror of grace and majesty divine,
Great lady of the greatest isle, whose light
Like Phoebus' lamp throughout the world doth shine,
Shed thy fair beams into my feeble eyne,°   *eyes*
And raise my thoughts, too humble and too vile,°   *common*
To think of that true glorious type° of thine,   *symbol*
The argument of mine afflicted° style;   *lowly*
The which to hear vouchsafe, O dearest dread,° awhile.   *one inspiring awe*

CANTO i

The patron° of true holiness   *representative*
Foul Error doth defeat;
Hypocrisy him to entrap,
Doth to his home entreat.

1 A gentle knight was pricking° on the plain,   *spurring*
Y-clad in mighty arms and silver shield,
Wherein old dents of deep wounds did remain,
The cruel marks of many a bloody field;
Yet arms till that time did he never wield.
His angry steed did chide° his foaming bit,   *was impatient of*
As much disdaining to the curb to yield.

iii.1 dreaded imp: Cupid, god of love, in some traditions the son of Jove. He and Venus are invoked, together with Mars (*iii.*7), to provide the "fierce wars and faithful loves" mentioned in *i.*9.

iv.1 goddess heavenly bright: Queen Elizabeth I.

iv.4 Phoebus' lamp: the sun.

iv.5 my: (1596). 1590 reads *mine.*

iv.7 true glorious type: Gloriana, the idealization of Elizabeth's beauty and majesty.

1.2 Y-clad: The prefix *y-* was, in the earlier form *ge-*, a common Anglo-Saxon verbal prefix denoting completion of action. By Spenser's time it had become an archaic feature of poetic diction, restricted mainly to past participles.

Full jolly° knight he seemed and fair did sit,   *handsome*
As one for knightly jousts and fierce encounters fit.

2   And on his breast a bloody cross he bore,
The dear remembrance of his dying lord,
For whose sweet sake that glorious badge he wore,
And dead as living ever him adored.
Upon his shield the like was also scored°   *painted*
For sovereign hope, which in his help he had.
Right faithful true he was in deed and word,
But of his cheer° did seem too solemn sad;°   *expression, grave*
Yet nothing did he dread, but ever was y-drad.°   *dreaded*

3   Upon a great adventure he was bond°   *bound*
That greatest Gloriana to him gave,
That greatest glorious queen of Faeryland,
To win him worship and her grace to have,
Which of all earthly things he most did crave.
And ever as he rode, his heart did earn°   *yearn*
To prove his puissance in battle brave
Upon his foe, and his new force to learn—
Upon his foe, a dragon horrible and stern.°   *merciless*

4   A lovely lady rode him fair beside
Upon a lowly ass more white than snow,
Yet she much whiter, but the same° did hide   *i.e. whiteness*
Under a veil that wimpled° was full low,   *hanging in folds*
And over all a black stole she did throw,
As one that inly mourned. So was she sad,
And heavy sat upon her palfrey slow;
Seemèd in heart some hidden care she had.
And by her in a line° a milk-white lamb she lad.°   *by a leash, led*

5   So pure and innocent as that same lamb
She was in life and every virtuous lore,
And by descent from royal lineage came
Of ancient kings and queens that had of yore
Their scepters stretched from east to western shore,
And all the world in their subjection held,

2.4 "I am he that liveth, and was dead; and, behold, I am alive for evermore . . ." (Revelation 1:18).

2.6 *sovereign:* having greatest effect or power, often applied to medical remedies.

2.8 *too solemn sad:* an indication that Red Cross depends too much on his own righteousness and not enough on the hope of grace.

3.1–3 *bond . . . faeryland:* These words rhymed for Spenser, the vowel probably being about like the *a* in *father*. Historically, *bound* meaning, as here, 'going,' 'headed,' is not related to *bound*, the past tense of *bind*. By Spenser's time they had fallen together in pronunciation, both words having the variant forms *bond* and *bound*. For our treatment of *bond* as the past tense of *bind*, see note to x.66.3.

Till that infernal fiend with foul uproar
Forwasted° all their land and them expelled;　　*destroyed*
Whom to avenge, she had this knight from far　　*completely*
　　compelled.°　　*summoned*

6　Behind her far away a dwarf did lag,
　　That lazy seemed in being ever last,
　　Or wearièd with bearing of her bag
　　Of needments at his back. Thus as they passed,
　　The day with clouds was sudden overcast,
　　And angry Jove an hideous storm of rain
　　Did pour into his leman's° lap so fast　　*mistress's*
　　That every wight° to shroud° it did constrain,°　　*creature, seek*
　　And this fair couple eke to shroud themselves were　　*cover, force*
　　　fain.°　　*eager*

7　Enforced to seek some covert nigh at hand,
　　A shady grove not far away they spied
　　That promised aid the tempest to withstand.
　　Whose lofty trees y-clad with summer's pride
　　Did spread so broad that heaven's light did hide,
　　Not pierceable with power of any star.
　　And all within were paths and alleys wide,
　　With footing worn and leading inward far.
　　Fair harbor that them seems,° so in they entered are.　　*seems to them*

8　And forth they pass, with pleasure forward led,
　　Joying to hear the birds' sweet harmony,
　　Which therein shrouded from the tempest dread
　　Seemed in their song to scorn the cruel sky.
　　Much can° they praise the trees so straight and high:　　*did*
　　The sailing pine, the cedar proud and tall,
　　The vine-prop elm, the poplar never dry,
　　The builder oak, sole king of forests all,
　　The aspen good for staves, the cypress funeral.

9　The laurel, meed° of mighty conquerors　　*prize*
　　And poets sage, the fir that weepeth still,°　　*always*
　　The willow worn of forlorn paramours,

　　6.6–7　*angry Jove . . . leman's lap:* a common metaphor in classical literature. "Then the lord omnipotent of Sky descends in fruitful showers into the lap of his laughing consort . . ." (Virgil, *Georgics,* II.325–326, trans. J. W. Mackail, Modern Library, p. 317).
　　8.5–9.9　This catalogue of trees has a long tradition in classical and medieval literature, originating in Ovid's *Meta-*morphoses, X.90–104 (trans. Mary M. Innes, Penguin Books, pp. 247–248, to which subsequent citations will refer). Spenser's most immediate source is probably Chaucer's *Parliament of Fowls,* 176–182.
　　8.6　*sailing pine:* used in shipbuilding.
　　8.7　*vine-prop elm:* used in staking up the grapes in vineyards.
　　8.8　*builder oak:* used in carpentry.

The yew obedient to the bender's will,
The birch for shafts, the sallow for the mill,
The myrrh sweet bleeding in the bitter wound,
The warlike beech, the ash for nothing ill,
The fruitful olive, and the platan° round,   *plane tree*
The carver holm,° the maple seldom inward sound.   *oak*

10 Led with delight, they thus beguile the way
Until the blustering storm is overblown;
When weening° to return whence they did stray,   *expecting*
They cannot find that path which first was shown,
But wander to and fro in ways unknown,
Furthest from end then when they nearest ween,
That makes them doubt° their wits be not their own.   *believe*
So many paths, so many turnings seen,
That which of them to take in diverse° doubt they been.   *distracting*

11 At last resolving forward still to fare
Till that some end they find or° in or out,   *either*
That path they take that beaten seemed most bare
And like to lead the labyrinth about;°   *out of*
Which when by tract° they hunted had throughout,   *tracks*
At length it brought them to a hollow cave
Amid the thickest woods. The champion stout
Eftsoons° dismounted from his courser brave,°   *then, splendid*
And to the dwarf awhile his needless spear he gave.

12 'Be well aware,' quoth then that lady mild,
'Lest sudden mischief ye too rash provoke.
The danger hid, the place unknown and wild,
Breeds dreadful doubts. Oft fire is without smoke,
And peril without show. Therefore your stroke,
Sir knight, withhold till further trial made.'
'Ah lady,' said he, 'shame were to revoke
The forward footing for° an hidden shade.   *because of*
Virtue gives herself light through darkness for to wade.'

13 'Yea, but,' quoth she, 'the peril of this place
I better wot° than you, though now too late   *know*
To wish you back return with foul disgrace;
Yet wisdom warns, whilst foot is in the gate,

9.4 *yew:* used to make bows.
9.5 *sallow:* willow. which grows along stream banks.
9.6 *myrrh:* Its resins, obtained by slashing the tree, were highly prized as perfume and incense.
9.9 *carver holm:* oak used for carving.

10.2–9 Red Cross and Una are in the Wandering Wood, reminiscent of the *selva oscura* of Dante's *Inferno*, I.2–3: "I woke to find myself in a dark wood/ Where the right road was wholly lost and gone" (trans. Dorothy L. Sayers, Penguin Books, p. 71).

To stay the step ere forcèd to retreat.
This is the Wandering Wood, this Error's den,
A monster vile whom God and man does hate.
Therefore I read° beware.' 'Fly, fly,' quoth then   *advise*
The fearful dwarf, 'this is no place for living men.'

14 But full of fire and greedy hardiment,°   *eager courage*
    The youthful knight could not for aught be stayed,
    But forth unto the darksome hole he went
    And lookèd in. His glistering armor made
    A little glooming light, much like a shade,
    By which he saw the ugly monster plain,
    Half like a serpent horribly displayed;
    But th' other half did woman's shape retain,
    Most loathsome, filthy, foul, and full of vile disdain.

15 And as she lay upon the dirty ground,
    Her huge long tail her den all overspread,
    Yet was in knots and many boughts° upwound,   *coils*
    Pointed with mortal sting. Of her there bred
    A thousand young ones, which she daily fed,
    Sucking upon her poisonous dugs, each one
    Of sundry shapes, yet all ill-favorèd.
    Soon as that uncouth° light upon them shone,   *unaccustomed*
    Into her mouth they crept, and sudden all were gone.

16 Their dam upstart, out of her den affrayed,°   *frightened*
    And rushèd forth, hurling her hideous tail
    About her cursèd head, whose folds displayed
    Were stretched now forth at length without entrail.°   *coils*
    She looked about, and seeing one in mail
    Armèd to point,° sought back to turn again;   *completely*
    For light she hated as the deadly bale,
    Aye° wont in desert darkness to remain,   *always*
    Where plain none might her see, nor she see any plain.

17 Which when the valiant elf perceived, he leapt
    As lion fierce upon the flying prey,
    And with his trenchant blade her boldly kept
    From turning back and forcèd her to stay.
    Therewith enraged she loudly gan to bray,
    And turning fierce,° her speckled tail advanced,   *fiercely*

13.6 *Wandering:* deviating from right, erring.
14.4–6 Red Cross's armor makes only a dim light because he is as yet weak and inexperienced. Contrast this glimmer with the blinding brightness of Arthur's shield (Canto viii.19–21).
14.7–15.9 Spenser's description of Error derives primarily from Hesiod's account of the Snake goddess in *Theogony*, 301. Some features of the monster probably come from Revelation 9:7–10.

Threatening her angry sting, him to dismay.
Who nought aghast, his mighty hand enhanced;° *raised*
The stroke down from her head unto her shoulder glanced.

18 Much daunted with that dint,° her sense was dazed, *stroke*
Yet, kindling rage, herself she gathered round,° *coiled up*
And all at once her beastly body raised
With doubled forces high above the ground.
Tho° wrapping up her wreathèd stern° around, *then, coiled tail*
Leapt fierce upon his shield, and her huge train° *tail*
All suddenly about his body wound,
That hand or foot to stir he strove in vain.
God help the man so wrapped in Error's endless train.° *deceit*

19 His lady, sad to see his sore constraint,
Cried out, 'Now, now, sir knight, show what ye be;
Add faith unto your force and be not faint!
Strangle her, else she sure will strangle thee.'
That when he heard, in great perplexity,
His gall did grate° for grief and high disdain, *he was enraged*
And knitting all his force got one hand free,
Wherewith he gripped her gorge° with so great pain *throat*
That soon to loose her wicked bands did her constrain.

20 Therewith she spewed out of her filthy maw° *stomach*
A flood of poison horrible and black,
Full of great lumps of flesh and gobbets raw.
Which stunk so vildly° that it forced him slack *vilely*
His grasping hold and from her turn him back.
Her vomit full of books and papers was,
With loathly frogs and toads which eyes did lack,
And creeping sought way in the weedy grass.
Her filthy parbreak° all the place defilèd has. *vomit*

21 As when old Father Nilus gins to swell
With timely° pride above th' Egyptian vale, *seasonal*
His fatty° waves do fertile slime outwell, *rich*
And overflow each plain and lowly dale.
But when his later spring° gins to avale,° *last flood, sink*
Huge heaps of mud he leaves, wherein there breed
Ten thousand kinds of creatures, partly male
And partly female, of his fruitful seed;
Such ugly monstrous shapes elsewhere may no man read.° *see*

20.1–9 The primary source of this stanza is Revelation 16:13: "And I saw three unclean spirits like frogs come out of the mouth of the dragon, and out of the mouth of the beast, and out of the mouth of the false prophet."

21.1–7 The force of this comparison, an epic simile which probably comes from Ovid's *Metamorphoses*, I.422–433 (p. 43), is that heresy is self-perpetuating just as it is self-destructive ultimately (see 26.9 below).

22   The same so sore annoyèd has the knight,
That well-nigh chokèd with the deadly stink,
His forces fail, ne° can no lenger° fight.   *nor, longer*
Whose courage when the fiend perceived to shrink,
She pourèd forth out of her hellish sink
Her fruitful° cursèd spawn of serpents small,   *numerous*
Deformèd monsters, foul and black as ink;
Which swarming all about his legs did crawl,
And him encumbered sore, but could not hurt at all.

23   As gentle shepherd in sweet eventide,
When ruddy Phoebus gins to welk° in west,   *fade*
High on an hill his flock to viewen wide
Marks which do bite their hasty supper best,
A cloud of cumbrous° gnats do him molest,   *harassing*
All striving to infix their feeble stings,
That from their noyance he nowhere can rest,
But with his clownish hands their tender wings
He brusheth oft, and oft doth mar their murmurings.

24   Thus ill bestead,° and fearful more of shame   *situated*
Than of the certain peril he stood in,
Half furious° unto his foe he came,   *insane*
Resolved in mind all suddenly to win
Or soon to lose before he once would lin;°   *leave off*
And struck at her with more than manly force,
That from her body full of filthy sin
He reft her hateful head without remorse.
A stream of coal-black blood forth gushèd from her corse.°   *body*

25   Her scattered brood, soon as their parent dear
They saw so rudely falling to the ground,
Groaning full deadly, all with troublous fear
Gathered themselves about her body round,°   *around her body*
Weening their wonted entrance to have found
At her wide mouth; but being there withstood,
They flockèd all about her bleeding wound
And suckèd up their dying mother's blood,
Making her death their life and eke her hurt their good.

26   That detestable sight him much amazed,
To see th' unkindly imps° of° heaven accursed   *monstrous*
Devour their dam. On whom while so he gazed,   *offspring, by*
Having all satisfied their bloody thirst,
Their bellies swollen he saw with fulness burst,
And bowels gushing forth. Well worthy end
Of such as drunk her life the which them nursed.

Now needeth him no lenger labor spend;
His foes have slain themselves with whom he should contend.

27   His lady, seeing all that chanced from far,
     Approached in haste to greet° his victory,   *commend*
     And said, 'Fair knight, born under happy star,
     Who see your vanquished foes before you lie,
     Well worthy be you of that armory°   *coat of arms*
     Wherein ye have great glory won this day,
     And proved your strength on a strong enemy,
     Your first adventure. Many such I pray,
     And henceforth ever wish that like° succeed° it may.'   *similar, follow*

28   Then mounted he upon his steed again
     And with the lady backward° sought to wend.°   *back, go*
     That path he kept which beaten was most plain,
     Ne ever would to any byway bend,
     But still° did follow one unto the end,   *always*
     The which at last out of the wood them brought.
     So forward on his way, with God to friend,
     He passèd forth and new adventure sought.
     Long way he travelèd before he heard of aught.

29   At length they chanced to meet upon the way
     An aged sire in long black weeds y-clad,
     His feet all bare, his beard all hoary gray;
     And by his belt his book he hanging had.
     Sober he seemed and very sagely sad,°   *grave*
     And to the ground his eyes were lowly bent,
     Simple in show and void of malice bad.
     And all the way he prayèd as he went,
     And often knocked his breast as one that did repent.

30   He fair the knight saluted, louting low,
     Who fair him quited,° as that courteous was,   *repaid in kind*
     And after askèd him if he did know
     Of strange adventures which abroad did pass.
     'Ah, my dear son,' quoth he, 'how should, alas,
     Silly° old man that lives in hidden cell,   *simple*
     Bidding his beads° all day for his trespass,   *praying*
     Tidings of war and worldly trouble tell?
     With holy father sits not° with such things to   *is not proper,*
        mell.°   *meddle*

29.1–9   ". . . when in a valley she met
a hermit whose beard came down to the
middle of his bosom, pious and venerable
in appearance. Thin from years and from
fasting . . . and more than anyone . . . he
looked precise and strict in conscience"
(*Orlando Furioso*, II.12–13). Ariosto's
hermit is also a deceiving black-magician.
This character is common in medieval
romance.

31 'But if of danger which hereby doth dwell,
And home-bred evil, ye desire to hear,
Of a strange man I can you tidings tell
That wasteth all this country far and near.'
'Of such,' said he, 'I chiefly do inquere,
And shall thee well reward to show the place
In which that wicked wight his days doth wear;°   *spend*
For to all knighthood it is foul disgrace
That such a cursèd creature lives so long a space.'

32 'Far hence,' quoth he, 'in wasteful° wilderness   *desolate*
His dwelling is, by which no living wight
May ever pass but thorough° great distress.'   *through*
'Now,' said the lady, 'draweth toward night,
And well I wot that of your later° fight   *recent*
Ye all forwearied be. For what so strong
But wanting rest will also want of might?
The sun, that measures heaven all day long,
At night doth bait° his steeds the ocean waves among.   *refresh*

33 'Then with the sun take, sir, your timely° rest,   *regular*
And with new day new work at once begin.
Untroubled night they say gives counsel best.'
'Right well, sir knight, ye have advisèd been,'
Quoth then that aged man. 'The way to win
Is wisely to advise.° Now day is spent;   *consider*
Therefore with me ye may take up your inn
For this same night.' The knight was well content;
So with that godly father to his home they went.

34 A little lowly hermitage it was,
Down in a dale, hard by a forest's side,
Far from resort of people that did pass
In travel to and fro. A little wide,°   *to one side*
There was an holy chapel edified,°   *built*
Wherein the hermit duly wont° to say   *was accustomed*
His holy things° each morn and eventide.   *offices*
Thereby a crystal stream did gently play,
Which from a sacred fountain wellèd forth alway.

35 Arrivèd there, the little house they fill,
Ne look for entertainment where none was.
Rest is their feast° and all things at their will;   *entertainment*

34.4–9 This is a description of the scene as it appeared to Red Cross. Spenser's narrator frequently attributes false values to the objects and personages he describes in order to present them as they seem to his characters. In fact, the chapel was not holy nor the fountain sacred. This narrative device is pervasive in *The Faerie Queene*.

35.3 *Rest is their* . . .: I.e., "Rest is sufficient, since they ask no more."

The noblest mind the best contentment has.
With fair discourse the evening so they pass;
For that old man of pleasing words had store,
And well could file his tongue° as smooth as glass.   *speak fluently*
He told of saints and popes, and evermore
He strowed° an *Ave Mary* after and before.   *scattered*

36 The drooping night thus creepeth on them fast,
And the sad humor° loading their eyelids,   *i.e. heaviness*
As messenger of Morpheus, on them cast
Sweet slumbering dew, the which to sleep them bids.
Unto their lodgings then his guests he rids;°   *conducts*
Where when all drowned in deadly° sleep he finds,   *deathlike*
He to his study goes, and there amids
His magic books and arts of sundry kinds,
He seeks out mighty charms to trouble sleepy minds.

37 Then choosing out few words most horrible—
Let none them read—thereof did verses frame,°   *make*
With which and other spells like° terrible,   *similarly*
He bade awake black Pluto's grisly dame,
And cursèd heaven and spake reproachful shame
Of highest God, the Lord of life and light.
A bold bad man that dared to call by name
Great Gorgon, prince of darkness and dead night,
At which Cocytus quakes and Styx is put to flight.

38 And forth he called out of deep darkness dread
Legions of sprites, the which like little flies
Fluttering about his ever-damnèd head,
Await whereto° their service he applies—   *wait to find out*
To aid his friends or fray° his enemies.   *where*
Of those he chose out two, the falsest two,   *frighten*
And fittest for to forge true-seeming lies;
The one of them he gave a message to,
The other by himself stayed other work to do.

39 He making speedy way through spersèd° air   *dispersed*
And through the world of waters wide and deep,

36.3 *Morpheus:* the god of sleep.
37.1–38.9 Spenser's description of Archimago is a conventional picture of the black-magician; for another renaissance description see Christopher Marlowe's *Dr. Faustus.*
37.4 *Pluto:* in classical myth the god of the dead and of the underworld; his wife is Persephone.
37.8 *Great Gorgon:* in renaissance interpretation the father of all the gods of classical mythology; in Christian writings he, like Pluto, is a type of Satan.
37.9 *Cocytus . . . Styx:* two of the five rivers which separate the underworld from the world of men.

To Morpheus' house doth hastily repair.
Amid the bowels of the earth full steep
And low, where dawning day doth never peep,
His dwelling is. There Tethys his wet bed
Doth ever wash, and Cynthia still° doth steep   *continually*
In silver dew his ever-drooping head,
Whiles sad Night over him her mantle black doth spread.

40   Whose double gates he findeth lockèd fast,
The one fair framed of burnished ivory,
The other all with silver overcast.
And wakeful dogs before them far do lie,
Watching to banish Care, their enemy,
Who oft is wont to trouble gentle sleep.
By them the sprite° doth pass in quietly,   *spirit*
And unto Morpheus comes, whom drownèd deep
In drowsy fit he finds. Of nothing he takes keep.°   *heed*

41   And more to lull him in his slumber soft,
A trickling stream from high rock tumbling down
And ever-drizzling rain upon the loft,°   *air*
Mixed with a murmuring wind much like the soun°   *sound*
Of swarming bees, did cast him in a swoun.°   *daze*
No other noise, nor people's troublous cries,
As still are wont t' annoy the wallèd town,
Might there be heard; but careless° Quiet lies   *free from worry*
Wrapped in eternal silence far from enemies.

42   The messenger approaching to him spake,
But his waste words returned to him in vain;
So sound he slept that nought mought° him awake.   *might*
Then rudely he him thrust and pushed with pain,
Whereat he gan to stretch. But he again
Shook him so hard that forcèd him to speak.
As one then in a dream, whose drier° brain   *too dry*
Is tossed with troubled sights and fancies weak,°   *insubstantial*
He mumbled soft, but would not all his silence break.   *images*

39.3–41.9 Most of the details of this description of the House of Morpheus come from Ovid's *Metamorphoses*, XI. 592–632 (pp. 285–286). Curiously, Spenser does not fully allegorize the two gates before the House, as had been done in both Virgil's *Aeneid*, VI.893 (p. 174) and Homer's *Odyssey*, XIX.563 (trans. E. V. Rieu, Penguin Books, p. 302, to which subsequent citations of the *Odyssey* will refer). The ivory gate (see 44.6 below) was the way by which false and deceiving dreams left and returned to the House, while the gate of horn (silver in 40.3) was traditionally the portal of dreams that truly foretold the future.

39.6 *Tethys:* a titaness, wife of the titan Ocean.

39.7 *Cynthia:* goddess of the moon, whose silver light descends nightly into the underworld. The moon goddess is associated for this reason with Persephone and Hecate (43.3), the goddess of dreams and of the arts of black magic, daughter of Night.

43 The sprite then gan more boldly him to wake,
    And threatened unto him the dreaded name
    Of Hecate. Whereat he gan to quake,
    And lifting up his lumpish head, with blame°   *impatience*
    Half angry, askèd him for what he came.
    'Hither,' quoth he, 'me Archimago sent,
    He that the stubborn sprites can wisely tame;
    He bids thee to him send for his intent°   *use*
    A fit false dream that can delude the sleeper's scent.'° *senses*

44 The god obeyed, and calling forth straightway
    A diverse° dream out of his prison dark,   *distracting*
    Delivered it to him and down did lay
    His heavy head, devoid of careful cark,°   *concern*
    Whose senses all were straight benumbed and stark.°   *paralyzed*
    He back returning by the ivory door,
    Remounted up as light as cheerful lark,
    And on his little wings the dream he bore
    In haste unto his lord, where he him left afore.

45 Who all this while with charms and hidden arts
    Had made a lady of that other sprite,
    And framed of liquid air her tender parts
    So lively and so like° in all men's sight,   *real*
    That weaker° sense it could have ravished quite.   *too weak*
    The maker self, for all his wondrous wit,
    Was nigh beguilèd with so goodly sight.
    Her all in white he clad, and over it
    Cast a black stole most like to seem for Una fit.

46 Now when that idle° dream was to him brought,   *unsubstantial*
    Unto that elfin knight he bade him fly
    Where he slept soundly, void of evil thought,
    And with false shows abuse his fantasy,°   *imagination*
    In sort as he him schoolèd privily;
    And that new creature born without her due,°   *unnaturally*
    Full of the maker's guile, with usage sly°   *cunning gestures*
    He taught to imitate that lady true,
    Whose semblance she did carry under feignèd hue.°   *sham appearance*

47 Thus well instructed, to their work they haste,
    And coming where the knight in slumber lay,

45.2–9 The spirit for which Archi-
mago fashions a body of air in the like-
ness of Una is a demon from hell. The
evil spirits, like the angels, are incorporeal
and must take on a body of air in order
to appear to men. See John Donne's
"Air and Angels" and the full account of
natural and aerial bodies given by Statius
in Dante's *Purgatorio*, XXV.22–108
(trans. Dorothy L. Sayers, Penguin
Books, pp. 263–266).

The one upon his hardy head him placed
And made him dream of loves and lustful play,
That nigh his manly heart did melt away,
Bathèd in wanton bliss and wicked joy.
Then seemèd him his lady by him lay
And to him plained how that false wingèd boy
Her chaste heart had subdued to learn Dame Pleasure's toy.

48   And she herself, of beauty sovereign queen,
Fair Venus, seemed unto his bed to bring
Her, whom he waking° evermore did ween   *when awake*
To be the chastest flower that aye° did spring   *ever*
On earthly branch, the daughter of a king,
Now a loose leman° to vile service bound.   *concubine*
And eke the graces seemèd all to sing
Hymen io Hymen, dancing all around,
Whilst freshest Flora her with ivy garland crowned.

49   In this great passion of unwonted° lust—   *unusual*
Or wonted fear of doing aught amiss—
He starteth up, as seeming to mistrust°   *suspect*
Some secret ill or hidden foe of his.
Lo, there before his face his lady is,
Under black stole hiding her baited hook;
And as half blushing, offered him to kiss
With gentle blandishment° and lovely look,   *soft appeal*
Most like that virgin true which for her knight him took.°   *chose him*

50   All clean dismayed to see so uncouth sight
And half enragèd at her shameless guise,
He thought have slain her in his fierce despite;
But hasty heat tempering with sufferance° wise,   *forebearance*
He stayed his hand, and gan himself advise
To prove° his sense and tempt° her feignèd truth.   *test, put to trial*
Wringing her hands in women's piteous wise,
Tho can° she weep to stir up gentle ruth,°   *then did,*
Both for her noble blood and for her tender youth.   *compassion*

51   And said, 'Ah sir, my liege lord and my love,
Shall I accuse the hidden cruel fate

47.8   *that false wingèd boy:* Eros, the god of sexual love.
48.7   *graces:* the three graces, Aglaia, Euphrosyne, and Thalia.
48.8   *Hymen io Hymen:* the call to sexual pleasure and the marriage feast. Spenser's source is probably Catullus' *Odi et Amo*, 61 (trans. Roy Arthur Swanson, Library of Liberal Arts, pp. 52–59, to which subsequent citations will refer).
48.9   *Flora:* goddess of flowers. In the Renaissance she is often a symbol of lust and adulterous love, having undergone the metamorphosis from a chaste nymph to a dissolute goddess as a result of being raped by Zephyrus, the god of the west wind. She is to be seen in both aspects in Botticelli's *Primavera*.

And mighty causes wrought in heaven above,
Or the blind god that doth me thus amate,°   *defeat*
For° hopèd love to win me certain hate?   *instead of*
Yet thus perforce° he bids me do, or die.   *forcibly*
Die is my due; yet rue my wretched state,
You, whom my hard avenging destiny
Hath made judge of my life or death indifferently.

52   'Your own dear sake forced me at first to leave
My father's kingdom. . . .' There she stopped with tears;
Her swollen heart her speech seemed to bereave.°   *seemed to rob her of speech*
And then again begun, 'My weaker years,
Captived to fortune and frail worldly fears,
Fly to your faith for succor and sure aid;
Let me not die in languor and long tears.'
'Why dame,' quoth he, 'what hath ye thus dismayed?
What frays° ye that were wont to comfort me afraid?'   *frightens*

53   'Love of yourself,' she said, 'and dear constraint°   *terrible compulsion*
Lets me not sleep, but waste the weary night
In secret anguish and unpitied plaint,°   *lamentation*
Whiles you in careless sleep are drownèd quite.'
Her doubtful° words made that redoubted knight   *questionable*
Suspect her truth. Yet since no untruth he knew,
Her fawning love with foul disdainful spite
He would not shend,° but said, 'Dear dame, I rue   *reproach*
That for my sake unknown° such grief unto you grew. *unknown to me*

54   'Assure yourself, it fell not all to ground;
For all so dear as life is to my heart
I deem your love, and hold me° to you bound;   *consider myself*
Ne let vain fears procure your needless smart
Where cause is none, but to your rest depart.'
Not all content, yet seemed she to appease
Her mournful plaints, beguilèd of her art
And fed with words that could not choose but please;
So sliding softly forth, she turned as to her ease.

55   Long after lay he musing at her mood,
Much grieved to think that gentle dame so light°   *frivolous*
For whose defence he was to shed his blood.
At last dull weariness of former fight
Having y-rocked asleep his irksome° sprite,   *tired and disgusted*
That troublous dream gan freshly toss his brain
With bowers° and beds and lady's dear delight;   *bedrooms*
But when he saw his labor all was vain,
With that misformèd° sprite he back returned again. *unnaturally created*

CANTO ii

The guileful great enchanter parts
The Red Cross Knight from Truth;
Into whose stead fair Falsehood steps,
And works him woeful ruth.°   *harm*

1   By this, the northern wagoner had set
    His sevenfold team behind the steadfast star
    That was in ocean waves yet never wet,
    But firm is fixed, and sendeth light from far
    To all that in the wide deep wandering are;
    And cheerful Chanticleer with his note shrill
    Had warnèd once that Phoebus' fiery car
    In haste was climbing up the eastern hill,
    Full envious that night so long his room did fill;

2   When those accursèd messengers of hell,
    That feigning dream and that fair-forgèd sprite,
    Came to their wicked master and gan tell
    Their bootless° pains and ill succeeding night.   *unsuccessful*
    Who all in rage to see his skillful might
    Deluded° so, gan threaten hellish pain   *frustrated*
    And sad Prosérpine's wrath them to affright.
    But when he saw his threatening was but vain,
    He cast about° and searched his baleful books again. *calculated*

3   Eftsoons he took that miscreated fair,°   *unnatural lady*
    And that false other sprite, on whom he spread
    A seeming body of the subtle air,
    Like a young squire in loves and lustihead°   *pleasure*
    His wanton days that ever loosely led,
    Without regard of arms and dreaded fight.
    Those two he took, and in a secret bed,
    Covered with darkness and misdeeming° night,   *deceiving*
    Them both together laid, to joy in vain delight.

4   Forthwith he runs with feignèd faithful haste
    Unto his guest, who after troublous sights
    And dreams gan now to take more sound repast,°   *rest*
    Whom suddenly he wakes with fearful frights,

1.1   *northern wagoner:* the constella-
tion Boötes.
    1.2   *sevenfold team:* the Big Dipper,
the seven stars in the constellation Ursa
Major, called the "Churl's Wain" (i.e.
peasant's wagon). The *steadfast star* is
Polaris, the North Star.
    1.7   *Phoebus:* god of the sun.

As one aghast with° fiends or damnèd sprites,   *terrified by*
And to him calls: 'Rise, rise, unhappy swain
That here wax° old in sleep whiles wicked wights   *grows*
Have knit themselves in Venus' shameful chain.
Come, see where your false lady doth her honor stain.'

5   All in amaze he suddenly upstart
With sword in hand, and with the old man went;
Who soon him brought into a secret part,
Where that false couple were full closely ment°   *joined*
In wanton lust and lewd embracèment.
Which when he saw, he burnt with jealous fire—
The eye of reason was with rage y-blent°—   *blinded*
And would have slain them in his furious ire,
But hardly° was restrainèd of that aged sire.   *with difficulty*

6   Returning to his bed in torment great
And bitter anguish of his guilty sight,°   *of the crime he*
He could not rest, but did his stout heart eat,   *has seen*
And waste his inward gall with deep despite,
Irksome of life and too long lingering night.
At last fair Hesperus in highest sky
Had spent his lamp and brought forth dawning light.
Then up he rose and clad him hastily;
The dwarf him brought his steed; so both away do fly.

7   Now when the rosy-fingered morning fair,
Weary of aged Tithon's saffron° bed,   *orange-yellow*
Had spread her purple robe through dewy air,
And the high hills Titan discoverèd,
The royal virgin shook off drowsihead,
And rising forth out of her baser° bower,   *humble*
Looked for her knight, who far away was fled,
And for her dwarf, that wont° to wait each hour;   *used*
Then gan she wail and weep to see that woeful stour.°   *plight*

8   And after him she rode with so much speed
As her slow beast could make, but all in vain;
For him so far had borne his light-foot steed,
Prickèd° with wrath and fiery fierce disdain,   *spurred*
That him to follow was but fruitless pain.

6.6   *Hesperus:* the evening star.
7.1–3   Spenser here conflates a number of classical sources. The famous epithet *rosy-fingered morning* is from Homer and almost every classical poet after him. The story of *Aurora* and *Tithon* originated in the Homeric "Hymn to Venus" and is found in a number of later classical poems.

The epithet *saffron* is applied to Aurora and to her robe by Virgil (*Aeneid*, VII.25, p. 175) and Ovid (*Metamorphoses*, VII. 703, p. 189). The purple robe is from *Metamorphoses*, III.184, p. 85, where *purpureae Aurorae* actually refers to a pinkish color.

Yet she her weary limbs would never rest,
But every hill and dale, each wood and plain,
Did search, sore grievèd in her gentle breast
He° so ungently left her whom she lovèd best.　　　　*that he*

9　But subtle Archimago, when his guests
He saw divided into double parts,
And Una wandering in woods and forests—
Th' end of his drift°—he praised his devilish arts,　　*his intention*
That had such might over true-meaning° hearts;　　*well-intentioned*
Yet rests not so, but other means doth make
How he may work unto her further smarts.
For her he hated as the hissing snake,
And in her many troubles did most pleasure take.

10　He then devised himself how to disguise;
For by his mighty science° he could take　　　　*knowledge*
As many forms and shapes, in seeming wise,°　　*in appearance*
As ever Proteus to himself could make—
Sometime a fowl, sometime a fish in lake,
Now like a fox, now like a dragon fell—
That of himself he oft for fear would quake,
And oft would fly away. O who can tell
The hidden power of herbs and might of magic spell?

11　But now seemed best, the person to put on
Of that good knight, his late beguilèd guest.
In mighty arms he was y-clad anon,
And silver shield; upon his coward breast
A bloody cross, and on his craven crest
A bunch of hairs discolored° diversely.　　　　*dyed*
Full jolly° knight he seemed and well addressed,°　*confident,*
　　　　　　　　　　　　　　　　　　　　　　　　equipped
And when he sat upon his courser free,°　　　*noble*
Saint George himself ye would have deemèd him to be.

12　But he, the knight whose semblant° he did bear,　*likeness*
The true Saint George, was wandered far away,
Still flying from his thoughts and jealous fear;
Will was his guide, and grief led him astray.
At last him chanced to meet upon the way
A faithless Saracen° all armed to point,°　　　*heathen,*
　　　　　　　　　　　　　　　　　　　　　　　completely

10.3–6　Demonic spirits inhabit each of the four elements of nature: air (fowl), water (fish), earth (fox), and fire (dragon). Thus Satan (Archimago) manifests himself in all aspects of creation, on earth as the fox, a conventional symbol of deceit, and in water as the "great fish" that swallowed Jonah. According to the renaissance mythographer Natalis Comes, *Proteus*, whose shape-changing is described in the *Odyssey*, IV.384 ff. (pp. 74–77), was enabled by the arts of magic to change his form at will.

In whose great shield was writ with letters gay
Sansfoy. Full large of limb and every joint
He was, and carèd not for God or man a point.

13   He had a fair companion of his way,
A goodly lady clad in scarlet red,
Purfled° with gold and pearl of rich assay,°   *trimmed, quality*
And like° a Persian mitre° on her head   *a thing like,*
                                                       turban
She wore, with crowns and ouches° garnishèd,   *gems*
The which her lavish lovers to her gave.
Her wanton palfrey all was overspread
With tinsel° trappings, woven like a wave,   *gold and silver*
Whose bridle rung with golden bells and bosses brave.°   *showy studs*

14   With fair disport° and courting dalliance   *playfulness*
She entertained her lover all the way;
But when she saw the knight his spear advance,
She soon left off her mirth and wanton play
And bade her knight address° him to the fray.   *prepare*
His foe was nigh at hand. He, pricked with pride
And hope to win his lady's heart that day,
Forth spurrèd fast; adown his courser's side
The red blood trickling stained the way as he did ride.

15   The Knight of the Red Cross, when him he spied
Spurring so hot with rage dispiteous,°   *merciless*
Gan fairly° couch° his spear and towards ride.   *expertly, lower*
Soon meet they both, both fell and furious,
That daunted° with their forces hideous,   *overcome*
Their steeds do stagger and amazèd stand,
And eke themselves, too rudely rigorous,
Astonied° with the stroke of their own hand,   *stunned*
Do back rebut,° and each to other yieldeth land.   *repel*

16   As when two rams, stirred with ambitious pride,
Fight for the rule of the rich fleecèd flock,
Their hornèd fronts so fierce on either side
Do meet, that with the terror of the shock
Astonied, both stand senseless as a block,
Forgetful of the hanging victory—
So stood these twain, unmovèd as a rock,
Both staring fierce and holding idèly°   *(idly) uselessly*
The broken relics of their former cruelty.

17   The Saracen, sore daunted with the buff,°   *blow*
Snatcheth his sword and fiercely to him flies;
Who well it wards° and quiteth° cuff with cuff.   *parries, returns*

Each other's° equal puissance envies,   *the other's*
And through their iron sides with cruel spies° *glances*
Does seek to pierce—repining courage yields
No foot to foe. The flashing fire flies
As from a forge out of their burning shields,
And streams of purple blood new dyes the verdant fields.

18 'Curse on that cross,' quoth then the Saracen,
  'That keeps thy body from the bitter fit.° *i.e. death*
  Dead long ago I wot thou haddest been
  Had not that charm from thee forwarnèd° it; *repelled*
  But yet I warn thee now, assurèd sit
  And hide thy head.' Therewith upon his crest
  With rigor so outragèous he smit
  That a large share it hewed out of the rest,
  And glancing down his shield, from blame° him fairly *harm,*
   blessed.°   *guarded*

19 Who thereat wondrous wroth, the sleeping spark
  Of native virtue° gan eftsoons revive, *strength*
  And at his haughty helmet making mark,
  So hugely struck that it the steel did rive° *split*
  And cleft his head. He tumbling down alive,
  With bloody mouth his mother earth did kiss,
  Greeting his grave; his grudging° ghost did strive *unwilling*
  With the frail flesh. At last it flitted is
  Whither the souls do fly of men that live amiss.

20 The lady, when she saw her champion fall
  Like the old ruins of a broken tower,
  Stayed not to wail his woeful funeral,
  But from him fled away with all her power;
  Who after her as hastily gan scour,° *run*
  Bidding the dwarf with him to bring away
  The Saracen's shield, sign of the conqueror.
  Her soon he overtook and bade to stay,
  For present cause was none of dread her to dismay.

21 She turning back with rueful countenance,
  Cried, 'Mercy, mercy, sir, vouchsafe to show
  On silly° dame, subject to hard mischance *helpless*
  And to your mighty will.' Her humbless° low, *humility*
  In so rich weeds and seeming glorious show,
  Did much emmove° his stout heroic heart, *move*
  And said,° 'Dear dame, your sudden overthrow *(he) said*
  Much rueth me; but now put fear apart,
  And tell both who ye be, and who that took your part.'

22 Melting in tears, then gan she thus lament:
    'The wretched woman whom unhappy hour
    Hath now made thrall to your commandèment,
    Before that angry heavens list° to lower°   *chose, frown*
    And fortune false betrayed me to your power,
    Was—O what now availeth that° I was!—   *what*
    Born the sole daughter of an emperor,
    He that the wide west under his rule has,
    And high hath set his throne where Tiberis doth pass.

23 'He, in the first flower of my freshest age,
    Betrothèd me unto the only heir
    Of a most mighty king most rich and sage.
    Was never prince so faithful and so fair,
    Was never prince so meek° and debonair.°   *kind, courteous*
    But ere my hopèd day of spousal° shone,   *marriage day*
    My dearest lord fell from high honor's stair
    Into the hands of his accursèd fone°   *foes*
    And cruelly was slain, that shall I ever moan.

24 'His blessed body, spoiled of lively breath,
    Was afterward, I know not how, conveyed°   *stolen*
    And fro me hid. Of whose most innocent° death   *undeserved*
    When tidings came to me, unhappy maid,
    O how great sorrow my sad soul assayed!°   *tried my soul*
    Then forth I went his woeful corse° to find,   *body*
    And many years throughout the world I strayed,
    A virgin widow, whose deep wounded mind
    With love long time did languish as the stricken hind.°   *female deer*

25 'At last it chancèd this proud Saracen
    To meet me wandering, who perforce° me led   *forcibly*
    With him away, but yet could never win
    The fort that ladies hold in sovereign dread.°   *greatest reverence*
    There lies he now with foul dishonor dead,
    Who whiles he lived was callèd proud Sansfoy,
    The eldest of three brethren, all three bred
    Of one bad sire, whose youngest is Sansjoy,
    And twixt them both was born the bloody bold Sansloy.

26 'In this sad plight, friendless, unfortunate,
    Now miserable I, Fidessa, dwell,
    Craving of you in pity of my state,
    To do none° ill if please ye not do well.'   *no*
    He in great passion all this while did dwell,
    More busying his quick eyes her face to view
    Than his dull ears to hear what she did tell;

And said, 'Fair lady, heart of flint would rue
The undeservèd woes and sorrows which ye shew.°   *show*

27   'Henceforth in safe assurance may ye rest,
Having both found a new friend you to aid
And lost an old foe that did you molest—
"Better new friend than an old foe" is said.'
With change of cheer° the seeming simple maid   *expression*
Let fall her eyne,° as shamefast,° to the earth,   *eyes, as if modest*
And yielding soft, in that she nought gainsaid,°   *opposed*
So forth they rode—he feigning seemly° mirth   *pleasing*
And she coy looks. So 'dainty,' they say, 'maketh dearth.'°   *coyness arouses
desire*

28   Long time they thus together travelèd,
Till weary of their way, they came at last
Where grew two goodly trees that fair did spread
Their arms abroad, with gray moss overcast;
And their green leaves trembling with every blast°   *breeze*
Made a calm shadow far in compass round.
The fearful shepherd often there aghast,
Under them never sat, ne wont there sound
His merry oaten pipe, but shunned th' unlucky ground.

29   But this good knight, soon as he them can° spy,   *did*
For the cool shade him thither hastily got;
For golden Phoebus now y-mounted high,
From fiery wheels of his fair chariot
Hurlèd his beam so scorching cruel hot
That living creature mote° it not abide;   *might*
And his new lady it endurèd not.°   *could not endure*
There they alight, in hope themselves to hide
From the fierce heat, and rest their weary limbs a tide.°   *while*

30   Fair seemly pleasance each to other makes
With goodly purposes° there as they sit;   *conversation*
And in his falsèd° fancy he her takes   *deceived*
To be the fairest wight that livèd yit;
Which to express, he bends° his gentle wit,   *applies*
And thinking of those branches green to frame
A garland for her dainty forehead fit,
He plucked a bough, out of whose rift° there came   *broken end*
Small drops of gory blood that trickled down the same.

30.8–43.9 The Fradubio episode is indebted to Ariosto's *Orlando Furioso* (VI.28–53) in which Astolfo, who has been transformed into a tree by the wicked enchantress Alcina, tells his story to Ruggiero. The original of both Ariosto and Spenser is the *Aeneid*, II.27–42 (pp. 75–77), in which the Trojan Polydorus, transformed into a bush, speaks to Aeneas. For a pictorial representation of a human transformed into a tree as a symbol of bondage to sin, see Mantegna's *Wisdom Overcoming the Vices*, reproduced in Seznec, *The Survival of the Pagan Gods*, p. 111.

31 Therewith a piteous yelling voice was heard,
   Crying, 'O spare with guilty hands to tear
   My tender sides in this rough rind embarred,°   *trapped*
   But fly, ah fly far hence away, for fear
   Lest to you hap that happened to me here,
   And to this wretched lady, my dear love—
   O too dear° love, love bought with death too dear.'   *costly*
   Astoned° he stood, and up his hair did hove,°   *paralyzed, rise*
   And with that sudden horror could no member move.

32 At last, whenas the dreadful passion°   *dread*
   Was overpassed and manhood well awake,
   Yet musing° at the strange occasion   *marveling*
   And doubting much his sense, he thus bespake:
   'What voice of damnèd ghost from Limbo lake
   Or guileful sprite wandering in empty air—
   Both which frail men do oftentimes mistake°—   *mislead*
   Sends to my doubtful ears these speeches rare°   *strange*
   And rueful plaints, me bidding guiltless blood to spare?'

33 Then groaning deep, 'Nor damnèd ghost,' quoth he,
   'Nor guileful sprite to thee these words doth speak,
   But once a man, Fradubio, now a tree—
   Wretched man, wretched tree—whose nature weak
   A cruel witch, her cursèd will to wreak,°   *inflict*
   Hath thus transformed and placed in open plains,
   Where Boreas doth blow full bitter bleak,
   And scorching sun does dry my secret° veins;   *hidden*
   For though a tree I seem, yet cold and heat me pains.'

34 'Say on Fradubio then, or° man or tree,'   *whether*
   Quoth then the knight, 'by whose mischievous arts
   Art thou misshapèd thus as now I see?
   He oft finds med'cine who his grief imparts;°   *makes known*
   But double griefs afflict concealing hearts,
   As raging flames who° striveth to suppress.'   *afflict him who*
   'The author then,' said he, 'of all my smarts
   Is one Duessa, a false sorceress
   That many errant knights hath brought to wretchedness.

35 'In prime of youthly years, when courage hot
   The fire of love and joy of chivalry
   First kindled in my breast, it was my lot
   To love this gentle lady, whom ye see
   Now not a lady but a seeming tree;

31.8–9 *Astoned he . . . member move:*
"I froze, my hair stiffened, and my voice   choked in my throat" (*Aeneid*, II.774,
   p. 74).
            33.7 *Boreas:* the north wind.

With whom as once I rode accompanied,
Me chancèd of a knight encountered be
That had a like° fair lady by his side—   *equally*
Like a fair lady, but did foul Duessa hide.

36   'Whose forgèd beauty he did take in hand°   *boast*
All other dames to have exceeded far.
I in defence of mine did likewise stand—
Mine, that did then shine as the morning star!
So both to battle fierce arrangèd are,
In which his harder° fortune was to fall   *very hard*
Under my spear. Such is the die of war.
His lady, left as a prize martial,°   *prize of war*
Did yield her comely person to be at my call.

37   'So doubly loved of ladies unlike° fair—   *in opposite ways*
Th' one seeming such, the other such indeed—
One day in doubt I cast for to compare°   *tried to decide*
Whether° in beauty's glory did exceed;   *which one*
A rosy garland was the victor's meed.
Both seemed to win, and both seemed won° to be,   *defeated*
So hard the discord was to be agreed.
Fraelissa was as fair as fair mote° be,   *could*
And ever false Duessa seemed as fair as she.

38   'The wicked witch now seeing all this while
The doubtful balance equally to sway,
What not by right, she cast to win by guile;
And by her hellish science raised straightway
A foggy mist that overcast the day
And a dull blast that, breathing on her face,
Dimmèd her former beauty's shining ray,
And with foul ugly form did her disgrace.°   *disfigure*
Then was she fair alone, when none was fair in place.

39   'Then cried she out, "Fie, fie, deformèd wight,
Whose borrowed beauty now appeareth plain
To have before bewitchèd all men's sight!
O leave her soon, or let her soon be slain."
Her loathly visage viewing with disdain,
Eftsoons I thought her such as she me told,
And would have killed her; but with feignèd pain,
The false witch did my wrathful hand withhold;
So left her where she now is turned to treèn mold.°   *form of a tree*

39.8   *The false witch . . . withhold:* Compare with Archimago's restraint of Red
Cross (5.8–9 above).

40   'Thenceforth I took Duessa for my dame,
    And in the witch unweeting° joyed° long   *unknowing,*
      time,   *delighted*
    Ne ever wist but that she was the same,°   *what she seemed*
    Till on a day—that day is every prime,°   *spring*
    When witches wont do penance for their crime—
    I chanced to see her in her proper hue,
    Bathing herself in origan and thyme.
    A filthy foul old woman I did view,
    That ever to have touched her I did deadly rue.

41   'Her nether° parts misshapen, monstruous,   *lower*
    Were hid in water that° I could not see,   *so that*
    But they did seem more foul and hideous
    Than woman's shape man would believe to be.
    Thenceforth from her most beastly company
    I gan refrain, in mind to slip away
    Soon as appeared safe opportunity;
    For danger great, if not assured decay,°   *certain*
    I saw before mine eyes if I were known to stray.   *destruction*

42   'The devilish hag by changes of my cheer°   *mood*
    Perceived my thought; and drowned in sleepy night,
    With wicked herbs and ointments did besmear
    My body all, through charms and magic might,
    That all my senses were bereavèd quite.
    Then brought she me into this desert waste°   *desolate place*
    And by my wretched lover's side me pight,°   *planted*
    Where now enclosed in wooden walls full fast,
    Banished from living wights, our weary days we waste.'

43   'But how long time,' said then the elfin knight,
    'Are you in this misformèd house to dwell?'
    'We may not change,' quoth he, 'this evil plight,
    Till we be bathèd in a living well.
    That is the term prescribèd by the spell.'
    'O how,' said he, 'mote I that well outfind
    That may restore you to your wonted well?'°   *well being*
    'Time and sufficèd° fates to former kind°   *satisfied, state*
    Shall us restore; none else from hence may us unbind.'

44   The false Duessa, now Fidessa hight,°   *called*
    Heard how in vain Fradubio did lament,
    And knew well all was true. But the good knight,
    Full of sad fear and ghastly dreariment,°   *grief*

40.7 *origan and thyme:* herbs con- See the description of Duessa in Canto
sidered remedies for itching and scabs. viii.47.

When all this speech the living tree had spent,
The bleeding bough did thrust into the ground,
That from the blood he might be innocent,
And with fresh clay did close the wooden wound.
Then turning to his lady, dead with fear her found.

45   Her seeming dead he found with feignèd fear,   *as though, un-*
    As° all unweeting° of that° well she knew,   *knowing, what*
    And pained himself with busy° care to rear   *anxious*
    Her out of careless° swoon. Her eyelids blue   *unconscious*
    And dimmèd sight with pale and deadly° hue   *deathlike*
    At last she up gan lift. With trembling cheer°   *expression*
    Her up he took, too simple° and too true,   *innocent*
    And oft her kissed. At length, all passèd fear,°   *all fear passed*
    He set her on her steed and forward forth did bear.

CANTO iii

      Forsaken Truth long seeks her love
        And makes the lion mild,
      Mars° Blind Devotion's mart,° and falls   *ruins, trade*
        In hand of lecher vild.°   *vile*

1   Nought is there under heaven's wide hollowness
    That moves more dear compassion of mind
    Than beauty brought t' unworthy° wretchedness   *undeserved*
    Through envy's snares or fortune's freaks° unkind.   *whims*
    I, whether lately through her brightness blind,
    Or through allegiance and fast fealty°   *loyalty*
    Which I do owe unto all womankind,
    Feel my heart pierced with so great agony,
    When such I see, that all for pity I could die.

2   And now it is impassionèd° so deep,   *moved*
    For fairest Una's sake of whom I sing,
    That my frail eyes these lines with tears do steep
    To think how she through guileful handèling°—   *treatment*
    Though true as touch,° though daughter of a king,   *touchstone*
    Though fair as ever living wight was fair,
    Though nor° in word nor deed ill meriting—   *neither*
    Is from her knight divorcèd in despair,
    And her due loves derived° to that vile witch's share.   *diverted*

3   Yet she, most faithful lady, all this while
    Forsaken, woeful, solitary maid,
    Far from all people's press° as in exile,   *gathering*

In wilderness and wasteful deserts strayed
To seek her knight; who subtilely betrayed
Through that late vision which th' enchanter wrought,
Had her abandoned. She, of nought afraid,
Through woods and wasteness° wide him daily sought;   *wasteland*
Yet wishèd tidings none° of him unto her brought.   *no one*

4 One day, nigh weary° of the irksome way,   *exhausted*
   From her unhasty beast she did alight,
   And on the grass her dainty limbs did lay
   In secret shadow,° far from all men's sight.   *secluded shade*
   From her fair head her fillet° she undight°   *headband, took off*
   And laid her stole aside. Her angel's face
   As the great eye of heaven shinèd bright
   And made a sunshine in the shady place.
   Did never mortal eye behold such heavenly grace.

5 It fortunèd out of the thickest wood
   A ramping° lion rushèd suddenly,   *raging*
   Hunting full greedy after savage blood.°   *wild game*
   Soon as the royal virgin he did spy,
   With gaping mouth at her ran greedily,
   To have at once devoured her tender corse.
   But to the prey whenas he drew more nigh,
   His bloody rage, assuagèd with remorse
   And with the sight amazed, forgot his° furious force.   *its*

6 Instead thereof he kissed her weary feet
   And licked her lily hands with fawning tongue,
   As° he her wrongèd innocence did weet.   *as though*
   O how can beauty master the most strong,
   And simple truth subdue avenging wrong!
   Whose yielded pride and proud submission,
   Still dreading death, when she had markèd long,
   Her heart gan melt in great compassion,
   And drizzling tears did shed for pure affection.

7 'The lion, lord of every beast in field,'
   Quoth she, 'his princely puissance doth abate,

4.1–9.9 The story of the fierce lion who becomes the loving companion and servant of a hero, lady, or saint is a commonplace of medieval literature. In *Bevis of Hamtoun*, Josian, a royal virgin like Una, is attacked by two lions who do not harm her because "the race of lions . . . can do no harm to a king's daughter who is a virgin. . . ." In the Percival story of Malory's *Morte d'Arthur*, the lion who befriends the hero is represented in a dream as the supporter of a beautiful young lady who is the "new law of holy church," that is, the true Christian church, as opposed to the church of the Jews. The lion, among the four emblems of the Evangelists (man, ox, lion, eagle), symbolized Christ's resurrection in medieval art. See Emile Male, *The Gothic Image*, trans. Dora Nussey, Harper Torchbooks, 1958, p. 37.

And mighty proud to humble weak does yield,
Forgetful of the hungry rage which late
Him pricked,° in pity of my sad estate.°   *goaded, condition*
But he, my lion and my noble lord,
How does he find in cruel heart to hate
Her that him loved and ever most adored
As the god of my life? Why hath he me abhorred?'

8 Redounding° tears did choke th' end of her plaint,   *overflowing*
Which softly echoed from the neighbor wood;
And sad to see her sorrowful constraint,°   *affliction*
The kingly beast upon her gazing stood.
With pity calmed, down fell his angry mood.
At last, in close° heart shutting up her pain,   *secret*
Arose the virgin born of heavenly brood,°   *ancestry*
And to her snowy palfrey got again,
To seek her strayèd champion if° she might attain.°   *whether, overtake*

9 The lion would not leave her desolate,
But with her went along as a strong guard
Of her chaste person, and a faithful mate
Of her sad troubles and misfortunes hard.
Still when she slept, he kept both watch and ward,
And when she waked, he waited diligent,
With humble service to her will prepared.
From her fair eyes he took commandèment,
And ever by her looks conceivèd° her intent.   *grasped*

10 Long she thus travelèd through deserts wide,
By which she thought her wandering knight should pass,
Yet never show of living wight espied;
Till that at length she found the trodden grass
In which the tract° of people's footing was,   *track*
Under the steep foot of a mountain hoar.°   *gray*
The same she follows till at last she has
A damsel spied, slow footing° her before,   *walking slowly*
That on her shoulders sad° a pot of water bore.   *drooping*

11 To whom approaching, she to her gan call
To weet if dwelling place were nigh at hand;
But the rude wench her answered nought at all.
She could not hear, nor speak, nor understand.
Till seeing by her side the lion stand,
With sudden fear her pitcher down she threw

10.8–11.9 Perhaps Spenser's description tion is influenced by John 4:7–22: "There cometh a woman of Samaria to draw water. . . ." The rest of the passage shows that this woman was both an adultress and an idolater.

And fled away; for never in that land
Face of fair lady she before did view,
And that dread lion's look her cast in deadly° hue.   *deathlike*

12 Full fast she fled ne ever looked behind,
As if her life upon the wager lay.°   *depended on it*
And home she came whereas her mother blind
Sat in eternal night. Nought could she say,
But sudden catching hold, did her dismay
With quaking hands and other signs of fear;
Who full of ghastly fright and cold affray,°   *terror*
Gan shut the door. By this, arrivèd there
Dame Una, weary dame, and entrance did requere.°   *request*

13 Which when none yielded, her unruly page
With his rude claws the wicket° open rent   *door*
And let her in. Where of his cruel rage
Nigh dead with fear and faint° astonishment,   *faint-producing*
She found them both in darksome corner pent,
Where that old woman day and night did pray
Upon her beads, devoutly penitent.
Nine hundred *Pater Nosters* every day,
And thrice nine hundred *Aves* she was wont to say.

14 And to augment her painful penance more,
Thrice every week in ashes she did sit,
And next her wrinkled skin rough sackcloth wore,
And thrice three times did fast from any bit.°   *food*
But now for fear her beads she did forget;
Whose needless dread for to remove away,
Fair Una framèd words and countenance fit;
Which hardly° done, at length she gan them pray   *with difficulty*
That in their cottage small that night she rest her may.

15 The day is spent and cometh drowsy night,
When every creature shrouded is in sleep;
Sad Una down her lays in weary plight,
And at her feet the lion watch doth keep.
Instead of rest, she does lament and weep
For the late loss of her dear lovèd knight,
And sighs and groans and evermore does steep
Her tender breast in bitter tears all night.
All night she thinks too long and often looks for light.

16 Now when Aldebaran was mounted high
Above the shiny Cassiopeia's Chair,

16.1 *Aldebaran:* a brilliant reddish   16.2 *Cassiopeia's Chair:* a constella-
star in the constellation Taurus.   tion of the northern hemisphere named

And all in deadly sleep did drownèd lie,
One knockèd at the door and in would fare.
He knockèd fast,° and often cursed and sware   *insistently*
That ready entrance was not at his call;
For on his back a heavy load he bare
Of nightly stealths and pillage several,
Which he had got abroad by purchase criminal.°   *robbery*

17 He was, to weet,° a stout and sturdy thief,   *in fact*
Wont to rob churches of their ornaments
And poor men's boxes° of their due relief,   *poor boxes*
Which given was to them for good intents.
The holy saints of their rich vestments
He did disrobe when all men careless slept,
And spoiled the priests of their habiliments.°   *vestments*
Whiles none the holy things in safety kept,
Then he by cunning sleights in at the window crept.

18 And all that he by right or wrong could find,
Unto this house he brought, and did bestow
Upon the daughter of this woman blind,
Abessa, daughter of Corceca slow,°   *dull*
With whom he whoredom used, that° few did know,   *which*
And fed her fat with feast of offerings
And plenty which in all the land did grow;
Ne sparèd he to give her gold and rings.
And now he to her brought part of his stolen things.

19 Thus long the door with rage and threats he bet,° *beat*
Yet of those fearful women none durst rise;
The lion frayèd° them him in to let.   *frightened*
He would no lenger stay him to advise,
But open breaks the door in furious wise
And entering is when that disdainful beast,
Encountering fierce, him sudden doth surprise,
And seizing° cruel claws on trembling breast,   *fastening*
Under his lordly foot him proudly hath suppressed.

20 Him booteth° not resist nor succor call;   *it helps*
His bleeding heart is in the venger's hand,

for the wicked mother-in-law of the hero Perseus. For her boastfulness her daughter Andromeda was chained to rocks and threatened by sea monsters. Perseus' rescue of Andromeda is a motif from pagan myth of striking similarity to the motif of St. George's rescuing the royal virgin. Cassiopeia is a type of Eve. For her treachery in attempting to have Perseus killed at his wedding feast Cassiopeia was stellified by Poseidon.

17.1–18.9 Kirkrapine is like the corrupt sons of Eli, who "lay with the women that assembled at the door of the tabernacle of the congregation" and made themselves "fat with the chiefest of all the offerings of Israel . . ." (I Samuel 2:22 and 29). The implication is that the corruption of the Jewish religion which Samuel records has invaded the Roman church also.

Who straight him rent in thousand pieces small
And quite dismembered hath. The thirsty land
Drunk up his life, his corse left on the strand.°   *ground*
His fearful friends wear out the woeful night,
Ne dare to weep nor seem to understand
The heavy hap° which on them is alight,°   *fortune, has*
Afraid, lest to themselves the like mishappen might.   *alighted*

21 Now when broad day the world discovered° has,   *uncovered*
Up Una rose, up rose the lion eke,
And on their former journey forward pass,
In ways unknown, her wandering knight to seek,
With pains° far passing that long wandering Greek   *trials*
That for his love refusèd deity.
Such were the labors of this lady meek,
Still seeking him that from her still did fly,
Then furthest from her hope when most she weenèd nigh.°   *she thought*
                                                                nearest

22 Soon as she parted thence, the fearful twain,
That blind old woman and her daughter dear,
Came forth; and finding Kirkrapine there slain,
For anguish great they gan to rend their hair,
And beat their breasts, and naked flesh to tear.
And when they both had wept and wailed their fill,
Then forth they ran like two amazèd deer,
Half mad through malice and revenging will,°   *desire for revenge*
To follow her that was the causer of their ill.

23 Whom overtaking, they gan loudly bray
With hollow howling and lamenting cry,
Shamefully at her railing all the way,
And her accusing of dishonesty°   *lewdness*
That was the flower of faith and chastity.
And still amidst her railing she° did pray   *i.e. Corceca*
That plagues and mischiefs and long misery
Might fall on her and follow all the way,
And that in endless error she might ever stray.

24 But when she saw her prayers nought prevail,
She back returnèd with some labor lost;
And in the way, as she did weep and wail,
A knight her met in mighty arms embossed,°   *encased*
Yet knight was not for all his bragging boast,

21.2 *Up Una rose . . .:* "Up rose the
sunne, and up rose Emilye" (Chaucer,
Knight's Tale, A.2273).
21.5–6 *that long wandering Greek:*
Odysseus, who gave up immortality and
the love of Calypso in order to return to
his wife Penelope.

But subtle Archimage, that Una sought
By trains° into new troubles to have tossed.   *tricks*
Of that old woman tidings he besought,
If that of such a lady she could tellen aught.

25 Therewith she gan her passion to renew,
And cry and curse and rail and rend her hair,
Saying that harlot she too lately knew
That caused her shed so many a bitter tear,
And so forth told the story of her fear.
Much seemèd he to moan° her hapless chance,   *sympathize with*
And after for that lady did inquere;
Which being taught, he forward gan advance
His fair enchanted steed and eke his charmèd lance.

26 Ere long he came where Una traveled slow,
And that wild champion waiting° her beside.   *attending*
Whom seeing such, for dread he durst not show
Himself too nigh at hand, but turnèd wide
Unto an hill; from whence when she him spied,
By his like-seeming shield, her knight by name°   *appearance*
She weened it was, and towards him gan ride.
Approaching nigh, she wist it was the same,
And with fair fearful humbless° towards him she came.   *humility*

27 And weeping said, 'Ah my long lackèd lord,
Where have ye been thus long out of my sight?
Much fearèd I to have been quite abhorred,
Or aught have done that ye displeasen might,
That° should as death unto my dear heart light.   *which*
For since mine eye your joyous sight did miss,
My cheerful day is turned to cheerless night,
And eke my night of death the shadow is;°   *is the shadow of death*
But welcome now my light and shining lamp of bliss.'

28 He thereto meeting said, 'My dearest dame,
Far be it from your thought, and fro my will,
To think that knighthood I so much should shame
As you to leave, that have me lovèd still,
And chose in faery court of mere° goodwill,   *pure*
Where noblest knights were to be found on earth.
The earth shall sooner leave her kindly skill°   *natural ability*
To bring forth fruit, and make eternal dearth,°   *famine*
Than I leave you, my lief,° y-born of heavenly birth.   *beloved*

26.6 *his like-seeming shield:* his shield looking like Red Cross's.

29 'And sooth to say, why I left you so long
    Was for to seek adventure in strange place,
    Where Archimago said a felon strong
    To many knights did daily work disgrace;
    But knight he now shall never more deface.
    Good cause of mine excuse, that° mote° ye please   *which, may it*
    Well to accept, and evermore embrace
    My faithful service, that by land and seas
    Have vowed you to defend. Now then your plaint appease.'

30 His lovely° words her seemed due recompense   *loving*
    Of all her passèd pains. One loving hour
    For many years of sorrow can dispense;°   *compensate*
    A dram of sweet is worth a pound of sour.
    She has forgot how many a woeful stour°   *hardship*
    For him she late endured; she speaks no more
    Of past. True is, that true love hath no power
    To looken back; his eyes be fixed before.
    Before her stands her knight, for whom she toiled so sore.

31 Much like as when the beaten mariner,
    That long hath wandered in the ocean wide—
    Oft soused° in swelling Tethys' saltish tear,   *soaked*
    And long time having tanned his tawny hide
    With blustering breath of heaven that none can bide
    And scorching flames of fierce Orion's hound—
    Soon as the port from far he has espied,
    His cheerful whistle merrily doth sound
    And Nereus crowns with cups: his mates him pledge°   *toast*
      around.

32 Such joy made Una when her knight she found.
    And eke th' enchanter joyous seemed no less
    Than the glad merchant that does view from ground
    His ship far come from watery wilderness;
    He hurls out vows and Neptune oft doth bless.
    So forth they passed, and all the way they spent
    Discoursing of her dreadful late distress,
    In which he asked her what the lion meant;
    Who told her all that fell° in journey, as she went.   *all that happened
                                                               to her*

33 They had not ridden far when they might see
    One pricking towards them with hasty heat,

31.6 *Orion's hound:* Sirius, the Dog
Star, in the constellation Canis Major;
scorching because that is what *Sirius*
means in Greek; the brightest star in the
heavens, its rising with the sun in summer
heralds the "dog days" of intolerably hot
and dry weather.
    31.9 *Nereus:* god of the Mediter-
ranean Sea.

Full strongly armed and on a courser free,
That through his fierceness foamèd all with sweat
And the sharp iron° did for anger eat,   *bit*
When his hot° rider spurred his chafèd side.   *angry*
His look was stern and seemèd still to threat
Cruel revenge which he in heart did hide,
And on his shield *Sansloy* in bloody lines was dyed.°   *painted*

34   When nigh he drew unto this gentle pair
And saw the red cross which the knight did bear,
He burnt in fire and gan eftsoons prepare
Himself to battle with his couchèd° spear.   *lowered*
Loath was that other, and did faint through fear,
To taste th' untrièd° dint of deadly steel;   *unexperienced*
But yet his lady did so well him cheer,
That hope of new good hap he gan to feel;
So bent° his spear and spurred his horse with iron heel.   *lowered*

35   But that proud paynim° forward came so fierce   *pagan*
And full of wrath, that with his sharp-head spear
Through vainly crossèd° shield he quite did pierce,   *bearing the cross*
And had his staggering steed not shrunk for fear,
Through shield and body eke he should him bear.°   *drive*
Yet so great was the puissance of his push
That from his saddle quite he did him bear.
He tumbling rudely down to ground did rush,
And from his gorèd wound a well of blood did gush.

36   Dismounting lightly from his lofty steed,
He to him leapt, in mind to reave his life,
And proudly said, 'Lo, there the worthy meed
Of him that slew Sansfoy with bloody knife.
Henceforth his ghost, freed from repining° strife,   *fretful*
In peace may passen over Lethe lake,
When mourning altars, purged° with enemy's life,   *cleansed*
The black infernal furies done aslake.°   *do calm*
Life from Sansfoy thou tookst, Sansloy shall from thee take.'

37   Therewith in haste his helmet gan unlace,
Till Una cried, 'O hold that heavy hand,
Dear sir, whatever that thou be in place.°   *rank*
Enough is that thy foe doth vanquished stand
Now at thy mercy. Mercy not withstand;°   *deny*
For he is one° the truest knight alive,   *one of*
Though conquered now he lie on lowly land,
And whilst him fortune favored, fair did thrive
In bloody field. Therefore of life him not deprive.'

38   Her piteous words might not abate his rage,
      But rudely rending up his helmet, would
      Have slain him straight;° but when he sees his age,   *immediately*
      And hoary head of Archimago old,
      His hasty hand he doth amazèd hold,
      And half ashamèd, wondered at the sight.
      For that old man well knew he, though untold,
      In charms and magic to have wondrous might,
      Ne ever wont in field ne in round lists to fight.

39   And said, 'Why, Archimago, luckless sire,
      What do I see? What hard mishap is this,
      That hath thee hither brought to taste mine ire?
      Or thine the fault, or mine the error is,
      Instead of foe to wound my friend amiss?'
      He answered nought but in a trance still lay,
      And on those guileful dazèd eyes of his
      The cloud of death did sit. Which done away,°   *vanished*
      He left him lying so, ne would no lenger stay.

40   But to the virgin comes, who all this while
      Amazèd stands, herself so mocked° to see   *deceived*
      By him, who has the guerdon° of his guile   *reward*
      For so misfeigning° her true knight to be.   *falsely pretending*
      Yet is she now in more perplexity,
      Left in the hand of that same paynim bold,
      From whom her booteth not at all to flee;
      Who by her cleanly garment catching hold,
      Her from her palfrey plucked, her visage to behold.

41   But her fierce servant full of kingly awe°   *rage*
      And high disdain, whenas his sovereign dame
      So rudely handled by her foe he saw,
      With gaping jaws full greedy at him came,
      And ramping on his shield, did ween° the same   *intend*
      Have reft away with his sharp rending claws.
      But he was stout, and lust did now inflame
      His courage more, that° from his gripping paws   *so that*
      He hath his shield redeemed, and forth his sword he draws.

42   O then too weak and feeble was the force
      Of savage beast, his puissance to withstand;
      For he was strong and of so mighty corse
      As ever wielded spear in warlike hand,
      And feats of arms did wisely understand.
      Eftsoons he piercèd through his chafèd° chest   *injured*
      With thrilling° point of deadly iron brand,°   *penetrating,*
                                                            sword

And launched° his lordly heart. With death oppressed   *pierced*
He roared aloud, whiles life forsook his stubborn breast.

43 Who now is left to keep the forlorn maid
From raging spoil of lawless victor's will—
Her faithful guard removed, her hope dismayed,
Herself a yielded° prey to save or spill?°   *helpless, destroy*
He, now lord of the field, his pride to fill,°   *satisfy*
With foul reproaches and disdainful spite
Her vildly entertains,° and will or nill,   *treats*
Bears her away upon his courser light.°   *quickly*
Her prayers nought prevail, his rage is more of might.

44 And all the way, with great lamenting pain
And piteous plaints she filleth his dull° ears,   *deaf*
That stony heart could riven have in twain;
And all the way she wets with flowing tears,
But he enraged with rancor, nothing hears.
Her servile beast yet would not leave her so,
But follows her far off, ne aught he fears
To be partaker of her wandering woe,
More mild in beastly kind° than that her beastly foe.   *nature*

CANTO iv

To sinful House of Pride Duess-
    a guides the faithful knight,
Where brother's death to wreak,° Sansjoy   *avenge*
    Doth challenge him to fight.

1 Young knight whatever that dost arms profess,
And through long labors huntest after fame,
Beware of fraud, beware of fickleness,
In choice and change of thy dear lovèd dame,
Lest thou of her believe too lightly blame,°   *evil*
And rash misweening,° do thy heart remove.   *mistaking*
For unto knight there is no greater shame
Than lightness and inconstancy in love;
That doth this Red Cross Knight's ensample° plainly prove.   *example*

2 Who after that he had fair Una lorn°   *lost*
Through light misdeeming° of her loyalty,   *hastily*
                              misjudging
And false Duessa in her stead had born°—   *placed*
Callèd Fidess and so supposed to be—
Long with her traveled, till at last they see
A goodly building, bravely garnishèd°—   *decorated*

The house of mighty prince it seemed to be—
And towards it a broad highway that led,
All bare through people's feet which thither travelèd.

3   Great troops of people traveled thitherward
Both day and night, of each degree and place,°   *status*
But few returnèd, having scapèd hard°   *escaped with*
    difficulty
With baleful beggary or foul disgrace,
Which° ever after in most wretched case   *who*
Like loathsome lazars° by the hedges lay.   *lepers*
Thither Duessa bade him bend his pace;
For she is weary of the toilsome way,
And also nigh consumèd is the lingering day.

4   A stately palace built of squarèd brick,
Which cunningly was without mortar laid,
Whose walls were high but nothing strong nor thick,
And golden foil all over them displayed,
That purest sky with brightness they dismayed.°   *overcame*
High lifted up were many lofty towers
And goodly galleries far over laid,°   *placed high above*
Full of fair windows and delightful bowers;
And on the top a dial told the timely hours.

5   It was a goodly heap° for to behold,   *structure*
And spake the praises of the workman's wit;°   *skill*

2.8–3.2 · "For wide is the gate, and broad is the way, that leadeth to destruction, and many there be which go in thereat" (Matthew 7:13–14). These lines are a signal that Red Cross is beginning an adventure analogous to his fight with Error: "That path they take that beaten seemed most bare" (Canto I.ii.3). The contrast between the two episodes is important too; for now, instead of truth, he has falsehood as his guide.

4.1–5.9 The description of the House of Pride is indebted to Ariosto's description of the city of Alcina in *Orlando Furioso*, VI.59: "From a distance was seen a long wall that circles around and shuts in much space, and seemingly its height reaches the sky and it is of gold from its high summit to the earth." Indeed, in general conception, the Red Cross Knight's disasterous sojourn in the House of Pride (Cantos iv and v), his adultery with Duessa, and his captivity by Orgoglio (Canto vii), his rescue by Arthur (Canto viii), and his recuperation in the House of Holiness (Canto x) depend heavily upon Ariosto's story of the hero Ruggiero's adventures, first in the city of the evil enchantress Alcina (Cantos vi and vii), then in the city of the wise and virtuous sister of Alcina, Logistilla (Canto x). Spenser's Duessa is clearly modeled upon Alcina, and Ariosto's Logistilla is comparable both to Caelia and Una in some respects. Ruggiero's adventures, even more clearly than Red Cross's are based upon the popular moral allegory of "Hercules at the Crossroads."

4.2 *without mortar laid:* "And one built up a wall, and, lo, others daubed it with untempered mortar. . . . So will I break down the wall that ye daubed with untempered mortar, and bring it down to the ground, so that the foundation thereof shall be discovered, and it shall fall, and ye shall be consumed in the midst thereof: and ye shall know that I am the Lord" (Ezekiel 13:10–14).

4.6 *many lofty towers:* a symbol of presumption since the Tower of Babel: "And they said one to another, go to, let us build us a city and a tower, whose top may reach unto heaven" (Genesis 11: 3–4).

4.9 The clock is the fit symbol of the City of Man, subject to the ravages of time.

But full great pity that so fair a mold°   *building*
Did on so weak foundation ever sit.
For on a sandy hill that still did flit°   *shift*
And fall away, it mounted was full high,
And every breath of heaven shakèd it;
That all the hinder° parts, that few could spy,   *back*
Were ruinous and old, but painted cunningly.

6 Arrivèd there they passèd in forthright;
But still to all° the gates stood open wide,   *everyone*
Yet charge of them was to a porter hight,°   *committed*
Called Malvenu, who entrance none denied.
Thence to the hall, which was on every side
With rich array and costly arras° dight;°   *tapestry,*
                                        furnished
Infinite sorts of people did abide
There, waiting long to win the wishèd sight
Of her that was the lady of that palace bright.

7 By them they pass, all gazing on them round,°   *from all sides*
And to the presence° mount, whose glorious view   *reception hall*
Their frail amazèd senses did confound.
In living prince's court none ever knew
Such endless richess and so sumptuous shew;
Ne Persia self,° the nurse of pompous pride,   *herself*
Like ever saw. And there a noble crew
Of lords and ladies stood on every side,
Which with their presence fair, the place much beautified.

8 High above all a cloth of state° was spread,   *canopy*
And a rich throne as bright as sunny day,
On which there sat most brave embellishèd
With royal robes and gorgèous array
A maiden queen, that° shone as Titan's ray,   *i.e. throne*
In glistering gold and peerless precious stone.
Yet her bright blazing beauty did assay°   *try*
To dim the brightness of her glorious throne,
As envying herself,° that° too exceeding shone.   *her, who*

9 Exceeding shone, like Phoebus' fairest child,
That did presume his father's fiery wain,°   *chariot*

5.3–7 "A foolish man . . . built his house upon the sand: and the rain descended, and the floods came, and the winds blew, and beat upon that house; and it fell" (Matthew 7:26).

5.8–9 Note the parallel between the hinder regions of the House of Pride and the nether regions of Duessa.

6.4 *Malvenu:* the opposite of welcome, Fr. *bienvenu.*

7.4–15.9 Compare the description of the pomp and vanity of Alcina's palace (*Orlando Furioso,* VII.31–32).

8.5 *Titan:* name used as an epithet for Phoebus Apollo, the sun, son of the titan Hyperion.

9.1 *Phoebus' fairest child:* Phaëthon, who, like Lucifera, strove to outdo the

And flaming mouths of steeds unwonted wild,
Through highest heaven with weaker° hand to rein.   *too weak*
Proud of such glory and advancement vain,
While flashing beams do daze his feeble eyne,°   *eyes*
He leaves the welkin° way most beaten plain,   *cloudy*
And rapt° with whirling wheels, inflames the skyne°   *carried away,*
With fire not made to burn, but fairly for to shine.   *skies*

10 So proud she shinèd in her princely state,
Looking to heaven—for earth she did disdain—
And sitting high—for lowly° she did hate.   *humility*
Lo, underneath her scornful feet was lain
A dreadful dragon with an hideous train.°   *tail*
And in her hand she held a mirror bright,
Wherein her face she often viewèd fain.°   *lovingly*
And in her self-loved semblance took delight;
For she was wondrous fair as any living wight.

11 Of grisly Pluto she the daughter was
And sad° Proserpina, the queen of hell;   *dismal*
Yet did she think her peerless worth to pass°   *surpass*
That parentage, with pride so did she swell;
And thundering Jove, that high in heaven doth dwell
And wield the world, she claimèd for her sire,
Or if° that any else did Jove excel.   *anyone if*
For to the highest she did still aspire,
Or if aught higher were than that, did it desire.

12 And proud Lucifera men did her call,
That made herself a queen and crowned to be;
Yet rightful kingdom she had none at all,
Ne heritage of native° sovereignty,   *inherited*
But did usurp with wrong and tyranny
Upon the scepter which she now did hold;
Ne ruled her realm with laws, but policy°   *cunning*
And strong advisement° of six wizards old,   *advice*
That with their counsels bad her kingdom did uphold.

13 Soon as the elfin knight in presence came,
And false Duessa, seeming lady fair,
A gentle usher, Vanity by name,
Made room, and passage for them did prepare.
So goodly brought them to the lowest stair

sun. Ovid's *Metamorphoses*, II.1–400 (pp.
54–63) tells the story of Phaëthon's
disasterous attempt to drive the chariot
of the sun, a story interpreted in medieval
tradition as a type of the revolt and fall
of Satan. Compare Revelation 9:1.
12.7 This and other details in the
description of the House of Pride show
the relation between Lucifera and Sansloy.

Of her high throne, where they on humble knee
Making obeisance did the cause declare
Why they were come her royal state to see:
To prove° the wide report of her great majesty.

determine the truth of

14   With lofty eyes, half loath to look so low,
She thankèd them in her disdainful wise,
Ne other grace vouchsafèd them to show
Of princess worthy—scarce them bade arise.
Her lords and ladies all this while devise°
Themselves to setten forth° to strangers' sight.
Some frounce their curlèd hair in courtly guise,°
Some prank° their ruffs, and others trimly dight
Their gay attire. Each others' greater pride does spite.

prepare
exhibit
elegant style
straighten

15   Goodly they all that knight do entertain,
Right glad with him to have increased their crew.
But to Duess each one himself did pain
All kindness and fair courtesy to shew;
For in that court whilom° her well they knew.
Yet the stout faery mongst the middest° crowd
Thought all their glory vain in knightly view,
And that great princess too exceeding proud,
That to strange knight no better countenance allowed.°

formerly
densest

showed

16   Sudden upriseth from her stately place
The royal dame and for her coach doth call.
All hurtlen° forth, and she with princely pace,
As fair Aurora in her purple pall°
Out of the east the dawning day doth call—
So forth she comes. Her brightness broad doth blaze;
The heaps of people thronging in the hall
Do ride each other upon her to gaze.
Her glorious glitterand° light doth all men's eyes amaze.

rush
robe

glittering

17   So forth she comes and to her coach does climb,
Adornèd all with gold and garlands gay,
That seemed as fresh as Flora in her prime
And strove to match in royal rich array

15.7–9   Red Cross's reaction to Lucifera's court is complex. He recognizes the vanity and snobbery of the place, but he is himself hurt that no attention is being paid him. That is, he is guilty of vanity.

17–36   The procession of the seven deadly sins is common in medieval literature and art. Spenser may have been influenced by the procession in John Gower's *Mirour de l'Omme*, but he was certainly influenced by the conventional iconography of the deadly sins in medieval and renaissance art. For the iconographical tradition see Samuel C. Chew, *The Pilgrimage of Life*, Yale University Press, 1962, pp. 79–113. For the medieval literary tradition see Morton W. Bloomfield, *The Seven Deadly Sins*, Michigan State University Press, 1952. Every detail of the portraits given here is significant.

Great Juno's golden chair, the which they say
The gods stand gazing on when she does ride
To Jove's high house through heaven's brass-paved way,
Drawn of fair peacocks, that excel in pride
And, full of Argus' eyes, their tails dispreaden wide.

18 But this was drawn of six unequal° beasts,   *different*
On which her six sage counselors did ride,
Taught to obey their bestial behests,
With like conditions to their kinds° applied.   *natures*
Of which the first, that all the rest did guide,
Was sluggish Idleness, the nurse of sin.
Upon a slothful ass he chose to ride,
Arrayed in habit black and amis° thin,   *hood*
Like to an holy monk, the service to begin.

19 And in his hand his portess° still he bare,   *breviary*
That much was worn but therein little read;
For of devotion he had little care,
Still drowned in sleep and most of his days dead.
Scarce could he once uphold his heavy head
To looken whether it were night or day.
May seem the wain was very evil led
When such an one had guiding of the way,
That knew not whether right he went or else astray.

20 From worldly cares himself he did esloin°   *withdraw*
And greatly shunnèd manly exercise;
From every work he challengèd essoin,°   *claimed*
For contemplation sake. Yet otherwise   *exemption*
His life he led in lawless riotize,°   *riotousness*
By which he grew to grievous malady;
For in his lustless° limbs, through evil guise,°   *feeble, behavior*
A shaking fever reigned continually.
Such one was Idleness, first of this company.

21 And by his side rode loathsome Gluttony,
Deformèd creature, on a filthy swine;
His belly was up-blown with luxury,
And eke with fatness swollen were his eyne,
And like a crane his neck was long and fine,°   *skinny*
With which he swallowed up excessive feast,
For want whereof poor people oft did pine.°   *starve*
And all the way, most like a brutish beast,
He spewèd up his gorge, that all did him detest.

21.1 *by his side:* The counselors are riding two-and-two.
21.5 *crane:* whose long throat sup-posedly allows it the maximum pleasure-able contact with its food.

22 In green vine leaves he was right fitly clad,
    For other clothes he could not wear for heat;
    And on his head an ivy garland had,
    From under which fast trickled down the sweat.
    Still as he rode, he somewhat° still did eat,   *something*
    And in his hand did bear a boozing can,
    Of which he supped so oft that on his seat
    His drunken corse he scarce upholden can,
    In shape and life more like a monster than a man.

23 Unfit he was for any worldly thing,
    And eke unable once° to stir or go,   *at all*
    Not meet to be of counsel to a king,
    Whose mind in meat and drink was drownèd so
    That from his friend he seldom knew his foe.
    Full of diseases was his carcass blue,°   *livid*
    And a dry° dropsy through his flesh did flow,   i.e. *causing thirst*
    Which by misdiet daily greater grew.
    Such one was Gluttony, the second of that crew.

24 And next to him rode lustful Lechery
    Upon a bearded goat whose rugged hair
    And whally° eyes (the sign of jealousy)   *greenish*
    Was like the person self° whom he did bear;   *the very person*
    Who rough and black and filthy did appear,
    Unseemly man to please fair lady's eye.
    Yet he of ladies oft was lovèd dear,
    When fairer faces were bid standen by.
    O who does know the bent of women's fantasy?

25 In a green gown he clothèd was full fair,
    Which underneath did hide his filthiness;
    And in his hand a burning heart he bare,
    Full of vain follies and newfangledness.°   *novelties*
    For he was false and fraught with fickleness,
    And learnèd had to love with secret looks,
    And well could° dance, and sing with ruefulness,   *knew how to*
    And fortunes tell, and read in loving° books,   *erotic*
    And thousand other ways to bait his fleshly hooks.

26 Inconstant man, that lovèd all he saw
    And lusted after all that he did love;
    Ne would his looser life be tied to law,
    But joyed weak women's hearts to tempt and prove°   *try*

22.1–3 Gluttony resembles Silenus, 89–99, pp. 270–271).
the drunken old satyr who was the tutor   24.1 *next:* behind, i.e., in the next pair
of Dionysus (Ovid, *Metamorphoses*, XI.   (so also in 30.1 below).

If from their loyal loves he might them move.
Which lewdness filled him with reproachful pain
Of that foul evil,° which all men reprove,   i.e. *syphilis*
That rots the marrow and consumes the brain.
Such one was Lechery, the third of all this train.

27   And greedy Avarice by him did ride
Upon a camel loaden all with gold;
Two iron coffers hung on either side,
With precious metal full as they might hold;
And in his lap an heap of coin he told;°   *counted*
For of his wicked pelf° his god he made,   *wealth*
And unto hell himself for money sold.
Accursèd usury was all his° trade,   *his only*
And right and wrong alike in equal balance weighed.

28   His life was nigh unto death's door y-placed,
And threadbare coat and cobbled shoes he ware,
Ne scarce good morsel all his life did taste;
But both from back and belly still did spare
To fill his bags and richess to compare.°   *acquire*
Yet child ne kinsman living had he none
To leave them to; but thorough° daily care   *through*
To get and nightly fear to lose his own,
He led a wretched life, unto himself, unknown.°   *friendless*

29   Most wretched wight, whom nothing might suffice,
Whose greedy lust did lack° in greatest store,°   *want, plenty*
Whose need had end, but no end covetise,°   *cupidity*
Whose wealth was want,° whose plenty made him poor,   *poverty*
Who had enough, yet wishèd ever more—
A vile disease. And eke in foot and hand
A grievous gout tormented him full sore,
That well he could not touch, nor go,° nor stand.   *walk*
Such one was Avarice, the fourth of this fair band.

30   And next to him malicious Envy rode
Upon a ravenous wolf, and still did chaw
Between his cankered° teeth a venomous toad,   *corroded*
That all the poison ran about his chaw.°   *jaw*
But inwardly he chawèd his own maw°   *guts*
At neighbors' wealth, that made him ever sad;
For death it was when any good he saw,
And wept that cause of weeping none he had;
But when he heard of harm, he waxèd wondrous glad.

27.3   *coffers:* (1596). 1590 reads *coffets.*

31 All in a kirtle° of discolored say°   *jacket, many-*
        He clothèd was, y-painted full of eyes;   *colored wool*
        And in his bosom secretly there lay
        An hateful snake, the which his tail upties
        In many folds and mortal sting implies.°   *covers up*
        Still as he rode, he gnashed his teeth to see
        Those heaps of gold with gripple° Covetise,   *grasping*
        And grudgèd° at the great felicity   *grumbled*
        Of proud Lucifera and his own company.

32 He hated all good words and virtuous deeds,
        And him no less that any like did use;°   *practice*
        And who with gracious bread the hungry feeds,
        His alms for want of faith he doth accuse;
        So every good to bad he doth abuse.°   *twist*
        And eke the verse of famous poets' wit
        He does backbite, and spiteful poison spews
        From leprous mouth on all that ever writ.
        Such one vile Envy was, that fifth in row did sit.

33 And him beside rides fierce revenging Wrath
        Upon a lion loath for to be led;
        And in his hand a burning brand° he hath,   *sword*
        The which he brandisheth about his head.
        His eyes did hurl forth sparkles fiery red,
        And starèd stern on all that him beheld,
        As ashes pale of hue and seeming dead;
        And on his dagger still his hand he held,
        Trembling through hasty rage when choler° in him swelled. *anger*

34 His ruffian° raiment all was stained with blood,   *disordered*
        Which he had split, and all to rags y-rent,
        Through unadvisèd rashness woxen wood;°   *grown insane*
        For of his hands he had no government,
        Ne cared for blood in his avengèment.
        But when the furious fit was overpassed,
        His cruel facts° he often would repent;   *deeds*
        Yet willful man, he never would forecast
        How many mischiefs should ensue his heedless haste.

35 Full many mischiefs follow cruel Wrath;
        Abhorrèd bloodshed and tumultuous strife,
        Unmanly° murder and unthrifty scath,°   *inhuman, damage*
        Bitter despite, with rancor's rusty knife,
        And fretting grief, the enemy of life.
        All these, and many evils mo,° haunt ire,   *more*
        The swelling spleen° and frenzy raging rife,   *temper*

The shaking palsy and Saint Francis' fire.
Such one was Wrath, the last of this ungodly tire.°   *procession*

36 And after all, upon the wagon beam°   *shaft*
  Rode Satan, with a smarting whip in hand,
  With which he forward lashed the lazy team
  So oft as Sloth still in the mire did stand.
  Huge routs of people did about them band,
  Shouting for joy; and still before their way
  A foggy mist had covered all the land;
  And underneath their feet all scattered lay
  Dead skulls and bones of men whose life had gone astray.

37 So forth they marchen in this goodly sort,
  To take the solace° of the open air,   *pleasure*
  And in fresh flowering fields themselves to sport;
  Amongst the rest rode that false lady fair,
  The foul Duessa, next unto the chair
  Of proud Lucifer', as one of the train.
  But that good knight would not so nigh repair,
  Himself estranging from their joyance vain,
  Whose fellowship seemed far unfit for warlike swain.

38 So having solacèd themselves a space,
  With pleasance of the breathing° fields y-fed,   *fragrant*
  They back returnèd to the princely place;
  Whereas an errant knight in arms y-cled°   *clad*
  And heathenish shield, wherein with letters red
  Was writ *Sansjoy*, they new arrivèd find.
  Inflamed with fury and fierce hardihead,
  He seemed in heart to harbor thoughts unkind,
  And nourish bloody vengeance in his bitter mind.

39 Who when the shamèd shield of slain Sansfoy
  He spied with that same faery champion's page,
  Bewraying° him that did of late destroy   *revealing*
  His eldest brother, burning all with rage
  He to him leapt, and that same envious gage°   *envied prize*
  Of victor's glory from him snatched away.
  But th' elfin knight, which ought° that warlike wage,°   *owned, reward*
  Disdained to loose the meed he won in fray,
  And him rencountering° fierce, rescued the noble prey.°   *engaging, prize*

40 Therewith they gan to hurtlen° greedily,   *rush together*
  Redoubted battle ready to deraign,°   *draw up for battle*

35.8 *Saint Francis' fire*: probably St. Anthony's fire, erysipelas.

40.1–9 The impetuous clash of the two knights, the royal restraint of them

And clash their shields and shake their swords on high,
That with their stir they troubled all the train;
Till that great queen, upon eternal pain
Of high displeasure that ensuen might,
Commanded them their fury to refrain;
And if that either to that shield had right,
In equal lists they should the morrow next it fight.

41 'Ah, dearest dame,' quoth then the paynim bold,
'Pardon the error of enragèd wight,
Whom great grief made forget the reins to hold
Of reason's rule—to see this recreant knight—
No knight, but treacher full of false despite
And shameful treason, who through guile hath slain
The prowest° knight that ever field did fight,   *most courageous*
Even stout Sansfoy—O who can then refrain?—
Whose shield he bears renverst° the more to heap disdain.   *reversed*

42 'And to augment the glory of his guile,
His° dearest love, the fair Fidessa, lo,   i.e. *Sansfoy's*
Is there possessèd of the traitor vile,
Who reaps the harvest sowen by his foe,
Sowen in bloody field and bought with woe.
That brother's hand shall dearly well requite,
So be,° O queen, you equal favor show.'   *if*
Him little answered th' angry elfin knight;
He never meant with words, but swords, to plead his right;

43 But threw his gauntlet as a sacred pledge,
His cause in combat the next day to try.
So been they parted both, with hearts on edge
To be avenged each on his enemy.
That night they pass in joy and jollity,
Feasting and courting° both in bower and hall;   *making love*
For steward was excessive Gluttony,
That of his plenty pourèd forth to all;
Which done, the chamberlain Sloth did to rest them call.

44 Now whenas darksome night had all displayed
Her coal-black curtain over brightest sky,
The warlike youths, on dainty couches laid,
Did chase away sweet sleep from sluggish eye,
To muse on means of hopèd victory.

---

in favor of a regulated joust in the future, as well as other details of the general situation amount almost to an ironic burlesque of Chaucer's *Knight's Tale:* Red Cross = Palamon; Sansjoy = Arcite; Duessa = Emily; Lucifera = Theseus; Night and the infernal powers = Saturn and the gods.

But whenas Morpheus had with leaden mace
Arrested all that courtly company,
Uprose Duessa from her resting place
And to the paynim's lodging comes with silent pace.

45 Whom broad awake she finds in troublous fit,
Forecasting how his foe he might annoy,
And him amoves° with speeches seeming fit.   *stirs*
'Ah dear Sansjoy, next dearest to Sansfoy,
Cause of my new grief, cause of my new joy,
Joyous to see his image in mine eye,
And grieved to think how foe did him destroy
That was the flower of grace and chivalry.
Lo, his Fidessa to thy secret faith° I fly.'   *loyalty*

46 With gentle words he can° her fairly greet,   *did*
And bade say on the secret of her heart.
Then sighing soft, 'I learn that little sweet
Oft tempered is,' quoth she, 'with muchel° smart;   *much*
For since my breast was launched° with lovely dart   *pierced*
Of dear Sansfoy, I never joyèd hour,
But in eternal woes my weaker heart
Have wasted, loving him with all my power,
And for his sake have felt full many an heavy stour.

47 'At last when perils all I weenèd past,
And hoped to reap the crop of all my care,
Into new woes unweeting I was cast
By this false faitor° who unworthy ware°   *impostor, wore*
His worthy shield, whom he with guileful snare
Entrappèd, slew, and brought to shameful grave.
Me silly° maid away with him he bare,   *helpless*
And ever since hath kept in darksome cave,
For that° I would not yield that° to Sansfoy I gave.   *because, what*

48 'But since fair sun hath spersed° that lowering° cloud,   *scattered, scowling*
And to my loathèd life now shows some light,
Under your beams I will me safely shroud
From dreaded storm of his disdainful spite.
To you th' inheritance belongs by right
Of brother's praise, to you eke longs° his love.   *belongs*
Let not his love, let not his restless sprite,
Be unrevenged, that calls to you above
From wandering Stygian shores, where it doth endless move.'

49 Thereto said he, 'Fair dame, be nought dismayed
For sorrows past; their grief is with them gone.

Ne yet of present peril be afraid;
For needless fear did never vantage none,°   *help anyone*
And helpless° hap it booteth not to moan.   *unavoidable*
Dead is Sansfoy, his vital pains are past,
Though grievèd ghost for vengeance deep do groan;
He lives that shall him pay his duties last,°   *last rites*
And guilty elfin blood shall sacrifice in haste.'

50 'O, but I fear the fickle freaks,'° quoth she,   *unpredictable*
'Of fortune false, and odds of arms in field.'   *tricks*
'Why dame,' quoth he, 'what odds can ever be,
Where both do fight alike, to win or yield?'
'Yea, but,' quoth she, 'he bears a charmèd shield
And eke enchanted arms that none can pierce;
Ne none can wound the man that does them wield.'
'Charmed or enchanted,' answered he then fierce,
'I no whit reck, ne you the like need to rehearse.°   *speak of*

51 'But fair Fidessa, sithens° fortune's guile   *since*
Or enemy's power hath now captivèd you,
Return from whence ye came and rest awhile
Till morrow next, that I the elf subdue,
And with Sansfoy's dead dowry you endue.'°   *endow*
'Ah me, that is a double death,' she said,
'With proud foe's sight my sorrow to renew.
Wherever yet I be, my secret aid
Shall follow you.' So passing forth she him obeyed.

CANTO v

The faithful knight in equal field
Subdues his faithless foe,
Whom false Duessa saves, and for
His cure to hell does go.

1 The noble heart, that harbors virtuous thought
And is with child of glorious great intent,
Can never rest until it forth have brought
Th' eternal brood of glory excellent.
Such restless passion did all night torment
The flaming courage of that faery knight,
Devising how that doughty tournament
With greatest honor he achieven° might.   *win*
Still did he wake, and still did watch for dawning light.

1.1–4   Spenser puts in Platonic terms (*Symposium*) the renaissance conviction that
virtue must be translated into action.

2 At last the golden oriental gate
   Of greatest heaven gan to open fair,
   And Phoebus fresh as bridegroom to his mate,
   Came dancing forth, shaking his dewy hair,
   And hurled his glistering beams through gloomy air.
   Which when the wakeful elf perceived, straightway
   He started up, and did himself prepare
   In sun-bright arms and battailous° array;   *warlike*
   For with the pagan proud he combat will that day.

3 And forth he comes into the common hall,
   Where early wait him many a gazing eye,
   To weet° what end to stranger knights may fall.   *find out*
   There many minstrels maken melody
   To drive away the dull melancholy,
   And many bards that to the trembling chord
   Can tune their timely voices cunningly,
   And many chroniclers that can record
   Old loves and wars for ladies done by many a lord.

4 Soon after comes the cruel Saracen,
   In woven mail all armèd warily,
   And sternly looks at him, who not a pin
   Does care for look of living creature's eye.
   They bring them wines of Greece and Araby
   And dainty spices fetched from furthest Ind,°   *India*
   To kindle heat of courage privily.°   *within*
   And in the wine a solemn oath they bind
   T' observe the sacred laws of arms that are assigned.°   *prescribed*

5 At last forth comes that far renowmèd queen
   With royal pomp and princely majesty;
   She is y-brought unto a palèd green,°   *fenced-in lawn*
   And placèd under stately canopy,
   The warlike feats of both those knights to see.
   On th' other side in all men's open view
   Duessa placèd is, and on a tree
   Sansfoy his° shield is hanged with bloody hue—   *Sansfoy's*
   Both those° the laurel garlands to the victor due.   *i.e. Duessa and*
                                                               shield

6 A shrilling trumpet sounded from on high
   And unto battle bade themselves address.

2.3 *Phoebus*: the sun. The bridegroom is reminiscent of Psalms 19:5.
3.4–9 Spenser may have thought of the minstrels as singing short fixed songs, the bards as reciting epic poems that they composed orally, and the chroniclers as reciting prose accounts (written or oral) of the heroic past. These were distinct narrative forms characteristic of various phases of medieval European culture.
3.7 *timely*: well-timed, measured.

Their shining shields about their wrists they tie,
And burning blades about their heads do bless,°   *wave*
The instruments of wrath and heaviness.
With greedy force each other doth assail,
And strike so fiercely that they do impress
Deep dinted furrows in the battered mail;
The iron walls to ward their blows are weak and frail.

7   The Saracen was stout and wondrous strong,
And heapèd blows like iron hammers great;
For after blood and vengeance he did long.
The knight was fierce and full of youthly heat,
And doubled° strokes like dreaded thunder's threat;   *returned*
For all for praise and honor he did fight.
Both stricken strike, and beaten both do beat,
That from their shields forth flyeth fiery light;
And helmets hewen° deep show marks of either's might.   *(hewn) battered*

8   So th' one for wrong, the other strives for right—
As when a griffon seizèd of° his prey   *in possession of*
A dragon fierce encountereth in his flight,
Through widest air making his idle way,
That would his rightful ravin° rend away;   *plunder*
With hideous horror both together smite,
And souse° so sore that they the heavens affray;   *strike*
The wise soothsayer, seeing so sad sight,
Th' amazèd vulgar° tells of wars and mortal fight.   *wide-eyed rabble*

9   So th' one for wrong, the other strives for right,
And each to deadly shame° would drive his foe;   *mortal defeat*
The cruel steel so greedily doth bite
In tender flesh that streams of blood down flow,
With which the arms that erst° so bright did show   *in the beginning*
Into a pure vermilion now are dyed.
Great ruth in all the gazers' hearts did grow,
Seeing the gorèd wounds to gape so wide,
That victory they dare not wish to either side.

10   At last the paynim chanced to cast his eye,
His sudden° eye, flaming with wrathful fire,   *rash*

7:9   *helmets hewen deep:* (1596). 1590
reads *hewen helmets deep.*
8.2–7   The griffon is a fabulous animal
having the head of an eagle and the body
of a lion. The griffon in medieval art is
likely to represent Christ and the forces
of good, as it does in Dante's *Purgatorio,*
XXXI–XXXII (pp. 315–330), where the
union of the two natures of Christ, divine
(bird) and human (animal), is intended.
Here the griffon is likened to Red Cross,
the dragon to Sansjoy.
8.8–9   Predicting future events from
the flights of birds was a common form
of augury in antiquity. See the famous
example in the *Odyssey,* II (pp. 41–42).
10.1–11.6   This scene is clearly in-
debted to the close of the *Aeneid* (XII.

Upon his brother's shield, which hung thereby.
Therewith redoubled was his raging ire,
And said, 'Ah wretched son of woeful sire,
Dost thou sit wailing by black Stygian lake
Whilst here thy shield is hanged for victor's hire?°   *reward*
And sluggish german,° dost° thy forces slake,°   *brother, dost thou,*
To after-send his foe, that him may overtake?   *slacken*

11 'Go caitive° elf, him quickly overtake,   *wretched*
And soon redeem from his long wandering woe.
Go guilty ghost, to him my message make
That I his shield have quit° from dying foe.'   *redeemed*
Therewith upon his crest he struck him so
That twice he reelèd, ready twice to fall;
End of the doubtful battle deemèd tho°   *then thought*
The lookers on, and loud to him gan call
The false Duessa, 'Thine the shield, and I, and all.'

12 Soon as the faery heard his lady speak,
Out of his swooning dream he gan awake;
And quickening faith, that erst was waxen weak,
The creeping deadly cold away did shake.
Tho moved with wrath and shame and lady's sake,°   *love of the lady*
Of all at once he cast° avenged to be,   *resolved*
And with so exceeding fury at him strake
That forcèd him to stoop upon his knee.
Had he not stoopèd so, he should have cloven be.°   *been*

13 And to him said, 'Go now, proud miscreant,
Thyself thy message do to german dear;
Alone he wandering thee too long doth want.
Go say his foe thy shield with his doth bear.'
Therewith his heavy hand he high gan rear,
Him to have slain, when, lo, a darksome cloud
Upon him fell. He nowhere doth appear,
But vanished is; the elf him calls aloud,
But answer none receives. The darkness him does shroud.

940–949, p. 338), where Aeneas, seeing the baldric of the dead Pallas upon the shoulder of the defeated Turnus, is infuriated and strikes his enemy dead.

10.6 *Stygian lake:* the river Styx. Sansjoy's infernal geography here does not quite square with Canto iii.36.6, where he imagines his brother on the shore of Lethe lake.

10.8–9 Sansjoy addresses himself as *sluggish german.*

11.3–4 This is a common type of victor's boast in medieval and renaissance heroic poetry. It probably derives from Pyrrhus' last words to the helpless Priam: "You shall be my messenger to Achilles my father; remember to tell him of my deplorable deeds. . . . Now die!" (*Aeneid*, II.547–548, p. 67).

13.5–9 This convenient "darksome cloud" has an ancient heritage in epic poetry: *Iliad*, III.380, V.345, XX.321; and *Aeneid*, V.810. See also Tasso's *Jerusalem Delivered*, VII.43–44.

14 In haste Duessa from her place arose,
  And to him running said, 'O prowest knight
  That ever lady to her love did choose,
  Let now abate the terror of your might,
  And quench the flame of furious despite
  And bloody vengeance. Lo, th' infernal powers,
  Covering your foe with cloud of deadly night,
  Have borne him hence to Pluto's baleful bowers.
  The conquest yours, I yours, the shield, and glory yours.'

15 Not all so satisfied, with greedy eye
  He sought all round about, his thirsty blade
  To bathe in blood of faithless enemy,
  Who all that while lay hid in secret shade.
  He stands amazèd how he thence should fade.
  At last the trumpets triumph sound on high;
  And running heralds humble homage made,
  Greeting him goodly with new victory,
  And to him brought the shield, the cause of enmity.

16 Wherewith he goeth to that sovereign queen,
  And falling her before on lowly knee,
  To her makes present of his service seen;°   *proved*
  Which she accepts with thanks and goodly gree,°   *goodwill*
  Greatly advancing° his gay chivalry.   *praising*
  So marcheth home, and by her takes the knight,
  Whom all the people follow with great glee,
  Shouting and clapping all their hands on height,°   *loudly*
  That all the air it fills and flies to heaven bright.

17 Home is he brought and laid in sumptuous bed,
  Where many skilfull leeches° him abide,°   *doctors, attend*
  To salve his hurts that yet still freshly bled.
  In wine and oil they wash his woundès wide,
  And softly gan embalm° on every side.   *anoint*
  And all the while, most heavenly melody
  About the bed sweet music did divide,
  Him to beguile of grief and agony.
  And all the while Duessa wept full bitterly.

18 As when a weary traveler that strays
  By muddy shore of broad seven-mouthèd Nile,

14.8 *Pluto's baleful bowers:* hell.
15.1–3 "For he [Aeneas] was on the track only of Turnus, searching for him everywhere in the dense murk and claiming him alone for combat" (*Aeneid,* XII. 466–467, p. 323).
17.7 *divide:* to vary the few essential notes of a tune by playing instead many smaller ones. Red Cross will hear such music again in Book III at Castle Joyous, where "all the while sweet music did divide / Her looser notes with Lydian harmony" (i.40.1–2).

Unweeting of the perilous wandering ways,
Doth meet a cruel crafty crocodile,
Which in false grief hiding his harmful guile,
Doth weep full sore and sheddeth tender tears—
The foolish man, that pities all this while
His mournful plight, is swallowed up unwares.
Forgetful of his own that minds another's cares.

19   So wept Duessa until eventide,
     That° shining lamps in Jove's high house were light;   *when*
     Then forth she rose ne lenger would abide,
     But comes unto the place where th' heathen knight,
     In slumbering swoond° nigh void of vital sprite,   *swoon*
     Lay covered with enchanted cloud all day.
     Whom when she found as she him left in plight,
     To wail his woeful case she would not stay,
     But to the eastern coast of heaven makes speedy way.

20   Where grisly Night with visage deadly sad,°   *dismal as death*
     That Phoebus' cheerful face durst never view,
     And in a foul black pitchy mantle clad,
     She finds forth coming from her darksome mew,°   *den*
     Where she all day did hide her hated hue.
     Before the door her iron chariot stood,
     Already harnessèd for journey new,
     And coal-black steeds y-born of hellish brood,
     That on their rusty bits did champ as they were wood.°   *insane*

21   Who when she saw Duessa sunny bright,
     Adorned with gold and jewels shining clear,
     She greatly grew amazèd at the sight,
     And th' unacquainted light began to fear—
     For never did such brightness there appear—
     And would have back retirèd to her cave,
     Until the witch's speech she gan to hear,
     Saying, 'Yet, O thou dreaded dame, I crave
     Abide till I have told the message which I have.'

22   She stayed, and forth Duessa gan proceed:
     'O thou most ancient grandmother of all,

18.6   *tender tears:* a part of medieval rather than ancient animal lore; crocodile tears have become a proverbial type of hypocrisy. Duessa is likened to the guileful beast who tricks his sympathetic prey into being swallowed.
     20.1–9   Infinitely suggestive of allegorical interpretation, Night is described largely as she appears in ancient poetry. She is the negation of created order, light, and truth, and the ancestor of all demonic powers. See Hesiod's *Theogony*, 211–225 (trans. Norman O. Brown, Liberal Arts Press, p. 59) for the beginning of the tradition. Spenser is closest to the renaissance mythographer Natalis Comes, *Mythologiae*, III.12 (see Henry G. Lotspeich, *Classical Mythology in the Poetry of Edmund Spenser*, Princeton Studies in English, X, 1932).

More old than Jove whom thou at first didst breed,
Or that great house of gods celestial,
Which wast° begot in Demogorgon's hall   *who were*
And sawst the secrets of the world unmade,°   *before it was*
Why sufferedst thou thy nephews dear to fall,   *created*
With elfin sword most shamefully betrayed?
Lo, where the stout Sansjoy doth sleep in deadly shade.

23   'And him before, I saw with bitter eyes
     The bold Sansfoy shrink underneath his spear;
     And now the prey of fowls in field he lies,
     Nor wailed of friends nor laid on groaning bier,
     That whilom was to me too dearly dear.°   *my lover*
     O, what of gods then boots it to be born,
     If old Aveugle's sons so evil hear?°   *are so poorly*
     Or who shall not great Night'ès children scorn,   *esteemed*
     When two of three her° nephews are so foul forlorn? *of her three*

24   'Up then, up dreary dame of darkness queen,
     Go gather up the relics° of thy race,   *i.e. bodies*
     Or else go them avenge and let be seen
     That dreaded Night in brightest day hath place,°   *high rank*
     And can the children of fair Light deface.'
     Her feeling speeches some compassion moved
     In heart, and change in that great mother's face.
     Yet pity in her heart was never proved°   *experienced*
     Till then; for evermore she hated, never loved.

25   And said, 'Dear daughter, rightly may I rue
     The fall of famous children born of me,
     And good successes which their foes ensue.°   *befall*
     But who can turn the stream of destiny,
     Or break the chain of strong necessity°   *cause and effect*
     Which fast is tied to Jove's eternal seat?
     The sons of Day he favoreth, I see,
     And by my ruins thinks to make them great.
     To make one great by other's loss is bad escheat.° *dishonest gain*

22.5 *Demogorgon:* a primeval creator, probably a corruption of Plato's Demiurge, whom Spenser borrows from Boccaccio, *De Genealogia Deorum,* I.21 (see Lotspeich). In Boccaccio he is viewed as a union of god (*demon*) and earth (*gorgon*); however, the ancient pre-Olympian powers were in Christian times usually identified with Satan and the demons of hell.
22.7 *nephews:* Latin *nepotes,* "grandsons."
23.4 "I beg you to remember me then and not to sail away and forsake me . . . nor leave me there unburied and unwept" (*Odyssey,* XI.53, p. 173).
23.7 *Aveugle:* blindness, the father of Sansfoy and son of Night.
24.5 *children of fair Light:* not specified here; they are also the "sons of Day" (25.7). They can be identified with the Olympian gods, who in medieval art became associated with aspects of God the Father, Christ, Mary, and the Holy Ghost, or the unfallen angels.

26 'Yet shall they not escape so freely all;
   For some shall pay the price of others' guilt.
   And he the man that made Sansfoy to fall
   Shall with his own blood price that° he hath spilt.   *pay for what*
   But what art thou that tellst of nephews kilt?'
   'I that do seem not I, Duessa am,'
   Quoth she, 'however now in garments gilt
   And gorgeous gold arrayed I to thee came.
   Duessa I, the daughter of Deceit and Shame.'

27 Then bowing down her aged back, she kissed
   The wicked witch, saying, 'In that fair face,
   The false resemblance of Deceit I wist
   Did closely° lurk; yet so true-seeming grace   *secretly*
   It carried, that I scarce in darksome place
   Could it discern, though I the mother be
   Of Falsehood, and root of Duessa's race.
   O welcome child, whom I have longed to see
   And now have seen unwares.° Lo, now I go with thee.'   *without recognizing*

28 Then to her iron wagon she betakes,
   And with her bears the foul well-favored° witch;   *beautiful*
   Through murksome air her ready° way she makes.   *easy*
   Her twifold° team, of which two black as pitch   *twofold*
   And two were brown, yet each to each unlich,°   *unlike*
   Did softly swim away, ne ever stamp
   Unless she chanced their stubborn mouths to twitch.
   Then foaming tar, their bridles they would champ,
   And trampling the fine element, would fiercely ramp.

29 So well they sped that they be come at length
   Unto the place whereas the paynim lay,
   Devoid of outward sense and native strength,
   Covered with charmèd cloud from view of day
   And sight of men since his late luckless fray.
   His cruel wounds, with cruddy° blood congealed,   *clotted*
   They binden up so wisely as they may,
   And handle softly till they can be healed.
   So lay him in her chariot, close in night concealed.

30 And all the while she stood upon the ground
   The wakeful dogs did never cease to bay,
   As giving warning of th' unwonted sound,
   With which her iron wheels did them affray
   And her dark grisly look them much dismay.
   The messenger of death, the ghastly owl,

27.7 Duessa and Sansfoy are therefore related, perhaps first cousins.

With dreary shrieks did also her bewray;°   *reveal*
And hungry wolves continually did howl
At her abhorrèd face, so filthy and so foul.

31   Thence turning back in silence soft they stole,
     And brought the heavy corse with easy pace
     To yawning gulf of deep Avernus hole.°   *cavern*
     By° that same hole an entrance dark and base,°   *by means of, low*
     With smoke and sulfur hiding all the place,
     Descends to hell. There creature never passed
     That back returnèd without heavenly grace,
     But dreadful furies which their chains have brast°   *burst*
     And damnèd sprites sent forth to make ill° men aghast.   *evil*

32   By that same way the direful dames do drive
     Their mournful chariot, filled with rusty blood,
     And down to Pluto's house are come belive.°   *soon*
     Which passing through, on every side them stood
     The trembling ghosts with sad amazèd mood,
     Chattering their iron teeth and staring wide
     With stony eyes. And all the hellish brood
     Of fiends infernal flocked on every side,
     To gaze on earthly wight that with the Night durst ride.

33   They pass the bitter waves of Acheron,
     Where many souls sit wailing woefully,
     And come to fiery flood of Phlegeton,
     Whereas the damnèd ghosts in torments fry,
     And with sharp shrilling shrieks do bootless cry,
     Cursing high Jove, the which them thither sent.
     The house of endless pain is built thereby,
     In which ten thousand sorts of punishment
     The cursèd creatures do eternally torment.

34   Before the threshold dreadful Cerberus
     His three deformèd heads did lay along,°   *down*
     Curlèd with thousand adders venomous,
     And lillèd forth° his bloody flaming tongue.   *hung out*
     At them he gan to rear his bristles strong
     And felly gnar,° until Day's enemy   *snarl savagely*
     Did him appease; then down his tail he hung

31.3 *Avernus:* a small lake near Naples; in poetry a cave, as here, through which is the entrance to hell. This description of the descent into hell derives from many classical poems, but especially *Aeneid,* VI.237–242.
31.7 Through Christ's harrowing of hell those souls possessing heavenly grace were allowed to return from hell.
33.1–3 *Acheron* and *Phlegeton:* two of the four rivers of hell.
34.1 *Cerberus:* the three-headed dog who guards the gate of hell.

And suffered them to passen quietly.
For she in hell and heaven had power equally.

35   There was Ixion turnèd on a wheel
For daring tempt the queen of heaven to sin,
And Sisyphus an huge round stone did reel°   *roll*
Against an hill, ne might from labor lin;°   *cease*
There thirsty Tantalus hung by the chin,
And Tityus fed a vulture on his maw;
Typhoeus' joints were stretchèd on a gin,°   *rack*
Theseus condemned to endless sloth by law,
And fifty sisters water in leak° vessels draw.   *leaky*

36   They all beholding worldly wights in place°   *there*
Leave off their work, unmindful of their smart,
To gaze on them. Who forth by them do pace
Till they be come unto the furthest part;
Where was a cave y-wrought by wondrous art,
Deep, dark, uneasy,° doleful, comfortless,   *disagreeable*
In which sad Aesculapius far apart
Imprisoned was in chains remediless,
For that° Hippolytus' rent corse he did redress.°   *because, revive*

37   Hippolytus a jolly° huntsman was,   *brave*
That wont in chariot chase the foaming boar;
He all his peers in beauty did surpass,
But ladies' love as loss of time forbore.
His wanton stepdame lovèd him the more,
But when she saw her offered sweets refused,
Her love she turned to hate, and him before
His father fierce of treason false° accused,   *falsely*
And with her jealous terms° his open° ears abused.   *words, trusting*

38   Who all in rage, his sea-god sire besought
Some cursèd vengeance on his son to cast.

35.1–9   The stories of *Ixion, Sisyphus, Tantalus, Tityus, Typhoeus, Theseus,* and the *fifty daughters* of Danaus are to be found in *Odyssey,* XI; *Aeneid,* VI; and *Metamorphoses,* IV and X. They were all guilty of presumption against the gods and as a group constitute a common topos in the classical and humanistic description of the punishments in hell.

36.7   *Aesculapius:* a son of Apollo whose healing arts were so great that he came dangerously close to giving man immortality. In classical myth the greatest benefactors of mankind were punished by the gods in order that man should not aspire to godhead. This story is told in *Aeneid,* VII, and *Metamorphoses,* XV.

37.1   *Hippolytus:* son of Theseus, king of Athens, and Hippolyta, queen of the Amazons. In addition to the Latin poems mentioned above, his story is dealt with fully in Euripides' *Hippolytus* and in Seneca's *Phaedra.*

37.5   *His wanton stepdame:* Phaedra, a subsequent wife of Theseus, who fell desperately in love with Hippolytus at the instigation of Venus. The goddess of love could not bear to see Hippolytus go unpunished for his chaste and single-minded devotion to Diana.

38.1   *his sea-god sire:* Neptune.

From surging gulf two monsters straight were brought;
With dread whereof his chasing steeds aghast,
Both chariot swift and huntsman overcast.
His goodly corpse, on ragged cliffs y-rent,
Was quite dismembered, and his members chaste
Scattered on every mountain as he went,
That of Hippolytus was left no monument.

39   His cruel stepdame seeing what was done,
Her wicked days with wretched knife did end,
In death avowing th' innocence of her son.
Which hearing, his rash sire began to rend
His hair, and hasty tongue that did offend.
Tho gathering up the relics of his smart
By Diane's means, who was Hippolyt's friend,
Them brought to Aesculape, that by his art
Did heal them all again, and joinèd every part.

40   Such wondrous science° in man's wit to reign   *skill*
When Jove avised,° that could the dead revive   *discovered*
And fates expirèd could renew again,
Of endless life he might him not deprive,
But unto hell did thrust him down alive,
With flashing thunderbolt y-wounded sore.
Where long remaining, he did always strive
Himself with salves to health for to restore,
And slake the heavenly fire that ragèd evermore.

41   There ancient Night arriving did alight
From her nigh weary° wain, and in her arms   *exhausted*
To Aesculapius brought the wounded knight;
Whom having softly disarrayed of arms,
Tho gan to him discover all his harms,
Beseeching him with prayer and with praise,
If either salves, or oils, or herbs, or charms
A fordone° wight from door of death mote raise,   *done for*
He would at her request prolong her nephew's days.

42   'Ah dame,' quoth he, 'thou temptest me in vain
To dare the thing which daily yet I rue,
And the old cause of my continued pain
With like attempt to like end to renew.
Is not enough, that thrust from heaven due,
Here endless penance for one fault I pay,
But that redoubled crime with vengeance new
Thou biddest me to eke?° Can Night defray   *increase*
The wrath of thundering Jove that rules both night and day?'

43 'Not so,' quoth she, 'but sith° that heaven's king   *since*
    From hope of heaven hath thee excluded quite,
    Why fearest thou that canst not hope for thing,
    And fearest not that more thee hurten might,
    Now in the power of everlasting Night?
    Go to, then, O thou far-renowmèd son
    Of great Apollo; show thy famous might
    In medicine that else° hath to thee won   *before*
    Great pains and greater praise, both never to be done.'°   *ended*

44 Her words prevailed. And then the learnèd leech°   *doctor*
    His cunning hand gan to his wounds to lay,
    And all things else the which his art did teach.
    Which having seen, from thence arose away
    The mother of dread darkness, and let stay
    Aveugle's son there in the leech's cure,
    And back returning took her wonted way
    To run her timely race,° whilst Phoebus pure   *nightly course*
    In western waves his weary wagon did recure.°   *refresh*

45 The false Duessa, leaving noyous° Night,   *harmful*
    Returned to stately palace of Dame Pride;
    Where when she came, she found the faery knight
    Departed thence, albe° his woundès wide   *although*
    Not throughly° healed, unready were to ride.   *thoroughly*
    Good cause he had to hasten thence away;
    For on a day his wary dwarf had spied
    Where in a dungeon deep huge numbers lay
    Of caitive° wretched thralls° that wailèd night and day.   *captive, slaves*

46 A rueful sight as could be seen with eye;
    Of whom he learnèd had in secret wise
    The hidden cause of their captivity:
    How mortgaging their lives to Covetise,
    Through wasteful Pride and wanton Riotise,
    They were by law of that proud tyranness°—   *i.e. Lucifera*
    Provoked° with Wrath and Envy's false surmise°—   *enraged,*
    Condemnèd to that dungeon merciless,   *suspicion*
    Where they should live in woe and die in wretchedness.

47 There was that great proud king of Babylon,
    That would compel all nations to adore

45.7 Common sense can see the miserable condition of those who have not resisted the sins and vanities of the world; most of the stories that follow are taken from ancient pre-Christian writers who had only the dwarf's kind of human reason to guide them.

46.6 *that proud tyranness:* Lucifera, whose law encourages the operation of the other sins in destroying man.

47.1 *proud king of Babylon:* Nebuchadnezzar (Daniel 3–4); Spenser may

And him as only god to call upon,
Till through celestial doom° thrown out of door,   *judgment*
Into an ox he was transformed of yore.
There also was king Croesus, that enhanced°   *exalted*
His heart too high through his great richess' store;
And proud Antiochus, the which advanced
His cursèd hand gainst God, and on his altars danced.

48   And them long time before, great Nimrod was,
      That first the world with sword and fire warrayed;°   *ravaged*
      And after, him old Ninus far did pass°   *surpass*
      In princely pomp, of all the world obeyed.
      There also was that mighty monarch, laid
      Low under° all, yet above all in pride,   *lower than*
      That name of native sire° did foul upbraid,°   *natural father, disgrace*
      And would as Ammon's son be magnified,
      Till scorned of God and man, a shameful death he died.

49   All these together in one heap were thrown,
      Like carcasses of beasts in butcher's stall.
      And in another corner wide were strown
      The antique ruins of the Romans' fall:
      Great Romulus, the grandsire of them all,
      Proud Tarquin and too lordly Lentulus,
      Stout Scipio and stubborn Hannibal,
      Ambitious Sylla and stern Marius,
      High Caesar, great Pompey, and fierce Antonius.

50   Amongst these mighty men were women mixed,
      Proud women, vain, forgetful of their yoke;°   *marriage bond*
      The bold Semiramis, whose sides transfixed

derive Nebuchadnezzar's unbiblical meta-
morphosis into an ox from John Gower's
Confessio Amantis, I.5. All of the follow-
ing princes who fell through pride were
cited by medieval writers in contexts simi-
lar to Spenser's. They are analogous to
the mythological group in 35 above. To
modern readers the best-known treatment
of these "tragedies" is Chaucer's *Monk's
Tale;* to medieval readers, first place was
held by Boccaccio's *De Casibus Virorum
Illustrium.*
47.6   *Croesus:* a king of Lydia in the
6th century, B.C., proverbial for his
wealth, who in medieval tradition died a
violent death.
47.8   *Antiochus:* king of Syria in the
2nd century, B.C. (*Maccabees* 1:1).
48.1   *great Nimrod:* according to
Flavius Josephus, *Antiquities of the Jews,*
I.4, the son of Ham and grandson of Noah
who incited his people to affront God by
building the Tower of Babel (Genesis
10:9), a crime in biblical history not un-

like those of Aesculapius and Prometheus
in Greek mythology.
48.3   *Ninus:* the eponymous founder
of Nineveh, husband (according to
legend) or son of Queen Semiramis, who
caused his death and reputedly built for
him a magnificent tomb. The tomb was
the meeting place of Pyramus and Thisbe
(*Metamorphoses,* IV.88, p. 104).
48.5–6   *mighty monarch:* Alexander the
Great, who also aspired to godhead in
claiming to be the son of Jove, worshipped
in Lybia as Jupiter *Ammon;* died igno-
miniously after an extended carousal (his-
torical) or of poisoning (legendary).
49.5–9   Proud military and political
leaders in earlier Roman history who led
violent lives and died violent deaths.
50.3 *Semiramis:* legendary queen of
Babylonia, wife of Ninus (48.3 above);
her sexual and military energy led to the
attraction of many interesting stories to
her name.

With son's own blade, her foul reproaches spoke;
Fair Sthenoboea, that herself did choke
With willful cord for wanting° of her will;   *not getting*
High minded Cleopatra, that with stroke
Of asp'ès sting herself did stoutly kill;
And thousands mo the like that did that dungeon fill,

51 Besides the endless routs of wretched thralls
Which thither were assembled day by day
From all the world, after their woeful falls
Through wicked pride and wasted wealth's decay.
But most of all which in that dungeon lay
Fell from high princes' courts or ladies' bowers,
Where they in idle pomp or wanton play
Consumèd had their goods and thriftless hours,
And lastly thrown themselves into these heavy stours.

52 Whose case whenas the careful° dwarf had told,   *sorrowful*
And made ensample° of their mournful sight   *given examples*
Unto his master, he no lenger would
There dwell in peril of like painful plight,
But early rose, and ere that dawning light
Discovered had the world to heaven wide,
He by a privy postern° took his flight,   *gate*
That of no envious° eyes he mote° be spied.   *malicious, might*
For doubtless death ensued if any him descried.

53 Scarce could he footing find in that foul way
For many corses, like a great lay-stall°   *rubbish heap*
Of murdered men, which therein strowèd lay
Without remorse or decent funeral.
Which all through that great princess' pride did fall
And came to shameful end. And them beside,
Forth riding underneath the castle wall,
A dunghill of dead carcasses he spied,
The dreadful spectacle° of that sad House of Pride. *emblem*

CANTO vi

From lawless lust by wondrous grace
  Fair Una is released;
Whom savage nation does adore
  And learns her wise behest.

50.5 *Sthenoboea:* more commonly called Anteia, wife of King Proetus, loved Bellerophon with an outcome similar to that of Phaedra's love for Hippolytus (*Iliad*, VI.160).

50.7 *Cleopatra:* like the other women mentioned here, finally destroyed through a combination of violent love and ambition.

1 As when a ship that flies fair under sail
   An hidden rock escapèd hath unwares,
   That lay in wait her wreck for to bewail,°   *bring about*
   The mariner yet half amazèd stares
   At peril passed, and yet in doubt ne dares
   To joy at his fool-happy° oversight—   *lucky*
   So doubly is distressed twixt joy and cares
   The dreadless courage of this elfin knight,
   Having escaped so sad ensamples in his sight.

2 Yet sad he was that his too hasty speed
   The fair Duess had forced him leave behind;
   And yet more sad that Una, his dear dreed,°   *(dread) beloved*
   Her truth had stained with treason so unkind.°   *unnatural*
   Yet crime in her could never creature find,
   But for his love and for her own self sake
   She wandered had° from one to other Ind   *would have*
   Him for to seek, ne ever would forsake
   Till her unwares the fierce Sansloy did overtake.

3 Who after Archimago's foul defeat,
   Led her away into a forest wild,
   And turning wrathful fire to lustful heat,
   With beastly sin thought her to have defiled
   And made the vassal of his pleasures vild.°   *vile*
   Yet first he cast by treaty° and by trains°   *persuasion, tricks*
   Her to persuade that stubborn fort to yield;
   For greater conquest of hard love he gains
   That works it to his will, than he that it constrains.

4 With fawning words he courted her awhile,
   And looking lovely° and oft sighing sore,   *lovingly*
   Her constant heart did tempt with diverse guile.
   But words and looks and sighs she did abhor,
   As rock of diamond steadfast evermore.
   Yet for to feed his fiery lustful eye,
   He snatched the veil that hung her face before;
   Then gan her beauty shine as brightest sky,
   And burnt his beastly heart t' efforce° her chastity.   *force*

5 So when he saw his flattering arts to fail
   And subtle engines beat from battery,
   With greedy force he gan the fort assail,
   Whereof he weened possessèd soon to be,
   And win rich spoil of ransacked chastity.

5.2 *And subtle engines beat from bat-*   (engines) destroyed itself in battering the
tery: a continuation of the military meta-   unyielding fort; i.e., his courtly advances
phor of 3.7. Sansloy's battering equipment   were frustrated.

Ah heavens, that do this hideous act behold,
And heavenly virgin thus outragèd see,
How can ye vengeance just so long withold,
And hurl not flashing flames upon that paynim bold?

6   The piteous maiden, careful comfortless,°   *desperately*
    Does throw out thrilling° shrieks and shrieking cries,   *anxious*
                                                              piercing
    The last vain help of women's great distress,
    And with loud plaints importuneth the skies,
    That molten stars do drop like weeping eyes.
    And Phoebus flying so most shameful sight,
    His blushing face in foggy cloud implies°   *wraps up*
    And hides for shame. What wit of mortal wight
    Can now devise to quit° a thrall from such a plight?   *free*

7   Eternal Providence, exceeding° thought,   *transcending*
    Where none appears can make herself a way.
    A wondrous way it for this lady wrought,
    From lion's claws to pluck the grippèd prey.
    Her shrill outcries and shrieks so loud did bray
    That all the woods and forests did resound;
    A troop of fauns and satyrs far away
    Within the wood were dancing in a round,
    Whiles old Sylvanus slept in shady arbor sound.

8   Who when they heard that piteous strainèd voice,
    In haste forsook their rural merriment,
    And ran towards the far rebounded noise
    To weet what wight so loudly did lament.
    Unto the place they came incontinent;°   *immediately*
    Whom when the raging Saracen espied—
    A rude, misshapen, monstrous rabblement,
    Whose like he never saw—he durst not bide,
    But got his ready steed and fast away gan ride.

9   The wild wood gods, arrivèd in the place,
    There find the virgin doleful desolate,
    With ruffled raiments and fair blubbered face,
    As her outrageous foe had left her late,
    And trembling yet through fear of former hate.°   *enemy*

6.5–8 Sympathetic nature partakes of this cosmic struggle between truth and lawlessness. Nature fell with Adam, and natural disturbances accompanied the crucifixion.

7.7 *fauns* (from Roman mythology) and *satyrs* (from Greek): wild creatures with men's bodies above and goats' bodies below. They followed the uninhibited desire for sensual pleasure.

7.9 *old Sylvanus:* the Roman god of fields and forests whose nature was similar to that of the fauns and satyrs, especially that of Dionysus' drunken old satyr, Silenus (see iv.22.1 above).

8.7–9 That Sansloy cannot face the monstrous crew is evidence that there is potential for natural goodness in the satyrs which their beastliness has not entirely subdued.

All stand amazèd at so uncouth° sight   *strange*
And gin to pity her unhappy state;
All stand astonied at her beauty bright,
In their rude eyes unworthy of° so woeful plight.   *not deserving*

10   She more amazed, in double dread doth dwell;
And every tender part for fear does shake—
As when a greedy wolf through hunger fell
A silly° lamb far from the flock does take,   *innocent*
Of whom he means his bloody feast to make,
A lion spies fast running towards him,
The innocent prey in haste he does forsake—
Which quit from death, yet quakes in every limb
With change of fear, to see the lion look so grim.

11   Such fearful fit assayed° her trembling heart,   *attacked*
Ne word to speak, ne joint to move she had.
The savage nation feel her secret smart
And read her sorrow in her countenance sad;
Their frowning foreheads, with rough horns y-clad,
And rustic horror° all aside do lay,   *roughness*
And gently grinning, show a semblance glad,
To comfort her and fear to put away.
Their backward bent knees teach° her humbly to obey.   *i.e. teach them*

12   The doubtful damsel dare not yet commit
Her single° person to their barbarous truth,°   *weak, sense of honor*
But still twixt fear and hope amazed does sit,
Late learned° what harm too hasty trust ensu'th.   *taught*
They in compassion of her tender youth
And wonder of her beauty sovereign,
Are won with pity and unwonted ruth,
And all prostrate upon the lowly plain,
Do kiss her feet and fawn on her with countenance fain.°   *happy*

13   Their hearts she guesseth by their humble guise°   *behaviour*
And yields her to extremity of time;°   *urgency of the present*
So from the ground she fearless doth arise
And walketh forth without suspect of crime.
They all as glad as birds of joyous prime,°   *morning*
Thence lead her forth, about her dancing round,
Shouting, and singing all a shepherd's rime,
And with green branches strowing all the ground,
Do worship her as queen, with olive garland crowned.

13.9 The satyrs' crowning Una is paralleled by a similar episode in Canto xii.8, where the maidens "crowned her twixt earnest and twixt game" with a garland. The difference is that the satyrs crown Una completely in earnest, that they worship the outward aspects of truth (physical beauty), of true religion (the institution of the church), and of religious teaching (the letter as opposed to the spirit of the word); and are thus guilty of idolatry.

14 And all the way their merry pipes they sound,
    That all the woods with doubled echo ring,
    And with their hornèd feet do wear the ground,
    Leaping like wanton kids in pleasant spring.
    So towards old Sylvanus they her bring;
    Who with the noise awakèd, cometh out
    To weet the cause, his weak steps governing
    And aged limbs on cypress stadle° stout,   *staff*
    And with an ivy twine his waist is girt about.

15 Far off he wonders what them makes so glad,
    Or° Bacchus' merry fruit they did invent,°   *whether, find*
    Or Cybele's frantic rites have made them mad.
    They drawing nigh, unto their god present
    That flower of faith and beauty excellent.
    The god himself, viewing that mirror rare,°   *paragon*
    Stood long amazed and burnt in his intent;°   *gaze*
    His own fair Dryope now he thinks not fair,
    And Pholoe foul, when her to this he doth compare.

16 The woodborn people fall before her flat
    And worship her as goddess of the wood;
    And old Sylvanus self bethinks° not what   *knows*
    To think of wight so fair, but gazing stood,
    In doubt to deem her born of earthly brood.
    Sometimes dame Venus self he seems to see,
    But Venus never had so sober mood;
    Sometimes Diana he her takes to be,
    But misseth bow and shafts and buskins° to her knee.   *boots*

17 By view of her he ginneth to revive
    His ancient love and dearest Cypariss,
    And calls to mind his portraiture alive°—   *picture when he*
    How fair he was and yet not fair to this;   *was alive*
    And how he slew with glancing dart amiss°   *accidentally*
    A gentle hind, the which the lovely boy
    Did love as life, above all worldly bliss;
    For grief whereof the lad n'ould° after joy,   *wouldn't*
    But pined away in anguish and self-willed annoy.°   *suffering*

15.2 *Bacchus' merry fruit:* wine grapes.
15.3 *Cybele:* Rhea, the mother of Jove, whose priests and priestesses, the Corybantes, worshipped her with frenzied shrieks and the clash of cymbals and drums.
15.8 *Dryope:* perhaps the same nymph as the one mentioned in *Aeneid,* X.551 (p. 268) as being the wife of Faunus.
15.9 *Pholoe:* a nymph beloved of Pan in classical myth. Spenser's reference to Dryope and Pholoe suggests a rough identification of Sylvanus with both Faunus and Pan.
17.2 *Cypariss:* a youth beloved of Sylvanus, who was changed into a cypress from grieving over the slain hind. Most of the details are to be found in Ovid's *Metamorphoses,* X.120–142 (pp. 248–249). Ovid, however, has it that it was Apollo who loved the youth; Spenser found his version in either Boccaccio or Natalis Comes, both of whom associate Cyparissus with Sylvanus (see Lotspeich).

18   The woody° nymphs, fair Hamadryades,   *forest*
     Her to behold do thither run apace,
     And all the troop of light-foot Naiades
     Flock all about to see her lovely face;
     But when they viewèd have her heavenly grace,
     They envy her in their malicious mind,
     And fly away for fear of foul disgrace.
     But all the satyrs scorn their woody kind,
     And henceforth nothing fair but her on earth they find.

19   Glad of such luck, the luckless lucky maid
     Did her content to please their feeble eyes,
     And long time with that savage people stayed,
     To gather breath in many miseries.
     During which time her gentle wit she plies°   *applies*
     To teach them truth, which worshipped her in vain,°   *foolishly*
     And made her th' image of idolatries;°   *made an idol*
                                                            of her
     But when their bootless zeal she did restrain
     From her own worship, they her ass would worship fain.° *gladly*

20   It fortunèd a noble warlike knight
     By just occasion° to that forest came,   *opportunity*
     To seek his kindred and the lineage right°   *true*
     From whence he took his well deservèd name.
     He had in arms abroad won muchel fame,
     And filled far lands with glory of his might—
     Plain, faithful, true, and enemy of shame,
     And ever loved to fight for lady's right,
     But in vainglorious frays he little did delight.

21   A satyr's son y-born in forest wild
     By strange adventure° as it did betide,   *chance*
     And there begotten of a lady mild,
     Fair Thyamis the daughter of Labryde,
     That was in sacred bands of wedlock tied
     To Therion, a loose unruly swain;
     Who had more joy to range the forest wide,
     And chase the savage beast with busy pain,
     Than serve his lady's love and waste in pleasures vain.

22   The forlorn maid did with love's longing burn,
     And could not lack° her lover's company,   *do without*
     But to the wood she goes to serve her turn°   *accomplish her*
                                                            desire

18.1 *Hamadryades:* wood nymphs, who were born and died with the trees they inhabited.
   18.3 *Naiades:* nymphs of fresh water.
   21.4 *Thyamis:* Greek *thymos,* "passion"; *Labryde:* Greek *labros,* "turbulent, greedy."
   21.6 *Therion:* Greek *therion,* "wild beast."

And seek her spouse, that from her still does fly
And follows other game and venery.°   *hunting*
A satyr chanced her wandering for to find,
And kindling coals of lust in brutish eye,
The loyal links of wedlock did unbind,
And made her person thrall unto his beastly kind.

23   So long in secret cabin there he held
      Her captive to his sensual desire,
      Till that with timely° fruit her belly swelled   *ripening*
      And bore a boy unto the savage sire.
      Then home he suffered her for to retire,
      For ransom leaving him the late born child;
      Whom till to riper years he gan aspire,°   *grow up*
      He nursled up in life and manners wild,
      Amongst wild beasts and woods, from laws of men exiled.

24   For all he taught the tender imp° was but   *child*
      To banish cowardice and bastard° fear;   *mean*
      His trembling hand he would him force to put
      Upon the lion and the rugged bear,
      And from the she-bear's teats her whelps to tear.
      And eke wild roaring bulls he would him make
      To tame, and ride their backs not made to bear,
      And the roebucks° in flight to overtake;   *male roedeer*
      That every beast for fear of him did fly and quake.

25   Thereby so fearless and so fell he grew
      That his own sire and master° of his guise°   *teacher, conduct*
      Did often tremble at his horrid view,°   *appearance*
      And oft for dread of hurt would him advise
      The angry beasts not rashly to despise,
      Nor too much to provoke; for he would learn°   *teach*
      The lion stoop to him in lowly wise—
      A lesson hard—and make the libbard° stern   *leopard*
      Leave roaring, when in rage he for revenge did earn.°   *yearn*

26   And for to make his power approvèd° more,   *to extend his*
      Wild beasts in iron yokes he would compel—   *power*
      The spotted panther and the tuskèd boar,
      The pardale° swift and the tiger cruel,   *leopard*
      The antelope and wolf both fierce and fell—
      And them constrain in equal° team to draw.   *paired*

    22.5 *venery:* probably a pun on "hunting" and "sexual activity."
    24.1–9 Satyrane's education is similar to that of the young Achilles at the hands of Chiron, his centaur teacher. It owes something to Ariosto's account of the education of Ruggiero (*Orlando Furioso,* VII.57).

Such joy he had their stubborn hearts to quell,
And sturdy courage tame with dreadful awe,
That his behest they fearèd as a tyrant's law.

27 His loving mother came upon a day
Unto the woods to see her little son,
And chanced unwares to meet him in the way,
After his sports and cruel pastime done,
When after him a lioness did run,
That roaring all with rage did loud requere°   *demand*
Her children dear, whom he away had won.
The lion whelps she saw how he did bear,
And lull in rugged arms withouten childish fear.

28 The fearful dame all quakèd at the sight,
And turning back, gan fast to fly away,
Until with love revoked° from vain affright,   *called back*
She hardly yet persuaded was to stay;
And then to him these womanish words gan say:
'Ah Satyrane, my darling and my joy,
For love of me leave off this dreadful play;
To dally thus with death is no fit toy;
Go find some other playfellows, mine own sweet boy.'

29 In these and like delights of bloody game
He trainèd was till riper years he raught,°   *reached*
And there abode, whilst any beast of name°   *known*
Walked in that forest whom he had not taught
To fear his force. And then his courage haught°   *high*
Desired of foreign foemen to be known,
And far abroad for strange adventures sought;
In which his might was never overthrown,
But through all Faeryland his famous worth was blown.

30 Yet evermore it was his manner fair,
After long labors and adventures spent,
Unto those native woods for to repair
To see his sire and ofspring° ancient.   *father*
And now he thither came for like intent;
Where he unwares the fairest Una found,
Strange lady in so strange habiliment,°   *clothes*
Teaching the satyrs, which her sat around,
True sacred lore, which from her sweet lips did redound.°   *flow*

31 He wondered at her wisdom heavenly rare,°   *excellent*
Whose like in women's wit he never knew;
And when her courteous deeds he did compare,°   *review*
Gan her admire and her sad sorrows rue,

Blaming of fortune, which such troubles threw
And joyed to make proof of her cruelty
On gentle dame, so hurtless and so true.
Thenceforth he kept her goodly company
And learned her discipline of faith and verity.

32 But she all vowed unto the Red Cross Knight,
His wandering peril closely° did lament,   *secretly*
Ne in this new acquaintance could delight,
But her dear heart with anguish did torment,
And all her wit in secret counsels spent
How to escape. At last in privy wise
To Satyrane she showèd her intent;
Who glad to gain such favor, gan devise
How with that pensive maid he best might thence arise.°   *depart*

33 So on a day when satyrs all were gone
To do their service to Sylvanus old,
The gentle virgin, left behind alone,
He led away with courage stout and bold.
Too late it was to satyrs to be told,
Or ever hope recover her again.
In vain he seeks that having cannot hold.
So fast he carried her with careful pain°   *painstaking care*
That they the woods are passed and come now to the plain.

34 The better part now of the lingering day
They traveled had whenas they far espied
A weary wight forwandering° by the way,   *trudging*
And towards him they gan in haste to ride,
To weet of news that did abroad betide,
Or tidings of her Knight of the Red Cross.
But he them spying gan to turn aside,
For fear as seemed, or for some feignèd loss;°   *supposed harm*
More greedy they of news, fast towards him do cross.

35 A silly man in simple weeds forworn°   *worn out*
And soiled with dust of the long drièd way;
His sandals were with toilsome travel torn,
And face all tanned with scorching sunny ray,
As he had traveled many a summer's day
Through boiling sands of Araby and Ind;
And in his hand a Jacob's staff° to stay   *pilgrim's staff*
His weary limbs upon. And eke behind
His scrip° did hang, in which his needments he did bind.   *bag*

33–48 The plot of the remainder of this canto is borrowed from the first two cantos
of *Orlando Furioso*.

36   The knight approaching nigh, of him inquered
     Tidings of war and of adventures new;
     But wars nor new adventures none he heard.
     Then Una gan to ask if aught he knew
     Or heard abroad of that her champion true,
     That in his armor bare a crosslet red.
     'Aye me, dear dame,' quoth he, 'well may I rue
     To tell the sad sight which mine eyes have read—
     These eyes did see that knight both living and eke dead.'

37   That cruel word her tender heart so thrilled
     That sudden cold did run through every vein,
     And stony horror all her senses filled
     With dying° fit, that down she fell for pain.   *deathlike*
     The knight her lightly rearèd up again
     And comforted with courteous kind relief;
     Then won from death, she bade him tellen plain
     The further process of her hidden grief.
     The lesser pangs can bear, who hath endured the chief.

38   Then gan the pilgrim thus, 'I chanced this day,
     This fatal day that shall I ever rue,
     To see two knights in travel on my way—
     A sorry sight—arranged in battle new,°   *just started*
     Both breathing vengeance, both of wrathful hue.
     My fearful flesh did tremble at their strife,
     To see their blades so greedily imbrue,°   *soak themselves*
                                                 in blood
     That drunk with blood, yet thirsted after life.
     What more? The Red Cross Knight was slain with paynim
       knife.'

39   'Ah dearest Lord,' quoth she, 'how might that be,
     And he the stoutest knight that ever won?'°   *fought*
     'Ah dearest dame,' quoth he, 'how might I see
     The thing that might not be, and yet was done?'
     'Where is,' said Satryane, 'that paynim's son
     That him of life and us of joy hath reft?'
     'Not far away,' quoth he, 'he hence doth won°   *stay*
     Forby° a fountain, where I late him left   *beside*
     Washing his bloody wounds, that through the steel were
       cleft.'

40   Therewith the knight thence marchèd forth in haste,
     Whiles Una with huge heaviness° oppressed,   *grief*
     Could not for sorrow follow him so fast;
     And soon he came, as he the place had guessed,

     39.7 *he:* (1596). 1590 reads *she.*

Whereas that pagan proud himself did rest
In secret shadow by a fountain side.
Even he it was that erst would have suppressed°   *forced down*
Fair Una; whom when Satyrane espied,
With foul reproachful words he boldly him defied.

41   And said, 'Arise thou cursèd miscreant,
That hast with knightless guile and treacherous train
Fair knighthood foully shamèd, and dost vaunt
That good Knight of the Red Cross to have slain.
Arise, and with like treason now maintain°   *defend*
Thy guilty wrong, or else thee guilty yield.'
The Saracen this hearing, rose amain,°   *at once*
And catching up in haste his three-square° shield   *triangular*
And shining helmet, soon him buckled to the field.

42   And drawing nigh him said, 'Ah misborn° elf,   *bastardly*
In evil hour thy foes thee hither sent,
Another's wrongs to wreak upon thyself.
Yet ill thou blamest me for having blent
My name with guile and traitorous intent.
That Red Cross Knight, perdie,° I never slew;   *in truth*
But had he been where erst his arms were lent,
Th' enchanter vain his error should not rue.
But thou his error shalt, I hope, now proven true.'

43   Therewith they gan, both furious and fell,
To thunder blows and fiercely to assail,
Each other bent his enemy to quell;°   *kill*
That with their force they pierced both plate and mail,
And made wide furrows in their fleshes frail,
That it would pity° any living eye.   *fill with pity*
Large floods of blood adown their sides did rail,°   *flow*
But floods of blood could not them satisfy;
Both hungered after death, both chose to win or die.

44   So long they fight and fell revenge pursue
That fainting each, themselves to breathen let,
And oft refreshèd, battle oft renew.
As when two boars, with rankling malice met,
Their gory sides fresh bleeding fiercely fret,°   *gnaw*
Till breathless both, themselves aside retire,
Where foaming wrath, their cruel tusks they whet

41.8 *three-square shield:* triangular
shield, straight across the top and pointed
at the bottom; prevalent from the 12th
through the 14th centuries.
42.7–9 I.e., "Had Red Cross been
where his arms were, the foolish enchanter
(Archimago) should not regret his error
(of fighting in Red Cross's place). But
you shall, I hope, confirm his (Archi-
mago's) error (of fighting me).
44.1 *fell:* (1596). 1590 reads *full.*

And trample th' earth, the whiles they may respire;°   *catch their breath*
Then back to fight again, new breathèd and entire°   *fresh and strong*

45   So fiercely when these knights had breathèd once,
They gan to fight return, increasing more
Their puissant force and cruel rage at once
With heapèd strokes more hugely than before,
That with their dreary° wounds and bloody gore,   *gory*
They both deformèd, scarcely could be known.
By this, sad Una fraught with anguish sore,
Led with their noise which through the air was thrown,
Arrived where they in earth their fruitless blood had sown.

46   Whom all so soon as that proud Saracen
Espied, he gan revive the memory
Of his lewd lusts and late attempted sin,
And left the doubtful battle hastily
To catch her, newly offered to his eye.
But Satyrane with strokes him turning, stayed,
And sternly bade him other business ply,
Than hunt the steps of pure unspotted maid.
Wherewith he all enraged, these bitter speeches said:

47   'O foolish faery's son, what fury mad
Hath thee incensed to haste thy doleful fate?
Were it not better I that lady had,
Than that thou hadst repented it too late?
Most senseless man he that himself doth hate
To love another. Lo then, for thine aid,
Here take thy lover's token on thy pate.'
So they to fight; the whiles the royal maid
Fled far away, of that proud paynim sore afraid.

48   But that false pilgrim which that leasing° told,   *lie*
Being indeed old Archimage, did stay
In secret shadow all this to behold,
And much rejoicèd in their bloody fray.
But when he saw the damsel pass away,
He left his stand and her pursued apace,
In hope to bring her to her last decay.
But for to tell her lamentable case,
And eke this battle's end, will need another place.

48.9 Sir Satyrane reappears in Book III, but nothing more is heard of *this bat-tle's end.*

CANTO vii

The Red Cross Knight is captive made,
    By giant proud oppressed;
Prince Arthur meets with Una, great-
    ly with those news distressed.

1   What man so wise, what earthly wit so ware,°   *wise*
    As to descry° the crafty cunning train   *discover*
    By which Deceit doth mask in visor fair,
    And cast° her colors dyèd deep in grain   *devise*
    To seem like Truth, whose shape she well can feign,
    And fitting gestures to her purpose frame,
    The guiltless man with guile to entertain?°   *make a fool of*
    Great mistress of her art was that false dame,
    The false Duessa, cloakèd with Fidessa's name.

2   Who when returning from the dreary Night
    She found not in that perilous House of Pride,
    Where she had left the noble Red Cross Knight,
    Her hopèd prey, she would no lenger bide,
    But forth she went to seek him far and wide.
    Ere long she found whereas he weary sate°   *sat*
    To rest himself forby° a fountain side,   *beside*
    Disarmèd all of iron-coated plate;
    And by his side his steed the grassy forage ate.

3   He feeds upon the cooling shade and bays°   *bathes*
    His sweaty forehead in the breathing wind,
    Which through the trembling leaves full gently plays,
    Wherein the cheerful birds of sundry kind
    Do chant sweet music to delight his mind.
    The witch approaching gan him fairly greet,
    And with reproach of carelessness unkind
    Upbraid for leaving her in place unmeet,°   *improper*
    With foul words tempering fair, sour gall with honey sweet.

4   Unkindness passed, they gan of solace treat,°   *talk of pleasure*
    And bathe in pleasance of the joyous shade,
    Which shielded them against the boiling heat,
    And with green boughs decking a gloomy glade,
    About the fountain like° a garland made;   *something like*
    Whose bubbling wave did ever freshly well,
    Ne ever would through fervent summer fade.

The sacred nymph which therein wont to dwell
Was out of Diane's favor, as it then befell.

5   The cause was this: One day when Phoebe fair
With all her band was following the chase,
This nymph, quite tired with heat of scorching air,
Sat down to rest in middest of the race.
The goddess wroth gan foully her disgrace,°   *disparage*
And bade the waters which from her did flow
Be such as she herself was then in place.°   *at that time*
Thenceforth her waters waxèd dull and slow,
And all that drink thereof do faint and feeble grow.

6   Hereof this gentle knight unweeting was,
And lying down upon the sandy grale,°   *gravel*
Drunk of the stream, as clear as crystal glass.
Eftsoons his manly forces gan to fail,
And mighty strong was turned to feeble frail.
His changèd powers at first themselves not felt,
Till crudled cold his courage° gan assail,   *vigor*
And cheerful° blood in faintness chill did melt,°   *lively, change*
Which like a fever fit through all his body swelt.°   *burned*

7   Yet goodly court he made still to his dame,
Poured out in looseness on the grassy ground,
Both careless of his health and of his fame;
Till at the last he heard a dreadful sound
Which through the wood loud bellowing did rebound,
That all the earth for terror seemed to shake,
And trees did tremble. Th' elf therewith astound,
Upstarted lightly from his looser make,°   *immoral*
And his unready weapons gan in hand to take.   *companion*

8   But ere he could his armor on him dight°   *put*
Or get his shield, his monstrous enemy
With sturdy steps came stalking in his sight,
An hideous giant, horrible and high,
That with his tallness seemed to threat the sky;

5.1 *Phoebe:* the moon goddess as Diana, chaste goddess of the hunt. Although the metamorphosis described in this stanza is in the pure Ovidian manner, it is apparently an invention of Spenser's, designed as a mythological emblem of Red Cross's sitting "down to rest in middest of the race."

8.4 *An hideous giant:* Orgoglio's parentage and gross carnality accord with ancient and medieval accounts of the giants. Spenser may have been conscious of the common (but false) etymology which derived Greek and Latin *gigas,* "giant," from Greek *gegenes,* "earthborn." Both George (see x.52.2) and Demogorgon (v.22.5) are names that were also thought to derive from the root *ge,* "earth." St. George encounters in the giant Orgoglio a symbol of his own pride in earthly flesh. Both Orgoglio and St. George are sons of earth.

The ground eke groanèd under him for dreed.
His living like saw never living eye,
Ne durst behold. His stature did exceed
The height of three the tallest sons of mortal seed.

9   The greatest Earth his uncouth mother was
And blustering Aeolus his boasted sire,
Who with his breath, which through the world doth pass,
Her hollow womb did secretly inspire,°   *breathe into*
And filled her hidden caves with stormy ire,
That she conceived; and trebling the due° time   *usual*
In which the wombs of women do expire,°   *deliver*
Brought forth this monstrous mass of earthly slime,
Puffed up with empty wind and filled with sinful crime.

10   So growen great through arrogant delight
Of th' high descent whereof he was y-born,
And through presumption of his matchless might,
All other powers and knighthood he did scorn.
Such now he marcheth to this man forlorn
And left to loss.° His stalking steps are stayed   *death*
Upon a snaggy oak which he had torn
Out of his mother's bowels, and it made
His mortal mace, wherewith his foemen he dismayed.°   *defeated*

11   That when the knight he spied, he gan advance
With huge force and insupportable main,°   *irresistable*
                                     strength
And towards him with dreadful fury prance;°   *stalk*
Who hapless and eke hopeless, all in vain
Did to him pace, sad battle to deraign°—   *fight*
Disarmed, disgraced, and inwardly dismayed,
And eke so faint in every joint and vein,
Through that frail° fountain which him feeble made,   *weakening*
That scarcely could he wield his bootless single blade.

12   The giant struck so mainly merciless
That could have overthrown a stony tower;
And were not heavenly grace, that him did bless,
He had been powdered all as thin as flour.
But he was wary of that deadly stour
And lightly leapt from underneath the blow;
Yet so exceeding was the villain's power,
That with the wind it did him overthrow
And all his senses stound,° that still he lay full low.   *stun*

11.9 *bootless single blade:* bootless (useless) because single (unaccompanied by shield,
spear, and armor).

13   As when that devilish iron engine wrought
     In deepest hell and framed by furies' skill,
     With windy niter and quick° sulfur fraught,°   *easily ignited,*
     And rammed with bullet round, ordained to kill,   *loaded*
     Conceiveth fire, the heavens it doth fill
     With thundering noise and all the air doth choke,
     That none can breath, nor see, nor hear at will,
     Through smoldery cloud of duskish stinking smoke,
     That th' only breath° him daunts, who hath escaped the   *the blast alone*
        stroke.

14   So daunted when the giant saw the knight,
     His heavy hand he heavèd up on high,
     And him to dust thought to have battered quite,
     Until Duessa loud to him gan cry:
     'O great Orgoglio, greatest under sky,
     O hold thy mortal hand for lady's sake.
     Hold for my sake, and do him not to die,
     But vanquished, thine eternal bondslave make,
     And me, thy worthy meed, unto thy leman° take.'   *mistress*

15   He hearkened, and did stay from further harms
     To gain so goodly guerdon° as she spake.°   *reward, promised*
     So willingly she came into his arms,
     Who her as willingly to grace did take,
     And was possessèd of his new found make.°   *lover*
     Then up he took the slumbered senseless corse,
     And ere he could out of his swoon awake,
     Him to his castle brought with hasty force
     And in a dungeon deep him threw without remorse.

16   From that day forth Duessa was his dear,
     And highly honored in his haughty eye;
     He gave her gold and purple pall° to wear,   *robe*
     And triple crown set on her head full high,
     And her endowed with royal majesty.
     Then for to make her dreaded more of men
     And people's hearts with awful terror tie,
     A monstrous beast y-bred in filthy fen
     He chose, which he had kept long time in darksome den.

17   Such one it was as that renowmèd snake
     Which great Alcides in Stremona slew,

16.3 "The woman was arrayed in pur-
ple and scarlet colour, and decked with
gold . . ." (**Revelation** 17:4).
     17.1–3 *that renowmèd snake:* the Ler-
nean Hydra, a nine-headed monster
whose lair was in a marsh near *Lerna* in
southern Greece; slain by Hercules (*Al-
cides:* descendant of Alcaeus) as one of
the twelve labors. Spenser sets the action
in Strymon (*Stremona*) a city in Thrace.

Long fostered in the filth of Lerna lake,
Whose many heads, out-budding ever new,
Did breed him endless labor to subdue.
But this same monster much more ugly was;
For seven great heads out of his body grew,
And iron breast, and back of scaly brass;
And all imbrued in blood,° his eyes did shine as glass.   *bloodshot*

18 His tail was strechèd out in wondrous length,
    That to the house of heavenly gods it raught;°   *reached*
    And with extorted° power and borrowed strength,   *stolen*
    The ever-burning lamps from thence it brought
    And proudly threw to ground, as things of nought.
    And underneath his filthy feet did tread
    The sacred things and holy hests° foretaught.   *commands*
    Upon this dreadful beast with sevenfold head
    He set the false Duessa, for more awe and dread.

19 The woeful dwarf, which saw his master's fall
    Whiles he had keeping of his grazing steed,
    And valiant knight become a caitive thrall,
    When all was past took up his forlorn weed°—   *abandoned*
    His mighty armor, missing most at need,   *equipment*
    His silver shield, now idle, masterless,
    His poignant spear, that many made to bleed—
    The rueful monuments of heaviness;
    And with them all departs to tell his great distress.

20 He had not traveled long when on the way
    He woeful lady, woeful Una, met,
    Fast flying from that paynim's greedy prey,°   *grasp*
    Whilst Satyrane him from pursuit did let.°   *prevent*
    Who when her eyes she on the dwarf had set
    And saw the signs that deadly tidings spake,
    She fell to ground for sorrowful regret,
    And lively breath her sad breast did forsake.
    Yet might her piteous heart be seen to pant and quake.

21 The messenger of so unhappy news
    Would fain have died. Dead was his heart within,
    Yet outwardly some little comfort shews.

17.7 *seven great heads:* "Behold a great red dragon, having seven heads and ten horns and seven crowns upon his heads" (Revelation 12:3).
18.1–5 "And his tail drew the third part of the stars from heaven, and did cast them to the earth . . ." (Revelation 12:4).

18.6–7 "And he opened his mouth in blasphemy against God, to blaspheme his name, and his tabernacle, and them that dwell in heaven" (Revelation 13:6).
18.8–9 "And I saw a woman sit upon a scarlet coloured beast, full of names of blasphemy, having seven heads and ten horns" (Revelation 17:3).

At last recovering heart, he does begin
To rub her temples and to chafe her chin,
And every tender part does toss and turn.
So hardly he the flitted life does win°   *persuade*
Unto her native prison° to return.   *i.e. body*
Then gins her grievèd ghost° thus to lament and mourn: *spirit*

22   'Ye dreary instruments° of doleful sight,   *i.e. eyes*
     That do this deadly spectacle behold,
     Why do ye lenger feed on loathèd light,
     Or liking° find to gaze on earthly mold,°   *pleasure, form*
     Sith cruel fates the careful° threads unfold,   *painful*
     The which my life and love together tied?
     Now let the stony dart of senseless cold
     Pierce to my heart and pass through every side,
     And let eternal night so sad sight fro me hide.

23   'O lightsome day, the lamp of highest Jove,
     First made by him, men's wandering ways to guide,
     When darkness he in deepest dungeon drove,
     Henceforth thy hated face forever hide,
     And shut up heaven's windows shining wide.
     For earthly sight can nought but sorrow breed
     And late repentance, which shall long abide.
     Mine eyes no more on vanity shall feed,
     But sealèd up with death, shall have their deadly meed.'°   *reward of death*

24   Then down again she fell unto the ground;
     But he her quickly rearèd up again.
     Thrice did she sink adown in deadly swound,
     And thrice he her revived with busy pain.
     At last when life recovered had the rein,
     And over-wrestled his strong enemy,
     With faltering tongue and trembling every vein,
     'Tell on,' quoth she, 'the woeful tragedy,
     The which these relics sad present unto mine eye.

25   'Tempestuous fortune hath spent all her spite,
     And thrilling sorrow thrown his utmost dart;
     Thy sad tongue cannot tell more heavy plight
     Than that I feel and harbor in mine heart.
     Who hath endured the whole can bear each part.
     If death it be, it is not the first wound
     That launchèd hath my breast with bleeding smart.
     Begin, and end the bitter baleful stound.°   *agony*
     If less than that° I fear, more favor I have found.'   *what*

22.9   *sight:* (1596). 1590 omits.

26   Then gan the dwarf the whole discourse declare:
     The subtle trains of Archimago old,
     The wanton loves of false Fidessa fair,
     Bought with the blood of vanquished paynim bold,
     The wretched pair transformed to treèn mold,°   *shape of trees*
     The House of Pride and perils round about,
     The combat which he with Sansjoy did hold,
     The luckless conflict with the giant stout,
     Wherein captived, of life or death he stood in doubt.

27   She heard with patience all unto the end,
     And strove to master sorrowful assay,°   *attack of sorrow*
     Which greater grew the more she did contend,
     And almost rent her tender heart in tway.
     And love fresh coals unto her fire did lay;
     For greater love, the greater is the loss.
     Was never lady lovèd dearer° day   *more dearly*
     Than she did love the Knight of the Red Cross,
     For whose dear sake so many troubles her did toss.

28   At last when fervent sorrow slakèd was,
     She up arose, resolving him to find
     Alive or dead, and forward forth doth pass,
     All as the dwarf the way to her assigned.°   *showed*
     And evermore in constant careful° mind   *tormented*
     She fed her wound with fresh renewèd bale.
     Long tossed with storms and beat with bitter wind,
     High over hills and low adown the dale,
     She wandered many a wood and measured many a vale.

29   At last she chancèd by good hap to meet
     A goodly knight, fair marching by the way
     Together with his squire, arrayèd meet.°   *properly*
     His glitterand armor shinèd far away
     Like glancing light of Phoebus' brightest ray.
     From top to toe no place appearèd bare
     That deadly dint of steel endanger may;
     Athwart his breast a baldric° brave he ware   *belt*
     That shined like twinkling stars with stones most precious
        rare.

30   And in the midst thereof one precious stone
     Of wondrous worth and eke of wondrous mights,

29.2   *A goodly knight:* Prince Arthur, the hero of *The Faerie Queene.* Both here and in Book II Arthur enters the story at the point where the hero of the individual book is unable to help himself. He is a type of Christ and of God's grace.

Shaped like a lady's head, exceeding shone,
Like Hesperus amongst the lesser lights,°   *stars*
And strove for to amaze the weaker sights.
Thereby his mortal blade full comely hung
In ivory sheath y-carved with curious sleights,°   *intricacies*
Whose hilts were burnished gold, and handle strong
Of mother pearl, and buckled with a golden tongue.°   *pin*

31 His haughty° helmet, horrid° all with gold,   *tall, bristling*
    Both glorious brightness and great terror bred.
    For all the crest a dragon did infold
    With greedy paws, and over all did spread
    His golden wings; his dreadful hideous head,
    Close couchèd on the beaver,° seemed to throw   *visor*
    From flaming mouth bright sparkles fiery red,
    That sudden horror to faint hearts did show;
    And scaly tail was stretched adown his back full low.

32 Upon the top of all his lofty crest,
    A bunch of hairs discolored° diversely,   *dyed*
    With sprinkled pearl and gold full richly dressed,
    Did shake and seemed to dance for jollity,
    Like to an almond tree y-mounted high
    On top of green Selinis all alone,
    With blossoms brave bedeckèd daintily,
    Whose tender locks do tremble every one
    At every little breath that under heaven is blown.

33 His warlike shield all closely covered was,
    Ne might of mortal eye be ever seen.
    Not made of steel nor of enduring brass—
    Such earthly metals soon consumèd been—
    But all of diamond perfect pure and clean
    It framèd was, one massy entire mold,°   *form*
    Hewn out of adamant rock° with engines° keen,   *diamond, instruments*

30.3 *Shaped like a lady's head:* that of the Faery Queen. This image on Arthur's baldric may have been suggested by the image of the Virgin Mary which traditionally decorated Arthur's shield.

30.4 *Hesperus:* the evening star.

31.1–9 Arthur's helmet is described in Geoffrey of Monmouth's *History of the Kings of Britain,* IX.4, as a "helm of gold graven with the semblance of a dragon" (trans. Sebastian Evans, Everyman's Library, 1958, p. 188). A close parallel with the fire-breathing dragon is to be found on the helmet of the Soldan in Tasso's *Jerusalem Delivered,* IX.25.

32.5–9 This simile appears almost verbatim in Marlowe's II *Tamburlaine,* 4096–4101, a play that was performed before *The Faerie Queene* was published in 1590. Marlowe must have read it in manuscript.

32.6 *Selinis:* Selinus, a town in Cilicia in Asia Minor (*Aeneid,* III.705).

32.8 *Whose:* (1596 and *Tamburlaine,* 4100). 1590 reads *Her.*

33.1 *His warlike shield:* Arthur's shield has many of the attributes of the shields of Atlanta (*Orlando Furioso,* II.55), of Athena (*Odyssey,* XVII, and *Iliad,* V), and of Perseus (*Metamorphoses,* IV and V). Like Red Cross's, it is the shield of faith in Ephesians 6:16.

That point of spear it never piercen could,
Ne dint of direful sword divide the substance would.

34 The same to wight he never wont disclose
 But° whenas monsters huge he would dismay,   *except*
 Or daunt unequal armies of his foes,
 Or when the flying heavens he would affray.
 For so exceeding shone his° glistering ray   *its*
 That Phoebus' golden face it did attaint,°   *darken*
 As when a cloud his beams doth over-lay;
 And silver Cynthia waxèd pale and faint,
 As when her face is stained with magic art's constraint.° *spells*

35 No magic arts hereof had any might,
 Nor bloody words of bold enchanter's call,°   *incantation*
 But all that was not such as seemed in sight
 Before that shield did fade and sudden fall.
 And when him list the rascal routs appall,
 Men into stones therewith he could transmew,° *change*
 And stones to dust, and dust to nought at all;
 And when him list the prouder° looks subdue, *most arrogant*
 He would them gazing blind, or turn to other hue.° *shape*

36 Ne let it seem that credence this exceeds,
 For he that made the same was known right well
 To have done much more admirable° deeds.   *amazing*
 It Merlin was, which whilom did excel
 All living wights in might of magic spell.
 Both shield and sword and armor, all, he wrought
 For this young prince when first to arms he fell;° *took up*
 But when he died, the Faery Queen it brought
 To Faeryland, where yet it may be seen if sought.

37 A gentle youth, his dearly lovèd squire,
 His spear of ebon wood° behind him bare,   *ebony*
 Whose harmful head, thrice heated in the fire,
 Had riven many a breast with pike-head square.
 A goodly person and could manage fair
 His stubborn steed with curbèd canon-bit,

34.8–9 *silver Cynthia . . . constraint:* a reference to the ancient belief that magicians could cause lunar eclipses.

35.1 *magic arts:* the instruments of "black magic," the supernatural power of evil spirits put at the disposal of a magician such as Archimago.

36.5 *magic spell:* Merlin's art is that of "white magic" (allegorically here the miracles of faith), which call upon the even stronger supernatural power of God to defeat the demonic forces employed by the black-magician.

36.9 *where yet it may be seen:* refers apparently to the magnificence of the heroes of Elizabeth's England and to the efficacy of their faith in defense of the Church of England.

37.1 *his dearly lovèd squire:* Timias (Greek *timieis,* "honored").

Who under him did trample as the air,°   *wind*
And chafed° that any on his back should sit;   *fretted*
The iron rowels° into frothy foam he bit.   *ends of the bit*

38   Whenas this knight nigh to the lady drew,
     With lovely court he gan her entertain;
     But when he heard her answers loath, he knew
     Some secret sorrow did her heart distrain;
     Which to allay and calm her storming pain,
     Fair feeling° words he wisely gan display,   *compassionate*
     And for her humor, fitting purpose feign,°   *make conversation*
     To tempt the cause itself for to bewray.
     Wherewith emmoved, these bleeding words she gan to say:

39   'What world's delight or joy of living speech
     Can heart so plunged in sea of sorrows deep
     And heapèd with so huge misfortunes reach?
     The careful cold beginneth for to creep,
     And in my heart his iron arrow steep,
     Soon as I think upon my bitter bale.°   *woe*
     Such helpless harms it's better hidden keep
     Than rip up grief where it may not avail;
     My last left comfort is, my woes to weep and wail.'

40   'Ah lady dear,' quoth then the gentle knight,
     'Well may I ween your grief is wondrous great;
     For wondrous great grief groaneth in my sprite
     Whiles thus I hear you of your sorrows treat.
     But woeful lady, let me you entreat
     For to unfold the anguish of your heart;
     Mishaps are mastered by advice discrete,
     And counsel mitigates the greatest smart.
     Found never help, who never would his hurts impart.'

41   'O but,' quoth she, 'great grief will not be told,
     And can more easily be thought than said.'
     'Right so,' quoth he, 'but he that never would,
     Could never; will to might gives greatest aid.'
     'But grief,' quoth she, 'does greater grow displayed,
     If then it find not help, and breeds despair.'
     'Despair breeds not,' quoth he, 'where faith is stayed.'°   *solid*
     'No faith so fast,' quoth she, 'but flesh does pair.'
     'Flesh may impair,' quoth he, 'but reason can repair.'

37.7 *trample:* (1596). 1590 reads *amble.*

38–42 Before Arthur can rescue Red Cross he must rescue Una from despair, teach her to renew her faith from within and urge her to a kind of confession. In contrast to the elaborate allegorical treatment of these themes in Cantos ix–xi, Spenser here adumbrates them with the somewhat typical romance exchange between the damsel in distress and her chivalrous rescuer.

42   His goodly reason and well guided° speech   *judicious*
      So deep did settle in her gracious thought
      That her persuaded to disclose the breach
      Which love and fortune in her heart had wrought;
      And said, 'Fair sir, I hope good hap hath brought
      You to inquire the secrets of my grief,
      Or that your wisdom will direct my thought,
      Or that your prowess can me yield relief.
      Then hear the story sad which I shall tell you brief.

43   'The forlorn maiden, whom your eyes have seen
      The laughing stock of fortune's mockeries,
      Am th' only daughter of a king and queen,
      Whose parents dear, whilst equal° destinies   *impartial*
      Did run about,° and their felicities   *revolve*
      The favorable heavens did not envy,
      Did spread their rule through all the territories
      Which Phison and Euphrates floweth by
      And Gehon's golden waves do wash continually.

44   'Till that their cruel cursèd enemy,
      An huge great dragon horrible in sight,
      Bred in the loathly lakes of Tartary,
      With murderous ravin° and devouring might   *destruction*
      Their kingdom spoiled and country wasted quite.
      Themselves, for fear into his jaws to fall,
      He forced to castle strong to take their flight;
      Where fast embarred in mighty brazen wall,
      He has them now four years besieged to make them thrall.

45   'Full many knights adventurous and stout
      Have enterprized that monster to subdue.
      From every coast that heaven walks about
      Have thither come the noble martial crew
      That famous hard achievements still pursue;
      Yet never any could that garland win,
      But all still shrank,° and still he greater grew.   *lost courage*
      All they for want of faith or guilt of sin
      The piteous prey of his fierce cruelty have been.

46   'At last y-led with far reported praise
      Which flying fame throughout the world had spread
      Of doughty knights whom Faeryland did raise—

43.4–5   *whilst equal destinies / Did run
about:* alluding to the notion that provi-
dential forces work through the influences
of the planets. Una's account of her par-
ents' fall from prosperity uses the secular

language of medieval and renaissance
tragedy.
      43.8–9   *Phison, Euphrates,* and *Gehon:*
three of the four rivers of Paradise
(Genesis 2:11–14).

That noble order hight° of Maidenhead—   *called*
Forthwith to court of Glorian I sped,
Of Glorian great queen of glory bright,
Whose kingdom's seat Cleopolis is read,°   *called*
There to obtain some such redoubted knight,
That parents dear from tyrant's power deliver might.

47   'It was my chance—my chance was fair and good—
     There for to find a fresh unprovèd knight
     Whose manly hands imbrued° in guilty blood   *stained*
     Had never been, ne ever by his might
     Had thrown to ground the unregarded° right.   *unrespected*
     Yet of his prowess proof he since hath made
     (I witness am) in many a cruel fight;
     The groaning ghosts of many one dismayed°   *defeated*
     Have felt the bitter dint of his avenging blade.

48   'And ye, the forlorn relics of his power—
     His biting sword and his devouring spear,
     Which have endurèd many a dreadful stour—
     Can speak his prowess, that did erst you bear
     And well could rule. Now he hath left you here
     To be the record of his rueful loss
     And of my doleful disaventurous dear.°   *disastrous loss*
     O heavy° record of the good Red Cross,   *mournful*
     Where have you left your lord that could so well you toss?°   *handle*

49   'Well hopèd I, and fair beginnings had,
     That he my captive langour° should redeem,   *slavery to sadness*
     Till all unweeting, an enchanter bad
     His sense abused, and made him to misdeem
     My loyalty, not such as it did seem,
     That° rather death desire than such despite.   *(I) who*
     Be judge, ye heavens, that all things right esteem,°   *judge correctly*
     How I him loved—and love—with all my might;
     So thought I eke of him, and think I thought aright.

50   'Thenceforth me desolate he quite forsook
     To wander where wild fortune would me lead;
     And other byways he himself betook,
     Where never foot of living wight did tread

46.4 *noble order:* the Most Noble Order of the Garter, the insignia of which shows St. George slaying the dragon.

46.5 *Forthwith . . . I sped:* "And the woman fled into the wilderness, where she has a place prepared by God, in which to be nourished for one thousand two hun-dred and sixty days" (Revelation 12:6). This is a little less than the rounder figure of four years given in 44.9 above.

46.7 *Cleopolis:* the Faeryland equivalent of London (Greek *kleos,* "fame," and *polis,* "city").

That brought not back the baleful body dead;
In which him chancèd false Duessa meet,
Mine only foe, mine only deadly dread,
Who with her witchcraft and misseeming sweet,°   grace
Inveigled him to follow her desires unmeet.°   improper

51   'At last by subtle sleights she him betrayed
Unto his foe, a giant huge and tall,
Who him disarmèd, dissolute, dismayed,
Unwares surprisèd. And with mighty maul
The monster merciless him made to fall
Whose fall did never foe before behold;
And now in darksome dungeon, wretched thrall,
Remediless for aye,° he doth him hold.   forever
This is my cause of grief, more great than may be told.'

52   Ere she had ended all, she gan to faint;
But he her comforted and fair bespake:
'Certes, madame, ye have great cause of plaint,
That stoutest heart, I ween, could cause to quake.
But be of cheer, and comfort to you take;
For till I have acquit° your captive knight,   freed
Assure yourself, I will you not forsake.'
His cheerful words revived her cheerless sprite;
So forth they went, the dwarf them guiding ever right.

CANTO viii

Fair virgin to redeem her dear
Brings Arthur to the fight;
Who slays the giant, wounds the beast,
And strips Duessa quite.

1   Ay me, how many perils do infold
The righteous man to make him daily fall,
Were not that heavenly grace doth him uphold
And steadfast truth acquit him out of all.
Her love is firm, her care continual,
So oft as he through his own foolish pride
Or weakness is to sinful bands made thrall.
Else should this Red Cross Knight in bands have died,
For whose deliverance she this prince doth thither guide.

2   They sadly traveled thus until they came
Nigh to a castle builded strong and high.
Then cried the dwarf, 'Lo, yonder is the same

In which my lord, my liege, doth luckless lie,
Thrall to that giant's hateful tyranny;
Therefore, dear sir, your mighty powers assay.'° *put to the test*
The noble knight alighted by and by
From lofty steed and bade the lady stay,
To see what end of fight should him befall that day.

3   So with his squire, th' admirer of his might,
He marchèd forth towards that castle wall;
Whose gates he found fast shut, ne living wight
To ward the same nor answer comer's call.
Then took that squire an horn of bugle° small,   *wild ox*
Which hung adown his side in twisted gold
And tassels gay. Wide wonders° over all   *marvelous tales*
Of that same horn's great virtues weren told,
Which had approvèd° been in uses° manifold.   *proved true,*
   instances

4   Was never wight that heard that shrilling sound
But trembling fear did feel in every vein;
Three miles it might be easy heard around,
And echoes three answered itself again.
No false enchantment nor deceitful train
Might once abide the terror of that blast,
But presently was void and wholly vain.
No gate so strong, no lock so firm and fast,
But with that piercing noise flew open quite or brast.°   *burst*

5   The same before the giant's gate he blew,
That all the castle quakèd from the ground,
And every door of free will open flew.
The giant self dismayèd with that sound,
Where he with his Duessa dalliance found,°   *made love*
In haste came rushing forth from inner bower
With staring countenance stern, as one astound,
And staggering steps, to weet what sudden stour
Had wrought that horror strange and dared his dreaded
   power.

6   And after him the proud Duessa came,
High mounted on her many-headed beast;

3.5 *an horn of bugle:* Beginning with the famous horn, Olifant, of the *Song of Roland*, enchanted horns became associated with Roland in heroic romance. Both Boiardo in the *Orlando Innamorato* (I.24.22) and Ariosto in *Orlando Furioso* (XV.14) provided models for Timias's horn described here. "And it shall come to pass, that when they make a long blast with the ram's horn, and when ye hear the sound of the trumpet, all the people shall shout with a great shout; and the wall of the city shall fall down flat" (Joshua 6:5). Joshua, the successor of Moses, is a type of Christ, and his destruction of Jericho a type of the harrowing of hell and the destruction of Babylon.

And every head with fiery tongue did flame,
And every head was crownèd on his crest,
And bloody mouthèd with late cruel feast.
That when the knight beheld, his mighty shield
Upon his manly arm he soon addressed,°   *adjusted*
And at him fiercely flew with courage filled;
And eager greediness° through every member thrilled.   *aggressiveness*

7 Therewith the giant buckled him to fight,
Inflamed with scornful wrath and high disdain,
And lifting up his dreadful club on height,
All armed with ragged snubs° and knotty grain,°   *snags, branches*
Him thought at first encounter to have slain.
But wise and wary was that noble peer,
And lightly leaping from so monstrous main,
Did fair avoid the violence him near.
It booted nought to think such thunderbolts to bear.

8 Ne shame he thought to shun so hideous might.
The idle° stroke, enforcing furious way,   *inaccurate*
Missing the mark of his misaimèd sight
Did fall to ground, and with his° heavy sway   *its*
So deeply dinted in the driven clay
That three yards deep a furrow up did throw.
The sad earth wounded with so sore assay°   *assault*
Did groan full grievous underneath the blow,
And trembling with strange fear, did like an earthquake
    show.

9 As when almighty Jove in wrathful mood,
To wreak° the guilt of mortal sins is bent,   *punish*
Hurls forth his thundering dart with deadly food,°   *(feud) hatred*
Enrolled in flames and smoldering dreariment,
Through riven clouds and molten firmament—
The fierce three-forkèd engine,° making way,   *i.e. weapon*
Both lofty towers and highest trees hath rent,
And all that might his° angry passage stay,   *its*
And shooting in the earth, casts up a mount of clay.

10 His boisterous° club, so buried in the ground,   *huge*
He could not rearen up again so light,°   *easily*
But that the knight him at advantage found,
And whiles he strove his cumbered club to quite°   *free*
Out of the earth, with blade all burning bright

8.2–9.9 The primary source of this image and the following simile is *Iliad*, XIV.414, where Ajax fells Hector with a huge stone. Spenser's comparison of Orgoglio's stroke with Jove's thunderbolt suggests simultaneously the earthly nature of Christ's suffering (i.e., at the hands of Orgoglio) and the fulfillment of divine judgment. Allegorically, Orgoglio is thus the fleshly nature of his opponent.

He smote off his left arm, which like a block
Did fall to ground, deprived of native might.
Large streams of blood out of the trunkèd stock°   *stub*
Forth gushèd like fresh water stream from riven rock.

11 Dismayèd with so desperate deadly wound
And eke impatient of° unwonted pain,   *unable to bear*
He loudly brayed with beastly yelling sound,
That all the fields rebellowèd again—
As great a noise as when in Cymbrian plain
An herd of bulls, whom kindly° rage doth sting,   *animal*
Do for the milky mothers' want complain
And fill the fields with troublous bellowing,
The neighbor woods around with hollow murmur ring.

12 That when his dear Duessa heard, and saw
The evil stound that dangered her estate,
Unto his aid she hastily did draw
Her dreadful beast, who swollen with blood of late,
Came ramping° forth with proud presumptuous gait   *raging*
And threatened all his heads like flaming brands.°   *torches*
But him the squire made quickly to retreat,
Encountering° fierce with single° sword in hand,   *attacking, only*
And twixt him and his lord did like a bulwark stand.

13 The proud Duessa, full of wrathful spite
And fierce disdain to be affronted so,
Enforced° her purple beast with all her might   *spurred*
That stop° out of the way to overthrow,   *obstacle*
Scorning the let° of so unequal foe.   *obstruction*
But nathemore would° that courageous swain   *still would not*
To her yield passage gainst his lord to go,
But with outrageous strokes did him restrain,
And with his body barred the way atwixt them twain.

14 Then took the angry witch her golden cup,
Which still she bore, replete° with magic arts;   *filled*

10.6 Striking off the enemy's arm is traditional in romance and epic; examples are found in *Beowulf, The Song of Roland,* and *Arthur of Little Britain.*

10.8–9 The metaphor shows that Arthur's attack on Orgoglio is a type of Christ's crucifixion: "And Moses lifted up his hand, and with his rod he smote the rock twice: and the water came out abundantly" (Numbers 20:11). During the Middle Ages this passage was understood as a foreshadowing of the crucifixion. The point seems to be that Arthur (Christ-God) wounds (crucifies) his own fleshly nature (Orgoglio-Christ-man).

11.1–9 The force of this simile is to compare the loud bellowing of Orgoglio to that of a whole herd of bulls in heat, separated from the newly calved cows.

11.5 *Cymbrian plain:* either the Cimbric Peninsula (modern Jutland), named for the Cimbri, a widely migratory Teutonic tribe: or the Tauric Peninsula (modern Crimea), at one time occupied by the Cimmerii, a quite distinct tribe with whom, however, the Cimbri were often confused.

Death and despair did many thereof sup,
And secret poison through their inner parts,
Th' eternal bale of heavy wounded hearts;
Which after charms and some enchantments said,
She lightly sprinkled on his weaker parts;
Therewith his sturdy courage soon was quayed,°   *subdued*
And all his senses were with sudden dread dismayed.

15 So down he fell before the cruel beast,
Who on his neck his bloody claws did seize,
That life nigh crushed out of his panting breast.
No power he had to stir, nor will to rise.
That when the careful° knight gan well avise,°   *watchful, became*
He lightly left the foe with whom he fought   *aware of*
And to the beast gan turn his enterprise;
For wondrous anguish in his heart it wrought
To see his lovèd squire into such thralldom brought.

16 And high advancing his bloodthirsty blade,
Struck one of those deformèd heads so sore
That of his puissance proud ensample made;
His monstrous scalp down to his teeth it tore
And that misformèd shape misshapèd more.
A sea of blood gushed from the gaping wound,
That° her gay garments stained with filthy gore   *which*
And overflowèd all the field around,
That° over shoes in blood he waded on the ground.   *so that*

17 Thereat he roarèd for exceeding pain,
That to have heard great horror would have bred,
And scourging th' empty air with his long train
Through great impatience° of his grievèd head,   *agony*
His gorgeous rider from her lofty stead°   *place*
Would have cast down and trod in dirty mire,
Had not the giant soon her succorèd;
Who all enraged with smart and frantic ire,
Came hurtling in full fierce and forced the knight retire.

18 The force which wont in two to be dispersed
In one alone left° hand he now unites,   *remaining*
Which is through rage more strong than both were erst;
With which his hideous club aloft he dights°   *raises*
And at his foe with furious rigor smites,
That strongest oak might seem to overthrow.

16.1–5 "And I saw one of his heads as it were wounded to death" (Revelation 13:3). Christ's wounding of the head of the serpent Satan at the crucifixion is a fulfillment of the prophecy in Genesis 3:15.

The stroke upon his shield so heavy lights
That to the ground it doubleth him full low.
What mortal wight could ever bear so monstrous blow?

19 And in his fall his shield, that covered was,
    Did loose his veil° by chance and open flew.   *its covering*
    The light whereof, that heaven's light did pass,
    Such blazing brightness through the air threw
    That eye mote° not the same endure to view.   *could*
    Which when the giant spied with staring° eye,   *awe-struck*
    He down let fall his arm and soft withdrew
    His weapon huge, that heavèd was on high
    For to have slain the man that on the ground did lie.

20 And eke the fruitful-headed° beast, amazed   *many-headed*
    At flashing beams of that sunshiny shield,
    Became stark blind and all his senses dazed,
    That down he tumbled on the dirty field,
    And seemed himself as conquerèd to yield.
    Whom when his mistress proud perceived to fall,
    Whiles yet his feeble feet for faintness reeled,
    Unto the giant loudly she gan call,
    'O help, Orgoglio, help, or else we perish all.'

21 At her so piteous cry was much amoved
    Her champion stout, and for to aid his friend
    Again his wonted angry weapon proved.°   *tried to use*
    But all in vain; for he has read his end
    In that bright shield, and all their forces spend
    Themselves in vain. For since that glancing° sight,   *flashing*
    He hath no power to hurt nor to defend;
    As where th' Almighty's lightning brand does light,
    It dims the dazèd eyne, and daunts the senses quite.

22 Whom when the prince, to battle new addressed
    And threatening high his dreadful stroke, did see,
    His sparkling blade about his head he blessed°   *waved*
    And smote off quite his right leg by the knee,
    That down he tumbled—as an aged tree,
    High growing on the top of rocky clift,
    Whose heartstrings with keen steel nigh hewen be,
    The mighty trunk half-rent with ragged rift,
    Doth roll adown the rocks and fall with fearful drift°—   *impact*

19.1–9 The blinding light of Arthur's unveiled shield, representing here the effect of the crucifixion, the outpouring of grace into the world, is an imitation of *Orlando Furioso*, XXII.84–86.

22.5–9 The simile is taken from *Aeneid*, II.626–631, where the fall of Troy is compared to the fall of an ancient ash.

23 Or as a castle rearèd high and round,
    By subtle engines and malicious sleight°   *magic*
    Is underminèd from the lowest ground°   *underneath*
    And her foundation forced° and feebled quite,   *blown up*
    At last down falls, and with her heapèd height
    Her hasty ruin does more heavy° make,   *great*
    And yields itself unto the victor's might—
    Such was this giant's fall, that seemed to shake
    The steadfast globe of earth as it for fear did quake.

24 The knight then lightly leaping to the prey,
    With mortal steel him smote again so sore
    That headless his unwieldy body lay,
    All wallowed in his own foul bloody gore,
    Which flowèd from his wounds in wondrous store.
    But soon as breath out of his breast did pass,
    That huge great body which the giant bore
    Was vanished quite, and of that monstrous mass
    Was nothing left, but like an empty bladder was.

25 Whose grievous fall when false Duessa spied,
    Her golden cup she cast unto the ground
    And crownèd mitre rudely threw aside;
    Such piercing grief her stubborn heart did wound
    That she could not endure that doleful stound,
    But leaving all behind her, fled away.
    The light-foot squire her quickly turned around,
    And by hard means enforcing her to stay,
    So brought unto his lord as his deservèd prey.

26 The royal virgin, which beheld from far,
    In pensive plight and sad perplexity,
    The whole achievement° of this doubtful war,   *action*
    Came running fast to greet his victory
    With sober gladness and mild modesty;
    And with sweet joyous cheer him thus bespake:
    'Fair branch of nobless, flower of chivalry,
    That with your worth the world amazèd make,
    How shall I quite the pains ye suffer for my sake?

27 'And you, fresh bud of virtue springing fast,°   *growing strong*
    Whom these sad eyes saw nigh unto death's door,
    What hath poor virgin for such peril passed

24.9 *but like an empty bladder was:*
apparently a standard metaphor for the
collapse of human power. Chaucer's *Sec-
ond Nun's Tale:* 'For every mortal mannes

power n'is / But like a bladder full of
wind, i-wis" (G.438–439).
    27.1 *fresh bud of virtue:* Una is ad-
dressing Timias.

Wherewith you to reward? Accept, therefore,
My simple self and service evermore.
And He that high does sit and all things see
With equal° eye, their merits to restore,° *impartial, pay*
Behold what ye this day have done for me,
And what I cannot quite, requite with usury.° *interest*

28 'But sith the heavens and your fair handèling
Have made you master of the field this day,
Your fortune master, eke, with governing,° *decisive action*
And well begun, end all so° well, I pray. *just as*
Ne let that wicked woman scape away,
For she it is that did my lord bethrall,
My dearest lord, and deep in dungeon lay,
Where he his better days hath wasted all.
O hear, how piteous he to you for aid does call.'

29 Forthwith he gave in charge unto his squire
That scarlet whore to keepen carefully,
Whiles he himself with greedy great desire
Into the castle entered forcibly,
Where living creature none he did espy.
Then gan he loudly through the house to call;
But no man cared to answer to his cry.
There reigned a solemn silence over all,
Nor voice was heard nor wight was seen in bower or hall.

30 At last with creeping crooked° pace forth came *crippled*
An old, old man, with beard as white as snow,
That on a staff his feeble steps did frame° *support*
And guide his weary gait both to and fro,
For his eyesight him failèd long ago.
And on his arm a bunch of keys he bore,
The which unusèd rust° did overgrow. *rust of disuse*
Those were the keys of every inner door,
But he could not them use, but kept them still in store.° *handy*

31 But very uncouth sight was to behold
How he did fashion his untoward° pace, *awkward*
For as he forward moved his footing old,
So backward still was turned his wrinkled face,
Unlike to men, who ever as they trace,° *walk*
Both feet and face one way are wont to lead.
This was the ancient keeper of that place
And foster father of the giant dead;
His name, Ignaro, did his nature right aread.° *signify*

32 His reverend hairs and holy gravity
    The knight much honored, as beseem\`ed well,°   *was proper*
    And gently asked where all the people be
    Which in that stately building wont to dwell.
    Who answered him full soft, he could not tell.
    Again he asked where that same knight was laid
    Whom great Orgoglio with his puissance fell
    Had made his caitive thrall; again he said,
    He could not tell, ne ever other answer made.

33 Then ask\`ed he which way he in might pass.
    He could not tell, again he answer\`ed.
    Thereat the courteous knight displeas\`ed was
    And said, 'Old sire, it seems thou hast not read
    How ill it sits° with that same silver head   *accords*
    In vain to mock, or mocked in vain to be.
    But if thou be, as thou art portray\`ed
    With nature's pen, in age's grave degree,°   *dignified status*
    Aread in graver wise what I demand of thee.'

34 His answer likewise was, he could not tell.
    Whose senseless speech and doted° ignorance   *idiotic*
    Whenas the noble prince had mark\`ed well,
    He guessed his nature by his countenance
    And calmed his wrath with goodly temperance.
    Then to him stepping, from his arm did reach
    Those keys and made himself free ent\`erance.
    Each door he opened without any breach;°   *forcing*
    There was no bar to stop, nor foe him to impeach.°   *challenge*

35 There all within full rich arrayed he found
    With royal arras° and resplendent gold,   *purple hangings*
    And did with store of everything abound
    That greatest prince's presence° might behold.   *court*
    But all the floor—too filthy to be told—
    With blood of guiltless babes and innocents true,
    Which there were slain as sheep out of the fold,
    Defil\`ed was, that dreadful was to view,
    And sacred ashes over it was strow\`ed new.

36 And there beside of marble stone was built
    An altar, carved with cunning imagery,
    On which true Christians' blood was often spilt

36.1–9 "I saw under the altar the souls of them that were slain for the word of God, and for the testimony which they held. And they cried with a loud voice saying, 'How long, O Lord, holy and true, dost thou not judge and avenge our blood on them that dwell on the earth'" (Revelation 6:9–10).

And holy martyrs often done to die°   *murdered*
With cruel malice and strong tyranny;
Whose blessed sprites from underneath the stone
To God for vengeance cried continually,
And with great grief were often heard to groan,
That hardest heart would bleed to hear their piteous moan.

37 Through every room he sought and every bower,
But nowhere could he find that woeful thrall.
At last he came unto an iron door
That fast was locked, but key found not at all
Amongst that bunch to open it withall;
But in the same a little grate was pight,°   *placed*
Through which he sent his voice and loud did call
With all his power, to weet if living wight
Were housèd therewithin whom he enlargen° might.   *set free*

38 Therewith an hollow, dreary, murmuring voice
These piteous plaints and dolors did resound:
'O who is that which brings me happy choice°   *opportunity*
Of death that here lie dying every stound,°   *minute*
Yet live perforce in baleful darkness bound?
For now three moons have changèd thrice their hue
And have been thrice hid underneath the ground
Since I the heavens' cheerful face did view.
O welcome thou, that dost of death bring tidings true.'

39 Which when that champion heard, with piercing point
Of pity dear° his heart was thrillèd sore,   *painful*
And trembling horror ran through every joint,
For ruth of gentle knight so foul forlore.
Which shaking off, he rent that iron door
With furious force and indignation fell;
Where entered in, his foot could find no floor,
But all a deep descent, as dark as hell,
That breathèd ever forth a filthy baneful smell.

40 But neither darkness foul nor filthy bands
Nor noyous smell his purpose could withhold—
Entire° affection hateth nicer° hands—   *complete, too*
But that with constant zeal and courage bold,   *dainty*
After long pains and labors manifold,
He found the means that prisoner up to rear;
Whose feeble thighs, unable to uphold
His pinèd° corse, him scarce to light could bear,   *wasted*
A rueful spectacle of death and ghastly drear.°   *despair*

41 His sad dull eyes, deep sunk in hollow pits,
     Could not endure th' unwonted sun to view;
     His bare thin cheeks, for want of better bits,°   *food*
     And empty sides, deceivèd° of their due,   *cheated*
     Could make a stony heart his hap to rue;
     His rawbone arms, whose mighty brawnèd bowers°   *muscles*
     Were wont to rive steel plates and helmets hew,
     Were clean consumed, and all his vital powers
     Decayed, and all his flesh shrunk up like withered flowers.

42 Whom when his lady saw, to him she ran
     With hasty joy. To see him made her glad,
     And sad to view his visage pale and wan
     Who erst in flowers of freshest youth was clad.
     Tho when her well of tears she wasted had,
     She said, 'Ah dearest lord, what evil star
     On you hath frowned and poured his influence bad,
     That of yourself ye thus berobbèd are,
     And this misseeming hue° your manly looks doth mar?   *unbecoming appearance*

43 'But welcome now, my lord in weal or woe,
     Whose presence I have lacked too long a day;
     And fie on Fortune, mine avowèd foe,
     Whose wrathful wreaks° themselves do now allay,   *injuries*
     And for these wrongs shall treble penance° pay   *restitution*
     Of treble good. Good grows of evil's prief.'°   *from enduring the test of evil*
     The cheerless man, whom sorrow did dismay,
     Had no delight to treaten° of his grief;   *in talking*
     His long endurèd famine needed more relief.

44 'Fair lady,' then said that victorious knight,
     'The things that grievous were to do or bear,
     Them to renew,° I wot, breeds no delight.   *recall*
     Best° music breeds delight in loathing ear   *better than anything*
     But th' only good that grows of passèd fear
     Is to be wise and ware of like again.
     This day's ensample hath this lesson dear
     Deep written in my heart with iron pen:
     That bliss may not abide in state of mortal men.

45 'Henceforth, sir knight, take to you wonted strength
     And master these mishaps with patient might.
     Lo, where your foe lies stretched in monstrous length,
     And lo, that wicked woman in your sight,°   *over there*
     The root of all your care and wretched plight,
     Now in your power to let her live or die.'
     'To do her die,' quoth Una, 'were despite,

And shame t' avenge so weak an enemy;
But spoil her of her scarlet robe and let her fly.'

46   So as she bade, that witch they disarrayed,
And robbed of royal robes and purple pall
And ornaments that richly were displayed;
Ne sparèd they to strip her naked all.
Then when they had dispoiled her tire° and caul,°   *attire, head-dress*
Such as she was their eyes might her behold,
That her misshapèd parts did them appall—
A loathly, wrinkled hag, ill favored, old,
Whose secret filth good manners biddeth not be told.

47   Her crafty head was altogether bald,
And as in hate of honorable eld,°   *old age*
Was overgrown with scurf and filthy scald;°   *scabs*
Her teeth out of her rotten gums were felled,
And her sour breath abominably smelled;
Her drièd dugs, like bladders lacking wind,
Hung down, and filthy matter from them welled;
Her wrizled° skin, as rough as maple rind,   *shrivelled*
So scabby was that would have loathed all womankind.

48   Her nether parts, the shame of all her kind,°   *i.e. womanhood*
My chaster muse for shame doth blush to write;
But at her rump she growing had behind
A fox's tail with dung all foully dight.°   *covered*
And eke her feet most monstrous were in sight;
For one of them was like an eagle's claw,
With gripping talons armed to greedy fight,
The other like a bear's uneven° paw.   *rough*
More ugly shape yet never living creature saw.

49   Which when the knights beheld, amazed they were
And wondered at so foul deformèd wight.
'Such then,' said Una, 'as she seemeth here,
Such is the face of falsehood, such the sight
Of foul Duessa, when her borrowed light
Is laid away and counterfeasance° known.'   *deceit*
Thus when they had the witch disrobèd quite
And all her filthy feature open shown,
They let her go at will and wander ways unknown.

50   She flying fast from heaven's hated face
And from the world that her discovered wide,°   *revealed to view*

46–48   The stripping of Duessa is similar to Ruggiero's disenchanted view of Alcina in *Orlando Furioso*, VII.71–73.

Fled to the wasteful wilderness apace
From living eyes her open shame to hide,
And lurked in rocks and caves long unespied.
But that fair crew of knights and Una fair
Did in that castle afterwards abide,
To rest themselves and weary powers repair,
Where store they found of all that dainty was and rare.

CANTO ix

His loves and lineage Arthur tells;
   The knights knit friendly bands.
Sir Trevisan flies from Despair,
   Whom Red Cross Knight withstands.

1   O goodly golden chain, wherewith y-fere°   *together*
   The virtues linkèd are in lovely wise,
   And noble minds of yore allièd were
   In brave pursuit of chivalrous emprise °   *adventure*
   That none did other's safèty despise
   Nor aid envy° to him in need that stands,   *begrudge*
   But friendly each did other's praise devise
   How to advance with favorable hands,
   As this good prince redeemed the Red Cross Knight from
      bands.

2   Who when their powers, impaired through labor long,
   With due repast they had recurèd well,
   And that weak captive wight now waxèd strong,
   Them list no lenger there at leisure dwell,
   But forward fare as their adventures fell.
   But ere they parted, Una fair besought
   That stranger knight his name and nation tell,
   Lest so great good as he for her had wrought
   Should die unknown and buried be in thankless thought.

3   'Fair virgin,' said the prince, 'ye me require
   A thing without the compass° of my wit;   *outside the*
                                                capability

1.1 *O goodly golden chain:* See Introduction. "Temperance and the Doctrine of Right Reason," pp. 48–53. The chain of love or concord by which all of the forces of the universe are bound in harmonious unity can, since the fall of man, be perceived and acted upon only by the noblest minds. The most influential statement of this principle of harmony is to be found in Boethius' *Consolation of Philosophy,*

II. Meter 8: "All this harmonious order of things is achieved by love which rules the earth and the seas, and commands the heavens. . . . Love binds together people joined by sacred bond. . . . O how happy the human race would be, if that love which rules the heavens ruled also your souls!" (trans. Richard Green, Library of Liberal Arts, Bobbs-Merrill, 1962, p. 41).

For both the lineage and the certain° sire   *true*
From which I sprung from me are hidden yit.
For all so soon as life did me admit
Into this world, and showèd heaven's light,
From mother's pap I taken was unfit,°   *unnaturally*
And straight delivered to a faery knight,
To be upbrought in gentle thews° and martial might.   *manners*

4   'Unto old Timon he me brought belive,°   *at once*
Old Timon, who in youthly years hath been
In warlike feats th' expertest man alive,
And is the wisest now on earth I ween.
His dwelling is low in a valley green,
Under the foot of Rauran, mossy hoar,
From whence the River Dee, as silver clean,°   *as clean as*
His tumbling billows rolls with gentle roar.
There all my days he trained me up in virtuous lore.

5   'Thither the great magician Merlin came,
As was his use, oft-times to visit me;
For he had charge my discipline to frame°   *plan*
And tutor's nuriture° to oversee.   *training*
Him oft and oft I asked in privity
Of what loins° and what lineage I did spring;   *parentage*
Whose answer bade me still assurèd be
That I was son and heir unto a king,
As time in her just term° the truth to light should bring.'   *due season*

6   'Well worthy imp,'° said then the lady gent,°   *heir, gentle*
'And pupil fit for such a tutor's hand.
But what adventure or what high intent
Hath brought you hither into Faeryland?
Aread, Prince Arthur, crown of martial band.'°   *knighthood*
'Full hard it is,' quoth he, 'to read aright
The course of heavenly cause, or understand
The secret meaning of th' eternal might
That rules men's ways and rules the thoughts of living wight.

7   'For whether He through fatal° deep foresight   *prophetic*
Me hither sent for cause to me unguessed,

3.8 *a faery knight:* presumably old Timon of the next stanza. In Malory's *Morte d'Arthur* the young prince is given over by Uther Pendragon, his father, to Sir Ector. Timon (Greek, "man of honor") is Spenser's invention.

4.5–9 Arthur—like Henry Tudor, the founder of Queen Elizabeth's royal family—was a Welshman. The Arthurian legend developed among the medieval Welsh from whence it passed through Latin, French, and English redactions into the mainstream of European literature. *Rauran:* a hill in Merionethshire, Wales. *The River Dee:* flowing generally northward from Merionethshire to the Irish Sea, forms along part of its length the boundary between England and Wales.

Or that fresh bleeding wound which day and night
Whilom° doth rankle in my riven breast,   *continually*
With forcèd fury following his° behest,   *its*
Me hither brought by ways yet never found,
You to have helped I hold myself yet blessed.'
'Ah courteous knight,' quoth she, 'what secret wound
Could ever find° to grieve the gentlest heart on ground?'   *succeed*

8   'Dear dame,' quoth he, 'you sleeping sparks awake,
     Which troubled once, into huge flames will grow,
     Ne ever will their fervent fury slake
     Till living moisture into smoke do flow,
     And wasted° life do lie in ashes low.   *consumed*
     Yet sithens° silence lesseneth not my fire,   *since*
     But told it flames, and hidden it does glow,
     I will reveal what ye so much desire.
     Ah Love, lay down thy bow, the whiles I may respire.°   *breathe*

9   'It was in freshest flower of youthly years,
     When courage first does creep in manly chest,
     Then first that coal of kindly° heat appears,   *natural*
     To kindle love in every living breast;
     But me had warned old Timon's wise behest°   *teaching*
     Those creeping flames by reason to subdue,
     Before their rage grew to so great unrest
     As miserable lovers use to rue,
     Which still wax old in woe whiles woe still waxeth new.

10   'That idle° name of love, and lover's life,   *empty*
     As loss of time and virtue's enemy
     I ever scorned, and joyed to stir up strife
     In middest of their mournful tragedy—
     Aye wont to laugh when them I heard to cry,
     And blow the fire which them to ashes brent.
     Their god himself, grieved at my liberty,
     Shot many a dart at me with fierce intent,
     But I them warded all with wary government.°   *self-control*

11   'But all in vain. No fort can be so strong,
     Ne fleshly breast can armèd be so sound,
     But will at last be won with battery° long,   *bombardment*
     Or unawares at disavantage found.

10.1–9 Arthur's sudden subjugation to the god of love is similar to that of Troilus in Chaucer's *Troilus and Criseyde*, I.167–210.

11.1–9 The metaphor of the besieged castle of chastity is a favorite with Spenser. Compare Sansloy's trial of Una's chastity in vi.5.1–5, above, and Chaucer's Wife of Bath's Prologue:
She may no while in chastity abide,
That is assailèd upon each a side. . . .
Thou sayst men may not keep a castle wall,
It may so long assailèd been o'er all.
(D.255–264)

Nothing is sure that grows on earthly ground;
And who most trusts in arm of fleshly might
And boasts in beauty's chain not to be bound
Doth soonest fall in disaventurous fight,
And yields his caitive neck to victor's most° despite.   *greatest*

12 'Ensample make of him, your hapless joy,°   *unfortunate lover*
And of myself now mated° as ye see;   *subdued*
Whose prouder° vaunt that proud avenging boy   *too proud*
Did soon pluck down and curbed my liberty.
For on a day, pricked° forth with jollity   *urged*
Of looser life and heat of hardiment,°   *boldness*
Ranging the forest wide on courser free,
The fields, the floods, the heavens with one consent
Did seem to laugh on me and favor mine intent.

13 'Forwearied with my sports, I did alight
From lofty steed and down to sleep me laid;
The verdant grass my couch did goodly dight,°   *cover*
And pillow was my helmet fair displayed.°   *spread out*
Whiles every sense the humor sweet embayed,°   *bathed*
And slumbering soft, my heart did steal away,
Me seemèd by my side a royal maid
Her dainty limbs full softly down did lay.
So fair a creature yet saw never sunny day.

14 'Most goodly glee° and lovely blandishment°   *entertainment,*
She to me made, and bade me love her dear,   *advances*
For dearly sure her love was to me bent,
As when just time expirèd° should appear.   *the right time*
But whether dreams delude or true it were,   *having come*
Was never heart so ravished with delight,
Ne living man like words did ever hear
As she to me delivered all that night;
And at her parting said she Queen of Faeries hight.°   *was called*

15 'When I awoke and found her place devoid,
And nought but pressèd grass where she had lyne,
I sorrowed all so much as erst I joyed,

13-15 Arthur's meeting with the Faery Queen is based on a very old romance tradition in which a mortal man yields to the frank and irresistible advances of an incredibly beautiful fairy princess. A popular medieval version of this motif is contained in Marie de France's *Lanval*. Arthur does not react to his dream of the beautiful and amorous woman with the righteous indignation with which Red Cross experienced his vision of the false Una. Nor does the Faery Queen propose that she and Arthur become lovers immediately, as had the false Una. In their controlled naturalness Arthur and the Faery Queen behave virtuously, while Red Cross and the false Una of his dream had, in their earlier meeting, performed an unnatural and sinful parody of this memorable vision.

And washèd all her place with watery eyne.
From that day forth I loved that face divine;
From that day forth I cast in careful mind
To seek her out with labor and long tine°   *affliction*
And never vowed to rest till her I find.
Nine months I seek in vain yet nill° that vow unbind.'°   *will not, break*

16 Thus as he spake, his visage waxèd pale,
    And change of hue great passion did bewray;°   *reveal*
    Yet still he strove to cloak his inward bale
    And hide the smoke that did his fire display,
    Till gentle Una thus to him gan say:
    'O happy Queen of Faeries, that hast found,
    Mongst many, one that with his prowess may
    Defend thine honor and thy foes confound.
    True loves are often sown, but seldom grow on ground.'

17 'Thine, O then,' said the gentle Red Cross Knight,
    'Next to that lady's love, shall be the place,
    O fairest virgin, full of heavenly light,
    Whose wondrous faith, exceeding earthly race,
    Was firmest fixed in mine extremest case.
    And you, my lord, the patron° of my life,   *savior*
    Of that great queen may° well gain worthy° grace.   *may you, deserved*
    For only worthy you, through prowess' prief°—   *test*
    If living man mote worthy be—to be her lief.'°   *love*

18 So diversely° discoursing of their loves,   *each one*
    The golden sun his glistering head gan shew,
    And sad remembrance now the prince amoves
    With fresh desire his voyage to pursue.
    Als° Una earned° her travel to renew.   *also, yearned*
    Then those two knights, fast friendship for to bind
    And love establish each to other true,
    Gave goodly gifts, the signs of grateful mind,
    And eke as pledges firm, right hands together joined.

19 Prince Arthur gave a box of diamond sure,°   *flawless*
    Embowed° with gold and gorgeous ornament,   *encircled*
    Wherein were closed few drops of liquor pure,
    Of wondrous worth and virtue excellent,
    That any wound could heal incontinent.°   *immediately*

16.6–9 Una gently chides Red Cross
with these words of praise for Arthur.
    17.1–5 I.e., "Your love, Una, shall
have the most deserving place next to
Gloriana's love, for your faithful love
was unswerving in my time of greatest
inconstancy."
    19.1–5 Arthur's gift of healing balm
is not unusual in the romances. Here it
may also represent the Eucharist.

Which to requite, the Red Cross Knight him gave
A book, wherein his Savior's Testament
Was writ with golden letters rich and brave,
A work of wondrous grace and able souls to save.

20 Thus been they parted, Arthur on his way
To seek his love, and th' other for to fight
With Una's foe, that all her realm did prey.
But she, now weighing the decayèd plight
And shrunken sinews of her chosen knight,
Would not awhile her forward course pursue,
Ne bring him forth in face of dreadful fight,
Till he recovered had his former hue.
For him to be yet weak and weary well she knew.

21 So as they traveled, lo, they gan espy
An armèd knight towards them gallop fast,
That seemèd from some fearèd foe to fly,
Or other grisly thing that him aghast.°   *terrified*
Still as he fled, his eye was backward cast
As if his fear still followed him behind;
Als flew his steed as he his bands had brast,
And with his wingèd heels did tread the wind
As he had been a foal of Pegasus's kind.°   *breed*

22 Nigh as he drew, they might perceive his head
To be unarmed, and curled uncombèd hairs
Upstaring stiff, dismayed with uncouth° dread.   *strange*
Nor drop of blood in all his face appears,
Nor life in limb. And to increase his fears,
In foul reproach° of knighthood's fair degree,°   *disgrace, status*
About his neck an hempen rope he wears,
That with his glistering arms does ill agree.
But he of rope or arms has now no memory.

23 The Red Cross Knight toward him crossèd fast
To weet what mister° wight was so dismayed.   *kind of*
There him he finds all senseless and aghast,
That of himself he seemed to be afraid;
Whom hardly he from flying forward stayed
Till he these words to him deliver might:
'Sir knight, aread who hath ye thus arrayed
And eke from whom make ye this hasty flight;
For never knight I saw in such misseeming° plight.'   *unbecoming*

19.6–9 Red Cross gives Arthur the
New Testament. The two gifts are the
Blood and Book of the new Covenant,
answering to those of the old (Exodus
24:6–8).

21.9 *Pegasus's kind:* i.e., a flying
horse, like Pegasus, the winged horse of
Bellerophon.

24 He answered nought at all, but adding new
    Fear to his first amazement—staring wide°   *wide-eyed*
    With stony eyes and heartless hollow hue°—   *cowardly vacant*
    Astonished stood as one that had espied   *expression*
    Infernal furies with their chains untied.
    Him yet again, and yet again, bespake
    The gentle knight; who nought to him replied,
    But trembling every joint, did inly quake;
    And faltering tongue at last these words seemed forth to
      shake:

25 'For God's dear love, sir knight, do me not stay;
    For lo, he comes, he comes fast after me.'
    Eft° looking back would fain have run away;   *again*
    But he him forced to stay and tellen free
    The secret cause of his perplexity.
    Yet nathemore° by his bold hearty speech   *not in the least*
    Could his blood-frozen heart emboldened be,
    But through his boldness, rather fear did reach;°   *succeed in rousing*
    Yet forced, at last he made through silence sudden breach.

26 'And am I now in safety sure,' quoth he,
    'From him that would have forcèd me to die?
    And is the point of death now turned fro me,
    That I may tell this hapless history?'
    'Fear nought,' quoth he, 'no danger now is nigh.'
    'Then shall I you recount a rueful case,'
    Said he, 'the which with this unlucky eye
    I late beheld, and had not greater grace
    Me reft from it, had been partaker of the place.

27 'I lately chanced—would I had never chanced—
    With a fair knight to keepen company,
    Sir Terwin hight, that well himself advanced
    In all affairs and was both bold and free,
    But not so happy as mote happy be.
    He loved, as was his lot, a lady gent,
    That him again° loved in the least degree;   *in return*
    For she was proud and of too high intent,°   *ambition*
    And joyed to see her lover languish and lament.

28 'From whom returning, sad and comfortless,
    As on the way together we did fare,
    We met that villain—God from him me bless!°—   *guard*
    That cursèd wight from whom I scaped whilere,°   *not long ago*
    A man of hell that calls himself Despair.
    Who first us greets and after fair areads

Of tidings strange and of adventures rare;
So creeping close as snake in hidden weeds,
Inquireth of our states and of our knightly deeds.

29 'Which when he knew, and felt our feeble hearts
Embossed° with bale° and bitter biting grief—   *stabbed, pain*
Which love had launchèd with his deadly darts—
With wounding words and terms of foul reprief,°   *insult*
He plucked from us all hope of due relief,
That erst us held in love of lingering life.
Then hopeless heartless, gan the cunning thief
Persuade us die to stint° all further strife;   *end*
To me he lent this rope, to him a rusty knife.

30 'With which sad instrument of hasty death
That woeful lover, loathing lenger light,
A wide way made to let forth living breath.
But I, more fearful or more lucky wight,
Dismayed with that deformèd dismal sight,
Fled fast away, half dead with dying° fear.   *fear of death*
Ne yet assured of life be you, sir knight,
Whose like infirmity like chance may bear.
But God you never let° his charmèd speeches hear.'   *may God never let you*

31 'How may a man,' said he, 'with idle speech
Be won to spoil the castle of his health?'
'I wot,' quoth he, 'whom trial° late did teach,   *experience*
That like° would not° for all this world'ès wealth.   *the like, would not do*
His subtle tongue, like dropping honey, melt'th
Into the heart and searcheth every vein,
That ere one be aware, by secret stealth
His power is reft and weakness doth remain.
O never, sir, desire to try his guileful train.'

32 'Certes,'° said he, 'hence shall I never rest   *certainly*
Till I that treacher's art have heard and tried.
And you, sir knight—whose name mote° I request—   *might*
Of grace do me unto his cabin guide.'
'I that hight Trevisan,' quoth he, 'will ride
Against my liking back to do you grace.
But nor for gold nor glee° will I abide   *glitter*
By you when ye arrive in that same place;
For liefer had I die than see his deadly face.'

33 Ere long they come where that same wicked wight
His dwelling has, low in an hollow cave,

30.7 *be:* 1590 and later editions read *by.*

Far underneath a craggy clift y-pight,°   *placed*
Dark, doleful, dreary, like a greedy grave
That still for carrion carcasses doth crave.
On top whereof aye dwelt the ghastly owl,
Shrieking his baleful note, which ever drave
Far from that haunt all other cheerful fowl.
And all about it wandering ghosts did wail and howl.

34   And all about old stocks and stubs of trees,
Whereon nor fruit nor leaf was ever seen,
Did hang upon the ragged rocky knees.°   *crags*
On which had many wretches hangèd been,
Whose carcasses were scattered on the green
And thrown about the cliffs. Arrivèd there,
That bare-head knight for dread and doleful teen°   *grief*
Would fain have fled, ne durst approachen near,
But th' other forced him stay and comforted in fear.

35   That darksome cave they enter, where they find
That cursèd man low sitting on the ground,
Musing full sadly in his sullen mind.
His griesy° locks, long growen and unbound,   *grey*
Disordered hung about his shoulders round
And hid his face. Through which his hollow eyne
Looked deadly dull, and starèd as astound.
His raw-bone cheeks through penury and pine°   *hunger*
Were shrunk into his jaws, as° he did never dine.   *as if*

36   His garment nought but many ragged clouts°   *cloths*
With thorns together pinned and patchèd was,
The which his naked sides he wrapped abouts.
And him beside, there lay upon the grass
A dreary corse whose life away did pass,
All wallowed in his own yet luke-warm blood,
That from his wound yet wellèd fresh, alas;
In which a rusty knife fast fixèd stood,
And made an open passage for the gushing flood.

37   Which piteous spectacle, approving° true   *proving*
The woeful tale that Trevisan had told,
Whenas the gentle Red Cross Knight did view,
With fiery zeal he burnt in courage bold
Him to avenge before his blood were cold;
And to the villain said, 'Thou damnèd wight,

33.3   *y-pight:* (1596). 1590 reads *yplight.*
35.1–36.3 Spenser's Despair has all the symptoms of acute melancholy. Robert Burton cites the following physical symptoms as typical of the disease: "lean, withered, hollow-eyed, look old, wrinkled, harsh, . . . hard, dejected looks, . . . little or no sleep. . . ." (*Anatomy of Melancholy,* p. 326).

The author of this fact° we here behold,   *deed*
What justice can but judge against thee right:
With thine own blood to price° his blood here shed in sight?'   *pay for*

38 'What frantic fit,' quoth he, 'hath thus distraught
Thee, foolish man, so rash a doom° to give?   *judgment*
What justice ever other judgment taught,
But he should die who merits not to live?
None else to death this man despairing driv°   *drove*
But his own guilty mind deserving death.
Is then unjust to each his due to give:
Or° let him die that loatheth living breath,   *either*
Or let him die at ease that liveth here uneath?°   *uneasy*

39 'Who travels by the weary wandering way
To come unto his wishèd home in haste,
And meets a flood that doth his passage stay,
Is not great grace to help him over passed,
Or free his feet that in the mire stick fast?
Most envious man, that grieves at neighbor's good,
And fond, that joyest in the woe thou hast,
Why wilt not let him pass that long hath stood
Upon the bank, yet wilt thyself not pass the flood?

40 'He there does now enjoy eternal rest
And happy ease, which thou dost want and crave,
And further from it daily wanderest.
What if some little pain the passage have
That makes frail flesh to fear the bitter wave?
Is not short pain well borne, that brings long ease,
And lays the soul to sleep in quiet grave?
Sleep after toil, port after stormy seas,
Ease after war, death after life does greatly please.'

38–47 Despair's marvelously subtle speech is an illogical mixture of ideas from the Old Testament and classical philosophy.
38.1–2 Despair demonstrates in the opening lines of his speech a mastery of classical rhetoric. He must calm the knight's anger if he is to persuade him to destroy himself. This he immediately does by putting Red Cross in the wrong and himself in the right, knowing that "people are mild if they think themselves to be in the wrong . . . for anger is not aroused by justice" (Aristotle, *Rhetoric*, II.3. p. 101).
38.8–9 This and other arguments in Despair's speech to the effect that one has the right to kill oneself rather than live out a painful life are derived from classical Stoicism. Seneca, the most influential of the Stoics, writes, "Nothing stands in the way of a man who wants to break loose and get away. Nature's corral is an open space, and when pressure reaches the allowable point a man can look around for an easy exit" ("Suicide," in *The Stoic Philosophy of Seneca*, trans. Moses Hadas, Doubleday Anchor Books, p. 206).
40–47 Having placated Red Cross, Despair proceeds to base his argument for suicide on the following appeals: appeal to pleasure and the desire to escape pain (40), appeal to necessity (42), appeal to the desire to escape pain (43–45), appeal to fear (46–47). All of these appeals are ancient and traditional rhetorical topics.

41   The knight much wondered at his sudden° wit,   *quick*
     And said, 'The term of life is limited,
     Ne may a man prolong nor shorten it.
     The soldier may not move from watchful stead,
     Nor leave his stand until his captain bed.'°   *commands*
     'Who life did limit by almighty doom,'
     Quoth he, 'knows best the terms establishèd;
     And he that points the sentinel his room
     Doth license him depart at sound of morning drum.

42   'Is not his deed, whatever thing is done,
     In heaven and earth? Did not he all create
     To die again? All ends that was begun.
     Their times in his eternal book of fate
     Are written sure, and have their certain date.
     Who then can strive with strong necessity,
     That holds the world in his° still changing state,   *its*
     Or shun the death ordained by destiny?
     When hour of death is come, let none ask whence nor why.

43   'The lenger life, I wot, the greater sin,
     The greater sin, the greater punishment.
     All those great battles which thou boasts to win
     Through strife and bloodshed and avengèment,
     Now praised, hereafter dear thou shalt repent.
     For life must life, and blood must blood repay.
     Is not enough thy evil life forspent?°   *utterly wasted*
     For he that once hath missèd the right way,
     The further he doth go, the further he doth stray.

44   'Then do no further go, no further stray,
     But here lie down and to thy rest betake,
     Th' ill to prevent that life ensuen° may.   *may follow life*
     For what hath life that may it lovèd make,
     And gives not rather cause it to forsake?
     Fear, sickness, age, loss, labor, sorrow, strife,
     Pain, hunger, cold that makes the heart to quake;
     And ever fickle fortune rageth rife.
     All which, and thousands mo, do make a loathsome life.

45   'Thou, wretched man, of death hast greatest need,
     If in true balance thou wilt weigh thy state;

41.2–5   Red Cross's argument against suicide is probably derived from Cicero's *De Senectute*, XX: "Pythagoras bids us stand like faithful sentries and not quit our post until God, our Captain, gives the word" (trans. William A. Falconer, Loeb Classical Library, p. 85).
42.1–9   If Despair's argument from necessity is valid, then suicide would be out of the question. That he would use such a clearly fallacious argument shows that he is sure of his man.
43.6   Genesis 9:6: "Whoso sheddeth man's blood, by man shall his blood be shed."

For never knight that darèd warlike deed
More luckless disadventures did amate.°   *overwhelm*
Witness the dungeon deep, wherein of late
Thy life shut up, for death, so oft did call.
And though good luck prolongèd hath thy date,°   *life span*
Yet death then would the like mishaps forestall,
Into the which hereafter thou mayst happen fall.

46 'Why then dost thou, O man of sin, desire
    To draw thy days forth to their last degree?
    Is not the measure of thy sinful hire°   *service to sin*
    High heapèd up with huge iniquity,
    Against the day of wrath° to burden thee?   *Judgment Day*
    Is not enough, that to this lady mild
    Thou falsèd hast thy faith with perjury,
    And sold thyself to serve Duessa vild,°   *vile*
    With whom in all abuse thou hast thyself defiled?

47 'Is not he just, that all this doth behold   *looks on impar-*
    From highest heaven and bears an equal eye?°   *tially*
    Shall he thy sins up in his knowledge fold,°   *assume*
    And guilty be of thine impiety?
    Is not his law "Let every sinner die;
    Die shall all flesh?" What then must needs be done,
    Is it not better to do willingly
    Than linger till the glass be all out run?
    Death is the end of woes. Die soon, O faery's son.'

48 The knight was much enmovèd with his speech,
    That as a sword's point through his heart did pierce
    And in his conscience made a secret breach—
    Well knowing true all that he did rehearse—
    And to his fresh remembrance did reverse°   *bring back*
    The ugly view of his deformèd crimes,
    That all his manly powers it did disperse,
    As he were charmèd with enchanted rimes,°   *incantation*
    That oftentimes he quaked, and fainted oftentimes.

49 In which amazement when the miscreant
    Perceivèd him to waver weak and frail,
    Whiles trembling horror did his conscience daunt

46.7 *falsèd:* (1596). 1590 reads *falsest.*
47.3–4 The answer to Despair's question should have been a resounding "yes," for Christ did take upon himself the sins of all men. His death on the cross was the atonement for the sin of mankind.
47.5 "The soul that sins shall die" (Ezekiel 18:4).
47.6 "All flesh shall perish together, and man shall turn again into dust" (Job 34:15).
48.2 "And a sword will pierce through your own soul also" (Luke 2:35).
49–50 Having stirred up Red Cross's emotions, Despair now caps his argument with strong visual appeals to the knight's disturbed imagination. Logically, the terrifying pictures of damned spirits in

And hellish anguish did his soul assail,
To drive him to despair and quite to quail,°   *destroy*
He showed him painted in a table° plain   *picture*
The damnèd ghosts that do in torments wail,
And thousand fiends that do them endless pain
With fire and brimstone, which forever shall remain.

50 The sight whereof so thoroughly him dismayed
That nought but death before his eyes he saw,
And ever burning wrath before him laid,
By righteous sentence of th' Almighty's law.
Then gan the villain him to overcraw,°   *exult over*
And brought unto him swords, ropes, poison, fire,
And all that might him to perdition draw,
And bade him choose what death he would desire.
For death was due to him that had provoked God's ire.

51 But whenas none of them he saw him take,
He to him raught° a dagger sharp and keen   *held out*
And gave it him in hand. His hand did quake
And tremble like a leaf of aspen green,
And troubled blood through his pale face was seen
To come and go with tidings from the heart,
As it a running messenger had been.
At last resolved to work his final smart,
He lifted up his hand, that back again did start.

52 Which whenas Una heard, through every vein
The crudled cold ran to her well of life°   *i.e. heart*
As in a swoon. But soon relived° again,   *revived*
Out of his hand she snatched the cursèd knife
And threw it to the ground, enragèd rife,°   *deeply*
And to him said, 'Fie, fie, faint-hearted knight,
What meanest thou by this reproachful strife?
Is this the battle which thou vauntst to fight
With that firemouthèd dragon, horrible and bright?

53 'Come, come away, frail, feeble, fleshly wight,
Ne let vain words bewitch thy manly heart,
Ne devilish thoughts dismay thy constant° sprite.   *resolute*
In heavenly mercies hast thou not a part?

---

hell should be powerful arguments against
despair and suicide, but as Burton points
out, "Many for fear of the judgment to
come . . . are desperate. . . . The terrible
meditation of hell-fire, and eternal punish-
ment, much torments a silly sinful soul"
(*Anatomy of Melancholy*, p. 940).
   53.1–9 Una's saving counsel is the
traditional antidote for despair. Again
see *Anatomy of Melancholy* on the cure
of despair, pp. 951–952.

Why shouldst thou then despair that chosen art?
Where justice grows, there grows eke greater grace,
The which doth quench the brand of hellish smart,
And that accursed handwriting doth deface.
Arise, sir knight, arise and leave this cursèd place.'

54   So up he rose and thence amounted° straight.   *mounted*
Which when the carl° beheld, and saw his guest   *churl*
Would safe depart for all his subtle sleight,
He chose an halter from among the rest,
And with it hung himself, unbid,° unblessed.   *unprayed for*
But death he could not work himself thereby;
For thousand times he so himself had dressed,°   *prepared*
Yet natheless it could not do him die°   *kill him*
Till he should die his last, that is eternally.

CANTO x

Her faithful knight fair Una brings
To House of Holiness,
Where he is taught repentance and
The way to heavenly bliss.

1   What man is he that boasts of fleshly might
And vain assurance of mortality,°   *mortal life*
Which all so soon as it doth come to fight
Against spiritual foes, yields by and by,
Or from the field most cowardly doth fly?
Ne let the man ascribe it to his skill,
That thorough grace hath gainèd victory.
If any strength we have, it is to ill,
But all the good is God's, both power and eke will.

2   By that which lately happened, Una saw
That this her knight was feeble and too faint,
And all his sinews waxen weak and raw°   *out of condition*
Through long imprisonment and hard constraint
Which he endurèd in his late restraint,
That yet he was unfit for bloody fight.
Therefore to cherish him with diets daint,°   *dainty*

53.8 "Blotting out the handwriting
of ordinances that was against us"
(Colossians 2:14). The new law of grace
and mercy replaces the old law of judg-
ment and punishment.
   1.1 "Cursed is the man who trusts in
man and makes flesh his arm" (Jeremiah
17:5).
   1.6–9 "For by grace you have been
saved through faith; and this is not your
own doing, it is the gift of God—not be-
cause of works, lest any man should
boast" (Ephesians 2:8–9).

She cast to bring him where he cheeren° might,
Till he recurèd° had his late decayèd plight.

regain cheerful-
ness

cured

3 There was an ancient house not far away,
Renowned throughout the world for sacred lore
And pure unspotted life, so well they say
It governed was and guided evermore,
Through wisdom of a matron grave and hoar,°
Whose only joy was to relieve the needs
Of wretched souls and help the helpless poor.
All night she spent in bidding of her beads,°
And all the day in doing good and godly deeds.

grey-haired

saying her
prayers

4 Dame Caelia men did her call, as thought
From heaven to come or thither to arise,
The mother of three daughters, well upbrought
In goodly thews° and godly exercise.
The eldest two, most sober, chaste, and wise—
Fidelia and Speranza—virgins were,
Though spoused, yet wanting wedlock's solemnize;
But fair Charissa to a lovely fere°
Was linkèd, and by him had many pledges dear.°

manners

mate

i.e. children

5 Arrivèd there, the door they find fast locked;
For it was warely watchèd night and day
For fear of many foes. But when they knocked,
The porter opened unto them straightway.
He was an aged sire, all hoary gray,
With looks full lowly cast and gait full slow,
Wont on a staff his feeble steps to stay,
Hight Humilta. They pass in stooping low;
For strait and narrow was the way which he did show.

3.8–9 *Bead* meant "prayer" in early English. The small pieces of glass on a rosary only stood for beads (prayers); later they were themselves called beads. Whether or not Spenser here means that the matron was using a rosary in saying her prayers, her solitary nocturnal devotion is contrasted with the (ironically) visual devotion of the blind Corceca (iii.13–14), for whom the material beads, sack cloth, and ashes became ends in themselves rather than mere visual show of true prayer and penance. The satire on blind devotion in Canto iii is as characteristic of such medieval poets as Dante, Langland, and Chaucer as it is of renaissance Protestant poets. Conversely, the matron's blending of contemplation with action, faith with good works is both a Catholic and Protestant ideal.

4.1 *Caelia:* "heavenly."

4.6 *Fidelia and Speranza:* "faith" and "hope."

4.8 *Charissa:* "charity," "spiritual love," "good works." "And now abideth faith, hope, charity, these three; but the greatest is charity" (I Corinthians 13:13).

5–7 The porter, the franklin, and the squire correspond to the porter Malvenu and the usher Vanity in the House of Pride.

5.3–4 "Knock and it shall be opened unto you" (Matthew 7:7).

5.9 "Strait is the gate, and narrow is the way, which leadeth unto life, and few there be that find it" (Matthew 7:14). This idea is found again in 10.3–6 below.

6   Each goodly thing is hardest to begin.
    But entered in, a spacious court they see,
    Both plain and pleasant to be walkèd in,
    Where them does meet a franklin° fair and free,°   *landowner,*
    And entertains with comely courteous glee.   *gracious*
    His name was Zeal, that him right well became,
    For in his speeches and behavior he
    Did labor lively° to express the same,   *with animation*
    And gladly did them guide till to the hall they came.

7   There fairly them receives a gentle squire,
    Of mild demeanor and rare courtesy,
    Right cleanly clad in comely sad° attire,   *dark-colored*
    In word and deed that° showed great modesty   *who*
    And knew his good° to all of each degree,   *the behavior*
    Hight Reverence. He them with speeches meet   *appropriate*
    Does fair entreat;° no courting nicety,   *converse with*
    But simple true° and eke unfeignèd sweet,°   *truth, sweetness*
    As might become a squire so great persons to greet.

8   And afterwards them to his dame he leads,
    That aged dame, the lady of the place,
    Who all this while was busy at her beads.
    Which done, she up arose with seemly grace
    And toward them full matronly did pace.
    Where when that fairest Una she beheld,
    Whom well she knew to spring from heavenly race,
    Her heart with joy unwonted inly swelled,
    As feeling wondrous comfort in her weaker eld.°   *old age*

9   And her embracing said, 'O happy earth,
    Whereon thy innocent feet do ever tread,
    Most virtuous virgin born of heavenly birth,
    That to redeem thy woeful parents' head
    From tyrant's rage and ever-dying dread°   *continual fear*
    Hast wandered through the world now long a day,   *of death*
    Yet ceasest not thy weary soles to lead,
    What grace hath thee now hither brought this way,
    Or done° thy feeble feet unweeting° hither stray?   *do, unwittingly*

10 'Strange thing it is an errant knight to see
    Here in this place, or any other wight
    That hither turns his steps. So few there be
    That choose the narrow path or seek the right.

    8–11 Compare Caelia's reception of   their lovers, and in both cases a journey
    Una with Night's meeting with Duessa.   is required. Many details of the two
    Both younger women seek the cure of   journeys correspond.

All keep the broad highway and take delight
With many rather for to go astray,
And be partakers of their evil plight,
Than with a few to walk the rightest way.
Of foolish men, why haste ye to your own decay?'

11 'Thyself to see and tired limbs to rest,
O matron sage,' quoth she, 'I hither came,
And this good knight his way with me addressed,
Led with thy praises and broad-blazèd fame,
That up to heaven is blown.' The ancient dame
Him goodly greeted in her modest guise,
And entertained them both, as best became,
With all the court'sies° that she could devise,   *courtesies*
Ne wanted aught to show her bounteous or wise.

12 Thus as they gan of sundry things devise,°   *talk*
Lo, two most goodly virgins came in place;
Y-linkèd arm in arm in lovely° wise,   *loving*
With countenance demure and modest grace,
They numbered even steps and equal pace.°   *walked in step*
Of which the eldest, that Fidelia hight,
Like sunny beams threw° from her crystal face,   *threw beams like*
That could have dazed the rash beholder's sight,   *the sun's*
And round about her head did shine like heaven's light.

13 She was arrayèd all in lily white,
And in her right hand bore a cup of gold,
With wine and water filled up to the height,
In which a serpent did himself infold,
That horror made to all that did behold;
But she no whit did change her constant mood.°   *expression*
And in her other hand she fast did hold
A book, that was both signed and sealed with blood,
Wherein dark things were writ, hard to be understood.

12.2 *two most goodly virgins:* As with the earlier portraits of the sins, the details in Spenser's description of Faith, Hope, and Charity are traditional. Emblem books, paintings, and tapestries in the Middle Ages and the Renaissance contained these portraits in detail. The literary technique involved in this kind of "verbal iconography" should be distinguished from the allegory of such episodes as the dream of Red Cross and Una's sojourn with the satyrs, where the more complex action is suggestive of spiritual and psychological experience rather than illustrative of static ideas. For some discussion of the most important details in Spenser's treatment of faith, hope, and charity, see Introduction, pp. 40–43.

13.1 According to Ariosto, "holy Fidelity is clothed in no other way than with a white garment completely covering her" (*Orlando Furioso*, XXIII.1).

13.6 *her constant mood:* "Let us hold fast the profession of our faith without wavering" (Hebrews 10:23).

13.8 *signed and sealed with blood:* The New Testament is signed and sealed with Christ's blood.

13.9 St. Peter says of the writings of St. Paul (II Peter 3:16) that they contain "some things hard to be understood." Jesus' disciples also found some of his parables hard to be understood.

14 Her younger sister, that Speranza hight,
    Was clad in blue, that her beseemèd well.
    Not all so cheerful seemèd she of sight°   *to look at*
    As was her sister; whether dread did dwell,
    Or anguish, in her heart is hard to tell.
    Upon her arm a silver anchor lay
    Whereon she leanèd ever, as befell;
    And ever up to heaven as she did pray,
    Her steadfast eyes were bent, ne swervèd other way.

15 They seeing Una, towards her gan wend,
    Who them encounters with like courtesy;
    Many kind speeches they between them spend
    And greatly joy each other well to see.
    Then to the knight with shamefast° modesty   *humble*
    They turn themselves, at Una's meek request,
    And him salute with well beseeming glee;°   *proper gladness*
    Who fair them quites, as him beseemèd best,
    And goodly gan discourse of many a noble gest.°   *deed of arms*

16 Then Una thus: 'But she your sister dear,
    The dear Charissa, where is she become,°   *where is she?*
    Or wants she health, or busy is elsewhere?'
    'Ah no,' said they, 'but forth she may not come;
    For she of late is lightened of her womb
    And hath increased the world with one son more,
    That her to see should be but troublesome.'
    'Indeed,' quoth she, 'that should her trouble sore,
    But thanked be God and her increase so° evermore.'   *in that way*

17 Then said the aged Caelia, 'Dear dame,
    And you, good sir, I wot that of your toil
    And labors long, through which ye hither came,
    Ye both forwearied be; therefore a while
    I read° you rest and to your bowers recoil.'°   *advise, withdraw*
    Then callèd she a groom that forth him led
    Into a goodly lodge, and gan despoil°   *undress*
    Of puissant arms and laid in easy bed.
    His name was meek Obedience, rightfully aread.°   *to tell the truth*

18 Now when their weary limbs with kindly rest,
    And bodies were refreshed with due repast,
    Fair Una gan Fidelia fair request
    To have her knight into her schoolhouse placed,

14.2 Blue is the color for hope in   title page device on renaissance books,
medieval color symbolism.   including *The Faerie Queene.*
    14.6 The *anchora spei* was a common   15.4 *well:* (1596). 1590 reads *for.*

That of her heavenly learning he might taste,
And hear the wisdom of her words divine.
She granted, and that knight so much agraced°
That she him taught celestial discipline,°
And opened his dull eyes, that light mote in them shine.

favored
divine laws

19 And that her sacred book, with blood y-writ,
That none could read except she did them teach,
She unto him disclosèd every whit,
And heavenly documents° thereout° did preach,
That weaker° wit of man could never reach—
Of God, of grace, of justice, of free will—
That wonder was to hear her goodly speech.
For she was able with her words to kill
And raise again to life the heart that she did thrill.°

doctrines, from it
too weak

pierce

20 And when she list pour out her larger sprite,°
She would command the hasty sun to stay,
Or backward turn his course from heaven's height;
Sometimes great hosts of men she could dismay;
Dry-shod to pass, she parts the floods in tway;
And eke huge mountains from their native seat
She would command themselves to bear away
And throw in raging sea with roaring threat.°
Almighty God her gave such power and puissance great.

i.e. spiritual power

threatening roar

21 The faithful knight now grew in little space,
By hearing her and by her sister's lore,
To such perfection of all heavenly grace
That wretched world he gan for to abhor
And mortal life gan loathe, as thing forlore,
Grieved with remembrance of his wicked ways,
And pricked with anguish of his sins so sore
That he desired to end his wretched days.
So much the dart of sinful guilt the soul dismays.

22 But wise Speranza gave him comfort sweet
And taught him how to take assurèd hold
Upon her silver anchor, as was meet;
Else had his sins so great and manifold
Made him forget all that Fidelia told.

19.6 These are traditional topics in Christian theology and the main topics of theological controversy in the Renaissance. They are the subjects of Milton's *Paradise Lost.*
20 Famous works of faith: Joshua commanded the sun to stand still (Joshua 10:12); Hezekiah reversed its direction (II Kings 20:10); Gideon's victory (Judges 7:7); Moses parted the waters of the Red Sea (Exodus 14:21–31); and Christ told his disciples that faith would give them power to move mountains (Matthew 21:21).
20.5 (1609). 1590 omits.

In this distressèd doubtful agony,
When him his dearest Una did behold—
Disdaining life, desiring leave to die—
She found herself assailed with great perplexity.

23 And came to Caelia to declare her smart,
Who well acquainted with that common plight
Which sinful horror° works in wounded heart,   *horror of sin*
Her wisely comforted all that she might
With goodly counsel and advisement right;
And straightway sent with careful diligence
To fetch a leech,° the which had great insight   *doctor*
In that disease of grievèd conscience,
And well could cure the same. His name was Patience.

24 Who coming to that soul-diseasèd knight,
Could hardly him intreat to tell his grief.
Which known, and all that noyed° his heavy sprite   *troubled*
Well searched,° eftsoons he gan apply relief   *probed*
Of salves and med'cines which had passing prief,°   *great power*
And thereto added words of wondrous might.
By which, to ease he him recurèd brief,°   *quickly*
And much assuaged the passion° of his plight,   *suffering*
That he his pain endured, as seeming now more light.

25 But yet the cause and root of all his ill,
Inward corruption and infected sin,
Not purged nor healed, behind remainèd still;
And festering sore did rankle yet within,
Close° creeping twixt the marrow and the skin.   *secretly*
Which to extirp,° he laid him privily   *root out*
Down in a darksome lowly place far in,
Whereas he meant his corsives° to apply,   *remedies*
And with strait° diet tame his stubborn malady.   *strict*

26 In ashes and sackcloth he did array
His dainty corse, proud humors° to abate;   *passions*

24.2 *to tell his grief:* Confession, whether public or private, general or individual, has always been a stage in the process of repentance. Both medieval Catholic and renaissance Protestant theologians agreed that confession is necessary to salvation. See for instance the discussion of confession in Martin Luther's *The Pagan Servitude of the Church* (*De Captivitate Babylonica Ecclesiae Praeludium*). The course of the Red Cross Knight's penance is the same, generally, as that advocated by medieval Catholic writers.

24.6 *words of wondrous might:* absolution.
25–26 Purgation follows contrition, confession, and absolution. During the Middle Ages public penance was common and must at times have been horrifying to behold. After the murder of Thomas Becket, Henry II had himself brutally scourged. A rigorous private penance was reinstituted by Protestants as a reaction against the late medieval practice of indulgences, which tended to by-pass purgation.

And dieted with fasting every day,
The swelling of his wounds to mitigate;
And made him pray both early and eke late.
And ever as superfluous flesh did rot,
Amendment ready still at hand did wait
To pluck it out with pincers fiery hot,
That soon in him was left no one corrupted jot.

27 And bitter Penance with an iron whip,
    Was wont him once to disc'ple° every day;   *discipline*
    And sharp Remorse his heart did prick and nip,
    That drops of blood thence like a well did play;
    And sad Repentance usèd to embay°   *bathe*
    His blameful body in salt water sore,
    The filthy blots of sin to wash away.
    So in short space they did to health restore
    The man that would not live, but erst° lay at death's door. *before*

28 In which his torment often was so great
    That like a lion he would cry and roar
    And rend his flesh and his own sinews eat.
    His own dear Una, hearing evermore
    His rueful shrieks and groanings, often tore
    Her guiltless garments and her golden hair
    For pity of his pain and anguish sore.
    Yet all with patience wisely she did bear;
    For well she wist, his crime could else be never clear.

29 Whom thus recovered by wise Patience
    And true Repentance, they to Una brought.
    Who joyous of his curèd conscience,
    Him dearly kissed and fairly eke besought
    Himself to cherish,° and consuming thought   *cheer up*
    To put away out of his careful breast.
    By this, Charissa, late in childbed brought,
    Was waxen strong and left her fruitful nest;
    To her fair Una brought this unacquainted guest.

30 She was a woman in her freshest age,
    Of wondrous beauty and of bounty rare,
    With goodly grace and comely personage,
    That was on earth not easy to compare.
    Full of great love, but Cupid's wanton snare
    As hell she hated, chaste in work and will.

27.1 *Penance:* probably "punishment."   avoid future sin. The salt in the water
27.3 *Remorse:* grief for past sins.   of expiatory ablution (Psalms 51:2 and
27.5 *Repentance:* the resolution to   Isaiah 1:16) was thought of as the tears
   of repentance.

Her neck and breasts were ever open bare,
That aye thereof her babes might suck their fill;
The rest was all in yellow robes arrayèd still.

31 A multitude of babes about her hung,
Playing their sports, that joyed her to behold,
Whom still she fed whiles they were weak and young,
But thrust them forth still as they waxèd old.
And on her head she wore a tire° of gold,   *head-dress*
Adorned with gems and ouches° wondrous fair,   *jewels*
Whose passing price uneath° was to be told;   *scarcely*
And by her side there sat a gentle pair
Of turtle doves, she sitting in an ivory chair.

32 The knight and Una entering, fair her greet
And bid her joy of that her happy brood;
Who them requites with court'sies seeming meet,
And entertains with friendly cheerful mood.
Then Una her besought to be so good
As in her virtuous rules to school her knight,
Now after all his torment well withstood,
In that sad house of Penance where his sprite
Had passed the pains of hell and long enduring night.

33 She was right joyous of her just request,
And taking by the hand that faery's son,
Gan him instruct in every good behest:
Of love, and righteousness, and well to done,°   *right doing*
And wrath and hatred warily to shun,
That drew on men God's hatred and his wrath,
And many souls in dolors° had fordone.°   *misery, destroyed*
In which when him she well instructed hath,
From thence to heaven she teacheth him the ready path.

34 Wherein his weaker wandering steps to guide,
An ancient matron she to her does call,
Whose sober looks her wisdom well descried.°   *made known*
Her name was Mercy, well known over all°   *all over*
To be both gracious and eke liberal.
To whom the careful charge of him she gave,
To lead aright, that he should never fall
In all his ways through this wide world'ès wave,°   *expanse*
That Mercy in the end his righteous soul might save.

35 The godly matron by the hand him bears
Forth from her presence by a narrow way,

30.9 Hymen, the god of marriage, is dressed in yellow in Ovid's *Metamorphoses*,
X.1.

Scattered with bushy thorns and ragged breres,°   *briers*
Which still before him she removed away,
That nothing might his ready passage stay.
And ever when his feet encumbered were,
Or gan to shrink, or from the right to stray,
She held him fast and firmly did upbear,
As careful nurse her child from falling oft does rear.

36   Eftsoons unto an holy hospital°   *retreat*
That was forby° the way she did him bring,   *beside*
In which seven beadmen° that had vowèd all   *men of prayer*
Their life to service of high heaven's King
Did spend their days in doing godly thing.°   *service*
Their gates to all were open evermore
That by the weary way were traveling,
And one sat waiting ever them before
To call in comers-by that needy were and poor.

37   The first of them, that eldest was and best,
Of all the house had charge and government,
As guardian and steward of the rest.
His office was to give entertainment
And lodging unto all that came and went—
Not unto such as could him feast again
And double quite° for that° he on them spent,   *repay, what*
But such as want of harbor° did constrain.   *shelter*
Those, for God's sake, his duty was to entertain.

38   The second was as almoner° of the place.   *distributor of alms*
His office was the hungry for to feed
And thirsty give to drink, a work of grace.
He feared not once himself to be in need,
Ne cared to hoard for those whom he did breed.°   *i.e. his family*
The grace of God he laid up still in store,
Which as a stock he left unto his seed;
He had enough, what need him care for more?
And had he less, yet some he would give to the poor.

39   The third had of their wardrobe custody,
In which were not rich tires° nor garments gay,   *clothes*
The plumes of pride and wings of vanity,

36–43 The seven holy men perform the seven corporal works of mercy, *opera misericordiae*, taught by the medieval church. There are also seven spiritual works of mercy: the conversion of sinners, teaching the ignorant, giving counsel to the doubtful, forgiving injuries, being patient under wrong, praying for the living and for the dead. The seven works of mercy here correspond to the seven deadly sins in the House of Pride.

36.3 *beadmen:* originally men who prayed for others in return for charity they received.

But clothès meet to keep keen cold away
And naked nature seemly to array;
With which, bare wretched wights he daily clad,
The images of God in earthly clay.
And if that no spare cloths to give he had,
His own coat he would cut, and it distribute glad.

40 The fourth appointed by his office was,
    Poor prisoners to relieve with gracious aid,
    And captives to redeem with price of brass°   *money*
    From Turks and Saracens, which them had stayed.°   *detained*
    And though they faulty were, yet well he weighed
    That God to us forgiveth every hour
    Much more than that why° they in bands were laid;   *for which*
    And he that harrowed hell with heavy stour
    The faulty souls from thence brought to his heavenly bower.

41 The fifth had charge sick persons to attend,
    And comfort those in point° of death which lay;   *on the point*
    For them most needeth comfort in the end,
    When sin, and hell, and death do most dismay
    The feeble soul departing hence away.
    All is but lost that, living, we bestow,
    If not well ended at our dying day.
    O man have mind of that last bitter throe;°   *agony*
    For as the tree does fall, so lies it ever low.

42 The sixth had charge of them now being dead,
    In seemly sort their corses to engrave,°   *bury*
    And deck with dainty flowers their bridal bed,
    That to their heavenly Spouse both sweet and brave°   *splendid*
    They might appear when he their souls shall save.
    The wondrous workmanship of God's own mold,°   *image*
    Whose face he made all beasts to fear, and gave
    All in his hand, even dead we honor should.
    Ah, dearest God, me grant I dead be not defouled.

43 The seventh, now after death and burial done,
    Had charge the tender orphans of the dead
    And widows aid, lest they should be undone.°   *harmed*
    In face of judgment° he their right would plead,   *in the law court*
    Ne aught the power of mighty men did dread
    In their defence, nor would for gold or fee

40.8 *harrowed hell:* refers to the exploits of Christ, recounted in the apocryphal Gospel of Nicodemus, during his descent into hell. These exploits were an extremely popular subject in medieval literature.

41.9 "In the place where the tree falleth, there it shall be" (Ecclesiastes 11:3).

Be won their rightful causes down to tread.
And when they stood in most necessity,
He did supply their want and gave them ever free.

44   There when the elfin knight arrivèd was,
The first and chiefest of the seven, whose care
Was guests to welcome, towards him did pass.
Where seeing Mercy, that his steps upbare
And always led, to her with reverence rare
He humbly louted° in meek lowliness,   *bowed*
And seemly welcome for her did prepare.
For of their order she was patroness,
Albe° Charissa were their chiefest founderess.   *although*

45   There she awhile him stays, himself to rest,
That to the rest° more able he might be.   *in continuing*
During which time, in every good behest
And godly work of alms and charity
She him instructed with great industry.
Shortly therein so perfect he became
That from the first unto the last degree°   *stage*
His mortal life he learnèd had to frame
In holy righteousness, without rebuke or blame.

46   Thence forward by that painful way they pass
Forth to an hill that was both steep and high,
On top whereof a sacred chapel was
And eke a little hermitage thereby,
Wherein an aged holy man did lie
That day and night said his devotion,
Ne other worldly business did apply.°   *carry on*
His name was Heavenly Contemplation;
Of God and goodness was his meditation.

47   Great grace that old man to him given had;°   *had been given*
For God he often saw from heaven's height,
All° were his earthly eyne both blunt° and bad   *although, dim*
And through great age had lost their kindly° sight,   *natural*

46 See Introduction, pp. 43–4 for comment on this and the previous stage in Red Cross's conversion. The knight's progress through the House of Holiness can be analyzed in three stages, corresponding to the three-fold mystical way of Purgation, Illumination, and Union. Spenser, however, despite the strong note of contempt for the world, *contemptus mundi*, which follows, was not essentially a mystic. And his allegory does not represent the last stage of the mystical way (Union). He believed too strongly in the simultaneous blending of the ideals of action and contemplation that was the hallmark of renaissance thought.

46.5 *an aged holy man:* contrasts with the false hermit Archimago, and the Hill of Contemplation with the lowly hermitage "down in a dale" in Canto i. In other respects he is contrasted with Ignaro, the mute porter of Orgoglio's palace in Canto viii.

Yet wondrous quick and persant° was his sprite,   *piercing*
As eagle's eye that can behold the sun.
That hill they scale with all their power and might,
That his frail thighs nigh weary and fordone
Gan fail, but by her help the top at last he won.

48   There they do find that godly aged sire,
With snowy locks adown his shoulders shed,
As hoary frost with spangles doth attire
The mossy branches of an oak half dead.
Each bone might through his body well be read
And every sinew seen, through° his long fast;   *as a result of*
For nought he cared his carcass long unfed;
His mind was full of spiritual repast,
And pined° his flesh to keep his body low and chaste.   *starved*

49   Who when these two approaching he espied,
At their first presence grew aggrievèd sore,
That forced him lay his heavenly thoughts aside.
And had he not that dame respected more,
Whom highly he did reverence and adore,
He would not once have movèd for the knight.
They him saluted standing far afore;°   *i.e. from afar*
Who well them greeting, humbly did requite,
And askèd to what end they clumb° that tedious height.   *had climbed*

50   'What end,' quoth she, 'should cause us take such pain
But that same end which every living wight
Should make his mark high heaven to attain?
Is not from hence the way that leadeth right
To that most glorious house that glistereth bright
With burning stars and everliving fire,
Whereof the keys are to thy hand behight°   *entrusted*
By wise Fidelia? She doth thee require
To show it to this knight, according° his desire.'   *granting*

51   'Thrice happy man,' said then the father grave,
'Whose staggering steps thy steady hand doth lead,
And shows the way his sinful soul to save.
Who better can the way to heaven aread°   *point out*
Than thou thyself that was both born and bred
In heavenly throne, where thousand angels shine?
Thou dost the prayers of the righteous seed
Present before the Majesty Divine,
And his avenging wrath to clemency incline.

50.7 *the keys:* i.e., to the kingdom of
heaven, in contrast to the apostolic keys
of St. Peter (Matthew 16:19); these keys
belong to contemplation, the love of God,
rather than to the church.

52   'Yet since thou bidst, thy pleasure shall be done.
     Then come, thou man of earth, and see the way
     That never yet was seen of faery's son,
     That never leads the traveler astray,
     But after labors long and sad delay,
     Brings them to joyous rest and endless bliss.
     But first thou must a season fast and pray,
     Till from her bands the sprite assoilèd° is,   *released*
     And have her strength recured° from frail infirmities.'   *recovered*

53   That done, he leads him to the highest mount;
     Such one as that same mighty man of God,
     That blood-red billows like a wallèd front°   *barrier*
     On either side disparted with his rod
     Till that his army dry-foot through them yod,°   *went*
     Dwelt forty days upon. Where, writ in stone
     With bloody letters by the hand of God,
     The bitter doom° of death and baleful moan   *judgment*
     He did receive, whiles flashing fire about him shone.

54   Or like that sacred hill whose head full high,
     Adorned with fruitful olives all around,
     Is—as it were for endless memory
     Of that dear Lord who oft thereon was found—
     Forever with a flowering garland crowned;
     Or like that pleasant mount that is for aye
     Through famous poets' verse eachwhere° renowned,   *everywhere*
     On which the thrice three learned ladies play
     Their heavenly notes and make full many a lovely lay.

55   From thence, far off he unto him did shew
     A little path that was both steep and long,
     Which to a goodly city led his view;
     Whose walls and towers were builded high and strong
     Of pearl and precious stone, that earthly tongue
     Cannot describe, nor wit of man can tell—
     Too high a ditty° for my simple song.   *subject*

52.2 *man of earth:* It is possible that Contemplation is punning on Red Cross's as yet undisclosed name, George (61.8), Greek *georgos*, "husbandman," from *gaia*, "earth" (cf. Virgil's *Georgics*). Although the knight has made a spiritual pilgrimage from the delusions and sins of his earthly condition ("a clownish young man," "frail, fleshly wight") and later becomes a type of Christ, still he remains a man only and, therefore, earthly.

53.2–9 Mt. Sinai, where Moses received the severe Mosaic law (Exodus 24 and 34).

54.1–5 the Mount of Olives.

54.6 *that pleasant mount:* Mt. Parnassus, the seat of the nine muses. All of these are in fact famous examples of divine inspiration and mystical vision. Although Mt. Parnassus may seem anticlimatic after the examples from the Old and New Testaments, Spenser is asserting a doctrine of poetry which renaissance critics took seriously. The doctrine goes back to Plato's *Ion.*

The City of the Great King hight it well,
Wherein eternal peace and happiness doth dwell.

56 As he thereon stood gazing, he might see
The blessed angels to and fro descend
From highest heaven in gladsome company,
And with great joy into that city wend
As commonly° as friend does with his friend.   *familiarly*
Whereat he wondered much and gan inquere
What stately building durst so high extend
Her lofty towers unto the starry sphere,
And what unknowèn nation there empeopled° were.   *settled*

57 'Fair knight,' quoth he, 'Jerusalem that is,
The New Jerusalem, that God has built
For those to dwell in that are chosen his,
His chosen people purged from sinful guilt
With precious blood, which cruelly was spilt
On cursèd tree, of that unspotted lamb
That for the sins of all the world was kilt.
Now are they saints all in that city sam,°   *together*
More dear unto their God than younglings to their dam.'

58 'Till now,' said then the knight, 'I weenèd well°   *was sure*
That great Cleopolis—where I have been—
In which that fairest Faery Queen doth dwell,
The fairest city was that might be seen;
And that bright tower all built of crystal clean,°   *clear*
Panthea, seemed the brightest thing that was.
But now by proof all otherwise I ween;
For this great city that° does far surpass,   *that one*
And this bright angels' tower quite dims that tower of glass.'

59 'Most true,' then said the holy aged man;
'Yet is Cleopolis for earthly frame°   *as man-made*
The fairest piece that eye beholden can.   *structures go*
And well beseems all knights of noble name,
That covet in th' immortal book of fame
To be eternizèd, that same to haunt,
And done their service to that sovereign dame,
That glory does to them for guerdon° grant.   *reward*
For she is heavenly born and heaven may justly vaunt.° *claim as home*

56.1–5 "And he [Jacob] dreamed, and behold a ladder set up on the earth, and the top of it reached to heaven: and behold the angels of God ascending and descending on it" (Genesis 28:12).
58.2 *Cleopolis:* the Faeryland equivalent of London.
58.6 *Panthea:* the Faeryland equivalent of Westminster Abbey, the burial place of Britain's illustrious rulers and heroes.

60 'And thou, fair imp, sprung out from English race,
    However now accounted elfin's son,
    Well worthy dost thy service for her grace,°   *favor*
    To aid a virgin desolate fordone.
    But when thou famous victory hast won,
    And high amongst all knights hast hung thy shield,
    Thenceforth the suit° of earthly conquest shun,   *pursuit*
    And wash thy hands from guilt of bloody field.
    For blood can nought but sin, and wars but sorrows yield.

61 'Then seek this path that I to thee presage,
    Which after all, to heaven shall thee send;
    Then peaceably thy painful pilgrimage
    To yonder same Jerusalem do bend,
    Where is for thee ordained a blessed end.
    For thou amongst those saints, whom thou dost see,
    Shalt be a saint, and thine own nation's friend
    And patron. Thou Saint George shall callèd be,
    Saint George of merry England, the sign of victory.'

62 'Unworthy wretch,' quoth he, 'of so great grace,
    How dare I think such glory to attain?'
    'These that have it attained were in like case,'
    Quoth he, 'as wretched, and lived in like pain.'
    'But deeds of arms must I at last be fain,°   *willing*
    And ladies' love to leave, so dearly bought?'
    'What need of arms where peace doth aye remain,'
    Said he, 'and battles none are to be fought?
    As for loose loves, they're vain and vanish into nought.'

63 'O let me not,' quoth he, 'then turn again
    Back to the world, whose joys so fruitless are;
    But let me here for aye in peace remain,
    Or straightway on that last long voyage fare,
    That nothing may my present hope impair.'
    'That may not be,' said he, 'ne mayst thou yit
    Forgo that royal maid's bequeathèd care,°   *trouble*
    Who did her cause into thy hand commit,
    Till from her cursèd foe thou have her freely quit.'°   *released entirely*

64 'Then shall I soon,' quoth he, 'so God me grace,
    Abet° that virgin's cause disconsolate,   *support*
    And shortly back return unto this place

61.8 *St. George:* For a discussion of   *as wretched men.*
the St. George legend see Introduction,   62.8 *battles none are to be fought:*
pp. 10–15.   (1596). 1590 reads *bitter battles all are*
    62.4 *as wretched:* (1596). 1590 reads *fought.*

To walk this way in pilgrim's poor estate.
But now aread, old father, why of late
Didst thou behight° me born of English blood,   *call*
Whom all a faery's son done nominate?'°   *do call*
'That word° shall I,' said he, 'avouchen° good,   i.e. *"English,"*
Sith to thee is unknown the cradle of thy brood.   *prove*

65 'For well I wot thou springst from ancient race
Of Saxon kings, that have with mighty hand
And many bloody battles fought in place°   *there*
High reared their royal throne in Britons' land,
And vanquished them unable to withstand.
From thence a faery thee unweeting reft,°   *secretly stole*
There as thou slepst in tender swadling band,
And her base elfin brood there for thee left.
Such, men do changelings call, so changed by faery's theft.

66 'Thence she thee brought into this Faeryland,
And in an heapèd furrow did thee hide,
Where thee a plowman all unweeting fand,°   *unexpectedly*
As he his toilsome team that way did guide,   *found*
And brought thee up in plowman's state to bide,
Whereof Georgos he thee gave to name.
Till pricked with courage and thy force's pride,
To faery court thou came'st to seek for fame,
And prove thy puissant arms, as seems thee best became.'

67 'O holy sire,' quoth he, 'how shall I quite
The many favors I with thee have found,
That hast my name and nation read° aright,   *told*
And taught the way that does to heaven bound?'° *go*
This said, adown he lookèd to the ground
To have returned, but dazèd were his eyne
Through passing° brightness, which did quite confound *surpassing*
His feeble sense and too exceeding shine.
So dark are earthly things compared to things divine.

65.3 *place:* (1596). 1590 reads *face.*

66.3 *fand:* Here and at the other places where we use the spelling *fand* for 'found' and *band* for 'bound' the early editions invariably read *fond* and *bond.* In Spenser's time they were perfect rhymes for such words as *land, stand, hand,* and *brand,* with which he used them frequently, the vowel probably being about like the *a* in *father.* In nearly all such cases the *–and* words were normalized by the early printers to *-ond,* adding "eye rhyme" to the already perfect phonetic rhyme. Our practice has been to normalize in the other direction, changing the spelling of the archaic forms to indicate their rhyme with the still current ones. *Fand* and *band* are not, it ought to be said, the phonetic ancestors of *found* and *bound;* they are alternative forms which have since become archaic. In early Middle English such verbs had both singular and plural past tense forms which frequently differed in root vowel. Modern English *found* and *bound* are from the plural forms, while Spenser's *fand* and *band* are from the singular forms.

68 At last whenas himself he gan to find,
To Una back he cast him to retire,
Who him awaited still with pensive mind.
Great thanks and goodly meed° to that good sire   *gift*
He thence departing gave for his pain's hire.°   *reward*
So came to Una, who him joyed to see,
And after little rest gan him desire
Of her adventure mindful for to be.
So leave they take of Caelia and her daughters three.

CANTO xi

The knight with that old dragon fights
    Two days incessantly;
The third him overthrows, and gains
    Most glorious victory.

1 High time now gan it wax for Una fair
To think of those her captive parents dear,
And their forwasted kingdom to repair;
Whereto whenas they now approachèd near,
With hardy words her knight she gan to cheer,
And in her modest manner thus bespake:
'Dear knight, as dear as ever knight was dear,
That all these sorrows suffer for my sake,
High heaven behold the tedious toil ye for me take.

2 'Now are we come unto my native soil
And to the place where all our perils dwell.
Here haunts that fiend and does his daily spoil;
Therefore, henceforth be at your keeping° well   *on your guard*
And ever ready for your foeman fell.
The spark of noble courage now awake
And strive your excellent self to excel;
That° shall ye evermore renowmèd make   *i.e. the excelling*
Above all knights on earth that battle undertake.'

3 And pointing forth, 'Lo, yonder is,' said she,
'The brazen tower in which my parents dear,
For dread of that huge fiend, imprisoned be,
Whom I from far see on the walls appear,
Whose sight my feeble° soul doth greatly cheer.   *melancholy*
And on the top of all I do espy

    3.1–9 (1596). 1590 omits.

The watchman waiting tidings glad to hear.
That,° O my parents, might I happily   *i.e. tidings*
Unto you bring, to ease you of your misery!'

4   With that they heard a roaring hideous sound
    That all the air with terror fillèd wide,
    And seemed uneath° to shake the steadfast ground.   *uneasily*
    Eftsoons that dreadful dragon they espied
    Where stretched he lay upon the sunny side
    Of a great hill, himself like a great hill.
    But all so soon as he from far descried
    Those glistering arms that heaven with light did fill,
    He roused himself full blithe and hastened them until.°   *to*

5   Then bade the knight his lady yede° aloof   *go*
    And to an hill herself withdraw aside,
    From whence she might behold that battle's proof°   *outcome*
    And eke be safe from danger far descried.
    She him obeyed and turned a little wide.°   *to the side*
    Now, O thou sacred muse, most learnèd dame,
    Fair imp° of Phoebus and his aged bride,   *child*
    The nurse of time and everlasting fame,
    That° warlike hands ennoblest with immortal name: *who*

6   O gently come into my feeble breast.
    Come gently, but not with that mighty rage
    Wherewith the martial troops thou dost infest,°   *make fierce*
    And hearts of great heroès dost enrage,
    That nought their kindled courage may assuage.
    Soon as thy dreadful trump begins to sound,
    The god of war, with his fierce equipage,
    Thou dost awake, sleep never he so sound,
    And scarèd nations dost with horror stern astound.

7   Fair goddess, lay that furious fit° aside   *mood*
    Till I of wars and bloody Mars do sing,
    And Briton fields with Saracen blood bedyed,
    Twixt that great Faery Queen and paynim king,
    That with their horror heaven and earth did ring—
    A work of labor long, and endless praise.

5.6   *sacred muse:* Calliope, the muse of heroic poetry.
5.7   *aged bride:* Mnemosyne(memory). Spenser's account of the parentage of the muse probably derives from medieval rather than classical sources.
7.2–5   Probably the song "of wars and bloody Mars" refers to the epic of the "politic virtues" which Spenser projects in the Letter to Raleigh. The present poem is concerned with the private virtues, in Spenser's mind analogous to the *Odyssey,* which was commonly understood in the Renaissance to be an allegory of the virtuous man.

But now a while let down that haughty° string   *high-keyed*
And to my tunes thy second° tenor raise,   *supporting*
That I this man of God his godly arms may blaze.°   *celebrate*

8   By this the dreadful beast drew nigh to hand,
    Half flying and half footing in his haste,
    That with his largeness measurèd much land
    And made wide shadow under his huge waist,
    As mountain doth the valley overcast.
    Approaching nigh, he rearèd high afore
    His body monstrous, horrible, and vast,
    Which to increase his wondrous greatness more,
    Was swollen with wrath, and poison, and with bloody gore.

9   And over,° all with brazen scales was armed   *over his back*
    Like plated coat of steel, so couchèd near°   *closely arranged*
    That nought mote pierce, ne might his corse be harmed
    With dint of sword nor push of pointed spear.
    Which as an eagle, seeing prey appear
    His airy plumes doth rouse,° full rudely dight,°   *shake, arranged*
    So shakèd he that horror was to hear.
    For as the clashing of an armor bright,
    Such noise his rousèd scales did send unto the knight.

10 His flaggy wings, when forth he did display,
    Were like two sails in which the hollow° wind   *insubstantial*
    Is gathered full and worketh° speedy way.   *makes*
    And eke the pens° that did this pinions° bind   *quills, feathers*
    Were like main yards with flying canvas lined,
    With which whenas him list the air to beat,
    And there by force unwonted passage find,
    The clouds before him fled for terror great,
    And all the heavens stood still, amazèd with his threat.

11 His huge long tail, wound up in hundred folds,
    Does overspread his long brass-scaly back,

7.7–9   The imagery of this invocation is probably based on Plato's *Republic*, III.398–399, and on renaissance ideas about Greek music, specifically about the modes or scales of Greek music. After some discussion with Glaucon, Socrates decides that only two modes, the Dorian and the Phrygian, have any usefulness in the state (*Republic*, trans. H. D. P. Lee, Penguin Books, p. 139). In some renaissance treatments, the Dorian mode is solemn and majestic while the Phrygian is wild and warlike, suitable to arouse the courage of armies. The "haughty" ("high-pitched) Phrygian is appropriate to an epic of the "politic virtues." Here Spenser invokes the lower-pitched ("second tenor") Dorian voice of his muse as more fitting to an epic of the private virtues. (On Greek modes in the Renaissance see John Hollander, *The Untuning of the Sky*, Princeton University Press, 1961.)

8–14   Spenser's description of the dragon is largely derived from medieval convention in art and literature, though some details may be derived from Ovid's description of the serpent of Mars (*Metamorphoses*, III, pp. 81–82). The dragon is a type of the great beast of Revelation.

10.5   *lined:* (1596). 1590 reads *kynd.*

Whose wreathèd boughts° whenever he unfolds   *coils*
And thick entangled knots adown does slack—
Bespotted as with shields of red and black—
It sweepeth all the land behind him far,
And of three furlongs does but little lack.
And at the point two stings infixèd are,
Both deadly sharp, that sharpest steel exceeden far.

12   But stings and sharpest steel did far exceed
The sharpness of his cruel rending claws;
Dead was it sure, as sure as death in deed,°   *in its result*
Whatever thing does touch his ravenous paws,
Or what within his reach he ever draws.
But his most hideous head my tongue to tell
Does tremble; for his deep devouring jaws
Wide gapèd like the grisly mouth of hell,
Through which into his dark abyss all ravin° fell.   *prey*

13   And that° more wondrous was, in either jaw   *what*
Three ranks of iron teeth enrangèd° were,   *arranged in files*
In which yet trickling blood and gobbets raw
Of late devourèd bodies did appear,
That sight thereof bred cold congealèd fear.
Which to increase and all at once to kill,
A cloud of smothering smoke and sulfur sear°   *burning*
Out of his stinking gorge forth steamèd still,
That all the air about with smoke and stench did fill.

14   His blazing eyes, like two bright shining shields,
Did burn with wrath and sparkled living fire.
As two broad beacons, set in open fields,
Send forth their flames far off to every shire,
And warning give that enemies conspire
With fire and sword the region to invade,
So flamed his eyne with rage and rancorous ire;
But far within, as in a hollow glade,
Those glaring lamps were set, that° made a dreadful shade.   *which*

15   So dreadfully he towards him did pass,
Forelifting up aloft his speckled breast,
And often bounding on the bruisèd grass,

11.8–9 "They had tails like unto scorpions, and there were stings in their tails" (Revelation 9:10). Perhaps the two stings may be glossed as sin and death.
12.1–2 I.e., "But the sharpness of his claws exceeded that of his stings and of the sharpest steel."

12.4 *ravenous paws:* "And the beast which I saw was like unto a leopard and his feet were as the feet of a bear" (Revelation 13:2).
12.6 *his most hideous head:* "And his mouth as the mouth of a lion" (Revelation 13:2).

As for great joyance of his new-come guest.
Eftsoons he gan advance his haughty crest,
As chafèd° boar his bristles doth uprear,   *angered*
And shook his scales, to battle ready dressed—
That made the Red Cross Knight nigh quake for fear—
As bidding bold defiance to his foeman near.

16 The knight gan fairly couch his steady spear
And fiercely ran at him with rigorous might.
The pointed steel, arriving rudely there,
His harder hide would neither pierce nor bite,
But glancing by, forth passèd forward right.°   *on by*
Yet sore amovèd with so puissant push,
The wrathful beast about him turnèd light,°   *quickly*
And him so rudely, passing by, did brush
With his long tail that horse and man to ground did rush.

17 Both horse and man up lightly rose again,
And fresh encounter towards him addressed;
But th' idle stroke yet back recoiled in vain,
And found no place his° deadly point to rest.   *its*
Exceeding rage inflamed the furious beast
To be avengèd of so great despite;
For never felt his impierceable breast
So wondrous force from hand of living wight.
Yet had he proved° the power of many a puissant knight.   *tested*

18 Then with his waving wings displayèd wide,
Himself up high he lifted from the ground,
And with strong flight did forcibly divide
The yielding air, which nigh too feeble found
Her flitting parts° and element unsound°   *moving particles,*
To bear so great a weight. He cutting way   *weak*
With his broad sails, about him soarèd round;
At last low stooping with unwieldy sway,
Snatched up both horse and man to bear them quite away.

19 Long he them bore above the subject plain,°   *plain below*
So far as yewen° bow a shaft may send,   *yew*
Till struggling strong did him at last constrain
To let them down before his flight'ès end.
As haggard° hawk, presuming to contend   *wild*
With hardy fowl above his able might,°   *beyond his ability*
His weary pounces° all in vain doth spend°   *claws, tire*
To truss° the prey too heavy for his flight;   *clutch*
Which coming down to ground, does free itself by fight.

20 He so disseizèd° of his gripping gross,°   *deprived, great*
    The knight his thrillant° spear again assayed   *clawfull*
                                                              piercing
    In his brass-plated body to emboss,°   *plunge*
    And three men's strength unto the stroke he laid.
    Wherewith the stiff beam° quakèd as afraid,   *spear*
    And glancing from his scaly neck, did glide
    Close under his left wing, then broad displayed.°   *spread out*
    The piercing steel there wrought a wound full wide,
    That with the uncouth smart the monster loudly cried.

21 He cried as raging seas are wont to roar
    When wintry storm his wrathful wreck does threat:
    The rolling billows beat the ragged shore
    As they the earth would shoulder from her seat,
    And greedy gulf does gape as he would eat
    His neighbor element° in his revenge;   *i.e. the earth*
    Then gin the blustering bretheren° boldly threat   *i.e. winds*
    To move the world from off his steadfast hinge,°   *axis*
    And boistrous battle make, each other to avenge.

22 The steely head stuck fast still in his flesh,
    Till with his cruel claws he snatched the wood
    And quite asunder broke. Forth flowèd fresh
    A gushing river of black gory blood
    That drownèd all the land whereon he stood;
    The stream thereof would drive a water-mill.
    Trebly augmented was his furious mood
    With bitter sense of his deep-rooted ill,°   *wound*
    That flames of fire he threw forth from his large nostril.

23 His hideous tail then hurlèd he about,
    And therewith all enwrapped the nimble thighs
    Of his froth-foamy steed, whose courage stout,
    Striving to loose the knot that fast him ties,
    Himself in straiter bands too rash implies,°   *entangles*
    That to the ground he is perforce constrained
    To throw his rider; who can° quickly rise   *did*
    From off the earth with dirty blood distained,°   *stained*
    For that reproachful fall right foully he disdained.

24 And fiercely took his trenchant blade in hand,
    With which he struck so furious and so fell

22.1–7 The description probably owes something to Ovid's description of Cadmus wounding the serpent of Mars (*Metamorphoses*, III.69–73, p. 82).

23.1–5 "Next they seized Laocoön . . . they bound him in the giant spirals of their scaly length, twice around his middle, twice around his throat; and still their heads and necks towered above him. His hands strove frantically to wrench the knots apart" (*Aeneid*, II.213–220, p. 57).

That nothing seemed the puissance could withstand.
Upon his crest the hardened iron fell,
But his more hardened crest was armed so well
That deeper dent therein it would not make;
Yet so extremely did the buff him quell
That from thenceforth he shunned the like to take,
But when he saw them come, he did them still forsake.

25 The knight was wroth to see his stroke beguiled,
And smote again with more outrageous might;
But back again the sparkling steel recoiled
And left not any mark where it did light,
As if in adamant rock it had been pight.°   *struck*
The beast, impatient of his smarting wound
And of so fierce and forcible despite,°   *powerful injury*
Thought with his wings to sty° above the ground,   *soar*
But his late wounded wing unserviceable found.

26 Then full of grief and anguish vehement,
He loudly brayed, that like was never heard,
And from his wide devouring oven sent
A flake of fire, that flashing in his beard,
Him all amazed and almost made afeard.
The scorching flame sore swingèd° all his face,   *singed*
And through his armor all his body seared,
That he could not endure so cruel case,
But thought his arms to leave and helmet to unlace.

27 Not that great champion of the antique world,
Whom famous poets' verse so much doth vaunt
And hath for twelve huge labors high extolled,
So many furies and sharp fits did haunt,
When him the poisoned garment did enchant,
With centaur's blood and bloody verses charmed,
As did this knight twelve thousand dolors° daunt, *pains*
Whom fiery steel now burnt that erst him armed,
That erst him goodly armed, now most of all him harmed.

26–27 Red Cross's ordeal by fire in
these stanzas is clearly a type of Christ's
death on the cross. Medieval and renais-
sance commentators sometimes treated
Hercules as a type of Christ, and Spenser
was no doubt aware of this tradition
through Ronsard's "The Christian Her-
cules." Commenting on the agony of
Hercules after putting on the burning
shirt of Nessus, which Spenser refers to
here, the 14th century author of the
Ovide Moralisé treats the poisoned shirt
as a type of human flesh which Christ
put on "to receive death and torment"
(*Ovide Moralisé*, IX.932–952). And Ron-
sard writes:

As Hercules his wife's apparel donned,
Christ Jesus did a thing to correspond:
He took upon himself the human form,
And loved his human church with love so
     warm
That cruel death in her behalf he died,
Since he did mortal form Himself provide.

("The Christian Hercules," trans. Fred
W. Bornhauser)

The story of Hercules and the shirt of
Nessus is told in Ovid's *Metamorphoses*,
IX.134–272, pp. 224–229.

28 Faint, weary, sore, emboilèd, grievèd, brent,°   *burned*
    With heat, toil, wounds, arms, smart, and inward fire,
    That never man such mischiefs did torment—
    Death better were, death did he oft desire;
    But death will never come when needs require.
    Whom so dismayed when that his foe beheld,
    He cast to suffer him no more respire,°   *rest*
    But gan his sturdy stern° about to weld,°   *tail, whip*
    And him so strongly struck that to the ground him felled.

29 It fortunèd—as fair it then befell—
    Behind his back unweeting,° where he stood,   *unnoticed*
    Of ancient time there was a springing well°   *spring*
    From which fast trickled forth a silver flood,
    Full of great virtues and for med'cine good.
    Whilom before that cursèd dragon got
    That happy land, and all with innocent blood
    Defiled those sacred waves, it rightly hot°   *was called*
    The Well of Life, ne yet his° virtues had forgot.   *its*

30 For unto life the dead it could restore,
    And guilt of sinful crimes clean wash away.
    Those that with sickness were infected sore
    It could recure,° and aged long decay   *cure*
    Renew,° as one were born that very day.   *make young*
    Both Silo, this, and Jordan did excel,
    And th' English Bath and eke the German Spa,
    Ne can Cephise nor Hebrus match this well.
    Into the same the knight back overthrown fell.

31 Now gan the golden Phoebus for to steep
    His fiery face in billows of the west,
    And his faint steeds watered in ocean deep
    Whiles from their journal° labors they did rest,   *daily*
    When that infernal monster, having cast
    His weary foe into that living well,
    Can° high advance his broad discolored breast   *did*
    Above his wonted pitch° with countenance fell,   *height*
    And clapped his iron wings, as victor he did dwell.°   *remain*

30.6–8 *Silo:* the river Siloam, in whose waters a blind man was told by Jesus to wash and was cured (John 9:7). *Jordan:* the river whose crossing signified the salvation of the Jews (Deuteronomy 27:2–9), in which Naaman was cured of leprosy (II Kings 5:10–14), and in which John the Baptist baptized Christ (Matthew 3:16). *Bath* and *Spa:* both famous watering places noted for the curative powers of their water. *Cephise:* a river in Greece which flows by the temple of Justice (Themis). *Hebrus:* the river in Thrace into which the head of the murdered Orpheus was thrown (*Metamorphoses*, XI.50, p. 269). Orpheus is often a type of Christ in medieval tradition. The two biblical rivers, and especially Jordan, were customarily treated as types of baptism in medieval and renaissance commentary.

32 Which when his pensive lady saw from far,
    Great woe and sorrow did her soul assay,°   *attack*
    As weening that the sad end of the war;
    And gan to highest God entirely° pray   *earnestly*
    That fearèd chance° from her to turn away.   *fate*
    With folded hands and knees full lowly bent,
    All night she watched, ne once adown would lay
    Her dainty limbs in her sad dreariment,
    But praying still did wake, and waking did lament.

33 The morrow next gan early to appear
    That° Titan rose to run his daily race;   *when*
    But early ere the morrow next gan rear
    Out of the sea fair Titan's dewy face,
    Up rose the gentle virgin from her place,
    And lookèd all about if she might spy
    Her lovèd knight to move° his manly pace.   *moving*
    For she had great doubt of his safèty
    Since late she saw him fall before his enemy.

34 At last she saw where he upstarted brave
    Out of the well, wherein he drenchèd lay.
    As eagle fresh out of the ocean wave,
    Where he hath left his plumes all hoary gray
    And decked himself with feathers youthly gay,
    Like eyas hawk° up mounts unto the skies,   *fledgling hawk*
    His newly budded pinions to assay,
    And marvels at himself still as he flies;
    So new this new-born knight to battle new did rise.

35 Whom when the damnèd fiend so fresh did spy,
    No wonder if he wondered at the sight
    And doubted whether his late enemy
    It were or other new-supplièd knight.
    He now to prove his late renewèd might,
    High brandishing his bright dew-burning° blade,   *sparkling with*
    Upon his crested scalp so sore did smite   *dew*
    That to the skull a yawning wound it made.
    The deadly dint his dullèd senses all dismayed.

33.2 *Titan:* the sun god, Phoebus Apollo.

34.2–8 "Bless the Lord . . . who redeemeth thy life from destruction . . . who satisficth thy mouth with good things; so that thy youth is renewed like the eagle's" (Psalms 103:1–5). The legend is that when the eagle grows old he flies up toward the sun and burns his old feathers off, then dives into a pure spring and dips himself in three times, and is renewed. Since the eagle is a conventional type of Christ, this legend was treated as an allegory of the crucifixion and resurrection of Christ. It was also, by extension, an allegory of the baptism and salvation of all Christians.

35.5–9 Here Red Cross accomplishes the same feat as Arthur had earlier (Canto viii.16) and thus proves his similarity to Arthur in holiness.

36 I wot not whether the revenging steel
    Were hardened with that holy water dew
    Wherein he fell, or sharper edge did feel,
    Or his baptizèd hands now greater grew,
    Or other secret virtue did ensue;
    Else never could the force of fleshly arm
    Ne molten metal in his blood imbrew.°   *dye itself*
    For till that stound° could never wight him harm,   *moment*
    By subtlety, nor sleight, nor might, nor mighty charm.

37 The cruel wound enragèd him so sore
    That loud he yelded° for exceeding pain,   *yelled*
    As hundred ramping lions seemed to roar,
    Whom ravenous hunger did thereto constrain.
    Then gan he toss aloft his stretchèd train,
    And therewith scourge the buxom° air so sore   *unresisting*
    That to his force to yielden it was fain;°   *forced*
    Ne aught his sturdy strokes might stand afore,
    That high trees overthrew and rocks in pieces tore.

38 The same advancing high above his head,
    With sharp intended° sting so rude him smot   *outstretched*
    That to the earth him drove, as stricken dead;
    Ne living wight would have him life behot.°   *judged him to be*
    The mortal sting his angry needle shot   *alive*
    Quite through his shield and in his shoulder seized,
    Where fast it stuck, ne would thereout be got.
    The grief° thereof him wondrous sore diseased,° *pain, discom-*
    Ne might his rankling pain with patience be appeased.   *forted*

39 But yet more mindful of his honor dear
    Than of the grievous smart which him did wring,° *torture*
    From loathèd soil he can him lightly rear,
    And strove to loose the far infixèd sting;
    Which when in vain he tried with struggèling,
    Inflamed with wrath his raging blade he heft,°   *lifted*
    And struck so strongly that the knotty string
    Of his huge tail he quite asunder cleft;
    Five joints thereoff he hewed, and but the stump him left.

40 Heart cannot think what outrage and what cries,
    With foul enfouldered° smoke and flashing fire, *black as a*
    The hell-bred beast threw forth unto the skies,   *thunder cloud*
    That all was coverèd with darkness dire.
    Then fraught with rancor and engorgèd° ire,   *ravenous*

38.1–9   Red Cross's wound is another clear type of the crucifixion of Christ, who
was wounded in the side on the cross.

He cast at once him to avenge for all,°   *once and for all*
And gathering up himself out of the mire
With his uneven° wings, did fiercely fall   *unsteady*
Upon his sun-bright shield, and gripped it fast withal.

41 Much was the man encumbered with his hold,
In fear to lose his weapon in his paw,
Ne wist yet how his talons to unfold;
Nor harder was from Cerberus' greedy jaw
To pluck a bone, than from his cruel claw
To reave by strength the grippèd gage° away.   *prize*
Thrice he assayed it from his foot to draw,
And thrice in vain to draw it did assay;
It booted nought to think to rob him of his prey.

42 Tho° when he saw no power might prevail,   *then*
His trusty sword he called to his last aid,°   *as a last resort*
Wherewith he fiercely did his foe assail,
And double blows about him stoutly laid,
That glancing fire out of the iron played,
As sparkles from the anvil use to fly
When heavy hammers on the wedge° are swayed.° *ingot, struck*
Therewith at last he forced him to untie
One of his grasping feet, him° to defend thereby. *himself*

43 The other foot, fast fixèd on his shield,
Whenas no strength nor strokes mote him constrain
To loose, ne yet the warlike pledge to yield,
He smote thereat with all his might and main,
That nought so wondrous puissance might sustain.
Upon the joint the lucky steel did light,
And made such way that hewed it quite in twain.
The paw yet missèd not his minished° might, *diminished*
But hung still on the shield, as it at first was pight.

44 For grief thereof and devilish despite,
From his infernal furnace forth he threw
Huge flames, that dimmèd all the heavens' light,
Enrolled in duskish smoke and brimstone blue—
As burning Aetna from his boiling stew°   *pot*
Doth belch out flames and rocks in pieces broke,° *broken*

41.4 *Cerberus:* the watch dog of Hades, defeated by Hercules (*Metamorphoses*, VII.410–415, p. 180). *Nor:* (1609). 1590 and 1596 read *For.*

44.5–9 "But close by Etna thunders and its affrighting showers fall. Sometimes it ejects up to high heaven a cloud of utter black, bursting forth in a tornado of pitchy smoke with white-hot lava, and shoots tongues of flame to lick the stars. Sometimes the mountain tears out the rocks which are its entrails and hurls them upwards" (*Aeneid*, III.570–577, p. 92).

And ragged ribs of mountains molten new,° *newly*
Enwrapped in coal-black clouds and filthy smoke,
That all the land with stench and heaven with horror choke.

45 The heat whereof and harmful pestilence
So sore him noyed° that forced him to retire *troubled*
A little backward for his best defence,
To save his body from the scorching fire,
Which he from hellish entrails did expire.° *exhale*
It chanced—eternal God that chance did guide—
As he recoilèd backward, in the mire
His nigh forwearied feeble feet did slide,
And down he fell, with dread of shame sore terrified.

46 There grew a goodly tree him fair beside,
Loaden with fruit and apples rosy red,
As they in pure vermilion had been dyed,
Whereof great virtues over all° were read.° *everywhere,*
For happy life to all which thereon fed *reported*
And life eke everlasting did befall.
Great God it planted in that blessed stead° *place*
With his almighty hand, and did it call
The Tree of Life, the crime of our first father's fall.

47 In all the world like was not to be found,
Save in that soil where all good things did grow
And freely sprung out of the fruitful ground
As incorrupted nature did them sow,
Till that dread dragon all did overthrow.
Another like fair tree eke grew thereby,
Whereof whoso did eat eftsoons did know
Both good and ill. O mournful memory!
That tree through one man's fault hath done us all to die.° *killed us*

48 From that first tree forth flowed, as from a well,
A trickling stream of balm, most sovereign

46.1–9 "And out of the ground made the Lord God to grow every tree that is pleasant to the sight, and good for food: the tree of life also in the midst of the garden, and the tree of knowledge of good and evil" (Genesis 2:9). Besides the Tree of Life in Paradise there is the other one in the New Jerusalem: "In the midst of the street of it, and on either side of the river, was there the tree of life . . . and the leaves of the tree were for the healing of the nations" (Revelation 22:2).

46.9 *the crime:* Adam's fall banished man from Paradise and subjected him to death. It is thus the loss of the Tree of

Life which is Adam's crime.

47.6–9 This is the Tree of Knowledge of Good and Evil, whose fruit Adam and Eve, disobeying God, ate, and fell (Genesis 3:1–6).

48.1–9 "My father Adam, the first-created, laid him down on a time to die, and sent me to make supplication unto God hard by the gate of paradise, that he would lead me by his angel unto the tree of mercy, and I should take the oil and anoint my father, and he should arise from his sickness. Which also I did; and after my prayer an angel of the Lord came and said unto me . . . Depart there-

And dainty dear,° which on the ground still fell   *precious*
And overflowèd all the fertile plain,
As it had dewèd been with timely° rain.   *seasonable*
Life and long health that gracious° ointment gave,   *full of grace*
And deadly wounds could heal, and rear again
The senseless corse appointed° for the grave.   *prepared*
Into that same he fell, which did from death him save.

49 For nigh thereto the ever-damnèd beast
    Durst not approach, for he was deadly made,°   *death was his*
    And all that life preservèd did detest;   *essence*
    Yet he it oft adventured° to invade.   *attempted*
    By this the drooping daylight gan to fade
    And yield his room to sad succeeding night,
    Who with her sable mantle gan to shade
    The face of earth and ways of living wight,
    And high her burning torch set up in heaven bright.

50 When gentle Una saw the second fall
    Of her dear knight, who weary of long fight
    And faint through loss of blood, moved not at all,
    But lay as in a dream of deep delight,
    Besmeared with precious balm, whose virtuous might°   *curative power*
    Did heal his wounds and scorching heat allay—
    Again she stricken was with sore affright,
    And for his safety gan devoutly pray,
    And watch the noyous° night, and wait for joyous day. *harmful*

51 The joyous day gan early to appear,
    And fair Aurora from the dewy bed
    Of aged Tithon gan herself to rear,
    With rosy cheeks, for shame as blushing red;
    Her golden locks for haste were loosely shed
    About her ears when Una her did mark
    Climb to her chariot, all with flowers spread,
    From heaven high to chase the cheerless dark.
    With merry note her loud salutes the mounting lark.

52 Then freshly up arose the doughty knight,
    All healèd of his hurts and woundès wide,

---

fore and say unto thy father, that after there are accomplished from the creation of the world five thousand five hundred years, then shall the only-begotten Son of God become man and come down upon the earth, and he shall anoint him with that oil, and he shall arise: and with water and the Holy Ghost shall he wash him and them that come of him. And then shall he be healed of every disease ... (The Gospel of Nicodemus, Part II, Chap. III (Greek text), trans. M. R. James, *The Apocryphal New Testament*, Oxford, 1924, pp. 127–128). The oil with which Seth is to anoint his father Adam is, like the balm in this stanza, the blood of Christ, which redeems man from a living death in hell.

And did himself to battle ready dight.
Whose early° foe, awaiting him beside   *early rising*
To have devoured so soon as day he spied,
When now he saw himself so freshly rear,
As if late fight had nought him damnified,°   *injured*
He wox dismayed and gan his fate to fear.
Nath'less° with wonted rage he him advancèd near.   *nevertheless*

53 And in his first encounter, gaping wide,
He thought at once him to have swallowed quite,
And rushed upon him with outrageous pride.
Who him rencountering fierce as hawk in flight,
Perforce rebutted° back. The weapon bright,   *drove*
Taking advantage of his open jaw,
Ran through his mouth with so importune° might   *terrible*
That deep empierced his darksome hollow maw;
And back retired, his life blood forth withal did draw.

54 So down he fell, and forth his life did breathe,
That vanished into smoke and cloudès swift;
So down he fell, that th' earth him underneath
Did groan, as feeble so great load to lift;
So down he fell, as an huge rocky clift,
Whose false foundation waves have washed away,
With dreadful poise° is from the mainland rift,°   *force, torn*
And rolling down, great Neptune doth dismay.
So down he fell, and like an heapèd mountain lay.

55 The knight himself even trembled at his fall,
So huge and horrible a mass it seemed;
And his dear lady that beheld it all
Durst not approach for dread, which she misdeemed.°   *mistakenly felt*
But yet at last, whenas the direful fiend
She saw not stir, off shaking vain affright,
She nigher drew and saw that joyous end.
Then God she praised and thanked her faithful knight,
That had achieved so great a conquest by his might.

CANTO xii

Fair Una to the Red Cross Knight
Betrothèd is with joy,
Though false Duessa it to bar
Her false sleights do employ.

1 Behold I see the haven nigh at hand,
To which I mean my weary course to bend.
Veer° the main sheet, and bear up with° the land,   *let out, move*
The which afore is fairly to be kenned,°   *toward*
    seen
And seemeth safe from storms that may offend.
There this fair virgin weary of her way
Must landed be, now at her journey's end;
There eke my feeble bark° awhile may stay,   *small ship*
Till merry wind and weather call her thence away.

2 Scarcely had Phoebus in the glooming east
Yet harnessèd his fiery-footed team,
Ne reared above the earth his flaming crest,
When the last deadly smoke aloft did steam,
That sign of last outbreathèd life did seem
Unto the watchman on the castle wall;
Who thereby dead that baleful beast did deem,
And to his lord and lady loud gan call,
To tell how he had seen the dragon's fatal fall.

3 Uprose with hasty joy and feeble speed
That aged sire, the lord of all that land,
And lookèd forth to weet if true indeed
Those tidings were as he did understand;
Which whenas true by trial he out fand,°   *found out*
He bade to open wide his brazen gate,
Which long time had been shut, and out of hand°   *immediately*
Proclaimèd joy and peace through all his state;
For dead now was their foe which them forayèd° late.   *raided*

4 Then gan triumphant trumpets sound on high,
That sent to heaven the echoèd report

1.1–9 "Part of my work remains, part now is made, / And here my ship is by her anchor stayed" (Ovid, *The Art of Love*, I.779–780). This narrative metaphor was extremely popular in Latin poetry, being used by Virgil (*Georgics*, IV.116–117), Statius (*Thebiad*, XII.809), and Juvenal (*Satires*, I.149–150) as well as by Ovid. It was imitated extensively in the Middle Ages and the Renaissance—by Dante, Chaucer, and Ariosto (Ernest R. Curtius, *European Literature and the Latin Middle Ages*, trans. Willard R. Trask, Harper Torchbooks, pp. 128–130).

4–13 This greatly, and rightly praised festival scene may reflect the celebration

Of their new joy and happy victory
Gainst him that had them long oppressed with tort°   *injury*
And fast imprisonèd in siegèd fort.
Then all the people, as in solemn feast,°   *sacred festival*
To him assembled with one full consort,°   *all together*
Rejoicing at the fall of that great beast,
From whose eternal bondage now they were released.

5   Forth came that ancient lord and aged queen,
    Arrayed in antique robes down to the ground
    And sad° habiliments right well beseen.°   *somber, attractive*
    A noble crew about them waited round
    Of sage and sober peers all gravely° gowned,   *solemnly*
    Whom far before did march a goodly band
    Of tall young men all able arms to sound,°   *to make swords*
    But now they laurel branches bore in hand—   *ring*
    Glad sign of victory and peace in all their land.

6   Unto that doughty conqueror they came,
    And him before themselves prostrating low,
    Their lord and patron° loud did him proclaim,   *protector*
    And at his feet their laurel boughs did throw.
    Soon after them all dancing on a row,
    The comely virgins came with garlands dight,°   *adorned*
    As fresh as flowers in meadow green do grow
    When morning dew upon their leaves doth light;
    And in their hands sweet timbrels° all upheld on height.   *tambourines*

7   And them before, the fry° of children young   *crowd*
    Their wanton° sports and childish mirth did play,   *frisky*
    And to the maidens' sounding timbrels, sung
    In well attunèd° notes a joyous lay,   *harmonious*
    And made delightful music all the way,
    Until they came where that fair virgin stood.
    As fair Diana in fresh summer's day
    Beholds her nymphs enranged° in shady wood—   *spread out*
    Some wrestle, some do run, some bathe in crystal flood—

8   So she beheld those maidens' merriment
    With cheerful view; who when to her they came,
    Themselves to ground with gracious humbless bent
    And her adored by honorable name,°   *illustrious title*
    Lifting to heaven her everlasting fame.

---

of Queen Elizabeth's triumphal entry into
London to assume the crown in 1559.
Sermons delivered on the queen's annual
accession day festival (November 17)
regularly compared her accession to the
defeat of Antichrist (the pope) and the
reestablishment of true religion in Eng-
land.

Then on her head they set a garland green
And crownèd her twixt earnest and twixt game;°   *half in fun*
Who in her self-resemblance° well beseen,°   *appearance,*
Did seem such as she was, a goodly maiden queen.   *attractive*

9 And after, all the rascal meinie° ran,   *common rabble*
Heapèd together in rude rabblement,
To see the face of that victorious man,
Whom all admirèd° as from heaven sent,   *marveled at*
And gazed upon with gaping° wonderment.   *open-mouthed*
But when they came where that dead dragon lay,
Stretched on the ground in monstrous large extent,
The sight with idle° fear did them dismay,   *senseless*
Ne durst approach him nigh, to touch or once assay.

10 Some feared and fled; some feared and well it feigned.°   *hid*
One that would wiser seem than all the rest
Warned him not touch,° for yet perhaps remained   *not to touch him*
Some lingering life within his hollow breast,
Or in his womb might lurk some hidden nest
Of many dragonetts, his fruitful seed;
Another said that in his eyes did rest
Yet sparkling fire, and bade thereof take heed;
Another said he saw him move his eyes indeed.

11 One mother, whenas her foolhardy child
Did come too near and with his talons play,
Half dead through fear her little babe reviled,°   *scolded*
And to her gossips° gan in counsel say,   *friends*
'How can I tell but that his talons may
Yet scratch my son or rend his tender hand?'
So diversely° themselves in vain they fray,°   *in various ways,*
Whiles some more bold, to measure him nigh stand,   *frighten*
To prove° how many acres he did spread of land.   *find out*

12 Thus flockèd all the folk him round about,
The whiles that hoary° king with all his train,   *ancient*
Being arrivèd where that champion stout
After his foe's defeasance° did remain,   *defeat*
Him goodly greets and fair does entertain
With princely gifts of ivory and gold,
And thousand thanks him yields for all his pain.
Then when his daughter dear he does behold,
Her dearly doth embrace and kisseth manifold.

13 And after to his palace he them brings,
With shawms° and trumpets and with clarions sweet;   *oboes*

And all the way the joyous people sings,
And with their garments strows the pavèd street.
Whence mounting up, they find purveyance° meet — *provisions*
Of all that royal prince's court became;° — *was fitting to*
And all the floor was underneath their feet
Bespread with costly scarlet° of great name,° — *scarlet cloth, fame*
On which they lowly sit and fitting purpose° frame. — *conversation*

14 What needs me tell their feast and goodly guise,° — *manners*
In which was nothing riotous nor vain?
What needs of dainty dishes to devise,
Of comely services° or courtly train?° — *tableware, attendants*
My narrow leaves cannot in them contain
The large discourse° of royal prince's state. — *full description*
Yet was their manner then but bare and plain,
For th' antique world excess and pride did hate;
Such proud luxurious pomp is swollen up but late.

15 Then when with meats and drinks of every kind
Their fervent° appetites they quenchèd had, — *strong*
That ancient lord gan fit occasion find
Of strange adventures and of perils sad,
Which in his travel him befallen had,
For to demand of his renowmèd guest.
Who then, with utterance grave and countenance sad,
From point to point, as is before expressed,
Discoursed his voyage long, according° his request. — *agreeing to*

16 Great pleasure mixed with pitiful° regard — *compassionate*
That godly king and queen did passionate,° — *express with emotion*
Whiles they his pitiful adventures heard,
That oft they did lament his luckless state,
And often blame the too importune° fate — *grievous*
That heaped on him so many wrathful wreaks.° — *injuries*
For never gentle knight, as he of late,
So tossèd was in fortune's cruel freaks.
And all the while salt tears bedewed the hearers' cheeks.

17 Then said that royal peer in sober wise:° — *manner*
'Dear son, great been the evils which ye bore
From first to last in your late enterprise,
That I n'ot whether° praise or pity more. — *don't know whether to*
For never living man, I ween, so sore
In sea of deadly dangers was distressed,
But since now safe ye seizèd° have the shore — *reached*

15.1–9 This situation is taken from   Odysseus tells the story of his adventures
Homer's *Odyssey*, VIII–IX, in which   to the king and queen of Phaeacia.

And well arrivèd are—high God be blessed—
Let us devise of ease and everlasting rest.'

18 'Ah dearest lord,' said then that doughty knight,
    'Of ease or rest I may not yet devise,
    For by the faith which I to arms have plight,
    I bounden° am straight after this emprise,°   *obliged, adventure*
    As that your daughter can ye well advise,
    Back to return to that great Faery Queen,
    And her to serve six years in warlike wise,
    Gainst that proud paynim king that works her teen;°   *does her harm*
    Therefore I ought° crave pardon till I there have been.' *must*

19 'Unhappy falls that hard necessity,'
    Quoth he, 'the troubler of my happy peace
    And vowèd foe of my felicity;
    Ne I against the same can justly preace.°   *plead*
    But since that band° ye cannot now release,   *obligation*
    Nor done, undo—for vows may not be vain—
    Soon as the term of those six years shall cease,
    Ye then shall hither back return again,
    The marriage to accomplish vowed betwixt you twain.

20 'Which for my part I covet to perform,
    In sort as° through the world I did proclaim—   *in the way*
    That whoso killed that monster most deform,
    And him in hardy battle overcame,
    Should have mine only daughter to his dame,°   *wife*
    And of my kingdom heir apparent be.
    Therefore since now to thee pertains° the same   *belongs*
    By due desert of noble chivalry,
    Both daughter and eke kingdom, lo, I yield to thee.'

21 Then forth he callèd that his daughter fair,
    The fairest Un', his only daughter dear,
    His only daughter and his only heir;
    Who forth proceeding with sad sober cheer,
    As bright as doth the morning star appear
    Out of the east with flaming locks bedight,
    To tell that dawning day is drawing near,
    And to the world does bring long wishèd light—
    So fair and fresh that lady showed herself in sight.

22 So fair and fresh as freshest flower in May;
    For she had laid her mournful stole aside,
    And widow-like sad wimple° thrown away,   *veil*
    Wherewith her heavenly beauty she did hide

Whiles on her weary journey she did ride.
And on her now a garment she did wear,
All lily white withouten spot or pride,°   *ornament*
That seemed like silk and silver woven near;°   *closely*
But neither silk nor silver therein did appear.

23 The blazing brightness of her beauty's beam,
And glorious light of her sunshiny face,
To tell were as to strive against the stream.
My ragged rhymes are all too rude and base
Her heavenly lineaments° for to enhance.°   *features, praise*
Ne wonder; for her own dear lovèd knight,
All° were she daily with himself in place,   *although*
Did wonder much at her celestial sight;
Oft had he seen her fair,° but never so fair dight.°   *beautifully, dressed*

24 So fairly dight when she in presence came,
She to her sire made humble reverence
And bowèd low, that° her right well became   *which*
And added grace unto her excellence.
Who with great wisdom and grave eloquence
Thus gan to say. . . . But ere he thus had said,
With flying speed and seeming great pretence,°   *importance*
Came running in, much like a man dismayed,
A messenger with letters which his message said.

25 All in the open hall amazèd stood
At suddenness of that unwary° sight,   *unexpected*
And wondered at his breathless hasty mood.
But he for nought would stay his passage right,°   *straight*
Till fast° before the king he did alight,   *close*
Where falling flat, great humbless he did make,
And kissed the ground whereon his foot was pight;
Then to his hands that writ° he did betake,°   *document, deliver*
Which he disclosing, read thus, as the paper spake:

26 'To thee, most mighty king of Eden fair,
Her greeting sends, in these sad lines addressed,
The woeful daughter and forsaken heir
Of that great emperor of all the west,
And bids thee be advisèd for the best,
Ere thou thy daughter link in holy band

23.1–5 Spenser here employs one of the most common devices of the rhetoric of praise (epideictic). Curtius calls this device and others based on or related to it in purpose "inexpressibility topoi" (Curtius, pp. 159–162). They are related also to the devices the narrator or orator employs to create an attractive ethos, called by Curtius the topos of "affected modesty" (pp. 83–85). Spenser uses both topoi often.

Of wedlock to that new unknowen guest;
For he already plighted his right hand°
Unto another love and to another land.

i.e. betrothed
himself

27 'To me sad maid, or rather widow sad,
He was affiancèd long time before,
And sacred pledges he both gave and had—
False errant knight, infamous and forswore!
Witness the burning altars, which° he swore,
And guilty heavens° of his bold perjury;
Which though he hath polluted oft of yore,
Yet I to them for judgment just do fly,
And them conjure° t' avenge this shameful injury.

by which
heavens receiving
the guilt

appeal to

28 'Therefore since mine he is, or° free or bond,
Or false or true, or living or else dead,
Withhold, O sovereign prince, your hasty hand
From knitting league° with him, I you aread.
Ne ween° my right with strength adown to tread
Through weakness of my widowhead° or woe;
For truth is strong her rightful cause to plead,
And shall find friends if need requireth so.
So bids thee well to fare,
      Thy neither friend nor foe,
        Fidessa.'

whether

forming an
alliance
don't think
widowhood

29 When he these bitter biting words had read,
The tidings strange did him abashèd make,
That still he sat long time astonishèd
As in great muse,° ne word to creature spake.
At last his solemn silence thus he brake,
With doubtful eyes fast° fixèd on his guest:
'Redoubted knight, that for mine only sake
Thy life and honor late adventurest,°
Let nought be hid from me that ought to be expressed.

abstraction

firmly

risked

30 'What mean these bloody vows and idle threats,
Thrown out from womanish impatient mind?
What heavens? What altars? What enragèd heats,°
Here heapèd up with terms of love unkind,°
My conscience clear with guilty bands° would bind?
High God be witness that I guiltless am.
But if yourself, sir knight, ye faulty find,
Or wrappèd° be in loves of former dame,
With crime do not it cover, but disclose the same.'

passions
cruel and
unnatural
perjured agree-
ments

involved

31 To whom the Red Cross Knight this answer sent:
'My lord, my king, be nought hereat dismayed,

Till well ye wot by grave intendiment°   *serious consider-*
What woman, and wherefore,° doth me upbraid   *ation*
With breach of love and loyalty betrayed.   *why she*
It was in my mishaps, as hitherward
I lately traveled, that unwares I strayed
Out of my way through perils strange and hard,
That day should fail me ere I had them all declared.

32   'There did I find, or rather I was found,
Of this false woman that Fidessa hight,
Fidessa hight the falsest dame on ground,
Most false Duessa, royal richly dight,
That easy was t' inveigle° weaker sight.   *to deceive*
Who by her wicked arts and wily skill,
Too false and strong for earthly skill or might,
Unwares me wrought unto her wicked will,
And to my foe betrayed when least I fearèd ill.'

33   Then steppèd forth the goodly royal maid,
And on the ground herself prostrating low,
With sober countenance thus to him said:
'O pardon me, my sovereign lord, to show
The secret treasons which of late I know
To have been wrought by that false sorceress.
She, only she it is, that erst did throw
This gentle knight into so great distress
That death him did await in daily wretchedness.

34   'And now it seems that she subornèd° hath   *bribed*
This crafty messenger with letters vain,
To work new woe and improvided scath°   *unforeseen harm*
By breaking of the band betwixt us twain;
Wherein she usèd hath the practic pain°   *cunning skill*
Of this false footman cloaked with simpleness,°   *innocence*
Whom if ye please for to discover plain,
Ye shall him Archimago find, I guess,
The falsest man alive. Who tries shall find no less.'

35   The king was greatly movèd at her speech;
And all with sudden indignation freight,°   *overwhelmed*
Bade on that messenger rude hands to reach.
Eftsoons the guard, which on his state° did wait,   *greatness*
Attached° that faitor° false and bound him strait.   *seized, impostor*
Who seeming sorely chafèd at his band,
As chainèd bear whom cruel dogs do bait,
With idle force did feign them to withstand,
And often semblance made to scape out of their hand.

36 But they him laid full low in dungeon deep,
And bound him hand and foot with iron chains,
And with continual watch did warely keep.
Who then would think that by his subtle trains
He could escape foul death or deadly pains?
Thus when that prince's wrath was pacified,
He gan renew the late forbidden banes,°   *marriage agree-*
And to the knight his daughter dear he tied   *ment*
With sacred rites and vows forever to abide.

37 His own two hands the holy knots did knit
That none° but death forever can divide.   *nothing*
His own two hands, for such a turn° most fit,   *purpose*
The housling° fire did kindle and provide,   *sacramental*
And holy water thereon sprinkled wide.
At which the bushy tead° a groom did light,   *torch*
And sacred lamp in secret° chamber hide,   *secluded*
Where it should not be quenchèd day nor night,
For fear of evil fates, but burnen ever bright.

38 Then gan they sprinkle all the posts with wine,
And made great feast to solemnize that day.
They all° perfumed with frankincense divine   *everything*
And precious odors fetched from far away,
That all the house did sweat with great array.
And all the while sweet music did apply
Her curious° skill the warbling notes to play,   *intricate*
To drive away the dull melancholy;
The whiles one° sung a song of love and jollity.   *someone*

39 During the which, there was an heavenly noise
Heard sound through all the palace pleasantly,
Like as it had been many an angel's voice,
Singing before th' eternal Majesty
In their trinal triplicities° on high;   *threefold classes*
of three
Yet wist no creature whence that heavenly sweet°   *delight*
Proceeded, yet each one felt secretly°   *inwardly*
Himself thereby reft of his senses meet,°   *proper*
And ravishèd° with rare impression° in his sprite.   *carried away,*
sensation

40 Great joy was made that day of young and old
And solemn feast° proclaimed throughout the land,   *great celebration*
That their exceeding mirth may not be told.

39.1–9 "I heard as it were the voice of a great multitude, and as the voice of many waters . . . saying, Alleluia: for the Lord God omnipotent reigneth. Let us be glad and rejoice, and give honor to him: for the marriage of the Lamb is come, and his wife hath made herself ready" (Revelation 19:6–7).

Suffice it here by signs° to understand   *small indications*
The usual joys at knitting of love's band.
Thrice happy man the knight himself did hold,
Possessèd of his lady's heart and hand,
And ever when his eye did her behold,
His heart did seem to melt in pleasures manifold.

41   Her joyous presence and sweet company
In full content he there did long enjoy;
Ne wicked envy ne vile jealousy
His dear delights were able to annoy.
Yet swimming in that sea of blissful joy,
He nought forgot how he whilom had sworn,
In case he could that monstrous beast destroy,
Unto his Faery Queen back to return.
The which he shortly did, and Una left to mourn.

42   Now strike° your sails, ye jolly mariners,   *lower*
For we be come unto a quiet road,°   *harbor*
Where we must land some of our passengers,
And light this weary vessel of her load.
Here she a while may make her safe abode,
Till she repairèd have her tackles spent,°   *worn out rigging*
And wants supplied. And then again abroad,
On the long voyage whereto she is bent.
Well may she speed, and fairly finish her intent.

THE SECOND BOOK OF
THE FAERIE QUEENE

Containing

The Legend of Sir Guyon, or of Temperance

i   Right well I wot,° most mighty sovereign,   *know*
     That all this famous antique history,
     Of° some th' abundance of an idle brain   *by*
     Will judgèd be, and painted forgery,
     Rather than matter of just° memory;   *worthy of*
     Sith none that breatheth living air does know
     Where is that happy land of faèry
     Which I so much do vaunt yet nowhere show,
     But vouch° antiquities, which nobody can know.   *assert*

ii But let that man with better sense advise°   *take note*
     That of the world least part to us is read;°   *revealed*
     And daily how through hardy enterprise,
     Many great regions are discoverèd,
     Which to late age were never mentionèd.
     Who ever heard of th' Indian Peru?
     Or who in venturous vessel measurèd
     The Amazons' huge river, now found true?
     Or fruitfullest Virginia, who did ever view?

iii Yet all these were, when no man did them know,
     Yet have from wisest ages hidden been;
     And later times things more unknown shall show.

ii.6–*iii*.9 The newly discovered lands of America were presented in renaissance writing as utopian paradises. The idea of life on the moon, also a favorite theme of renaissance utopian writers, exercised some of the most original minds of the period, including the German, Nicholas of Cusa, and the Italian, Giordano Bruno.

Why then should witless man so much misween°   *think wrongly*
That nothing is but that which he hath seen?
What if within the moon's fair shining sphere—
What if in every other star unseen
Of other worlds he happily° should hear?   *by chance*
He wonder would much more; yet such to some appear.

iv Of Faeryland yet if he more inquire,
By certain signs here set in sundry place
He may it find; ne let him then admire,
But yield his sense to be too blunt and base,
That n'ot° without an hound fine footing° trace.   *does not know how, tracks*
And thou, O fairest princess under sky,
In this fair mirror° mayst behold thy face,   *i.e. Gloriana*
And thine own realms in land of faèry,
And in this antique image° thy great ancestry.   *i.e. the poem*

v   The which O pardon me thus to enfold
In covert veil, and wrap in shadow's light,
That feeble eyes your glory may behold,
Which else could not endure those beamès bright,
But would be dazzled with exceeding light.
O pardon, and vouchsafe with patient ear
The brave adventures of this faery knight,
The good Sir Guyon, graciously to hear,
In whom great rule of temperance goodly doth appear.

CANTO i

Guyon by Archimage abused,°   *tricked*
    The Red Cross Knight awaits,
Finds Mordant and Amavia slain
    With pleasure's poisoned baits.

1   That cunning architect of cankered guile,
Whom prince's late displeasure left in bands
For falsèd° letters and subornèd° wile,   *forged, perjured*
Soon as the Red Cross Knight he understands
To been departed out of Eden lands,
To serve again his sovereign elfin queen,

iv.6 *fairest princess:* Queen Elizabeth.
iv.9 See particularly the parallel chronicles of England and Faeryland in Canto x.
v.1–5 Spenser turns an apology for his allegorical method into a hyperbolical compliment to Queen Elizabeth. Her blinding glory, too bright to be represented directly, is compared, by implication, to that of God, truth, Zeus, and the sun, all symbols or analogies of kingship in medieval and renaissance thought.
1.1 *architect of . . . guile:* Archimago.

His arts he moves, and out of caitiffs'° hands   *wretches'*
Himself he frees by secret means unseen—
His shackles empty left, himself escapèd clean.

2   And forth he fares full of malicious mind
To worken mischief and avenging woe
Wherever he that godly knight may find,
His only heartsore and his only foe,
Sith Una now he algates° must forgo,   *completely*
Whom his° victorious hands did erst° restore   *i.e. Red Cross's,*
                                                                         formerly
To native crown and kingdom late y-go;°   *lately*
Where she enjoys sure peace for evermore,
As weather-beaten ship arrived on happy shore.

3   Him therefore now the object of his spite
And deadly feud he makes; him to offend
By forgèd treason or by open fight
He seeks, of all his drift° the aimèd end.°   *scheming, object*
Thereto his subtle engines he does bend,
His practic wit° and his fair filèd° tongue,   *cunning, eloquent*
With thousand other sleights. For well he kenned°   *knew*
His credit now in doubtful balance hung;
For hardly could be hurt, who was already stung.

4   Still° as he went he crafty stales° did lay   *continually, baits*
With cunning trains° him to entrap unwares,   *snares*
And privy spials° placed in all his way   *secret agents*
To weet° what course he takes and how he fares,   *find out*
To catch him at avantage° in his snares.   *opportune time*
But now so wise and wary was the knight,
By trial° of his former harms and cares,   *through experi-*
                                                                   ence
That he descried and shunnèd still his sleight.
The fish that once was caught, new bait will hardly bite.

5   Nath'less° th' enchanter would not spare his pain,°   *nevertheless, effort*
In hope to win occasion to his will;
Which when he long awaited had in vain,
He changed his mind from one to other ill,
For to all good he enemy was still.
Upon the way him fortunèd to meet,
Fair marching underneath a shady hill,
A goodly knight, all armed in harness meet,°   *appropriate*
That from his head no place appearèd to his feet.

6   His carriage was full comely and upright,
His countenance demure and temperate,

3.7–9   Archimago knew that it was   Cross. Once injured by him, Red Cross
going to be difficult to restore the balance   would be exceedingly wary.
(win revenge) in his warfare with Red

But yet so stern and terrible in sight
That cheered his friends and did his foes amate.°   *dismay*
He was an elfin° born of noble state°   *elf, rank*
And mickle worship° in his native land;   *great honor*
Well could he tourney and in lists debate,°   *fight*
And knighthood took of good Sir Huon's hand,
When with King Oberon he came to Faeryland.

7   Him als° accompanied upon the way   *also*
    A comely° palmer, clad in black attire,   *dignified*
    Of ripest years and hairs all hoary gray,
    That with a staff his feeble steps did stire,°   *steer*
    Lest his long way his aged limbs should tire.
    And if by looks one may the mind aread,
    He seemed to be a sage and sober sire,
    And ever with slow pace the knight did lead,
    Who taught his trampling steed with equal steps° to tread. *even gait*

8   Such whenas Archimago them did view,
    He weenèd well to work some uncouth° wile.   *strange*
    Eftsoons untwisting his deceitful clew,°   *plot*
    He gan to weave a web of wicked guile,
    And with fair countenance and flattering style, .
    To them approaching, thus the knight bespake:
    'Fair son of Mars, that seek with warlike spoil
    And great achievements great yourself to make,
    Vouchsafe to stay your steed for humble miser's sake.'

9   He stayed his steed for humble miser's sake,
    And bade tell on the tenor of his plaint;
    Who feigning then in every limb to quake
    Through inward fear, and seeming pale and faint,
    With piteous moan his piercing speech gan paint:
    'Dear lady, how shall I declare thy case,
    Whom late I left in langorous constraint?
    Would God thyself now present were in place°   *here*
    To tell this rueful tale! Thy sight could win thee grace.

10 'Or rather would, O would it so had chanced,
    That you, most noble sir, had present been
    When that lewd ribald,° with vile lust advanced,°   *lecher, moved*
    Laid first his filthy hands on virgin clean,
    To spoil her dainty corpse° so fair and sheen,   *body*
    As on the earth, great mother of us all,

6.8–9 For Oberon, a faery king, see   hero of the very popular late medieval
Canto x.76. Sir Huon, befriended by King   romance, *Huon of Bordeaux.*
Oberon and brought to Faeryland, is the

With living eye more fair was never seen
Of chastity and honor virginal.
Witness ye heavens, whom she in vain to help did call.'

11 'How may it be,' said then the knight half wroth,
  'That knight should knighthood ever so have shent?'°   *disgraced*
  'None but that saw,' quoth he, 'would ween° for troth   *think*
  How shamefully that maid he did torment.
  Her looser° golden locks he rudely rent,   *flowing*
  And drew her on the ground, and his sharp sword
  Against her snowy breast he fiercely bent,
  And threatened death with many a bloody word.
  Tongue hates to tell the rest, that eye to see abhorred.'

12 Therewith amovèd from his sober mood,
  'And lives he yet,' said he, 'that wrought this act,
  And done° the heavens afford him vital food?'   *do*
  'He lives,' quoth he, 'and boasteth of the fact,°   *deed*
  Ne yet hath any knight his courage cracked.'
  'Where may that treacher then,' said he, 'be found,
  Or by what means may I his footing tract?'
  'That shall I show,' said he, 'as sure as hound
  The stricken deer doth challenge° by the bleeding wound.' *track*

13 He stayed not lenger° talk, but with fierce ire   *longer*
  And zealous haste away is quickly gone
  To seek that knight, where him that crafty squire
  Supposed to be. They do arrive anon
  Where sat a gentle lady all alone,
  With garments rent and hair dishevelèd,
  Wringing her hands and making piteous moan;
  Her swollen eyes were much disfigurèd,
  And her fair face with tears was foully blubberèd.

14 The knight approaching nigh, thus to her said,
  'Fair lady, through foul sorrow ill bedight,°   *afflicted*
  Great pity is to see you thus dismayed,
  And mar the blossom of your beauty bright;
  Forthy° appease your grief and heavy plight,   *therefore*
  And tell the cause of your conceivèd° pain.   *obvious*
  For if he live that hath you done despite,
  He shall you do due recompense again,
  Or else his wrong with greater puissance maintain.'

15 Which when she heard, as in despiteful wise,
  She willfully her sorrow did augment,
  And offered hope of comfort did despise.

Her golden locks most cruelly she rent,
And scratched her face with ghastly dreariment,
Ne would she speak ne see, ne yet be seen,
But hid her visage, and her head down bent,
Either for grievous shame or for great teen,°   *grief*
As if her heart with sorrow had transfixèd° been.   *pierced*

16 Till her that squire bespake, 'Madame my lief,°   *dear*
For God's dear love be not so willful bent,
But do vouchsafe now to receive relief,
The which good fortune doth to you present.
For what boots it to weep and to waiment°   *lament*
When ill is chanced, but doth the ill increase
And the weak mind with double woe torment?'
When she her squire heard speak, she gan appease
Her voluntary° pain, and feel some secret ease.   *willful*

17 Eftsoon she said, 'Ah gentle trusty squire,
What comfort can I woeful wretch conceive,
Or why should ever I henceforth desire
To see fair heaven's face, and life not leave,
Sith that false traitor did my honor reave?'°   *steal*
'False traitor certes,' said the faery knight,
'I read the man that ever would deceive
A gentle lady, or her wrong through might.
Death were too little pain for such a foul despite.°   *injury*

18 'But now, fair lady, comfort to you make,
And read° who hath ye wrought this shameful plight,   *tell*
That short revenge the man may overtake
Whereso he be, and soon upon him light.'
'Certes,' said she, 'I wot not how he hight,°   *what his name is*
But under him a gray steed he did wield,
Whose sides with dappled circles weren dight;
Upright he rode, and in his silver shield
He bore a bloody cross that quartered all the field.'

19 'Now by my head,' said Guyon, 'much I muse°   *wonder*
How that same knight should do so foul amiss,
Or ever gentle damsel so abuse;
For may I boldly say, he surely is
A right good knight, and true of word y-wis.°   *certainly*
I present was, and can it witness well,
When arms he swore, and straight did enterpriss°   *undertake*
Th' adventure of the Errant Damosel,
In which he hath great glory won, as I hear tell.

    19.8 *Errant Damosel*: Una.

20 'Nath'less he shortly shall again be tried,
   And fairly quite him of th' imputed blame,
   Else be ye sure he dearly shall abide,°   *suffer*
   Or make you good amendment for the same.
   All wrongs have mends, but no amends of shame.
   Now therefore, lady, rise out of your pain
   And see the salving of your blotted name.'
   Full loath she seemed thereto, but yet did feign;
   For she was inly° glad her purpose so to gain.   *secretly*

21 Her purpose was not such as she did feign
   Ne yet her person such as it was seen,°   *as it appeared*
   But under simple show and semblant plain°   *honest appear-*
   Lurked false Duessa, secretly unseen,   *ance*
   As a chaste virgin that had wrongèd been.
   So had false Archimago her disguised,
   To cloak her guile with sorrow and sad teen;°   *grief*
   And eke himself had craftily devised
   To be her squire, and do her service well aguised.°   *costumed*

22 Her late forlorn and naked he had found
   Where she did wander in waste wilderness,
   Lurking in rocks and caves far under ground,
   And with green moss covering her nakedness
   To hide her shame and loathly filthiness,
   Sith her Prince Arthur of proud ornaments
   And borrowed beauty spoiled. Her natheless,°   *nevertheless*
   Th' enchanter finding fit for his intents,
   Did thus revest,° and decked with due habiliments.°   *clothe, dress*

23 For all he did, was to deceive good knights
   And draw them from pursuit of praise and fame,
   To slug in sloth and sensual delights,
   And end their days with irrenowmèd shame.
   And now exceeding grief him overcame
   To see the Red Cross thus advancèd high;
   Therefore this crafty engine° he did frame,°   *plot, invent*
   Against his praise to stir up enmity
   Of such as virtues like mote unto him ally.

24 So now he Guyon guides an uncouth° way   *strange*
   Through woods and mountains, till they came at last
   Into a pleasant dale that lowly lay
   Betwixt two hills, whose high heads overplaced

20.7 *blotted:* (1596). 1590 reads *blot-*   enmity of those whose similar virtues
ting.   might naturally ally them with holiness.
23.8–9   *to stir . . . ally:* to stir up the

The valley did with cool shade overcast;
Through midst thereof a little river rolled,
By which there sat a knight with helm unlaced,
Himself refreshing with the liquid cold,
After his travel long and labors manifold.

25 'Lo yonder he,' cried Archimage aloud,
'That wrought the shameful fact which I did shew,°   *show*
And now he doth himself in secret shroud,
To fly the vengeance for his outrage due;
But vain, for ye shall dearly do him rue,°   *make him repent*
So° God ye speed and send you good success,   *if*
Which we far off will here abide to view.'
So they him left, inflamed with wrathfulness,
That straight against that knight his spear he did address.

26 Who seeing him from far so fierce to prick,
His warlike arms about him gan embrace,°   *put on*
And in the rest his ready spear did stick;
Tho° whenas still he saw him towards pace,   *then*
He gan rencounter° him in equal race.   *charge*
They been y-met,° both ready to affrap,°   *met, strike*
When suddenly that° warrior gan abase°   *the other, lower*
His threatened spear, as if some new mishap
Had him betid,° or hidden danger did entrap.   *happen to*

27 And cried, 'Mercy, sir knight, and mercy lord,
For mine offense and heedless hardiment,°   *recklessness*
That had almost committed crime abhorred,
And with reproachful shame mine honor shent,°   *disgraced*
Whiles cursèd steel against that badge I bent,
The sacred badge of my Redeemer's death,
Which on your shield is set for ornament.'
But his fierce foe his steed could stay uneath,°   *with difficulty*
Who pricked with courage keen did cruel battle breathe.

28 But when he heard him speak, straightway he knew
His error, and himself inclining said,
'Ah, dear Sir Guyon, well becometh you,
But me behooveth rather to upbraid,
Whose hasty hand so far from reason strayed
That almost it did heinous violence
On that fair image of that heavenly maid
That decks and arms your shield with fair defense;
Your court'sy takes on you another's due offense.'

29 So been° they both at one, and done° uprear   *are, do*
Their beavers bright, each other for to greet;

28.7   *heavenly maid:* Gloriana, the Faery Queen.

Goodly comportance° each to other bear,   *behavior*
And entertain themselves with court'sies meet.
Then said the Red Cross Knight, 'Now mote I weet,°   *might I know*
Sir Guyon, why with so fierce saliance°   *assault*
And fell intent ye did at erst me meet;
For sith I know your goodly governance,°   *conduct*
Great cause, I ween,° you guided, or some uncouth chance.'   *assume*

30 'Certes,' said he, 'well mote I shame to tell
The fond encheason° that me hither led.   *foolish cause*
A false infamous faitor° late befell   *villain*
Me for to meet, that seemèd ill bestead,°   *in trouble*
And plained° of grievous outrage, which he read°   *complained, said*
A knight had wrought against a lady gent;
Which to avenge, he to this place me led,
Where you he made the mark of his intent,
And now is fled. Foul shame him follow where he went.'

31 So can° he turn his earnest unto game   '   *did*
Through goodly handling and wise temperance.
By this, his aged guide in presence came;
Who soon as on that knight his eye did glance,
Eftsoons of him had perfect cognizance°—   *recognized him*
Sith him in faery court he late avised°—   *saw*
And said, 'Fair son, God give you happy chance,
And that dear cross upon your shield devised,
Wherewith above all knights ye goodly seem aguised.°   *armed*

32 'Joy you may have, and everlasting fame,
Of late most hard achievement by you done,
For which enrollèd is your glorious name
In heavenly registers above the sun,
Where you a saint with saints your seat have won.
But wretched we, where ye have left your mark,
Must now anew begin, like° race to run;   *a similar*
God guide thee, Guyon, well to end thy wark,°   *work*
And to the wishèd haven bring thy weary bark.'

33 'Palmer,' him answerèd the Red Cross Knight,
'His be the praise that this achievement wrought,
Who made my hand the organ of His might.
More than goodwill to me attribute nought;
For all I did, I did but as I ought.
But you, fair sir, whose pageant next ensues,
Well mote ye thee° as well can wish your thought,   *prosper*
That home ye may report thrice happy news;
For well ye worthy been for worth and gentle thews.'°   *manners*

33.8 *thrice:* (1596). 1590 reads *these.*

34   So courteous congé° both did give and take   *farewell*
     With right hands plighted, pledges of good will.
     Then Guyon forward gan his voyage make
     With his black palmer, that him guided still;°   *always*
     Still he him guided over dale and hill,
     And with his steady staff did point his way.
     His race° with reason, and with words his will,   *movements*
     From foul intemperance he oft did stay,
     And suffered not in wrath his hasty steps to stray.

35   In this fair wise they traveled long y-fere,°   *together*
     Through many hard assays° which did betide;°   *trials, happen*
     Of which he honor still away did bear,
     And spread his glory through all countries wide.
     At last, as chanced them by a forest side
     To pass, for succor from the scorching ray,
     They heard a rueful voice, that dernly° cried   *dismally*
     With piercing shrieks and many a doleful lay;°   *moan*
     Which to attend, awhile their forward steps they stay.

36   'But if that careless heavens,' quoth she, 'despise
     The doom of just revenge, and take delight
     To see sad pageants of men's miseries—
     As bound° by them to live in lives' despite—   *condemned*
     Yet can they not warn death from wretched wight.
     Come then, come soon, come sweetest death to me,
     And take away this long lent loathèd light;
     Sharp be thy wounds, but sweet the med'cines be
     That long captivèd souls from weary thraldom free.

37   'But thou, sweet babe, whom frowning froward° fate   *hostile*
     Hath made sad witness of thy father's fall,
     Sith heaven thee deigns to hold in living state,
     Long mayst thou live, and better thrive withal
     Than to thy luckless parents did befall.
     Live thou, and to thy mother dead attest
     That clear she died from blemish criminal;
     Thy little hands imbrued° in bleeding breast   *stained*
     Lo I for pledges leave. So give me leave to rest.'

38   With that a deadly shriek she forth did throw
     That through the wood re-echoèd again,
     And after gave a groan so deep and low

34.5–9   It is thus clear that Sir Guyon is not an allegorical representative of perfect temperance, but of the achievement of temperance through right reason (the palmer).

35.7   *a rueful voice:* that of Amavia, whose story—one of the most important allegorical episodes in Book II—occupies the remainder of Canto i.

That seemed her tender heart was rent in twain,
Or thrilled° with point of thorough-piercing° pain;   *pierced, (through-)*
As gentle hind—whose sides with cruel steel
Through launchèd, forth her bleeding life does rain,
Whiles the sad pang° approaching she does feel—   *i.e. death*
Brays out her latest breath, and up her eyes doth seal.

39   Which when that warrior heard, dismounting straight
From his tall steed, he rushed into the thick,
And soon arrivèd where that sad portrait
Of death and dolor lay, half dead, half quick;
In whose white alabaster breast did stick
A cruel knife that made a grisly wound,
From which forth gushed a stream of gore-blood thick,
That all her goodly garments stained around,
And into a deep sanguine° dyed the grassy ground.   *red*

40   Pitiful spectacle of deadly smart,
Beside a bubbling fountain low she lay,
Which she increasèd with her bleeding heart,
And the clean waves with purple gore did ray.°   *discolor*
Als° in her lap a lovely babe did play   *also*
His cruel sport, instead of sorrow due;
For in her streaming blood he did embay°   *bathe*
His little hands, and tender joints imbrue°—   *soak*
Pitiful spectacle as ever eye did view.

41   Besides them both, upon the soilèd grass
The dead corse° of an armèd knight was spread,   *body*
Whose armor all with blood besprinkled was.
His ruddy lips did smile, and rosy red
Did paint his cheerful cheeks, yet being dead;
Seemed to have been a goodly personage,
Now in his freshest flower of lustihead,
Fit to inflame fair lady with love's rage,
But that fierce fate did crop the blossom of his age.

42   Whom when the good Sir Guyon did behold,
His heart gan wax as stark° as marble stone,   *stiff*
And his fresh blood did freeze with fearful cold,
That all his senses seemed bereft at one.°   *at once*
At last his mighty ghost° gan deep to groan,   *soul*
As lion grudging° in his great disdain   *complaining*
Mourns inwardly and makes to himself moan;
Till ruth and frail affection did constrain
His stout courage to stoop, and show his inward pain.

43 Out of her gorèd wound the cruel steel
    He lightly snatched, and did the floodgate stop
    With his fair garment; then gan softly feel
    Her feeble pulse to prove if any drop
    Of living blood yet in her veins did hop;°   *pulse*
    Which when he felt to move, he hopèd fair
    To call back life to her forsaken shop.°   *form*
    So well he did her deadly wounds repair
    That at the last she gan to breathe out living air.

44 Which he perceiving greatly gan rejoice,
    And goodly counsel (that for wounded heart
    Is meetest med'cine) tempered with sweet voice:
    'Ay me, dear lady, which the image art
    Of rueful pity and impatient smart,
    What direful chance, armed with avenging fate,
    Or cursèd hand hath played this cruel part,
    Thus foul to hasten your untimely date?
    Speak, O dear lady, speak; help never comes too late.'

45 Therewith her dim eyelids she up gan rear,
    On which the dreary death did sit, as sad°   *heavy*
    As lump of lead, and made dark clouds appear;
    But whenas him all in bright armor clad
    Before her standing she espièd had,
    As one out of a deadly dream affright
    She weakly started, yet she nothing drad.°   *dreaded*
    Straight down again herself in great despite
    She groveling threw to ground, as hating life and light.

46 The gentle knight her soon with careful pain
    Uplifted light, and softly did uphold;
    Thrice he her reared, and thrice she sunk again,
    Till he his arms about her sides gan fold,
    And to her said, 'Yet if the stony cold
    Have not all seizèd on your frozen heart,
    Let one word fall that may your grief unfold,
    And tell the secret of your mortal smart.
    He oft finds present help who does his grief impart.'

47 Then casting up a deadly look, full low
    She sighed from bottom of her wounded breast,
    And after, many bitter throbs did throw;
    With lips full pale and faltering tongue oppressed,
    These words she breathèd forth from riven chest:
    'Leave, ah leave off, whatever wight thou be,
    To let° a weary wretch from her due rest,   *keep*

And trouble dying soul's tranquility.
Take not away now got, which none would give to me.'

48   'Ah far be it,' said he, 'dear dame, fro me
To hinder soul from her desirèd rest,
Or hold sad life in long captivity;
For all I seek is but to have redressed
The bitter pangs that doth your heart infest.
Tell then, O lady, tell what fatal prief°   *experience*
Hath with so huge misfortune you oppressed,
That I may cast to compass° your relief,   *plan to*
Or die with you in sorrow and partake your grief.'   *accomplish*

49   With feeble hands then stretchèd forth on high,
As heaven accusing guilty of her death,
And with dry drops congealèd in her eye,
In these sad words she spent her utmost breath:
'Hear then, O man, the sorrows that uneath°   *hardly*
My tongue can tell, so far all sense they pass.
Lo this dead corpse that lies here underneath,
The gentlest knight that ever on green grass
Gay steed with spurs did prick, the good Sir Mordant was.

50   'Was—ay the while, that he is not so now—
My lord, my love— my dear lord, my dear love—
So long as heavens just with equal° brow   *impartial*
Vouchsafèd to behold us from above.
One day when him high courage did emmove,
As wont ye knights, to seek adventures wild,
He prickèd forth his puissant force to prove;°   *test*
Me then he left enwombèd of this child,
This luckless child, whom thus ye see with blood defiled.

51   'Him fortunèd—hard fortune ye may guess—
To come where vile Acrasia does won,°   *live*
Acrasia a false enchantèress,
That many errant knights hath foul fordone.°   *destroyed*
Within a wandering island that doth run
And stray in perilous gulf her dwelling is.
Fair sir, if ever there ye travel, shun
The cursèd land where many wend amiss,
And know it by the name: it hight° the Bower of Bliss.   *is called*

52   'Her bliss is all in pleasure and delight,
Wherewith she makes her lovers drunken mad,

49.9 *Mordant:* death-giving, as explained in Stanza 55.
50.8 *this child:* Ruddymane, the bloody-handed babe.

51.3–4 *Acrasia:* from the Greek *akratos*, 'powerless, not having command over a thing; incontinent, lacking power or control over oneself.'

And then with words and weeds° of wondrous might,   *herbs*
On them she works her will to uses bad.
My liefest° lord she thus beguilèd had,   *dearest*
For he was flesh—all flesh doth frailty breed.
Whom when I heard to been so ill bestad,°   *situated*
Weak wretch I wrapped myself in palmer's weed°   *habit*
And cast to seek him forth through danger and great dreed.°   *dread*

53   'Now had fair Cynthia by even turns
Full measurèd three quarters of her year,
And thrice three times had filled her crooked horns,
Whenas my womb her burden would forbear,°   *give up*
And bade me call Lucina to me near.
Lucina came: a man child forth I brought.
The woods, the nymphs, my bowers, my midwives were—
Hard help at need. So dear the babe I bought,
Yet nought too dear I deemed, while so my dear I sought.

54   'Him so I sought, and so at last I found,
Where him that witch had thrallèd to her will,
In chains of lust and lewd desires y-bound,
And so transformèd from his former skill°   *intelligence*
That me he knew not, neither his own ill;
Till through wise handling and fair governance,
I him recurèd to a better will,
Purgèd from drugs of foul intemperance.
Then means I gan devise for his deliverance.

55   'Which when the vile enchantèress perceived,
How that my lord from her I would reprive,°   *rescue*
With cup thus charmed, him parting she deceived:
"Sad verse, give death to him that death does give,
And loss of love to her that loves to live,
So soon as Bacchus with the nymph does link."
So parted we and on our journey driv,°   *drove*
Till coming to this well, he stooped to drink.
The charm fulfilled, dead suddenly he down did sink.

56   'Which when I wretch . . . .' Not one word more she said;
But breaking off the end for want of breath,
And sliding soft, as down to sleep her laid,
And ended all her woe in quiet death.
That seeing, good Sir Guyon could uneath°   *hardly*

53.5 *Lucina:* Diana or Juno as pre-
siding goddesses of childbirth.
53.7 I.e., "The woods were my
bowers, the nymphs were my midwives."
That Ruddymane was born under such

chaste, natural auspices is allegorically
significant.
54.5 Ignorance, the darkening of rea-
son, was one of the chief effects of the
fall of Adam.

From tears abstain, for grief his heart did grate;°   *quake*
And from so heavy sight his head did wreath,°   *turn*
Accusing fortune and too cruel fate,
Which plungèd had fair lady in so wretched state.

57   Then turning to his palmer said, 'Old sire,
    Behold the image of mortality,
    And feeble nature clothed with fleshly tire,
    When raging passion with fierce tyranny
    Robs reason of her due regality,
    And makes it servant to her basest part.
    The strong it weakens with infirmity,
    And with bold fury arms the weakest heart.
    The strong through pleasure soonest falls, the weak through
      smart.'

58   'But temperance,' said he, 'with golden squire°   *square*
    Betwixt them both can measure out a mean:
    Neither to melt in pleasure's hot desire,
    Nor fry in heartless grief and doleful teen.
    Thrice happy man who fares them both atween.
    But sith this wretched woman overcome
    Of anguish, rather than of crime, hath been,
    Reserve her cause to her eternal doom,
    And in the mean° vouchsafe her honorable tomb.'   *meantime*

59   'Palmer,' quoth he, 'death is an equal doom
    To good and bad, the common inn of rest;
    But after death the trial is to come,
    When best shall be to them that livèd best.
    But both alike, when death hath both suppressed,
    Religious reverence doth burial teen.°   *allot*
    Which whoso wants,° wants so much of his rest;   *lacks*
    For all so great shame after death I ween,
    As self to dyen bad, unburied bad to been.'

60   So both agree their bodies to engrave.°   *bury*
    The great earth's womb they open to the sky,
    And with sad cypress seemly it embrave;°   *decorate*
    Then covering with a clod their closèd eye,
    They lay therein those corses tenderly,
    And bid them sleep in everlasting peace.
    But ere they did their utmost obsequy,

57.4–6 I.e., "when raging passion usurps the ruling function of reason and makes reason the subject rather than the governor of the emotions."

58.1 *squire:* the set-square, a common renaissance emblem of temperance.

59.6–7 Sir Guyon's attitude toward burial and the ensuing ceremony seem more Greek or Roman than Christian.

Sir Guyon more affection to increase,
Benempt° a sacred vow, which none should aye° release.   *took, ever*

61   The dead knight's sword out of his sheath he drew,
With which he cut a lock of all their hair,
Which medling with their blood and earth, he threw
Into the grave, and gan devoutly swear:
'Such and such evil, God on Guyon rear,
And worse and worse, young orphan, be thy pain,
If I or thou due vengeance do forbear,
Till guilty blood her guerdon° do obtain.'   *reward*
So shedding many tears, they closed the earth again.

CANTO ii

Babe's bloody hands may not be cleansed;
    The face of Golden Mean.
Her sisters, two extremities,
    Strive her to banish clean.

1   Thus when Sir Guyon with his faithful guide
Had with due rites and dolorous lament
The end of their sad tragedy uptied,
The little babe up in his arms he hent;°   *took*
Who with sweet pleasance° and bold blandishment,   *pleasure*
Gan smile on them, that rather ought to weep,
As careless of his woe or innocent
Of that° was done, that ruth empiercèd deep   *what*
In that knight's heart, and words with bitter tears did steep.

2   'Ah luckless babe, born under cruel star,
And in dead parents' baleful ashes bred,
Full little weenest thou what sorrows are
Left thee for portion of thy livelihead,°   *livelihood*
Poor orphan in the wide world scatterèd,
As budding branch rent from the native tree,
And thrown forth till it be witherèd.
Such is the state of men: thus enter we
Into this life of woe, and end with misery.'

3   Then soft himself inclining on his knee
Down to that well, did in the water ween°—   *think*

60.8 *more affection to increase:* to
arouse in himself more determination.
61.8 *guilty blood:* The blood of Ama-
via, spilled through the guilt of Acrasia,
will be rewarded by the destruction of
Acrasia.

2.2 *baleful ashes bred:* an allusion to
the phoenix, a fabulous bird that dies in
flames and is reborn out of its own ashes.
Literally, this appears to contradict
Amavia's story of Ruddymane's birth,
Canto i.

So love does loathe disdainful nicety°—   *cold fastidious-*
His° guilty hands from bloody gore to clean.   *ness*
He washed them oft and oft, yet nought they been *i.e. Ruddymane's*
For all his washing cleaner. Still he strove,
Yet still the little hands were bloody seen;
The which him into great amazement drove,
And into diverse doubt his wavering wonder clove.

4 He wist not whether blot of foul offence
    Might not be purged with water nor with bath;
    Or that high God, in lieu of innocence,
    Imprinted had that token of his wrath
    To show how sore blood-guiltiness he hat'th;°   *hateth*
    Or that the charm and venom which they drunk,
    Their blood with secret filth infected hath,
    Being diffusèd through the senseless trunk,
    That through the great contagion direful deadly stunk.

5 Whom thus at gaze, the palmer gan to board°   *speak to*
    With goodly reason, and thus fair bespake:
    'Ye been right hard amated,° gracious lord,   *dismayed*
    And of your ignorance great marvel make,
    Whiles cause not well conceivèd° ye mistake.   *understood*
    But know that secret virtues are infused
    In every fountain and in every lake,
    Which who hath skill them rightly to have choosed,
    To proof of° passing wonders hath full often used.   *in causing*

6 'Of those some were so from their source° endued°   *beginning,*
    By great Dame Nature, from whose fruitful pap   *endowed*
    Their well-heads spring and are with moisture dewed;
    Which feeds each living plant with liquid sap,
    And fills with flowers fair Flora's painted lap.
    But other some by gift of later grace,
    Or by good prayers, or by other hap,
    Had virtue poured into their waters base,
    And thenceforth were renowmed, and sought from place to
      place.

4.8 *the senseless trunk:* For the use of a singular noun to denote a plural referent, compare Canto i.60.4, "Then covering with a clod their closèd eye."

4.9 The stench of the so recently dead corpses of Mordant and Amavia appears to confirm at least the last of Guyon's speculations about the unwashable blood on Ruddymane's hands.

6.2 *Dame Nature:* For the importance and meaning of nature in medieval and renaissance allegory, see especially Alanus de Insulis, *De Planctu Naturae*, trans. D. M. Moffat, Yale Studies in English, 36, 1908; Jean de Meun, *The Romance of the Rose*, pp. 365–413; *The Faerie Queene*, Book III, Canto vi; also "Mutability Cantos," vii, and notes.

6.5 *fair Flora's painted lap:* For a typical representation of Flora, the goddess of flowers, in renaissance painting, see Botticelli's *Primavera*. See Book I.i.48.9,n.

7 'Such is this well, wrought by occasion strange,
   Which to her nymph befell. Upon a day,
   As she the woods with bow and shafts did range,
   The heartless° hind and roebuck to dismay,   *timid*
   Dan Faunus chanced to meet her by the way,
   And kindling fire at her fair burning eye,
   Inflamèd was to follow beauty's chase,°   *hunt*
   And chasèd her, that fast from him did fly;
   As hind from her, so she fled from her enemy.

8 'At last when failing breath began to faint,
   And saw no means to scape, of shame afraid, ,
   She set her down to weep for sore constraint,°   *distress*
   And to Diana calling loud for aid,
   Her dear besought to let her die a maid.
   The goddess heard, and sudden where she sate,
   Welling out streams of tears and quite dismayed
   With stony fear of that rude rustic mate,
   Transformed her to a stone from steadfast virgin's state.

9 'Lo now she is that stone, from whose two heads,
   As from two weeping eyes, fresh streams do flow,
   Yet° cold through fear and old conceivèd dreads.   *still*
   And yet the stone her semblance seems to show,
   Shaped like a maid, that such ye may her know;
   And yet her virtues in her water bide,
   For it is chaste and pure, as purest snow,
   Ne° lets her waves with any filth be dyed,   *nor*
   But ever like herself unstainèd hath been tried.°   *found*

10 'From thence it comes that this babe's bloody hand
   May not be cleansed with water of this well.
   Ne certes, sir, strive you it to withstand,
   But let them still be bloody as befell,
   That they his mother's innocence may tell,
   As she bequeathed in her last testament;
   That as a sacred symbol it may dwell

7-9 The palmer's story of the nymph's well is a conscious Spenserian imitation of an Ovidian metamorphosis; see *Metamorphoses*, I (Daphne), IX (Byblis), XIII (Acis). Spenser's most immediate source for the story appears to have been an allegorical myth in Giovanni Giorgio Trissino's *L'Italia Liberata da Gotti*, IV.

7.5 *Dan Faunus:* in Roman myth, often treated as the equivalent of Pan, the satyr god of nature. See Book I.vi. 15–17.

7.7 *Chase* is emended by most editors to *prey* in order to preserve the rhyme. There are, however, four other passages in Book II, and nine altogether in *The Faerie Queene*, in which the early editions give a non-rhyming word in a position where an obvious synonym would rhyme. Spenser was apparently indulging in intentional metrical imperfection. The other imperfect rhymes in Book II are at ii.42.6, iii.28.7, viii.29.7, and xii.54.7.

8.4 *Diana:* virgin goddess of chastity and the hunt.

In her son's flesh to mind° revengèment,   *remind of*
And be for all chaste dames an endless monument.'

11 He harkened to his reason, and the child
    Uptaking, to the palmer gave to bear;
    But his sad father's arms with blood defiled,
    An heavy load, himself did lightly rear.
    And turning to that place in which whilere°   *before*
    He left his lofty steed with golden sell°   *saddle*
    And goodly gorgeous barbs,° him found not there.   *armor*
    By other accident that erst befell
    He is conveyed, but how or where, here fits not tell.

12 Which when Sir Guyon saw, all were he° wroth,   *although he was*
    Yet algates° mote° he soft himself appease   *regardless, must*
    And fairly fare on foot, however loath;
    His double burden did him sore disease.°   *discomfort*
    So long they travelèd with little ease,
    Till that at last they to a castle came,
    Built on a rock adjoining to the seas;
    It was an ancient work of antique fame,
    And wondrous strong by nature and by skillful frame.°   *design*

13 Therein three sisters dwelt of sundry° sort,   *differing*
    The children of one sire by mothers three;
    Who dying whilom° did divide this fort   *sometime before*
    To them by equal shares in equal fee.°   *right of ownership*
    But strifeful mind and diverse quality
    Drew them in parts, and each made others' foe.
    Still° did they strive and daily disagree;   *continually*
    The eldest did against the youngest go,
    And both against the middest meant to worken woe.

14 Where when the knight arrived, he was right well
    Received—as knight of so much worth became—
    Of° second sister, who did far excel   *by*
    The other two. Medina was her name,
    A sober sad and comely courteous dame;
    Who rich arrayed, and yet in modest guise,°   *fashion*
    In goodly garments that her well became,
    Fair marching forth in honorable wise,
    Him at the threshold met and well did enterprise.°   *entertain*

15 She led him up into a goodly bower,
    And comely courted with meet modesty;

12.8 *fame:* (1596). 1590 reads *frame.*   the soul, as described in Plato's *Republic,*
13.2 *by mothers three:* the rational,   IX.580–581 (p. 355).
the appetitive, and the ireful powers of   14.4 *Medina:* the golden mean.

Ne in her speech, ne in her havior,
Was lightness seen or looser° vanity,   *too loose*
But gracious womanhood and gravity,
Above the reason of her youthly years.
Her golden locks she roundly did uptie
In braided trammels, that no looser hairs
Did out of order stray about her dainty ears.

16 Whilst she herself thus busily did frame°   *apply*
Seemly to entertain her new-come guest,
News hereof to her other sisters came,
Who all this while were at their wanton rest,
According° each her friend with lavish fest.   *entertaining*
They were two knights of peerless puissance,
And famous far abroad for warlike gest,°   *deed*
Which to these ladies love did countenance,°   *show*
And to his mistress each himself strove to advance.

17 He that made love unto the eldest dame
Was hight Sir Huddibras, an hardy man;
Yet not so good of deeds as great of name,
Which he by many rash adventures wan,°   *won*
Since errant arms to sue° he first began.   *pursue*
More huge in strength than wise in works he was,
And reason with foolhardice overran;
Stern melancholy did his courage pass,°   *surpass*
And was for terror more all armed in shining brass.

18 But he that loved the youngest was Sansloy,
He that fair Una late foul outragèd,
The most unruly and the boldest boy
That ever warlike weapons managèd,
And to all lawless lust encouragèd
Through strong opinion of his matchless might.
Ne aught he cared whom he endamagèd
By tortuous wrong, or whom bereaved of right.
He now this lady's champion chose for love to fight.

19 These two gay knights, vowed to so diverse loves,
Each other does envy with deadly hate,
And daily war against his foeman moves,
In hope to win more favor with his mate,
And th' other's pleasing service to abate°   *diminish*
To magnify his own. But when they heard

18.1 *Sansloy:* the would-be rapist who   18.9 *this lady's champion:* i.e., "as
attacked Una when she had been forsaken   this lady's champion."
by Red Cross.

How in that place strange knight arrivèd late,
Both knights and ladies forth right angry fared,
And fiercely unto battle stern themselves prepared.

20 But ere they could proceed unto the place
Where he abode, themselves at discord fell,
And cruel combat joined in middle space.
With horrible assault and fury fell,
They heaped huge strokes, the scornèd life to quell,
That all on uproar from her settled seat
The house was raised, and all that in did dwell;
Seemed that loud thunder with amazement great
Did rend the rattling skies with flames of fouldering° heat.   *thundering*

21 The noise thereof called forth that stranger knight
To weet° what dreadful thing was there in hand;   *find out*
Where whenas two brave knights in bloody fight
With deadly rancor he enrangèd° fand,°   *poised, found*
His sunbroad shield about his wrist he band,°   *bound*
And shining blade unsheathed, with which he ran
Unto that stead,° their strife to understand;   *place*
And at his first arrival, them began
With goodly means to pacify well as he can.

22 But they him spying, both with greedy force
At once upon him ran, and him beset
With strokes of mortal steel without remorse,
And on his shield like iron sledges bet.°   *beat*
As when a bear and tiger being met
In cruel fight on Lybic ocean wide,
Espy a traveler with feet surbet,°   *bruised*
Whom they in equal prey hope to divide,
They stint their strife, and him assail on every side.

23 But he, not like a weary traveler,
Their sharp assault right boldly did rebut,
And suffered not their blows to bite him near,
But with redoubled buffs them back did put.
Whose grievèd minds, which choler° did englut,   *anger*
Against themselves turning their wrathful spite,
Gan with new rage their shields to hew and cut;
But still when Guyon came to part their fight,
With heavy load on him they freshly gan to smite.

24 As a tall ship tossèd in troublous seas—
Whom raging winds, threatening to make the prey

22.6 *Lybic ocean:* the undulating sand dunes of the Lybian desert.

Of the rough rocks, do diversely disease°— *afflict*
Meets two contrary billows by the way
That her on either side do sore assay,° *attack*
And boast to swallow her in greedy grave;
She scorning both their spites does make wide way,
And with her breast breaking the foamy wave,
Does ride on both their backs, and fair herself doth save.

25   So boldly he him bears, and rusheth forth
Between them both, by conduct° of his blade. *skillful use*
Wondrous great prowess and heroic worth
He showed that day, and rare ensample° made, *example*
When two so mighty warriors he dismayed.
At once he wards and strikes, he takes and pays,
Now forced to yield, now forcing to invade,
Before, behind, and round about him lays.
So double was his pains, so double be his praise.

26   Strange sort of fight, three valiant knights to see
Three combats join in one, and to deraign° *engage in*
A triple war with triple enmity,
All for their ladies' froward° love to gain, *perverse*
Which gotten was but hate. So Love does reign
In stoutest minds and maketh monstrous war;
He maketh war, he maketh peace again,
And yet his peace is but continual jar.
O miserable men, that to him subject are.

27   Whilst thus they mingled were in furious arms,
The fair Medina with her tresses torn
And naked breast, in pity of their harms,
Amongst them ran, and falling them beforn,
Besought them by the womb which them had borne,
And by the loves which were to them most dear,
And by the knighthood which they sure had sworn,
Their deadly cruel discord to forbear,
And to her just conditions of fair peace to hear.

28   But her two other sisters standing by,
Her loud gainsaid, and both their champions bade
Pursue the end of their strong enmity,
As° ever of their loves they would be glad. *if*
Yet she with pithy words and counsel sad,° *sober*
Still strove their stubborn rages to revoke,
That at the last suppressing fury mad,
They gan abstain from dint of direful stroke,
And hearken to the sober speeches which she spoke:

28.2   *their:* (1596). 1590 reads *her.*

29   'Ah puissant lords, what cursèd evil sprite
     Or fell Erinys in your noble hearts
     Her hellish brand hath kindled with despite,
     And stirred you up to work your willful smarts?
     Is this the joy of arms? Be these the parts
     Of glorious knighthood, after blood to thrust,°   *thirst*
     And not regard due right and just deserts?
     Vain is the vaunt, and victory unjust,
     That more to mighty hands than rightful cause doth trust.

30   'And were there rightful cause of difference,
     Yet were not better fair it to accord°   *reconcile*
     Than with blood-guiltiness to heap offence,
     And mortal vengeance join to crime abhorred?
     O fly from wrath, fly, O my liefest° lord.   *dearest*
     Sad be the sights and bitter fruits of war,
     And thousand furies wait on wrathful sword;
     Ne aught the praise of prowess more doth mar
     Than foul revenging rage and base contentious jar.

31   'But lovely concord and most sacred peace
     Doth nourish virtue, and fast friendship breeds;
     Weak she makes strong, and strong thing does increase
     Till it the pitch of highest praise exceeds.
     Brave be her wars and honorable deeds,
     By which she triumphs over ire and pride,
     And wins an olive garland for her meeds.°   *rewards*
     Be therefore, O my dear lords, pacified,
     And this misseeming° discord meekly lay aside.'   *unseemly*

32   Her gracious words their rancor did appall,
     And sunk so deep into their boiling breasts
     That down they let their cruel weapons fall,
     And lowly did abase their lofty crests
     To her fair presence and discreet behests.
     Then she began a treaty to procure,
     And stablish terms betwixt both their requests,
     That as a law forever should endure;
     Which to observe in word of knights they did assure.

33   Which to confirm, and fast to bind their league,
     After their weary sweat and bloody toil,
     She them besought, during their quiet treague,°   *truce*
     Into her lodging to repair awhile,

29.2 *Erinys:* here the spirit of irrational fury in man. In Greek and Roman mythology, the Erinyes, also called the Furies or Eumenides, were spirits of retribution. See Aeschylus, *The Eumenides.*

To rest themselves and grace to reconcile.
They soon consent; so forth with her they fare,
Where they are well received and made to spoil
Themselves of soilèd arms, and to prepare
Their minds to pleasure and their mouths to dainty fare.

34 And those two froward sisters, their fair loves,
Came with them eke, all were they wondrous loath,
And feignèd cheer, as for the time° behooves,   *occasion*
But could not color yet so well the troth
But that their natures bad appeared in both.
For both did at their second sister grutch°   *complain*
And inly grieve, as doth an hidden moth
The inner garment fret, not th' utter° touch;   *outer*
One thought her cheer too little, th' other thought too much.

35 Elissa—so the eldest hight—did deem
Such entertainment base; ne aught would eat,
Ne aught would speak, but evermore did seem
As discontent for want of mirth or meat.
No solace could her paramour entreat
Her once to show, ne court nor dalliance;
But with bent lowering brows, as she would threat,
She scowled and frowned with froward countenance,
Unworthy of fair lady's comely governance.°   *behavior*

36 But young Perissa was of other mind,
Full of disport,° still laughing, loosely light,   *playfulness*
And quite contrary to her sister's kind;
No measure in her mood, no rule of right,
But pourèd out in pleasure and delight.
In wine and meats she flowed above the bank,
And in excess exceeded her own might;
In sumptuous tire she joyed herself to prank,°   *display*
But of her love too lavish—little have she thank.

37 Fast by her side did sit the bold Sansloy,
Fit mate for such a mincing minion,°   *affected mistress*
Who in her looseness took exceeding joy;
Might not be found a franker franion,°   *looser rake*
Of her lewd parts° to make companion.   *behavior*
But Huddibras, more like a malcontent,
Did see and grieve at his bold fashion;
Hardly could he endure his hardiment,
Yet still he sat and inly did himself torment.

35.1 *Elissa:* deficiency, from Greek   *perissos*, "excesses in relation to the
elleipsis, "deficiency in moral virtue."   mean."
36.1 *Perissa:* excess, from Greek

38 Betwixt them both the fair Medina sate
    With sober grace and goodly carriage.
    With equal measure she did moderate
    The strong extremities of their outrage:
    That forward pair she ever would assuage
    When they would strive due reason to exceed;
    But that same froward twain would accourage,°   *enliven*
    And of her plenty add unto their need.
    So kept she them in order, and herself in heed.°   *authority*

39 Thus fairly she attemperèd° her feast,   *regulated*
    And pleased them all with meet satiety.
    At last when lust of meat and drink was ceased,
    She Guyon dear besought of courtesy
    To tell from whence he came through jeopardy,
    And whither now on new adventure bound.
    Who with bold grace and comely gravity,
    Drawing to him the eyes of all around,
    From lofty siege° began these words aloud to sound: *seat*

40 'This thy demand, O lady, doth revive
    Fresh memory in me of that great queen,
    Great and most glorious virgin queen alive,
    That with her sovereign power and scepter sheen°   *bright*
    All Faeryland does peaceably sustain.
    In widest ocean she her throne does rear,
    That over all the earth it may be seen;
    As morning sun her beams dispreaden° clear,   *spread out*
    And in her face fair peace and mercy doth appear.

41 'In her the richess° of all heavenly grace   *wealth*
    In chief degree are heapèd up on high;
    And all that else this world's enclosure base
    Hath great or glorious in mortal eye
    Adorns the person of her majesty,
    That men beholding so great excellence
    And rare perfection in mortality,
    Do her adore with sacred reverence,
    As th' idol° of her Maker's great magnificence.   *symbol*

42 'To her I homage and my service owe,
    In number of° the noblest knights on ground,   *along with*

38.5 *forward pair*: Perissa and Sans-
loy.
38.7 *twain*: Elissa and Huddibras.
39–46 Spenser early establishes Gu-
yon's kinship with the heroes of the
Odyssey and, especially, the *Aeneid*.

Here Guyon's account of his adventures
is paralleled by the accounts of Odysseus
and Aeneas in *Odyssey*, IX–XII, and
Aeneid, II–III.
40.5 *peaceably*: (1596). 1590 reads
peaceable.

Mongst whom on me she deignèd to bestow
Order of Maidenhead, the most renowned
That may this day in all the world be found.
An yearly solemn feast she wonts° to make   *is accustomed*
The day that first doth lead the year around,
To which all knights of worth and courage bold
Resort, to hear of strange adventures to be told.

43   'There this old palmer showed himself that day,
And to that mighty princess did complain
Of grievous mischieves, which a wicked fay°   *fairy*
Had wrought and many whelmed° in deadly pain,   *crushed*
Whereof he craved redress. My sovereign,
Whose glory is in gracious deeds, and joys
Throughout the world her mercy to maintain,
Eftsoons devised redress for such annoys;
Me all unfit for so great purpose she employs.

44   'Now hath fair Phoebe with her silver face
Thrice seen the shadows of the nether world
Sith last I left that honorable place
In which her royal presence° is introlled.°   *court, established*
Ne ever shall I rest in house nor hold°   *shelter*
Till I that false Acrasia have won;°   *defeated*
Of whose foul deeds, too hideous to be told,
I witness am, and this their wretched son,
Whose woeful parents she hath wickedly fordone.'°   *destroyed*

45   'Tell on, fair sir,' said she, 'that doleful tale,
From which sad ruth does seem you to restrain,
That we may pity such unhappy bale
And learn from pleasure's poison to abstain.
Ill by ensample good doth often gain.'
Then forward he his purpose gan pursue,
And told the story of the mortal pain
Which Mordant and Amavia did rue,
As with lamenting eyes himself did lately view.

46   Night was far spent, and now in ocean deep,
Orion, flying fast from hissing snake,

42.4 *Order of Maidenhead:* probably an allusion to the Order of the Garter.

42.6 *make:* see note at 7.7 for imperfect rhyme. Most editions have emended to *hold.*

42.7 *The day that first doth lead the year around:* March 25th, not January 1st. The New Year was associated with Easter in the Middle Ages rather than with Christmas. Dante's adventures in *The Divine Comedy* begin on Good Friday, a day from which the time sequences of many romances, most notably perhaps

Wolfram von Eschenbach's *Parzival,* are reckoned.

44.1–2 *Phoebe:* Diana, the moon, has completed three cycles. It is now about the beginning of summer. The astronomical allusions here and in 46 below are conventional characteristics of medieval allegorical poetry.

46.2 *Orion . . . snake:* the constellation Orion sets as Scorpio rises. For the myth of Orion's death in battle with a scorpion, see Ovid, *Fasti,* 5.

His flaming head did hasten for to steep,
When of his piteous tale he end did make;
Whilst with delight of that° he wisely spake,   *that which*
Those guests, beguilèd, did beguile their eyes
Of kindly sleep, that did them overtake.
At last when they had marked the changèd skies,
They wist° their hour was spent; then each to rest him hies.   *knew*

CANTO iii

> Vain Braggadochio getting Guy-
> on's horse is made the scorn
> Of knighthood true, and is of fair
> Belphoebe foul forlorn.°   *defeated*

1 Soon as the morrow fair with purple beams
Dispersed the shadows of the misty night,
And Titan playing on the eastern streams
Gan clear the dewy air with springing light,
Sir Guyon mindful of his vow y-plight,°   *sworn*
Uprose from drowsy couch and him addressed
Unto the journey which he had behight.°   *vowed*
His puissant arms about his noble breast,
And many-folded shield he bound about his wrist.

2 Then taking congé° of that virgin pure,   *farewell*
The bloody-handed babe unto her truth°   *trust*
Did earnestly commit, and her conjure
In virtuous lore to train his tender youth,
And all that gentle nuriture° ensu'th;°   *training, pertains to*
And that so soon as riper years he raught,°   *reached*
He might for memory of that day's ruth
Be callèd Ruddymane, and thereby taught
T' avenge his parents' death on them that had it wrought.

3 So forth he fared, as now befell, on foot,
Sith his good steed is lately from him gone;
Patience perforce—helpless, what may it boot
To fret for anger or for grief to moan?
His palmer now shall foot no more alone.
So fortune wrought, as under green wood's side
He lately heard that dying lady groan,

1.9 *many-folded shield:* "And now Aias drew near, carrying a shield like a tower, made of bronze and seven layers of leather" (*Iliad*, VII.220, p. 137). ". . . it passed through the outer circle of the seven fold shield . . ." (*Aeneid*, XII.923, p. 337).

He left his steed without and spear beside,
And rushèd in on foot to aid her ere she died.

4   The whiles a losel° wandering by the way,   *scoundrel*
     One that to bounty° never cast his mind,   *virtue and valor*
     Ne thought of honor ever did assay°   *test*
     His baser° breast, but in his kestrel kind°   *cowardly, coarse*
                                                                   nature
     A pleasing vein of glory° he did find,   *boastfulness*
     To which his flowing tongue and troublous sprite
     Gave him great aid and made him more inclined—
     He that brave steed there finding ready dight,
     Purloined both steed and spear and ran away full light.°   *quickly*

5   Now gan his heart all swell in jollity,
     And of himself great hope and help conceived,
     That puffèd up with smoke of vanity
     And with self lovèd personage° deceived,   *image*
     He gan to hope of men to be received
     For such as he him thought, or fain would be.
     But for° in court gay portance° he perceived   *because, bearing*
     And gallant show to be in greatest gree,°   *favor*
     Eftsoons to court he cast t' advance his first degree.

6   And by the way he chancèd to espy
     One sitting idle on a sunny bank,
     To whom avaunting° in great bravery,°   *advancing,*
                                                                   bravado
     As peacock that his painted plumes doth prank,°   *display*
     He smote his courser in the trembling flank,
     And to him threatened his heart-thrilling spear.
     The silly man seeing him ride so rank,°   *fiercely*
     And aim at him, fell flat to ground for fear,
     And crying mercy loud, his piteous hands gan rear.

7   Thereat the scarecrow waxèd wondrous proud
     Through fortune of his first adventure fair,
     And with big thundering voice reviled him loud:
     'Vile caitiff, vassal of dread and despair,
     Unworthy of the common breathèd air,
     Why livest thou, dead dog, a lenger° day,   *longer*
     And dost not unto death thyself prepare?
     Die, or thyself my captive yield for aye;
     Great favor I thee grant, for answer thus to stay.'

4.1 *losel:* Braggadochio, an amusing variation on the type of the braggart soldier, a literary convention that passed into renaissance literature through Roman comedy. Particularly fine examples of this type are Pistol in Shakespeare's *Henry V* and Captain Bobadill in Jonson's *Every Man in His Humor.* Compare Braggadochio's ranting rhetoric with Pistol's; it is a sure sign of his cowardice.

5.9 *first degree:* the first stage in the education of a knight.

8   'Hold, O dear lord, hold your dead-doing° hand,'   *killing*
    Then loud he cried, 'I am your humble thrall.'
    'Ah wretch,' quoth he, 'thy destinies withstand
    My wrathful will and do for mercy call.
    I give thee life; therefore prostrated fall,
    And kiss my stirrup. That thy homage be.'
    The miser° threw himself, as an offal,   *wretch*
    Straight at his foot in base humility,
    And clepèd° him his liege, to hold of him in fee.   *called*

9   So happy peace they made and fair accord.
    Eftsoons this liegeman gan to wax more bold,
    And when he felt the folly of his lord,
    In his own kind° he gan himself unfold;°   *nature, show*
    For he was wily-witted and grown old
    In cunning sleights and practic° knavery.   *skillful*
    From that day forth he cast for to uphold
    His idle humor° with fine flattery,   *foolish obsession*
    And blow the bellows to his swelling vanity.

10 Trompart, fit man for Braggadochio,
    To serve at court in view of vaunting eye.
    Vainglorious man, when fluttering wind does blow
    In his light wings, is lifted up to sky—
    The scorn of knighthood and true chivalry,
    To think without desert of gentle deed
    And noble worth to be advancèd high.
    Such praise is shame; but honor, virtue's meed,
    Doth bear the fairest flower in honorable seed.

11 So forth they pass, a well-consorted° pair,   *matched*
    Till that at length with Archimage they meet;
    Who seeing one that shone in armor fair,
    On goodly courser thundering with his feet,
    Eftsoons supposèd him a person meet
    Of his revenge to make the instrument.
    For since the Red Cross Knight he erst did weet
    To been with Guyon knit in one consent,
    The ill which erst to him, he now to Guyon meant.

8.9   *to hold of him in fee:* i.e., to be his vassal.

10.1   *Trompart:* representing flattery, a fit servant to vainglory in that it nourishes vanity.

10.8–9   Braggadochio's vainglory is made especially ludicrous by his low birth, and at the same time his low birth becomes the explanation of his cowardice and bragging. For Spenser and for many renaissance humanists great acts of bravery were appropriate only to the aristocracy, who were created for the express purpose of achieving glorious feats. Braggadochio must be a fraud, simply because of his peasant birth. This doctrine of the superiority of the nobility is developed in considerable detail in Book VI of *The Faerie Queene.*

11.3   How Braggadochio comes by his armor is not explained. He had stolen only Guyon's horse and spear.

12   And coming close to Trompart, gan inquere
     Of him what mighty warrior that mote° be   *might*
     That rode in golden sell° with single° spear,   *saddle, only a*
     But wanted sword to wreak his enmity.
     'He is a great adventurer,' said he,
     'That hath his sword through hard assay° forgone,°   *combat, lost*
     And now hath vowed, till he avengèd be
     Of that despite,° never to wearen none;   *outrage*
     That spear is him enough to done a thousand groan.'

13   Th' enchanter greatly joyèd in the vaunt,
     And weenèd well ere long his will to win,
     And both his fone° with equal foil° to daunt.   *foes, defeat*
     Tho° to him louting° lowly, did begin   *then, bowing*
     To plain of wrongs which had committed been
     By Guyon and by that false Red Cross Knight,
     Which two through treason and deceitful gin,°   *plot (engine)*
     Had slain Sir Mordant and his lady bright.
     That mote him honor win, to wreak° so foul despite.   *avenge*

14   Therewith all suddenly he seemed enraged,
     And threatened death with dreadful countenance,
     As if their lives had in his hand been gaged;°   *left as pledge*
     And with stiff force shaking his mortal lance,
     To let him weet his doughty valiance,
     Thus said: 'Old man, great sure shall be thy meed,°   *reward*
     If where those knights for fear of due vengeance
     Do lurk thou certainly to me aread,°   *tell*
     That I may wreak on them their heinous hateful deed.'

15   'Certes, my lord,' said he, 'that shall I soon,
     And give you eke good help to their decay.
     But mote I wisely you advise to doon:°   *act (do)*
     Give no odds to your foes, but do purvey°   *provide*
     Yourself of sword before that bloody day;
     For they be two the prowest° knights on ground,   *most valiant*
     And oft approved° in many hard assay;   *tried*
     And eke of surest steel that may be found
     Do arm yourself against that day, them to confound.'

12.6–8 Both Trompart's story of
Braggadochio's forgone sword and Brag-
gadochio's later and different account are
reminiscent of the Tartar, Mandricardo,
in Ariosto's *Orlando Furioso*: "He does
not carry sword or mace, for when he
gained the arms that belonged to Trojan
Hector, since he found that the sword was
missing from them he swore ... that until
he took the sword of Orlando, he would
not lay hand on any other" (XIV.43).
Mandricardo is cruel and arrogant, but
not a coward.
  12.9 *done a thousand groan:* cause a
thousand (foes) to groan.
  15.3 I.e., "May I advise you to act
wisely."

16 'Dotard,' said he, 'let be thy deep advise;
   Seems that through many years thy wits thee fail,
   And that weak eld° hath left thee nothing° wise,   *old age, not at all*
   Else never should thy judgment be so frail
   To measure manhood by the sword or mail.
   Is not enough four quarters of a man,°   *i.e. one whole man*
   Withouten sword or shield, an host to quail?
   Thou little wotest° what this right hand can: *knowest*
   Speak they° which have beheld the battles which it wan.'°   *Let them speak, won*

17 The man was much abashèd at his boast;
   Yet well he wist that whoso would contend
   With either of those knights on even coast°   *on equal terms*
   Should need of all his arms, him to defend;
   Yet fearèd lest his boldness should offend,
   When Braggadochio said, 'Once I did swear,
   When with one sword seven knights I brought to end,
   Thenceforth in battle never sword to bear
   But it were that which noblest knight on earth doth wear.'

18 'Perdie, sir knight,' said then th' enchanter blive,°   *promptly*
   'That shall I shortly purchase to your hand;
   For now the best and noblest knight alive
   Prince Arthur is, that wones° in Faeryland.   *lives*
   He hath a sword that flames like burning brand;
   The same by my device I undertake
   Shall by tomorrow by thy side be fand.'
   At which bold word that boaster gan to quake,
   And wondered in his mind what mote that monster make.°   *perform that marvel*

19 He stayed not for more bidding, but away
   Was sudden vanishèd out of his sight.
   The northern wind his wings did broad display°   *spread out*
   At his command, and rearèd him up light
   From off the earth to take his airy flight.
   They looked about, but nowhere could espy
   Tract of his foot. Then dead through great affright
   They both nigh were, and each bade other fly;
   Both fled at once, ne ever back returnèd eye,

20 Till that they come unto a forest green,
   In which they shroud themselves from causeless fear.
   Yet fear them follows still, whereso they been;°   *are*
   Each trembling leaf and whistling wind they hear,
   As ghastly bug° does greatly them affear;   *goblin*

19.3   Satan is identified with the north   *Tale* he dwells "fer in the north contree"
in medieval folklore. In Chaucer's *Friar's*   (D.1413). See Isaiah 14:13–14.

Yet both do strive their fearfulness to feign.°   *conceal*
At last they heard a horn that shrillèd clear
Throughout the wood, that echoèd again,
And made the forest ring as it would rive in twain.

21 Eft through the thick they heard one rudely rush;
With noise whereof he from his lofty steed
Down fell to ground, and crept into a bush
To hide his coward head from dying dreed.°   *dread of death*
But Trompart stoutly stayed to taken heed
Of what might hap. Eftsoon there steppèd forth
A goodly lady clad in hunter's weed,
That seemed to be a woman of great worth,
And by her stately portance,° borne of heavenly birth.   *bearing*

22 Her face so fair, as° flesh it seemèd not,   *that*
But heavenly portait of bright angel's hue,
Clear as the sky, withouten blame or blot,
Through goodly mixture of complexions due;
And in her cheeks the vermeil red did shew
Like roses in a bed of lilies shed,
The which ambrosial odors from them threw,
And gazer's sense with double pleasure fed,
Able to heal the sick and to revive the dead.

23 In her fair eyes two living lamps did flame,
Kindled above at th' heavenly maker's light,
And darted fiery beams out of the same,
So passing persant° and so wondrous bright   *piercing*
That quite bereaved the rash beholder's sight.
In them the blinded god his lustful fire

21.7 *A goodly lady:* Belphoebe. She represents, as Spenser says in the Letter to Raleigh, Queen Elizabeth in her private character of "a most virtuous and beautiful lady." Much of the imagery of the description of Belphoebe is the conventional language of Petrarchan and Neoplatonic love poetry, as well as that of *The Song of Solomon.* From the beginning, Spenser is at pains to show that Belphoebe is not simply a virgin foster-daughter of Diana, the virgin goddess, though she is that primarily. More than once he implies through subtle literary allusion that she is a sort of Diana-Venus, infinitely attractive and unattainable. Through this treatment of Belphoebe he pays an elaborate compliment to Elizabeth. Her virginity does not represent hostility toward love; indeed she is a virgin goddess of love who inspires worship in virtuous men, though only lust in fools like Braggadochio. Her encounter with Braggadochio is a conscious Spenserian imitation of Venus's meeting with her son Aeneas in Book I of the *Aeneid:* "Under the trees his mother met him. She had a maiden's countenance and a maiden's guise, and carried a maiden's weapons, like some Spartan girls . . ." (314–316, p. 37).

22.4 *complexions:* humors or temperaments produced by the mixture of four bodily "humors." Belphoebe is a physical paragon equivalent to the more obviously allegorical Medina.

23.6 *blinded god:* the blind Cupid, god of animal passion. In medieval and renaissance love poetry the eyes allowed easiest access to the lover's heart. The Platonic light in Belphoebe's eyes is in direct contrast to the passion provoked in "the rash beholder's sight" by Acrasia's Bower of Bliss.

To kindle oft assayed, but had no might;
For with dread majesty and awful ire,
She broke his wanton darts and quenchèd base desire.

24   Her ivory forehead, full of bounty brave,
Like a broad table° did itself dispread,   *tablet*
For Love his lofty triumphs to engrave
And write the battles of his great godhead.
All good and honor might therein be read,
For there their dwelling was. And when she spake,
Sweet words like dropping honey she did shed,
And twixt the pearls and rubins° softly brake°   *rubies, broke*
A silver sound that heavenly music seemed to make.

25   Upon her eyelids many graces sate,
Under the shadow of her even brows,
Working belgards° and amorous retrait,°   *beautiful looks,*
And every one her with a grace endows;   *expression*
And every one with meekness to her bows.
So glorious mirror of celestial grace
And sovereign monument of mortal vows,
How shall frail pen descrive° her heavenly face, *write down*
For fear through want of skill her beauty to disgrace?

26   So fair, and thousand thousand times more fair,
She seemed when she presented was to sight,
And was y-clad, for heat of scorching air,
All in a silken camis° lily white,   *chemise*
Purfled upon° with many a folded plight;°   *decorated, pleat*
Which all above besprinkled was throughout
With golden aigulets,° that glistered bright   *spangles*
Like twinkling stars; and all the skirt about
Was hemmed with golden fringe . . . .

27   Below her ham° her weed° did somewhat train, *thigh, garment*
And her straight legs most bravely were embailed° *enclosed*
In gilden buskins of costly cordwain,°   *cordovan*
All barred with golden bands, which were entailed° *carved*
With curious antics,° and full fair amailed.°   *fantastic figures,*
Before, they fastened were under her knee   *enamelled*
In a rich jewel, and therein entrailed°   *coiled*
The ends of all their knots, that none might see
How they within their foldings close enwrappèd be.

28   Like two fair marble pillars they were seen,
Which do the temple of the gods support,

27–28 ". . . her tunic's flowing folds   were bare" (*Aeneid*, I.319–320, p. 37).
were caught up and tied, and her knees   27.8 *their:* (1596). 1590 reads *the.*

Whom all the people deck with garlands green
And honor in their festival resort.
Those same with stately grace and princely port°   *dignity*
She taught to tread, when she herself would grace;
But with the woody nymphs when she did play,
Or when the flying libbard° she did chase,   *leopard*
She could them nimbly move, and after fly apace.

29   And in her hand a sharp boar-spear she held,
And at her back a bow and quiver gay,
Stuffed with steel-headed darts, wherewith she quelled°   *killed*
The savage beasts in her victorious play,
Knit with a golden baldric which forelay
Athwart her snowy breast and did divide
Her dainty paps; which like young fruit in May
Now little gan to swell, and being tied,°   *bound*
Through her thin weed their places only signified.

30   Her yellow locks, crispèd like golden wire,
About her shoulders weren loosely shed,
And when the wind amongst them did inspire,°   *breathe*
They wavèd like a pennon wide dispread,
And low behind her back were scatterèd.
And whether art it were or heedless hap,
As through the flowering forest rash she fled,
In her rude° hairs sweet flowers themselves did lap,°   *disordered,*
And flourishing fresh leaves and blossoms did enwrap.   *enfold*

31   Such as Diana by the sandy shore
Of swift Eurotas or on Cynthus green,
Where all the nymphs have her unwares forlore,
Wandereth alone with bow and arrows keen
To seek her game; or as that famous queen
Of Amazons whom Pyrrhus did destroy,

28.7   *play:* imperfect rhyme. The later editions read *sport.* See note on ii.7.7.

29.2–4   "Slung ready on her shoulder she carried a bow as a huntress would . . ." (*Aeneid,* I.317–318, p. 37).

30.1–4   ". . . and she had let her hair stream in the wind" (*Aeneid,* I.318, p. 37).

31.1–5   "She was like Diana when she keeps her dancers dancing on the banks of Eurotas or along the slopes of Cynthus, with a thousand mountain-nymphs following in bands on this side and on that . . ." (*Aeneid,* I.498–500, p. 43). In the *Aeneid,* this simile is applied to Dido, who destroys herself because of her passion for Aeneas, much as Amavia destroys herself at the loss of Mordant. Belphoebe's beauty and her greatness are to be compared with the beauty and greatness of Dido, but her chastity makes her both greater and more fortunate than the Carthaginian queen.

31.5–9   "And battle-mad Penthesilea was there, leading the charge of Amazons carrying their crescent-shields; in the midst of thousands she blazed, showing her breast uncovered with a gold girdle clasped below, a warrior maid daring the shock of combat against men" (*Aeneid,* I.490–493, p. 42). Aeneas sees this scene pictured on the walls of Dido's temple of Juno. With the comparison to Penthesilea, Queen of the Amazons, Spenser veers slightly from his intention to reflect in Belphoebe the private character of Elizabeth as a virtuous and beautiful

The day that first of Priam she was seen
Did show herself in great triumphant joy,
To succor the weak state of sad afflicted Troy.

32 Such whenas heartless° Trompart her did view,   *cowardly*
    He was dismayèd in his coward mind,
    And doubted whether he himself should shew,
    Or fly away, or bide alone behind.
    Both fear and hope he in her face did find,
    When she at last him spying thus bespake:
    'Hail, groom. Didst not thou see a bleeding hind
    Whose right haunch erst my steadfast arrow strake?°   *struck*
    If thou didst, tell me, that I may her overtake.'

33 Wherewith revived, this answer forth he threw:
    'O goddess, for such I thee take to be—
    For neither doth thy face terrestrial shew,
    Nor voice sound mortal—I avow to thee
    Such wounded beast as that I did not see,
    Sith erst into this forest wild I came.
    But mote thy goodlihead forgive it me
    To weet° which of the gods I shall thee name,   *know*
    That unto thee due worship I may rightly frame.'ᶜ   *direct*

34 To whom she thus . . . . But ere her words ensued,
    Unto the bush her eye did sudden glance,
    In which vain Braggadochio was mewed,°   *hidden*
    And saw it stir. She left her piercing lance,
    And towards gan a deadly shaft advance,
    In mind to mark° the beast. At which sad stour,   *shoot*
    Trompart forth stepped to stay° the mortal chance,   *stop*
    Out crying, 'O whatever heavenly power
    Or earthly wight thou be, withhold this deadly hour.°   *catastrophe*

35 'O stay thy hand for yonder is no game
    For thy fierce arrows, them to exercise,
    But lo my lord, my liege, whose warlike name

---

lady. The point of this comparison, and
to a lesser extent that of the Diana-Dido
simile, is to stress her public character
as a virtuous and powerful queen. Again
Elizabeth-Belphoebe is superior to Pen-
thesilea because she does save Troy
(England). Penthesilea's death at the
hands of Achilles' son Pyrrhus, an un-
Homeric idea which Spenser inherited
from the medieval tradition of the Trojan
story, is contrasted with Belphoebe's
easy victory over the blustering Bragga-
dochio, proving again her superiority.

32.7–9 See the similar salutation of
Venus in *Aeneid,* I.321–324, p. 37.
   33.2–9 Trompart's reply to Belphoebe
is a clear imitation of Aeneas' reply to
Venus: "No, I . . . only, how am I to
speak to you? You have not the counte-
nance of human kind and your voice has
no tones of mortality. . . . Goddess! For
a goddess surely you must be" (*Aeneid,*
I.326–328, p. 37). That Trompart answers
emphasizes Braggadochio's cowardice:
our Aeneas is too frightened to play his
part.

Is far renowned through many bold emprise;°   *deed*
And now in shade he shrowded yonder lies.'
She stayed; with that he crawled out of his nest,
Forth creeping on his caitiff hands and thighs,
And standing stoutly up, his lofty crest
Did fiercely shake and rouse, as coming late from rest.

36 As fearful fowl that long in secret cave
    For dread of soaring hawk herself hath hid,
    Not caring how her silly° life to save,   *harmless*
    She, her gay painted plumes disorderèd,
    Seeing at last herself from danger rid,
    Peeps forth, and soon renews her native pride;
    She gins her feathers foul disfigurèd
    Proudly to prune and set on every side,
    So shakes off shame, ne thinks how erst° she did her hide.   *before*

37 So when her goodly visage he beheld,
    He gan himself to vaunt; but when he viewed
    Those deadly tools which in her hand she held,
    Soon into other fits° he was transmewed,°   *impulses, changed*
    Till she to him her gracious speech renewed:
    'All hail, sir knight, and well may thee befall,
    As all thee like° which honor have pursued   *like you*
    Through deeds of arms and prowess martial;
    All virtue merits praise, but such the most of all.'

38 To whom he thus: 'O fairest under sky,
    True be thy words, and worthy of thy praise
    That warlike feats dost highest glorify.
    Therein have I spent all my youthly days,
    And many battles fought, and many frays
    Throughout the world, whereso they might be found,
    Endeavoring my dreaded name to raise
    Above the moon, that Fame may it resound
    In her eternal trump, with laurel garland crowned.

39 'But what art thou, O lady, which dost range
    In this wild forest where no pleasure is,
    And dost not it for joyous court exchange,
    Amongst thine equal peers, where happy bliss
    And all delight does reign much more than this?

38.1–9 Aeneas' boast (*Aeneid*, I.379, p. 39) that "beyond the sky my fame is known" is justified. Braggadochio's answer is ludicrous by comparison. The implied comparison between Braggadochio and Aeneas sets going a similarly incongruous comparison between Guyon and Braggadochio, since Guyon has been pointedly compared with Aeneas in the Castle of Medina episode.

38.4 *have I:* (1596). 1590 reads *I have.*

There thou mayst love, and dearly lovèd be,
And swim in pleasure, which thou here dost miss;
There mayst thou best be seen, and best mayst see.
The wood is fit for beasts, the court is fit for thee.'

40 'Whoso in pomp of proud estate,' quoth she,
'Does swim, and bathes himself in courtly bliss,
Does waste his days in dark obscurity,
And in oblivion ever buried is.
Where ease abounds, it's eath° to do amiss;   *easy*
But who his limbs with labors, and his mind
Behaves° with cares, cannot so easy miss.   *exercises*
Abroad in arms, at home in studious kind,°   *way of life*
Who seeks with painful toil shall Honor soonest find.

41 'In woods, in waves, in wars she wonts to dwell,
And will be found with peril and with pain;
Ne can the man that molds in idle cell
Unto her happy mansion attain.
Before her gate high God did sweat ordain
And wakeful watches ever to abide.
But easy is the way and passage plain
To Pleasure's palace; it may soon be spied,
And day and night her doors to all stand open wide.

42 'In prince's court . . . .' The rest she would have said,
But that the foolish man, filled with delight
Of her sweet words, that all his sense dismayed,°   *overpowered*
And with her wondrous beauty ravished quite,
Gan burn in filthy lust; and leaping light,°   *quickly*
Thought in his bastard arms her to embrace.
With that she swerving back, her javelin bright
Against him bent, and fiercely did menace.
So turnèd her about and fled away apace.

43 Which when the peasant saw, amazed he stood
And grievèd at her flight; yet durst he not
Pursue her steps through wild unknowèn wood;
Besides he feared her wrath and threatened shot
Whiles in the bush he lay, not yet forgot.
Ne cared he greatly for her presence vain,
But turning said to Trompart, 'What foul blot
Is this to knight, that lady should again
Depart to woods untouched and leave so proud disdain?'

44 'Perdie,' said Trompart, 'let her pass at will,
Lest by her presence danger mote befall.

For who can tell—and sure I fear it ill—
But that she is some power celestial?
For whiles she spake, her great words did apall
My feeble courage, and my heart oppress,
That yet I quake and tremble over all.'
'And I,' said Braggadochio, 'thought no less,
When first I heard her horn sound with such ghastliness.

45 'For from my mother's womb this grace I have
Me given by eternal destiny:
That earthly thing may not my courage brave
Dismay with fear, or cause on foot to fly,
But either hellish fiends or powers on high.
Which was the cause, when erst that horn I heard,
Weening it had been thunder in the sky,
I hid myself from it as one afeard;
But when I other° knew, myself I boldly reared.   *otherwise*

46 'But now for fear of worse that may betide,
Let us soon hence depart.' They soon agree;
So to his steed he got, and gan to ride
As one unfit therefor, that all might see
He had not trainèd been in chivalry.°   *horsemanship*
Which well that valiant courser did discern;
For he despised to tread in due degree,
But chafed and foamed with courage fierce and stern,
And to be eased of that base burden still did earn.

CANTO iv

Guyon does Furor bind in chains
And stops Occasion,
Delivers Phedon, and therefore
By Strife is railed upon.

1 In brave pursuit of honorable deed,
There is I know not what great difference
Between the vulgar and the noble seed,

Argument.3 *Phedon:* (1596). 1590 reads *Phaon.*

1.1–9 An elaboration of the notion implied in Canto iii.10 that only the noble are capable of honorable and great actions. In *The Defense of Poesy* (2nd paragraph), Sir Philip Sidney cites his riding master's view that "soldiers were the noblest estate of mankind, and horsemen the noblest of soldiers. He said they were the masters of war and ornaments of peace, speedy goers and strong abiders, triumphers both in camps and courts; nay, to so unbelieved a point he proceeded, as that no earthly thing bred such wonder to a prince as to be a good horseman." No doubt this is a professional's exaggeration, but most renaissance writers on the education of the aristocracy place great emphasis on horsemanship.

Which unto things of valorous pretence
Seems to be born by native influence,
As feats of arms and love to entertain;°   *engage in*
But chiefly skill to ride seems a science
Proper to gentle blood. Some others feign
To manage steeds, as did this vaunter,° but in vain.   *braggart*

2 But he the rightful owner of that steed,
   Who well could manage and subdue his pride,
   The whiles on foot was forcèd for to yede°   *go*
   With that black palmer, his most trusty guide,
   Who suffered not his wandering feet to slide;
   But when strong passion or weak fleshliness
   Would from the right way seek to draw him wide,
   He would, through temperance and steadfastness,
   Teach him the weak to strengthen, and the strong suppress.

3 It fortunèd forth faring on his way,
   He saw from far, or seemèd for to see,
   Some troublous uproar or contentious fray,
   Whereto he drew in haste it to agree.°   *settle*
   A madman, or that feignèd mad to be,
   Drew by the hair along upon the ground
   A handsome stripling with great cruelty,
   Whom sore he beat and gored with many a wound,
   That cheeks with tears, and sides with blood did all abound.

4 And him behind, a wicked hag did stalk
   In ragged robes and filthy disarray;
   Her other leg was lame, that she n'ot° walk,   *couldn't*
   But on a staff her feeble steps did stay.
   Her locks that loathly were and hoary gray,
   Grew all afore, and loosely hung unrolled;
   But all behind was bald and worn away,
   That none° thereof could ever taken hold,   *no one*
   And eke her face ill favored, full of wrinkles old.

5 And ever as she went, her tongue did walk°   *move*
   In foul reproach and terms of vile despite,
   Provoking him by her outrageous talk
   To heap more vengeance on that wretched wight;

2.9 *the weak to strengthen, and the
strong suppress:* an echo of the Mordant
and Amavia episode.
    3.5 *A madman, or that feignèd mad to
be:* Furor, named in Stanza 2. Spenser's
Furor is wrath, the extreme excess of the
irascible power carried to the point of
insanity. In the next two cantos and in
part of Canto vi, Guyon's enemies are all
representatives of excessive anger.
    4.1–9 The *wicked hag* is Occasion, spe-
cifically the occasions on which men are
tempted to wrath. Her hair-do illustrates
the proverbial advice to "seize occasion
by the forelock."

Sometimes she raught° him stones wherewith to smite,   *handed*
Sometimes her staff, though it her one leg were,
Withouten which she could not go upright.
Ne any evil means she did forbear
That might him move to wrath, and indignation rear.°   *arouse*

6   The noble Guyon moved with great remorse,
Approaching, first the hag did thrust away,
And after, adding more impetuous force,
His mighty hands did on the madman lay,
And plucked him back; who all on fire straightway,
Against him turning all his fell intent,
With beastly brutish rage gan him assay,°   *attack*
And smote and bit and kicked and scratched and rent,
And did he wist not what in his avengèment.°   *vengeance*

7   And sure he was a man of mickle° might,   *great*
Had he had governance it well to guide;
But when the frantic fit inflamed his sprite,
His force was vain, and struck more often wide
Than at the aimèd mark which he had eyed;
And oft himself he chanced to hurt unwares,
Whilst reason, blent° through passion, nought descried;°   *blinded, saw*
But as a blindfold bull at random fares,
And where he hits, nought knows, and whom he hurts,
    nought cares.

8   His rude assault and rugged handèling
Strange seemèd to the knight, that aye with foe
In fair defense and goodly managing
Of arms was wont to fight; yet nathemo°   *not at all*
Was he abashèd now not fighting so;
But more enfiercèd through his currish play,
Him sternly gripped, and haling° to and fro,   *dragging*
To overthrow him strongly did assay;
But overthrew himself unwares, and lower lay.

9   And being down, the villain sore did beat
And bruise with clownish fists his manly face;
And eke the hag, with many a bitter threat,
Still called upon to kill him in the place.
With whose reproach and odious menace,
The knight, emboiling° in his haughty° heart,   *boiling, noble*
Knit all his forces and gan soon unbrace°   *unfasten*

8.9 Guyon's mistake is that he attempts to fight Furor on his own terms, letting his own anger do the work of his reason. He is temporarily the victim of his own wrath.

His grasping hold; so lightly did upstart,
And drew his deadly weapon to maintain his part.

10 Which when the palmer saw, he loudly cried,
'Not so, O Guyon, never think that so
That monster can be mastered or destroyed;
He is not, ah, he is not such a foe
As steel can wound or strength can overthrow.
That same is Furor, cursèd cruel wight,
That unto knighthood works much shame and woe;
And that same hag, his aged mother, hight
Occasion, the root of all wrath and despite.

11 'With her, whoso will raging Furor tame
Must first begin, and well her amenage:°   *tame*
First her restrain from her reproachful blame
And evil means, with which she doth enrage
Her frantic son and kindles his courage;
Then when she is withdrawn or strong withstood,
It's eath° his idle fury to assuage,   *easy*
And calm the tempest of his passion wood.°   *mad*
The banks are overflown when stoppèd° is the flood.'   *dammed up*

12 Therewith Sir Guyon left his first emprise,°   *undertaking*
And turning to that woman, fast her hent°   *seized*
By the hoar locks that hung before her eyes,
And to the ground her threw. Yet n'ould she stent°   *she wouldn't stop*
Her bitter railing and foul revilement,
But still provoked her son to wreak° her wrong;   *avenge*
But natheless he did her still torment,
And catching hold of her ungracious tongue,
Thereon an iron lock did fasten firm and strong.

13 Then whenas use of speech was from her reft,
With her two crooked hands she signs did make,
And beckoned him, the last help she had left;
But he that last left help away did take,
And both her hands fast bound unto a stake,
That she n'ot° stir. Then gan her son to fly   *couldn't*
Full fast away, and did her quite forsake;
But Guyon after him in haste did hie,
And soon him overtook in sad perplexity.

14 In his strong arms he stiffly him embraced,
Who him gainstriving,° nought at all prevailed,   *struggling against him*

11.9 Furor, intemperate anger, must be defeated by controlling the occasion for anger.

For all his power was utterly defaced,
And furious fits at erst° quite weren quailed.   *immediately*
Oft he renforced,° and oft his forces failed,   *strained*
Yet yield he would not, nor his rancor slack.
Then him to ground he cast and rudely haled,°   *pushed*
And both his hands fast bound behind his back,
And both his feet in fetters to an iron rack.

15   With hundred iron chains he did him bind,
And hundred knots that did him sore constrain;
Yet his great iron teeth he still did grind
And grimly gnash, threatening revenge in vain.
His burning eyne,° whom bloody streaks did stain,   *eyes*
Starèd full wide and threw forth sparks of fire;
And more for rank despite than for great pain,
Shaked his long locks, colored like copper wire,
And bit his tawny beard to show his raging ire.

16   Thus whenas Guyon Furor had captived,
Turning about, he saw that wretched squire,
Whom that madman of life nigh late deprived,
Lying on ground, all soiled with blood and mire;
Whom whenas he perceivèd to respire,
He gan to comfort and his wounds to dress.
Being at last recured,° he gan inquire   *recovered*
What hard mishap him brought to such distress,
And made that caitiff's thrall, the thrall of wretchedness.

17   With heart then throbbing, and with watery eyes,
'Fair sir,' quoth he, 'what man can shun the hap°   *fate*
That hidden lies unwares him to surprise?
Misfortune waits advantage° to entrap   *opportunity*
The man most wary in her whelming lap.°   *enfolding garment*
So me weak wretch, of many weakest one,
Unweeting, and unware of such mishap,
She brought to mischief through occasion,
Where this same wicked villain did me light upon.

18   'It was a faithless squire that was the source
Of all my sorrow, and of these sad tears;
With whom from tender dug° of common nurse   *breast*
At once I was upbrought; and eft when years

16.2   *wretched squire:* Phedon, whose story, probably taken from Ariosto's *Orlando Furioso,* Canto IV, is very similar to the main plot of Shakespeare's *Much Ado. About Nothing.* The plot has numerous analogues in renaissance Italian novelle.
17.6   *one:* (1596). 1590 reads *wretch.*
17.8   *occasion:* (1596). 1590 reads *her guileful trech.*
17.9   *light upon:* (1596). 1590 reads *wandering ketch.*

More ripe us reason lent to choose our peers,
Ourselves in league of vowèd love we knit.
In which we long time without jealous fears
Or faulty thoughts continued, as was fit;
And for my part I vow, dissembled not a whit.

19 'It was my fortune, common to that age,
To love a lady fair of great degree,
The which was born of noble parentage,
And set in highest seat of dignity,
Yet seemed no less to love than loved to be.
Long I her served and found her faithful still,
Ne ever thing could cause us disagree—
Love that two hearts makes one, makes eke one will—
Each strove to please, and other's pleasure to fulfill.

20 'My friend, hight Philemon, I did partake°   *confide in*
Of all my love and all my privity;°   *secret thoughts*
Who greatly joyous seemèd for my sake,
And gracious to that lady as to me.
Ne ever wight that mote so welcome be
As he to her, withouten blot or blame;
Ne ever thing that she could think or see
But unto him she would impart the same.
O wretched man, that would abuse so gentle dame.

21 'At last such grace I found, and means I wrought,
That I that lady to my spouse had won.
Accord of friends, consent of parents sought,
Affiance made, my happiness begun,
There wanted nought but few rites to be done
Which marriage make. That day too far did seem.
Most joyous man on whom the shining sun
Did show his face myself I did esteem,
And that my falser° friend did no less joyous deem.   *most false*

22 'But ere that wishèd day his beam disclosed,
He either envying my toward° good,   *approaching*
Or of himself to treason ill disposed,
One day unto me came in friendly mood,
And told for secret how he understood
That lady whom I had to me assigned
Had both distained° her honorable blood,   *stained*
And eke the faith which she to me did bind;
And therefore wished me stay till I more truth should find.

23 'The gnawing anguish and sharp jealousy,
Which his sad speech infixèd in my breast,

Rankled so sore and festered inwardly
That my engrievèd mind could find no rest,
Till that the truth thereof I did outwrest;°   *extract*
And him besought, by that same sacred band
Betwixt us both, to counsel me the best.
He then with solemn oath and plighted hand
Assured ere long the truth to let me understand.

24 'Ere long with like again he boarded me,
Saying he now had bolted° all the flour,   *sifted*
And that it was a groom of base degree
Which of my love was partner paramour,
Who usèd in a darksome inner bower
Her oft to meet. Which better to approve,
He promisèd to bring me at that hour
When I should see that° would me nearer move,   *that which*
And drive me to withdraw my blind abusèd love.

25 'This graceless man for furtherance of his guile
Did court the handmaid of my lady dear;
Who glad t' embosom° his affection vile,   *cherish*
Did all she might, more pleasing to appear.
One day to work her to his will more near,
He wooed her thus: "Pryenè"—so she hight—
"What great despite doth Fortune to thee bear,
Thus lowly to abase thy beauty bright,
That it should not deface all others' lesser light?

26 ' "But if she had her least help to thee lent
T' adorn thy form according thy desert,
Their blazing pride thou wouldest soon have blent,
And stained their praises with thy least good part;
Ne should fair Claribell with all her art,
Though she thy lady be, approach thee near.
For proof thereof, this evening, as thou art,
Array thyself in her most gorgeous gear,
That I may more delight in thy embracement dear."

27 'The maiden, proud through praise and mad through love,
Him hearkened to, and soon herself arrayed,
The whiles to me the treachor did remove
His crafty engine, and (as he had said)
Me leading, in a secret corner laid,
The sad spectator of my tragedy;
Where left, he went and his own false part played,

27.3–5 I.e., "Meanwhile the traitor turned his scheming plot to me, and lead- ing me (as he had promised), laid me in a hidden corner."

Disguisèd like that groom of base degree
Whom he had feigned th' abuser of my love to be.

28 'Eftsoons he came unto th' appointed place,
And with him brought Pryenè, rich arrayed
In Claribella's clothes. Her proper face
I not discernèd in that darksome shade,
But weened it was my love with whom he played.
Ah God, what horror and tormenting grief
My heart, my hands, mine eyes, and all assayed.°   *afflicted*
Me liefer were ten thousand deathès' prief
Than wound of jealous worm and shame of such reprief.°   *reproof*

29 'I home returning—fraught with foul despite,
And chawing vengeance all the way I went—
Soon as my loathèd love appeared in sight,
With wrathful hand I slew her, innocent.
That after soon I dearly did lament;
For when the cause of that outrageous deed,
Demanded, I made plain and evident,
Her faulty handmaid, which that bale did breed,
Confessed how Philemon her wrought to change her weed.

30 'Which when I heard, with horrible affright
And hellish fury all enraged, I sought
Upon myself that vengeable despite°   *injury*
To punish; yet it better first I thought
To wreak my wrath on him that first it wrought.
To Philemon, false faitour° Philemon,   *villain*
I cast to pay that° I so dearly bought;   *repay what*
Of deadly drugs I gave him drink anon,
And washed away his guilt with guilty potion.

31 'Thus heaping crime on crime and grief on grief,
To loss of love adjoining loss of friend,
I meant to purge both with a third mischief,
And in my woe's beginner it to end:
That was Pryenè; she did first offend,
She last should smart. With which cruel intent,
When I at her my murderous blade did bend,
She fled away with ghastly dreariment,
And I pursuing my fell purpose after went.

32 'Fear gave her wings, and rage enforced my flight;
Through woods and plains so long I did her chase,
Till this madman, whom your victorious might

28.8 Literally, "more pleasant to me would be ten thousand deaths' painful experience."

Hath now fast bound, me met in middle space;
As I her, so he me pursued apace,
And shortly overtook. I breathing ire,
Sore chaféd at my stay° in such a case,   *hindrance*
And with my heat kindled his cruel fire;
Which kindled once, his mother did more rage inspire.

33 'Betwixt them both they have me done to die,°   *killed*
Through wounds, and strokes, and stubborn handèling,
That death were better than such agony
As grief and fury unto me did bring;
Of which in me yet sticks the mortal sting
That during life will never be appeased.'
When he thus ended had his sorrowing,
Said Guyon, 'Squire, sore have ye been diseased;
But all your hurts may soon through temperance be eased.'

34 Then gan the palmer thus: 'Most wretched man,
That to affections does the bridle lend.
In their beginning they are weak and wan,
But soon through sufferance grow to fearful end.
Whiles they are weak betimes° with them contend;   *right away*
For when they once to perfect strength do grow,
Strong wars they make and cruel battery bend
Gainst fort of reason, it to overthrow.
Wrath, jealousy, grief, love this squire have laid thus low.

35 'Wrath, jealousy, grief, love do thus expell:
Wrath is a fire and jealousy a weed,
Grief is a flood and love a monster fell;
The fire of sparks, the weed of little seed,
The flood of drops, the monster filth did breed.
But sparks, seed, drops, and filth do thus delay:
The sparks soon quench, the springing seed outweed,
The drops dry up, and filth wipe clean away.
So shall wrath, jealousy, grief, love die and decay.'

36 'Unlucky squire,' said Guyon, 'sith thou hast
Fallen into mischief through intemperance,
Henceforth take heed of that thou now hast passed,
And guide thy ways with wary governance,
Lest worse betide thee by some later chance.
But read° how art thou named, and of what kin.'   *tell*
'Phedon I hight,' quoth he, 'and do advance

34–35 In pointing the moral of Phe-   36.7 *Phedon:* (1596). 1590 reads
don's story, the palmer gives advice on   *Phaon.*
mastering the occasions to wrath.

Mine ancestry from famous Coradin,
Who first to raise our house to honor did being.'

37 Thus as he spake, lo far away they spied
A varlet running towards hastily,
Whose flying feet so fast their way applied
That round about a cloud of dust did fly,
Which mingled all with sweat, did dim his eye.
He soon approachèd, panting, breathless, hot,
And all so soiled that none could him descry;°   *make out*
His countenance was bold, and bashèd° not   *retreated*
For Guyon's looks, but scornful eye-glance at him shot.

38 Behind his back he bore a brazen shield,
On which was drawen fair in colors fit
A flaming fire in midst of bloody field,
And round about the wreath this word was writ:
Burnt I Do Burn. Right well beseemèd it
To be the shield of some redoubted knight;
And in his hand two darts exceeding flit°   *swift*
And deadly sharp he held, whose heads were dight°   *coated*
In poison and in blood, of malice and despite.

39 When he in presence came, to Guyon first
He boldly spake: 'Sir knight, if knight thou be,
Abandon this forestallèd° place at erst°   *reserved, at once*
For fear of further harm, I counsel thee,
Or bide the chance° at thine own jeopardy.'   *take the risk*
The knight at his great boldness wonderèd,
And though he scorned his idle vanity,
Yet mildly him to purpose° answerèd;   *on the subject*
For not to grow of nought he it conjecturèd.

40 'Varlet, this place most due to me I deem,
Yielded by him that held it forcibly.
But whence should come that harm which thou dost seem
To threat to him that minds° his chance t' aby?'°   *intends, to take*
'Perdie,' said he, 'here comes, and is hard by,
A knight of wondrous power and great assay,
That never yet encountered enemy
But did him deadly daunt or foul dismay;
Ne thou for better hope, if thou his presence stay.'°   *hinder*

37.2 *A varlet running:* Atin, named in Stanza 42. He is a descendant of Ate, goddess of strife: "Ate, the eldest daughter of Zeus, who blinds us all, accursed spirit that she is, never touching the ground with those insubstantial feet of hers, but flitting through men's heads, corrupting them . . ." (*Iliad*, XIX.91–93, p. 356).

38.1–6 The shield of his master, Pyrochles, who is introduced in Stanza 41.

41　'How hight he then,' said Guyon, 'and from whence?'
　　'Pyrochles is his name, renowmèd far
　　For his bold feats and hardy confidence,
　　Full oft approved° in many a cruel war;　　　　　　　　*proved*
　　The brother of Cymochles, both which are
　　The sons of old Acrates and Despite,
　　Acrates, son of Phlegeton and Jar;
　　But Phlegeton is son of Erebus and Night,
　　But Erebus son of Æternity is hight.

42　'So from immortal race he does proceed
　　That mortal hands may not withstand his might,
　　Drad° for his derring-do and bloody deed;　　　　　*dreaded*
　　For all in blood and spoil is his delight.
　　His am I, Atin, his in wrong and right,
　　That matter make for him to work upon,
　　And stir him up to strife and cruel fight.
　　Fly therefore, fly this fearful stead° anon,　　　　　*place*
　　Lest thy foolhardice° work thy sad confusion.'　　*foolhardiness*

43　'His be that care whom most it doth concern,'
　　Said he, 'but whither with such hasty flight
　　Art thou now bound? For well mote I discern
　　Great cause that carries thee so swift and light.'
　　'My lord,' quoth he, 'me sent, and straight behight
　　To seek Occasion, whereso she be;
　　For he is all disposed to bloody fight,
　　And breathes out wrath and heinous cruelty.
　　Hard is his hap that first falls in his jeopardy.'

44　'Madman,' said then the palmer, 'that does seek
　　Occasion to wrath and cause of strife.
　　She comes unsought and, shunnèd, follows eke.
　　Happy who can abstain when rancor rife
　　Kindles revenge and threats° his rusty knife;　　*threatens with*
　　Woe never wants where every cause is caught,
　　And rash Occasion makes unquiet life.'
　　'Then lo, where bound she sits whom thou hast sought,'
　　Said Guyon. 'Let that message to thy lord be brought.'

41.2–9 *Pyrochles:* from the Greek *pyr*, "fire," and *ochleon*, "moved." He represents the choleric man, habitually disposed to anger and violence. *Cymochles* from the Greek *kyma*, "wave," and *ochleon*, "moved," represents the completely incontinent, uncontrolled man. *Acrates*, from Greek *akrates*, "ungovernable." *Despite*, malice. *Phlegeton*, an infernal god and one of the rivers of Hades: ". . . a river sweeping round with a current of white-hot flames and boulders that spun and roared; this was Tartarean Phlegethon, the Burning River of Hell" (*Aeneid*, VI.550–551, pp. 163–164). *Jar*, discord, perhaps Ate. *Erebus*, in Virgil a name for the infernal regions. Hesiod makes Erebus the brother and husband of Night (*Theogony*, 123). *Aeternity*, Spenser probably got this name from Boccaccio's *De Genealogia Deorum*, I; she is perhaps the same as Hesiod's Chaos (see Lotspeich).

45 That when the varlet heard and saw, straightway
   He waxèd wondrous wroth and said, 'Vile knight,
   That knights and knighthood dost with shame upbray,°   *disgrace*
   And show'st th' ensample of thy childish might
   With silly weak old woman thus to fight,
   Great glory and gay spoil sure hast thou got,
   And stoutly proved thy puissance here in sight;
   That shall Pyrochles well requite, I wot,
   And with thy blood abolish so reproachful blot.'

46 With that, one of his thrillant° darts he threw,   *piercing*
   Headed with ire and vengeable despite;
   The quivering steel his aimèd end° well knew,   *mark*
   And to his breast itself intended right.
   But he was wary, and ere it empight°   *plunged*
   In the meant mark, advanced his shield atween,
   On which it seizing, no way enter might,
   But back rebounding, left the fork-head keen;
   Eftsoons he fled away and might nowhere be seen.

CANTO v

Pyrochles does with Guyon fight,
And Furor's chain unbinds;
Of whom sore hurt, for his revenge
Atin Cymochles finds.

1 Whoever doth to temperance apply
  His steadfast life, and all his actions frame,
  Trust me, shall find no greater enemy
  Than stubborn perturbation to the same;
  To which right well the wise do give that name,
  For it the goodly peace of stayèd° minds   *steadfast*
  Does overthrow and troublous war proclaim—
  His own woe's author, whoso bound it finds
  As did Pyrochles, and it willfully unbinds.

45.5 *thus to:* (1596). 1590 reads *that did.*
46.8 The shaft rebounded, but the sharp two-pronged head remained in Guyon's shield.
Argument.2 *unbinds:* (1596). 1590 reads *unties.*
Argument.3 *Of whom sore hurt, for his revenge:* (1596). 1590 reads *Who him sore wounds, whiles Atin to*
Argument.4 *Atin Cymochles finds:*

(1596). 1590 reads *Cymochles for aid flies.*
1.4 *stubborn perturbation:* ". . . this thunder and lightning of perturbation, which causeth such violence and speedy alterations in this our Microcosm, and many times subverts the good estate and temperance of it" (Robert Burton, *The Anatomy of Melancholy*, p. 217).
1.8–9 I.e., "Perturbation brings woe to him who, finding it bound as did Pyrochles, willfully unbinds it."

2 After that varlet's flight, it was not long
   Ere on the plain fast pricking Guyon spied
   One in bright arms embatteled° full strong,   *armed*
   That as the sunny beams do glance and glide
   Upon the trembling wave, so shinèd bright,
   And round about him threw forth sparkling fire
   That seemed him to inflame on every side.
   His steed was bloody red, and foamèd ire
   When with the mastering spur he did him roughly stire.°   *incite*

3 Approaching nigh, he never stayed to greet,
   Ne chaffer° words, proud courage to provoke,   *exchange*
   But pricked so fierce that underneath his feet
   The smoldering dust did round about him smoke,
   Both horse and man nigh able for to choke.
   And fairly couching his steel-headed spear,
   Him first saluted with a sturdy stroke;
   It booted nought Sir Guyon, coming near,
   To think such hideous puissance on foot to bear.

4 But lightly shunnèd it, and passing by,
   With his bright blade did smite at him so fell
   That the sharp steel, arriving forcibly
   On his broad shield, bit not, but glancing fell
   On his horse' neck before the quilted sell,°   *saddle*
   And from the head the body sundered quite.
   So him dismounted low, he did compel
   On foot with him to matchen° equal fight;   *match*
   The trunkèd° beast fast bleeding, did him foully dight.°   *truncated, defile*

5 Sore bruisèd with the fall, he slow uprose,
   And all enragèd, thus him loudly shent:°   *insulted*
   'Disleal° knight, whose coward courage chose   *disloyal*
   To wreak itself on beast all innocent,
   And shunned the mark at which it should be meant!
   Thereby thine arms seem strong, but manhood frail.
   So hast thou oft with guile thine honor blent;°   *stained*

2.1 *that varlet's flight:* i.e., Atin's.
5.3–9 According to the chivalric code,
injuring a horse, even an enemy's, was to
be avoided if at all possible. On the
poem's fictional level, then, Guyon can
be accused of a regrettable incompetence
if not a technical cowardice. Like Atin's
indictment (iv.45) of Guyon for mistreat-
ing a helpless old woman (Occasion),
Pyrochles' charge of cowardice is a power-
ful incitement to anger. Twice now Guyon
has been maneuvered into actions that
seem to violently abuse the chivalric code.

When we consider the allegorical sig-
nificance of Occasion and Pyrochles, how-
ever, Guyon's behavior has been perfectly
justified. A tension thus develops between
Guyon's fictional commitment to the
chivalric code and the demands on him
of the allegory. Guyon defends himself
against neither Atin's nor Pyrochles' un-
just accusation. By leaving his hero in-
articulate, Spenser increases the effect of
frustration. He allows the reader no re-
lease from the mounting shame, injustice,
and anger.

But little may such guile thee now avail
If wonted force and fortune do me not much fail.'

6   With that he drew his flaming sword and struck
     At him so fiercely that the upper marge°   *edge*
     Of his seven-folded shield away it took,
     And glancing on his helmet, made a large
     And open gash therein. Were not his targe,°   *for his shield*
     That broke the violence of his intent,
     The weary soul from thence it would discharge;
     Nath'less so sore a buff to him it lent,
     That made him reel, and to his breast his beaver° bent.   *helmet*

7   Exceeding wroth was Guyon at thàt blow,
     And much ashamed that stroke of living arm
     Should him dismay and make him stoop so low,
     Though otherwise it did him little harm.
     Tho hurling high his iron-bracèd arm,
     He smote so manly on his shoulder plate
     That all his left side it did quite disarm;
     Yet there the steel stayed not, but inly bate°   *bit*
     Deep in his flesh and opened wide a red floodgate.

8   Deadly dismayed with horror of that dint
     Pyrochles was, and grievèd eke entire.°   *entirely*
     Yet nathemore did it his fury stint,
     But added flame unto his former fire,
     That well-nigh molt° his heart in raging ire.   *melted*
     Ne thenceforth his approvèd skill to ward°   *parry*
     Or strike or hurtle round in warlike gyre°   *circle*
     Remembered he, ne cared for his safeguard,
     But rudely raged and like a cruel tiger fared.

9   He hewed, and lashed, and foined,° and thundered blows,   *thrust*
     And every way did seek into his life;
     Ne plate, ne mail could ward so mighty throws,°   *thrusts*
     But yielded passage to his cruel knife.
     But Guyon, in the heat of all his strife,
     Was wary wise and closely° did await   *secretly*
     Avantage, whilst his foe did rage most rife;
     Sometimes athwart, sometimes he struck him straight,
     And falsèd° oft his blows t' illude° him with such bait —   *feinted, to deceive*

10   Like as a lion, whose imperial power
     A proud rebellious unicorn defies,

6.3 *seven-folded shield:* see note on
Book II.iii.1.9.
8.6–9 Note the loss of control which
characterizes both Pyrochles and Furor.

10.1–9 This account of the lion's
tactics in defeating the unicorn is found
commonly in medieval bestiaries and
natural histories.

T' avoid the rash assault and wrathful stour°   *combat*
Of his fierce foe, him° to a tree applies,   *himself*
And when him running in full course° he spies,   *full speed*
He slips aside; the whiles that furious beast
His precious horn, sought of his enemies,
Strikes in the stock, ne thence can be released,
But to the mighty victor yields a bounteous feast—

11 With such fair sleight him Guyon often failed,°   *deluded*
Till at the last, all breathless, weary, faint
Him spying, with fresh onset he assailed,
And kindling new his courage, seeming quent,°   *quenched*
Struck him so hugely that through great constraint°   *force*
He made him stoop perforce unto his knee,
And do unwilling worship to the saint
That on his shield depainted he did see;
Such homage till that instant never learnèd he.

12 Whom Guyon seeing stoop, pursuèd fast
The present offer of fair victory,
And soon his dreadful blade about he cast,
Wherewith he smote his haughty crest so high°   *fiercely*
That straight on ground made him full low to lie;
Then on his breast his victor foot he thrust.
With that he cried, 'Mercy, do me not die,°   *do not kill me*
Ne deem thy force, by fortune's doom unjust,
That hath, maugré° her spite, thus low me laid in dust.'   *damn*

13 Eftsoons his cruel hand Sir Guyon stayed,
Tempering the passion with advisement° slow   *reflection*
And mastering might on enemy dismayed;
For th' equal die of war he well did know.
Then to him said, 'Live and allegiance owe
To him that gives thee life and liberty,
And henceforth by this day's ensample trow°   *believe*
That hasty wroth and heedless hazardry°   *rashness*
Do breed repentance late° and lasting infamy.   *slow moving*

14 So up he let him rise, who with grim look
And countenance stern upstanding,° gan to grind   *standing up*
His grated° teeth for great disdain, and shook   *clenched*
His sandy locks, long hanging down behind,
Knotted in blood and dust, for grief of mind
That he in odds of arms° was conquerèd;   *combat*
Yet in himself some comfort he did find

11.7–8 *the saint:* Gloriana.   force with the unjust decree of fortune
12.8 I.e., "Nor confuse your [weak]   which was the real cause of my [defeat]."

That him so noble knight had masterèd,
Whose bounty, more than might, yet both, he wonderèd.°   *marveled at*

15 Which Guyon marking said, 'Be nought aggrieved,
Sir knight, that thus ye now subduèd are.
Was never man who most conquests achieved
But sometimes had the worse and lost by war.
Yet shortly gained that loss exceeded far.
Loss is no shame, nor to be less than foe;
But to be lesser than himself doth mar
Both loser's lot and victor's praise also.
Vain others' overthrows, who self doth overthrow.

16 'Fly, O Pyrochles, fly the dreadful war
That in thyself thy lesser parts do move,
Outrageous anger and woe-working jar,°   *discord*
Direful impatience and heart-murdering love;
Those, those thy foes, those warriors far remove,
Which thee to endless bale° captivèd lead.   *woe*
But sith in might, thou didst my mercy prove,°   *experience*
Of courtesy to me the cause aread
That thee against me drew with so impetuous dreed.'°   *dreadfulness*

17 'Dreadless,' said he, 'that shall I soon declare:
It was complained that thou hadst done great tort°   *wrong*
Unto an aged woman, poor and bare,
And thrallèd her in chains with strong effort,
Void of all succor and needful comfort.
That ill beseems° thee, such as I thee see,   *becomes*
To work such shame; therefore I thee exhort
To change thy will and set Occasion free,
And to her captive son yield his first° liberty.'   *original*

18 Thereat Sir Guyon smiled: 'And is that all,'
Said he, 'that thee so sore displeasèd hath?
Great mercy sure, for to enlarge a thrall
Whose freedom shall thee turn to greatest scath.°   *harm*
Nath'less now quench thy hot emboiling wrath.
Lo, there they be; to thee I yield them free.'
Thereat he wondrous glad, out of the path
Did lightly leap, where he them bound did see,
And gan to break the bands of their captivity.

17–20 Pyrochles' constitutional intemperance blinds him to right action. Unlike the incontinent man, the intemperate man does not even see the right course. Although his defeat at Guyon's hands is sufficient "occasion" for wrath, Pyrochles has from the first been sincerely convinced that Guyon is a villain. Under the influence of his bodily choler he blindly perseveres in freeing the "harmless" old woman whom Guyon, by Pyrochles' lights, has so unchivalrously mistreated.

19 Soon as Occasion felt herself untied,
   Before her son could well assoilèd° be,   *set free*
   She to her use° returned, and straight defied   *habitual practice*
   Both Guyon and Pyrochles, th' one, said she,
   Because he won, the other because he
   Was won. So matter did she make of nought,
   To stir up strife and gar° them disagree.   *make*
   But soon as Furor was enlarged, she sought
   To kindle his quenched fire, and thousand causes wrought.

20 It was not long ere she inflamed him so
   That he would algates° with Pyrochles fight,   *by all means*
   And his redeemer challenged for° his foe   *as*
   Because he had not well maintained his right,
   But yielded had to that same stranger knight.
   Now gan Pyrochles wax as wood° as he,   *insane*
   And him affronted° with impatient might;   *attacked*
   So both together fierce engraspèd be,
   Whiles Guyon standing by, their uncouth strife does see.

21 Him all that while Occasion did provoke
   Against Pyrochles, and new matter framed°   *built*
   Upon the old, him stirring to be wroke°   *avenged*
   Of his late wrongs, in which she oft him blamed
   For suffering such abuse as knighthood shamed
   And him disabled quite. But he was wise,
   Ne would with vain occasions be inflamed;
   Yet others she more urgent did devise,
   Yet nothing could him to impatience entice.

22 Their fell contention still increasèd more,
   And more thereby increasèd Furor's might,
   That he his foe has hurt and wounded sore,
   And him in blood and dirt deformèd quite.
   His mother eke, more to augment his spite,
   Now brought to him a flaming fire-brand,
   Which she, in Stygian lake aye° burning bright,   *forever*
   Had kindled; that° she gave into his hand,   *which*
   That armed with fire, more hardly he mote him withstand.

23 Tho gan that villain wax so fierce and strong
   That nothing might sustain his furious force;

19.4 *she:* (1596). 1590 reads *he.*
21.4–6 Occasion reminds Guyon of Atin's and Pyrochles' unjust accusations.
22.1–23.5 Pyrochles' battle with Furor, a shameful temper tantrum, illustrates the madness which unchecked anger leads to. All renaissance authorities agree that choler in excess leads to frenzy and, eventually, to death. For a detailed portrait of a pathologically choleric man, see Christopher Marlowe's *Tamburlaine*, Part II.

He cast him down to ground, and all along
Drew him through dirt and mire without remorse,
And foully batterèd his comely corse,
That Guyon much disdained so loathly sight.
At last he was compelled to cry perforce,°   *of necessity*
'Help, O Sir Guyon, help most noble knight,
To rid a wretched man from hands of hellish wight.'

24   The knight was greatly movèd at his plaint,
And gan him dight° to succor his distress,   *prepare*
Till that the palmer, by his grave restraint,
Him stayed from yielding pitiful redress,
And said, 'Dear son, thy causeless ruth repress,
Ne let thy stout heart melt in pity vain.
He that his sorrow sought through willfulness,
And his foe, fettered, would release again,
Deserves to taste his folly's fruit—repented pain.'

25   Guyon obeyed. So him away he drew
From needless trouble of renewing fight
Already fought, his voyage to pursue.
But rash Pyrochles' varlet, Atin hight,
When late he saw his lord in heavy plight
Under Sir Guyon's puissant stroke to fall,
Him deeming dead, as then he seemed in sight,
Fled fast away to tell his funeral
Unto his brother, whom Cymochles men did call.

26   He was a man of rare redoubted might,
Famous throughout the world for warlike praise
And glorious spoils, purchased in perilous fight.
Full many doughty knights he in his days
Had done to death, subdued in equal frays,
Whose carcasses, for terror of his name,
Of fowls and beasts he made the piteous preys,
And hung their conquered arms for more defame°   *insult*
On gallow trees, in honor of his dearest dame.

27   His dearest dame is that enchantèress,
The vile Acrasia, that with vain delights
And idle pleasures in her Bower of Bliss,

24.9 *repented pain:* represented by
Pyrochles' admission in 23.8–9 that
Furor is a hellish wight.

25.2–3 *fight / Already fought:* Guyon
has defeated the temptation to immod-
erate anger (Furor) which external causes
(Occasion) place in his way, as well as
the tendency toward excessive anger

which lies in his own constitution (Pyro-
chles).

27–34 Acrasia resembles Homer's
Circe (*Odyssey*, X). The description of
the Bower of Bliss here and in Canto xii
owes even more to Torquato Tasso's
Jerusalem Delivered, Cantos XV–XVI.

Does charm her lovers, and the feeble sprites
Can call out of the bodies of frail wights;
Whom then she does transform to monstrous hues°   *forms*
And horribly misshapes with ugly sights,°   *appearances*
Captived eternally in iron mews°   *cages*
And darksome dens, where Titan his face never shews.

28 There Atin found Cymochles sojourning
  To serve his leman's° love; for he by kind° *mistress', nature*
  Was given all to lust and loose living,
  Whenever his fierce hands he free mote find.
  And now he has poured out his idle mind
  In dainty delices° and lavish joys,   *delights*
  Having his warlike weapons cast behind,
  And flows in pleasures and vain pleasing toys,
  Mingled amongst loose ladies and lascivious boys.

29 And over him, art striving to compare°   *be equal*
  With nature, did an arbor green dispread,
  Framèd of wanton ivy flowering fair,
  Through which the fragrant Eglantine did spread
  His prickling arms entrailed° with roses red, *entwined*
  Which dainty odors round about them threw,
  And all within with flowers was garnishèd,
  That when mild Zephyrus amongst them blew,
  Did breathe out bounteous smells, and painted colors shew.

30 And fast beside, there trickled softly down
  A gentle stream, whose murmuring wave did play
  Amongst the pumice-stones and made a soun° *sound*
  To lull him soft asleep that by it lay;
  The weary traveler, wandering that way,
  Therein did often quench his thirsty heat,
  And then by it his weary limbs display,°   *spread out*
  Whiles creeping slumber made him to forget
  His former pain, and wiped away his toilsome sweat.

31 And on the other side, a pleasant grove
  Was shot up high, full of the stately tree
  That dedicated is t' Olympic Jove,
  And to his son, Alcides, whenas he
  In Nemus gainèd goodly victory;

29.8 *Zephyrus:* the gentle west wind.
31.2 *stately tree:* the oak.
31.4–5 *Alcides:* Hercules, who in his first trial killed the Nemean lion and in memory of his victory planted the Nemean Wood. See Robert Graves, *The Greek Myths*, Penguin Books, II, 103–105.

Therein the merry birds of every sort
Chanted aloud their cheerful harmony
And made amongst themselves a sweet consort,°   *concert*
That quickened the dull sprite with musical comfort.

32 There he him found all carelessly displayed
In secret shadow from the sunny ray,
On a sweet bed of lilies softly laid,
Amidst a flock of damsels fresh and gay,
That round about him dissolute did play
Their wanton follies and light merriments;
Every of which did loosely disarray
Her upper parts of meet habiliments,°   *proper clothing*
And showed them naked, decked with many ornaments.

33 And every of them strove with most delights
Him to aggrate,° and greatest pleasures shew.   *please*
Some framed fair looks, glancing like evening lights,
Others sweet words, dropping like honey dew;
Some bathèd kisses and did soft imbrue°   *soak*
The sugared liquor through his melting lips.
One boasts her beauty and does yield to view
Her dainty limbs above her tender hips;
Another her outboasts, and all for trial° strips.   *proof*

34 He like an adder lurking in the weeds,
His wandering thought in deep desire does steep,
And his frail eye with spoil° of beauty feeds.   *denuding*
Sometimes he falsely feigns himself to sleep,
Whiles through their lids his wanton eyes do peep
To steal a snatch of amorous conceit,°   *image*
Whereby close° fire into his heart does creep.   *secret*
So he them deceives, deceived in his deceit,
Made drunk with drugs of dear voluptuous receipt.°   *recipe*

35 Atin arriving there, when him he spied
Thus in still waves of deep delight to wade,
Fiercely approaching, to him loudly cried,

31.6–9 Compare the song of the birds in the garden of the enchantress Armida in *Jerusalem Delivered:*

The joyous birds, hid under greenwood shade,
Sung merry notes on every branch and bough;
The wind, that in the leaves and waters played,
With murmur sweet now sang, and whistled now;
Ceased the birds, the wind loud answer made,
And while they sung it rumbled soft and low.

(XVI.12, trans. Edward Fairfax)

'Cymochles! O no, but Cymochles' shade,
In° which that manly person late did fade;   *into*
What is become of great Acrates' son?
Or where hath he hung up his mortal° blade,   *deadly*
That hath so many haughty conquests won?
Is all his force forlorn, and all his glory done?'

36   Then pricking him with his sharp-pointed dart,
     He said, 'Up, up, thou womanish weak knight
     That here in ladies' lap entombèd art—
     Unmindful of thy praise and prowest° might,   *most valiant*
     And weetless° eke of lately wrought despite—   *ignorant*
     Whiles sad Pyrochles lies on senseless ground
     And groaneth out his utmost grudging sprite,°   i.e. *last breath*
     Through many a stroke and many a streaming wound,
     Calling thy help in vain that here in joys art drowned.'

37   Suddenly out of his delightful dream
     The man awoke, and would have questioned more;
     But he would not endure that woeful theme
     For to dilate at large, but urgèd sore
     With piercing words and pitiful implore
     Him hasty to arise. As one affright
     With hellish fiends or Furies' mad uproar,
     He then uprose, inflamed with fell despite,
     And callèd for his arms; for he would algates fight.

38   They been y-brought. He quickly does him dight;
     And lightly mounted, passeth on his way.
     Ne ladies' loves, ne sweet entreaties might
     Appease his heat or hasty passage stay,
     For he has vowed to been avenged that day—
     That day itself him seemèd all too long—
     On him that did Pyrochles dear dismay.
     So proudly pricketh on his courser strong,
     And Atin aye him pricks with spurs of shame and wrong.

35.4–36.9   Atin's speech to Cymochles
is modeled after Mercury's speech to
Aeneas in *Aeneid*, IV.265–276, p. 105.
See also Ubaldo's speech to Rinaldo,
Jerusalem Delivered, XVI.33; and *Orlando
Furioso*, VII.56–64.
    37.3–4   I.e., "Atin would not patiently
retell his woeful story in detail."
    37.6–9   "Aeneas was struck dumb by
the vision. He was out of his wits, his hair
bristled with a shiver of fear, and his
voice was checked in his throat" (*Aeneid*,
IV.279–280, p. 105).

CANTO vi

Guyon is of immodest Mirth
Led into loose desire,
Fights **with** Cymochles, whiles his bro-
ther burns in furious fire.

1 A harder lesson to learn continence
In joyous pleasure than in grievous pain.
For sweetness doth allure the weaker sense
So strongly that uneaths it can refrain
From that which feeble nature covets fain;
But grief and wrath, that be her enemies,
And foes of life, she better can abstain.
Yet virtue vaunts in both her° victories,   *their*
And Guyon in them all shows goodly masteries.

2 Whom bold Cymochles traveling to find,
With cruel purpose bent to wreak on him
The wrath which Atin kindled in his mind,
Came to a river by whose utmost brim
Waiting to pass, he saw whereas did swim
Along the shore, as swift as glance of eye,
A little gondolay° bedeckèd trim   *gondola*
With boughs and arbors woven cunningly,
That like a little forest seemèd outwardly.

3 And therein sat a lady fresh and fair,
Making sweet solace to herself alone;
Sometimes she sung as loud as lark in air,
Sometimes she laughed, that nigh her breath was gone;
Yet was there not with her else anyone
That to her might move cause of merriment.
Matter of mirth enough, though there were none,
She could devise, and thousand ways invent
To feed her foolish humor and vain jolliment.

4 Which when far off Cymochles heard and saw,
He loudly called to such as were aboard,

1.1–9 This stanza is based on Aris-
totle's *Ethics*, II.3: ". . . it is hard to
fight against anger, but it is harder still
to fight against pleasure. Yet to grapple
with the harder has always been the
business, as of art, so of goodness, success
in a task being proportionate to its diffi-
culty" (p. 60).
    3.1 *lady fresh and fair:* Phaedria,
from Greek *phaidros*, "glittering."
    3.4 *that nigh . . . was gone:* (1596).
1590 reads *as merry as Pope Joan.*

The little bark unto the shore to draw,
And him to ferry over that deep ford.
The merry mariner unto his word
Soon hearkened, and her painted boat straightway
Turned to the shore, where that same warlike lord
She in received; but Atin by no way
She would admit, albe° the knight her much did pray.   *although*

5 Eftsoons her shallow ship away did slide
More swift than swallow shears the liquid sky,
Withouten oar or pilot it to guide,
Or wingèd canvas with the wind to fly;
Only she turned a pin, and by and by
It cut away upon the yielding wave,
Ne carèd° she her course for to apply.°   *bothered, steer*
For it was taught the way which she would have,
And both from rocks and flats itself could wisely save.

6 And all the way, the wanton damsel found
New mirth, her passenger to entertain.
For she in pleasant purpose° did abound,   *talk*
And greatly joyèd merry tales to feign,
Of which a storehouse did with her remain,
Yet seemèd nothing well they her became;
For all her words she drowned with laughter vain,
And wanted grace in uttering of the same,
That turnèd all her pleasance to a scoffing game.

7 And other whiles, vain toys° she would devise   *pastimes*
As her fantastic wit did most delight:
Sometimes her head she fondly would aguise°   *array*
With gaudy garlands, or fresh flowerets dight
About her neck, or rings of rushes plight;°   *braid*
Sometimes to do° him laugh, she would assay°   *make, pretend*
To laugh at shaking of the leavès light,
Or to behold the water work and play
About her little frigate therein making way.

8 Her light behavior and loose dalliance
Gave wondrous great contentment to the knight,
That of his way he had no souvenance°   *remembrance*
Nor care of vowed revenge and cruel fight,

4.8–9 Atin and, later, the palmer are excluded from Phaedria's boat and from her island because both are opposed to idleness, which supports excessive mirth. Atin stirs men to vicious action; right reason leads away from excess to virtuous action.

5.1–9 Phaedria's ship is like the Phaeacian ships in *Odyssey*, VIII.555 (p. 137).

But to weak wench did yield his martial might.
So easy was to quench his flamèd mind
With one sweet drop of sensual delight;
So easy is t' appease the stormy wind
Of malice in the calm of pleasant womankind.

9   Diverse discourses in their way they spent,
Mongst which Cymochles of her questionèd
Both what she was, and what that usage meant
Which in her cot° she daily practisèd.   *boat*
'Vain man,' said she, 'that wouldst be reckonèd
A stranger in thy home, and ignorant
Of Phaedria—for so my name is read—
Of Phaedria, thine own fellow servant;
For thou to serve Acrasia thyself dost vaunt.

10   'In this wide inland sea, that hight by name
The Idle Lake, my wandering ship I row,
That knows her port and thither sails by aim;
Ne care, ne fear I how the wind do blow,
Or whether swift I wend or whether slow;
Both slow and swift alike do serve my turn.
Ne swelling Neptune ne loud thundering Jove
Can change my cheer or make me ever mourn;
My little boat can safely pass this perilous bourn.'°   *obstacle*

11   Whiles thus she talkèd and whiles thus she toyed,
They were far past the passage which he spake,
And come unto an island waste and void°   *uninhabited*
That floated in the midst of that great lake.
There her small gondolay her port did make,
And that gay pair issuing on the shore
Disburdened her. Their way they forward take
Into the land that lay them fair before,
Whose pleasance she him showed and plentiful great store.

12   It was a chosen plot of fertile land,
Amongst wide waves set like a little nest,
As if it had by Nature's cunning hand
Been choicely pickèd out from all the rest,
And laid forth for ensample of the best.
No dainty flower or herb that grows on ground,
No arboret° with painted blossoms dressed   *shrub*
And smelling sweet, but there it might be found
To bud out fair, and throw her sweet smells all around.

11.3–4 The floating island is reminiscent of the island of Aeolia in *Odyssey*, X (p. 155), and also of Delos, which according to legend floated around the Aegean Sea until Zeus chained it to the bottom of the ocean.

13 No tree whose branches did not bravely spring,
    No branch whereon a fine bird did not sit,
    No bird but did her shrill notes sweetly sing,
    No song but did contain a lovely dit;
    Trees, branches, birds, and songs were framèd fit
    For to allure frail mind to careless° ease.   *untroubled*
    Careless the man soon wox,° and his weak wit   *became*
    Was overcome of thing that did him please;
    So pleasèd, did his wrathful purpose fair appease.°   *subside*

14 Thus when she had his eyes and senses fed
    With false delights and filled with pleasures vain,
    Into a shady dale she soft him led,
    And laid him down upon a grassy plain;
    And her sweet self without dread or disdain
    She set beside, laying his head disarmed
    In her loose lap, it softly to sustain,
    Where soon he slumbered, fearing not be harmed,
    The whiles with a love-lay she thus him sweetly charmed:

15 'Behold, O man, that toilsome pains dost take,
    The flowers, the fields, and all that pleasant grows,
    How they themselves do thine ensample make,
    Whiles, nothing envious, Nature them forth throws
    Out of her fruitful lap—how, no man knows,
    They spring, they bud, they blossom fresh and fair,
    And deck the world with their rich pompous shows;
    Yet no man for them taketh pains or care,
    Yet no man to them can his careful pains compare.

16 'The lily, lady of the flowering field,
    The flower-de-luce,° her lovely paramour,   *fleur-de-lis*

15–17 Phaedria's song is modeled after the song of Tasso's enchantress Armida in *Jerusalem Delivered*, who lulls the hero Rinaldo to sleep:

Ye happy youths, whom April fresh and May
Attire in flowering green of lusty age,
For glory vain or virtue's idle ray
Do not your tender limbs to toil engage;
In calm streams fishes, birds in sunshine play,
Who followeth pleasure he is only sage;
So nature saith, yet 'gainst her sacred will
Why still rebel you, and why strive you still?

O fools, who youth possess yet scorn the same,
A precious but a short-abiding treasure;
Virtue itself is but an idle name,
Prized by the world 'bove reason all and measure;

And honor, glory, praise, renown, and fame,
That men's proud hearts bewitch with tickling pleasure,
An echo is, a shade, a dream, a flower,
With each wind blasted, spoiled with every shower.

But let your happy souls in joy possess
The ivory castles of your bodies fair,
Your passed harms salve with forgetfulness,
Haste not your coming ills with thought and care,
Regard no blazing star with burning tress,
Nor storm, nor threatening sky, nor thundering air;
This wisdom is, good life, and worldly bliss,
Kind teacheth us, nature commands us this.
                                        (XIV.62–64)
The argument of the two songs is the same: Look at nature, it does not toil

Bid thee to them thy fruitless labors yield,
And soon leave off this toilsome weary stour;°   *conflict*
Lo, lo how brave she decks her bounteous bower
With silken curtains and gold coverlets,
Therein to shroud her sumptuous belamour,°   *lover*
Yet neither spins nor cards, ne cares nor frets,
But to her mother, Nature, all her care she lets.

17 'Why then dost thou, O man, that of them all
Art lord, and eke of Nature sovereign,
Willfully make thyself a wretched thrall
And waste thy joyous hours in needless pain,
Seeking for danger and adventures vain?
What boots it all to have, and nothing use?
Who shall him rue that swimming in the main
Will die for thirst, and water doth refuse?
Refuse such fruitless toil, and present pleasures choose.'

18 By this she had him lullèd fast asleep,
That of no worldly thing he care did take;
Then she with liquors strong his eyes did steep,
That nothing should him hastily awake.
So she him left, and did herself betake
Unto her boat again, with which she cleft
The slothful wave of that great grisy° lake;   *grey*

---

nor strive; give up the pursuit of honor and virtue and live the life of pleasure. The language of Spenser's song, however, is based on the Sermon on the Mount, Matthew 6:25-34: "Therefore I say unto you, Take no thought for your life, what ye shall eat, or what ye shall drink; nor yet for your body, what ye shall put on. Is not the life more than meat, and the body than raiment? Behold the fowls of the air: for they sow not, neither do they reap, nor gather into barns; yet your heavenly Father feedeth them. Are ye not much better than they? Which of you by taking thought can add one cubit unto his stature? And why take ye thought for raiment? Consider the lilies of the field, how they grow; they toil not, neither do they spin: And yet I say unto you, That even Solomon in all his glory was not arrayed like one of these. Wherefore, if God so clothe the grass of the field, which today is, and tomorrow is cast into the oven, shall he not much more clothe you, O ye of little faith? Therefore take no thought, saying, What shall we eat? or, What shall we drink? or Wherewithal shall we be clothed? (For after all these things do the Gentiles seek:) for your heavenly Father knoweth that ye have need of all these things. But seek ye first the kingdom of God, and his righteousness; and all these things shall be added unto you. Take therefore no thought for the morrow; for the morrow shall take thought for the things of itself. Sufficient unto the day is the evil thereof." Phaedria sings a blasphemous parody of Christ's sermon. Christ argues that man should seek "the kingdom of God, and his righteousness" and not material needs, which God will supply. Phaedria's argument is almost opposite—set your mind on pleasure and not on virtue and honor. Christ wants men to rise above ordinary human nature; Phaedria wants men to sink to a state of nature below the human. The song also sounds a note opposed to another of Guyon's temptations, fruitless avarice (Canto vii). Even the image of the swimmer will be repeated in the struggling Tantalus (vii.58-59). The temperate man must steer a course between these two extremes. In Christian terms, he must avoid both fruitless ease (Phaedria) and fruitless toil (Mammon) that he may be fruitful in good works (Christ).

18.2 *worldly:* (1596). 1590 reads *wordly.*

Soon she that island far behind her left,
And now is come to that same place where first she weft.°   *floated*

19 By this time was the worthy Guyon brought
Unto the other side of that wide strand
Where she was rowing, and for passage sought.
Him needed not long call; she soon to hand
Her ferry brought, where him she biding fand°   *found*
With his sad° guide. Himself she took aboard,   *grave*
But the black palmer suffered still to stand,
Ne would for price or prayers once afford
To ferry that old man over the perilous ford.

20 Guyon was loath to leave his guide behind,
Yet being entered, might not back retire;
For the flit bark, obeying to her mind,
Forth launchèd quickly, as she did desire,
Ne gave him leave to bid that aged sire
Adieu, but nimbly ran her wonted course
Through the dull billows thick as troubled mire,
Whom neither wind out of their seat could force,
Nor timely° tides did drive out of their sluggish source.   *periodic*

21 And by the way as was her wonted guise,°   *custom*
Her merry fit she freshly gan to rear
And did of joy and jollity devise,
Herself to cherish,° and her guest to cheer.   *endear*
The knight was courteous, and did not forbear
Her honest mirth and pleasance to partake;
But when he saw her toy and gibe and jeer
And pass the bonds° of modest merrimake,   *bounds*
Her dalliance he despised, and follies did forsake.

22 Yet she still followèd her former style,
And said and did all that mote° him delight,   *might*
Till they arrivèd in that pleasant isle,
Where sleeping late she left her other knight.
But whenas Guyon of that land had sight,
He wist himself amiss, and angry said,
'Ah Dame, perdie ye have not done me right
Thus to mislead me, whiles I you obeyed;
Me little needed from my right way to have strayed.'

23 'Fair sir,' quoth she, 'be not displeased at all.
Who fares on sea may not command his way,
Ne wind and weather at his pleasure call.
The sea is wide and easy for to stray,

The wind unstable and doth never stay.
But here awhile ye may in safety rest,
Till season serve new passage to assay;
Better safe port than be in seas distressed.'
Therewith she laughed, and did her earnest end in jest.

24   But he half discontent, mote° natheless   *could*
Himself appease, and issued forth on shore;
The joys whereof and happy fruitfulness,
Such as he saw, she gan him lay before,
And all, though pleasant, yet she made much more.
The fields did laugh, the flowers did freshly spring,
The trees did bud and early blossoms bore,
And all the choir of birds did sweetly sing,
And told that garden's pleasures in their caroling.

25   And she more sweet than any bird on bough,
Would oftentimes amongst them bear a part,
And strive to pass°—as she could well enow—   *surpass*
Their native music by her skillful art.
So did she all that might his constant heart
Withdraw from thought of warlike enterprise
And drown in dissolute delights apart,
Where noise of arms or view of martial guise°   *military equip-*
Might not revive desire of knightly exercise.   *ment*

26   But he was wise and wary of her will,
And ever held his hand upon his heart;
Yet would not seem so rude and thewèd ill°   *ill mannered*
As to despise so courteous-seeming part°   *conduct*
That gentle lady did to him impart;°   *show*
But fairly tempering, fond desire subdued
And ever her desirèd to depart.
She list° not hear, but her disports pursued,   *would*
And ever bade him stay till time the tide renewed.

27   And now by this, Cymochles' hour was spent,
That he awoke out of his idle dream,
And shaking off his drowsy dreariment,
Gan him avise how ill did him beseem
In slothful sleep his molten heart to steam,
And quench the brand of his conceivèd ire.
Tho up he started, stirred with shame extreme,
Ne stayèd for his damsel to inquire,
But marchèd to the strand, there passage to require.

26.2   *And ever held his hand upon his heart:* i.e., to keep Phaedria from stealing
it away.

28 And in the way he with Sir Guyon met,
    Accompanied with Phaedria the fair.
    Eftsoons he gan to rage and inly fret,
    Crying, 'Let be that lady debonaire,
    Thou recreant° knight, and soon thyself prepare   *cowardly*
    To battle if thou mean her love to gain.
    Lo, lo already, how the fowls in air
    Do flock, awaiting shortly to obtain
    Thy carcass for their prey, the guerdon of thy pain.'

29 And therewithal he fiercely at him flew
    And with importune° outrage him assailed;   *severe*
    Who soon prepared to field, his sword forth drew,
    And him with equal value° countervailed.   *valor*
    Their mighty strokes their habergeons° dismailed,   *coats of mail*
    And naked made each other's manly spalls;°   *shoulders*
    The mortal steel despiteously entailed°   *carved*
    Deep in their flesh, quite through the iron walls,
    That a large purple stream adown their jambeaux° falls. *leg armor*

30 Cymochles, that had never met before
    So puissant foe, with envious despite
    His proud presumèd force increasèd more,
    Disdaining to be held so long in fight;
    Sir Guyon grudging not so much his might
    As those unknightly railings which he spoke,
    With wrathful fire his courage kindled bright,
    Thereof devising shortly to be wroke,°   *avenged*
    And doubling all his powers, redoubled every stroke.

31 Both of them high at once their hands enhanced,°   *raised*
    And both at once their huge blows down did sway.°   *swing*
    Cymochles' sword on Guyon's shield y-glanced,
    And thereof nigh one quarter sheared away;
    But Guyon's angry blade so fierce did play
    On th' other's helmet, which as Titan° shone,   *i.e. the sun*
    That quite it clove his plumèd crest in tway,
    And barèd all his head unto the bone;
    Wherewith astonished, still he stood as senseless stone.

32 Still as he stood, fair Phaedria, that beheld
    That deadly danger, soon atween them ran
    And at their feet herself most humbly felled,

32–36 The fight between Guyon and Cymochles and the calming speech of Phaedria are intentionally imitated from the fight between Guyon, Huddibras, and Sansloy and the calming speech of Medina. A detailed comparison of the two scenes would illuminate the allegory greatly.

Crying with piteous voice and countenance wan,
'Ah welaway, most noble lords, how can
Your cruel eyes endure so piteous sight,
To shed your lives on ground? Woe worth° the man   *come to*
That first did teach the cursèd steel to bite
In his own flesh, and make way to the living sprite.

33 'If ever love of lady did empierce
Your iron breasts, or pity could find place,
Withhold your bloody hands from battle fierce,
And sith for me ye fight, to me this grace
Both yield: to stay° your deadly strife a space.'   *stop*
They stayed awhile, and forth she gan proceed:
'Most wretched woman and of wicked race,
That am the author of this heinous deed,
And cause of death between two doughty knights do breed.

34 'But if for me ye fight or me will serve,
Not this rude kind of battle nor these arms
Are meet, the which do° men in bale° to starve,°   *cause, misery, die*
And doleful sorrow heap with deadly harms.
Such cruel game my scarmoges° disarms.   *skirmishes*
Another war and other weapons I
Do love, where love does give his sweet alarms
Without bloodshed, and where the enemy
Does yield unto his foe a pleasant victory.

35 'Debateful strife and cruel enmity
The famous name of knighthood foully shend;°   *disgrace*
But lovely peace and gentle amity,
And in amours the passing hours to spend,
The mighty martial hands do most commend;
Of love they ever greater glory bore
Than of their arms. Mars is Cupido's friend,
And is for Venus' loves renowmèd more
Than all his wars and spoils, the which he did of yore.'

36 Therewith she sweetly smiled. They though full bent
To prove extremities of bloody fight,°   i.e. *fight to the finish*

32.5 *welaway:* an exclamation of grief.
35.7–9 Although the love of Mars and Venus was a famous Neoplatonic symbol of concord in the soul, it was also a symbol of shame and sensual excess, as in the story recited in *Odyssey*, VIII.266 ff. (pp. 129–131).
36.1–9 Guyon is calmed by the reasonable elements in Phaedria's plea, those elements most similar to Medina's speech. Cymochles is calmed by the appeal to pleasure. The narrator's praise of Phaedria's speech is only half serious: the susceptability to the power of "pleasing words" is Cymochles'; the courteous clemency is Guyon's, whose "gentle heart" is an attribute of the gentleman. This concept, the core of the courtly love tradition, is most memorably expressed in the canzone "The Gentle Heart," by the thirteenth-century Italian poet Guido Guinicelli.

Yet at her speech their rages gan relent,
And calm the sea of their tempestuous spite;
Such power have pleasing words; such is the might
Of courteous clemency in gentle heart.
Now after all was ceased, the faery knight
Besought that damsel suffer him depart,
And yield him ready passage to that other part.

37 She no less glad than he desirous was
Of his departure thence; for of her joy
And vain delight she saw he light did pass,°   *disregard*
A foe of folly and immodest toy,
Still solemn sad or still disdainful coy,
Delighting all in arms and cruel war,
That her sweet peace and pleasures did annoy,
Troubled with terror and unquiet jar,
That she well pleasèd was thence to amove him far.

38 Tho him she brought aboard, and her swift boat
Forthwith directed to that further strand;
The which on the dull waves did lightly float
And soon arrivèd on the shallow sand,
Where gladsome Guyon sallied forth to land,
And to that damsel thanks gave for reward.
Upon that shore he spièd Atin stand,
There by his master left when late he fared
In Phaedria's flit bark over that perilous shard.°   *obstacle*

39 Well could he him remember, sith of late
He with Pyrochles sharp debatement made;
Straight gan he him revile and bitter rate,
As shepherd's cur that in dark evening's shade
Hath tracted forth some savage beast'ès trade:°   *track*
'Vile miscreant,' said he, 'whither dost thou fly
The shame and death which will thee soon invade?
What coward hand shall do° thee next to die,   *cause*
That art thus foully fled from famous enemy?'

40 With that he stiffly shook his steel-head dart.
But sober Guyon, hearing him so rail,
Though somewhat movèd in his mighty heart,
Yet with strong reason mastered passion frail,
And passèd fairly forth. He turning tail,
Back to the strand retired and there still stayed
Awaiting passage, which him late did fail;
The whiles Cymochles with that wanton maid
The hasty heat of his avowed revenge delayed.

41   Whilst there the varlet stood, he saw from far
An armèd knight that towards him fast ran.
He ran on foot, as if in luckless war
His forlorn steed from him the victor wan;
He seemèd breathless, heartless, faint, and wan,
And all his armor sprinkled was with blood
And soiled with dirty gore, that no man can
Discern the hue thereof. He never stood,
But bent his hasty course towards the idle flood.

42   The varlet saw, when to the flood he came,
How without stop or stay he fiercely leapt,
And deep himself beduckèd in the same,
That in the lake his lofty crest was stept;°   *steeped*
Ne of his safety seemèd care he kept,
But with his raging arms he rudely flashed°   *splashed*
The waves about, and all his armor swept,
That all the blood and filth away was washed;
Yet still he bet° the water and the billows dashed.   *beat*

43   Atin drew nigh to weet what it mote be,
For much he wondered at that uncouth sight.
Whom should he but his own dear lord there see,
His own dear lord, Pyrochles, in sad plight,
Ready to drown himself for fell despite.
'Harrow now out' and 'welaway,' he cried,
'What dismal day hath lent this cursèd light,
To see my lord so deadly damnified?
Pyrochles, O Pyrochles, what is thee betide?'

44   'I burn, I burn, I burn,' then loud he cried,
'O how I burn with implacable fire;
Yet nought can quench mine inly flaming side,
Nor° sea of liquor cold nor lake of mire;   *neither*
Nothing but death can do° me to respire.'   *cause*
'Ah be it,' said he, 'from Pyrochles far
After° pursuing death once to require,°   *for, ask*
Or think that aught those puissant hands may mar.
Death is for wretches born under unhappy star.'

45   'Perdie, then is it fit for me,' said he,
'That am, I ween, most wretched man alive,
Burning in flames, yet no flames can I see,
And dying daily, daily yet revive.

42.5 I.e., "It seemed he was not con-   43.7 Atin curses the day in whose
cerned with his safety."   light he sees his master's agony.
43.6 *Harrow:* an exclamation of alarm.

O Atin, help to me last death to give.'
The varlet at his plaint was grieved so sore
That his deep wounded heart in two did rive,
And his own health remembering now no more,
Did follow that ensample which he blamed afore.

46 Into the lake he leapt, his lord to aid—
So love the dread of danger doth despise—
And of him catching hold him strongly stayed
From drowning. But more happy he than wise,
Of that sea's nature did him not avise.
The waves thereof so slow and sluggish were,
Engrossed with mud which did them foul agrise,°   *make horrible*
That every weighty thing they did upbear.
Ne aught mote ever sink down to the bottom there.

47 Whiles thus they struggled in that idle wave
And strove in vain, the one himself to drown,
The other both from drowning for to save,
Lo, to that shore one in an ancient gown,
Whose hoary locks great gravity did crown,
Holding in hand a goodly arming sword,
By fortune came, led with the troublous soun;°   *sound*
Where drenchèd deep he found in that dull ford
The careful° servant striving with his raging lord.   *conscientious*

48 Him Atin spying, knew right well of yore,
And loudly called, 'Help, help, O Archimage,
To save my lord, in wretched plight forlore;
Help with thy hand or with thy counsel sage.
Weak hands, but counsel is most strong in age.'
Him when the old man saw, he wondered sore
To see Pyrochles there so rudely rage;
Yet sithence° help, he saw, he needed more   *since*
Than pity, he in haste approachèd to the shore,

49 And called, 'Pyrochles, what is this I see?
What hellish fury hath at erst° thee hent?°   *now, seized*
Furious ever I thee knew to be,
Yet never in this strange astonishment.'
'These flames, these flames,' he cried, 'do me torment.'
'What flames,' quoth he, 'when I thee present see
In danger rather to be drent than brent?'

46.2 This line is an echo of ii.3.3 where
Guyon, loathing "disdainful nicety,"
kneels down to wash the blood from
Ruddymane's hands. The similarity of
situation implies a contrast between the
Lake of Idleness and the nymph's well.
Pyrochles is outwardly but not inwardly
cleansed.
47.6 *arming sword:* the kind of heavy
sword worn as part of a knight's armor.

'Harrow, the flames which me consume,' said he,
'Ne can be quenched, within my secret bowels be.

50   'That cursèd man, that cruel fiend of hell,
Furor, O Furor, hath me thus bedight.
His deadly wounds within my liver swell,
And his hot fire burns in mine entrails bright,
Kindled through his infernal brand of spite,
Sith late with him I battle vain would boast;
That now I ween Jove's dreaded thunder light
Does scorch not half so sore, nor damnèd ghost
In flaming Phlegeton does not so felly° roast.'   *grievously*

51   Which whenas Archimago heard, his grief
He knew right well, and him at once disarmed,°   *stripped of armor*
Then searched his secret wounds, and made a prief°   *an examination*
Of every place that was with bruising harmed
Or with the hidden fire inly warmed.
Which done, he balms and herbs thereto applied,
And evermore with mighty spells them charmed,
That in short space he has them qualified,
And him restored to health that would have algates died.

CANTO vii

Guyon finds Mammon in a delve,°   *ravine*
Sunning his treasure hoar;°   *ancient*
Is by him tempted, and led down
To see his secret store.

1   As pilot well expert in perilous wave
That to a steadfast star his course hath bent,°   *directed*
When foggy mists or cloudy tempests have
The faithful light of that fair lamp y-blent°   *blinded*
And covered heaven with hideous dreriment,
Upon his card° and compass firms his eye—   *chart*
The masters of his long experiment°—   *experience*
And to them does the steady helm apply,
Bidding his wingèd vessel fairly forward fly:

2   So Guyon having lost his trusty guide,
Late left beyond that Idle Lake, proceeds
Yet on his way, of none° accompanied;   *by no one*

50.9 *Phlegeton:* the infernal river which in iv.41 was said to be Pyrochles' grand-father.

And evermore himself with comfort feeds
Of his own virtues and praiseworthy deeds.
Long so he yode,° yet no adventure found   *went*
Which Fame of her shrill trumpet worthy reads;°   *declares*
For still he traveled through wide wasteful ground,
That nought but desert wilderness showed all around.

3   At last he came unto a gloomy glade,
Covered with boughs and shrubs from heaven's light,
Whereas he sitting found in secret shade
An uncouth, savage, and uncivil° wight,   *uncivilized*
Of grisly hue° and foul ill-favored sight.°   *shape, appear-*
His face with smoke was tanned and eyes were bleared,   *ance*
His head and beard with soot were ill bedight,°   *covered*
His coal-black hands did seem to have been seared
In smith's fire-spitting forge, and nails like claws appeared.

4   His iron coat all overgrown with rust
Was underneath envelopèd with gold,
Whose glistering gloss, darkened with filthy dust,
Well yet appearèd to have been of old
A work of rich entail° and curious mold,°   *carving, design*
Woven with antics° and wild imagery.   *grotesque figures*
And in his lap a mass of coin he told°   *counted*
And turnèd upside down, to feed his eye
And covetous desire with his huge treasury.

5   And round about him lay on every side
Great heaps of gold, that never could be spent.
Of which some were rude ore, not purified
Of Mulciber's devouring element;
Some others were new driven° and distent°   *beaten, drawn out*
Into great ingoes° and to wedges square;   *ingots*
Some in round plates withouten monument;°   *stamped image*

2.4–5 *himself with comfort feeds / Of his own virtues:* Many critics have been distressed by Guyon's insufferable self-righteousness here. Spenser is making an allegorical and ethical point, however, at the apparent expense of the fictional characterization. The whole episode of Mammon's temptation of Sir Guyon is similar at many points (beginning with the "desert wilderness" in which Guyon wanders) to Satan's temptation of Christ (Matthew 4:1–11). As Christ suffered the temptations in the wilderness in his human nature, without the help of his divinity, Guyon is tempted without the help of reason. Neither Phaedria nor Mammon could even pose temptations to the man guided by right reason. Later he will need the active support of both divine grace and right reason, but this adventure tests solely his love of virtue and "proper pride" in his accomplishments. According to Aquinas (*Summa Theologica*, II.132.1): "Now it is not a sin to know and approve one's own good. . . . Likewise it is not a sin to be willing to approve one's own good works. . . ."

4.1 Spenser's continued allusion to the Sermon on the Mount links the temptation of Mammon to the song of Phaedria. "Lay not up for yourselves treasures upon earth, where moth and rust doth corrupt . . ." (Matthew 6:19).

5.4 *Mulciber's devouring element:* fire. Mulciber is another name for Vulcan.

But most were stamped, and in their metal bare
The antique shapes of kings and kaisers° strange and rare.   *caesars*

6 Soon as he Guyon saw, in great affright
And haste he rose for to remove aside
Those precious hills from stranger's envious sight,
And down them pourèd through an hole full wide
Into the hollow earth, them there to hide.
But Guyon lightly to him leaping, stayed
His hand, that trembled as one terrified;
And though himself werc at the sight dismayed,
Yet him perforce° restrained, and to him doubtful said: *by force*

7 'What art thou man—if man at all thou art—
That here in desert hast thine habitance,
And these rich hills of wealth dost hide apart
From the world's eye and from her right usance?'
Thereat with staring eyes fixèd askance,
In great disdain he answered, 'Hardy elf,
That darest view my direful countenance,
I read thee rash and heedless of thyself
To trouble my still seat and heaps of precious pelf.

8 'God of the world and wordlings I me call,
Great Mammon, greatest god below the sky,
That of my plenty pour out unto all,
And unto none my graces do envy.
Riches, renowm, and principality,
Honor, estate, and all this world'ès good,
For which men swink° and sweat incessantly,   *labor*
Fro me do flow into an ample flood,
And in the hollow earth have their eternal brood.°   *breeding place*

9 'Wherefore if me thou deign to serve and sue,
At thy command, lo, all these mountains be;
Or if to thy great mind or greedy view
All these may not suffice, there shall to thee
Ten times so much be numbered frank and free.'
'Mammon,' said he, 'thy godhead's vaunt° is vain,   *boast of divinity*
And idle offers of thy golden fee;°   *reward*
To them that covet such eye-glutting gain
Proffer thy gifts, and fitter servants entertain.

6.1–5 "Lay not up for yourselves treasures upon earth . . . where thieves break through and steal" (Matthew 6:19).

8.1–2 *Mammon*: from the Syriac "wealth." The Syriac word was misunderstood by some early commentators on the Gospels who interpreted it as the name of one of the fallen angels and, from the New Testament context, the god of earthly wealth. In the Gospels he is the antithesis of God: "No man can serve two masters: for either he will hate the one, and love the other; or else he will hold to the one, and despise the other. Ye cannot serve God and mammon" (Matthew 6:24).

10   'Me ill besits, that in der-doing° arms   *courageous*
     And honor's suit° my vowèd days do spend,   *pursuit*
     Unto thy bounteous baits and pleasing charms—
     With which weak men thou witchest—to attend.
     Regard of wordly muck doth foully blend°   *stain*
     And low abase the high heroic sprite,
     That joys for crowns and kingdoms to contend.
     Fair shields, gay steeds, bright arms be my delight;
     Those be the riches fit for an adventurous knight.'

11   'Vainglorious elf,' said he, 'dost not thou weet
     That money can thy wants at will supply?
     Shields, steeds, and arms, and all things for thee meet
     It can purvey in twinkling of an eye,
     And crowns and kingdoms to thee multiply.
     Do not I kings create, and throw the crown
     Sometimes to him that low in dust doth lie,
     And him that reigned into his room thrust down,
     And whom I lust° do heap with glory and renown?'   *please*

12   'All otherwise,' said he, 'I riches read,°   *regard*
     And deem them root of all disquietness.
     First got with guile, and then preserved with dreed,
     And after spent with pride and lavishness,
     Leaving behind them grief and heaviness;°   *misery*
     Infinite mischiefs of them do arise:
     Strife and debate, bloodshed and bitterness,
     Outrageous wrong and hellish covetise;
     That noble heart in great dishonor doth despise.

13   'Ne thine be kingdoms, ne the scepters thine;
     But realms and rulers thou dost both confound,
     And loyal truth to treason dost incline.
     Witness the guiltless blood poured oft on ground,
     The crownèd often slain, the slayer crowned,
     The sacred diadem in pieces rent,
     And purple robe gorèd with many a wound,
     Castles surprised, great cities sacked and brent:
     So mak'st thou kings and gainest wrongful government.

12.1–9 "But they that will be rich fall into temptation and a snare, and into many foolish and hurtful lusts, which drown men in destruction and perdition. For the love of money is the root of all evil . . ." (1 Timothy 6:9–10). Spenser's list of the mischiefs arising from riches is conventional; see the similar listing of the "daughters of covetousness" in *Summa Theologica*, II.118.8.

13.1–9 The political evils resulting from excessive love of wealth are forms of injustice, acts done for gain (*Ethics*, V, p. 143). A vivid and detailed picture of the political evils of the love of money is found in Wiiliam Langland's *Piers Plowman*, Passus 3–4 (B text). Medieval political thought, but to a far greater extent that of the Renaissance, is characterized especially by a phobia of treason and revolution.

14 'Long were to tell the troublous storms that toss
   The private state° and make the life unsweet;   i.e. *private man*
   Who° swelling sails in Caspian Sea doth cross,   *he who*
   And in frail wood on Adrian Gulf doth fleet,°   *float*
   Doth not, I ween, so many evils meet.'
   Then Mammon waxing wroth, 'And why then,' said,
   'Are mortal men so fond° and undiscrete   *foolish*
   So evil thing to seek unto their aid,
   And having not, complain, and having it, upbraid?'

15 'Indeed,' quoth he, 'through foul intemperance
   Frail men are oft captived to covetise.
   But would they think with how small allowance
   Untroubled nature doth herself suffice,
   Such superfluities they would despise,
   Which with sad cares impeach° our native joys.   *impair*
   At the well-head the purest streams arise;
   But mucky filth his° branching arms annoys,   *its*
   And with uncomely weeds the gentle wave accloys.°   *clogs*

16 'The antique° world, in his first flowering youth,   *ancient*
   Found no defect in his Creator's grace,
   But with glad thanks and unreprovèd truth,
   The gifts of sovereign Bounty did embrace.
   Like angels' life was then men's happy case;
   But later ages' pride, like corn-fed steed,
   Abused her plenty and fat swollen increase
   To all licentious lust, and gan exceed
   The measure of her mean, and natural first need.

17 'Then gan a cursèd hand the quiet womb
   Of his great grandmother with steel to wound,
   And the hid treasures in her sacred tomb
   With sacrilege to dig. Therein he found
   Fountains of gold and silver to abound,

14.4   *Adrian Gulf:* the Adriatic Sea, which, like the Caspian, was famous for its "troublous storms."

15.3–9   The statement of this important idea, the distinction between what is necessary to sustain life and a superfluity of wealth, comes from Boethius: "No doubt the fruits of the earth are given to animals and men for their food; but, if you simply wish to satisfy the demands of nature, there is no reason why you should struggle for the superfluities of Fortune. For nature's needs are few and small; if you try to glut yourself with too many things, you will find your excesses either unpleasant or positively harmful" (*The Consolation of Philosophy*, II. Prose 5, pp. 31–32). Spenser may also have had in mind Aristotle's distinction between natural wealth and unnatural wealth, the latter being an end in itself, the former a means to the preservation of life (*Politics*, I.8–9).

16–17   Guyon alludes to the myth of the Golden Age. Again the ultimate source may be Boethius, *The Consolation of Philosophy*, II. Meter 5 (pp. 33–34). Chaucer, too, adapted these verses in his poem "The Former Age." For the myth in classical form see Ovid, *Metamorphoses*, I (pp. 33–35).

Of which the matter of his huge desire
And pompous pride eftsoons° he did compound;   *presently*
Then avarice gan through his veins inspire°   *breathe*
His greedy flames and kindled life-devouring fire.'

18 'Son,' said he then, 'let be thy bitter scorn,
And leave the rudeness of that antique age
To them that lived therein in state forlorn;
Thou that dost live in later times, must wage°   *do*
Thy works for wealth, and life for gold engage.°   *hire out*
If then thee list my offered grace to use,
Take what thou please of all this surplusage;
If thee list not, leave have thou to refuse,
But thing refusèd, do not afterward accuse.'

19 'Me list not,' said the elfin knight, 'receive
Thing offered till I know it well be got,
Ne wot° I but thou didst these goods bereave   *know*
From rightful owner by unrighteous lot,°   *division*
Or that blood-guiltiness or guile them blot.'
'Perdie,'° quoth he, 'yet never eye did view,   *in truth*
Ne tongue did tell,° ne hand these handled not,   *count*
But safe I have them kept in secret mew°   *cell*
From heaven's sight, and power of all which them puurse.'

20 'What secret place,' quoth he, 'can safely hold
So huge a mass, and hide from heaven's eye?
Or where hast thou thy wone,° that so much gold   *home*
Thou canst preserve from wrong and robbery?'
'Come thou,' quoth he, 'and see.' So by and by
Through that thick covert he him led, and found
A darksome way, which no man could descry,°   *discover*
That deep descended through the hollow ground
And was with dread and horror compassèd around.

21 At length they came into a larger space
That stretched itself into an ample plain,
Through which a beaten broad highway did trace,
That straight did lead to Pluto's grisly reign.°   *horrible kingdom*
By that way's side there sat infernal Pain,

19.1–5 Again the fictional character-
ization of Guyon seems to suffer for the
sake of Spenser's doctrine. This is a clear
reflection of the idea in Aristotle's *Ethics*,
IV: "One may infer from what has been
said that another trait of the liberal man
will be this. He will not accept money
from a tainted source—receipts of that
sort are impossible to one who sets little
store by riches" (p. 111).

20.3–5 *Come thou . . . and see:* an
ironic echo of Christ's invitation: "Rabbi
. . . where dwellest thou? He saith unto
them, Come and see" (John 1:38–39).
21.5–25 This description of the sub-
urbs of hell depends primarily on the
Aeneid, VI.273–281: "In front of the very
Entrance Hall, in the very Jaws of Hades,
Grief and Resentful Care have laid their
beds. Shapes terrible of aspect have their

And fast beside him sat tumultuous Strife;
The one in hand an iron whip did strain,°   *grip*
The other brandishèd a bloody knife,
And both did gnash their teeth, and both did threaten life.

22 On th' other side in one consort° there sate   *group*
Cruel Revenge and rancorous Despite,
Disloyal Treason and heart-burning Hate,
But gnawing Jealousy out of their sight
Sitting alone, his bitter lips did bite,
And trembling Fear still to and fro did fly,
And found no place where safe he shroud° him might;   *hide*
Lamenting Sorrow did in darkness lie,
And Shame his ugly face did hide from living eye.

23 And over them sad Horror with grim hue
Did always soar, beating his iron wings;
And after him owls and night-ravens flew,
The hateful messengers of heavy° things,   *woeful*
Of death and dolor telling sad tidings;
Whiles sad Celaeno, sitting on a clift,°   *cliff*
A song of bale and bitter sorrow sings,
That heart of flint asunder could have rift.°   *split*
Which having ended, after him she flyeth swift.

24 All these before the gates of Pluto lay,
By whom they passing, spake unto them nought.
But th' elfin knight with wonder all the way
Did feed his eyes and filled his inner thought.
At last him to a little door he brought
That to the gate of hell, which gapèd wide,
Was next adjoining; ne them parted aught.°   *nothing separated*
Betwixt them both was but a little stride,   *them*
That did the House of Richess from hell-mouth divide.

---

dwelling there, pallid Disease, Old Age forlorn, Fear, Hunger, the Counsellor Evil, ugly Poverty, Death, and Pain. Next is Sleep who is close kin to Death, and Joy of Sinning and, by the threshold in front, Death's harbinger, War. And the iron chambers of the Furies are there, and Strife the insane, with a bloody ribbon binding her snaky hair. . . . There are besides many monstrous hybrid beasts, Centaurs stabled at the gate, Scyllas half-human, Briareus the hundredfold, Lerna's Beast with its horrifying hiss, and the Chimaera, weaponed with flames; next Gorgons, Harpies, and the shadowy shape of the three-bodied Geryon" (pp. 155–156). Spenser's owls (23.3) are to be found in a similar description in Seneca's *Hercules Furens*, 686–696.

21.5 *infernal:* (1596). 1590 reads *internal.*

23.6 *sad Celaeno:* one of the harpies, a beast with face and breasts of a woman, wings and talons of a bird of prey. "Celaeno herself, perching high on a rock, broke silence and spoke to us like a prophetess of doom . . ." (*Aeneid*, III. 245–246, p. 82). Celaeno is associated with avarice by some renaissance commentators on Virgil.

24.7 *aught:* (1596). 1590 reads *nought.*

25   Before the door sat self-consuming Care,
    Day and night keeping wary watch and ward,
    For fear lest Force or Fraud should unaware
    Break in and spoil the treasure there in guard.
    Ne would he suffer Sleep once thitherward
    Approach, albe his drowsy den were next;°   *adjoining*
    For next to Death is Sleep to be compared.
    Therefore his house is unto his annexed;
    Here Sleep, there Richess, and hell-gate them both betwext.

26   So soon as Mammon there arrived, the door
    To him did open and afforded way;
    Him followed eke Sir Guyon evermore,
    Ne darkness him ne danger might dismay.
    Soon as he entered was, the door straightway
    Did shut, and from behind it forth there leapt
    An ugly fiend, more foul than dismal day,
    The which with monstrous stalk behind him stepped,
    And ever as he went, due watch upon him kept.

27   Well hopèd he ere long that hardy guest—
    If ever covetous hand or lustful eye
    Or lips he laid on thing that liked° him best,   *pleased*
    Or ever sleep his eyestrings did untie—
    Should be his prey. And therefore still° on high   *always*
    He over him did hold his cruel claws,
    Threatening with greedy grip to do him die
    And rend in pieces with his ravenous paws,
    If ever he transgressed the fatal Stygian laws.

28   That house's form within was rude and strong,
    Like an huge cave hewn out of rocky clift,
    From whose rough vault the ragged breaches° hung,   *stalactites*
    Embossed with massy gold of glorious gift,°   *quality* ·
    And with rich metal loaded every rift,°   *crack*
    That heavy ruin they did seem to threat;
    And over them Arachne high did lift
    Her cunning web and spread her subtle° net,   *artful*
    Enwrappèd in foul smoke and clouds more black than jet.

26.6–27 Spenser's "ugly fiend" may owe something to Pausanius' Eurynomous: ". . . Eurynomus, said by the Delphian guides to be one of the demons in hades, who eats off all the flesh of the corpses, leaving only their bones. . . . He is of a color between blue and black, like that of meat flies; he is showing his teeth and is seated— and under him is spread vulture's skin" (*Description of Greece*, X.28.7, Loeb ed., IV, p. 533). Still more likely he is based on the fury who follows behind the initiate in the Eleusinian rites. The "fatal Stygian laws" also suggest an initiation.

26.7 *dismal day:* an unlucky day; *dismal* from Latin *dies mali*, "evil days," of which in medieval lore there were supposed to be two in each month, the first and the seventh from last.

29   Both roof and floor and walls were all of gold,
But overgrown with dust and old decay
And hid in darkness, that none could behold
The hue thereof. For view of cheerful day
Did never in that house itself display,
But a faint shadow of uncertain light,
Such as a lamp whose life does fade away,
Or as the moon clothèd with cloudy night,
Does show to him that walks in fear and sad affright.

30   In all that room was nothing to be seen
But huge great iron chests and coffers strong,
All barred with double bands, that none could ween°   *think*
Them to efforce° by violence or wrong;   *force open*
On every side they placèd were along.
But all the ground with skulls was scatterèd,
And dead men's bones which round about were flung,
Whose lives, it seemèd, whilom° there were shed,   *in the past*
And their vile carcasses now left unburièd.

31   They forward pass, ne Guyon yet spoke word
Till that they came unto an iron door
Which to them opened of his own accord,
And showed of richess such exceeding store
As eye of man did never see before;
Ne ever could within one place be found,
Though all the wealth which is, or was of yore,
Could gathered be through all the world around,
And that above were added to that under ground.

32   The charge thereof unto a covetous sprite
Commanded was, who thereby did attend,
And warily awaited day and night
From other covetous fiends it to defend,
Who it to rob and ransack did intend.
Then Mammon turning to that warrior said,

29.6–9 ". . . as men walk through a wood under a fitful moon's ungenerous light when Jupiter has hidden the sky in shade and a black night has stolen the color from the world" (*Aeneid*, VI.270–272, p. 155).

30–50 The temptations to wealth and power which Guyon successfully overcomes are analogous to the temptations to worldliness and avarice conquered by Christ in Milton's *Paradise Regained*, II.406–IV.194. Although Milton was probably influenced in his description of the second of Christ's temptations (according to Matthew) by Spenser's description of the Cave of Mammon, there was a large and detailed literature on the temptations in the work of medieval and renaissance theologians. The second temptation of Christ was generally treated as the temptations of the world (as opposed to the sins of the flesh and the devil) and was related specifically to the deadly sin of avarice, which, as Chaucer's Parson says, "is not only greed for land and property, but also at times for learning and for glory and for every outrageous thing" (*Canterbury Tales*, I.743).

'Lo here the world'ès bliss, lo here the end
To which all men do aim—rich to be made.
Such grace now to be happy is before thee laid.'

33   'Certes,' said he, 'I n'ill° thine offered grace,   *do not want*
     Ne to be made so happy do intend.
     Another bliss before mine eyes I place,
     Another happiness, another end.
     To them that list, these base regards° I lend;°   *concerns, relin-*
     But I in arms and in achievements brave   *quish*
     Do rather choose my flitting hours to spend,
     And to be lord of those that riches have,
     Than them to have myself, and be their servile slave.'

34   Thereat the fiend his gnashing teeth did grate,
     And grieved so long to lack his greedy° prey;   *greedily desired*
     For well he weenèd° that so glorious bait   *thought*
     Would tempt his guest to take thereof assay.°   *test*
     Had he so done, he had him snatched away
     More light than culver° in the falcon's fist.   *dove*
     Eternal God thee save from such decay.°   *death*
     But whenas Mammon saw his purpose missed,
     Him to entrap unwares° another way he wist.°   *unsuspecting,*
                                                                          knew

35   Thence forward he him led and shortly brought
     Unto another room, whose door forthright
     To him did open, as it had been taught.
     Therein an hundred ranges weren pight,°   *placed*
     And hundred furnaces all burning bright;
     By every furnace many fiends did bide,
     Deformèd creatures, horrible in sight,
     And every fiend his busy pains applied
     To melt the golden metal ready to be tried.°   *purified*

36   One with great bellows gathered filling air,
     And with forced wind the fuel did inflame;
     Another did the dying brands° repair   *burning sticks*
     With iron tongs, and sprinkled oft the same
     With liquid waves, fierce Vulcan's rage to tame,
     Who mastering them renewed his former heat.
     Some scummed the dross that from the metal came,
     Some stirred the molten ore with ladles great;
     And everyone did swink,° and everyone did sweat.   *labor*

35.1–36.9   Mammon's forge is based   clopses (*Aeneid*, VIII.418–454, pp. 213–
on Virgil's description of the underground   214).
forge of Vulcan operated by the Cy-   35.5   See notes on ix.28–30.

37 But when an earthly wight they present saw,
    Glistering in arms and battailous array,
    From their hot work they did themselves withdraw
    To wonder at the sight; for till that day,
    They never creature saw that came that way.
    Their staring eyes, sparkling with fervent fire,
    And ugly shapes did nigh the man dismay,
    That were it not for shame he would retire,
    Till that him thus bespake their sovereign lord and sire:

38 'Behold, thou faery's son, with mortal eye
    That° living eye before did never see.   *what*
    The thing that thou didst crave so earnestly,
    To weet whence all the wealth late showed by me
    Proceeded, lo now is revealed to thee.
    Here is the fountain of the world'ès good.
    Now therefore, if thou wilt enrichèd be,
    Advise thee well and change thy willful mood,
    Least thou perhaps hereafter wish, and be withstood.'

39 'Suffice it then, thou money god,' quoth he,
    'That all thine idle offers I refuse.
    All that I need I have; what needeth me
    To covet more than I have cause to use?
    With such vain shows thy worldlings vile abuse;
    But give me leave to follow mine emprise.'°   *adventure*
    Mammon was much displeased, yet n'ot° he choose   *he could not*
    But bear the rigor of his bold misprise,°   *contempt*
    And thence him forward led, him further to entice.

40 He brought him through a darksome narrow strait,
    To a broad gate all built of beaten gold.
    The gate was open, but therein did wait
    A sturdy villain, striding stiff and bold
    As if that highest God defy he would.
    In his right hand an iron club he held,
    And he himself was all of iron mold,
    Yet had both life and sense, and well could weld°   *wield*
    That cursèd weapon when his cruel foes he quelled.

41 Disdain he callèd was, and did disdain
    To be so called and whoso did him call.

37.6–8 In his shame Guyon shows the part of temperance called "shamefacedness, fear of doing a disgraceful deed . . ." (*Summa Theologica*, II.144.2).

41.1–9 *Disdain:* Disdain is arrogance, the proper guardian of the Court of Ambition. He represents the pride of the rich and powerful, those who have all the ornaments of greatness except the virtue without which greatness is impossible. Aristotle says of such people that "those who can boast of these advantages only are apt to be supercilious and overweening, for without virtue it is hard to bear good fortune modestly" (*Ethics*, IV.3, p. 123).

Stern was his look and full of stomach° vain,   *arrogance*
His portance° terrible, and stature tall,   *bearing*
Far passing th' height of men terrestrial;
Like an huge giant of the Titans' race,
That made him scorn all creatures great and small,
And with his pride all others' power deface.°   *destroy*
More fit amongst black fiends than men to have his place.

42   Soon as those glitterand arms he did espy,
That with their brightness made that darkness light,
His harmful club he gan to hurtle high,
And threaten battle to the faery knight;
Who likewise gan himself to battle dight,°   *prepare*
Till Mammon did his hasty hand withold,
And counseled him abstain from perilous fight;
For nothing might abash the villain bold,
Ne mortal steel empierce his miscreated mold.

43   So having him with reason pacified,
And the fierce carl° commanding to forbear,   *villain*
He brought him in. The room was large and wide,
As it some guild° or solemn temple were.   *guild hall*
Many great golden pillars did upbear
The massy roof, and riches huge sustain,
And every pillar deckèd was full dear°   *richly*
With crowns and diadems and titles vain,
Which mortal princes wore whiles they on earth did reign.

44   A rout of people there assembled were
Of every sort and nation under sky,
Which with great uproar pressèd to draw near
To th' upper part, where was advancèd high
A stately siege° of sovereign majesty;   *throne*
And thereon sat a woman gorgeous gay
And richly clad in robes of royalty,

42.1–43.1 Disdain threatens Guyon not only because he is virtuous, but also because he is not rich and powerful. The force of Mammon's playing the part of the palmer and pacifying Guyon with reason is ironic. It is all too true that the virtuous man has no chance against the arrogance of the wealthy. Spenser also wishes to imply that Disdain, like the monsters against whom Hercules and Aeneas drew their swords, is insubstantial, based on nothing real (*Aeneid*, VI. 290–291, p. 156, and Robert Graves, *The Greek Myths*, II, 153).
43.3–47.9 Spenser's picture of frantic

obsession with wealth and power as ends in themselves, though based largely on conventional materials, is fairly descriptive of court life in the Renaissance and possibly arises partly from his own, unsuccessful, efforts to gain favor at court. The Court of Philotime is the natural home of Braggadochio.
44.6 *a woman gorgeous gay:* Philotime (named in Stanza 49), from Greek, *philotimia*—love of honor. She is remarkably like Langland's Lady Meed: "I saw a woman richly clothed, covered with the finest furs, wearing a crown better than the king's. Her fingers were fashionably

That never earthly prince in such array
His glory did enhance, and pompous pride display.

45   Her face right wondrous fair did seem to be,
That her broad beauty's beam great brightness threw
Through the dim shade, that all men might it see.
Yet was not that same her own native hue,°   *form*
But wrought by art and counterfeited shew,
Thereby more lovers unto her to call;
Nath'less most heavenly fair in deed and view°   *appearance*
She by creation was, till she did fall;
Thenceforth she sought for helps to cloak her crime withal.

46   There as in glistering glory she did sit,
She held a great gold chain y-linkèd° well,   *linked*
Whose upper end to highest heaven was knit
And lower part did reach to lowest hell;
And all that press° did round about her swell   *crowd*
To catchen hold of that long chain, thereby
To climb aloft and others to excel;
That was Ambition, rash desire to sty,°   *rise*
And every link thereof a step of dignity.

47   Some thought to raise themselves to high degree
By riches and unrightèous reward,
Some by close shouldering,° some by flattery,   *secret intrigue*
Others through friends, others for base regard;° *bribes*
And all by wrong ways for themselves prepared.
Those that were up themselves kept others low,
Those that were low themselves held others hard,

---

covered with golden rings whose settings were rubies . . . and the most expensive diamonds, and two kinds of sapphire. . . . Her costume ravished me; I never saw such wealth" (*Piers Plowman*, B.II.8–17). Philotime is an anti-Gloriana.

46.1–9 The great golden chain of Ambition, held by Philotime, is derived from the *Iliad*, VIII.19–22: "Suspend a golden rope from heaven and lay hold of the end of it, all of you together. Try as you may, you will never draw Zeus the High Counsellor down from heaven to the ground" (p. 145). Greek and Christian philosophers developed Homer's image into one of the most important symbols in Western thought. The golden chain attached to the throne of Zeus represents the rational order imposed upon creation by God, as well as the law according to which an orderly universe was created and is sustained. This law is divine reason made manifest in nature. For the renaissance mythographer Natalis Comes, the golden chain represents "sometimes avarice and sometimes ambition . . ." (*Mythologiue*, 2.4). See Lotspeich, p. 64. Spenser combines both interpretations to suggest that the obsession with the false honor that derives from wealth and power corrupts the rational order of the universe, especially, of course, the rational structure of society.

46.9 *a step of dignity:* literally a rank in society. Elizabethan society was an aristocracy based upon numerous legally sanctioned class distinctions. The hierarchical society was thought to be analogous to the order of nature, and its structure was thought to be sanctioned by divine law. Ambition may be generally defined as a rebellion against the law of nature, an attempt to take a higher place in nature than one was created to occupy. Satan, who attempted to usurp the throne of God, was the first ambitious spirit.

Ne suffered them to rise or greater grow,
But everyone did strive his fellow down to throw.

48 Which whenas Guyon saw, he gan inquire
What meant that press about that lady's throne,
And what she was that did so high aspire.
Him Mammon answerèd, 'That goodly one
Whom all that folk with such contention
Do flock about, my dear, my daughter is;
Honor and dignity from her alone
Derivèd are, and all this world'ès bliss
For which ye men do strive. Few get, but many miss.

49 'And fair Philotimè she rightly hight,°   *is called*
The fairest wight that woneth° under sky,   *dwells*
But that this darksome nether world her light
Doth dim with horror and deformity,
Worthy of heaven and high felicity,
From whence the gods have her for envy thrust.
But sith thou hast found favor in mine eye,
Thy spouse I will her make—if that thou lust°—   *desire*
That she may thee advance for works and merits just.'

50 'Gramercy Mammon,' said the gentle knight,
'For so great grace and offered high estate.
But I, that am frail flesh and earthly wight,
Unworthy match for such immortal mate
Myself well wot, and mine unequal fate;
And were I not, yet is my troth y-plight
And love avowed to other lady late,°   *lately*
That to remove the same I have no might.
To change love causeless° is reproach to warlike knight.' *without cause*

51 Mammon enmovèd was with inward wrath;
Yet forcing it to feign,° him forth thence led   *hiding his anger*
Through grisly shadows by a beaten path
Into a garden goodly garnishèd
With herbs and fruits, whose kinds mote not be read°—   *told*
Not such as earth out of her fruitful womb
Throws forth to men, sweet and well-savorèd,
But direful deadly black, both leaf and bloom,
Fit to adorn the dead and deck the dreary tomb.

50.1–9 Guyon's answer shows not only that he is tactful (*Ethics*, IV.6, pp. 130–131) but also that he has proper ambition. He is not the excessively ambitious man who "shows an inordinate desire for honor or desires it from an improper source . . ." (*Ethics*, IV.4, p. 126).

51.8 *But direful deadly black:* Spenser's black garden derives ultimately from the Grove of Persephone in *Odyssey*, X (p. 169); the black herbs derive probably from commentaries on *Aeneid*, VI.281–283 (p. 155).

52 There mournful cypress grew in greatest store,
    And trees of bitter gall and ebon° sad,   *ebony*
    Dead-sleeping poppy and black hellebore,
    Cold coloquintida and tetra mad,
    Mortal samnitis and cicuta bad,
    With which th' unjust Athenians made to die
    Wise Socrates, who thereof quaffing glad,
    Poured out his life and last philosophy
    To the fair Critias, his dearest belamy.°   *friend*

53 The Garden of Proserpina this hight;°   *was called*
    And in the midst thereof a silver seat
    With a thick arbor goodly overdight,°   *placed overhead*
    In which she often used from open heat
    Herself to shroud, and pleasures to entreat.°   *entertain herself*
    Next thereunto did grow a goodly tree,   *with*
    With branches broad dispread and body great,
    Clothèd with leaves, that none the wood mote see,
    And loaden all with fruit as thick as it might be.

54 Their fruit were golden apples glistering bright,
    That goodly was their glory to behold.
    On earth like never grew, ne living wight
    Like ever saw, but° they from hence were sold;°   *unless, brought*
    For those which Hercules with conquest bold

52.1–9 The plants in the Garden of
Proserpina are all either poisons or sym-
bols of death because Proserpina (Per-
sephone) in her role as Queen of Hades
is goddess of poisons (Pausanius, *Descrip-
tion of Greece*, X.28.5). Among the plants
mentioned, Cypress is traditionally asso-
ciated with funerals. *Coloquintida* is
colocynth, *tetra* is perhaps deadly night-
shade, and *samnitis* has not been identi-
fied. For the death of Socrates, about
which Spenser is not accurate, see Plato's
Phaedo. Because of the circumstances of
Socrates' death and the doctrine of life
after death found in the *Phaedo*, Socrates
was treated as type of Christ by many
authors.
   52.6 *With which:* (1596). 1590 reads
Which with.
   53.2 *silver seat:* the Chair of Forget-
fulness, in which the hero Theseus was
persuaded to sit by Pluto. Theseus' flesh
grew to the chair and he remained a cap-
tive until Hercules invaded hell and
rescued him (Robert Graves, *The Greek
Myths*, I, 363–364). Hercules' rescue of
Theseus is a type of Christ's rescue of
Adam from hell. Perhaps also Spenser
intends an allusion to the forbidden seat
of Ceres in the Eleusinian rite of initiation.
   53.6–54.4 The golden apple tree of

Persephone is taken from Claudian's
Rape of Proserpine, II: "There is, more-
over, a precious tree in the leafy groves
whose curving branches gleam with living
ore—a tree consecrate to thee" (*Claudian*,
trans. Maurice Platnauer, 2 vols., Loeb
Classical Library, II, 339). Pluto promises
the tree as well as other gifts to Persephone
as he takes her to Hades. This is probably
the same tree from which Persephone took
the apple which, when she ate it, con-
demned her to spend a part of each year
in Hades. Persephone's fate is a type of
the fall of Eve.
   54.5–6 Hercules' eleventh labor, ac-
cording to some authorities, was to get
fruit from the golden apple-tree cared for
by the Hesperides, daughters of Atlas. In
order to get the fruit he had first to kill a
dragon which guarded the tree. The
labors of Hercules were widely allegorized
as types of Christ's conquest of evil, as
in Pierre de Ronsard's *Hercule Chrétien*.
Although Ronsard does not mention the
apples of the Hesperides, other writers
compare Hercules' killing the dragon
which guarded the tree to Christ's victory
over Satan, who assumed the form of a
serpent to tempt Eve to eat the apple of
the Tree of Knowledge.

Got from great Atlas' daughters hence began,
And planted there, did bring forth fruit of gold;
And those with which th' Euboean young man wan°   *won*
Swift Atalanta, when through craft he her outran.

55 Here also sprung that goodly golden fruit
With which Acontius got his lover true,
Whom he had long time sought with fruitless suit.
Here eke that famous golden apple grew,
The which amongst·the gods false Ate threw;
For which th' Idaean ladies disagreed,
Till partial Paris dempt° it Venus' due,°   *judged, rightful*
And had of her fair Helen for his meed,   *prize*
That many noble Greeks and Trojans made to bleed.

56 The warlike elf much wondered at this tree
So fair and great that shadowed all the ground;
And his broad branches, laden with rich fee,°   *prizes*
Did stretch themselves without° the utmost bound   *beyond*
Of this great garden, compassed with a mound,
Which over-hanging, they themselves did steep
In a black flood which flowed about it round;
That is the river of Cocytus deep,
In which full many souls do endless wail and weep.

57 Which to behold, he clumb up to the bank,
And looking down, saw many damnèd wights
In those sad waves, which direful deadly stank,
Plungèd continually of° cruel sprites,   *by*
That with their piteous cries and yelling shrights°   *shrieks*
They made the further shore resounden° wide.   *echo*
Amongst the rest of those same rueful sights,
One cursèd creature he by chance espied
That drenchèd lay full deep under the garden side.

54.8–55.3 The story of Atalanta and Hippomenes is told in Ovid's *Metamorphoses*, X.560–680, pp. 261–266; the story of Acontius and Cydippe can be found in Ovid's *Heroides*, XX and XXI. Both stories, relating the trickery of a maiden by means of a piece of fruit and a subsequent loss of chastity, are probably types of Eve's fall through the temptation of the apple. The chaste Atalanta was a huntress much like Belphoebe.

55.4–9 For the story of the golden apple which Ate, the goddess of discord, threw into the midst of the wedding banquet of Peleus and Thetis see Robert Graves, *The Greek Myths*, II, 269. Paris, who awarded the apple to Venus as the fairest, was given Helen as his prize, and his abduction of Helen precipitated the Trojan War.

56.8–9 *Cocytus:* a river in Hades for which see *Aeneid*, VI.131–139, 295–330 (pp. 151, 156–157). Spenser's conception of Cocytus probably comes from the medieval tradition. Virgil's description of Cocytus suggests that the Lake of Idleness into which Pyrochles and Atin jump is a Cocytus in disguise: "There in mud and murk seethes the Abyss, enormous and engulfing, choking forth all its sludge into Cocytus" (p. 156).

57.8–60.5 The description of Tantalus is based on the *Odyssey*, XI (p. 187). In medieval literature the punishment of Tantalus is a common symbol of avarice. Spenser relates him specifically to ambi-

58 Deep was he drenchèd to the upmost chin,
    Yet gaped still, as coveting to drink
    Of the cold liquor which he waded in,
    And stretching forth his hand, did often think
    To reach the fruit which grew upon the brink;
    But both the fruit from hand and flood from mouth
    Did fly aback and made him vainly swink,°   *labor*
    The whiles he starved with hunger and with drouth.
    He daily died, yet never throughly° dyen couth.°   *thoroughly,*
                                                         could

59 The knight him seeing labor so in vain,
    Asked who he was and what he meant thereby;
    Who groaning deep, thus answered him again:
    'Most cursèd of all creatures under sky,
    Lo Tantalus, I here tormented lie;
    Of whom high Jove wont whilom° feasted be,   *was accustomed*
    Lo here I now for want of food do die.   *formerly*
    But if that thou be such as I thee see,
    Of grace I pray thee, give to eat and drink to me.'

60 'Nay, nay, thou greedy Tantalus,' quoth he,
    'Abide the fortune of thy present fate,
    And unto all that live in high degree°   *eminent positions*
    Ensample be of mind intemperate,
    To teach them how to use their present state.'
    Then gan the cursèd wretch aloud to cry,
    Accusing highest Jove and gods ingrate,
    And eke blaspheming heaven bitterly
    As author of unjustice, there to let him die.

61 He looked a little further and espied
    Another wretch, whose carcass deep was drent°   *submerged*
    Within the river, which the same did hide.
    But both his hands most filthy feculent°   *soiled*
    Above the water were on high extent,°   *extended*
    And feigned to wash themselves incessantly;
    Yet nothing cleaner were for such intent,
    But rather fouler seemèd to the eye,
    So lost his labor vain and idle° industry.   *futile*

---

tion probably because of the myth that
Tantalus served up his own son Pelops
as a banquet to the gods. Another story
has it that Tantalus was punished be-
cause he stole ambrosia and nectar from
the gods. Both myths are related in
Pindar's *Olympia* I (*Odes of Pindar*, trans.
Richmond Lattimore, University of Chi-
cago Press, pp. 2–3). Tantalus' son was
restored to life by the gods.
    60.4 *intemperate:* (1596). 1590 reads
more temperate.

61–62 The figure of Pontius Pilate is
an indication that Guyon's ordeal, espe-
cially the Garden of Proserpina, is not
simply a pagan fiction. The cave of
Mammon, the garden, the tree, even the
mythological allusions, are all suggestive
of Christian history, and cannot be under-
stood except in the light of its chief
events. Tantalus and Pilate are similar in
their murderous acts, as are the resurrec-
tions of Pelops and Christ.

62 The knight him calling, askèd who he was,
Who lifting up his head, him answered thus:
'I Pilate am, the falsest judge, alas,
And most unjust, that by unrightèous
And wicked doom to Jews despiteous
Delivered up the Lord of Life to die,
And did acquit a murderer felonous;
The whiles my hands I washed in purity,
The whiles my soul was soiled with foul iniquity.'

63 Infinite mo,° tormented in like pain   *more*
He there beheld, too long here to be told.
Ne Mammon would there let him long remain,
For terror of the tortures manifold
In which the damnèd souls he did behold,
But roughly him bespake: 'Thou fearful fool,
Why takest not of that same fruit of gold,
Ne sittest down on that same silver stool
To rest thy weary person in the shadow cool?'

64 All which he did to do him deadly fall
In frail intemperance through sinful bait;
To which if he inclinèd had at all,
That dreadful fiend which did behind him wait
Would him have rent in thousand pieces straight.°   *immediately*
But he was wary wise in all his way,
And well perceivèd his deceitful sleight,
Ne suffered lust his safety to betray;
So goodly did beguile the guiler of his prey.

65 And now he has so long remained there
That vital powers gan wax both weak and wan
For want of food and sleep, which two upbear
Like mighty pillars this frail life of man,
That none without the same enduren can.
For now three days of men were full outwrought°   *completed*
Since he this hardy enterprise began;
Forthy° great Mammon fairly he besought   *therefore*
Into the world to guide him back, as he him brought.

66 The god, though loath, yet was constrained t' obey;
For lenger time than that no living wight
Below the earth might suffered be to stay;
So back again him brought to living light.
But all so soon as his enfeebled sprite
Gan suck this vital air into his breast,
As overcome with too exceeding might,
The life did flit away out of her nest,
And all his senses were with deadly fit oppressed.

CANTO viii

Sir Guyon laid in swoon is by
Acrates' sons despoiled,
Whom Arthur soon hath rescuèd
And paynim° brethren foiled.   *heathen*

1   And is there care in heaven? And is there love
    In heavenly spirits to these creatures base,
    That may compassion of their evils move?
    There is; else much more wretched were the case
    Of men than beasts. But O, th' exceeding grace
    Of highest God, that loves his creatures so,
    And all his works with mercy doth embrace,
    That blessèd angels he sends to and fro
    To serve to wicked man, to serve his wicked foe.

2   How oft do they their silver bowers leave
    To come to succor us that succor want!°   *lack*
    How oft do they with golden pinions° cleave   *wings*
    The flitting° skies, like flying pursuivant,°   *insubstantial,*
    Against foul fiends to aid us militant!°   *messenger*
    They for us fight, they watch and duly ward,   *militantly*
    And their bright squadrons round about us plant;
    And all for love, and nothing for reward.
    O why should heavenly God to men have such regard?

3   During the while that Guyon did abide
    In Mammon's house, the palmer, whom whilere°   *before*
    That wanton maid of passage had denied,
    By further search had passage found elsewhere;
    And being on his way, approachèd near
    Where Guyon lay in trance, when suddenly
    He heard a voice that callèd loud and clear,
    'Come hither, come hither, O come hastily,'
    That all the fields resounded with the rueful cry.

4   The palmer lent his ear unto the noise
    To weet who callèd so importunely;
    Again he heard a more efforcèd° voice,   *forceful*

1.8–9 "Are they not all ministering
spirits, sent forth to minister for them
who shall be heirs of salvation" (Hebrews
1:14). Guardian angels are instruments of
God's love and grace.

2.9 "Lord, what is man, that thou
takest knowledge of him! or the son of
man, that thou makest account of him!"
(Psalms 144:3).

That bade him come in haste. He by and by
His feeble feet directed to the cry;
Which to that shady delve him brought at last
Where Mammon erst° did sun his treasury.   *before*
There the good Guyon he found slumbering fast
In senseless dream; which sight at first him sore aghast.°   *terrified*

5   Beside his head there sat a fair young man
    Of wondrous beauty and of freshest years,
    Whose tender bud° to blossom new began   *youth*
    And flourish fair above his equal peers.
    His snowy front° curlèd with golden hairs,   *forehead*
    Like Phoebus' face adorned with sunny rays,
    Divinely shone; and two sharp wingèd shears,°   *blades*
    Deckèd with diverse° plumes like painted jays,   *different colored*
    Were fixèd at his back to cut his airy ways.

6   Like as Cupido on Idaean hill,
    When having laid his cruel bow away,
    And mortal arrows wherewith he doth fill
    The world with murderous spoils and bloody prey,
    With his fair mother he him dights° to play   *attires*
    And with his goodly sisters, Graces three—
    The goddess pleasèd with his wanton play,
    Suffers herself through sleep beguiled to be,
    The whiles the other ladies mind their merry glee.

7   Whom when the palmer saw, abashed he was
    Through fear and wonder, that he nought could say,
    Till him the child bespoke: 'Long lacked, alas,
    Hath been thy faithful aid in hard assay,°   *trial*
    Whiles deadly fit thy pupil doth dismay.

5.1–6.9 Spenser's description of the
angel owes something to Tasso's portrait
of Gabriel:

Like to a man in show and shape he fared,
But full of heavenly majesty and might;
A stripling seemed he, thrice five winters
  old,
And radiant beams adorned his locks of
  gold.

Of silver wings he took a shining pair,
Fringed with gold, unwearied, nimble,
  swift,
With these he parts the winds, the clouds,
  the air
And over seas and earth himself doth lift.
    (*Jerusalem Delivered* I.13–14)

But Spenser owes even more to late
medieval and renaissance distinctions be-
tween "sacred love" and "profane love."

In medieval and renaissance art the
blinded love (Cupid) of Canto iii who
attempted to inflame Belphoebe's eyes
represents the lust of the appetite. The
seeing love (Cupid) represents spiritual
love. Spenser's description appears to de-
pend more on the medieval tradition of
art and mythography than on the renais-
sance Neoplatonic tradition—especially
the description of Cupid as a youth.
Medieval commentators often use such a
figure of Cupid as a symbol of God's love
for man. See Panofsky, *Studies in Iconol-
ogy*, pp. 95–169.
    6.1 *Idaean hill:* Mount Ida, where the
"judgment of Paris" took place.
    7.1–2 The palmer is abashed because
God's love and grace transcend nature
and right reason and are not compre-
hended by them. Note that only the
palmer, not Guyon, sees the angel.

Behold this heavy° sight, thou reverend sire,   *woeful*
But dread of death and dolor do away;°   *cast off*
For life ere long shall to her home retire,
And he that breathless seems shall courage bold respire.

8 'The charge which God doth unto me aret°   *entrust*
Of his dear safety, I to thee commend;
Yet will I not forgo, ne yet forget
The care thereof myself unto the end,
But evermore him succor and defend
Against his foe and mine. Watch thou I pray,
For evil is at hand him to offend.'
So having said, eftsoons he gan display°   *spread*
His painted nimble wings and vanished quite away.

9 The palmer seeing his left empty place,°   *place left empty*
And his slow eyes beguilèd of their sight,
Wox° sore afraid, and standing still a space,   *became*
Gazed after him as fowl escaped by flight.
At last him turning to his charge behight,°   *entrusted*
With trembling hand his troubled pulse gan try;
Where finding life not yet dislodgèd quite,
He much rejoiced and cured° it tenderly,   *cared for*
As chicken newly hatched, from dreaded destiny.

10 At last he spied where towards him did pace
Two paynim° knights all armed as bright as sky,   *heathen*
And them beside an aged sire did trace,°   *walk*
And far before a lightfoot page did fly
That breathèd strife and troublous enmity.
Those were the two sons of Acrates old,
Who meeting erst° with Archimago sly   *earlier*
Forby that idle strand,° of him were told   *stream*
That he which erst them combated was Guyon bold.

11 Which to avenge on him they dearly° vowed,   *earnestly*
Wherever that on ground they mote him find.
False Archimage provoked their courage proud,
And strifeful Atin in their stubborn mind
Coals of contention and hot vengeance tined.°   *kindled*
Now been they come whereas the palmer sate

8.3–6 The continuing cooperating grace of God is needed for perseverance in virtue in the face of the "shocks of temptation" (*Summa Theologica*, I.109. 10).

9.1–4 The palmer's reaction is compared with Braggadochio's at the flight of Archimago (iii.19). The differences as well as the similarity are significant.

10.2 *Two paynim knights:* Pyrochles and Cymochles. For the first time the two brothers are described as "paynims" —enemies of God and of true religion. In the earlier cantos they had represented irrational tendencies or types of human nature.

Keeping that slumbered corse° to him assigned;   *body*
Well knew they both his person, sith of late
With him in bloody arms they rashly did debate.

12 Whom when Pyrochles saw, inflamed with rage,
That sire he foul bespake: 'Thou dotard vile,
That with thy bruteness° shendst° thy comely age,   *stupidity, shames*
Abandon soon, I read, the caitiff spoil°   *miserable wreck*
Of that same outcast carcass that erewhile
Made itself famous through false treachery,
And crowned his coward crest with knightly style.°   *title of knighthood*
Lo where he now inglorious doth lie
To prove he livèd ill that did thus foully die.'

13 To whom the palmer fearless answerèd,
'Certes, sir knight, ye been too much to blame
Thus for to blot the honor of the dead,
And with foul cowardice his carcass shame
Whose living hands immortalized his name.
Vile is the vengeance on the ashes cold,
And envy base to bark at sleeping fame.
Was never wight that treason of him told;
Yourself his prowess proved and found him fierce and bold.'

14 Then said Cymochles, 'Palmer, thou dost dote,
Ne canst of prowess ne of knighthood deem,°   *judge*
Save as thou seest or hear'st; but well I wot
That of his puissance trial made extreme.
Yet gold all is not that doth golden seem,
Ne all good knights that shake well spear and shield.
The worth of all men by their end esteem,
And then due praise or due reproach them yield;
Bad therefore I him deem that thus lies dead on field.'

15 'Good or bad,' gan his brother fierce reply,
'What do I reck, sith that he died entire?°   *completely*
Or what doth his bad death now satisfy
The greedy hunger of revenging ire,
Sith wrathful hand wrought not her own desire?
Yet since no way is left to wreak my spite,
I will him reave° of arms, the victor's hire,°   *strip, reward*
And of that shield, more worthy of good knight;
For why should a dead dog be decked in armor bright?'

16 'Fair, sir,' said then the palmer suppliant,
'For knighthood's love, do not so foul a deed,

14.7-9 Cymochles misapplies a famous saying of Solon the lawgiver, reported in
Herodotus.

Ne blame° your honor with so shameful vaunt   *stain*
Of vile revenge—to spoil the dead of weed°   *clothing*
Is sacrilege and doth all sins exceed—
But leave these relics of his living might
To deck his hearse and trap° his tomb-black steed.'   *decorate*
'What hearse or steed,' said he, 'should he have dight,°   *prepared*
But be entombèd in the raven or the kite?'

17 With that, rude hand upon his shield he laid,
And th' other brother gan his helm unlace,
Both fiercely bent to have him disarrayed;
Till that they spied where towards them did pace
An armèd knight of bold and bounteous grace,
Whose squire bore after him an ebon° lance   *ebony*
And covered shield. Well kenned him so far space
Th' enchanter by his arms and amenance,°   *bearing*
When under him he saw his Lybian steed to prance;

18 And to those brethren said, 'Rise, rise belive,°   *immediately*
And unto battle do yourselves address;
For yonder comes the prowest knight alive,
Prince Arthur, flower of grace and nobiless,°   *nobility*
That hath to paynim knights wrought great distress,
And thousand Saracens foully done to die.'
That word so deep did in their hearts impress
That both eftsoons upstarted furiously,
And gan themselves prepare to battle greedily.

19 But fierce Pyrochles lacking his own sword,
The want° thereof now greatly gan to plain,°   *lack, complain*
And Archimage besought, him that afford
Which he had brought for Braggadocchio vain.
'So would I,' said th' enchanter, 'glad and fain
Beteem° to you this sword, you to defend,   *grant*

16.4–5 Not only was it considered a shameful violation of the chivalric code to steal a dead knight's armor; it was also the sacrilege which Christ's executioners committed (Mark 15:24).
16.8–9 "And the Philistine said to David, Come to me, and I will give thy flesh unto the fowls of the air, and to the beasts of the field" (I Samuel 17:44).
17.5 *An armèd knight:* Arthur, whose function in the structure of *The Faerie Queene* is to demonstrate in each book the perfect state of the virtue which is the subject of that book. By the end of the poem, as projected, Arthur would have represented the perfect hero, possessed of all virtues.

17.7 *covered shield:* In Book I, Arthur's shield is accidentally uncovered and its brilliant light completely paralyzes the giant Orgoglio, with whom Arthur is fighting. The uncovered shield in Book I is generally interpreted as divine grace. That it remains covered throughout the battle with Pyrochles and Cymochles suggests that, like Christ, Arthur is fighting his demonic enemies in his humanity without the special miraculous power of grace. This is not to say that he does not have the strength of faith and the ordinary grace which belongs to him as a Christian. He had the shield, he simply does not uncover it.

Or aught that else your honor might maintain,
But that this weapon's power I well have kenned°   *learned*
To be contrary to the work which ye intend.

0   'For that same knight's own sword this is of yore,
Which Merlin made by his almighty art
For that his nursling, when he knighthood swore,
Therewith to done his foes eternal smart.
The metal first he mixed with medaewort,
That no enchantment from his dint° might save,   *stroke*
Then it in flames of Aetna wrought apart,°   *worked into shape*
And seven times dipped in the bitter wave
Of hellish Styx, which hidden virtue° to it gave.   *power*

21 'The virtue is that neither steel nor stone
The stroke thereof from entrance may defend;
Ne ever may be usèd by his fone,°   *foes*
Ne forced his rightful owner to offend,
Ne ever will it break, ne ever bend.
Wherefore Morddure it rightfully is hight.
In vain therefore, Pyrochles, should I lend
The same to thee, against his lord to fight,
For sure it would deceive thy labor and thy might.'

22 'Foolish old man,' said then the pagan wroth,
'That weenest words or charms may force withstand.
Soon shalt thou see, and then believe for troth,
That I can carve with this enchanted brand°   *sword*
His lord's own flesh.' Therewith out of his hand
That virtuous steel he rudely snatched away,
And Guyon's shield about his wrist he band—
So ready dight fierce battle to assay°   *engage in*
And match his brother proud in battailous array.

23 By this that stranger knight in presence came
And goodly salued° them; who nought again   *saluted*
Him answerèd as courtesy became,
But with stern looks and stomachous° disdain   *arrogant*
Gave signs of grudge and discontentment vain.
Then turning to the palmer, he gan spy
Where at his feet, with sorrowful demain°   *demeanor*

20.1–21.6 Arthur's marvelous sword is a literary descendant of the many enchanted weapons which fill the medieval romances. It probably owes something to the *Aeneid*, where the sword of Turnus was also said to have been "tempered . . . while still white-hot in waters of Styx" (XII.90–91, p. 312). The name "Morddure" is probably imitated from *Orlando Furioso*, where the sword of the hero Orlando is called "Durlindana." Morddure translates *bite cruelly*.

20.5 *medaewort:* medic, a clover-like plant similar to alfalfa.

And deadly hue,° an armèd corse did lie,　　　　　　*deathlike appear-*
In whose dead face he read great magnanimity.　　　*ance*

24　Said he then to the palmer, 'Reverend sire,
　　What great misfortune hath betid° this knight?　*happened to*
　　Or did his life her fatal date expire,
　　Or did he fall by treason or by fight?
　　However, sure I rue his piteous plight.'
　　'Not one nor other,' said the palmer grave,
　　'Hath him befallen, but clouds of deadly night
　　Awhile his heavy eyelids covered have,
　　And all his senses drownèd in deep senseless wave.

25　'Which, those his cruel foes that stand hereby,
　　Making advantage, to revenge their spite
　　Would him disarm and treaten shamefully,
　　Unworthy usage of redoubted knight.
　　But you, fair sir, whose honorable sight°　　　　*appearance*
　　Doth promise hope of help and timely grace,
　　Mote I beseech to succor his sad plight,
　　And by your power protect his feeble case.
　　First praise of knighthood is foul outrage to deface.'

26　'Palmer,' said he, 'no knight so rude, I ween,
　　As to done outrage to a sleeping ghost;
　　Ne was there ever noble courage seen
　　That in advantage would his puissance boast.
　　Honor is least where odds appeareth most.
　　May be that better reason will assuage
　　The rash revengers' heat. Words well dispost°　　*disposed*
　　Have secret power t' appease inflamèd rage.
　　If not, leave unto me thy knight's last patronage.'°　*protection*

27　Tho° turning to those brethren, thus bespoke:　　*then*
　　'Ye warlike pair, whose valorous great might
　　It seems just wrongs to vengeance do provoke—
　　To wreak your wrath on this dead-seeming knight—
　　Mote aught° allay the storm of your despite　　*can anything*
　　And settle patience in so furious heat?
　　Not to debate the challenge of your right,
　　But for this carcass pardon I entreat,
　　Whom fortune hath already laid in lowest seat.'

23.9　*great magnanimity:* Magnanim-　　which [Guyon's faint], those cruel foes
ity is the crowning virtue in Aristotle's　　that stand hereby would disarm and treat
Ethics.　　　　　　　　　　　　　　　him shamefully to revenge their spite."
25.1–3　I.e., "Taking advantage of

28 To whom Cymochles said, 'For what art thou
    That mak'st thyself his daysman° to prolong   *lawyer*
    The vengeance prest?° Or who shall let° me now   *at hand, hinder*
    On this vile body from to wreak my wrong,
    And make his carcass as the outcast dung?
    Why should not that dead carrion satisfy
    The guilt, which if he livèd had thus long,
    His life for due revenge should dear abuy?°   *pay for*
    The trespass still doth live, albe° the person die.'   *although*

29 'Indeed,' then said the prince, 'the evil done
    Dies not when breath the body first doth leave,
    But from the grandsire to the nephew's° son   *grandson's*
    And all his seed the curse doth often cleave,
    Till vengeance utterly the guilt bereave:°   *take away*
    So straitly° God doth judge. But gentle knight   *rigorously*
    That doth against the dead his hand uprear,
    His honor stains with rancor and despite,
    And great disparagement makes to his former might.'

30 Pyrochles gan reply the second time,
    And to him said, 'Now felon, sure I read
    How that thou art partaker of his crime;
    Therefore, by Termagant, thou shalt be dead.'
    With that, his hand more sad° than lump of lead   *heavy*
    Uplifting high, he weenèd with Morddure—
    His own good sword Morddure—to cleave his head.
    The faithful steel such treason n'ould° endure,   *would not*
    But swerving from the mark, his lord's life did assure.

31 Yet was the force so furious and so fell
    That horse and man it made to reel aside.
    Nath'less the prince would not forsake his sell,°   *saddle*
    For well of yore he learnèd had to ride,
    But full of anger fiercely to him cried,
    'False traitor miscreant,° thou broken hast   *infidel*
    The law of arms, to strike foe undefied.°   *unchallenged*
    But thou thy treason's fruit, I hope, shalt taste
    Right sour, and feel the law the which thou hast defaced.'

32 With that, his baleful spear he fiercely bent
    Against the pagan's breast, and therewith thought

29.1–6 "For I the Lord thy God am a jealous God, visiting the iniquity of the fathers upon the children unto the third and fourth generation of them that hate me" (Exodus 20:5). Pyrochles and Cymochles are proof of Arthur's unintentionally ironic words—see their ancestry in iv.41.
    29.7 *uprear:* imperfect rhyme. Later editions read *upheave.* See note on ii.7.7.
    30.4 *Termagant:* A conventional oath of pagan knights in medieval romances; the origin of the term is not known.

His cursèd life out of her lodge have rent;
But ere the point arrivèd where it ought,
That sevenfold shield which he from Guyon brought
He cast between to ward the bitter stound.°   *blow*
Through all those folds the steel head passage wrought
And through his shoulder pierced; wherewith to ground
He groveling fell, all gorèd in his gushing wound.

33   Which when his brother saw, fraught with great grief
And wrath, he to him leapèd furiously,
And foully said, 'By Mahoun, cursèd thief,
That direful stroke thou dearly shalt abuy.'
Then hurling up his harmful blade on high,
Smote him so hugely on his haughty crest
That from his saddle forcèd him to fly;
Else mote it needs down to his manly breast
Have cleft his head in twain, and life thence dispossessed.

34   Now was the prince in dangerous distress,
Wanting his sword when he on foot should fight.
His single spear could do him small redress
Against two foes of so exceeding might,
The least of which was match for any knight.
And now the other, whom he erst did daunt,
Had reared himself again to cruel fight,
Three times more furious and more puissant,
Unmindful of his wound, of his fate ignorant.

35   So both at once him charge on either side
With hideous strokes and importable° power,   *unbearable*
That forcèd him his ground to traverse wide
And wisely watch to ward that deadly stour.°   *peril of death*
For in his shield as thick as stormy shower
Their strokes did rain, yet did he never quail
Ne backward shrink. But as a steadfast tower,
Whom foe with double battery° doth assail,   *artillery*
Them on her bulwark bears and bids them nought avail,

36   So stoutly he withstood their strong assay;°   *attack*
Till that at last, when he advantage spied,
His poignant spear he thrust with puissant sway°   *force*
At proud Cymochles whiles his shield was wide,°   *to one side*
That through his thigh the mortal steel did gride.°   *pierce*
He swerving with the force, within his flesh
Did break the lance, and let the head abide.
Out of the wound the red blood flowèd fresh,
That underneath his feet soon made a purple plesh.°   *pool*

33.3 *Mahoun:* Mohammed.

37 Horribly then he gan to rage and rail,
    Cursing his gods, and himself damning deep.
    Als° when his brother saw the red blood rail°   *also, flow*
    Adown so fast and all his armor steep,
    For very fellness loud he gan to weep,
    And said, 'Caitiff,° curse on thy cruel hand   *villain*
    That twice hath sped;° yet shall it not thee keep   *succeeded*
    From the third brunt of this my fatal brand.
    Lo where the dreadful death behind thy back doth stand.'

38 With that he struck, and th' other struck withal,°   *at the same time*
    That nothing seemed mote bear so monstrous might.
    The one upon his covered shield did fall,
    And glancing down would not his owner bite;
    But th' other did upon his truncheon smite,
    Which hewing quite asunder, further way
    It made and on his haqueton° did light;   *underjacket*
    The which dividing with importune sway,
    It seized in his right side; and there the dint did stay.°   *stop*

39 Wide was the wound, and a large lukewarm flood,
    Red as the rose, thence gushèd grievously;
    That when the paynim spied, the streaming blood
    Gave him great heart and hope of victory.
    On th' other side, in huge perplexity
    The prince now stood, having his weapon broke.
    Nought could he hurt, but still at ward° did lie;   *on guard*
    Yet with his truncheon he so rudely stroke
    Cymochles twice that twice him forced his foot revoke.

40 Whom when the palmer saw in such distress,
    Sir Guyon's sword he lightly to him raught,°   *reached*
    And said, 'Fair son, great God thy right hand bless
    To use that sword so well as he it ought.'°   *who owns it*
    Glad was the knight and with fresh courage fraught,
    Whenas again he armèd felt his hand.
    Then like a lion which hath long time sought
    His robbèd whelps, and at the last them fand
    Amongst the shepherd swains, then waxeth wood and yond,° *furious*

41 So fierce he laid about him and dealt blows
    On either side that neither mail could hold
    Ne shield defend the thunder of his throws.
    Now to Pyrochles many strokes he told;

40.7–8 "I will meet them as a bear
that is bereaved of her whelps, and will
rend the caul of their heart, and there
will I devour them as a lion . . ." (Hosea
13:8).

Eft to Cymochles twice so many fold.
Then back again turning his busy hand,
Them both at once compelled with courage bold
To yield wide way to his heart-thrilling brand;
And though they both stood stiff, yet could not both with-
    stand.

42   As savage bull whom two fierce mastiffs bait,
When rancor doth with rage him once engore,
Forgets with wary ward them to await,
But with his dreadful horns them drives afore
Or flings aloft or treads down in the floor,
Breathing out wrath and bellowing disdain,
That all the forest quakes to hear him roar—
So raged Prince Arthur twixt his foemen twain,
That neither could his mighty puissance sustain.

43   But ever at Pyrochles when he smit,°   *struck*
Who Guyon's shield cast ever him before,
Whereon the Faery Queen's portrait was writ,
His hand relented and the stroke forbore,
And his dear° heart the picture gan adore,   *loving*
Which oft the paynim saved from deadly stour.°   *blow*
But him henceforth the same can save no more;
For now arrivèd is his fatal hour,
That n'ot° avoided be by earthly skill or power.   *can not*

44   For when Cymochles saw the foul reproach
Which them appeachèd,° pricked with guilty shame   *accused*
And inward grief, he fiercely gan approach,
Resolved to put away that loathly blame°   *disgusting blemish*
Or die with honor and desert of fame;
And on the hauberk stroke the prince so sore
That quite disparted all the linkèd frame
And piercèd to the skin, but bit no more,
Yet made him twice to reel that never moved afore.

45   Whereat renfierced with wrath and sharp regret,
He struck so hugely with his borrowed blade
That it empierced the pagan's burgonet,
And cleaving the hard steel, did deep invade
Into his head, and cruel passage made

42.1–7 "He who has seen in the square a fierce bull, dogged and goaded and beaten all day, break out of his stockade around which the dense crowd flows, so that the people flee in terror, and he lifts on his horns now one and now another, may imagine that such or more terrible was the cruel African as he came on" (*Orlando Furioso*, XVIII.19).
    44.8 *no more:* (1596). 1590 reads *not thore.*

Quite through his brain. He tumbling down on ground
Breathed out his ghost, which to th' infernal shade
Fast flying, there eternal torment found
For all the sins wherewith his lewd life did abound.

46 Which when his german° saw, the stony fear   *brother*
Ran to his heart and all his sense dismayed;
Ne thenceforth life ne courage did appear,
But as a man whom hellish fiends have frayed,°   *frightened*
Long trembling still he stood. At last thus said:
'Traitor, what hast thou done? How ever may
Thy cursèd hand so cruelly have swayed
Against that knight? Harrow, and welaway,
After so wicked deed why livst thou lenger° day?'   *longer*

47 With that, all desperate, as loathing light,
And with revenge desiring soon to die,
Assembling all his force and utmost might,
With his own sword he fierce at him did fly
And struck and foined° and lashed outrageously,   *thrust*
Withouten reason or regard. Well knew
The prince with patience and sufferance sly
So hasty heat soon coolèd to subdue.
Tho when this breathless wox, that battle gan renew.

48 As when a windy tempest bloweth high,
That nothing may withstand his stormy stour,°   *turmoil*
The clouds, as things afraid, before him fly;
But all so soon as his outrageous power
Is laid,° they fiercely then begin to shower,   *calmed*
And as in scorn of his spent stormy spite,
Now all at once their malice forth do pour—
So did Prince Arthur bear himself in fight,
And suffered rash Pyrochles waste his idle might.

49 At last whenas the Saracen perceived
How that strange sword refused to serve his need,
But when he struck most strong the dint deceived,
He flung it from him, and devoid of dreed,
Upon him lightly leaping without heed,
Twixt his two mighty arms engraspèd fast,

48.8 *Prince Arthur:* (1596). 1590 reads *Sir Guyon.*
49.1–7 These lines are probably imitated from a combat in *Jerusalem Delivered:*

His sword at last he let hang by the chain,
And grip'd his hardy foe in both his hands;

In his strong arms Tancred caught him again,
And thus each other held and wrapt in bands.
With greater might Alcides did not strain
The giant Antaeus on the Lybian sands.
(XIX.17)

Thinking to overthrow and down him tread.
But him in strength and skill the prince surpassed,
And through his nimble sleight did under him down cast.

50 Nought booted it the paynim then to strive.
For as a bittor° in the eagle's claw   *bittern*
That may not hope by flight to scape alive
Still waits for death with dread and trembling awe,
So he now subject to the victor's law,
Did not once move nor upward cast his eye
For vile disdain and rancor, which did gnaw
His heart in twain with sad melancholy,
As one that loathèd life, and yet despised to die.

51 But full of princely bounty and great mind,
The conqueror nought carèd him to slay,
But casting wrongs and all revenge behind,
More glory thought to give life than decay,
And said, 'Paynim, this is thy dismal day;
Yet if thou wilt renounce they miscreance,°   *infidelity*
And my true liegeman yield thyself for aye,°   *forever*
Life will I grant thee for thy valiance,
And all thy wrongs will wipe out of my souvenance.'°   *remembrance*

52 'Fool,' said the pagan, 'I thy gift defy.
But use thy fortune as it doth befall,
And say that I not overcome do die,
But in despite of life for death do call.'
Wroth was the prince and sorry yet withal
That he so willfully refusèd grace;
Yet sith his fate so cruelly did fall,
His shining helmet he gan soon unlace,
And left his headless body bleeding all the place.

53 By this Sir Guyon from his trance awaked,
Life having masterèd her senseless foe,
And looking up, whenas his shield he lacked
And sword saw not, he waxèd wondrous woe.°   *sorrowful*
But when the palmer, whom he long ago
Had lost, he by him spied, right glad he grew,
And said, 'Dear sir, whom wandering to and fro

50.1–4 "As easily as the sacred falcon, taking wing from some high rock, will overtake a dove far up in the clouds, grasp it, hold it, and with hooked talons disembowel it, while blood and out-torn feathers float down from the sky" (*Aeneid*, XI.721–724, p. 301).

52.2 *use thy fortune as it doth befall:* This is adapted from the famous last speech of Turnus: "Enjoy the fortune which falls to you" (*Aeneid*, XII.932, p. 338). Arthur in his defeat of Pyrochles is compared to Aeneas in the culminating triumph of his life.

I long have lacked, I joy thy face to view;
Firm is thy faith, whom danger never fro me drew.

54 'But read what wicked hand hath robbèd me
    Of my good sword and shield?' The palmer glad,
    With so fresh hue° uprising him to see,   *color*
    Him answerèd: 'Fair son, be no whit sad
    For want of weapons; they shall soon be had.'
    So gan he to discourse the whole debate
    Which that strange knight for him sustainèd had,
    And those two Saracens confounded late,
    Whose carcasses on ground were horribly prostrate.

55 Which when he heard, and saw the tokens true,
    His heart with great affection was embayed,°   *suffused*
    And to the prince bowing with reverence due,
    As to the patron of his life, thus said:
    'My lord, my liege, by whose most gracious aid
    I live this day and see my foes subdued,
    What may suffice to be for meed° repaid   *reward*
    Of so great graces as ye have me shewed,
    But to be ever bound. . . .'

56 To whom the infant thus: 'Fair sir, what need
    Good turns be counted as a servile band,
    To bind their doers to receive their meed?
    Are not all knights by oath bound to withstand
    Oppressors' power by arms and puissant hand?
    Suffice that I have done my due in place.'°   *here*
    So goodly purpose they together fand°   *found*
    Of kindness and of courteous aggrace;°   *goodwill*
    The whiles false Archimage and Atin fled apace.

CANTO ix

The House of Temperance, in which
    Doth sober Alma dwell
Besieged of many foes, whom stranger
    Knights to flight compel.

1   Of all God's works which do this world adorn,
    There is no one more fair and excellent
    Than is man's body both for power and form,

55.3 *bowing with:* (1596). 1590 reads   56.1 *infant:* from Spanish *infante,*
with bowing.   "noble young man or prince."

Whiles it is kept in sober government;
But none than it more foul and indecent,
Distempered through misrule and passions base.
It grows a monster, and incontinent
Doth lose his dignity and native grace.
Behold, who list, both one and other in this place.

2   After the paynim brethren conquered were,
The Briton prince recovering his stolen sword
And Guyon his lost shield, they both y-fere°   *together*
Forth passèd on their way in fair accord,
Till him the prince with gentle court did board:°   *address*
'Sir knight, mote I of you this court'sy read,
To weet° why on your shield so goodly scored°   *know, drawn*
Bear ye the picture of that lady's head?
Full lively is the semblant,° though the substance dead.'   *likeness*

3   'Fair sir,' said he, 'if in that picture dead
Such life ye read, and virtue in vain shew,
What mote ye ween if the true livelihead
Of that most glorious visage ye did view?
But if the beauty of her mind ye knew,
That is her bounty° and imperial power,   *goodness*
Thousand times fairer than her mortal hue,
O how great wonder would your thoughts devour,
And infinite desire into your spirit pour!

4   'She is the mighty queen of Faèry
Whose fair retrait° I in my shield do bear;   *portrait*
She is the flower of grace and chastity,
Throughout the world renowmèd far and near,
My lief, my liege, my sovereign, my dear,
Whose glory shineth as the morning star,
And with her light the earth enlumines clear.
Far reach her mercies, and her praises far,
As well in state of peace, as puissance in war.'

5   'Thrice happy man,' said then the Briton knight,
'Whom gracious lot and thy great valiance

1.9 Spenser does not fulfill the promise of this line satisfactorily in Canto ix. The main subject is the Castle of Alma, the excellence of the body while "it is kept in sober government." The monster "distempered through misrule and passions base" is introduced briefly as the leader of a motley band attacking the Castle of Alma. He becomes the villain of Canto xi.

3.1–7.9 This passage is another encomium of Queen Elizabeth, this time in her role as a powerful and virtuous ruler—Gloriana. At the same time it allows Arthur to reveal that he is searching for Gloriana so that he may serve her. Book I recounts how Arthur saw Gloriana in a vision and loved her. His search was to have ended successfully when all of Spenser's knights had finished their quests.

Have made thee soldier of that princess bright,
Which with her bounty and glad countenance
Doth bless her servants and them high advance!
How may strange knight hope ever to aspire
By faithful service and meet amenance°   *proper conduct*
Unto such bliss? Sufficient were that hire
For loss of thousand lives, to die at her desire.'

6   Said Guyon, 'Noble lord, what meed° so great   *reward*
Or grace of earthly prince so sovereign°   *excellent*
But by your wondrous worth and warlike feat
Ye well may hope and easily attain?
But were your will her sold° to entertain,°   *pay, accept*
And numbered be mongst Knights of Maidenhead,
Great guerdon,° well I wot, should you remain,°   *reward, repay*
And in her favor high be reckonèd,
As Arthegall and Sophy now been honorèd.

7   'Certes,' then said the prince, 'I God avow
That sith I arms and knighthood first did plight,°   *profess in vows*
My whole desire hath been, and yet is now,
To serve that queen with all my power and might.
Now hath the sun with his lamp-burning light
Walked round about the world, and I no less,
Sith of that goddess I have sought the sight,
Yet nowhere can her find. Such happiness
Heaven doth to me envy, and fortune favorless.'

8   'Fortune, the foe of famous chevisance,°   *achievement*
Seldom,' said Guyon, 'yields to virtue aid,
But in her way throws mischief and mischance,
Whereby her course is stopped and passage stayed.
But you, fair sir, be not herewith dismayed,
But constant keep the way in which ye stand;
Which were it not that I am else delayed
With hard adventure which I have in hand,
I labor would to guide you through all Faeryland.'

9   'Gramercy sir,' said he, 'but mote I weet
What strange adventure do ye now pursue?
Perhaps my succor or advisement meet
Mote stead you much your purpose to subdue.'°   *achieve*

6.9 *Arthegall:* the hero of Book V of   7.5 *Now hath:* (1596). 1590 reads
The Faerie Queene, the Knight of Justice.   *Seven times.*
Sophy, from Greek *sophia,* "wisdom."   7.6 *Walked round:* (1596). 1590 reads
Probably he or she was to have been the   *Hath walked.*
central character of a projected, perhaps   9.1 *weet:* (1596). 1590 reads *wote.*
lost, book of the poem.

Then gan Sir Guyon all the story shew
Of false Acrasia and her wicked wiles,
Which to avenge, the palmer him forth drew
From faery court. So talkèd they the whiles
They wasted° had much way and measured many miles.   *traveled*

10   And now fair Phoebus gan decline in haste
His weary wagon to the western vale,
Whenas they spied a goodly castle, placed
Foreby° a river in a pleasant dale,   *next to*
Which choosing for that evening's hospital,
They thither marched; but when they came in sight,
And from their sweaty coursers did avale,°   *dismount*
They found the gates fast barrèd long ere night,
And every loop° fast locked, as fearing foe's despite.   *loophole*

11   Which when they saw, they weenèd foul reproach°   *insult*
Was to them done, their entrance to forestall,
Till that the squire gan nigher to approach
And wind his horn under the castle wall,
That with the noise it shook as it would fall.
Eftsoons forth lookèd from the highest spire
The watch, and loud unto the knights did call
To weet what they so rudely did require.
Who gently answerèd they entrance did desire.

12   'Fly, fly, good knights,' said he, 'fly fast away
If that your lives ye love, as meet ye should;
Fly fast, and save yourselves from near decay.
Here may ye not have entrance, though we would.
We would and would again if that we could,
But thousand enemies about us rave,
And with long siege us in this castle hold.
Seven years this wise they us besiegèd have,
And many good knights slain that have us sought to save.'

13   Thus as he spoke, lo with outrageous cry
A thousand villeins° round about them swarmed   *low-born rascals*
Out of the rocks and caves adjoining nigh—
Vile caitiff wretches, ragged, rude, deformed,

12.8 *Seven years:* This may be simply a conventional expression of romance. On the other hand, it might suggest the seven ages of man since the fall of Adam.

13.1–15.9 These are the troops of Maleger, the monster mentioned in the first stanza of this canto. Two things should be noted about Maleger's troops: their ragged and wild disorder, and their insubstantiality. For the temperate man the base passions which attack and destroy the body have no reality. Many critics have remarked a similarity between Maleger's troops and Spenser's description of Irish rebel bands in *View of the Present State of Ireland*, a prose tract.

All threatening death, all in strange manner armed,
Some with unwieldy clubs, some with long spears,
Some rusty knives, some staves in fire warmed.
Stern was their look, like wild amazèd steers,
Staring with hollow eyes and stiff upstanding hairs.

14 Fiercely at first those knights they did assail,
And drove them to recoil; but when again
They gave fresh charge, their forces gan to fail,
Unable their encounter to sustain.
For with such puissance and impetuous main
Those champions broke on them that forced them fly,
Like scattered sheep, whenas the shepherd's swain
A lion and a tiger doth espy
With greedy pace forth rushing from the forest nigh.

15 Awhile they fled, but soon returned again
With greater fury than before was found;
And everymore their cruel capitain
Sought with his rascal routs t' enclose them round
And overrun, to tread them to the ground.
But soon the knights with their bright-burning blades
Broke their rude troops and orders° did confound,   *ranks*
Hewing and slashing at their idle° shades;   *empty*
For though they bodies seem, yet substance from them fades.

16 As when a swarm of gnats at eventide
Out of the fens of Allan do arise,
Their murmuring small trumpets sounden wide,
Whiles in the air their clustering army flies,
That as a cloud doth seem to dim the skies;
Ne man nor beast may rest or take repast
For their sharp wounds and noyous° injuries,   *annoying*
Till the fierce northern wind with blustering blast
Doth blow them quite away, and in the ocean cast.

17 Thus when they had that troublous rout dispersed,
Unto the castle gate they come again,
And entrance craved which was denièd erst.
Now when report of that their perilous pain
And cumbrous conflict, which they did sustain,
Came to the lady's ear which there did dwell,
She forth issuèd with a goodly train
Of squires and ladies equipagèd well,
And entertainèd them right fairly, as befell.

16.1–9 The simile comes directly from Spenser's Irish experience. The fens of Allan
are in Central Ireland.

18 Alma she callèd was, a virgin bright,
    That had not yet felt Cupid's wanton rage;
    Yet was she wooed of many a gentle knight
    And many a lord of noble parentage,
    That sought with her to link in marriage;
    For she was fair as fair mote ever be,
    And in the flower now of her freshest age,
    Yet full of grace and goodly modesty,
    That even heaven rejoicèd her sweet face to see.

19 In robe of lily white she was arrayed
    That from her shoulder to her heel down raught,°   *reached*
    The train whereof loose far behind her strayed,
    Branchèd° with gold and pearl most richly wrought,   *embroidered*
    And borne of two fair damsels which were taught
    That service well. Her yellow golden hair
    Was trimly woven and in tresses wrought;
    Ne other tire she on her head did wear,
    But crownèd with a garland of sweet rosier.°   *sweetbriar*

20 Goodly she entertained those noble knights,
    And brought them up into her castle hall;
    Where gentle court° and gracious delight   *entertainment*
    She to them made, with mildness virginal,
    Showing herself both wise and liberal.
    There when they rested had a season due,
    They her besought, of favor special,
    Of that fair castle to afford them view;
    She granted, and them leading forth, the same did shew.

21 First she them led up to the castle wall,
    That was so high as foe might not it climb,

18.1–19.9 Alma is the rational soul, and like all the heroines of Book II she is a virgin to show her freedom from earthly passion. Spenser's description of her owes something to medieval allegories of courtly love such as *The Romance of the Rose* as well as to allegories of the soul such as the fourteenth century English poem *The Pearl*. The roses on Alma's head are sacred to Venus. If Spenser means to suggest that Alma is a kind of Venus, he certainly has in mind the "heavenly Venus" of medieval and renaissance Neoplatonism. She represents spiritual love, the love of God. Alma's virginity is due, then, to the fact that she, like all human souls, is betrothed to Christ.

20.9 Alma's castle is an allegorical anatomy of the mortal part of man, not just of the body. Such allegorical castles are common in medieval literature. Spen-

ser's most immediate source was probably the *Divine Weeks* of the French renaissance poet Guillaume de Salluste Du Bartas, which also influenced Milton's *Paradise Lost* importantly. (See the English translation of Josuah Sylvester, "First Week, Sixth Day.") Other works containing castles with which Spenser may have been familiar are John Gower's *Mirour de L'Omme* and Stephen Hawes' *The Pastime of Pleasure*. See also the Castle of Anima in Langland's *Piers Plowman* (Passus IX, 1–57).

21.1–9 The castle wall is the body, made of material like Egyptian slime because "the Lord God formed man of the dust of the ground . . ." (Genesis 2:7). Ninus and his wife Semiramus were legendary founders of Babylon; the Tower of Babel was built of brick "and slime had they for mortar" (Genesis 11:3).

21.1 *them:* (1596). 1590 reads *him.*

And all so fair and fensible° withal—   *fortified*
Not built of brick ne yet of stone and lime,
But of thing like to that Egyptian slime
Whereof King Nine whilom built Babel tower.
But O great pity that no lenger time
So goodly workmanship should not endure.
Soon it must turn to earth; no earthly thing is sure.

22   The frame thereof seemed partly circular
And part triangular—O work divine.
Those two the first and last proportions° are—   *figures*
The one imperfect, mortal, feminine,
Th' other immortal, perfect, masculine—
And twixt them both a quadrate° was the base,   *rectangle*
Proportioned equally by seven and nine;
Nine was the circle set in heaven's place,
All which compacted made a goodly diapase.°   *harmony*

23   Therein two gates were placèd seemly well.
The one before, by which all in did pass,
Did th' other far in workmanship excel;
For not of wood nor of enduring brass,
But of more worthy substance framed it was;
Doubly disparted, it did lock and close,
That when it lockèd, none might thorough° pass,   *through*

22.1–9   The meaning of this stanza is difficult. In a simple physical sense the head may be compared to a circle, the trunk of the body to a rectangle (quadrant), and the legs spread to a triangle. But these physical figures of the body are symbolic of the union of matter with form or spirit in man. The chief sources of such symbolism in the Middle Ages and the Renaissance were Plato's *Timaeus* and Macrobius' *In Somnium Scipionis*, where geometrical figures and numbers are given allegorical interpretation. In some interpretations the three figures represent the three "souls" which were said to compose man. The triangle represents the vegetable soul, which contains the faculties of growth and reproduction; the rectangle represents the sensible soul, which contains the four humors and is the seat of man's emotional life; and the circle represents the most perfect part of man, the rational soul. For Plato and later followers the circle is a perfect figure, symbolic of form and spirit. It is without beginning and without end and therefore represents eternity and God. The triangle, in Pythagorean number theory the first figure generated by the One, represents matter, which is weak and imperfect. Created beings like man are a union of form or spirit and matter—of the circle and the triangle. Matter is characterized in the *Timaeus* as "the mother" and is, therefore, feminine. The form or spirit which imposes itself upon matter is masculine. The dimensions of the rectangle are mystical symbols of body and spirit. The seven is related in the *Republic* to the gestation period of man and is, therefore, a symbol of the vegetable soul and of matter. The nine, like the circle, was considered a perfect number. (See *Republic*, VIII.546, pp. 315–316.) There are nine heavenly spheres, the ninth of which is a symbol of divinity. According to the *Republic* the human creature is developed in seven steps analogous to the seven divisions of the musical scale; and the nine celestial spheres of the universe create their own musical harmony as they rotate. The union of body and soul is a harmony of earthly and heavenly music. Spenser's elaborate allegory in this stanza amounts to a hymn in praise of the marvelous workmanship of the human body, and of the heavenly creator. The form of the body is a symbol of the perfection of God's work.

23.1   The two gates are the mouth and the anus.

And when it opened, no man might it close,
Still open to their friends, and closèd to their foes.

24   Of hewen stone the porch was fairly wrought,
Stone more of value and more smooth and fine
Than jet or marble far from Ireland brought;
Over the which was cast a wandering vine,
Enchasèd° with a wanton ivy twine.   *ornamented*
And over it a fair portcullis hung,
Which to the gate directly did incline,
With comely compass° and compacture° strong,   *proportion,*
Neither unseemly short, nor yet exceeding long.   *structure*

25   Within the barbican a porter sate,
Day and night duly keeping watch and ward,
Nor wight nor word mote pass out of the gate,
But in good order and with due regard;
Utterers of secrets he from thence debarred,
Babblers of folly, and blazers° of crime.   *heralds*
His larum-bell might loud and wide be heard
When cause required, but never out of time;°   *untimely*
Early and late it rung, at evening and at prime.°   *daybreak*

26   And round about the porch on every side
Twice sixteen warders sat, all armèd bright
In glistering steel and strongly fortified;
Tall yeomen seemèd they, and of great might,
And were enrangèd ready still° for fight.   *always*
By them as Alma passèd with her guests,
They did obeisance, as beseemèd right,
And then again returnèd to their rests;
The porter eke to her did lout with humble gests.°   *gestures*

27   Thence she them brought into a stately hall,
Wherein were many tables fair° dispread,   *appealingly*
And ready dight with drapets° festival,   *cloths*
Against° the viands should be ministered.   *for when*
At th' upper end there sat, y-clad in red
Down to the ground, a comely personage,
That in his hand a white rod managèd.
He steward was, hight Diet, ripe of age,
And in demeanor sober and in counsel sage.

24.1   *porch:* the chin probably.
24.4   *wandering vine:* beard.
24.5   *ivy twine:* moustache.
24.6   *portcullis:* nose
25.1   The tongue (*porter*) sits within
the oral cavity (*barbican*).
26.2   *Twice sixteen warders:* the teeth.
27.1–28.6   The dining hall with the

steward, Diet, and the marshal, Appetite,
is less a part of the allegory of the body
than it is an allegory of temperance in
the choice and quantity of food and drink
eaten. Appetite, the demand of the stom-
ach for food, is governed by Diet, reason-
able satisfaction of desire.

28   And through the hall there walkèd to and fro
      A jolly yeoman, marshal of the same,
      Whose name was Appetite; he did bestow°   *dispose*
      Both guests and meat whenever in they came,
      And knew them how to order without blame,
      As him the steward bade. They both at one
      Did duty to their lady, as became;
      Who passing by, forth led her guests anon
      Into the kitchen room, ne spared for niceness° none.   *squeamishness*

29   It was a vault y-built for great dispense,°   *liberality*
      With many ranges reared along the wall,
      And one great chimney whose long tunnel thence
      The smoke forth threw. And in the midst of all
      There placèd was a cauldron wide and tall
      Upon a mighty furnace, burning hot—
      More hot than Aetna or flaming Mongiball;
      For day and night it brent,° ne ceasèd not   *burned*
      So long as anything it in the cauldron got.

30   But to delay° the heat, lest by mischance   *moderate*
      It might break out and set the whole on fire,
      There added was by goodly ordinance
      An huge great pair of bellows, which did stire°   *move*
      Continually, and cooling breath inspire.°   *breathe in*

28.8–30.9 These two stanzas are an allegory of the stomach and its functions. It produces nourishment for the entire body and sustains the soul itself. Spenser contrasts the furnace and cauldron of the stomach with the furnaces in the Cave of Mammon. The stomach and its functions are the obedient servants of Alma and are under her control; the furnaces of Mammon produce gold as an end in itself. They are characterized by disorder. Perhaps Mammon's forge represents the diseased physical nature of the avaricious man. His obsession with wealth turns even his physical organs into a gold-producing machine. Spenser's allegory depends ultimately upon the doctrines of the Greek medical writer Galen of Pergamum (born 129 A.D.). Galen was by far the most authoritative medical writer for the Renaissance. Two of his famous renaissance followers were Thomas Linacre (1460–1524), founder of the Royal College of Physicians and friend of Erasmus and Sir Thomas More, and François Rabelais (1494–1553), author of *Pantagruel* and *Gargantua*. For the influence of Galen in medieval and renaissance medicine see George Sarton, *The Appreciation of Ancient and Medieval Science During the Renaissance*, University of Pennsylvania, 1955, pp. 17–33.

29.1–7 "And if one considers along with this the adjacent viscera, like a lot of burning hearths around a great cauldron —to the right the liver, to the left the spleen, the heart above, and along with it the diaphragm . . . you may believe what an extraordinary alteration it is which occurs in the food taken into the stomach" (Galen, *On the Natural Faculties*, III, Loeb ed., p. 255).

29.7 This comparison of the digestive heat of the stomach to the volcanic heat of Mount Aetna is playfully alluded to by Galen: "This is as if we were to suppose that it was necessary to put the fires of Etna under the stomach before it could manage to alter the food" (*On the Natural Faculties*, III, p. 259).

30.4–5 In *Hippocrates et Platon*, Galen refers to the doctrine of Hippocrates that "inspiration [breathing in] takes place for the purpose of cooling the native heat [of the stomach] and expiration in order that fulginous superfluities may be discharged and breathed out "(VII.9, quoted from *Variorum*, II. 292). Spenser's comparison of the lungs to bellows is, then, appropriate.

About the cauldron many cooks accoiled,°   *gathered*
With hooks and ladles, as need did require;
The whiles the viands in the vessel boiled,
They did about their business sweat, and sorely toiled.

31 The master cook was called Concoction,
    A careful man and full of comely guise.°   *conduct*
    The kitchen clerk, that hight Digestion,
    Did order all th' achates° in seemly wise   *provisions*
    And set them forth° as well he could devise.   *arranged them*
    The rest had several offices assigned:
    Some to remove the scum as it did rise,
    Others to bear the same away did mind,
    And others it to use according to his kind.°   *nature*

32 But all the liquor which was foul and waste,
    Not good nor serviceable else for aught,
    They in another great round vessel placed,
    Till by a conduit pipe it thence were brought.
    And all the rest that noyous° was and nought,°   *harmful, worthless*
    By secret ways, that none might it espy,
    Was close° conveyed and to the back gate brought,   *privately*
    That clepèd° was Port Esquiline, whereby   *named*
    It was avoided° quite and thrown out privily.   *ejected*

33 Which goodly order and great workman's skill
    Whenas those knights beheld, with rare delight
    And gazing wonder they their minds did fill;
    For never had they seen so strange a sight.
    Thence back again fair Alma led them right,°   *immediately*
    And soon into a goodly parlor brought,
    That was with royal arras° richly dight,   *scarlet tapestry*
    In which was nothing portrayèd nor wrought,
    Not wrought nor portrayèd, but easy to be thought.

30.8 Galen compares the digestive process to boiling (*On the Natural Faculties*, III, p. 259).

31.1–5 Spenser makes a distinction between "concoction" and "digestion" which Galen does not appear to make. Spenser's concoction corresponds to Galen's "digestion," the mixing and boiling of the food in the stomach, and the transformation of the food into a liquid "chyle." Spenser's digestion appears to be the distribution of the "chyle" to the various organs of the body, which turn it into the humors which sustain the body.

32.3–4 *great round vessel:* the bladder; *conduit pipe:* the urinary canal.

32.8 *Port Esquiline:* the anus. The Esquiline gate in imperial Rome was a sort of common dump for trash and offal.

33.6–35.8 The goodly parlor is the heart, seat of the passions. The order which prevails in Alma's parlor is contrasted with the frantic activity of Philotime's court. Alma's parlor is an allegory of the harmony between the concupiscible and irascible powers of the soul in the temperate man. The young men and women singing, laughing, playing and relaxing are the various tendencies of the concupiscible power; those who are frowning, blushing, seeming envious or coy are the tendencies of the irascible power. All of these tendencies are under control.

33.8–9 The meaning of these lines is obscure. In medieval courtly love poetry the walls of chambers are usually decorated with rich tapestries depicting

34 And in the midst thereof upon the floor,
A lovely bevy of fair ladies sate,
Courted of many a jolly paramour,
The which them did in modest wise amate,°   *respond to*
And each one sought his lady to aggrate.°   *please*
And eke amongst them little Cupid played
His wanton sports, being returnèd late
From his fierce wars and having from him laid
His cruel bow, wherewith he thousands hath dismayed.

35 Diverse delights they found themselves to please:
Some sung in sweet consort,° some laughed for joy,   *harmony*
Some played with straws,° some idly sat at ease.   *jackstraws*
But other some could not abide to toy,°   *play*
All pleasance was to them grief and annoy:
This frowned, that fawned,° the third for shame did blush, *cringed*
Another seemèd envious or coy,
Another in her teeth did gnaw a rush.
But at these strangers' presence everyone did hush.

36 Soon as the gracious Alma came in place,
They all at once out of their seats arose,
And to her homage made with humble grace.
Whom when the knights beheld, they gan dispose
Themselves to court, and each a damsel chose.
The prince by chance did on a lady light
That was right fair and fresh as morning rose,
But somewhat sad and solemn eke in sight,
As if some pensive thought constrained her gentle sprite.

37 In a long purple pall, whose skirt with gold
Was fretted all about, she was arrayed,
And in her hand a poplar branch did hold.
To whom the prince in courteous manner said,
'Gentle madam, why been ye thus dismayed,
And your fair beauty do with sadness spill?
Lives any that you hath thus ill apaid?
Or done° you love, or done you lack your will?   *do*
Whatever be the cause, it sure beseems you ill.'

38 'Fair sir,' said she half in disdainful wise,
'How is it that this word° in me ye blame,   i.e. *sadness*
And in yourself do not the same advise?°   *perceive*
Him ill beseems another's fault to name

---

mythological subjects. Perhaps Spenser
means that the objects of the passions do
not originate in the sensible soul but in
the imagination, which creates images
from sense data.

That may unwares be blotted with the same.
Pensive I yield I am, and sad in mind,
Through great desire of glory and of fame;
Ne aught I ween are ye therein behind,
That have twelve months sought one, yet nowhere can her
  find.'

39 The prince was inly° movèd at her speech,   *secretly*
Well weeting true what she had rashly told,
Yet with fair semblant sought to hide the breach
Which change of color did perforce unfold,
Now seeming flaming hot, now stony cold.
Tho turning soft aside, he did inquire
What wight she was, that poplar branch did hold;
It answered was, her name was Praise-desire,
That by well doing sought to honor to aspire.

40 The whiles, the faery knight did entertain
Another damsel of that gentle crew,
That was right fair and modest of demain,°   *behavior*
But that too oft she changed her native hue.°   *complexion*
Strange was her tire, and all her garment blue,
Close round about her tucked with many a plight.°   *pleat*
Upon her fist the bird which shunneth view
And keeps in coverts close from living wight
Did sit, as yet ashamed how rude° Pan did her dight.° *unattractively,*
                                                   dress

41 So long as Guyon with her commonèd,°   *accompanied*
Unto the ground she cast her modest eye,
And ever and anon with rosy red
The bashful blood her snowy cheeks did dye;
That her became as polished ivory,
Which cunning craftsman's hand hath overlaid
With fair vermilion or pure castory.°   *a red dye*
Great wonder had the knight to see the maid
So strangely passionèd, and to her gently said,

42 'Fair damsel, seemeth by your troubled cheer
That either me too bold ye ween, this wise

38.9 *twelve months:* (1596). 1590 reads *three years.*

39.8 *Praise-desire:* the desire of honor, the essential motivating force in Arthur's life. Her purple and golden robe is a sign of majesty, the highest glory (Gloriana). The poplar is sacred to Hercules. Here the allusion to Hercules represents not only Christian temperance but also "superhuman virtue—moral goodness on the heroic or godlike scale" (Aristotle, *Ethics,* VII.1, p. 193). The highest honor belongs to the highest virtue.

40.7–9 This bird has not been identified, perhaps the mourning dove.

41.2–7 This simile comes ultimately from the *Iliad.* It was imitated over and over in classical and medieval poetry. Spenser knew it from the *Aeneid,* Ovid's *Amores* and the *Metamorphoses.* (See *Aeneid,* XII.64–69, p. 311.)

42.1 *cheer:* (1596). 1590 reads *clear.*

You to molest, or other ill to fear
That in the secret of your heart close lies,
From whence it doth as cloud from sea arise.
If it be I, of pardon I you pray;
But if aught else that I mote not devise,°   *guess*
I will, if please you it discure,° assay   *discover*
To ease you of that ill so wisely as I may.'

43   She answered nought, but more abashed for shame,
      Held down her head, the whiles her lovely face
      The flashing blood with blushing did inflame,
      And the strong passion marred her modest grace,
      That Guyon marvelled at her uncouth° case;   *strange*
      Till Alma him bespake: 'Why wonder ye,
      Fair sir, at that which ye so much embrace?
      She is the fountain of your modesty;
      You shamefast are, but Shamefastness itself is she.'

44   Thereat the elf did blush in privity,
      And turned his face away; but she the same
      Dissembled fair and feigned to oversee.°   *overlook*
      Thus they awhile with court and goodly game
      Themselves did solace each one with his dame,
      Till that great lady thence away them sought
      To view her castle's other wondrous frame.
      Up to a stately turret she them brought,
      Ascending by ten steps of alablaster wrought.

45   That turret's frame most admirable was,
      Like highest heaven compassèd around
      And lifted high above this earthly mass,
      Which it surveyed as hills done lower ground.
      But not on ground mote like to this be found—
      Not that which antique Cadmus whilom built
      In Thebes which Alexander did confound;°   *bring to ruin*
      Nor that proud tower of Troy, though richly gilt,
      From which young Hector's blood by cruel Greeks was spilt.

46   The roof hereof was archèd overhead,
      And decked with flowers and arbors daintily.
      Two goodly beacons set in watch's stead

43.9 *Shamefastness:* Aristotle's shame-facedness, the fear of doing a dishonorable act. The essential motivation of Guyon's quest appears to be negative in comparison with the "praise-desire" which moves Arthur.
44.8–47.5 Alma's turret is the head, the seat of the mind and its faculties. Of all man's physical parts it is the noblest, analogous to reason in the rational soul, the king in the state, and God in creation. As the noblest of God's creations it is superior to all man-made structures.
45.6–7 The story of the founding of Thebes by Cadmus is told in Ovid's *Metamorphoses*, III.1–137 (pp. 80–83).

Therein gave light and flamed continually;
For they of living fire most subtilely
Where made and set in silver sockets bright,
Covered with lids devised of substance sly,
That readily they shut and open might.
O who can tell the praises of that Maker's might!

47 Ne can I tell, ne can I stay to tell
This part's great workmanship and wondrous power,
That all this other world's work doth excel,
And likest is unto that heavenly tower
That God hath built for his own blessed bower.
Therein were divers rooms and divers stages;
But three the chiefest and of greatest power,
In which there dwelt three honorable sages,
The wisest men, I ween, that livèd in their ages.

48 Not he whom Greece, the nurse of all good arts,
By Phoebus' doom the wisest thought alive
Might be compared to these by many parts;
Nor that sage Pylian sire which did survive
Three ages such as mortal men contrive,°   *wear out*
By whose advice old Priam's city fell,
With these in praise of policies mote strive.
These three in these three rooms did sundry° dwell,   *apart*
And counsellèd fair Alma how to govern well.

49 The first of them could things to come foresee,
The next could of things present best advise,
The third things past could keep in memory,
So that no time nor reason could arise

47.8–9 The three wise men are the three interior senses of the mind: imagination, judgment, and memory. These faculties arise from the sensible soul and the judgment here allegorized is different from reason or understanding, a faculty of the rational soul. Spenser's allegory of the three interior senses is an emblem of prudence (practical wisdom) and of the three ages of man (youth, maturity, old age). For the three ages of man see Aristotle's *Rhetoric*, II (pp. 132–137). Spenser's association of the three divisions of time with the three ages of man and the three interior senses of the mind shows that he means his three sages together to represent practical wisdom, the wisdom which is derived from sense experience and which is concerned with particular events and objects, not with general principles or with laws of nature. For a brief survey, with illustrations, of the allegory

of prudence in the Renaissance see Erwin Panofsky, *Meaning in the Visual Arts*, Doubleday Anchor Books, 1955, pp. 146–168. From the Aristotelian text and from Titian's allegorical painting of prudence (Panofsky, Illustration 28), it may be gathered that Spenser's middle figure, judgment, is to be regarded as the mean between the other two figures.

48.1–3 Socrates explains in the *Apology* that the oracle of Phoebus at Delphi had said that no one was wiser than he (Plato, *The Last Days of Socrates*, Penguin Books, p. 23).

48.3 *these:* (1596). 1590 reads *this*.

48.4–6 Nestor "that master of the courteous word, the clear-voiced orator from Pylos, whose speech ran sweeter than honey off his tongue. He had already seen two generations come to life, grow up, and die in sacred Pylos, and now he ruled the third" (*Iliad*, I.248–252, p. 29).

But that the same could one of these comprise.°   *understand*
Forthy° the first did in the forepart sit,   *therefore*
That nought mote hinder his quick prejudize.°   *forejudgment*
He had a sharp foresight and working° wit   *energetic*
That never idle was, ne once could rest a whit.

50 His chamber was dispainted all within
With sundry colors, in the which were writ
Infinite shapes of things dispersèd thin°—   *i.e. as vapor*
Some such as in the world were never yit,°   *yet*
Ne can devisèd be of mortal wit,
Some daily seen and knowen by their names,
Such as in idle fantasies do flit:
Infernal hags, centaurs, fiends, hippodames,°   *sea-horses*
Apes, lions, eagles, owls, fools, lovers, children, dames.

51 And all the chamber fillèd was with flies,
Which buzzèd all about and made such sound
That they encumbered all men's ears and eyes,
Like many swarms of bees assembled round
After their hives with honey do abound.
All those were idle thoughts and fantasies,
Devices,° dreams, opinions unsound,   *images*
Shows, visions, sooth-says, and prophesies;
And all that feignèd° is, as leasings,° tales, and lies.   *counterfeit, lies*

52 Amongst them all sat he which wonèd° there,   *lived*
That hight Phantastes by his nature true,
A man of years, yet fresh° as mote appear,   *youthful*
Of swarth complexion and of crabbèd° hue,   *morose*
That him full of melancholy did shew—
Bent hollow beetle brows, sharp staring eyes,
That mad or foolish seemed. One by his view°   *appearance*
Mote deem him born with ill disposèd skies,
When oblique Saturn sat in th' house of agonies.

49.6–52.9 "Phantasy, or imagination, which some call estimative . . . is an inner sense which doth more fully examine the species perceived by common sense, of things present or absent, and keeps them longer, recalling them to mind again, or making new of his own. In time of sleep this faculty is free and many times conceives strange, stupend, absurd shapes, as in sick men we commonly observe. . . . In *melancholy* men this faculty is most powerful and strong, and often hurts, producing many monstrous and prodigious things . . ." (Burton, *The Anatomy of Melancholy*, pp. 139–140). Burton's account of fantasy (Phantastes) does not agree at all points with Spenser's, largely because Burton's "common sense" is something quite different from Spenser's second sage, "judgment." Spenser conceives of fantasy as a primary receiver of sense impressions, with the creative function of combining such data into images. The monsters which fantasy creates come about through the uncritical combination of impressions which have no relation to each other in reality. Note Burton's emphasis on the melancholic tendency of fancy.

49.9 *could:* (1596). 1590 reads *would.*
52.9 Saturn was one of the planets which were thought to dispose men to melancholy (*The Anatomy of Melancholy*, pp. 180–181). "The house of agonies" is probably one of the signs of the zodiac. It has not been identified so far.

53 Whom Alma having showèd to her guests,
    Thence brought them to the second room, whose walls
    Were painted fair with memorable gests
    Of famous wizards, and with pictorals
    Of magistrates, of courts, of tribunals,
    Of commonwealths, of states, of policy,
    Of laws, of judgments, and of decretals°—   *decrees*
    All arts, all science, all philosophy,
    And all that in the world was aye° thought wittily.   *ever*

54 Of those that room was full, and them among
    There sat a man of ripe° and perfect age   *mature*
    Who did them meditate all his life long,
    That through continual practice and usage,
    He now was grown right wise and wondrous sage.
    Great pleasure had those stranger knights to see
    His goodly reason and grave personage,
    That his disciples both desired to be;
    But Alma thence them led to th' hindmost room of three.

55 That chamber seemèd ruinous and old,
    And therefore was removèd far behind;
    Yet were the walls that did the same uphold
    Right firm and strong, through somewhat they declined.°   *leaned*
    And therein sat an old, old man, half blind
    And all decrepit in his feeble corse;°   *body*
    Yet lively vigor rested in his mind
    And recompensed him with a better scorse.°   *exchange*
    Weak body well is changed for mind's redoubled force.

56 This man of infinite remembrance was,
    And things foregone through many ages held,
    Which he recorded still as they did pass,
    Ne suffered them to perish through long eld—
    As all things else the which this world doth weld°—   *govern*
    But laid them up in his immortal scrine,°   *roll*

53.1–54.5 The occupant of the second room seems to be Aristotle's *phronesis*, prudence or common sense. The faculty is to be understood as a judging faculty. It has reference to practical affairs. "Practical wisdom [*phronesis*] is a rational faculty exercised for the attainment of truth in things that are humanly good and bad. . . . In the popular mind prudence is more associated with the self and the individual—a usurpation of the title of prudence, which actually belongs to all forms and kinds, including those designated as domestic economy, constitution-building, the art of the lawgiver, and political science, which again is subdivided into deliberative and judicial science" (*Ethics*, VI.5–8, pp. 177–181). The difference between this faculty of judgment and reason is that "intelligence [reason] apprehends the truth of definitions which cannot be proved by argument, while prudence involves knowledge of the ultimate particular thing . . ." (*Ethics*, VI.8, p. 182). Note the concern of Spenser's second sage with politics.

56.1–58.9 The third interior faculty, memory, is said by almost all authorities to be located at the back of the brain, as is Eumnestes.

Where they forever incorrupted dwelled.
The wars he well remembered of King Nine,
Of old Assaracus, and Inachus divine.

57 The years of Nestor nothing were to his,
Ne yet Methusalem, though longest lived;
For he remembered both their infancies.
Ne wonder then if that he were deprived
Of native strength now, that he them survived.
His chamber all was hanged about with rolls
And old records from ancient times derived.
Some made in books, some in long parchment scrolls
That were all worm-eaten and full of canker holes.

58 Amidst them all he in a chair was set,
Tossing and turning them withouten end.
But for he was unable them to fet,°   *fetch*
A little boy did on him still attend,
To reach whenever he for aught did send;
And oft when things were lost or laid amiss,
That boy them sought and unto him did lend.
Therefore he Anamnestes clepèd is,
And that old man Eumnestes, by their properties.

59 The knights there entering did him reverence due,
And wondered at his endless exercise.
Then as they gan his library to view
And antique registers for to avise,°   *examine*
There chancèd to the prince's hand to rise
An ancient book, hight *Briton Monuments*,
That of this land's first conquest did devise,°   *tell*
And old division into regiments°   *kingdoms*
Till it reducèd was to one man's governments.

60 Sir Guyon chanced eke on another book,
That hight *Antiquity of Faeryland*.
In which when as he greedily did look,
Th' offspring° of elves and faeries there he fand,   *lineage*
As it delivered was from hand to hand.
Whereat they burning both with fervent fire,
Their countries' ancestry to understand,
Craved leave of Alma and that aged sire
To read those books, who gladly granted their desire.

56.8 *Nine:* Ninus, the legendary founder of the Babylonian empire.

56.9 *Assaracus:* son of Tros and, after his father, king of Troy. *Inachus:* a river god, whose daughter Io was raped by Zeus and transformed into a cow. Spenser chooses names which represent a time much earlier even than the Trojan war.

57.2 See Genesis 5:27.

58.8 *Anamnestes:* probably from Greek, *ana*—again; *mnestes*—memory.

58.9 *Eumnestes:* Greek, *eu*—good. Since Spenser's sage is housed in the Castle of Alma, he is more than simply memory; he is memory at its best.

CANTO x

A chronicle of Briton kings
From Brute to Uther's reign,
And rolls° of elfin emperors   *records*
Till time of Gloriane.

1 Who now shall give unto me words and sound
   Equal unto this haughty enterprise?
   Or who shall lend me wings with which from ground
   My lowly verse may loftily arise
   And lift itself unto the highest skies?
   More ample spirit than hitherto was wont
   Here needs me, whiles the famous ancestries
   Of my most dreaded sovereign I recount,
   By which all earthly princes she doth far surmount.

2 Ne under sun that shines so wide and fair,
   Whence all that lives does borrow life and light,
   Lives aught that to her lineage may compare,
   Which though from earth it be derivèd right
   Yet doth itself stretch forth to heaven's height,
   And all the world with wonder overspread—
   A labor huge, exceeding far my might.
   How shall frail pen, with fear disparagèd,°   *discouraged*
   Conceive such sovereign glory and great bountihead?° *virtue*

3 Argument worthy of Maeonian quill,
   Or rather worthy of great Phoebus' rote,°   *harp*
   Whereon the ruins of great Ossa hill
   And triumphs of Phlegraean Jove he wrote,

Argument. *Brute:* the legendary eponymous founder of Britain (stanzas 9–13); *Uther:* Arthur's father (stanza 68). The two kingdoms—Britain, with its capital at Troynovant, and Faeryland, with its capital at Cleopolis—are types of Spenser's England. By introducing the theme of the political application of temperance, Spenser fulfills his promise in the Proem to Book II (stanza 4) to show Queen Elizabeth her great ancestry. The Chronicle of Briton Kings has no single source. It is based mainly on the legendary material in Geoffrey of Monmouth's *Historia Regum Britanniae* (1139) with eclectic borrowings from John Hardyng's *Chronicle of England* (1543), *The Mirror for Magistrates* (1559), Raphael Holinshed's *Chronicles* (1577), John Stow's *Chronicles of England* (1580), and half a dozen less important sources. The chief authority is Carrie A. Harper, *The Sources of the British Chronicle History in Spenser's "Faerie Queene,"* Bryn Mawr, 1910.

3.1 *Maeonian quill:* either the plectrum with which Homer struck the lyre, the pipe he played, or (least likely) his pen. Homer was at one time thought to have come from Maeonia, an ancient country in Asia Minor.

3.3 *Ossa:* a mountain in Thessaly from which the giants attempted to climb Mt. Olympus.

3.4 *Phlegraean Jove:* so called because of his victory over the giants at Phlegra.

That all the gods admired his lofty note.
But if some relish° of that heavenly lay   *flavor*
His learned daughters would to me report
To deck my song withal, I would assay
Thy name, O sovereign queen, to blazon far away.

4   Thy name, O sovereign queen, thy realm and race,
From this renownèd prince derivèd are,
Who mightily upheld that royal mace
Which now thou bear'st, to thee descended far
From mighty kings and conquerors in war—
Thy fathers and great-grandfathers of old,
Whose noble deeds above the northern star
Immortal fame forever hath enrolled;
As in that old man's book they were in order told.

5   The land which warlike Britons now possess,
And therein have their mighty empire raised,
In antique times was savage wilderness,
Unpeopled, unmanured, unproved, unpraised;
Ne was it island then, ne was it peised°   *poised*
Amid the ocean waves, ne was it sought
Of merchants far for profits therein praised,
But was all desolate, and of some thought
By sea to have been from the Celtic mainland brought.

6   Ne did it then deserve a name to have,
Till that the venturous mariner that way—
Learning his ship from those white rocks to save,
Which all along the southern seacoast lay,
Threatening unheedy° wreck and rash° decay—   *unexpected, quick*
For safèty that same his sea-mark made,
And named it Albion. But later day,
Finding in it fit ports for fisher's trade,
Gan more the same frequent, and further to invade.°   *penetrate*

7   But far inland a savage nation dwelt,
Of hideous giants and half beastly men
That never tasted grace nor goodness felt,
But like wild beasts lurking in loathsome den
And flying fast as roebuck through the fen,
All naked without shame or care of cold,
By hunting and by spoiling° livèden;   *plunder*

3.7   *His learned daughters:* Phoebus'
daughters, the nine muses.
4.2   *this renownèd prince:* i.e., Arthur.
7.1–9   The legendary giants, like the
etymology of the name Albion from Latin
albus, "white," in the stanza above, are
found in most of Spenser's sources.

Of stature huge and eke of courage bold,
That sons of men amazed, their sternness to behold.

8   But whence they sprung or how they were begot   *impossible, be*
     Uneath° is to assure°—uneath to ween°   *sure, believe*
     That monstrous error, which doth some assot,°   *stupify*
     That Dioclesian's fifty daughters sheen°   *beautiful*
     Into this land by chance have driven been,
     Where companing° with fiends and filthy sprites   *copulating*
     Through vain illusion of their lust unclean,
     They brought forth giants and such dreadful wights
     As far exceeded men in their immeasured mights.

9   They held this land and with their filthiness
     Polluted this same gentle soil long time—
     That their own mother loathed their beastliness
     And gan abhor her brood's unkindly° crime,   *unnatural*
     All were they born of her own native slime—
     Until that Brutus anciently derived
     From royal stock of old Assarac's line,
     Driven by fatal error, here arrived,
     And them of their unjust possession deprived.

10 But ere he had establishèd his throne
     And spread his empire to the utmost shore,
     He fought great battles with his savage fone,°   *foes*
     In which he them defeated evermore,
     And many giants left on groaning floor.°   *ground*
     That well can witness yet unto this day
     The western Hoe, besprinkled with the gore
     Of mighty Goèmot, whom in stout fray
     Corineus conquerèd and cruelly did slay.

11 And eke that ample pit, yet far renowned
     For the large leap which Debon did compel
     Còulin to make—being eight lugs° of ground—   *rods*
     Into the which, returning back, he fell.
     But those three monstrous stones do most excell

8.4 *Dioclesian:* a king of Syria, whose thirty (or thirty-three) daughters were confused with the fifty daughters of Danaus—the Danaides of Greek myth— as progenitors of the giants in British legend.
9.7 *Assarac:* Assaracus, the great-grandfather of Aeneas and founder of the Trojan dynasty.
9.8 *fatal error:* his banishment from Italy as a punishment for accidentally killing his father on a hunting trip.

10.7–9 The Hoe, a hill overlooking the harbor in Plymouth, is the legendary site of Corineus' slaying of the giant Gogmagog. For a version of the story similar in many details to Spenser's see Geoffrey of Monmouth, *History of the Kings of Britain,* I.16 (pp. 26–27).
11.1–9 The sources of Spenser's stories of Debon and Coulin and of Canutus and Godmer are not known. Holinshed tells at length of Hercules' killing Albion in France.

Which that huge son of hideous Albion,
Whose father Hercules in France did quell,°   kill
Great Godmer, threw, in fierce contention,
At bold Canutus; but of him was slain anon.

12 In meed of° these great conquests by them got,   reward for
Corineus had that province utmost west
To him assignèd for his worthy lot,
Which of his name and memorable gest°   deed(s)
He callèd Cornwail, yet so callèd best;°   most properly
And Debon's share was that is Devonshire;
But Canute had his portion from the rest,°   apart
The which he called Canutium, for his hire°—   reward
Now Cantium, which Kent we commonly inquire.°   call

13 Thus Brute this realm unto his rule subdued
And reignèd long in great felicity,
Loved of his friends and of his foes eschewed.°   avoided
He left three sons, his famous progeny,
Born of fair Inogene of Italy,
Mongst whom he parted his imperial state,
And Locrine left chief lord of Britanny.
At last ripe age bade him surrender late
His life and long good fortune unto final fate.

14 Locrine was left the sovereign lord of all;
But Albanact had all the northern part,
Which of himself Albania he did call;
And Camber did possess the western quart,
Which Severn now from Logris doth depart.°   separate
And each his portion peaceably enjoyed,
Ne was there outward breach nor grudge in heart
That once their quiet government annoyed,
But each his pains° to others' profit still employed. labors

15 Until a nation strange, with visage swart°   swarthy
And courage fierce that all men did affray,°   frighten
Which through the world then swarmed in every part
And overflowed all countries far away,
Like Noah's great flood, with their importune sway,° irresistible force
This land invaded with like violence,
And did themselves through all the north display,°   spread
Until that Locrine for his realm's defense
Did head against them make, and strong munificence.° fortification

12.1-9 Geoffrey, I.12-16 (pp. 20, 26), makes Corineus the eponymous ruler of Cornwall, a pattern Spenser adopts with his own Debon and Canute.
13-20 The story of Locrine and Gwendolen follows Geoffrey, II.1-6 (pp. 29-33), closely.
15.1 *a nation strange:* Geoffrey's Huns.

16   He them encountered, a confusèd rout,
    Forby the river that whilom was hight
    The ancient Abus, where with courage stout
    He them defeated in victorious fight,
    And chased so fiercely after fearful flight
    That forced their chieftain for his safety's sake—
    Their chieftain Humber namèd was aright—
    Unto the mighty stream him to betake,
    Where he an end of battle and of life did make.

17   The king returnèd proud of victory,
    And insolent wox° through unwonted ease,   *became*
    That shortly he forgot the jeopardy
    Which in his land he lately did appease,°   *calm*
    And fell to vain voluptuous disease.
    He loved fair Lady Estrild, lewdly loved,
    Whose wanton pleasures him too much did please,
    That quite his heart from Guendolene removed,
    From Guendolene his wife, though always faithful proved.

18   The noble daughter of Corineus
    Would not endure to be so vile disdained,
    But gathering force and courage valorous,
    Encountered him in battle well ordained,°   *planned*
    In which him, vanquished, she to fly constrained.
    But she so fast pursued that him she took,
    And threw in bands where he till death remained;
    Als° his fair leman, flying through a brook,   *also*
    She overhent,° nought movèd with her piteous look.   *overtook*

19   But both herself and eke her daughter dear,
    Begotten by her kingly paramour,
    The fair Sabrina, almost dead with fear,
    She there attackèd, far from all succor.
    The one she slew in that impatient stour;°   *conflict*
    But the sad virgin innocent of all,
    Adown the rolling river she did pour,
    Which of her name now Severn men do call.
    Such was the end that to disloyal love did fall.

20   Then for° her son, which she to Locrine bore,   *because*
    Madan, was young, unmeet the rule to sway,
    In her own hand the crown she kept in store
    Till riper years he raught° and stronger stay;°   *reached, state*
    During which time her power she did display°   *extend*

16.3   *Abus:* a river not in Geoffrey;   19.5   *in that . . . stour:* (1596). 1590
perhaps taken from the *Mirror for Magis-*   reads *upon the present flour.*
trates, I.55.

Through all this realm, the glory of her sex,
And first taught men a woman to obey.
But when her son to man's estate did wex,°   *grow*
She it surrendered, ne herself would lenger vex.

21 Tho° Madan reigned, unworthy of his race;   *then*
For with all shame that sacred throne he filled.
Next Memprise, as unworthy of that place,
In which being consorted° with Manild,   *allied*
For thirst of single kingdom him he killed.
But Ebranck salvèd both their infamies
With noble deeds, and warrayed on Brunchild
In Hainaut, where yet of his victories
Brave monuments remain, which yet that land envies.°   *angers*

22 An happy man in his first days he was,
And happy father of fair progeny,
For all so many weeks as the year has,
So many children he did multiply;
Of which were twenty sons, which did apply
Their minds to praise and chivalrous desire.
Those germans° did subdue all Germany—   *brothers*
Of° whom it hight.° But in the end their sire   *for, is named*
With foul repulse from France was forcèd to retire.

23 Which blot, his son succeeding in his seat,
The second Brute—the second both in name
And eke in semblance° of his puissance great—   *resemblance*
Right well recured, and did away that blame
With recompence of everlasting fame.
He with his victor sword first openèd
The bowels of wide France, a forlorn dame,
And taught her first how to be conquerèd;
Since which, with sundry spoils° she hath been ransackèd.   *devastations*

24 Let Scaldis tell, and let tell Hania,
And let the marsh of Esthambruges tell
What color were their waters that same day
And all the moor twixt Elversham and Dell,
With blood of Hainalois, which therein fell.

20.7 *taught men a woman to obey:*
Gwendolen would have been recognized
by renaissance historians as a type of
Queen Elizabeth.
21.6–22 The account of Ebranck fol-
lows Stow's *Chronicles.*
24.1–9 The rivers Scaldis and Hania
and the marsh of Esthambruges in
Hainaut, as well as the name Brutus

Greenshield, are in Stow. No source has
been found for Elversham and Dell or the
Welsh words that rather surprisingly turn
up here. In some copies of the first edition
of *The Faerie Queene* (1590), the Welsh
words are missing. Brunchild, prince of
Hainaut, was mentioned in 21.7–8 above.

How oft that day did sad Brunchildis see
The green shield dyed in dolorous vermeil,
That not *Scuith guiridh*° he mote seem to be,   i.e. *green shield*
But rather *y Scuith gogh*,° sign of sad cruelty?   i.e. *the red shield*

25   His son King Leill, by father's labor long,
Enjoyed an heritage of lasting peace,
And built Cairleill and built Cairleon strong.
Next Huddibras his realm did not increase,
But taught the land from weary wars to cease.
Whose footsteps Bladud following, in arts
Excelled at Athens all the learnèd press,°   *crowd*
From whence he brought them to these savage parts,
And with sweet science° mollified their stubborn hearts.   *knowledge*

26   Ensample° of his wondrous faculty,   *as an example*
Behold the boiling baths at Cairbadon,
Which seethe with secret fire eternally
And in their entrails, full of quick brimstone,°   *hot sulphur*
Nourish the flames which they are warmed upon,
That to their people wealth they forth do well,
And health to every foreign nation.
Yet he at last, contending to excel
The reach of men through flight, into fond mischief fell.

27   Next him King Lear in happy peace long reigned,
But had no issue male him to succeed,
But three fair daughters which were well uptrained
In all that seemèd fit for kingly seed,
Mongst whom his realm he equally decreed
To have divided. Tho when feeble age
Nigh to his utmost date he saw proceed,
He called his daughters, and with speeches sage
Inquired which of them most did love her parentage.

28   The eldest, Goneril, gan to protest
That she much more than her own life him loved;
And Regan greater love to him professed
Than all the world, whenever it were proved;°   *tested*
But Cordeill said she loved him as behoved.
Whose simple answer, wanting colors fair°   *lacking ornate*
                                                                   style

25.3 *Cair* means city. *Cairleill*, Carlisle; *Cairleon* (City of the Legion), Chester.
25.4 *Huddibras:* from Geoffrey. Among many other variants of the name, he is known to later chroniclers as Lud.
26.2–7 *Cairbadon:* Bath, where the curative wells have been a health resort from Roman times till the present. Such phenomena were referred to by the palmer in discussing the nymph's well (ii.5), but he did not mention that their virtues might be infused through such agencies as Bladud's "arts."
27–32 Spenser's version of *King Lear* follows Geoffrey, II.11–14 (pp. 36–42).

To paint it forth, him to displeasance moved,
That in his crown he counted her no heir,
But twixt the other twain his kingdom whole did share.

29 So wedded th' one to Maglan, king of Scots,
And th' other to the king of Cambria,
And twixt them shared his realm by equal lots.
But without dower the wise Cordelia
Was sent to Aganip of Celtica.
Their aged sire, thus easèd of his crown,
A private life led in Albania
With Goneril, long had in great renown,
That nought him grieved to been from rule deposèd down.

30 But true it is that when the oil is spent
The light goes out, and wick is thrown away.
So when he had resigned his regiment,°   *rule*
His daughter gan despise his drooping day,
And weary wax of his continual stay.
Tho to his daughter Regan he repaired,
Who him at first well usèd every way;
But when of his departure she despaired,
Her bounty she abated, and his cheer impaired.

31 The wretched man gan then avise° too late   *perceive*
That love is not where most it is professed—
Too truly tried in his extremest state.
At last resolved likewise to prove the rest,
He to Cordelia himself addressed,
Who with entire affection him received,
As for her sire and king her seemèd best.
And after all an army strong she leaved°   *levied*
To war on those which him had of his realm bereaved.°   *robbed*

32 So to his crown she him restored again,
In which he died, made ripe for death by eld,
And after willed it should to her remain;
Who peaceably the same long time did weld,°   *govern*
And all men's hearts in due obedience held,
Till that her sisters' children, woxen strong
Through proud ambition, against her rebelled
And, overcomen, kept in prison long,
Till weary of that wretched life, herself she hung.

33 Then gan the bloody brethren both to reign.
But fierce Cundah gan shortly to envy

29.2–7 *Cambria:* Wales; *Celtica:* France; *Albania:* Scotland.

His brother Morgan, pricked with proud disdain
To have a peer in part of sovereignty;
And kindling coals of cruel enmity,
Raised war, and him in battle overthrew.
Whence as he to those woody hills did fly—
Which hight of him Glamorgan—there him slew.
Then did he reign alone, when he none equal knew.

34 His son Rivall his dead room did supply,
In whose sad time blood did from heaven rain;
Next great Gurgustus, then fair Caecily,
In constant peace their kingdoms did contain;
After whom Lago and Kinmarke did reign,
And Gorbogud till far in years he grew.
Then his amtitious sons unto them twain
Arraught° the rule, and from their father drew°—   *usurped, rebelled*
Stout Ferrex and stern Porrex him in prison threw.

35 But O, the greedy thirst of royal crown,
That knows no kinred° nor regards no right,   *family*
Stirred Porrex up to put his brother down;
Who unto him assembling foreign might,
Made war on him and fell himself in fight;
Whose death t' avenge, his mother merciless,
Most merciless of women, Wyden hight,
Her other son fast sleeping did oppress,°   *surprise*
And with most cruel hand him murdered pitiless.

36 Here ended Brutus' sacred progeny,
Which had seven hundred years this scepter borne
With high renowm and great felicity;
The noble branch from th' antique stock was torn
Through discord, and the royal throne forlorn.
Thenceforth this realm was into factions rent,
Whilst each of Brutus boasted to be born,
That in the end was left no monument
Of Brutus, nor of Britons' glory ancient.

37 Then up arose a man of matchless might
And wondrous wit to manage high affairs,

34.3 *fair Caecily:* Geoffrey's Sisillius (II.16, p. 43), whom Spenser seems to have feminized. This stanza and the next follow Geoffrey closely.

36.1–9 The *great felicity* of the adultery, treason, and murder characterizing the first seven hundred years of British rule must surely be felicitous only by its contrast to the condition of the island's previous subhuman inhabitants. The narrator seems throughout the Chronicle of Briton Kings to adopt a point of view appropriate to the functions of memory, which sees the past as worthy of preservation in its own right, without regard to its moral significance.

37.1 *a man of matchless might* introduces what might be considered Part II of the Chronicle of Briton Kings, in which the lawlessness of the previous dynasty is brought under control.

Who stirred with pity of the stressèd° plight   *distressed*
Of this sad realm—cut into sundry shares
By such as claimed themselves Brute's rightful heirs—
Gathered the princes of the people loose°   *disunified*
To taken counsel of their common cares;°   *problems*
Who with his wisdom won, him straight did choose
Their king, and swore him fealty° to win or lose.   *loyalty*

38   Then made he head° against his enemies,   *attacked*
And Ymner slew, of Logris miscreate;°   *unlawful ruler*
Then Ruddoc and proud Stater, both allies—
This of Albany newly nominate°   *named*
And that of Cambry king confirmèd late—
He overthrew through his own valiance;
Whose countries he reduced to quiet state
And shortly brought to civil governance,
Now one, which erst° were many made through variance.°   *before, discord*

39   Then made he sacred laws, which some men say
Were unto him revealed in vision,
By which he freed the traveler's highway,
The Church's part, and plowman's portion,
Restraining stealth and strong extortion—
The gracious Numa of Great Britanny.
For till his days, the chief dominion
By strength was wielded without policy;°   *legal authority*
Therefore he first wore crown of gold for dignity.

40   Donwallo died—for what may live for ay?—
And left two sons, of peerless prowess both,
That° sackèd Rome too dearly did assay°—   *which, experience*
The recompence of their perjurèd oath—
And ransacked Greece well tried,° when they were wroth,   *experienced*
Besides subjected France and Germany,
Which yet their praises speak, all be they loath,
And inly tremble at the memory
Of Brennus and Belinus, kings of Britanny.

38.2–5   *Logris:* England; *Albany:* Scotland; *Cambry:* Wales.

39.1–2   *sacred laws:* Dunwallo the lawgiver is a type of Moses, who, in turn, is a type of Christ. This characteristically medieval historical pattern would not be lost, however, on a renaissance audience which was trained to view the Old Testament as a foreshadowing of the New, and secular history an imitation of sacred.

39.6   *Numa:* an apt parallel in Roman history to Dunwallo. Numa Pompilus (died 622 B.C.) was Romulus' successor to the throne of Rome after a similarly chaotic interregnum. He established many of the legal and religious institutions of ancient Rome. See Livy, *A History of Rome,* I.18–21.

40.2–9   I.e., sacked Rome and ransacked Greece experienced the prowess of Brennus and Belinus. Geoffrey (II.9, pp. 54–56) tells the story of the Romans' breaking their treaty with the brothers, but he does not record their conquest of Greece. The later chronicles do.

41 Next them did Gurgiunt, great Belinus' son,
In rule succeed, and eke in father's praise;
He Easterland subdued and Denmark won,
And of them both did foy° and tribute raise,   *allegiance*
The which was due in his dead father's days.
He also gave to fugitives of Spain,
Whom he at sea found wandering from their ways,
A seat in Ireland safely to remain,
Which they should hold of him, as subject to Britain.

42 After him reignèd Guitheline his heir,
The justest man and truest in his days,
Who had to wife Dame Mertia the fair,
A woman worthy of immortal praise,
Which for this realm found° many goodly lays,°   *devised, laws*
And wholesome statutes to her husband brought.
Her many deemed to have been of the fays,
As was Aegeria that Numa taught;
Those yet of her be Mertian laws both named and thought.

43 Her son Sisillus after her did reign,
And then Kimarus, and then Danius;
Next whom Morindus did the crown sustain,
Who, had he not with wrath outrageous
And cruel rancor dimmed his valorous
And mighty deeds, should matchèd have the best—
As well in that same field victorious
Against the foreign Morands he expressed.
Yet lives his memory, though carcass sleep in rest.

44 Five sons he left begotten of one wife,
All which successively by turns did reign:
First Gorboman, a man of virtuous life;
Next Archigald, who for his proud disdain
Deposèd was from princedom sovereign,
And piteous Elidure put in his stead;
Who shortly it to him restored again,
Till by his death he it recoverèd;
But Peridure and Vigent him disthronizèd.

45 In wretched prison long he did remain,
Till they outreignèd had their utmost date,

41.3 *Easterland:* not mentioned by Geoffrey or the later chronicles, perhaps Austria.
43.9 *though carcass sleep in rest:* an apparent contradiction of the chronicles' account of Morindus' being swallowed by a sea-monster, a story that should have appealed to Spenser.
44.2–9 The five sons of Morindus treat each other about as well as did the rulers in Part I of Spenser's Chronicles. The progress from the subhuman giants to Arthur is an uneven one.

And then therein reseizèd° was again,   *reinstated*
And rulèd long with honorable state,
Till he surrendered realm and life to fate.
Then all the sons of these five brethren reigned
By due success,° and all their nephews late,   *regular succession*
Even thrice eleven descents° the crown retained,   *generations*
Till aged Hely by due heritage it gained.

46 He had two sons, whose eldest, callèd Lud,
    Left of his life most famous memory
    And endless monuments of his great good.
    The ruined walls he did re-edify°   *rebuild*
    Of Troynovant, gainst force of enemy,
    And built that gate which of his name is hight,
    By which he lies entombèd solemnly.°   *grandly*
    He left two sons too young to rule aright,
    Androgeus and Tenantius, pictures of his might.

47 Whilst they were young, Cassibalane their eme°   *uncle*
    Was by the people chosen in their stead,
    Who on him took the royal diadem
    And goodly well long time it governèd,
    Till the proud Romans him disquieted,
    And warlike Caesar, tempted with the name
    Of this sweet island, never conquerèd,
    And envying the Britons' blazèd° fame—   *heralded*
    O hideous hunger of dominion°—hither came.   *for power*

48 Yet twice they were repulsèd back again,
    And twice renforced° back to their ships to fly,   *forced*
    The whiles with blood they all the shore did stain,
    And the gray ocean into purple dye.
    Ne had they footing found at last, perdie,°   *in fact*
    Had not Androgeus, false to native soil
    And envious of uncle's sovereignty,
    Betrayed his country unto foreign spoil.
    Nought else but treason from the first this land did foil.

49 So by him Caesar got the victory
    Through great bloodshed and many a sad assay,°   *heavy assault*
    In which himself was chargèd heavily
    Of° hardy Nennius, whom he yet did slay,   *by*
    But lost his sword, yet to be seen this day.
    Thenceforth this land was tributary made
    T' ambitious Rome, and did their rule obey,
    Till Arthur all that reckoning° defrayed;°   *tribute, paid off*
    Yet oft the Briton kings against them strongly swayed.° *attacked*

46.5 *Troynovant*: London.

50 Next him Tenantius reigned, then Kimbeline,
     What time° th' eternal Lord in fleshly slime   *at the time*
     Enwombèd was, from wretched Adam's line
     To purge away the guilt of sinful crime.
     O joyous memory of happy time
     That heavenly grace so plentiously displayed—
     O too high ditty° for my simple rime!   *theme*
     Soon after this the Romans him warrayed,°   *attacked*
     For that their tribute he refused to let be paid.

51 Good Claudius, that next was emperor,
     An army brought, and with him battle fought,
     In which the king was by a treachetor°   *traitor*
     Disguisèd slain ere any thereof thought.
     Yet ceasèd not the bloody fight for aught,
     For Arvirage his brother's place supplied
     Both in his arms and crown, and by that draught°   *trick*
     Did drive the Romans to the weaker side,
     That they to peace agreed. So all was pacified.

52 Was never king more highly magnified°   *praised*
     Nor dread of Romans than was Arvirage,
     For which the emperor to him allied
     His daughter Genuiss' in marriage.
     Yet shortly he renounced the vassalage
     Of Rome again, who hither hastily sent
     Vespasian, that with great spoil and rage
     Forwasted° all, till Genuissa gent°   *destroyed, noble*
     Persuaded him to cease, and her lord to relent.

53 He died; and him succeeded Marius,
     Who joyed his days in great tranquillity,
     Then Coyll, and after him good Lucius,
     That first receivèd Christianity,
     The sacred pledge of Christ's evangely.°   *gospel*
     Yet true it is that long before that day
     Hither came Joseph of Arimathy,
     Who brought with him the Holy Grail, they say,
     And preached the truth; but since it greatly did decay.

54 This good king shortly without issue died,
     Whereof great trouble in the kingdom grew,
     That did herself in sundry parts divide
     And with her power her own self overthrew,

51.1 *Good* seems a strange adjective to apply to Claudius, Caesar's successor.
53.7–9 None of the chronicles mention the Holy Grail, although they do name Joseph of Arimathea, with whom the Grail is associated in legend and romance.

Whilst Romans daily did the weak subdue.
Which seeing, stout Bunduca up arose,
And taking arms, the Britons to her drew;
With whom she marchèd straight against her foes,
And them unwares besides the Severn did enclose.°   *surround*

55 There she with them a cruel battle tried,
Not with so good success as she deserved,
By reason that the captains on her side,
Corrupted by Paulinus, from her swerved.
Yet such as were through former flight preserved
Gathering again, her host she did renew,
And with fresh courage on the victor served;°   *attacked*
But being all defeated save a few,
Rather than fly or be captived, herself she slew.

56 O famous monument of women's praise,
Matchable either to Semiramis,
Whom antique history so high doth raise,
Or to Hypsipyl' or to Tomyris—
Her host two hundred thousand numbered is!
Who whiles good fortune favorèd her might,
Triumphèd oft against her enemies;
And yet though overcome in hapless° fight,   *luckless*
She triumphèd on death, in enemies' despite.

57 Her relics° Fulgent having gatherèd,   *remnants of her*
Fought with Severus and him overthrew,   *army*
Yet in the chase was slain of them that fled;
So made them victors whom he did subdue.
Then gan Carausius tyrannize anew,
And gainst the Romans bent their proper power,°   *own troops*
But him Allectus treacherously slew,
And took on him the robe of emperor—
Nath'less the same enjoyèd but short happy hour;

58 For Asclepiodate him overcame,
And left inglorious on the vanquished plain,
Without or° robe or rag to hide his shame.   *either*

54.6 *Bunduca:* the Boudicca of Taci-
tus (*Agricola,* XVI, Penguin Books, p.
66) and Boadicea of popular legend, not
mentioned in Geoffrey's *History.* Her ex-
ploits against the Romans in A.D. 61
were well known to the later chroniclers.
The interpolation of a type of the female
ruler is especially appropriate to Spenser's
Chronicle. From this point on, Spenser
follows Geoffrey in the main, but sup-
presses some things and takes other, non-
Galfridian elements from the later chron-
icles.
55.4 *Paulinus:* a Roman general
(Tacitus, *Agricola,* XVI, p. 66).
56.1–4 Bunduca's likeness to *Semira-
mis* (as well known for her sexual as her
military prowess), *Hysipyle,* and *Tomyris*
is not particularly flattering. They are
types of the female ruler who rose to
earthly power through crime as well as
virtue. For Semiramis see Book I.v.50.3.

Then afterwards he in his stead did reign,
But shortly was by Coyll in battle slain;
Who after long debate, since Lucius' time,
Was of the Britons first crowned sovereign.
Then gan this realm renew her passèd prime;° *youth*
He of his name Coylchester built of stone and lime.

59 Which when the Romans heard, they hither sent
Constantius, a man of mickle° might, *great*
With whom king Coyll made an agreement,
And to him gave for wife his daughter bright,° *beautiful*
Fair Helena, the fairest living wight;
Who in all godly thews° and goodly praise *qualities*
Did far excel, but was most famous hight° *known*
For skill in music of all in her days,
As well in curious° instruments as cunning lays. *difficult*

60 Of whom he did great Constantine beget,
Who afterward was emperor of Rome.
To which,° whiles absent he his mind did set,° *i.e. emperorship, concentrate*
Octavius here leapt into his room
And it usurpèd by unrighteous doom.° *illegal judgment*
But he his title justified by might,
Slaying Traherne and having overcome
The Roman legion in dreadful fight;
So settled he his kingdom and confirmed his right.

61 But wanting issue male, his daughter dear
He gave in wedlock to Maximian,
And him with her made of his kingdom heir;
Who soon by means thereof the empire won,
Till murdered by the friends of Gratian.
Then gan the Huns and Picts invade this land
During the reign of Maximinian;
Who dying left none heir them to withstand,
But that they overran all parts with easy hand.

62 The weary Britons, whose war-able youth
Was by Maximian lately led away,
With wretched miseries and woeful ruth° *sorrow*
Were to those pagans made an open prey
And daily spectacle of sad decay—
Whom Roman wars, which now four hundred years
And more had wasted,° could no whit dismay— *devastated*

60.1 *great Constantine:* joint ruler of Rome and Britain (Geoffrey, V.7–8, pp. 95–97) with whose reign the British and Roman destinies are reunited. This reunification can be thought to begin Part III.
61.7 *Maximinian:* a variant form of the name Maximian in line 2 above.

Till by consent of commons and of peers
They crowned the second Constantine with joyous tears.

63 Who having oft in battle vanquishèd
Those spoilful Picts and swarming Easterlings,
Long time in peace his realm establishèd,
Yet oft annoyed with sundry bordragings°   *raids*
Of neighbor Scots and foreign scatterlings,°   *roving bands*
With which the world did in those days abound.
Which to outbar,° with painful pionings°   *keep out, digging*
From sea to sea he heaped a mighty mound
Which from Alcluid to Panwelt did that border bound.

64 Three sons he dying left—all under age—
By means whereof their uncle Vortiger
Usurped the crown during their pupilage;
Which th' infants' tutors gathering to fear,°   *judging to be*
Them closely° into Armoric did bear.   *dangerous*
                                                 secretly
For dread of whom, and for those Picts' annoys,
He sent to Germany strange° aid to rear,   *foreign*
From when eftsoons arrivèd here three hoys°   *small ships*
Of Saxons, whom he for his safèty employs.

65 Two brethren were their capitans, which hight
Hengist and Horsus, well approved° in war,   *experienced*
And both of them men of renowmèd might;
Who making vantage of their civil jar,°   *discord*
And of those foreigners which came from far,
Grew great, and got large portions of land;
That in the realm ere long they stronger are
Than they which sought at first their helping hand,
And Vortiger have forced the kingdom to aband.°   *abandon*

66 But by the help of Vortimere his son,
He is again unto his rule restored;
And Hengist seeming sad for that was done,
Receivèd is to grace and new accord
Through his fair daughter's face and flattering word;
Soon after which, three hundred lords he slew
Of British blood, all sitting at his board;
Whose doleful monuments who list to rue,°   *wants to mourn*
Th' eternal marks of treason may at Stonehenge view.

63.2 *Easterlings:* probably proto-Viking Norwegians and Danes.
64.5 *Armoric:* Armorica, continental Britanny.
66.9 *Stonehenge:* a neolithic assemblage of massive stones set up on the Salisbury Plain, probably for religious observations and sacrifices that were made at times determined by astronomical sightings through the stones. According to an account in Geoffrey (VIII.10–12, pp. 163–167), the magician Merlin brought the stones from Ireland and erected Stonehenge as a monument to the slain British nobles.

67 By this the sons of Constantine, which fled,
    Ambrose and Uther, did ripe years attain,
    And here arriving, strongly challengèd
    The crown which Vortiger did long detain;
    Who flying from his guilt, by them was slain,
    And Hengist eke soon brought to shameful death.
    Thenceforth Aurelius peaceably did reign,
    Till that through poison stoppèd was his breath;
    So now entombèd lies at Stonehenge by the heath.

68 After him, Uther, which Pendragon hight,
    Succeeding . . . . There abruptly it did end,
    Without full point° or other caesure right,°   *period, proper*
    As if the rest some wicked hand did rend,   *caesura*
    Or th' author self could not at least attend°   *stay*
    To finish it. That so untimely breach°   *break*
    The prince himself half seemèd to offend,
    Yet secret pleasure did offence impeach,°   *hinder*
    And wonder of antiquity long stopped his speech.

69 At last, quite ravished with delight to hear
    The royal offspring° of his native land,   *pedigree*
    Cried out, 'Dear country, O how dearly dear°   *precious*
    Ought thy remembrance and perpetual band°   *bond*
    Be to thy foster-child, that from thy hand
    Did common breath and nouriture° receive!   *nurture*
    How brutish° is it not to understand   *stupid*
    How much to her we owe that all us gave,
    That gave unto us all, whatever good we have!'

70 But Guyon all this while his book did read,
    Ne yet has ended; for it was a great
    And ample volume, that doth far exceed
    My leisure so° long leaves here to repeat.   *such*
    It told how first Prometheus did create
    A man, of many parts from beasts derived,°   *taken*
    And then stole fire from heaven to animate
    His work, for which he was by Jove deprived
    Of life himself, and heart-strings of an eagle rived.° *torn*

71 That man so made he callèd Elf, to weet,°   *to wit*
    "Quick," the first author of all elfin kind;

67.1–9 Follows Geoffrey (VIII.1–14, pp. 153–169) accuraetly.

69.1–9 Arthur's patriotic enthusiasm is extreme, even for an Elizabethan. He seems to relish earthly glory, the product of human memory, beyond all else.

70.5–9 *Prometheus:* in Natalis Comes the creator of man, who combined in man's nature the characteristics of the hare, the wolf, peacock, tiger, and lion (*Mythologiae*, IV.6). After long suffering Prometheus was redeemed by Hercules. The very act of creating man involved a fall and subsequent salvation. See Lotspeich, p. 103.

Who wandering through the world with weary feet,
Did in the Gardens of Adonis find
A goodly creature, whom he deemed in mind
To be no earthly wight, but either sprite
Or angel, th' author of all woman kind;
Therefore a Fay he her according° hight,   *appropriately*
Of whom all faeries spring and fetch their lineage right.°   *directly*

72   Of these a mighty people shortly grew,
And puissant kings which all the world warrayed°   *waged war on*
And to themselves all nations did subdue.
The first and eldest which that scepter swayed
Was Elfin; him all India obeyed
And all that now America men call.
Next him was noble Elfinan, who laid
Cleopolis' foundation first of all;
But Elfiline enclosed it with a golden wall.

73   His son was Elfinell, who overcame
The wicked Gobbelines in bloody field;
But Elfant was of most renowmèd fame,
Who all of crystal did Panthea build.
Then Elfar, who two brethren giants killed,
The one of which had two heads, th' other three.
Then Elfinor, who was in magic skilled;
He built by art upon the glassy sea
A bridge of brass, whose sound heaven's thunder seemed to
    be.

74   He left three sons, the which in order reigned,
And all their offspring in their due descents,
Even seven hundred princes, which maintained
With mighty deeds their sundry governments;
That were too long their infinite contents
Here to record, ne much material.°   *to the point*
Yet should they be most famous monuments
And brave ensample, both of martial
And civil rule to kings and states imperial.

75   After all these, Elficleos did reign—
The wise Elficleos in great majesty,

71.4 *Garden of Adonis:* described fully in Book III, Canto vi.
72.8 *Cleopolis:* the Faeryland equivalent of Troynovant and London.
73.2 *Gobbelines:* opposed to the elfs in a feud suggestive of that between the medieval Italian Guelfs and Ghibellines.
73.4 *Panthea:* the Faeryland equivalent of Westminster Abbey.
74.1–9 Note the contrast with the turbulence of the Chronicle of Briton Kings.
75–76 The most recent entries in the Roll of Elfin Emperors are patent idealizations of the Tudor monarchs. *Elficleos:* Henry VII; *Elferon:* Prince Arthur, eldest

Who mightily that scepter did sutsain,
And with rich spoils and famous victory
Did high advance the crown of Faèry.
He left two sons, of which fair Elferon,
The eldest brother, did untimely die;
Whose empty place the mighty Oberon
Doubly supplied, in spousal and dominion.°   *marriage and rule*

76 Great was his power and glory over° all   *greater than*
Which him before that sacred seat did fill,
That yet remains his wide memorial.
He dying left the fairest Tanaquill
Him to succeed therein, by his last will.
Fairer and nobler liveth none this hour,
Ne like° in grace, ne like in learned skill;   *comparable*
Therefore they Glorian call that glorious flower—
Long mayst thou Glorian live, in glory and great power.

77 Beguiled thus with delight of novelties
And natural desire° of country's state,   *desire to know*
So long they read in those antiquities
That how the time was fled they quite forgate,°   *forgot*
Till gentle Alma seeing it so late,
Perforce their studies broke and them besought
To think how supper did them long await.
So half unwilling from their books them brought,
And fairly feasted, as to noble knights she ought.°   *owed*

CANTO xi

The enemies of Temperance
  Besiege her dwelling place;
Prince Arthur them repels, and foul
  Maleger doth deface.°   *destroy*

1 What war so cruel or what siege so sore
As that which strong affections do apply
Against the fort of reason evermore

---

son of Henry VII and brother of Henry VIII; *Oberon:* Henry VIII, who married Arthur's widow Katherine; *Tanaquill:* Elizabeth I. Spenser omits elfin parallels with the reigns of Edward VI and Mary, who ruled between Henry VIII and Elizabeth. On this level of topical allegory, Mary had served as one meaning of Duessa in Book I.

1.1–2.9 "Let not sin therefore reign in your mortal body, that ye should obey it in the lusts thereof. Neither yield ye your members as instruments of unrighteousness unto sin" (Romans 6:12–13). "As ye have yielded your members servants to uncleanliness and to iniquity unto iniquity; even so now yield your members servants to righteousness unto holiness" (Romans 6:19).

To bring the soul into captivity?
Their force is fiercer through infirmity
Of the frail flesh, relenting to their rage,
And exercise most bitter tyranny
Upon the parts brought into their bondage.
No wretchedness is like to sinful villeinage.°   *slavery to sin*

2   But in a body which doth freely yield
His parts to reason's rule obedient,
And letteth her that ought the scepter wield,
All happy peace and goodly government
Is settled there in sure establishment.
There Alma like a virgin queen most bright
Doth flourish in all beauty excellent,
And to her guests doth bounteous banquet dight,°   *prepare*
Attempered° goodly well for health and for delight.   *seasoned*

3   Early before the morn with crimson ray
The windows of bright heaven opened had,
Through which into the world the dawning day
Might look, that maketh every creature glad,
Uprose Sir Guyon, in bright armor clad,°
And to his purposed journey him prepared.
With him the palmer eke in habit sad°   *sober*
Himself addressed to that adventure hard;
So to the river's side they both together fared;

4   Where them awaited ready at the ford
The ferryman, as Alma had behight,°   *commanded*
With his well riggèd boat. They go aboard,
And he eftsoons gan launch his bark forthright.
Ere long they rowèd were quite out of sight,
And fast the land behind them fled away.
But let them pass whiles wind and weather right
Do serve their turns; here I awhile must stay
To see a cruel fight done by the prince this day.

5   For all so soon as Guyon thence was gone
Upon his voyage with his trusty guide,
That wicked band of villeins fresh began

5.3–15.9 The siege of the Castle of Alma is a variant of the allegorical attack of sin on the soul by way of the body. This allegory has a long tradition in European literature and probably derives from Jewish commentaries on the sacred scriptures. The notion of the sins attacking the soul through the five senses was treated allegorically by the Jewish philosopher Philo Judaeus, a contemporary of Jesus, and became a common theme in medieval treatments of the seven deadly sins. Three late versions of the allegorical attack on the castle are found in *Ancrene Riwle* (ca. 1300), *Piers Plowman* (ca. 1380), and the morality play *The Castle of Perseverance* (ca. 1425).

That castle to assail on every side,
And lay strong siege about it far and wide.
So huge and infinite their numbers were
That all the land they under them did hide,
So foul and ugly that exceeding fear
Their visages impressed when they approachèd near.

6   Them in twelve troops their captain did dispart,°   *divide*
    And round about in fittest steads° did place,   *positions*
    Where each might best offend his proper part
    And his contrary object most deface,
    As every one seemed meetest in that case.
    Seven of the same against the castle gate
    In strong entrenchments he did closely place,
    Which with incessant force and endless hate
    They battered day and night, and entrance did await.

7   The other five, five sundry ways he set
    Against the five great bulwarks of that pile,°   *building*
    And unto each a bulwark did aret°   *assign*
    T' assail with open force or hidden guile,
    In hope thereof to win victorious spoil.
    They all that charge did fervently apply
    With greedy malice and importune° toil,   *frenzied*
    And planted there their huge artillery,
    With which they daily made most dreadful battery.

8   The first troop was a monstrous rabblement
    Of foul misshapen wights, of which some were
    Headed like owls, with beaks uncomely bent,
    Others like dogs, others like griffons drear,°   *horrible*
    And some had wings, and some had claws to tear,
    And every one of them had lynx's eyes,
    And every one did bow and arrows bear.

6.6–9   The seven troops which attack the castle gate are the seven deadly sins: pride, envy, anger, avarice, sloth, gluttony, lechery. For a conventional exposition of the seven deadly sins see Chaucer's *Parson's Tale*. The castle gate is the heart.

7.1–2   "The heart's wardens are the five senses: sight, hearing, speaking, and smelling, and every limb's feeling" (*Ancrene Riwle*, ed. Mabel Day, Early English Text Society, p. 21).

8.1–9   The association of animals with sins and vices is common in medieval literature; however, there was not any great consistency in the association from author to author. The same animals might represent as many as five or six of the cardinal sins in the work of different authors. Spenser's dogs are commonly associated with envy, his owl and griffon less commonly with covetousness and lechery. (See Bloomfield, *The Seven Deadly Sins*, pp. 245–249). The association of lust with the eyes is probably traditional (see *Ancrene Riwle*, pp. 22 ff.). The assailants of the eyes carry bows in *Ancrene Riwle*: "Whoso is wise and good let her guard against the shooting—that is, guard her eyes well. For all the evil that ever is comes of the eye-arrows. And is she not too bold or too foolhardy that holds her head boldly forth in the open battlements, the while men assail the castle from outside with crossbow-arrows" (pp. 26–27).

All those were lawless lusts, corrupt envies,
And covetous aspects, all cruel enemies.

9   Those same against the bulwark of the sight
Did lay strong siege and battailous assault,
Ne once did yield it respite day nor night;
But soon as Titan gan his head exalt
And soon again as he his light withhalt,°   *withheld*
Their wicked engines they against it bent—
That is, each thing by which the eyes may fault;°   *sin*
But two than all more huge and violent,
Beauty and money, they that bulwark sorely rent.

10   The second bulwark was the hearing sense,
Gainst which the second troop designment makes,
Deformèd creatures in strange difference—
Some having heads like harts, some like to snakes,
Some like wild boars late roused out of the brakes°—   *thickets*
Slanderous reproaches and foul infamies,
Leasings,° backbitings, and vainglorious crakes,°   *lies, boasts*
Bad counsels, praises, and false flatteries.
All those against that fort did bend their batteries.

11   Likewise, that same third fort, that is the smell,
Of that third troop was cruelly assayed;°   *attacked*
Whose hideous shapes were like to fiends of hell—
Some like to hounds, some like to apes dismayed,°   *berserk*
Some like to puttocks° all in plumes arrayed—   *kites*
All shaped according° their conditions.   *in agreement with*
For by those ugly forms weren portrayed
Foolish delights and fond abusions,°   *deceptions*
Which do that sense besiege with light illusions.

12   And that fourth band, which cruel battery bent
Against the fourth bulwark, that is the taste,
Was as the the rest, a grisy° rabblement—   *hideous*
Some mouthed like greedy ostriches, some faced
Like loathly toads, some fashioned in the waist
Like swine; for so deformed is luxury,

9.8–9 The eyes' attraction to beauty
and money open the way not only to lust
and covetousness, but also to the other
sins as well. Lucifer fell in love with his
own beauty and opened the way for pride,
for which he was cast into hell (*Ancrene
Riwle*, p. 22).
  9.9 *that bulwark . . . rent:* (1596).
1590 reads *against that bulwark lent.*
  10.4–9 Snakes are specifically associ-
ated with backbiting and slander in
Ancrene Riwle (p. 36), and the vices which
assail the sense of hearing in *Ancrene
Riwle* are with few exceptions the ones
listed by Spenser: foul speech, heresy, out
and out lying, backbiting, and flattery
(p. 35).
  12.6 For swine associated with glut-
tony see Bloomfield, p. 248.

Surfeit, misdiet, and unthrifty waste,
Vain feasts, and idle superfluity.
All those this sense's fort assail incessantly.

13 But the fifth troop, most horrible of hue°   *shape*
    And fierce of force, is dreadful to report;
    For some like snails, some did like spiders shew,
    And some like ugly urchins° thick and short.   *hedgehogs*
    Cruelly they assayèd that fifth fort,
    Armèd with darts of sensual delight,
    With stings of carnal lust, and strong effort
    Of feeling° pleasures, with which day and night   *tactile*
    Against that same fifth bulwark they continued fight.

14 Thus these twelve troops with dreadful puissancce
    Against that castle restless° siege did lay,   *continual*
    And evermore their hideous ordinance°   *ordnance*
    Upon the bulwarks cruelly did play,°   *batter*
    That now it gan to threaten near decay.
    And evermore their wicked capitain
    Provokèd them the breaches to assay,
    Sometimes with threats, sometimes with hope of gain
    Which by the ransack of that piece they should attain.

15 On th' other side, th' assiegèd castle's ward°   *guard*
    Their steadfast stands did mightily maintain,
    And many bold repulse and many hard
    Achievement wrought with peril and with pain,
    That goodly frame from ruin to sustain.
    And those two brethren giants did defend
    The walls so stoutly with their sturdy main,°   *might*
    That never entrance any durst pretend,°   *attempt*
    But° they to direful death their groaning ghosts did send. *unless*

16 The noble virgin, lady of the place,
    Was much dismayèd with that dreadful sight,
    For never was she in so evil case;
    Till that the prince seeing her woeful plight,
    Gan her recomfort from so sad affright,
    Offering his service and his dearest° life   *most precious*
    For her defense, against that carl° to fight   *boor*
    Which was their chief and th' author of that strife.
    She him remercied° as the patron° of her life.   *thanked, protector*

13.3–4 None of these animals is con-   ation of touch.
ventionally associated with the sin of lust,   15.6 *two brethren giants:* the eyes? the
but they have an artistic rightness in that arms?
they all represent some loathsome sens-

17　Eftsoons himself in glitterand arms he dight,
　　And his well provèd weapons to him hent;°　　　　　*took*
　　So taking courteous congé,° he behight°　　　　　　*farewell, com-*
　　Those gates to be unbarred, and forth he went.　　　*manded*
　　Fair mote he thee,° the prowest and most gent°　　　*prosper, noble*
　　That ever brandishèd bright steel on high;
　　Whom soon as that unruly rabblement
　　With his gay squire issuing did espy,
　　They reared a most outrageous dreadful yelling cry.

18　And therewith all at once at him let fly
　　Their fluttering arrows thick as flakes of snow,
　　And round about him flock impetuously,
　　Like a great water flood that, tumbling low
　　From the high mountains, threats to overflow
　　With sudden fury all the fertile plain,
　　And the sad husbandman's long hope doth throw
　　Adown the stream and all his vows make vain;
　　Nor bounds nor banks his headlong ruin may sustain.°　*hold back*

19　Upon his shield their heapèd hail he bore,
　　And with his sword dispersed the rascal flocks,
　　Which fled asunder and him fell before
　　As withered leaves drop from their d](ried stocks
　　When the wroth° western wind does reave° their locks;　*angry, tear*
　　And underneath him his courageous steed,
　　The fierce Spumador, trod them down like docks°—　　*weeds*
　　The fierce Spumador born of heavenly seed,
　　Such as Laomedon of Phoebus' race did breed.

20　Which sudden horror and confusèd cry
　　Whenas their captain heard, in haste he yode°　　　　*went*

17.9–18.6 "Then with a sudden shout, they leapt forward, cheering on their horses till they were battle-mad, and pouring as they galloped a shower of shafts from every side, thick as snow-flakes . . ." (*Aeneid*, XI.610–611, p. 298). ". . . more fiercely, even, than some foaming river which breaks its banks and leaps over them in a swirling torrent, and defeats every barrier, till the mad piled water charges on the ploughland and sweeps away with it cattle and their stalls over miles of country" (*Aeneid*, II.495–499, p. 66). Spenser's use of these two similes is significant. The first is used in the *Aeneid* in a battle scene between Aeneas' forces and the army of Latinum, the second to describe the destruction of Troy by the Greeks. In the present context the first simile implies the eventual triumph of Arthur, who has already been compared with Aeneas, over Maleger; the second establishes the heartless cruelty of his enemies.

19.7–9 *Spumador:* frothing. ". . . concentrate on the horses of Aeneas. Seize them and drive them out of the Trojan lines into our own. For I tell you, they are bred from the same stock as those that all-seeing Zeus gave Tros in return for his boy Ganymedes. . . . Later, Prince Anchises stole the breed by putting mare to them without Laomedon's consent" (*Iliad*, V.263–269, p. 99). Boccaccio says that Laomedon promised these horses, born of divine seed, to Hercules (*De Genealogia Deorum*, VI.6). Again Spenser identifies Arthur with the two chief ancient heroes whose deeds lie behind most of the action of Book II.

20.1–23.9 Most of Spenser's description of Maleger is conventional material in devil lore. As he states in the opening stanzas of Canto ix, Spenser intends

The cause to weet and fault to remedy.
Upon a tiger swift and fierce he rode,
That as the wind ran underneath his load,
Whiles his long legs nigh raught° unto the ground.   *reached*
Full large he was of limb and shoulders broad,
But of such subtle substance and unsound,
That like a ghost he seemed, whose grave-clothes were
  unbound.

21 And in his hand a bended bow was seen,
And many arrows under his right side,
All deadly dangerous, all cruel keen,
Headed with flint, and feathers bloody dyed,
Such as the Indians in their quivers hide.
Those could he well direct and straight as line,
And bid them strike the mark which he had eyed;
Ne was there salve, ne was there medicine
That mote recure their wounds, so inly° they did tine.°   *deeply, injure*

22 As pale and wan as ashes was his look,
His body lean and meager as a rake,
And skin all withered like a drièd rook,
Thereto° as cold and dreary as a snake,   *in addition*
That seemed to tremble evermore and quake.
All in a canvas thin he was bedight,°   *dressed*
And girded with a belt of twisted brake;°   *brush*
Upon his head he wore an helmet light,
Made of a dead man's skull, that seemed a ghastly sight.

23 Maleger was his name, and after him
There followed fast at hand two wicked hags,
With hoary locks all loose and visage grim,
Their feet unshod, their bodies wrapt in rags,
And both as swift on foot as chasèd stags.

Maleger to represent the corrupt body grown a monster through base passions. Partly for this reason Maleger, literally "desperately diseased," is characterized by horrible disease. But the equation of disease with sin in the Bible and in medieval literature generally suggests that Maleger also represents original sin. Other features of the description strongly suggest both Satan, the author of sin, and Death, its wages. In most allegorical attacks on the Castle of the Soul the leader of the sins is either pride or Satan (which are much the same in medieval thought). Satan in some of these attacks carries a bow and arrows which represent the cardinal sins and death. The comparison of Maleger to a snake also sug-

gests Satan. The subtlety of Maleger's substance may have something to do with the idea that sin is a privation of good, that is, nothing in itself, but rather a lack of something. Milton is indebted to this idea in his treatment of Satan in *Paradise Lost* as a spirit progressively diminishing in strength and character. (See Bloomfield, *The Seven Deadly Sins*, Index: "arrow," "disease," "Satan," "sin.") Spenser's Maleger is then a composite symbol of the demonic opposition of sin, in the form of moral and physical disease, to the soul. The two hags attendant on Maleger represent the traditional tribulations (impotence and impatience) of the dying man. Disease is an occasion of sin as well as a result.

And yet the one her other° leg had lame,   *left*
Which with a staff all full of little snags
She did support, and Impotence her name;
But th' other was Impatience, armed with raging flame.

24 Soon as the carl from far the prince espied,
Glistering in arms and warlike ornament,
His beast he felly° pricked on either side,   *fiercely*
And his mischievous bow fully ready bent,
With which at him a cruel shaft he sent;
But he was wary, and it warded well
Upon his shield, that it no further went,
But to the ground the idle quarrel° fell;   *harmless arrow*
Then he another and another did expel.

25 Which to prevent, the prince his mortal spear
Soon to him raught, and fierce at him did ride
To be avengèd of that shot whilere.°   *immediately*
But he was not so hardy to abide
That bitter stound, but turning quick aside
His light-foot beast, fled fast away for fear;
Whom to pursue, the infant° after hied   *prince*
So fast as his good courser could him bear;
But labor lost it was to ween° approach him near.   *think to*

26 For as the wingèd wind his tiger fled,
That view of eye could scarce him overtake,
Ne scarce his feet on ground were seen to tread.
Through hills and dales he speedy way did make,
Ne hedge ne ditch his ready passage brake;°   *hindered*
And in his flight the villein turned his face—
As wonts the Tartar by the Caspian lake
Whenas the Russian him in fight does chase—
Unto his tiger's tail, and shot at him apace.°   *swiftly*

27 Apace he shot, and yet he fled apace
Still as the greedy knight nigh to him drew,
And oftentimes he would relent his pace,
That him his foe more fiercely should pursue.
Who when his uncouth manner° he did view,   *strange behavior*
He gan avise° to follow him no more,   *resolve*

26.6–9 "And ye shall understand that it is a great dread for to pursue the Tartars if they flee in battle. For in fleeing they shoot behind them and slay both men and horses" (*The Travels of Sir John Mandeville*, ed., A. W. Pollard, London, 1900, p. 196). Spenser also undoubtedly refers to the fighting habits of the Parthians (Virgil, *Georgics*, III.31). This method of fighting expresses the essential deceitfulness of sin and Satan and death, but Spenser seems almost to be writing from some well known emblem or maxim, which has not so far been identified.
27.5 *Who:* (1596). 1590 reads *But.*

But keep his standing,° and his shafts eschew   *stand his ground*
Until he quite had spent his perilous store,
And then assail him fresh ere he could shift for more.

28   But that lame hag, still as abroad he strew
His wicked arrows, gathered them again
And to him brought, fresh battle to renew;
Which he espying, cast° her to restrain   *considered how*
From yielding succor to that cursèd swain,
And her attacking, thought her hands to tie.
But soon as him dismounted on the plain
That other hag did far away espy
Binding her sister, she to him ran hastily,

29   And catching hold of him as down he lent,
Him backward overthrew, and down him stayed
With their rude hands and grisly° grapplement,   *horrible*
Till that the villein coming to their aid,
Upon him fell and load upon him laid.
Full little wanted° but he had him slain,   *lacked*
And of the battle baleful end had made,
Had not his gentle squire beheld his pain
And comen to his rescue ere his bitter bane.°   *death*

30   So greatest and most glorious thing on ground
May often need the help of weaker hand;
So feeble is man's state and life unsound°   *insecure*
That in assurance it may never stand
Till it dissolvèd be from earthly band.°   *bond*
Proof be thou prince, the prowest man alive
And noblest born of all in Britain land;
Yet thee fierce Fortune did so nearly drive
That had not grace thee blessed, thou shouldest not survive.

31   The squire arriving, fiercely in his arms
Snatched first the one and then the other jade,
His chiefest lets° and authors of his harms,   *hinderances*
And them perforce° withheld with threatened blade   *forcibly*
Lest that his lord they should behind invade;
The whiles the prince, pricked with reproachful shame,
As one awaked out of long slumbering shade,°   *shadow*
Reviving thought of glory and of fame,
United all his powers to purge himself from blame.

32   Like as a fire the which in hollow cave
Hath long been underkept and, down suppressed,

32.1–9 Arthur's rage is compared to the eruption of a volcano. The volcanic fire strives to reach the sphere of fire, in ancient cosmology a sphere encircling the spheres of the earth, the waters, and the atmosphere.

With murmurous disdain doth inly rave
And grudge, in so strait prison to be pressed,
At last breaks forth with furious infest°   *hostility*
And strives to mount unto his native seat;
All that did erst it hinder and molest
It now devours with flames and scorching heat
And carries into smoke with rage and horror great—

33 So mightily the Briton prince him roused
    Out of his hold and broke his caitiff° bands,   *captive*
    And as a bear whom angry curs have toused,°   *worried*
    Having off-shaked them and escaped their hands,
    Becomes more fell,° and all that him withstands   *fierce*
    Treads down and overthrows. Now had the carl
    Alighted from his tiger, and his hands
    Dischargèd° of his bow and deadly quarrel,°   *emptied, arrow*
    To seize upon his foe flat lying on the marl.°   *ground*

34 Which now him turned to disavantage dear,°   *costly*
    For neither can he fly nor other harm,
    But trust unto his strength and manhood mere,
    Sith now he is far from his monstrous swarm,
    And of his weapons did himself disarm.
    The knight yet wrothful for his late disgrace,
    Fiercely advanced his valorous right arm,
    And him so sore smote with his iron mace
    That groveling to the ground he fell and filled his place.

35 Well weenèd he that field was then his own
    And all his labor brought to happy end,

33.2–4 See viii.42. Bearbaiting rivaled the theater as an entertainment in Elizabethan England.

34.6–46.9 Arthur's battle with and defeat of Maleger is in imitation of Hercules' defeat of Antaeus. Antaeus was the son of Poseidon and Mother Earth and was king of Libya. He forced strangers and travelers in his land to wrestle him, and when they were exhausted he killed them and used their skulls to build a temple to Poseidon. On his way back from the labor of the apples of the Hesperides, Hercules wrestled Antaeus. He threw the giant twice, but deriving strength from his mother, he got up stronger each time. Finally Hercules cracked Antaeus' ribs and held him aloft until he died (Robert Graves, *The Greek Myths*, II, 146–147). The battle of Hercules and Antaeus was one of the most popular subjects of renaissance art. Boccaccio, following medieval authorities, allegorizes Antaeus as the "lust of the flesh"—a common term for original sin (*De Genealogia Deorum*, I.15). And Milton, following the tradition of the Christian Hercules, compares Christ's victory over the temptations of Satan to the defeat of Antaeus (*Paradise Regained*, IV.562–568). There is not the least doubt that Spenser is combining these two interpretations, and that Arthur is a type of Christ and that his victory represents Christ's victory over sin and Satan. But there is some evidence that Spenser goes even further. Arthur's killing Maleger, if it represents the death of sin, is meant to suggest baptism, in which the old Adam is killed and the new man quickened. As such it is related to the washing of Ruddymane's hands in Canto ii. Arthur's faintness after his ordeal is obviously related to Guyon's faint in Canto vii, but it probably represents the crucifixion of Christ rather than the ambiguous triumph of virtue which Guyon's faith symbolizes.

When sudden up the villein overthrown
Out of his swoon arose, fresh to contend,
And gan himself to second battle bend
As hurt he had not been. Thereby there lay
An huge great stone, which stood upon one end
And had not been removèd many a day—
Some landmark seemed to be, or sign of sundry way.°   *branching road*

36   The same he snatched, and with exceeding sway
Threw at his foe, who was right well aware
To shun the engine of his meant decay;
It booted not to think that throw to bear,
But ground he gave and lightly leapt arear.
Eft fierce returning—as a falcon fair
That once hath failèd of her souse° full near°   *swoop, barely*
Remounts again into the open air,
And unto better fortune doth herself prepare—

37   So brave returning, with his brandished blade
He to the carl himself again addressed,
And struck at him so sternly that he made
An open passage through his riven breast,
That half the steel behind his back did rest;
Which drawing back, he lookèd evermore
When the heart blood should gush out of his chest,
Or his dead corse should fall upon the floor;
But his dead corse upon the floor fell nathemore.°   *not at all*

38   Ne drop of blood appearèd shed to be,
All° were the wound so wide and wonderous   *although*
That through his carcass one might plainly see.
Half in amaze with horror hideous,
And half in rage to be deluded thus,
Again through both the sides he struck him quite,
That made his sprite to groan full piteous;
Yet nathemore forth fled his groaning sprite,
But freshly as at first prepared himself to fight.

39   Thereat he smitten was with great affright,
And trembling terror did his heart appall;
Ne wist he what to think of that same sight,
Ne what to say, ne what to do at all.
He doubted lest it were some magical
Illusion that did beguile his sense,
Or wandering ghost that wanted funeral,
Or airy spirit under false pretense,
Or hellish fiend raised up through devilish science.°   *i.e. black magic*

40 His wonder far exceeded reason's reach,
    That he began to doubt his dazzled sight,
    And oft of error did himself appeach.°   *accuse*
    Flesh without blood, a person without sprite,
    Wounds without hurt, a body without might,
    That could do harm, yet could not harmèd be,
    That could not die, yet seemed a mortal wight,
    That was most strong in most infirmity—
    Like did he never hear, like did he never see.

41 Awhile he stood in this astonishment,
    Yet would he not for all his great dismay
    Give over° to effect his first intent,   *stop trying*
    And th' utmost means of victory assay—
    Or th' utmost issue° of his own decay.°   *final outcome,*
    His own good sword Morddure, that never failed   *defeat*
    At need till now, he lightly threw away,
    And his bright shield that nought him now availed,
    And with his naked hands him forcibly assailed.

42 Twixt his two mighty arms him up he snatched,
    And crushed his carcass so against his breast
    That the disdainful soul he thence dispatched,
    And th' idle breath all utterly expressed.°   *pressed out*
    Tho when he felt him dead, adown he cast
    The lumpish corse unto the senseless ground.
    Adown he cast it with so puissant wrest°   *heave*
    That back again it did aloft rebound,
    And gave against his mother earth a groanful sound;

43 As when Jove's harness-bearing bird from high
    Stoops° at a flying heron with proud disdain,   *dives*
    The stone-dead quarry° falls so forcibly   *prey*
    That it rebounds against the lowly plain,
    A second fall redoubling back again.
    Then thought the prince all peril sure was passed
    And that he victor only did remain;
    No sooner thought than that the carl as fast
    Gan heap huge strokes on him as ere° he down was cast.   *before*

44 Nigh his wits' end then wox° th' amazèd knight,   *became*
    And thought his labor lost and travail vain
    Against this lifeless shadow so to fight;
    Yet life he saw, and felt his mighty main,
    That whiles he marvelled still, did still him pain.
    Forthy° he gan some other ways advise   *therefore*
    How to take life from that dead-living swain,

Whom still he markèd freshly to arise
From th' earth, and from her womb new spirits to reprise.°   *take again*

45 He then remembered well that had been said
How th' earth his mother was and first him bore;
She eke so often as his life decayed
Did life with usury to him restore,
And raised him up much stronger than before
So soon as he unto her womb did fall.
Therefore to ground he would him cast no more
Ne him commit to grave terrestrial,
But bear him far from hope of succor usual.

46 Tho up he caught him twixt his puissant hands,
And having scruzed out of his carrion corse
The loathful life, now loosed from sinful bands,°   *bondage to sin*
Upon his shoulders carried him perforce
Above three furlongs, taking his full course,°   *measuring exactly*
Until he came unto a standing lake;
Him thereinto he threw without remorse,
Ne stirred till hope of life did him forsake.
So end of that carl's days and his own pains did make.

47 Which when those wicked hags from far did spy,
Like two mad dogs they ran about the lands;
And th' one of them with dreadful yelling cry,
Throwing away her broken chains and bands,
And having quenched her burning fire brands,
Headlong herself did cast into that lake;
But Impotence with her own willful hands
One of Maleger's cursèd darts did take;
So rived her trembling heart, and wicked end did make.

48 Thus now alone he conqueror remains.
Tho° coming to his squire, that kept his steed,   *then*
Thought to have mounted; but his feeble veins
Him failed thereto° and servèd not his need,   *in the attempt*
Through loss of blood which from his wounds did bleed,
That he began to faint, and life° decay.   *his life*
But his good squire him helping up with speed,
With steadfast hand upon his horse did stay,
And led him to the castle by the beaten way;

49 Where many grooms and squires ready were
To take him from his steed full tenderly,
And eke the fairest Alma met him there
With balm and wine and costly spicery

To comfort him in his infirmity.
Eftsoons she caused him up to be conveyed,
And of his arms despoilèd easily;
In sumptuous bed she made him to be laid,
And all the while his wounds were dressing, by him stayed.

CANTO xii

Guyon by palmer's governance
Passing through perils great,
Doth overthrow the Bower of Bliss
And Acrasy defeat.

1   Now gins this goodly frame° of temperance   *structure*
Fairly to rise, and her adornèd head
To prick° of highest praise forth to advance,   *point*
Formerly grounded and fast settelèd
On firm foundation of true bountihead.
And that brave knight, that for this virtue fights,
Now comes to point of that same perilous stead
Where pleasure dwells in sensual delights,
Mongst thousand dangers and ten thousand magic mights.

2   Two days now in that sea he sailèd has,
Ne ever land beheld, ne living wight,
Ne aught save peril still as he did pass.
Tho when appearèd the third morrow bright
Upon the waves to spread her trembling light,
An hideous roaring far away they heard
That all their senses fillèd with affright,
And straight they saw the raging surges reared
Up to the skies, that them of drowning made afeared.

3   Said then the boatman, 'Palmer, steer aright
And keep an even course, for yonder way
We needs must pass—God do us well acquite!°—   *deliver*
That is the Gulf of Greediness, they say,
That deep engorgeth all this world'ès prey;

Argument.1 *by:* (1596). 1590 reads *through.*
Argument.2 *passing through* (1596). 1590 reads *through passing.*
2–38 Guyon's voyage to the Bower of Bliss is modeled primarily upon the wanderings of Odysseus as they came down to Spenser in literary tradition, including Virgil's *Aeneid.* An allegorical trip through perilous waters that are haunted by fantastic monsters, wandering rocks and islands, whirlpools and quicksands, and are made more dangerous still by seductive women, is a standard feature of dozens of myths, commentaries, romances, travel narratives, and courtly love allegories known to Spenser.
3.4 *Gulf of Greediness:* Homer's (*Odyssey*, XII) and Virgil's (*Aeneid*, III) Charybdis.

Which having swallowed up excessively,
He soon in vomit up again doth lay,
And belcheth forth his superfluity,
That all the seas for fear do seem away to fly.

4　'On th' other side an hideous rock is pight
　　Of mighty magnes-stone,° whose craggy clift　　　　lodestone
　　Depending° from on high, dreadful to sight,　　　　hanging
　　Over the waves his rugged arms doth lift
　　And threateneth down to throw his ragged rift°　　fragment
　　On whoso cometh nigh. Yet nigh it draws
　　All passengers, that none from it can shift;
　　For whiles they fly that gulf's devouring jaws,
　　They on this rock are rent, and sunk in helpless wawes.'°　waves

5　Forward they pass, and strongly he them rows,
　　Until they nigh unto that gulf arrive,
　　Where stream more violent and greedy grows.
　　Then he with all his puissance doth strive
　　To strike his oars, and mightily doth drive
　　The hollow vessel through the threatful wave,
　　Which gaping wide to swallow them alive
　　In th' huge abyss of his engulfing grave,
　　Doth roar at them in vain and with great terror rave.

6　They passing by, that grisly mouth did see
　　Sucking the seas into his entrails deep,
　　That seemed more horrible than hell to be,
　　Or that dark dreadful hole of Tartare steep
　　Through which the damnèd ghosts done often creep
　　Back to the world, bad livers° to torment.　　　　sinners
　　But nought that falls into this direful deep,
　　Ne that approacheth nigh the wide descent,
　　May back return, but is condemnèd to be drent.

7　On th' other side, they saw that perilous rock,
　　Threatening itself on them to ruinate,
　　On whose sharp clifts the ribs of vessels broke;
　　And shivered ships which had been wreckèd late
　　Yet stuck, with carcasses exanimate°　　　　　　dead
　　Of such as, having all their substance spent
　　In wanton joys and lusts intemperate,
　　Did afterwards make shipwrack violent,
　　Both of their life and fame forever foully blent.

　　4.1　*an hideous rock:* Homer's Scylla　leading to Tartarus, the region of punish-
(*Odyssey*, XII).　　　　　　　　　　　ment below Hades.
　　6.4　*hole of Tartare:* the mouth of hell

8   Forthy this hight The Rock of vile Reproach,
    A dangerous and detestable place,
    To which nor fish nor fowl did once approach,
    But yelling mews° with sea gulls hoarse and base   *gulls*
    And cormorants with birds of ravenous race,
    Which still sat waiting on that wasteful clift
    For spoil of wretches whose unhappy case,
    After lost credit and consumèd thrift,
    At last them driven hath to this despairful drift.°   *end*

9   The palmer seeing them in safety passed,
    Thus said: 'Behold th' ensamples in our sights
    Of lustful luxury and thriftless waste.
    What now is left of miserable wights
    Which spent their looser days in lewd delights
    But shame and sad reproach, here to be read
    By these rent relics, speaking their ill plights?
    Let all that live, hereby be counsellèd
    To shun Rock of Reproach, and it as death to dread.'

10 So forth they rowèd, and that ferryman
    With his stiff oars did brush the sea so strong
    That the hoar waters from his frigate ran,
    And the light bubbles dancèd all along
    Whiles the salt brine out of the billows sprung.
    At last far off they many islands spy
    On every side, floating the floods among.
    Then said the knight, 'Lo I the land descry;
    Therefore, old sire, thy course do thereunto apply.'

11 'That may not be,' said then the ferryman,
    'Lest we unweeting hap to be fordone;
    For those same islands, seeming° now and then,   *appearing*
    Are not firm land, nor any certain wone,°   *fixed place*
    But straggling plots which to and fro do run
    In the wide waters; therefore are they hight
    The Wandering Islands. Therefore do them shun,
    For they have oft drawn many a wandering wight
    Into most deadly danger and distressèd plight.

12 'Yet well they seem to him that far doth view,
    Both fair and fruitful, and the ground dispread
    With grassy green of delectable hue,

10.1 *that ferryman:* probably sug-
gested by the mythographers who inter-
preted the classical Charon, ferryman on
the River Styx, as clearness of conscience.

11–13 *The Wandering Islands:* like
that of Phaedria in vii.II. The *Odyssey*,
X.2 (p. 155) has the floating island of
Aeolia, home of the winds.

And the tall trees with leaves apparellèd
Are decked with blossoms dyed in white and red,
That mote the passengers thereto allure;
But whosoever once hath fastenèd
His foot thereon may never it recure,°   *recover*
But wandereth evermore, uncertain and unsure.

13 'As th' isle of Delos, whilom men report,
Amid th' Aegean Sea long time did stray,
Ne made for shipping any certain port,
Till that Latona traveling that way,
Flying from Juno's wrath and hard assay,
Of her fair twins was there deliverèd,
Which afterwards did rule the night and day;
Thenceforth it firmly was establishèd,
And for Apollo's temple highly herièd.'°   *praised*

14 They to him hearken as beseemeth meet,
And pass on forward. So their way does lie
That one of those same islands which do fleet
In the wide sea they needs must passen by,
Which seemed so sweet and pleasant to the eye
That it would tempt a man to touchen there.
Upon the bank they sitting did espy
A dainty damsel dressing of her hair,
By whom a little skippet° floating did appear.   *skiff*

15 She them espying, loud to them can° call,   *did*
Bidding them nigher draw unto the shore,
For she had cause to busy them withal,
And therewith loudly laughed. But nathemore
Would they once turn, but kept on as afore.
Which when she saw, she left her locks undight,
And running to her boat withouten oar,
From the departing land it launchèd light,
And after them did drive with all her power and might.

16 Whom overtaking, she in merry sort
Them gan to board and purpose diversely,°   *talk of various*
Now feigning dalliance and wanton sport,   *things*
Now throwing forth lewd words immodestly;
Till that the palmer gan full bitterly
Her to rebuke for being loose and light;
Which not abiding, but more scornfully

13.4–9 *Latona*: Leto, the mother of
Apollo and Diana in *Metamorphoses*,
VI.185–217 (pp. 156–157). See Lotspeich
p. 77, for Natalis Comes (*Mythologiae*,
IX.6), the version closest to Spenser's.

Scoffing at him that did her justly wite,°   *rebuke*
She turned her boat about, and from them rowèd quite.

17 That was the wanton Phaedria, which late
Did ferry him over The Idle Lake.
Whom nought regarding, they kept on their gate°   *path*
And all her vain allurements did forsake,
When them the wary boatman thus bespake:
'Here now behooveth us well to avise,
And of our safèty good heed to take;
For here before a perilous passage lies,
Where many mermaids haunt, making false melodies.

18 'But by the way there is a great quicksand
And a whirlpool of hidden jeopardy;
Therefore, sir palmer, keep an even hand,
For twixt them both the narrow way doth lie.'
Scarce had he said when hard at hand they spy
That quicksand nigh with water coverèd,
But by the checkèd° wave they did descry   *checkered*
It plain, and by the sea discolorèd.
It callèd was The Quicksand of Unthriftihead.

19 They passing by, a goodly ship did see,
Laden from far with precious merchandize
And bravely furnishèd as ship might be,
Which through great disadventure of misprize°   *blunder*
Herself had run into that hazardize;
Whose mariners and merchants with much toil
Labored in vain to have recured° their prize,   *recovered*
And the rich wares to save from piteous spoil;
But neither toil nor travail might her back recoil.°   *push*

20 On th' other side they see that perilous pool
That callèd was The Whirlpool of Decay,
In which full many had with hapless dool°   *grief*
Been sunk, of whom no memory did stay.
Whose circled waters rapt with whirling sway,°   *motion*
Like to a restless wheel still running round,
Did covet as they passèd by that way
To draw their boat within the utmost bound
Of his wide labyrinth, and then to have them drowned.

21 But th' heedful boatman strongly forth did stretch
His brawny arms, and all his body strain,
That th' utmost sandy breach they shortly fetch,

21.1 *heedful:* (1596). 1590 reads *earnest.*   water mixed with sand just at the edge
21.3 I.e., "They soon reach the broken   of the quicksand."

Whiles the dread danger does behind remain.
Sudden they see from midst of all the main
The surging waters like a mountain rise,
And the great sea puffed up with proud disdain
To swell above the measure of his guise,°   habit
As threatening to devour all that his power despise.

22 The waves come rolling, and the billows roar
Outrageously, as they enragèd were,
Or wrathful Neptune did them drive before
His whirling chariot for exceeding fear.
For not one puff of wind there did appear
That all the three thereat wox much afraid,
Unweeting what such horror strange did rear.°   cause
Eftsoons they saw an hideous host arrayed
Of huge sea monsters, such as living sense dismayed.

23 Most ugly shapes and horrible aspects,
Such as Dame Nature self mote fear to see,
Or shame, that ever should so foul defects
From her most cunning hand escapèd be,
All dreadful portraits of deformity—
Spring-headed hydras and sea-shouldering whales;
Great whirlpools which all fishes made to flee;
Bright scolopendras armed with silver scales;
Mighty monoceros with immeasurèd tails;

24 The dreadful fish that hath deserved the name
Of death, and like him looks in dreadful hue;
The grisly wasserman, that makes his game
The flying ships with swiftness to pursue;
The horrible sea satyr, that doth shew
His fearful face in time of greatest storm;
Huge ziffius, whom mariners eschew
No less than rocks, as travelers inform;
And greedy rosmarines with visages deform—

25 All these, and thousand thousands many more,
And more deformèd monsters thousand fold,
With dreadful noise and hollow rumbling roar,
Came rushing in the foamy waves enrolled,
Which seemed to fly for fear, them to behold.

23.6–24.9 *spring-headed hydras:* sea monsters imaged as spouting like whales; *whirlpools:* spouting whales; *scolopendras:* oceangoing centipedes; *monoceros:* oceangoing unicorns, probably by analogy with seahorses; *death:* a playful translation of the morse or walrus as if it were Latin *mors,* "death"; *wasserman:* German for water man, i.e., merman; *sea satyr:* another type of merman; *ziffius:* the sword fish, Greek *xiphias; rosmarines:* walruses.

No wonder if these did the knight appall,
For all that here on earth we dreadful hold
Be but as bugs to fearen babes withal,
Comparèd to the creatures in the sea's entrail.°   *interior*

26   'Fear nought,' then said the palmer well avised,
'For these same monsters are not these indeed,
But are into these fearful shapes disguised
By that same wicked witch, to work us dreed
And draw from on this journey to proceed.'
Tho lifting up his virtuous staff on high,
He smote the sea, which calmèd was with speed,
And all that dreadful army fast gan fly
Into great Tethys' bosom, where they hidden lie.

27   Quit from that danger, forth their course they kept,
And as they went they heard a rueful cry
Of one that wailed and pitifully wept,
That through the sea the resounding plaints did fly.
At last they in an island did espy
A seemly maiden sitting by the shore,
That with great sorrow and sad agony
Seemèd some great misfortune to deplore,
And loud to them for succor callèd evermore.

28   Which Guyon hearing, straight his palmer bade
To steer the boat towards that doleful maid,
That he might know and ease her sorrow sad.
Who him avising better, to him said,
'Fair sir, be not displeased if disobeyed;
For ill it were to hearken to her cry.
For she is inly nothing ill apaid,°   *ill pleased*
But only womanish fine forgery,
Your stubborn° heart t' affect with frail infirmity.   *steadfast*

29   'To which when she your courage° hath inclined   *heart*
Through foolish pity, then her guileful bait
She will embosom deeper in your mind,
And for your ruin at the last await.'
The knight was rulèd, and the boatman straight

26.6 *his virtuous staff:* much like the magical rod of Moses or the caduceus of the divine messenger Hermes. Ubaldo, who invades the garden of Armida in *Jerusalem Delivered* (XIV.73), also carries such a wand. The palmer takes on the aspect of a traditional magician that he may counteract the "magic" of Acrasia. Without the help of Hermes, Odysseus could not have defeated Circe (*Odyssey*, X, p. 163).
26.9 *Tethys:* a titaness identified with the sea, wife of the titan Oceanus.
27.6 *A seemly maiden:* The experience with this maiden is a recapitulation of Guyon's failure to see through the deceit of Duessa.

Held on his course with stayèd steadfastness,
Ne ever shrunk, ne ever sought to bate°   *ease*
His tirèd arms for toilsome weariness,
But with his oars did sweep the watery wilderness.

30   And now they nigh approachèd to the stead
Whereas those mermaids dwelt. It was a still
And calmy bay, on th' one side shelterèd
With the broad shadow of an hoary hill;
On th' other side an high rock towered still,
That twixt them both a pleasant port they made,   *something like,*
And did like° an half theater fulfill.°   *occupy*
There those five sisters had continual trade,°   *occupation*
And used to bathe themselves in that deceitful shade.

31   They were fair ladies, till they fondly strived
With th' Heliconian maids for mastery;
Of whom they, overcomen, were deprived
Of their proud beauty, and th' one moiety°   *part*
Transformed to fish for their bold surquidry,°   *presumption*
But th' upper half their hue° retainèd still,   *shape*
And their sweet skill in wonted melody—
Which ever after they abused to ill,
T' allure weak travelers, whom gotten they did kill.

32   So now to Guyon as he passèd by,
Their pleasant tunes they sweetly thus applied:
'O thou fair son of gentle faèry,
That art in mighty arms most magnified
Above all knights that ever battle tried,
O turn thy rudder hitherward awhile.
Here may thy storm-beat vessel safely ride;
This is the port of rest from troublous toil,
The world's sweet inn from pain and wearisome turmoil.'

33   With that, the rolling sea resounding soft,
In his big bass them fitly answerèd,
And on the rock the waves breaking aloft,
A solemn mean unto them measurèd,

30–32 *mermaids:* Spenser's sirens are analogous to Homer's, but show the influence of a long tradition intervening between the *Odyssey* and *The Faerie Queene.* The three classical Sirens were part women and part birds—not part fish as are medieval and modern mermaids. Spenser increases their number to five, corresponding to the five senses to which they appeal. The singing contest with the Heliconian maids (the muses) is a myth not found in classical writers. The Sirens of *Odyssey,* XII, appeal to Odysseus' curiosity for wisdom rather than offering him only a rest from toil. For Natalis Comes' identification of the Sirens with voluptuous desire (*Mythologiae,* VII.13), see Lotspeich, p. 81.

33.4 *mean:* the middle part (tenor or alto) in a musical composition.

The whiles sweet Zephyrus loud whistelèd
His treble—a strange kind of harmony;
Which Guyon's senses softly tickelèd,
That he the boatman bade row easily,
And let him hear some part of their rare melody.

34   But him the palmer from that vanity
With temperate advice discounsellèd,
That they it passed, and shortly gan descry
The land to which their course they levelèd.°   *directed*
When suddenly a gross fog overspread
With his dull vapor all that desert has,°   i.e. *has overspread*
And heaven's cheerful face envelopèd,
That all things one, and one as nothing was,
And this great universe seemed one confusèd mass.

35   Thereat they greatly were dismayed, ne wist
How to direct their way in darkness wide,
But feared to wander in that wasteful mist
For tumbling into mischief unespied.
Worse is the danger hidden than descried.
Suddenly an innumerable flight
Of harmful fowls about them fluttering cried,
And with their wicked wings them oft did smite
And sore annoyèd, groping in that grisly night.

36   Even all the nation of unfortunate°   *ill-omened*
And fatal birds about them flockèd were,
Such as by nature men abhor and hate—
The ill-faced owl, death's dreadful messenger,
The hoarse night-raven, trump of doleful drear,
The leather-wingèd bat, day's enemy,
The rueful strich,° still waiting on the bier,   *screech owl*
The whistler shrill, that whoso hears doth die,
The hellish harpies, prophets of sad destiny—

37   All those, and all that else does horror breed
About them flew and filled their sails with fear.
Yet stayed they not, but forward did proceed,
Whiles th' one did row and th' other stiffly steer;

33.5   *Zephyrus:* the warm west wind that stimulates the growth of living things and the sexual impulse; his presence is a standard element in the rhetorical topoi of the spring morning and the amorous garden. He is best known to students of English literature from Chaucer's lines,

Whan Zephirus eek with his sweete breeth
Inspired hath in every holt and heeth
The tendre croppes . . .
              (*Canterbury Tales*, A.5–7).

Compare v.29.8. where Zephyrus appears in the description of Cymochles in the Bower of Bliss.

34.5–9   *a gross fog:* perhaps taken from the *Legend of St. Brandan*, in which several adventures parallel features of Guyon's voyage.

36.8   *whistler:* the plover or pewit.

Till that at last the weather gan to clear,
And the fair land itself did plainly show.
Said then the palmer, 'Lo where does appear
The sacred° soil where all our perils grow;   *cursed*
Therefore, sir knight, your ready arms about you throw.'

38   He harkened, and his arms about him took,
The whiles the nimble boat so well her sped
That with her crooked° keel the land she struck.   *curved*
Then forth the noble Guyon sallièd,
And his sage palmer, that him governèd;
But th' other by his boat behind did stay.
They marchèd fairly forth, of nought y-dread,
Both firmly armed for every hard assay,
With constancy and care gainst danger and dismay.

39   Ere long they heard an hideous bellowing
Of many beasts that roared outrageously,
As if that hunger's point or Venus' sting
Had them enragèd with fell surquidry.°   *arrogance*
Yet nought they feared, but passed on hardily,
Until they came in view of those wild beasts;
Who all at once, gaping full greedily
And rearing fiercely their upstaring° crests,   *bristling*
Ran towards° to devour those unexpected guests.   *forward*

40   But soon as they approached with deadly threat,
The palmer over them his staff upheld,
His mighty staff that could all charms defeat.
Eftsoons their stubborn courages were quelled,
And high advancèd crests down meekly felled;
Instead of fraying they themselves did fear,
And trembled as them passing they beheld.
Such wondrous power did in that staff appear,
All monsters to subdue to him that did it bear.

41   Of that same wood it framed was cunningly
Of which Caduceus whilom was made,
Caduceus the rod of Mercury,
With which he wonts the Stygian realms invade

39–40 The beasts are men trans-
formed by Acrasia's magic. The same
animals are to be found about the dwell-
ing of Circe in *Odyssey*, X; *Aeneid*, VII;
and *Metamorphoses*, XIV. As with the
voyage and its traditional hazards, the
enchantress Acrasia is the product of
fourteen hundred years' epic tradition
rather than a direct imitation of Homer's
Circe. Spenser's most immediate source
was Giangiorgio Trissino's *L'Italia Libe-
rata dai Goti* (1548). Books IV and V
contain many parallels to Spenser's plot,
including figures corresponding to Ama-
via, Phaedria, and the Palmer. Most
significant, however, Trissino's enchan-
tress is named Acratia.

Through ghastly horror and eternal shade;
Th' infernal fiends with it he can assuage,
And Orcus tame whom nothing can persuade,
And rule the furies when they most do rage—
Such virtue in his staff had eke this palmer sage.

42 Thence passing forth, they shortly do arrive
Whereas the Bower of Bliss was situate—
A place picked out by choice of best alive
That nature's work by art can imitate;
In which whatever in this worldly state
Is sweet and pleasing unto living sense,
Or that may daintest fantasy aggrate,
Was pourèd forth with plentiful dispense
And made there to abound with lavish affluence.

43 Goodly it was enclosèd round about,
As well their° entered guests to keep within   *i.e. the inmates'*
As those unruly beasts to hold without;
Yet was the fence thereof but weak and thin.
Nought feared their force that fortilage° to win   *small fort*
But wisdom's power and temperance's might,
By which the mightest° things efforcèd° been.   *mightiest, over-*
And eke the gate was wrought of substance light,   *powered*
Rather for pleasure than for battery or fight.

44 It framèd was of precious ivory,
That seemed a work of admirable wit;
And therein all the famous history
Of Jason and Medea was y-writ—
Her mighty charms, her furious loving fit,
His goodly conquest of the golden fleece,
His falsèd faith, and love too lightly flit,
The wondered° Argo, which in venturous piece°   *wonderful, con-*
First through the Euxine seas bore all the flower of Greece.   *struction*

41.7 *Orcus:* Pluto, the ruler of the classical underworld.

42–87 The description of the Bower of Bliss is most directly influenced by Cantos XV and XVI of Tasso's *Jerusalem Delivered*. In fact, so close are the parallels between some lines that Tasso's translator Edward Fairfax used Spenser's phrases in translating the Italian. For the significance, in terms of the sources, of Spenser's having taken his plot from Trissino and his description from Tasso, see Graham Hough, *A Preface to "The Faerie Queene,"* pp. 161–163.

42.3–4 I.e., "a place selected by the best artisans alive." This is in contrast to Phaedria's island (vi.12), which was picked out by "Nature's cunning hand."

43.5–6 I.e., "The inmates did not fear the physical force of Guyon; they feared the power of wisdom and the might of temperance."

44.1 *precious ivory:* suggested by Trissino (*L'Italia Liberata,* V.165).

44.4 Jason is a type of the heroic man overcome by the magic of a passionate woman. For a full treatment of Jason's expedition to capture the golden fleece and his falling in love with the enchantress Medea, see Apollonius of Rhodes, *The Voyage of the Argo* (trans. E. V. Rieu, Penguin Books).

45   Ye might have seen the frothy billows fry
     Under the ship, as thorough them she went,
     That seemed the waves were into ivory
     Or ivory into the waves were sent;
     And otherwhere the snowy substance sprent°   *sprinkled*
     With vermeil, like the boy's blood therein shed,
     A piteous spectacle did represent;
     And otherwhiles with gold besprinkelèd,
     It seemed th' enchanted flame which did Creüsa wed.

46   All this and more might in that goodly gate
     Be read, that ever open stood at all
     Which thither came. But in the porch there sate
     A comely personage of stature tall
     And semblance pleasing, more than natural,
     That travelers to him seemed to entice.
     His looser garment to the ground did fall,
     And flew about his heels in wanton wise,
     Not fit for speedy pace or manly exercise.

47   They in that place him Genius did call—
     Not that celestial power to whom the care
     Of life and generation of all
     That lives pertains in charge° particular,   *belongs by assign-*
     Who wondrous things concerning our welfare   *ment*
     And strange phantoms doth let us oft foresee,
     And oft of secret ill bids us beware;
     That is our self, whom though we do not see,
     Yet each doth in himself it well perceive to be.

48   Therefore a god him sage antiquity
     Did wisely make, and good Agdistes call.
     But this same was to that quite contrary:

45.5–9   The ivory was sprinkled with vermilion like the blood of Apsyrtus, Medea's brother, whom she had Jason kill; it was sprinkled with gold like the flames which enveloped Creüsa, Jason's betrothed, when she put on the wedding gown cursed by the enchantress.

47–48   A short lucid discussion of the two Geniuses in medieval and renaissance poetry is to be found in C. S. Lewis, *The Allegory of Love*, Oxford University Press, 1936, pp. 361–363. The usual conception, from which Spenser here departs slightly, includes a universal generative principle (Spenser's Agdistes) and individual personal genii presiding over places and persons (Spenser's Genius of the Bower of Bliss). Lewis conveniently labels Agdistes "Genius A" and the Genius of the Bower "Genius B." The conventional conception assigns personal genii, both good and bad, only to Genius B. But Spenser imagines both the good Genius A and the false Genius B as manifesting themselves in individual personal genii as well as maintaining their universal, cosmic natures. Genius A, the generative principle in nature, figures importantly in Book III. vi.31–33. The closest analogue to the cosmic Genius B is Spenser's Archimago and the False Semblant of Jean de Meun's *Romance of the Rose*. Scholars have not yet isolated, studied, and documented this medieval and renaissance concept of a cosmic principle of false-seeming and deceit. It is the philosophical equivalent of the Christian conception of Satan.

The foe of life, that good envies to all,
That secretly doth us procure to fall
Through guileful semblants which he makes us see.
He of this garden had the governal,
And pleasure's porter was devised to be,
Holding a staff in hand for more formality.

49 With divers flowers he daintily was decked
And strowèd round about, and by his side
A mighty mazer° bowl of wine was set,   *hard-wood*
As if it had to him been sacrified;
Wherewith all new-come guests he gratified.
So did he eke Sir Guyon passing by,
But he his idle courtesy defied,
And overthrew his bowl disdainfully,
And broke his staff with which he charmèd semblants sly.

50 Thus being entered, they behold around
A large and spacious plain, on every side
Strowèd with pleasance, whose fair grassy ground
Mantled with green and goodly beautified
With all the ornaments of Flora's pride,
Wherewith her mother Art—as half in scorn
Of niggard Nature—like a pompous bride
Did deck her and too lavishly adorn,
When forth from virgin bower she comes in th' early morn.

51 Thereto the heavens always jovial
Looked on them lovely, still in steadfast state;
Ne suffered storm nor frost on them to fall,
Their tender buds or leaves to violate,
Nor scorching heat nor cold intemperate
T' afflict the creatures which therein did dwell;
But the mild air with season moderate
Gently attempered, and disposed so well
That still it breathèd forth sweet spirit and wholesome smell.

52 More sweet and wholesome than the pleasant hill
Of Rhodope, on which the nymph that bore

48.7 *of this:* (1596). 1590 reads *oft his.*
49.3 *mazer bowl of wine:* Genius's drinking bowl, like the golden cup of Excess in 56 below, is reminiscent of the enchanted cup Mordant drank at the hands of Acrasia. The cup of Circe is the type of all these lesser cups of enchantment, so abundant in romance and other-world literature. It is the anti-type of the cup of the Eucharist and as such is identified with the whore of Babylon's cup of abominations (Revelation 17:4).

51.1 *Thereto:* (1596). 1590 reads *Therewith.*
51.1 *jovial:* literally, under the influence of the planet Jupiter.
52.2 *Rhodope:* a mountain in Thrace where Orpheus attracted all the trees in the world by the music of his lyre. The nymph Rhodope, who was transformed into the mountain as a punishment for calling herself Juno, bore a giant child by Neptune.

A giant babe herself for grief did kill;
Or the Thessalian Tempe, where of yore
Fair Daphne Phoebus' heart with love did gore;
Or Ida, where the gods loved to repair
Whenever they their heavenly bowers forlore;
Or sweet Parnass, the haunt of muses fair;
Or Eden self, if aught with Eden mote compare.

53 Much wondered Guyon at the fair aspect
Of that sweet place, yet suffered no delight
To sink into his sense nor mind affect,
But passèd forth and looked still forward right,
Bridling his will and mastering his might,
Till that he came unto another gate—
No gate, but like one, being goodly dight
With boughs and branches which did broad dilate
Their clasping arms in wanton wreathings intricate.

54 So fashionèd a porch with rare device,
Arched overhead with an embracing vine
Whose bunches hanging down seemed to entice
All passersby to taste their luscious wine,
And did themselves into their hands incline,
As freely offering to be gatherèd—
Some deep empurpled as the hyacint,°   *hyacinth (sap-*
Some as the rubine° laughing sweetly red,   *phire)*
Some like fair emeralds, not yet well ripenèd.   *ruby*

55 And them amongst, some were of burnished gold,
So made by art to beautify the rest,
Which did themselves amongst the leaves enfold,
As lurking from the view of covetous guest,
That the weak boughs, with so rich load oppressèd,
Did bow adown, as over-burdenèd.
Under that porch a comely dame did rest,
Clad in fair weeds, but foul disorderèd,
And garments loose, that seemed unmeet for womanhead.

56 In her left hand a cup of gold she held,
And with her right the riper fruit did reach,
Whose sappy liquor, that with fullness swelled,
Into her cup she scruzed° with dainty breach   *squeezed*
Of her fine fingers, without foul impeach,°   *hindrance*

52.4 *Tempe:* the valley where Daphne, to escape the embrace of Phoebus, was transformed into a laurel.
54.7 *hyacint:* See note on ii.7.7 for imperfect rhyme. The sapphire, ruby, and emerald are used primarily to indicate the color of the grapes in various states of ripeness. The simile emphasizes their appearance at the expense of their fruitfulness.

That so fair wine press made the wine more sweet.
Thereof she used to give to drink to each
Whom passing by she happenèd to meet.
It was her guise all strangers goodly so to greet.

57   So she to Guyon offered it to taste,
Who taking it out of her tender hand,
The cup to ground did violently cast,
That all in pieces it was broken fand,°   *found*
And with the liquor stainèd all the land.
Whereat Excess exceedingly was wroth,
Yet n'ot° the same amend, ne yet withstand,   *could not*
But suffered him to pass, all were she loath—
Who nought regarding her displeasure forward go'th.

58   There the most dainty paradise on ground
Itself doth offer to his sober eye,
In which all pleasures plenteously abound
And none does other's happiness envy—
The painted flowers, the trees upshooting high,
The dales for shade, the hills for breathing space,
The trembling groves, the crystal running by.
And that which all fair works doth most aggrace,
The art which all that wrought, appearèd in no place.

59   One would have thought—so cunningly the rude
And scornèd parts were mingled with the fine—
That nature had for wantonness ensued°   *imitated*
Art, and that art at nature did repine.°   *grumble*
So striving each th' other to undermine,
Each did the other's work more beautify;
So differing both in wills, agreed in fine;°   *in the end*
So all agreed through sweet diversity
This garden to adorn with all variety.

60   And in the midst of all, a fountain stood,
Of richest substance that on earth might be,
So pure and shiny that the silver flood
Through every channel running one might see.
Most goodly it with curious imagery
Was overwrought, and shapes of naked boys,
Of which some seemed with lively jollity
To fly about, playing their wanton toys,
Whilst others did themselves embay° in liquid joys.   *bathe*

61   And over all, of purest gold was spread
A trail of ivy in his native hue;

For the rich metal was so colorèd
That wight who did not well-advised it view
Would surely deem it to be ivy true.
Low his lascivious arms adown did creep,
That themselves dipping in the silver dew,
Their fleecy flowers they tenderly did steep,
Which drops of crystal seemed for wantonness to weep.

62 Infinite streams continually did well
Out of this fountain, sweet and fair to see,
The which into an ample laver fell,
And shortly grew to so great quantity
That like a little lake it seemed to be;
Whose depth exceeded not three cubits height,
That through the waves one might the bottom see,
All paved beneath with jasper shining bright,
That seemed the fountain in that sea did sail upright.

63 And all the margent round about was set
With shady laurel trees, thence to defend°   *ward off*
The sunny beams which on the billows bet,°   *beat*
And those which therein bathèd mote offend.
As Guyon happened by the same to wend,
Two naked damsels he therein espied,
Which therein bathing seemèd to contend
And wrestle wantonly, ne cared to hide
Their dainty parts from view of any which them eyed.

64 Sometimes the one would lift the other quite
Above the waters, and then down again
Her plunge, as over-masterèd by might,
Where both awhile would coverèd remain,
And each the other from to rise restrain;
The whiles their snowy limbs, as through a veil
So through the crystal waves, appearèd plain;
Then suddenly both would themselves unheal,°   *uncover*
And th' amorous sweet spoils to greedy eyes reveal.

65 As that fair star, the messenger of morn,
His° dewy face out of the sea doth rear,   *its*
Or as the Cyprian goddess, newly born
Of th' ocean's fruitful froth, did first appear,
Such seemèd they, and so their yellow hair
Crystalline humor droppèd down apace.

61.8 *tenderly:* (1596). 1590 reads *fear-fully.*
65.1–4 *fair star:* the planet Venus; the mentioning of which leads by association to the myth of the birth of the goddess from the ocean.

Whom such when Guyon saw, he drew him near,
And somewhat gan relent his earnest pace,
His stubborn breast gan secret pleasance to embrace.

66 The wanton maidens him espying, stood
Gazing awhile at his unwonted guise;
Then th' one herself low duckèd in the flood,
Abashed that her a stranger did avise;
But th' other rather higher did arise,
And her two lily paps aloft displayed,
And all that might his melting heart entice
To her delights she unto him bewrayed.°   *displayed*
The rest hid underneath, him more desirous made.

67 With that, the other likewise up arose,
And her fair locks, which formerly were bound
Up in one knot, she low adown did loose,
Which flowing long and thick, her clothed around,
And th' ivory in golden mantle gowned,
So that fair spectacle from him was reft;
Yet that which reft it no less fair was found.
So hid in locks and waves from looker's theft,
Nought but her lovely face she for his looking left.

68 Withal she laughèd, and she blushed withal,
That blushing to her laughter gave more grace,
And laughter to her blushing, as did fall.
Now when they spied the knight to slack his pace
Them to behold, and in his sparkling face
The secret signs of kindled lust appear,
Their wanton merriments they did increase,
And to him beckoned to approach more near,
And showed him many sights that courage cold could rear.

69 On which when gazing him the palmer saw,
He much rebuked those wandering eyes of his,
And, counselled well, him forward thence did draw.
Now are they come nigh to the Bower of Bliss—
Of her fond favorites so named amiss—
When thus the palmer: 'Now, sir, well avise,
For here the end of all our travail is;
Here wons° Acrasia, whom we must surprise,   *lives*
Else she will slip away and all our drift despise.'°   *scorn our plans*

70 Eftsoons they heard a most melodious sound
Of all that mote delight a dainty ear,
Such as at once might not on living ground,
Save in this paradise, be heard elsewhere.
Right hard it was for wight which did it hear
To read° what manner music that mote be,   *tell*

For all that pleasing is to living ear
Was there consorted in one harmony—
Birds, voices, instruments, winds, waters, all agree.

71 The joyous birds, shrouded in cheerful shade,
Their notes unto the voice attempered sweet;
Th' angelical soft trembling voices made
To th' instruments divine respondence meet;
The silver sounding instruments did meet
With the base murmur of the water's fall;
The water's fall with difference discreet,
Now soft, now loud, unto the wind did call;
The gentle warbling wind low answerèd to all.

72 There, whence that music seemèd heard to be,
Was the fair witch herself now solacing
With a new lover, whom through sorcery
And witchcraft she from far did thither bring.
There she had him now laid aslumbering
In secret shade, after long wanton joys;
Whilst round about them pleasantly did sing
Many fair ladies and lascivious boys,
That ever mixed their song with light licentious toys.

73 And all that while, right over him she hung,
With her false eyes fast fixèd in his sight,
As seeking medicine whence she was stung,
Or greedily depasturing° delight;   *devouring*
And oft inclining down with kisses light,
For fear of waking him, his lips bedewed,
And through his humid eyes did suck his sprite,°   *spirit*
Quite molten into lust and pleasure lewd;
Wherewith she sighèd soft, as if his case she rued.

74 The whiles someone did chant this lovely lay:
'Ah see, who so fair thing dost fain to see,
In springing flower the image of thy day;
Ah see the virgin rose, how sweetly she
Doth first peep forth with bashful modesty,
That fairer seems the less ye see her may;
Lo see soon after, how more bold and free
Her barèd bosom she doth broad display;
Lo see soon after, how she fades and falls away.

73.7 Without waking him, Acrasia "sucks" her lover's spirit with her eyes as she kisses his lips.

74–75 This song is one of the most memorable examples in English literature of the literary topos called, from Horace's phrase, *carpe diem*, "seize the day." Later examples are Marvell's "To His Coy Mistress" and Herrick's famous "To the Virgins, To Make Much of Time," beginning:

Gather ye rosebuds while ye may,
Old Time is still a-flying;
And this same flower that smiles today,
Tomorrow will be dying.

75   'So passeth in the passing of a day
     Of mortal life the leaf, the bud, the flower,
     Ne more doth flourish after first decay,
     That erst was sought to deck both bed and bower
     Of many a lady, and many a paramour.
     Gather, therefore, the rose whilst yet is prime,
     For soon comes age, that will her pride deflower.
     Gather the rose of love whilst yet is time,
     Whilst loving thou mayst lovèd be with equal crime.'

76   He ceased, and then gan all the choir of birds
     Their diverse notes t' attune unto his lay,
     As in approvance of his pleasing words.
     The constant pair heard all that he did say,
     Yet swervèd not, but kept their forward way
     Through many covert groves and thickets close,
     In which they creeping did at last display°   *see*
     That wanton lady with her lover loose,
     Whose sleepy head she in her lap did soft dispose.

77   Upon a bed of roses she was laid,
     As faint through heat, or dight to pleasant sin,
     And was arrayed, or rather disarrayed,
     All in a veil of silk and silver thin
     That hid no whit her alablaster skin,
     But rather showed more white, if more might be.
     More subtle web Arachne can not spin,
     Nor the fine nets which oft we woven see
     Of scorchèd dew do not in th' air more lightly flee.

78   Her snowy breast was bare to ready spoil
     Of hungry eyes, which n'ot° therewith be filled;   *could not*
     And yet through languor of her late sweet toil,
     Few drops more clear than nectar forth distilled,
     That like pure orient pearls adown it trilled;
     And her fair eyes, sweet smiling in delight,
     Moistened their fiery beams, with which she thrilled
     Frail hearts, yet quenchèd not; like starry light,
     Which sparkling on the silent waves does seem more bright.

79   The young man sleeping by her seemed to be
     Some goodly swain of honorable place,
     That certes it great pity was to see
     Him his nobility so foul deface.
     A sweet regard and amiable grace,
     Mixèd with manly sternness, did appear
     Yet sleeping in his well proportioned face,
     And on his tender lips the downy hair
     Did now but freshly spring, and silken blossoms bear.

80 His warlike arms, the idle instruments
    Of sleeping praise, were hung upon a tree,
    And his brave shield, full of old monuments,
    Was foully rased,° that none the signs might see.   *erased*
    Ne for them, ne for honor carèd he,
    Ne aught that did to his advancement tend,
    But in lewd loves and wasteful luxury
    His days, his goods, his body he did spend.
    O horrible enchantment, that him so did blend.°   *blind*

81 The noble elf and careful palmer drew
    So nigh them, minding nought but lustful game,
    That sudden forth they on them rushed, and threw
    A subtle° net, which only for the same   *finely woven*
    The skillful palmer formally° did frame.   *symmetrically*
    So held them under fast, the whiles the rest
    Fled all away for fear of fouler shame.
    The fair enchantress, so unwares oppressed,
    Tried all her arts and all her sleights thence out to wrest.

82 And eke her lover strove. But all in vain,
    For that same net so cunningly was wound
    That neither guile nor force might it distrain.
    They took them both, and both them strongly bound
    In captive bands, which there they ready found.
    But her in chains of adamant he tied,
    For nothing else might keep her safe and sound;
    But Verdant—so he hight—he soon untied,
    And counsel sage instead thereof to him applied.

83 But all those pleasant bowers and palace brave
    Guyon broke down with rigor pitiless;
    Ne aught their goodly workmanship might save
    Them from the tempest of his wrathfulness,
    But that their bliss he turned to balefulness.
    Their groves he felled, their gardens did deface,
    Their arbors spoil, their cabinets° suppress,   *summer houses*
    Their banquet houses burn, their buildings rase,°   *raze*
    And of the fairest late, now made the foulest place.

84 Then led they her away, and eke that knight
    They with them led, both sorrowful and sad;
    The way they came, the same returned they right,
    Till they arrivèd where they lately had

81.3–9 The Palmer's subtle net is reminiscent of the net with which Hephaestus captures his wife Aphrodite in bed with Ares (*Odyssey*, VIII.276–281, pp. 131–132).

82.8 The first of Acrasia's lovers the reader meets is Mordant, "death giving," and the last Verdant, "green" or perhaps "spring giving." Mythically, Mordant and Verdant are the same young man who has abandoned his pursuit of honor for intemperate indulgence in sensual pleasure. Mordant fell and gave death. Verdant lives and gives life.

Charmed those wild beasts that raged with fury mad.
Which now awaking, fierce at them gan fly,
As in their mistress' rescue, whom they led;
But them the palmer soon did pacify.
Then Guyon asked what meant those beasts which there did
    lie.

85 Said he, 'These seeming beasts are men indeed,
Whom this enchantress hath transformèd thus—
Whilom her lovers which her lusts did feed,
Now turnèd into figures hideous,
According to their minds like monstruous.'
'Sad end,' quoth he, 'of life intemperate,
And mournful meed of joys delicious.
But, palmer, if it mote thee so aggrate,
Let them returnèd be unto their former state.'

86 Straightway he with his virtuous staff them struck,
And straight of beasts they comely men became;
Yet being men they did unmanly look,
And starèd ghastly, some for inward shame
And some for wrath to see their captive dame.
But one above the rest in special,
That had an hog been late, hight Grill by name,
Repinèd greatly and did him miscall
That had from hoggish form him brought to natural.

87 Said Guyon, 'See the mind of beastly man
That hath so soon forgot the excellence
Of his creation, when he life began,
That now he chooseth, with vile difference,
To be a beast and lack intelligence.'
To whom the palmer thus: 'The dunghill kind
Delights in filth and foul incontinence:
Let Grill be Grill, and have his hoggish mind.
But let us hence depart, whilst weather serves and wind.'

85.5 *According to their minds like monstruous:* Unlike Homer's Circe, who changed Odysseus' companions into the bodies of swine though they kept the minds of men, Acrasia changes her lovers into the bodies of those animals which their minds most nearly resemble. The physical metamorphosis is thus only an outward representation of an essentially psychological transformation. The daemonic power of False Seeming (Genius B) and Excess (of emotion) unite in Acrasia to rob "reason of her due regality" and subject the minds of men to their brutish impulses. Spenser's allegorical conception of the Circe myth was clearly suggested by renaissance mythographers and the commentators on the *Odyssey*.

86.7 *Grill:* said by Plutarch, in his dialogue *Whether the Beasts Have the Use of Reason,* to be a companion of Odysseus who refused to be restored to his human shape. An English translation in 1557 of Giovambattista Gelli's *Circe* (1548) gave currency to Plutarch's Gryllus.

The Mutability Cantos

INTRODUCTION

"Two Cantos of Mutability" and the first two stanzas of a third were printed for the first time in the 1609 edition of *The Faerie Queene*. Although the fragment is labelled with canto numbers (vi, vii, and viii), the questions of how it was preserved during the decade following Spenser's death and what role, if any, he intended it to play in the completed *Faerie Queene* have never been answered. Like the *Four Hymns*, the "Mutability Cantos" reflect Spenser's interest in metaphysical speculation. Unlike the more discursive and oratorical hymns, however, they also illustrate the poet's supreme mastery of allegorical narrative as an instrument of philosophical analysis.

The long speeches and descriptions aside, the narrative structure of the "Mutability Cantos" is simple. The Titaness Mutability (Change), having won domination over the world, seeks to control the gods as well. She rises up to the sphere of the moon and attempts to cast Cynthia from her throne. At this outrage the gods gather in council, bringing Mutability before them to know the cause of her ambition. She explains that her lineage is more ancient than theirs, going back to the Titans who were expelled from power by Saturn; that they are the usurpers, not she. Although Jove disputes her claim he cannot dismiss it, and adjudication before the goddess Nature is agreed upon. In a digression, the narrator (who identifies himself with the poet Colin) tells a mythological tale about Arlo Hill in Ireland, where the goddess Nature is to hear Mutability's plea. The digression over, the scene shifts to the court of Nature, where Mutability presents her case before a full assembly of gods and natural creatures. She argues that the four elements and everything living in them are all subject to her sway. Then she brings forth a pageant of the four seasons, the twelve months of the year, day and night, the hours, and life and death, all of whom obey her laws of change. In answer to Jove's objection that such change is regulated by time and that time is regulated by the gods (i.e. the sun and moon and planets), Mutability claims that even the planets are mortal, subject to changes in their appearance and their courses. In the end, Nature decides simply that all change is but a process of fulfillment ordained by fate and ruled over by Nature. The two stanzas of

Canto viii consist of the narrator's somber reflection on what has taken place. In view of Mutability's undoubted earthly power, he is greatly consoled by Nature's statement that all things will someday come to rest with God.

Coming to the "Mutability Cantos," or to any renaissance philosophical allegory, with the assumptions which modern readers ordinarily bring to a reading of modern literature is not the ideal approach. The modern literary imagination is fascinated by the interplay of myth with a detailed representation of objective reality. Spenser's concern in the "Mutability Cantos," as in *The Faerie Queene* generally, is just the reverse. He attempts to rationalize myth, to give it philosophical meaning, and to generalize the representation of the real world to the point at which it coincides with the mythical. Before considering the "Mutability Cantos" in detail, therefore, it may be profitable to reconstruct something of their historical context.

As an antidote to the practice of judging literary works solely by the quality of the ideas they set forth, modern critics insist on making a clear distinction between philosophy and poetry. They point out that as a philosopher St. Thomas Aquinas was far greater than Dante, but that Dante was immeasurably better than Aquinas as a poet. Similarly, when Shakespeare is read solely for his philosophical ideas he turns out to be an undistinguished compounder of conventional commonplaces and contemporary conservatism. Invariably, when we read the poets for their philosophical ideas, we are disappointed at their lack of both rigor and originality. Any attempt to defend poetry as being the highest embodiment of philosophical thought is thus to abandon poetry to the enemy.

There are some kinds of poetry and some kinds of philosophical writing, however, for which a hard and fast distinction between poetry and philosophy is more likely to be an unhelpful critical cliché than a reliable statement of universal truth. The most obvious instances are the Homeric epics and other traditional narratives which were produced when no discursive philosophical methods existed. Most of the Bible illustrates narrative literature in which the philosophical and poetic content is undifferentiated. As we have pointed out in our Introduction to *The Faerie Queene*, discursive philosophical writing in both ancient Greece and the Christian West seems to have begun as commentary on such undifferentiated narratives as the Homeric epics and the Bible. An assumption underlying philosophical commentary of this sort was, of course, that the literary text contained within it certain hidden truths; that it was, in other words, a mode of philosophical writing; and that its interpretation provided a reliable instrument for discovering truth.

During the early Middle Ages the philosophical treatise had not been a common literary form. Some of the writings of Aristotle were available as models in the Latin translations made by Boethius in the sixth century, but not until the thirteenth century did a tradition of rigorous intellectual prose develop out of the oral methods of scholastic teachers. The sermon, history, letter, and gloss were the chief vehicles of philosophical thought. Except for the gloss, or commentary, which was the most important of these genres, medieval intellectual writing tended to be rhetorically elaborate, its thought and language highly figurative. It tended to preserve intact rather than to analyze the traditional images and metaphors it inherited from the past. Even in theology, the best work during this period was done in the form of scriptural commentary, applying the ideas of the Church Fathers to biblical texts. Some of this commentary was brilliant, resulting in genuine theological progress. But as a method, it reflected six hundred years of repeating essentially the same intellectual exercises. In secular philosophy, the methods of Aristotle were revolutionary when they began filtering through Arabic translations into twelfth-century medical schools and lecture halls. As a scientific method, however, even Aristotle's writings did not universally challenge the vaguely Neoplatonic empirical mysticism of medieval alchemy and folk science until the sixteenth century.

In ancient Greece, Plato's successful attack on the poets and their allegorical commentators signalled the triumph of that state of mind which recognizes a sharp distinction between the aims and methods of philosophy and poetry. Because he was a philosopher, Plato conceived of truth and the discovery of truth in philosophical terms, and had little more than contempt for poetry as a philosophical tool. Between the sixth and the twelfth centuries in Western Europe, however, Plato's distinction was yet to be convincingly made. Even when it did come, with the brilliant new theology and the more or less secular metaphysics of the thirteenth century scholastics, it was not announced with a single, sudden blast on the trumpet of Sapience, nor was it followed by universal enlightenment. Its most powerful impact on the English mind came between Spenser and Dryden, when it drove the opening wedge between what C. P. Snow has called the "two cultures." The insistence upon a clear distinction between philosophy and poetry is a trademark of the two cultures; each feels it gains in dignity by excluding the other.

If we should attempt to put ourselves into the mind of a pre-Socratic Greek or a non-scholastic Western European, trying to unravel the mysteries of God, man, and nature by mastering every nuance of a traditional text as it was being recited, we should probably feel that we were attempting to discover some significance in the literary images other than, or in addition to, the significance they had as representations of the actual world. Having discovered that when the poet mentioned Zeus he also intended the sun, or that when the Bible mentioned Adam and Eve it also intended man's reason and will, we should teach this signification to others. At this early stage, philosophical doctrine would amount essentially to attaching meanings to literary images, meanings the images could not have had as mere representations of actuality.

When many such extra-representational meanings had accumulated through generations of allegorical commentary, it would be possible to reverse the interpretive process, enabling authors to compose new narratives in which the images (e.g., Zeus or Adam and Eve) had an allegorical significance (e.g., the sun or reason and will) beyond their meaning as mere images of the actual world. Both aspects of this allegorizing method, the interpretive and the creative, are the result of a rationalizing impulse. They are both attempts either (1) to relate the mysteries of a traditional text to the observed facts of experience, thus illuminating the meaning of the text, or (2) to relate the mysteries of experience to the conventions of literary tradition, thus illuminating the meaning of experience. The extended metaphors of allegorical narrative and the elaborate conceits of lyric poetry which are related to them were, during the later Middle Ages and the Renaissance, methods of discovering truth. They were alternatives to the methods of the newer, more rigorous authors of discursive philosophy. Topics such as the relative roles of reason and the appetites were explored endlessly by both narrative and lyric poets. For anticipation of the discoveries of modern psychiatry in the Middle Ages and the Renaissance it is to the poets that we should have to turn. We should find there, in such works as *The Romance of the Rose* and the sonnets of Petrarch, close analogues to the modern metaphors of *id*, *ego*, and *superego*.

When a more or less conscious rivalry developed in the thirteenth century between the older philosopher-poets and the newer followers of the rediscovered Aristotle, it took on characteristics reminiscent of Plato's dispute with traditional poetry and its commentators. The attitudes of the two groups toward imaginative literature, especially toward the authors of classical antiquity, reflect their differences. The older group were humanists, cherishing their Ovid and Cicero and insisting upon the "poetic truth" of the ancient mythology. The newer group tended to dismiss the writings of the ancient poets as only so many lies. C. H. Haskins has demonstrated the enormous debt which subsequent literary tradition owes to twelfth-century humanism and to its epitome, the school of Chartres.[1]

Among the brilliant philosopher-poets of the school of Chartres, one in particular stands out for his profound learning and influence on later literature. He is Alain de Lille (Alanus de Insulis, 1128–1202), the author of two important Latin poems, *Anticlaudianus* and *De Planctu Naturae* (*The Complaint of Nature*), in addition to other works on theology, rhetoric, and doctrinal controversy.[2] As a philosopher he was the last of a vanishing breed, but as a philosophical poet he was to remain a potent influence even into the seventeenth century. "For the first time in the history of Western European philosophy and poetry," writes Friedrich Heer, "we find here [i.e., in the works of Alain and the other members of the school at Chartres] the idea of 'nature' as cosmic power, the goddess *Natura* (in Goethe's sense), radiant and beguiling, the demonic-divine mother of all things."[3] "Alain," Heer continues, "enthroned *natura* in opposition to . . . pseudo-spirituality: let *natura* create a perfect man, 'the youth,' the new man, who shall live in harmony with the cosmos, and the Golden Age will return. Alain conceived his work as an 'encyclopedia,' a formative doctrine of 'catholic' application for the instruction of all mankind. Christ played no part in the process he described. Alain held that *natura* was not concerned with theology, but that this was of no consequence; the teachings of *natura* and theology were not contrary but diverse, *non adversa sed diversa*."[4]

By two or three generations into the thirteenth century the medieval mind

[1] *The Renaissance of the 12th Century* (Harvard University Press, 1927; Meridian Books, 1957).

[2] The *Anticlaudianus* has been translated with a useful introduction by W. H. Cornog (Philadelphia, 1935), and *The*

Complaint of Nature by D. M. Moffat (Yale Studies in English, XXXVI, Henry Holt, 1908).

[3] *The Medieval World*, trans. Janet Sondheimer (Mentor Books, 1963), p. 118.

[4] *Ibid.*, p. 120.

had closed itself against the radically naturalistic and deliberately profane thought of Alain and the school of Chartres. Not until the second great flowering of humanism and secular thought in the Renaissance was it possible to again explore the possibility of man's regaining his lost happiness and rectitude in nature. In particular, it was nature as an intermediary between the apparently haphazard and irrational events of the physical universe and the ordered unity of the mind of God which appealed to the humanistic imagination of the philosophical poets.

In the "Mutability Cantos" Spenser explicitly recalls Alain de Lille, his conception of *natura*, and the ancient allegorical method of rationalizing the mysteries of experience by relating them to the conventional images of literary tradition (vii.9). The two stanzas of the third canto of Mutability (viii) point to Spenser's unwillingness to leave *natura* unrelated to theology. Cantos vi and vii go as far as Spenser is able to in seeking a principle of order and permanence outside of Christian faith. Even in the goddess Nature's refutation of the claims of the Titaness Mutability to rule the whole visible universe, Nature looks forward to the cessation of change ("But time shall come that all shall changèd be, / And from thenceforth, none no more change shall see," vii.59.4–5). Spenser is clearly writing from a more conservative position than Alain's. Whereas the men of the school of Chartres were looking forward to a time when the assumptions of modern science would be tolerated by Christian doctrine, Spenser seems to be saying that the time is not yet. Whether we agree with them or not, we must grant the crucial importance of essentially philosophical ideas in Spenser's poetry. The allegory is designed to lead us toward them, not to a sharply focussed prose statement of them, of course, but to an awareness of their presence as a rational structure behind the mysteries of myth and experience. By using the methods of the allegorizing poet-philosophers of the Middle Ages, Spenser allies himself with the old humanistic notion that Truth cannot be divided between philosophical (including scientific) truth on one hand and poetic truth on the other. As beautiful and mysterious as his images are in themselves, they are not just pretty pictures of bygone times. Without their consciously controlled structure of philosophical ideas, Spenser's allegories would not be poetry at all.

If the times were ripe for Spenser to return to the method of Alain, they were ripe for others to return to Alain's doctrine, and to press it considerably further with the new tools of accurate observation, mathematics, and Aristotelian logic. If the "Mutability Cantos" do not refer explicitly to Christ and to Christian mystery, they also omit direct consideration of man's part in the controversy between change and the gods. Others in the Renaissance were willing to speculate, however, as Alain had done, that one possibility for man's happiness lay exclusively in discovering and following natural law. Books I and II of *The Faerie Queene* amply demonstrate how remote such ideas were from Spenser's thought. But leaving aside man and his spiritual nature, considering only the physical universe (as Spenser seems to intend by equating the gods with the planets and by omitting human characters from his narrative), the apparently haphazard change that overtakes everything in nature is a fact that must be accounted for.

One way of stating Spenser's problem might be to posit two alternatives, both of which he must reject. The first is that no rational principle governs the physical universe (Mutability's claim). The second is that natural law is the controlling principle and that no higher God is necessary (the claim of what might be called renaissance scientific atheism). Spenser sides with science in rejecting Mutability's claim, but then goes beyond science in asserting through Nature that all things will eventually come to rest eternally with God. A doctrine of the final resurrection and perfection of the physical universe permits Spenser to avoid a dualism of matter and spirit and thereby to magnify and dignify Nature and her rule.

Because the images out of which the "Mutability Cantos" are constructed are so traditional, individual sources are difficult to identify. As is usually the case, Spenser's myth comes from Ovid and from the allegorizing commentators such as Boccaccio and Natalis Comes.[5] E. R. Curtius has outlined the history of the goddess Natura, and Spenser seems to have drawn on nearly the whole tradition, from the Orphic Hymns of Hellenistic Greece to Chaucer's *Parliament of Fowls*.[6] For the mythological digression in Canto vi about Faunus, Diana, and the Irish rivers, Spenser no doubt drew on Irish tradition and his own invention in addition to Ovid. But for such images as the signs of the zodiac, the personification of the seasons and the months, the council of the gods, and the allegorical debate, dozens of analogues in medieval plastic and literary art make source hunting unnecessary.

Two classical texts, both differing from Spenser's in form and content, may yet have been his main sources for the details of Mutability's claim that all things change. In Book XV of the *Metamorphoses*, Ovid brings his collection of mythical changes into a quite explicit philosophical context by introducing the ancient philosopher Pythagoras as a character and by putting into his mouth a brilliant poetic statement of the transmigration of souls and the transmutation of matter from one changing and impermanent form to another.[7] According to Pythagoras, nothing is constant and nothing perishes. The other text is Book V of Lucretius' *De Rerum Natura*, in which the change and decay in nature is cited as proof that the earth and all physical nature is mortal, merely a chance collocation of atoms.[8] The ideas of Lucretius, which were essentially unknown during the Middle Ages, were making themselves felt with renewed vigor in Spenser's day, proof that Mutability represents a contemporary threat to the kind of synthesis between science and theology that Spenser seems to propose at the end of the "Mutability Cantos." Although Spenser would have rejected Lucretius out of hand as an atheistic materialist, such a rejection does not argue against his putting Lucretian doctrine in the

[5] For the nature and general availability of such commentaries in the Renaissance, see Jean Seznec, *The Survival of the Pagan Gods* (Pantheon Books for the Bollingen Foundation, 1953; Harper Torchbooks, 1961), pp. 312–315. For the specific details of Spenser's dependence on them, see H. G. Lotspeich, *Classical Mythology in the Poetry of Edmund Spenser* (Princeton, 1932).

[6] *European Literature and the Latin Middle Ages* (Pantheon Books for the Bollingen Foundation, 1953; Harper Torchbooks, 1964), pp. 106–127.

[7] Ovid, *Metamorphoses*, trans. Mary M. Innes (Penguin Books, 1955), pp. 364–377.

[8] Lucretius, *The Nature of the Universe* [*De Rerum Natura*], trans. R. E. Latham (Penguin Books, 1951), pp. 171–216, to which all subsequent references will be made.

mouth of Mutability. It is not change that is being debated in the poem, but the implications of change. The victory of Mutability would have meant the victory of Lucretian *chance*, haphazard and undirected change.

The "Mutability Cantos" reflect the inability of the Middle Ages and the Renaissance to regard change as a source of good. Change for most conservative renaissance thinkers could mean only a deterioration of original perfection. The most usual conception of this doctrine was, of course, the Christian myth of the fall of man. Stating the same idea in secular terms could be accomplished in allegorical poetry, however, by referring to the classical myth of the revolt of the Titans against Uranus and of the end of the Golden Age with Jove's revolt against Saturn. And this is precisely the mythic background of the "Mutability Cantos." Spenser probably knew Natalis Comes' interpretation of the myth of the revolt of the Titans as "*elementorum mutationes*," i.e., the changes of the elements, as well as countless other naturalistic interpretations of the classical myths. The pagan gods are not, therefore, to be understood as the true godhead, but as allegorical representations of natural phenomena.

Inevitably, such correspondences will lead to a somewhat fantastic literal narrative. The wagon drawn by a team of fish in vii.42 or the nymphs of Canto vi who are now girls and now rivers do not directly represent anything found in nature. The logic of their appearance in the poem is not derived from our experience of real fish and real girls. Instead it is derived from our knowledge of the traditional allegorical interpretation of such images in classical myth. When he wants to write about the last month of winter or the scenery near his home in Ireland, Spenser is able to reverse the interpretive process and create his own allegorically significant myths. This reversal of traditional allegorical interpretation is the basis of Spenser's great mythopoeic power. He is the most fertile inventor of myths in the Ovidian manner in the history of English literature, not because he imitated the unrationalized myth of classical antiquity, but because for him the images of traditional narrative had become the most significant terms in which to represent the meaning of human experience.

Two Cantos of Mutability
Which, both for form and matter, appear
to be parcel of some following book of the
Faerie Queene
Under the Legend of Constancy

CANTO vi

Proud Change, not pleased in mortal things
    Beneath the moon to reign,
Pretends, as well of gods as men,
    To be the sovereign.

1   What man that sees the ever-whirling wheel
Of Change, the which all mortal things doth sway,°   *rule*
But that thereby doth find, and plainly feel,
How Mutability in them doth play
Her cruel sports, to many men's decay?°   *ruin*
Which that° to all may better yet appear,   *so that*
I will rehearse that whilom° I heard say,   *what lately*
How she at first herself began to rear
Gainst all the gods, and th' empire sought from them to
    bear.

2   But first, here falleth fittest to unfold
Her antique race and lineage ancient,
As I have found it registered of old
In Faeryland mongst records permanent.
She was, to weet,° a daughter by descent   *to wit*
Of those old Titans that did whilom° strive   *in the past*
With Saturn's son for heaven's regiment;°   *rule*
Whom though high Jove of kingdom did deprive,
Yet many of their stem long after did survive.

1–2   *Change ... Mutability:* two names for the same thing; represented allegorically as a Titaness. The Titans were children of Uranus (sky) and Gaea (earth). When they revolted against their father they placed Saturn (Cronus) on the throne in his place. In time he was overcome by his son Jove (Zeus), who cast those of the Titans who had sided with Saturn into Tartarus. Other Titans and their descendants were spared. Mutability summarizes her ancestry in 26.4–27.9 below.

3   And many of them afterwards obtained
    Great power of Jove, and high authority:
    As Hecate, in whose almighty hand
    He placed all rule and principality,
    To be by her disposèd diversely
    To gods and men, as she them list° divide;   *wished to*
    And drad° Bellona, that doth sound on high   *dread*
    Wars and alarums unto nations wide,
    That makes both heaven and earth to tremble at her pride.

4   So likewise did this Titaness aspire,
    Rule and dominion to herself to gain,
    That as a goddess men might her admire,
    And heavenly honors yield, as to them twain.
    And first, on earth she sought it to obtain;
    Where she such proof and sad examples shewed°   *showed*
    Of her great power, to many one's great pain,
    That not men only—whom she soon subdued—
    But eke all other creatures her bad doings rued.

5   For she the face of earthly things so changed
    That all which Nature had established first
    In good estate,° and in meet order ranged,°   *condition,*
    She did pervert, and all their statutes burst.   *arranged*
    And all the world's fair frame, which none yet durst
    Of gods or men to alter or misguide,
    She altered quite, and made them all accursed
    That God had blessed and did at first provide°   *intend*
    In that still° happy state forever to abide.   *always*

6   Ne she the laws of Nature only brake,
    But eke of Justice and of Policy,°   *good government*
    And wrong of right, and bad of good did make,
    And death for life exchangèd foolishly;
    Since which, all living wights° have learned to die,   *creatures*
    And all this world is woxen° daily worse.   *grown*
    O piteous work of Mutability!
    By which we all are subject to that curse,
    And death, instead of life, have suckèd from our nurse.

3.3 *Hecate:* the daughter of the Titan Perses and Phoebe's daughter Asteria. Hecate received great powers at the hands of Zeus. She is described by Hesiod (*Theogony*, 411–453, pp. 65–66) as the chief deity of witches and the dreadful underworld aspect of the triple moongoddess.
    3.7 *Bellona:* not a Titaness in classical tradition, but the sister, daughter, or wife of Mars; Enyo in Greek mythology. See 32.4–8 below.
    4.4 *them twain:* i.e., Hecate and Bellona.
    5–6 The effects of Mutability's ambition, which are enumerated in these two stanzas, constitute an allegorical version of what in sober Christian doctrine was held to be the result of Adam's fall.

7   And now, when all the earth she thus had brought
     To her behest, and thrallèd to her might,
     She gan to cast° in her ambitious thought   *resolved*
     T' attempt the empire of the heavens' height,
     And Jove himself to shoulder from his right.
     And first, she passed the region of the air,
     And of the fire, whose substance thin and slight
     Made no resistance, ne could her contrair,°   *oppose*
     But ready passage to her pleasure did prepare.

8   Thence to the circle of the Moon she clamb,°   *climbed*
     Where Cynthia reigns in everlasting glory,
     To whose bright shining palace straight she came,
     All fairly decked with heaven's goodly story;°   *architecture*
     Whose silver gates, by which there sat an hoary
     Old aged sire with hourglass in hand,
     Hight° Time, she entered, were he lief or sorry.°   *named, willing
                                                                      or not*
     Ne° stayed till she the highest stage° had scanned,   *nor, floor*
     Where Cynthia did sit, that never still did stand.

9   Her sitting on an ivory throne she found,
     Drawn of two steeds, th' one black, the other white,
     Environed with ten thousand stars around,
     That duly her attended day and night.
     And by her side there ran her page, that hight
     Vesper, whom we the evening star intend,°   *call*
     That with his torch, still twinkling like twilight,
     Her lightened all the way where she should wend,°   *go*
     And joy to weary wandering travelers did lend.

10   That when the hardy Titaness beheld
     The goodly building of her palace bright,
     Made of the heavens' substance, and upheld
     With thousand crystal pillars of huge height,
     She gan to burn in her ambitious sprite,
     And t' envy her that in such glory reigned.
     Eftsoons she cast by force and tortious° might   *wicked*
     Her to displace, and to herself to have gained
     The kingdom of the night, and waters by her waned.°   *diminished*

8–19 Mutability's flight upward to the palace of Cynthia (Phoebe, Diana), the moon, parallels in several respects Ovid's description (*Metamorphoses*, II) of Phaeton's journey to the palace of Apollo, the sun. In both instances, the resultant disorder caused misery on earth and the intervention of the gods to re-establish the ordered course of heavenly motion.

9.1–2 The two steeds, one black and one white, which draw Cynthia's chariot have been identified by Henry G. Lotspeich as traditional medieval mythology. They appear in Boccaccio's *De Genealogia Deorum*, IV.16, and Natalis Comes' *Mythologiae*, III.17 (*Classical Mythology in the Poetry of Edmund Spenser*, p. 54).

10.9 *waters by her waned*: i.e., waters of the oceans, whose tides are subject to the moon's dominion.

11 Boldly she bid the goddess down descend
    And let herself into that ivory throne;
    For she herself more worthy thereof wend,°   considered
    And better able it to guide alone.
    Whether to men, whose fall she did bemoan,
    Or unto gods, whose state she did malign,
    Or to th' infernal powers her need give loan
    Of her fair light and bounty most benign,
    Herself of all that rule she deemèd most condign.°   worthy

12 But she that had to her that sovereign seat
    By highest Jove assigned, therein to bear
    Night's burning lamp, regarded not her threat,
    Ne yielded aught for favor or for fear;
    But with stern countenance and disdainful cheer,°   mood
    Bending her hornèd brows, did put her back,
    And boldly blaming her for coming there,
    Bade her at once from heaven's coast to pack,
    Or at her peril bide the wrathful thunder's wrack.

13 Yet nathemore° the giantess forbear;   not in the least
    But boldly pressing on, raught° forth her hand   reached
    To pluck her down perforce° from off her chair,   by force
    And therewith lifting up her golden wand,
    Threatened to strike her if she did withstand.
    Whereat the stars, which round about her blazed,
    And eke° the Moon's bright wagon still did stand,   also
    All being with so bold attempt amazed,
    And on her uncouth habit and stern look still gazed.

14 Meanwhile the lower world, which nothing knew
    Of all that chancèd here, was darkened quite;
    And eke the heavens and all the heavenly crew
    Of happy wights, now unpurveyed of° light,   not supplied with
    Were much afraid, and wondered at that sight—
    Fearing lest Chaos broken had his chain
    And brought again on them eternal night—
    But chiefly Mercury, that next doth reign,
    Ran forth in haste, unto the king of gods to plain.°   complain

15 All ran together with a great outcry
    To Jove's fair palace, fixed in heaven's height,

    11.7 *th' infernal powers:* recipients of
    the moon's light while it is not visible on
    earth.
    14.8 *Mercury, that next doth reign:* The
    planet Mercury was thought to occupy
    the next higher sphere from the moon in
    the Ptolemaic cosmology. As they are in
    many medieval allegories such as Chau-
    cer's "Complaint of Mars," the pagan
    gods are here understood simultaneously
    as planets and as traditional mythological
    personages. Mercury (Hermes) is the
    messenger of the gods.

And beating at his gates full earnestly,
Gan call to him aloud with all their might
To know what meant that sudden lack of light.
The father of the gods, when this he heard,
Was troubled much at their so strange affright,
Doubting lest Typhon were again upreared,
Or other his old foes, that once him sorely feared.°   *frightened*

16   Eftsoons° the son of Maia forth he sent   *immediately*
Down to the circle of the Moon to know
The cause of this so strange astonishment,
And why she did her wonted course forslow;°   *delay*
And if that any were on earth below
That did with charms or magic her molest,
Him to attach,° and down to hell to throw.   *capture*
But if from heaven it were, then to arrest
The author and him bring before his presence prest.°   *quickly*

17   The winged-foot god so fast his plumes did beat
That soon he came whereas the Titaness
Was striving with fair Cynthia for her seat;
At whose strange sight and haughty hardiness°   *boldness*
He wondered much, and fearèd her no less.
Yet laying fear aside to do his charge,°   *carry out his*
                                                             assignment
At last he bade her with bold steadfastness
Cease to molest° the Moon to walk at large,   *hinder*
Or come before high Jove, her doings to discharge.°   *justify*

18   And therewithal he on her shoulder laid
His snaky-wreathèd mace, whose awful power
Doth make both gods and hellish fiends afraid.
Whereat the Titaness did sternly lower,
And stoutly answered that in evil hour
He from his Jove such message to her brought,
To bid her leave fair Cynthia's silver bower,
Sith she his Jove and him esteemèd nought,
No more than Cynthia's self, but all their kingdoms sought.

19   The heavens' herald stayed not to reply,
But passed away, his doings to relate
Unto his lord, who now in th' highest sky
Was placèd in his principal estate,

15.8   *Typhon:* a huge monster born of
Earth and Tartarus; eventually confined
by Zeus under Mount Aetna, from
whence he continues to send up fire and
smoke. See 29.6 below.
16.1   *the son of Maia:* Mercury (Her-
mes).

18.2   *snaky-wreathèd mace:* the cadu-
ceus. In *The Faerie Queene,* II.xii.41, the
powers of the caduceus are listed in the
description of the Palmer's staff.

With all the gods about him congregate.
To whom when Hermes had his message told,
It did them all exceedingly amate,°   *dismay*
Save Jove, who changing nought his countenance bold,
Did unto them at length these speeches wise unfold:

20 'Harken to me awhile, ye heavenly powers.
    Ye may remember since° th' Earth's cursèd seed   *before this*
    Sought to assail the heavens' eternal towers,
    And to us all exceeding fear did breed.
    But how we then defeated all their deed
    Ye all do know, and them destroyèd quite;
    Yet not so quite but that there did succeed
    An offspring of their blood, which did alight
    Upon the fruitful earth, which doth us yet despite.

21 'Of that bad seed is this bold woman bred
    That now with bold presumption doth aspire
    To thrust fair Phoebe from her silver bed,
    And eke ourselves from heaven's high empire,
    If that her might were match to her desire.
    Wherefore it now behooves us to advise°   *consider*
    What way is best to drive her to retire;
    Whether by open force or counsel wise,
    Aread,° ye sons of God, as best ye can devise.'   *advise*

22 So having said, he ceased. And with his brow—
    His black eyebrow, whose doomful dreaded beck°   *movement*
    Is wont° to wield the world unto his vow,°   *accustomed, will*
    And even the highest powers of heaven to check—
    Made sign to them in their degrees° to speak;   *order of rank*
    Who straight gan cast° their counsel grave and wise. *consider*
    Meanwhile th' Earth's daughter, though she nought did reck
    Of Hermes' message, yet gan now advise
    What course were best to take in this hot bold emrpise.° *undertaking*

23 Eftsoons she thus resolved: that whilst the gods—
    After return of Hermes' embassy—
    Were troubled, and amongst themselves at odds,
    Before they could new counsels re-ally,°   *form again*
    To set upon them in that ecstasy,°   *astonishment*

20.2 *th' Earth's cursèd seed:* the
Titans.
20.8 *An offspring of their blood:* The
destruction of the giants and the en-
gendering of men from their blood is told
by Ovid in *Metamorphoses,* I.151–162 (pp.
35–36). Spenser's account of Mutability's

ancestry blends the traditions of the
Titans and the later giants.
21.9 *ye sons of God:* a phrase which
suggests that the Olympians are inferior
to a higher God.
22.2 *His black eyebrow:* Iliad, I.528,
quoted in note to 30.6–8 below.

And take what fortune, time, and place would lend.
So forth she rose, and through the purest sky
To Jove's high palace straight cast to ascend
To prosecute her plot. Good onset bodes good end.

24   She there arriving, boldly in did pass;
     Where all the gods she found in council close,°   *secret*
     All quite unarmed, as then their manner was.
     At sight of her they sudden all arose
     In great amaze, ne wist° what way to choose.   *nor knew*
     But Jove, all fearless, forced them to aby;°   *stay*
     And in his sovereign throne gan straight dispose°   *arrange*
     Himself more full of grace and majesty,
     That mote° encheer his friends, and foes mote terrify.   *would*

25   That when the haughty Titaness beheld,
     All were she° fraught with pride and impudence,   *although she was*
     Yet with the sight thereof was almost quelled;
     And inly quaking, seemed as reft of sense
     And void of speech in that drad° audience.   *dread*
     Until that Jove himself herself bespake:
     'Speak, thou frail woman, speak with confidence.
     Whence art thou, and what dost thou here now make?°   *do*
     What idle errand hast thou, earth's mansion to forsake?'

26   She half confusèd with his great command,
     Yet gathering spirit of her nature's pride,
     Him boldly answered thus to his demand:
     'I am a daughter, by the mother's side,
     Of her that is grandmother magnified
     Of all the gods, great Earth, great Chaos' child.
     But by the father's (be it not envied)
     I greater am in blood (whereon I build)
     Than all the gods, though wrongfully from heaven exiled.

27   'For Titan (as ye all acknowledge must)
     Was Saturn's elder brother by birthright,
     Both, sons of Uranus. But by unjust
     And guileful means, through Corybantes' sleight,°   *trickery*

27.1–9 According to Hesiod and the usual classical mythographers, Saturn devoured his children lest the prophecy that one of them would depose him should come true. However, Natalis Comes gives an account (*Mythologiae*, VI.20) similar to Mutability's, in which Saturn kills his children as a condition to his remaining on the throne of heaven in his elder brother's place.

27.4 *Corybantes' sleight:* The Cory-bantes, originally attendants of the Great Mother in Eastern cults, were identified in classical times with the Curetes, attendants of Rhea. Ovid (*Fasti*, IV.201–246) tells that when Zeus was born, Rhea deceived Saturn by giving him a stone to swallow instead of the newborn child. To muffle the infant's cries, the Corybantes beat on shields and helmets, thus insti-tuting what Spenser calls (*Faerie Queene*, I.vi.15.3) "Cybele's [Rhea's] frantic rites."

The younger thrust the elder from his right;
Since which, thou, Jove, injuriously hast held
The heavens' rule from Titan's sons by might,
And them to hellish dungeons down hast felled.
Witness, ye heavens, the truth of all that I have telled.'

28 Whilst she thus spake, the gods, that gave good ear
To her bold words and markèd well her grace—
Being of stature tall as any there
Of all the gods, and beautiful of face
As any of the goddesses in place° —   *there*
Stood all astonied; like a sort° of steers   *herd*
Mongst whom some beast of strange and foreign race
Unwares is chanced, far straying from his peers.
So did their ghastly gaze bewray° their hidden fears.   *reveal*

29 Till having paused awhile, Jove thus bespake:
'Will never mortal thoughts cease to aspire
In this bold sort to heaven claim to make,
And touch celestial seats with earthly mire?
I would have thought that bold Procrustes' hire,°   *punishment*
Or Typhon's fall, or proud Ixion's pain,
Or great Prometheus' tasting of our ire
Would have sufficed the rest for to restrain,
And warned all men, by their example, to refrain.

30 'But now this offscum of that cursèd fry
Dare to renew the like bold enterprise,
And challenge th' heritage of this our sky;
Whom what should hinder but that we likewise
Should handle as the rest of her allies,
And thunder-drive to hell?' With that, he shook

27.5 *younger . . . elder:* Jove . . . Saturn.

29.5 *Procrustes:* a robber who killed his house guests either by lopping off or by stretching out their limbs until they fit perfectly into the bed in which they slept. His punishment was to be fit into his own "Procrustian" bed by Theseus. Why Spenser includes him among those who aspire to make claim to heaven is not clear.

29.6 *Typhon:* See note to 15.8 above.

29.6 *Ixion:* bound to an incessantly turning fiery wheel for attempting to seduce Hera.

29.7 *Prometheus:* the wisest of the Titans and the creator of mankind. For giving fire to man he was bound to a pillar in the Caucasian mountains, where every day a vulture tore at his liver and every night it grew whole again (Hesiod, *Theogony*, 521–616, pp. 68–70, Aeschylus, *Prometheus Bound*, and Spenser's own variant version in *Faerie Queene*, II.x. 70.5–9).

30.1 *this offscum of that cursèd fry:* a somewhat mixed metaphor if taken too literally (the filthy scum of fish's spawn). But the reference of the metaphor is none too clear either: *offscum* probably refers to Mutability, despite the verb *dare*, and *that cursèd fry* probably refers to mankind generally, the offspring of the Titans and giants.

30.6–8 "Zeus, as he finished, bowed his sable brows. The ambrosial locks rolled forward from the immortal head of the King, and high Olympus shook" (*Iliad*, I.528–530, p. 37).

His nectar-dewèd locks, with which the skies
And all the world beneath for terror quoke,°   *quaked*
And eft° his burning levin-brand° in hand he took.   *then, flash of*
                                                                    lightning

31 But when he lookèd on her lovely face,
    In which fair beams of beauty did appear
    That could the greatest wrath soon turn to grace
    (Such sway° doth beauty even in heaven bear),   *power*
    He stayed his hand; and having changed his cheer,°   *mood*
    He thus again in milder wise began:
    'But ah, if gods should strive with flesh y-fere,°   *i e. against flesh*
    Then shortly should the progeny of man
    Be rooted out, if Jove should do still° what he can.   *always*

32 'But thee, fair Titan's child, I rather ween,°   *think*
    Through some vain error, or inducement light°   *frivolous*
    To see that° mortal eyes have never seen;   *what*
    Or through ensample of thy sister's might,
    Bellona, whose great glory thou dost spite,°   *envy*
    Since thou hast seen her dreadful power below
    Mongst wretched men, dismayed with her affright,
    To bandy° crowns, and kingdoms to bestow—   *toss around*
    And sure thy worth no less than hers doth seem to show.

33 'But wot° thou this, thou hardy Titaness,   *know*
    That not the worth of any living wight
    May challenge aught in heaven's interess,°   *control*
    Much less the title of old Titan's right.
    For we by conquest of our sovereign might,
    And by eternal doom of Fates' decree,
    Have won the empire of the heavens bright;
    Which to ourselves we hold, and to whom we
    Shall worthy deem partakers of our bliss to be.

34 'Then cease thy idle claim, thou foolish girl,
    And seek by grace and goodness to obtain
    That place from which by folly Titan fell;
    Thereto thou mayst perhaps, if so thou fain,°   *wish*
    Have Jove thy gracious lord and sovereign.'
    So having said, she thus to him replied:
    'Cease, Saturn's son, to seek by proffers vain
    Of idle hopes t' allure me to thy side,
    For to° betray my right before I have it tried.   *in order to*

35 'But thee, O Jove, no equal° judge I deem   *disinterested*
    Of my desert, or of my dueful right,

31.7–9 "My spirit shall not always   33.6 *eternal doom of Fates' decree:* alle-
strive with man, for that he also is flesh"   gorically the divine order, to which the
(Genesis 6:3).   Olympians themselves are subject.

That in thine own behalf mayst partial seem.
But to the highest him, that is behight°   *called*
Father of gods and men by equal might,°   *equal power over both*
To weet,° the god of nature, I appeal.'   *to wit*
Thereat Jove waxèd wroth,° and in his sprite   *angry*
Did inly grudge,° yet did it well conceal,   *complain*
And bade Dan Phoebus Scribe her appellation° seal.   *appeal*

36 Eftsoons the time and place appointed were
Where all, both heavenly powers and earthly wights,
Before great Nature's presence should appear
For trial of their titles and best rights.
That was, to weet, upon the highest heights
Of Arlo Hill (Who knows not Arlo Hill?)
That is the highest head,° in all men's sights,   *peak*
Of my old Father Mole, whom shepherd's quill
Renowmèd° hath with hymns fit for a rural skill.   *made famous*

37 And were it not ill-fitting for this file,°   *recital*
To sing of hills and woods mongst wars and knights,
I would abate the sterness of my style,
Mongst these stern stounds° to mingle soft delights,   *battles*
And tell how Arlo through Diana's spites—
Being of old the best and fairest hill
That was in all this holy island's heights—
Was made the most unpleasant and most ill.
Meanwhile, O Clio, lend Calliope thy quill.

38 Whilom° when Ireland flourishèd in fame   *long ago*
Of wealths and goodness, far above the rest

35.4 *the highest him:* the god of nature, beyond whom Mutability recognizes no higher authority; he appears later in the form of the goddess Nature, whose sex, however, no creature can determine (vii.5 below).

35.9 *Dan Phoebus Scribe:* a homely archaism, in which Phoebus Apollo is, quite contrary to mythological tradition, given the title and office of secretary to the gods. The tone is unmistakably ironic, of a piece with Jove's susceptibility to Mutability's feminine charm in stanza 31 above.

36.6 *Arlo Hill:* Galtymore, a mountain of over 3000 feet in County Limerick, Ireland; called Arlo Hill by Spenser from the fact that it overlooks the beautiful Vale of Aherlow in County Tipperary. The river Aherlow flows into the Suir (50.9 below). Galtymore was the scene of innumerable events in Irish myth and folk belief.

36.8 *my old Father Mole:* Spenser's pastoral persona, Colin Clout, described himself as sitting "Under the foot of Mole, that mountain hoar" in *Colin Clout's Come Home Again,* 57. By Mole Spenser meant the whole range of mountains running from Buttevant in County Cork eastward to their "highest head," Galtymore (Arlo Hill). Spenser's own residence in Ireland, Kilcolman Castle, was situated at the western end of this range, south of the Ballyhoura Hills in County Cork. The "shepherd's quill" that "renowmed hath" old Father Mole is thus his own, and the force of the allusion is to remind us that frequently throughout *The Faerie Queene,* but especially in the "Mutability Cantos," Spenser's narrative voice is that of the shepherd Colin.

37.1–3 *And were it not . . . I would:* I.e., "And if it is not . . . I will."

37.9 *Clio . . . Calliope:* The narrator's epic muse Calliope will now use the pen of Clio, the muse of history, to write the "true story" of Faunus and the Irish rivers which follows.

38.1 *when Ireland flourishèd:* History still attests to the fact that from the 6th to the 9th century the Irish were preeminent in art and learning throughout Northern Europe.

Of all that bear the British Islands' name,
The gods then used, for pleasure and for rest,
Oft to resort thereto, when seemed them best.
But none of all therein more pleasure found
Than Cynthia, that is sovereign queen professed
Of woods and forests, which therein abound,
Sprinkled with wholesome waters more than most on
    ground.°   *on earth*

39 But mongst them all, as fittest for her game,°   *play*
Either for chase of beasts with hound or bow,
Or for to shroud in shade from Phoebus' flame,
Or bathe in fountains that do freshly flow,
Or° from high hills or from the dales below,   *either*
She chose this Arlo; where she did resort
With all her nymphs enrangèd on a row,
With whom the woody gods did oft consort;
For with the nymphs the satyrs love to play and sport.

40 Amongst the which there was a nymph that hight
Molanna, daughter of old Father Mole
And sister unto Mulla, fair and bright,
Unto whose bed false Bregog whilom° stole,   *one time*
That Shepherd Colin dearly° did condole,   *lovingly*
And made her luckless loves well-known to be.
But this Molanna, were she not so shoal,°   *shallow*
Were no less fair and beautiful than she;
Yet as she is, a fairer flood° may no man see.   i.e *than Mulla*

41 For first she springs out of two marble rocks
On which a grove of oaks high-mounted grows,
That as a garland seems to deck the locks
Of some fair bride, brought forth with pompous° shows   *splendid*
Out of her bower,° that many flowers strows;   *bedroom*
So through the flowery dales she tumbling down
Through many woods and shady coverts° flows,   *thickets*
That on each side her silver channel crown,
Till to the plain she come, whose valleys she doth drown.

42 In her sweet streams Diana usèd oft,
After her sweaty chase and toilsome play,

38.7 *Cynthia:* Diana, the virgin huntress in classical myth.

40.2 *Molanna:* the river Behanna; renamed by Spenser as a combination of *Mole* and *Behanna*, although Molanna is a place name in the district. According to visitors to the site, Spenser's mythological countryside bears a remarkably accurate resemblance to the environs of Kilcolman Castle.

40.3 *Mulla:* the river Awbeg near Kilcolman, which Spenser renames from Kilnemullah, the ancient name of Buttevant, a village on the Awbeg. The story of Mulla's affair with the river Bregog ('deceitful' in Irish) is told in *Colin Clout's Come Home Again,* 104–155.

42–55 The following story combines elements of three Ovidian myths: Actaeon and Diana (*Metamorphoses,* III.173–252,

To bathe herself; and after, on the soft
And downy grass, her dainty limbs to lay
In covert shade, where none behold her may.
For much she hated sight of living eye.
Foolish god Faunus, though full many a day
He saw her clad, yet longèd foolishly
To see her naked mongst her nymphs in privity.

43 No way he found to compass° his desire   *accomplish*
But to corrupt Molanna, this her maid,
Her to discover° for some secret hire.°   *reveal, payment*
So her with flattering words he first assayed;°   *tempted*
And after, pleasing gifts for her purveyed,°   *supplied*
Queen-apples° and red cherries from the tree,   *quinces*
With which he her allurèd and betrayed
To tell what time he might her lady see
When she herself did bathe, that he might secret° be. *hidden*

44 Thereto he promised, if she would him pleasure
With this small boon,° to quit° her with a better: *favor, requite*
To weet, that whereas she had out of measure
Long loved the Fanchin, who by nought did set° her, *was indifferent to*
That he would undertake for this to get her
To be his love, and of him likèd well.
Besides all which, he vowed to be her debtor
For many mo° good turns than he would tell,   *more*
The least of which this little pleasure should excel.

45 The simple maid did yield to him anon,
And eft him placèd where he close might view
That° never any saw, save only one,   *what*
Who, for his hire° to so foolhardy due,   *punishment*
Was of his hounds devoured in hunter's hew.°   *slaughter*
Tho,° as her manner was on sunny day,   *then*
Diana, with her nymphs about her, drew
To this sweet spring; where, doffing her array,
She bathed her lovely limbs, for Jove a likely prey.

pp. 85–87), Diana's punishment of the nymph Calisto (*Ibid.*, II.463–465, p. 67), and the love of the river Alpheus for the nymph Arethusa, who was herself changed into a river (*Ibid.*, V.577–641, pp. 142–144). But such myths were also known to Spenser from Irish sources. In several traditional stories the Irish fertility and water goddess Aine plays a part corresponding to Diana's here (Roland M. Smith, "Spenser's Irish River Stories," *PMLA*, L(1935), 1047–1056). More important than the exact source of the myth, however, is the fact that Spenser's allegory refers accurately to the natural setting of a particular locality while at the same time it illustrates the sort of mutability in natural forms for which a satisfying philosophical explanation was badly needed in the Renaissance.

42.7 *god Faunus:* in Roman myth a god of nature and patron of agriculture; confused in literary tradition with the similar gods Pan and Sylvanus.

44.4 *Fanchin:* the river Funsheon, into which the Behanna (Molanna) flows.

45.3 *only one:* i.e., Actaeon.

46   There Faunus saw that pleasèd much his eye,
    And made his heart to tickle in his breast;
    That for great joy of somewhat° he did spy,   *something*
    He could him not contain in silent rest,
    But breaking forth in laughter, loud professed
    His foolish thought. A foolish faun indeed,
    That couldst not hold thyself, so hidden, blessed,
    But wouldest needs thine own conceit° aread!°   *thought, make*
                                        known
    Babblers unworthy been of so divine a meed.°   *reward*

47   The goddess, all abashèd with that noise,
    In haste forth started from the guilty brook;
    And running straight whereas she heard his voice,
    Enclosed the bush about, and there him took
    Like darèd lark, not daring up to look   *trapped*
    On her whose sight before so much he sought.
    Thence forth they drew him by the horns, and shook
    Nigh all to pieces, that they left him nought;
    And then into the open light they forth him brought.

48   Like as an huswife° (that with busy care   *housewife*
    Thinks of her dairy to make wondrous gain)
    Finding whereas some wicked beast unware°   *secretly*
    That breaks into her dair'house there doth drain
    Her creaming pans, and frustrate all her pain,°   *effort*
    Hath, in some snare or gin° set close behind,   *trap*
    Entrappèd him, and caught into her train,°   *snare*
    Then thinks what punishment were best assigned,
    And thousand deaths deviseth in her vengeful mind—

49   So did Diana and her maidens all
    Use silly Faunus, now within their bail.°   *custody*
    They mock and scorn him, and him foul miscall;
    Some by the nose him plucked, some by the tail,
    And by his goatish beard some did him hail.
    Yet he (poor soul) with patience all did bear,
    For nought against their wills might countervail;°   *prevail*
    Ne° aught he said, whatever he did hear,   *nor*
    But hanging down his head, did like a mome° appear.   *fool*

50   At length, when they had flouted him their fill,
    They gan to cast what penance him to give.

47.7 *horns:* the goat horns usually decorating the heads of pans, sylvans, satyrs, and fauns. When Actaeon was cursed by Diana he began sprouting the horns of a stag.

48.4 *dair'house:* an unhistorical form which conflates two Middle English synonyms, *daiehouse* and *dairy*. The *dai* element means 'dairy maid,' and the *ry* is the French locative suffix found in *pantry*, *nunnery*, *nursery*, and *vestry*.

Some would have gelt him, but that same° would spill°   i.e. *gelding,*
The wood god's breed, which must forever live;   *destroy*
Others would through the river him have driv
And duckèd deep, but that seemed penance light.
But most agreed, and did this sentence give,
Him in deer's skin to clad, and in that plight
To hunt him with their hounds, himself save how he might.

51   But Cynthia's self, more angry than the rest,
Thought not enough to punish him in sport,
And of her shame to make a gamesome jest,
But gan examine him in straiter° sort,   *stricter*
Which of her nymphs, or other close consort,°   *companions*
Him thither brought and her to him betrayed.
He, much afeared, to her confessèd short
That 'twas Molanna which her so bewrayed.°   *betrayed*
Then all at once their hands upon Molanna laid.

52   But him, according as they had decreed,
With a deer's skin they covered, and then chased
With all their hounds, that after him did speed;
But he, more speedy, from them fled more fast
Than any deer, so sore him dread aghast.°   *terrified*
They after followed all with shrill outcry,
Shouting as° they the heavens would have brast,°   *as though, burst*
That all the woods and dales where he did fly
Did ring again, and loud re-echo to the sky.

53   So they him followed till they weary were.
When back returning to Molann' again,
They, by commandment of Diana, there
Her whelmed with stones. Yet Faunus, for her pain,°   *effort*
Of her beloved Fanchin did obtain
That her he would receive unto his bed.
So now her waves pass through a pleasant plain
Till with the Fanchin she herself do wed,
And, both combined, themselves in one fair river spread.

54   Nath'less° Diana, full of indignation,   *nevertheless*
Thenceforth abandoned her delicious brook,
In whose sweet stream, before that bad occasion,
So much delight to bathe her limbs she took.

53.4 *Her whelmed with stones:* explaining why the river is now "so shoal" (40.7). A similar fate was the lot of Bregog, into whose waters old Father Mole rolled such massive stones that today the river disappears underground before converging with the Awbeg (Mulla) (*Colin Clout's Come Home Again,* 148–155). Folklorists call such stories explaining why something is the way it is *pour-quoi* stories.

Ne only her, but also quite forsook
All those fair forests about Arlo hid,
And all that mountain, which doth overlook
The richest champaign° that may else be read,   *field*
And the fair Shure, in which are thousand salmons bred.

55 Them all, and all that she so dear did weigh,°   *consider*
Thenceforth she left; and parting from the place,
Thereon an heavy hapless curse did lay:
To weet, that wolves where she was wont to space°   *roam*
Should harbored be, and all those woods deface,
And thieves should rob and spoil that coast around.
Since which, those woods, and all that goodly chase,°   *hunting ground*
Doth to this day with wolves and thieves abound;
Which too, too true that land's indwellers° since have found. *inhabitants*

CANTO vii

Pealing° from Jove to Nature's bar,°   *appealing, court*
    Bold Alteration° pleads   i.e. *Mutability*
Large° evidence. But Nature soon   *extensive*
    Her righteous doom° areads.°   *decision, renders*

1 Ah! whither dost thou now, thou greater° muse,   *very great*
Me from these woods and pleasing forests bring?
And my frail spirit—that doth oft refuse°   *turn back from*
This too high flight, unfit for her weak wing—
Lift up aloft, to tell of heaven's king
(Thy sovereign sire) his° fortunate success,   i.e. *heaven's king's*
And victory in bigger° notes to sing,   *louder*
Which he obtained against that Titaness,
That him of heaven's empire sought to dispossess?

2 Yet sith° I needs must follow thy behest,   *since*
Do thou my weaker wit with skill inspire

54.8–9 *The richest champaign:* the Golden Vale in County Tipperary, watered by the river Suir (*Shure*); one of Ireland's most fertile agricultural regions.
55.3–9 *an heavy hapless curse:* an unhappy reminder that the common people of Spenser's Ireland had been reduced by poverty and political turmoil to the direst extremes of misery. That this is a heavy curse indeed to result from such an apparently trivial episode has led some critics to speculate that the story of Faunus and the Irish rivers is more than a *pour-quoi* story, that is a serious moral

and political allegory of the causes of Ireland's woes. Diana as a symbol of Elizabeth I in particular and of English rectitude in general is a possibility.
1–2 *thou greater muse:* either Calliope or Urania, the muse of heavenly wisdom whose nature Spenser described in his poem *Tears of the Muses* (481–540) in the *Complaints* volume of 1591. All nine of the muses are said to be daughters of Apollo, and hence "y-born of heaven and heavenly sire." Similar addresses to his muse occur in each of the *Four Hymns*.

Fit for this turn;° and in my feeble breast   *performance*
Kindle fresh sparks of that immortal fire
Which learned minds inflameth with desire
Of heavenly things. For who but thou alone,
That art y-born of heaven and heavenly sire,
Can tell things done in heaven so long y-gone,°   *ago*
So far past memory of man that may be known?

3   Now at the time that was before agreed,
     The gods assembled all on Arlo Hill,
     As well those that are sprung of heavenly seed
     As those that all the other° world do fill,   *i.e. earthly*
     And rule both sea and land unto their will.
     Only th' infernal powers might not appear,
     As well for horror of their countenance ill
     As for th' unruly fiends which they did fear;
     Yet Pluto and Proserpina were present there.

4   And thither also came all other creatures,
     Whatever life or motion do retain,
     According to their sundry kinds of features,
     That Arlo scarcely could them all contain,
     So full they fillèd every hill and plain.
     And had not Nature's sergeant, that is Order,
     Them well disposèd by his busy pain,°   *care*
     And rangèd far abroad in every border,
     They would have causèd much confusion and disorder.

5   Then forth issued—great goddess—great Dame Nature
     With goodly port and gracious majesty,
     Being far greater and more tall of stature
     Than any of the gods or powers on high.
     Yet certes by her face and physnomy,°   *countenance*
     Whether she man or woman inly were

3.9 *Pluto and Proserpina:* the king and queen of the underworld, the story of whose marriage was an important fertility myth (Claudian, *De Raptu Proserpina*) which Alanus de Insulis associated with the goddess Natura in his *Anticlaudianus*.
4.6 *Nature's sergeant, that is Order:* a significant allegorical detail when it is recalled that Mutability has perverted "all which Nature had established first / In good estate, and in meet order ranged" (vi.5.2–3 above). The operation of natural law (Order) is the aspect of Nature most threatened by Mutability, for it manifests continual change in the physical universe.

5.3 *more tall of stature:* an allegorical detail not in Chaucer or Alanus. It points to Nature's superior power over the symbols of the visible universe, earthly and celestial alike.
5.5–9 The veil suggesting the ambiguity of Nature's sex is an attribute of the goddesses Isis (Plutarch, *De Iside et Osiride,* IX) and Venus (*Faerie Queene,* IV.x.41.6) in the role of Great Mother, a hermaphroditic divinity in whom the contrary sexes had not yet been sundered. A refusal to describe Nature seems to have been part of the convention; Jean de Meun takes 75 lines of *The Romance of the Rose* to say that he cannot describe her (16,172–16,248, pp. 345–346).

That could not any creature well descry;
For with a veil that wimpled° everywhere,   *hung in folds*
Her head and face was hid, that mote° to none appear.   *might*

6   That, some do say, was so by skill devised
    To hide the terror of her uncouth hue°   *appearance*
    From mortal eyes, that should be sore agrised,°   *horrified*
    For that her face did like a lion shew,
    That eye of wight could not endure to view.
    But others tell that it so beauteous was,
    And round about such beams of splendor threw,
    That it the sun a thousand times did pass,°   *surpass*
    Ne could be seen but° like an image in a glass.° *except*, mirror

7   That well may seemen true. For well I ween
    That this same day, when she on Arlo sat,
    Her garment was so bright and wondrous sheen
    That my frail wit cannot devise to what
    It to compare, nor find like stuff to that.
    As those three sacred saints, though else most wise,
    Yet on Mount Tabor quite their wits forgat
    When they their glorious Lord in strange disguise
    Transfigured saw; his garments so did daze their eyes.

8   In a fair plain upon an equal hill
    She placèd was in a pavilion;
    Not such as craftsmen by their idle° skill   *vain*
    Are wont for princes' states to fashion.
    But th' Earth herself, of her own motion,
    Out of her fruitful bosom made to grow
    Most dainty trees, that shooting up anon,°   *straight*
    Did seem to bow their blossoming heads full low,
    For homage unto her, and like a throne did show.°   *appear*

9   So hard it is for any living wight
    All her array and vestiments to tell
    That old Dan Geoffrey, in whose gentle sprite°   *noble spirit*

6.4 *her face did like a lion shew:* perhaps suggested by the lion depicted in the first stone of Nature's diadem (i.e. the zodiac) in Alanus (Prose I, p. 7).

7.6 *three sacred saints:* Peter, James, and John, who witnessed the transfiguration of Christ in a radiance of glory (Matthew 17:1–8). As the transfiguration was a sign of Christ's resurrection and eternal life, so the radiance of Nature is a sign of her divinity and eventual union with God.

8.1–9 And in a land, upon an hill of flowers,
Was set this noble goddessè Nature.
Of branches were her hallès and her bowers
Y-wrought, after her cast and her measure.
(Chaucer, *Parliament of Fowls*, 302–305.)
9.3–7 And right as Alain, in the *Plaint of Kind*,
Deviseth Nature of array and face,
In such array men might her therè find. (*Ibid.*, 316–318.)

The pure wellhead of poesy did dwell,
In his *Fowls' Parley* durst not with it mell,°   *involve himself*
But it transferred to Alan, who he thought
Had in his *Plaint of Kind's* described it well.
Which who will read set forth so as it ought,
Go seek he out that Alan where he may be sought.

10 And all the earth far underneath her feet
Was dight with flowers, that voluntary° grew   *uncultivated*
Out of the ground, and sent forth odors sweet—
Ten thousand mores° of sundry scent and hue,   *plants*
That might delight the smell or please the view,
The which the nymphs from all the brooks thereby
Had gathered, which they at her footstool threw—
That richer seemed than any tapestry
That princes' bowers adorn with painted imagery.

11 And Mole himself, to honor her the more,
Did deck himself in freshest fair attire;
And his high head, that seemeth always hoar
With hardened frosts of former winters' ire,
He with an oaken garland now did tire,°   *attire*
As if the love of some new nymph late seen
Had in him kindled youthful fresh desire,
And made him change his gray attire to green.
Ah, gentle Mole, such joyance hath thee well beseen.°   *ornamented*

12 Was never so great joyance since the day
That all the gods whilom assembled were
On Haemus Hill in their divine array
To celebrate the solemn bridal cheer
Twixt Peleus and Dame Thetis pointed° there;   *held*
Where Phoebus' self, that° god of poets hight,°   *who, is called*
They say did sing the spousal hymn full clear,
That all the gods were ravished with delight
Of his celestial song, and music's wondrous might.

13 This great grandmother of all creatures bred,°   *born*
Great Nature—ever young yet full of eld,

10.8 *tapestry:* The commonest wall decoration in very wealthy renaissance homes were tapestries, such as the seven magnificent Unicorn tapestries now at the Cloisters in New York City. Such works depicted in their backgrounds hundreds of species of plants and animals in astonishingly realistic detail.

12.5 *Peleus and Dame Thetis:* the father and mother of Achilles. Ancient authorities place their wedding on Mount Pelion rather than Haemus (12.3). At this famous assembly of the gods, Eris rolled the golden apple of discord, inscribed 'To the Fairest,' among Hera, Athene, and Aphrodite, initiating the series of events that culminated in the Trojan War.

13.1–4 Nature as an intermediary between the one and the many, the ideal and the actual, God and his creation, must be described in apparent paradoxes, with the attributes of both the permanent, invisible source of life and the

Still moving, yet unmovèd from her stead,
Unseen of any, yet of all beheld—
Thus sitting in her throne, as I have telled,
Before her came Dame Mutability;
And being low before her presence felled,
With meek obeisance and humility,
Thus gan her plaintive plea with words to amplify:

14 'To thee, O greatest goddess, only great,
An humble suppliant, lo, I lowly fly,
Seeking for right, which I of thee entreat,
Who right to all dost deal indifferently,°   *impartially*
Damning all wrong and tortious° injury   *wicked*
Which any of thy creatures do to other,
Oppressing them with power, unequally,°   *i.e. as their*
Sith of them all thou art the equal mother,   *superior*
And knittest each to each, as brother unto brother.

15 'To thee therefore of this same Jove I plain,°   *complain*
And of his fellow gods that feign to be,
That challenge° to themselves the whole world's reign,   *claim*
Of which the greatest part is due to me,
And heaven itself by heritage in fee.
For heaven and earth I both alike do deem,
Sith heaven and earth are both alike to thee;
And gods no more than men thou dost esteem,
For even the gods to thee, as men to gods do seem.

16 'Then weigh, O sovereign goddess, by what right
These gods do claim the world's whole sovereignty,
And that° is only due unto thy might   *that which*
Arrogate° to themselves ambitiously.   *appropriate*
As for the gods' own principality,°   *office of prince*
Which Jove usurps unjustly, that to be
My heritage Jove's self cannot deny,
From my great grandsire Titan unto me
Derived by due descent—as is well known to thee.

17 'Yet mauger° Jove, and all his gods beside,   *despite*
I do possess the world's most regiment,°   *strongest rule*

changing, visible forms in which it is manifested. Although different in meaning and intention the terms of the description are strikingly similar to those used of the pagan goddess Natura in the Orphic hymn to Physis (Curtius, pp. 106–107; *Variorum,* VI, 295–296).
    15.2 I.e., "And of those who pretend to be his fellow gods."

15.6–9 Mutability argues that Nature controls both heaven (i.e., the visible heaven of stars and planets, which Spenser allegorizes as the domain of the gods) and earth. Therefore, they are worlds of a similar kind. Since Mutability already reigns on earth she has an equal right to reign in heaven.

As, if ye please it into parts divide
And every part's inholders° to convent,°
Shall to your eyes appear incontinent.°
And first, the Earth, great mother of us all,
That only° seems unmoved and permanent
And unto Mutability not thrall,
Yet is she changed in part, and eke in general.

*tenants, call
together*
immediately

alone

18 'For all that from her springs and is y-bred,
However fair it flourish for a time,
Yet see we soon decay, and being dead,
To turn again unto their earthly slime.
Yet out of their decay and mortal crime°
We daily see new creatures to arise,
And of their winter spring another prime,
Unlike in form and changed by strange disguise;
So turn they still about, and change in restless wise.

corruption

19 'As for her tenants, that is, man and beasts,
The beasts we daily see massacred die
As thralls and vassals unto men's behests.
And men themselves do change continually,
From youth to eld, from wealth to poverty,
From good to bad, from bad to worst of all.
Ne do their bodies only flit and fly;
But eke their minds, which they immortal call,
Still change and vary thoughts as new occasions fall.

20 'Ne is the water in more constant case,
Whether those same on high or these below.
For th' ocean moveth still from place to place,
And every river still° doth ebb and flow;
Ne any° lake that seems most still and slow,
Ne pool so small, that can his smoothness hold

continually
nor is there any

17–25 The illustration of universal mutability through examples suggested by the four elements (earth, water, air, and fire) follows the order and many of the details of Lucretius' *The Nature of the Universe*, V.257–305 (pp. 178–180).
17.6–18.9 "Whatever earth contributes to feed the growth of others is restored to it. It is an observed fact that the universal mother is also the common grave. Earth, therefore, is whittled away and renewed with fresh increment" (*Ibid.*, V.257–260, p. 178).
18.7 I.e., "And from their winter arise another spring."
19.2–3 "You cannot appease the hungry cravings of your wicked gluttonous stomachs, except by destroying

some other life!" (*Metamorphoses*, XV. 94–95, p. 366).
19.4–6 "Our bodies are always ceaselessly changing, and what we have been, or now are, we shall not be tomorrow" (*Ibid.*, 214–216, p. 370).
19.7–9 "Mind and body are born together, grow up together and together decay" (*The Nature of the Universe*, III.445–446, p. 109).
20.1–9 "Come now, admit that even water gives and takes new forms" (*Metamorphoses*, XV.308–309, p. 372). "As for water, it needs no words to show that sea and river and springs are perennially replenished and the flow of fluid is unending" (*The Nature of the Universe*, V.261–265, pp. 178–179).

When any wind doth under heaven blow;
With which the clouds are also tossed and rolled,
Now like great hills, and straight° like sluices them unfold.°   *immediately, open*

21 'So likewise are all watery living wights
Still tossed and turnèd with continual change,
Never abiding in their steadfast plights.
The fish, still floating,° do at random range   *continually*
And never rest, but evermore exchange   *swimming*
Their dwelling places as the streams them carry.
Ne have the watery fowls a certain grange°   *fixed dwelling*
Wherein to rest, ne in one stead° do tarry,   *place*
But flitting still do fly, and still their places vary.

22 'Next is the air; which who feels not by sense—
For of all sense it is the middle mean—
To flit still, and with subtle influence
Of his° thin spirit, all creatures to maintain   *its*
In state of life? O weak life, that does lean
On thing so tickle° as th' unsteady air,   *unstable*
Which every hour is changed and altered clean
With every blast that bloweth foul or fair.
The fair doth it prolong; the foul doth it impair.

23 'Therein the changes infinite behold
Which to her creatures every minute chance:
Now boiling hot, straight° freezing deadly cold;   *immediately*
Now fair sunshine, that makes all skip and dance,
Straight bitter storms and baleful countenance,
That makes them all to shiver and to shake.
Rain, hail, and snow do pay them sad penance,
And dreadful thunderclaps, that make them quake,
With flames and flashing lights that thousand changes make.

24 'Last is the fire; which though it live forever
Ne can be quenchèd quite, yet every day
We see his parts, so soon as they do sever,
To lose their heat, and shortly to decay—
So makes himself his own consuming prey.
Ne any living creatures doth he breed,
But all that are of others bred doth slay,

22.1–9 "Now a word about air, whose whole mass undergoes innumerable transformations hour by hour. All the effluences that objects are for ever shedding are swept into the vast ocean of air. Unless this in turn gave back matter to objects and rebuilt their ever-flowing shapes, they would all by now have been dissolved and turned into air" (*Ibid.*, V.273–278, p. 17).

24.1–9 "Fed by their burning, they [the flames] race to supply new light, pressing onward, onward, with ever-flickering flames, leaving no gap in the unbroken stream of brilliance: flame from every fire" (*Ibid.*, V.297–299, p. 180).

And with their death his cruel life doth feed,
Nought leaving but their barren ashes, without seed.

25 'Thus all these four, the which the groundwork be
Of all the world and of all living wights,°   *creatures*
To thousand sorts of change we subject see.
Yet are they changed, by other wondrous sleights,°   *devices*
Into themselves, and lose their native mights:
The fire to air, and th' air to water sheer,
And water into earth. Yet water fights
With fire, and air with earth, approaching near;
Yet all are in one body, and as one appear.

26 'So in them all reigns Mutability,
However these, that gods themselves do call,
Of them do claim the rule and sovereignty:
As Vesta, of the fire ethereal;
Vulcan, of this° with us so usual;   i.e. *earthly fire*
Ops, of the earth; and Juno, of the air;
Neptune, of seas; and nymphs, of rivers all.
For all those rivers to me subject are.
And all the rest which they usurp be° all my share.   *are*

27 'Which to approven° true, as I have told,   *prove*
Vouchsafe, O goddess, to thy presence call
The rest which do the world in being hold,
As times and seasons of the year that fall.
Of all the which demand in general,
Or judge thyself by verdict of thine eye,
Whether to me they are not subject all.'
Nature did yield thereto, and by and by
Bade Order call them all before her majesty.

28 So forth issued the seasons of the year.
First, lusty Spring, all dight in leaves of flowers

25.1–9 "Even the things we call elements do not remain constant. ... Though they are distinct from each other in space, yet they are all derived from one another, and are resolved back again into themselves. Earth is broken up and refined into liquid water, water becoming still less substantial, changes into air and wind, and air too, being already of the finest texture, flashes upwards when it loses weight, into the fiery atmosphere above. Then the process is reversed, and the elements are restored again in the same order" (*Metamorphoses*, XV.237–249, pp. 370–371). Lucretius scorns this doctrine of the transmutation of the four elements, a fact which argues against Spenser's heavy reliance on the *De Rerum Natura* for Mutability's philosophy of natural change.

26.4 *fire ethereal:* celestial fire, the fire of the heavenly bodies; hence sacred fire.
26.6 *Ops:* an Italian earth-goddess, identified by medieval mythographers with Rhea, the mother of the gods and wife of Saturn.
27.4 *times and seasons of the year:* Ovid's Phythagoras also illustrates his doctrine that "everything is in a state of flux" by referring to the passage of time as reflected in the stars and to the four seasons, which he relates to the four ages of man (*Metamorphoses*, XV.186–213, pp. 369–370).
28 In this stanza and in 44 below Spenser uses only two rhymes.
28–46 No single source for the pageants which follow has been identified.

That freshly budded and new blossoms did bear,
In which a thousand birds had built their bowers,
That sweetly sung to call forth paramours.
And in his hand a javelin he did bear;
And on his head, as fit for warlike stours,°   *conflicts*
A gilt engraven morion° he did wear,   *helmet*
That° as some did him love, so others did him fear.   *so that*

29   Then came the jolly Summer, being dight
     In a thin silken cassock colored green,
     That was unlinèd all, to be more light.
     And on his head a garland well beseen°   *handsome*
     He wore, from which, as he had chafèd° been,   *heated*
     The sweat did drop; and in his hand he bore
     A bow and shafts, as he in forest green
     Had hunted late the libbard° or the boar,   *leopard*
     And now would bathe his limbs, with labor heated sore.

30   Then came the Autumn, all in yellow clad,
     As though he joyèd in his plenteous store,
     Laden with fruits that made him laugh, full glad
     That he had banished hunger, which to-fore
     Had by the belly oft him pinchèd sore.
     Upon his head a wreath that was enrolled
     With ears of corn of every sort he bore;
     And in his hand a sickle he did hold
     To reap the ripened fruits the which the earth had yold.°   *yielded*

31   Lastly came Winter, clothèd all in frieze,
     Chattering his teeth for cold that did him chill,
     Whilst on his hoary beard his breath did freeze,
     And the dull drops that from his purpled bill
     As from a limbec° did adown distill.   *alembic*
     In his right hand a tippèd staff he held,
     With which his feeble steps he stayèd still;
     For he was faint with cold and weak with eld,
     That scarce his loosèd° limbs he able was to weld.° *weakened, control*

32   These, marching softly,° thus in order went,   *slowly*
     And after them the months all riding came.

While the general conception is classical (*Metamorphoses*, II.25–30, pp. 54–55; *The Nature of the Universe*, V.737–747, pp. 193–194), the wealth of conventional detail comes from the later Middle Ages, when such pageants were actually performed or were subjects for the art of the tapestry maker, painter, wood carver, and worker in stained glass. Each of the stanzas devoted to the months (32–43) includes an allegorical figure representing both the month's chief agricultural occupation and a stage in the life of man. This figure is then associated with a symbol of the particular "house" of the zodiac which was occupied by the sun during that month, a connection being made in at least eight of the stanzas between the ascendant constellation and an event in classical myth. At least in popular belief and literary tradition the planets were felt to exert strong influences on the earth below.

First, sturdy March, with brows full sternly bent,
And armèd strongly, rode upon a ram—
The same which over Hellespontus swam.
Yet in his hand a spade he also hent,°   *held*
And in a bag all sorts of seeds y-sam,°   *together*
Which on the earth he strowèd as he went,
And filled her womb with fruitful hope of nourishment.

33 Next came fresh April, full of lustihead,
And wanton as a kid whose horn new buds.
Upon a bull he rode, the same which led
Europa floating through th' Argolic floods.
His horns were gilden all with golden studs,
And garnishèd with garlands goodly dight°   *fashioned*
Of all the fairest flowers and freshest buds
Which th' earth brings forth; and wet he seemed in sight
With waves, through which he waded for his love's delight.

34 Then came fair May, the fairest maid on ground,
Decked all with dainties of her season's pride,
And throwing flowers out of her lap around.
Upon two brethren's shoulders she did ride,
The twins of Leda, which on either side
Supported her like to their sovereign queen.
Lord, how all creatures laughed when her they spied,
And leapt and danced as they had ravished been.
And Cupid self about her fluttered all in green.

35 And after her came jolly June, arrayed
All in green leaves, as he a player° were;   *actor*
Yet in his time he wrought° as well as played,   *worked*
That by his plow-irons° mote right well appear.   *colter and plow-*
Upon a crab he rode,˙ that him did bear   *share*
With crooked crawling steps an uncouth pace,
And backward yode,° as bargemen wont to fare,   *went*
Bending their force contrary to their face,
Like that ungracious crew which feigns demurest grace.

32.3 *First, sturdy March:* because until the middle of the 18th century the new year began officially in March. Popular tradition, however, was inconsistent; *The Shepherd's Calendar* begins with January.

32.4–5 The ram is Aries, the constellation of the zodiac which is in the ascendant during late March and April. Zeus is said to have taken the form of a ram with golden fleece in order to rescue/seduce Helle. In some stories she falls from his back into the Hellespont, which was named for her (Graves, *The Greek Myths*, I, 225–231).

33.3–4 The bull is Taurus, the second sign of the zodiac; here identified (as in Ovid's *Fasti*, V.617) with the bull in whose shape Zeus carried off Europa (*Metamorphoses*, II.836–875, pp. 78–79). *Argolic:* i.e., Greek.

34.5 *The twins of Leda:* Castor and Pollux, the Gemini.

35.2 *a player:* i.e., costumed as a savage man.

35.5 *a crab:* Cancer, in which the sun at midsummer begins to move "backward," away from its most northerly course.

35.9 *that ungracious crew:* flattering hypocrites who feign humility by leaving a room without turning the back.

36   Then came hot July boiling like to fire,
      That all his garments he had cast away.
      Upon a lion raging yet with ire
      He boldly rode, and made him to obey;
      It was the beast that whilom did foray
      The Nemaean forest, till th' Amphitryonide
      Him slew, and with his hide did him° array.   *himself*
      Behind his back a scythe, and by his side
      Under his belt he bore a sickle circling wide.

37   The sixth was August, being rich arrayed
      In garment all of gold down to the ground.
      Yet rode he not, but led a lovely maid
      Forth by the lily hand, the which was crowned
      With ears of corn, and full her hand was found.
      That was the righteous virgin which of old
      Lived here on earth, and plenty made abound;
      But after wrong was loved and justice sold,
      She left th' unrighteous world and was to heaven extolled.°   *raised*

38   Next him, September marchèd eke on foot;
      Yet was he heavy laden with the spoil
      Of harvests' riches, which he made his boot,°   *booty*
      And him enriched with bounty of the soil.
      In his one hand, as fit for harvest's toil,
      He held a knife-hook; and in th' other hand
      A pair of weights, with which he did assoil°   *determine*
      Both more and less, where it in doubt did stand,
      And equal gave to each as justice duly scanned.°   *measured*

39   Then came October full of merry glee.
      For yet his noule° was totty° of the must°   *head, dizzy, new*
      Which he was treading in the wine vat's sea,   *wine*
      And of the joyous oil, whose gentle gust°   *taste*
      Made him so frolic and so full of lust.
      Upon a dreadful scorpion he did ride,
      The same which by Diana's doom unjust

36.3–7 Leo is identified with the Nemaean lion, slain by Hercules, the son of Amphitryon (*th' Amphitryonide*), as his first labor.

37.6 *the righteous virgin:* Virgo, identified with the Roman goddess of justice, Astraea, whose departure from earth at the coming of the Age of Iron is described in *Metamorphoses*, I.140–150 (p. 35). The medieval depiction of Virgo with corn and other signs of plenty may be reminiscent of her identification much earlier with the Babylonian fertility goddess Ishtar.

38.7 *a pair of weights:* Libra, the Balance, usually explained as symbolizing the equality of night and day at the autumnal equinox.

39.6–8 *a dreadful scorpion:* Scorpio, identified with the scorpion which, in one form of a very ancient myth, killed the hunter Orion. In attributing Orion's death to "Diana's doom unjust" Spenser may be indebted to Natalis Comes (*Variorum*, VI, 306).

Slew great Orion; and eke by his side
He had his plowingshare and colter ready tied.

40   Next was November, he full gross and fat,
As fed with lard, and that right well° might seem.   *reasonably*
For he had been a-fatting hogs of late,
That yet his brows with sweat did reek and steam,
And yet the season was full sharp and breem;°   *cold*
In planting eke he took no small delight.
Whereon he rode, not easy was to deem;
For it a dreadful centaur was in sight,
The seed of Saturn and fair Nais, Chiron hight.°   *named*

41   And after him came next the chill December.
Yet he, through merry feasting which he made
And great bonfires, did not the cold remember—
His Savior's birth his mind so much did glad.
Upon a shaggy-bearded goat he rad,°   *rode*
The same wherewith Dan Jove in tender years,
They say, was nourished by th' Idaean maid;
And in his hand a broad deep bowl he bears,
Of which he freely drinks an health to all his peers.

42   Then came old January, wrappèd well
In many weeds to keep the cold away;
Yet did he quake and quiver like to quell,°   *die*
And blow his nails to warm them if he may.
For they were numbed with holding all the day
An hatchet keen, with which he fellèd wood
And from the trees did lop the needless spray.°   *branch*
Upon an huge great earth-pot steen° he stood,   *urn*
From whose wide mouth there flowèd forth the Roman flood.

43   And lastly came cold February, sitting
In an old wagon, for he could not ride,
Drawn of two fishes for the season fitting,
Which through the flood before did softly slide
And swim away. Yet had he by his side

40.8–9 *a dreadful centaur:* Sagittarius, identified with the centaur Chiron, whose parents according to Apollonius (*Argonautica*, II.1238–1241) were Saturn and Philyra. *Nais* is a variant of the word *naias*, 'water-nymph' in Greek.

41.5–6 *a shaggy-bearded goat:* Capricorn, identified with the goat which nourished Zeus while he was being hidden from Saturn. The story has many variants (Graves, *The Greek Myths*, I, 39–43), but in most of them "th' Idaean maid,"

Amalthea, is herself in the shape of a goat, and it is she whom Zeus stellified as Capricorn.

42.8–9 January and the "earth-pot steen" upon which he stands together represent Aquarius, the water bearer. The Roman flood has not been identified. A stream of water was sometimes represented as flowing from the mouth of Aquarius's urn to the constellation *Piscis australis.*

43.3 *two fishes:* Pisces.

His plow and harness fit to till the ground,
And tools to prune the trees, before the pride
Of hasting prime° did make them burgeon round.   *spring*
So passed the twelve months forth, and their due places
    found.

44   And after these there came the Day and Night,
     Riding together both with equal pace,
     Th' one on a palfrey black, the other white.
     But Night had covered her uncomely face
     With a black veil, and held in hand a mace,
     On top whereof the moon and stars were pight,°   *placed*
     And Sleep and Darkness round about did trace.°   *walk*
     But Day did bear upon his scepter's height
     The goodly sun, encompassed all with beamès bright.

45   Then came the Hours, fair daughters of high Jove
     And timely Night, the which were all endued°   *endowed*
     With wondrous beauty fit to kindle love;
     But they were virgins all, and love eschewed,
     That might forslack° the charge to them foreshewed   *cause neglect of*
     By mighty Jove, who did them porters make
     Of heaven's gate, whence all the gods issued;
     Which they did daily watch, and nightly wake°   *guard*
     By even turns, ne ever did their charge forsake.

46   And after all came Life, and lastly Death.
     Death with most grim and grisly visage seen,
     Yet is he nought but parting of the breath,
     Ne aught to see, but like a shade to ween,°   *understand*
     Unbodièd, unsouled, unheard, unseen.
     But Life was like a fair young lusty boy,
     Such as they feign Dan Cupid to have been,
     Full of delightful health and lively joy,
     Decked all with flowers, and wings of gold fit to employ.

47   When these were past, thus gan the Titaness:
     'Lo, mighty mother, now be judge, and say
     Whether in all thy creatures more and less
     Change doth not reign and bear the greatest sway.
     For who sees not that Time on all doth prey?
     But times do change and move continually.

45.1 *the Hours:* "The Gates of Heaven . . . are kept by the Hours, the Wardens of the broad sky and of Olympus, whose task it is to close the entrance or to roll away the heavy cloud" (*Iliad*, V.748-750, p. 112). Originally three in number, the Hours were agricultural and weather deities. In Hesiod they are the daughters of Zeus and Themis [law] (*Theogony*, 901, p. 78). They became associated with the divisions of the day in Roman times.

So nothing here long standeth in one stay.
Wherefore this lower world who can deny
But to be subject still to Mutability?'

48   Then thus gan Jove: 'Right true it is that these
And all things else that under heaven dwell
Are changed of° Time, who doth them all disseize°   *by, deprive*
Of being. But who is it, to me tell,
That Time himself doth move and still compel
To keep his course? Is not that namely we,
Which pour that virtue from our heavenly cell°   i.e. *planet*
That moves them all, and makes them changèd be?
So them we gods do rule, and in them also thee.'

49   To whom thus Mutability: 'The things
Which we see not how they are moved and swayed
Ye may attribute to yourselves as kings,
And say they by your secret power are made.
But what we see not, who shall us persuade?
But were they so, as ye them feign to be,
Moved by your might, and ordered by your aid,
Yet what if I can prove that even ye
Yourselves are likewise changed, and subject unto me?

50   'And first, concerning her that is the first—
Even you, fair Cynthia— whom so much ye make
Jove's dearest darling: she was bred and nursed
On Cynthus Hill, whence she her name did take.
Then is she mortal born, howso ye crake.°   *brag*
Besides, her face and countenance every day
We changèd see, and sundry forms partake,
Now horned, now round, now bright, now brown and gray;
So that "as changeful as the moon" men use to say.

51   'Next Mercury, who though he less appear
To change his hue, and always seem as one,
Yet he his course doth alter every year,
And is of late far out of order gone.
So Venus eke, that goodly paragon,
Though fair all night, yet is she dark all day;

50–53 The gods are described in their roles both as mythological personages and as planets. The traditional Ptolemaic order of the planetary orbits, starting nearest the earth, was the moon, Mercury, Venus, the sun, Mars, Jupiter, and Saturn.

50.4 *Cynthus Hill:* a peak on the island of Delos, which was said to be the birthplace of Apollo and Diana.

51.3 *his course doth alter:* The assumption that the planets moved in circular orbits made their courses (especially that of Mars) appear irregular. The law of elliptical orbits was not established until the publication of Johannes Kepler's *De Motibus Stellae Martis* (Prague, 1609).

And Phoebus self, who lightsome° is alone,   *radiant*
Yet is he oft eclipsèd by the way,
And fills the darkened world with terror and dismay.

52 'Now Mars, that valiant man, is changèd most.
For he sometimes so far runs out of square
That he his way doth seem quite to have lost,
And clean without° his usual sphere to fare,   *outside*
That even these stargazers stonished are
At sight thereof, and damn their lying books.
So likewise grim Sir Saturn oft doth spare°   *dispense with*
His stern aspect, and calm his crabbèd looks.
So many turning cranks° these have, so many crooks.°   *windings, bend-*
                                                                   ings

53 'But you, Dan Jove, that only constant are,
And king of all the rest, as ye do claim,
Are you not subject eke to this misfare?
Then let me ask you this withouten blame:
Where were ye born? Some say in Crete by name,
Others in Thebes, and others otherwhere.
But wheresoever, they comment the same:
They all consent that ye begotten were
And born here in this world, ne other° can appear.   *otherwise*

54 'Then are ye mortal born, and thrall to me,
Unless the kingdom of the sky ye make
Immortal and unchangeable to be.
Besides, that power and virtue which ye spake,
That ye here work, doth many changes take,
And your own natures change. For each of you,
That virtue have or° this or that to make,   *either*
Is checked and changèd from his nature true
By others' opposition or obliquid view.

55 'Besides, the sundry motions of your spheres,
So sundry ways and fashions as clerks feign,°   *imagine*
Some in short space, and some in longer years—
What is the same but alteration plain?
Only the starry sky doth still remain;
Yet do the stars and signs therein still move,

54.6–9 The astrological influence, or "virtue," of an individual planet depended upon its position with relation to the fixed stars and to the other planets, which could be in houses opposite to or at an oblique angle from that occupied by the planet in question.

55.1 *sundry motions:* orbits of various sizes.

55.6–8 The "fixed" stars were thought to be stationary only with respect to each other, the whole heaven appearing to advance gradually from east to west, completing one revolution during the course of a year. Mutability may refer here, however, to gradual changes in the relative positions of individual stars and constellations which were not accounted for in astronomical theories of the time and which therefore caused increasing uneasiness.

And even itself is moved, as wizards sayn.°   *wisemen say*
But all that moveth doth mutation love;
Therefore both you and them to me I subject prove.

56 'Then since within this wide great universe
Nothing doth firm and permanent appear,
But all things tossed and turnèd by transverse,°   *haphazardly*
What then should let° but I aloft should rear   *prevent*
My trophy, and from all the triumph bear?
Now judge then, O thou greatest goddess true,
According as thyself dost see and hear,
And unto me adoom that° is my due;   *decide what*
That is the rule of all, all being ruled by you.'

57 So having ended, silence long ensued;
Ne Nature to or fro spake for a space,°   *time*
But with firm eyes affixed, the ground still viewed.
Meanwhile, all creatures, looking in her face,
Expecting° th' end of this so doubtful case,   *awaiting*
Did hang in long suspense what would ensue,
To whether° side should fall the sovereign place.   *which*
At length, she looking up with cheerful view,
The silence brake, and gave her doom in speeches° few: *sentences*

58 'I well consider all that ye have said,
And find that all things steadfastness do hate,
And changèd be. Yet being rightly weighed,
They are not changèd from their first estate,°   *original nature*
But by their change their being do dilate,°   *evolve*
And turning to themselves at length again,
Do work their own perfection so by fate.
Then over them Change doth not rule and reign;
But they reign over Change, and do their states maintain.

59 'Cease therefore, daughter, further to aspire,
And thee content thus to be ruled by me;
For thy decay thou seekst by thy desire.
But time shall come that all shall changèd be,

58 Nature's mysterious answer to Mutability's elaborate argument echoes both Plato and Aristotle. Countless passages from the works of the two philosophers and from their ancient, medieval, and renaissance followers could be adduced as sources and analogues. In homage to his greatness, we here cite only Boethius: "The generation of all things, and the whole course of mutable natures and of whatever is in any way subject to change, take their causes, order, and forms from the unchanging mind of God. . . . When this government is regarded as belonging to the purity of the divine mind, it is called Providence; but when it is considered with reference to the things which it moves and governs, it has from very early times been called Fate' " (*Consolation of Philosophy*, IV.Prose 6, p. 91).

59.4–5 "For the trumpet shall sound, and the dead shall be raised incorruptible, and we shall be changed (1 Corinthians 15:52).

And from thenceforth none no more change shall see.'
So was the Titaness put down and whist,°   *silenced*
And Jove confirmed in his imperial see.°   *throne*
Then was that whole assembly quite dismissed,
And Nature's self did vanish, whither no man wist.°   *knew*

CANTO viii

(Unfinished)

1   When I bethink me on that speech whilere°   *just past*
Of Mutability, and well it weigh,
Me seems that though she all unworthy were
Of the heaven's rule, yet very sooth to say,
In all things else she bears the greatest sway.
Which makes me loathe this state of life so tickle,°   *unstable*
And love of things so vain to cast away;
Whose flowering pride, so fading and so fickle,
Short Time shall soon cut down with his consuming sickle.

2   Then gin I think on that which Nature said,
Of that same time when no more change shall be,
But steadfast rest of all things, firmly stayed
Upon the pillars of eternity,
That is contrair° to Mutability.   *the opposite of*
For all that moveth doth in change delight;
But thenceforth all shall rest eternally
With him that is the God of Sabaoth hight.°   *called*
O that great Sabaoth God, grant me that Sabbath's sight.

2.8–9 *Sabaoth . . . Sabbath:* In the original edition (1609) these lines read: "With Him that is the God of Sabbaoth hight: / O! that great Sabbaoth God, grant me that Sabaoths sight." Spenser seems to be playing on *Sabbath,* 'a time of rest,' and *Sabaoth* in the Hebrew phrase *Yahweh Sabaoth,* 'Lord of Hosts.' The 'hosts' were sometimes thought of as armies of angels, the instruments of the divine will in nature. Both conceptions, the God of eternal rest and the God of all inferior powers, seem appropriate to the context. Because of the *Sabbaoth-Sabaoth* variant in the first edition, Spenser's great editor John Upton suggested the normalization of the text that we have adopted.

The November Eclogue

From

The Shepherd's Calendar

INTRODUCTION

One of the paradoxes of literary history is that the most strikingly original works in any age are those which depend most heavily on antecedent literary traditions. One thinks in our own time of Eliot's *Waste Land* and Joyce's *Ulysses*, and in the age of Elizabeth of Spenser's *Shepherd's Calendar*. Spenser must have felt, even more profoundly than did Eliot and Joyce, that the serious poet's most important function was to redefine both the tradition to which English literature ought to belong and the relationship a practising writer ought to establish to this tradition.

To begin with the latter question, the poet's relationship to his tradition, nothing reveals so well as do the opening lines of *The Faerie Queene* Spenser's reasons for launching his poetic career with a pastoral poem.

> Lo I, the man whose muse whilom did mask,
> As time her taught, in lowly shepherd's weeds,
> Am now enforced a far unfitter task:
> For trumpets stern to change mine oaten reeds. . . .

is a loose paraphrase of the opening of Virgil's *Aeneid* as it was printed in renaissance editions ("I am that poet who in times past made the light melody of pastoral poetry. . . . But now I turn to the terrible strife of Mars" [p. 27]). Not only did the tradition that Spenser chose for himself, and for English poetry in general, dictate that the epic poem was, in Dryden's words, "the greatest work which the soul of man is capable to perform"; it also dictated that the epic poet must begin as a writer of pastorals. To sing well of shepherds was a license to attempt the higher song, and behind the mask of modest "Immerito" was an apprentice poet who longed desperately to "sing of knights' and ladies' gentle deeds."

The Shepherd's Calendar consists of twelve pastoral eclogues, one for each month of the year, together with an introduction and commentary written by a certain E.K. By Spenser's time, the eclogue had become a specific pastoral genre. Like Virgil's pastoral poems, which later editors have called his *Eclogues*, Spenser's eclogues are poetical dialogues between shepherds. They take up a variety of subjects, including love, poetry, social and ecclesiastical criticism, and, in the case of the "November Eclogue," the death of a beautiful girl.

The somewhat pedantic and obtrusive commentary of E.K. was by no means as tiresome to the Elizabethan reader as to the modern. Above all, it served the function, as does Mr. Eliot's commentary on *The Waste Land*, of educating the audience to the poet's tradition. Convincing enough cases can be made out both for Spenser's authorship of E.K.'s commentary and for authorship by a second person that the question remains open. Together with the poems, the commentary demonstrates that Spenser went about the task of making himself into a pastoral poet neither half-heartedly nor slavishly.

Rather than adopting, as a modern poet might, the classical Virgil as his model, Spenser made himself instead a part of the renaissance Virgilian tradition. It was, in other words, the Renaissance, not Virgil, that dictated he become a pastoral poet; and it was renaissance pastoral poetry, not Virgilian, that he set up for his model. The pastoral tradition was consciously held by all the learned poets who worked in it to have descended from the Greeks (Theocritus, Bion, Moschus) and Virgil; and the classical pastoral tradition was indeed one of its major components. But in Spenser's case, at least, there is little evidence to show that he was directly influenced by the Greeks at all, and even his Virgil is that which was taken over by the tradition. The classical conventions had become commonplaces in the Renaissance. These included the rural setting, the rustic occupations of the speakers, the singing match with a sheep or kid as prize, the love-sick shepherd singing his mistress's beauty or his own despair of ever enjoying her charms, and the lament for the death of a beloved shepherd or shepherdess. This last convention, the pastoral elegy, took on a separate life of its own in English literature. From the "November Eclogue," the first classical elegy (in the manner of Moschus and Virgil) in English, can be traced such well known examples as Milton's *Lycidas*, Shelley's *Adonais*, and Arnold's *Thyrsis*. The pastoral elegy is itself made up of conventional elements, most of which are illustrated in the "November Eclogue."

Just as *The Faerie Queene* is not merely an imitation of the *Aeneid*, *The Shepherd's Calendar* is not merely an imitation of any previous collection of pastoral eclogues, ancient or modern. In both cases, Spenser's relationship to his tradition is more subtle than simply a degree of dependence on, or independence of, a given source. It is, therefore, a relationship easily misunderstood by modern readers. Spenser's originality consists of creating complex and imaginative poetry out of the materials supplied to him by his whole adopted tradition, a tradition which has since his time come to be recognized as the mainstream of Western literature.

A second component of the renaissance pastoral tradition, inherited in large measure from the Middle Ages, was supplied by biblical pastoral imagery and its ancillary commentary. Such Middle English works as *Piers Plowman* and *The Second Shepherds' Play* illustrate the variety of significance figures like the farmer and the shepherd could have for the Middle Ages. Supreme among them is Christ as the Good Shepherd who protects his flock from the wolves of Satan.

Into this rich medieval pastoral tradition was inevitably absorbed a certain amount of ancient Northern European folk belief and mythology, an element still somewhat neglected in studies of late medieval pastoral. Common to both the biblical and the classical pastoral traditions as they were inherited by the Renaissance was a sometimes harsh satire. The figure of Piers the Plowman, for example, became a symbol of social and religious revolution in the fifteenth and sixteenth centuries. Life in both the courts of princes and the higher reaches of the ecclesiastical hierarchy was often held up in bitterly critical contrast to the millennial ideal of pastoral existence. This pastoral ideal was a kind of synthesis of Christian apocalypse, Stoic ethical values, and the classical myth of the Golden Age. It represented, in the simplest Christian terms, the social perfection that would be achieved only with the captivity and destruction of Satan and his worldly agents—a resurrected Garden of Eden. Among Spenser's continental sources, the pastoral eclogues of Baptista Spanuoli (1448–1516), called Mantuan from his birthplace Mantua, were noted especially for their satire.

A third component of the tradition came from romance. The pastoral romance provided both a country setting for the strong passions of so-called "courtly" love and a complex plot. This element of the pastoral tradition, however, is not as important in *The Shepherd's Calendar* as in other renaissance works such as Sir Philip Sidney's prose romance *Arcadia* or Shakespeare's *The Winter's Tale*. In *The Shepherd's Calendar* the love of Colin for Rosalind utilizes some of the eroticism but none of the intricacy of plot supplied by romance. Instead of a plot, we have merely the situation of the shepherd-poet-lover Colin Clout longing for the love of his disdainful mistress, the country lass Rosalind. Rosalind herself never appears, nor is there any particular reason for identifying her with an actual person in Spenser's life.

That Colin, on the other hand, is to be identified with Spenser in his traditional role as apprentice poet is clear enough. Whereas a modern poet must actually go out into the country to experience the rural life before he can write about it, a renaissance pastoral poet needed only to cast himself as a shepherd in the slight fiction of his eclogues in order to establish a sufficient identity between himself and his subject. The pastoral role of Colin Clout, with its traditional rhetoric of humility, was congenial to Spenser. It may seem remarkable to us that neither the first edition of *The Shepherd's Calendar* in 1579 nor the other four editions to appear during the poet's lifetime mentioned that Spenser was the author. Dedicated to "the noble and virtuous gentleman most worthy of all titles both of learning and chivalry, M. Philip Sidney," the most significant poem to be written by an Englishman since Chaucer is ascribed simply to "Immerito." Of course Sidney and the literary circle about him, the so-called Areopagus, knew the identity of " the undeserving one" and praised his work lavishly.

Part of the function of *The Shepherd's Calendar* was the projection of an extra-textual fictional character named Colin, who could be identified consistently with Spenser from poem to poem in his subsequent career. In even the most elevated passages of *The Faerie Queene* and the *Four Hymns* the pastoral convention of the humble shepherd-poet contributes to the ethos of Spenser's public voice. Like Chaucer two centuries earlier, but quite unlike any conceivable present-day analogue, Spenser used a more or less consistent mask from poem to poem, continually reminding the reader of his unworthiness and modest abilities. Colin in *The Shepherd's Calendar* is an important and complex element in the development of this public mask. Complex, because, as we shall see in the "November Eclogue," while he is only a lowly shepherd, he is, within his little pastoral world, universally acclaimed as a master singer. If the pastoral world is not a pattern of the actual world, it is a pattern of how the actual world ought to be. The image of Colin Clout, then, is relevant to the whole poetic career which Spenser projected for himself in the late 1570's. A mixture of traditional humility and somewhat less traditional poetic mastery, the figure of Colin Clout is one of the unifying fictional elements of *The Shepherd's Calendar* as a whole.

The name Colin Clout had been the satirical mask of an earlier English poet, John Skelton (1460–1529), in his *Book of Colin Clout* (*ca.* 1519). Appropriately, too, Colin and Thenot, the names of the two speakers in the "November Eclogue," were the names used by Clément Marot (1497–1544) in his *Complaint de Madame Loyse de Savoye* (1531), a pastoral elegy of which the "November Eclogue" is an extremely close imitation. The name Colin itself, therefore, exemplifies the synthesis of native English pastoral satire with the highest renaissance tradition of classical pastoral which characterizes *The Shepherd's Calendar*. But the greatest work of the synthesis in Spenser's poem can only be touched on here: the unification of the twelve quite separate pastoral eclogues, with their diverse metrical forms and subjects, in the form of a calendar or almanac.

Calendar poems are at least as old as Ovid's *Fasti*. Hundreds of examples, from ancient and medieval treatises on the six days of creation to the Book of Common Prayer, can be found of the ritual and theological uses of the calendar and the cycle of time. Two works only can be mentioned here. The first lent its name and the second its framework of ideas to *The Shepherd's Calendar*. The very popular French work, *Le Compost et Kalendrier des bergiers* (Paris, 1493), was translated into English as *The Kalender of Shepherdes* and published in seven editions before the appearance of Spenser's poem. In addition to the emblems illustrating the occupations of the seasons and their associated lore (which were imitated in the woodcuts illustrating Spenser's eclogues), *The Kalender* contained moral, religious, scientific, and other types of useful instruction on a variety of subjects arranged according to the months of the year and stated with a crudeness that readily appealed to simple minds. It was genuinely pastoral, and the use of its name and format alone were enough to bestow an air of authenticity on Spenser's poem. The second book, a satirical and philosophical calendar poem by Marcellus Palingenius (Pier Angelo Manzolli) called *Zodiacus Vitae* (Basel, 1543), was translated into English by Barnabe Googe, himself a writer of pastoral eclogues, as *The Zodiake of Life* (1565). *The Zodiake of Life* illustrated for Spenser the diversity of material that could be unified in the calendar scheme. Hundreds of analogies were available to link the humble thoughts and labors of shepherds and farmers to the most significant images in Western thought. Infinite discord became eternal concord in the unchanging cycle of seasonal change.

From the time of E.K.'s Dedicatory Epistle onward, *The Shepherd's Calendar's* most controversial (and least favorably received) feature has been its language. Typical is the remark of Sir Philip Sidney in his *Apology for Poetry* (written in the 1580's, first ed. 1595) that although "*The Shepherd's Calendar* hath much poetry in his eclogues, indeed worthy the reading . . . that same framing of his style to an old rustic language I dare not allow. . . ." At this remove in time an intelligent contribution to the controversy is scarcely possible. We can be sure neither of the degree of rusticity in Spenser's language nor of its effect on an Elizabethan audience. Since the Romantic Movement, a consciously artificial poetic diction has earned automatic condemnation. On the other hand, the use of authentic regional dialect is considered by the canons of modern taste to be a virtue.

Only two historical comments can be made here. First, Spenser was quite consciously following the somewhat nationalistic poetic theory of the Pléiade, enunciated in du Bellay's *Deffense et Illustration de la Langue Francayse*, when he attempted to create an illusion of genuine Englishness by using regional and archaic linguistic forms. In this respect, he looked back, correctly from an historical point of view, to Chaucer as the originator of his poetic tradition in English, including its dialect. Secondly, the degree of archaism and rusticity in both *The Shepherd's Calendar* and Spenser's poetry in general can be easily exaggerated by those who are not thoroughly familiar with English poetry of the 1570's and 80's.

Even though it has occasionally led us into the awkward position of writing a commentary on a commentary, we have incorporated most of E.K.'s notes to the "November Eclogue" in our glosses and notes. Spenser's imitation of Marot is so close that we have drawn attention in the notes to its departures from, rather than its accordance with, the French original. And finally, we have joined the large majority of critics from Dryden onward who have construed Spenser's spelling *Shepheardes* in the title of the poem to be the equivalent of the modern spelling *Shepherd's*. Convincing enough arguments can be advanced for the spelling *Shepherds'*, however, that we should have, in this one instance, been grateful for the easy lot of the old-spelling editor.

NOVEMBER ECLOGUE

Argument

In this eleventh eclogue he bewaileth the death of some maiden of great blood whom he calleth Dido. The personage is secret and to me altogether unknown, albe [even though] of himself I often required [asked about] the same. This eclogue is made in imitation of Marot his [Marot's] song which he made upon the death of Lois, the French queen; but far passing his reach [surpassing Marot's achievement], and in mine opinion all other the eclogues of this book. [E.K.]

Thenot

Colin my dear, when shall it please thee sing,
As thou were wont, songs of some jovisance?°   *joviality*
Thy muse too long slumbreth in sorrowing,
Lullèd asleep through love's misgovernance.
Now somewhat° sing whose endless souvenance°   *something,*
Among the shepherds' swains may aye remain,   *memory*
Whether thee list° thy lovèd lass advance°   *you want to,*
Or honor Pan with hymns of higher vein.   *praise*

Colin

Thenot, now n'is° the time of merrymake,   *isn't*
10   Nor Pan to hery,° nor with love to play.   *praise*
Sik° mirth in May is meetest for to make,   *such*
Or summer shade under the cockèd° hay.   *stacked*
But now sad° winter welkèd° hath the day,   *somber, dimmed*
And Phoebus, weary of his yearly task,
Y-stabled hath his steeds in lowly lea°   *meadow*
And taken up his inn° in fish's hask.°   *residence, weir*
Thilk° sullen season sadder plight doth ask,°   *this, require*
And loatheth sik delights as thou dost praise.

5–8 Spenser would have recognized Marot's imitation of Virgil's Eclogue V. 10–12: "Lead off, Mopsus, with any song you know. Let it be *Phyllis and her Loves,* or *In Praise of Alcon,* or *Cadrus Quarrelling.* Begin: our kids are feeding; Tityrus will keep his eye on them" (*Pastoral Poems,* trans. E. V. Rieu, Penguin Books, 1954, pp. 60–61).

13–16 The general sense is that with the shorter days of approaching winter, the sun (Phoebus) appears to have sunk below the horizon (stabled his steeds) in subterranean fields and waters.

16 *in fish's hask:* "The sun reigneth, that is, in the sign of Pisces all November. A hask is a wicker pad, wherein they use to carry fish" [E.K.]. The sun occupies the zodiacal sign of Pisces in February, not November. E.K.'s mistake has led some scholars to conjecture that the "November Eclogue" was at one time intended for February. The context indicates, however, that Colin is complaining of the beginning, not the end, of winter.

The mournful muse in mirth now list ne mask
20 As she was wont in youngth° and summer days.   *youth*
But if thou algate° lust° light virelays   *anyway, want*
And looser songs of love to underfong,°   *undertake*
Who but thyself deserves sik poet's praise?
Relieve° thy oaten pipes that sleepen long.   *take up again*

Thenot

The nightingale is sovereign of song;
Before him sits° the titmouse silent be.   *is fitting*
And I unfit to thrust in skillful throng°   *compete in trials*
Should Colin make judge of my foolery.   *of skill*
Nay, better learn of hem° that learned be   *them*
30 And han be watered° at the muses' well.   *have been given*
The kindly dew drops from the higher tree,   *drink*
And wets the little plants that lowly dwell.
But if sad winter's wrath and season chill
Accord not with thy muse's merriment,
To sadder times thou mayst attune thy quill,°   *pipe*
And sing of sorrow and death's dreariment.
For dead is Dido, dead alas and drent°—   *drowned*
Dido, the great shepherd his° daughter sheen.°   *shepherd's,*
The fairest may° she was that ever went;°   *beautiful*
                                                                     maiden, walked
40 Her like she has not left behind I ween.°   *believe*
And if thou wilt bewail my woeful teen,°   *grief*
I shall thee give yond cosset for thy pain.°   *trouble*
And if thy rhymes as round and rueful been
As those that did thy Rosalind complain,

19 *list ne mask:* doesn't want to masquerade.

21 *virelays:* "a light kind of song" [E.K.]. Technically, a stanzaic poem of various line lengths, the long lines of one stanza employing the same rhymes as the short lines of another and *vice versa*.

24 *oaten pipes:* The shepherd's pipe, made of oat straw, is a commonplace of the pastoral convention. It may have originated in the *tenui avena* (thin oat) of Virgil's Eclogue I.2.

26 *titmouse:* Marot's bird is the *pivert*, green woodpecker; Spenser's titmouse is a proverbial English antithesis of the melodious nightingale.

30 *be watered:* "For it is a saying of poets that they have drunk of the muses' well Castalas" [E.K.]. The Castalian Well on Mount Parnasus in Greece was sacred to Apollo and the muses, and in literary tradition has come to represent a source of poetic inspiration.

38 *the great shepherd:* "some man of high degree, and not, as some vainly suppose, God Pan. The person both of

the shepherd and of Dido is unknown and closely buried in the author's conceit. But out of doubt I am that it [Dido] is not Rosalind, as some imagine; for he speaketh soon after of her also" [E.K.]. See line 113 and note for 113 below.

41–46 The promise of a reward for singing is to be found in Theocritus, Virgil, and their imitators. It is related to the prize or wager for which the shepherds compete in the conventional singing matches. Theocritus, Idyll I.23–25: "If you but sing as you sang that day in the match with Chromis of Libya, I'll not only give you three milkings of a twinner goat that for all her young yields two pailfuls, but . . . a fine mazer to boot" (*The Greek Bucolic Poets*, trans. J. M. Edmonds, Loeb Classical Library, 1912, pp. 10–11).

42 *cosset:* "a lamb brought up without the dam" [E.K.].

44 *Rosalind:* The name in Marot is Ysabeau, understood to refer to Diane of Poitier, the lady whom Marot served. Both in the slight fiction that runs through

Much greater gifts for guerdon° thou shalt gain   *reward*
Than kid or cosset which I thee benempt.°   *promised*
Then up, I say, thou jolly shepherd swain,
Let not my small demand° be so contempt.°   *request, scorned*

Colin

Thenot, to that° I choose thou dost me tempt;   *that which*
50 But, ah, too well I wot° my humble vein,°   *know, quality*
And how my rhymes been° rugged and unkempt.   *are*
Yet as I can, my cunning° I will strain: *ability*

Up then, Melpomene, thou mournfulst muse of nine!
Such cause of mourning never hadst afore.
Up, grisly ghosts, and up, my rueful rhyme!
Matter of mirth now shalt thou have no more.
For dead she is that mirth thee made of yore.
    Dido my dear, alas, is dead,
    Dead and lieth wrapped in lead.
60   O heavy hearse,°   *funeral service*
Let streaming tears be pourèd out in store.
    O careful° verse.   *full of pain*

Shepherds that by your flocks on Kentish downs abide,
Wail ye this woeful waste° of nature's wark.°   *decay, work*
Wail we the wight° whose presence was our pride.   *person*
Wail we the wight whose absence is our cark.°   *misery*
The sun of all the world is dim and dark.
    The earth now lacks her wonted light,
    And all we dwell in deadly night,
70   O heavy hearse.
Break we our pipes that shrilled as loud as lark,
    O careful verse.

Why do we longer live—ah why live we so long?—
Whose better days death hath shut up in woe?

The Shepherd's Calendar and in the poem *Colin Clout's Come Home Again* Rosalind is Colin's unrelenting mistress. Whether she represents anything more substantial in Spenser's life is not known.

51 *unkempt;* "*incompti;* not combed; that is, rude and unhandsome" [E.K.].

53–62 With this elaborate and minutely irregular stanza form, the elegy proper begins.

53 *Melpomene:* "the sad and wailful muse used of [by] poets in honor of tragedies; as saith Virgil, '*Melpomene tragico proclamat maesta boatu* [sorrowing Melpomene cries out with tragic wail]' " [E.K.]. This verse from the anonymous poem *De Musis* was widely attributed to Virgil in the Renaissance.

55 *Up, grisly ghosts:* "the manner of tragical poets, to call for help of furies and damned ghosts; so is Hecuba of [by] Euripides and Tantalus brought in of [by] Seneca; and the rest of [by] the rest" [E.K.]. *Hecuba,* in fact, is the name of the play in which Euripides "brings in" the ghost of Polydorus.

60 *hearse:* "the solemn obsequy in funerals" [E.K.].

73 *ah why:* "an elegant epanorthosis; as also soon after, 'Nay, time was long ago' " [E.K.]. An epanorthosis is a rhetorical figure in which a preceding statement is corrected.

The fairest flower our garland all among
Is faded quite and into dust y-go.°   *gone*
Sing now, ye shepherds' daughters, sing no mo°   *more*
   The songs that Colin made in her praise,
   But into weeping turn your wanton lays,
80   O heavy hearse,
Now is° time to die. Nay, time was long ago,   *that it is*
   O careful verse.

Whence is it that the floweret of the field doth fade,
And lieth buried long in winter's bale,°   *harm*
Yet soon as spring his° mantle hath displayed,°   *its, spread out*
It flowereth fresh, as it should never fail?
But thing on earth that is of most avail,
   As° virtue's branch and beauty's bud,   *such as*
   Reliven° not for any good.   *revive*
90   O heavy hearse,
The branch once dead, the bud eke° needs must quail,° *also, wither*
   O careful verse.

She, while she was—that 'was' a woeful word to sayn°— *to say*
For beauty's praise and pleasance had no peer;
So well she couth° the shepherds entertain   *knew how to*
With cakes and cracknels° and such country cheer.°   *cookies, food*
Ne would she scorn the simple shepherd's swain,
   For she would call hem° often hame°   *them, home*
   And give hem curds and clouted° cream.   *thickened*
100   O heavy hearse,
Als° Colin Clout she would not once disdain.   *also*
   O careful verse.

83–92 Behind Marot's less elaborate
original of these lines is a lengthy elegiac
tradition. Two ancient sources, both
known to Spenser, may have contributed
to his statement of the mortality of the
individual human character in contrast
to the immortality of natural forms: "Ay
me! when the mallows and the fresh green
parsley and the springing crumpled anise
perish in the garden, they live yet again
and grow another year; but we men that
are so tall and strong and wise, soon as
ever we be dead, unhearing there in a
hole of the earth, sleep we both sound and
long a sleep that is without end or
waking" (Moschus, Idyll III.99–104, *The
Greek Bucolic Poets*, pp. 452–453). "For
there is hope of a tree, if it be cut down,
that it will sprout again, and that the
tender branch thereof will not cease.
Though the root thereof wax old in the
earth, and the stock thereof die in the
ground; yet through the scent of water it
will bud and bring forth boughs like a
plant. But man dieth, and wasteth away:
yea, man giveth up the ghost, and where
is he?" (Job 14:1–17).

83 *floweret:* "a diminutive for 'a little
flower.' This is a notable and sententious
comparison *a minore ad majus* [from the
lesser to the greater]" [E.K.].

89 *Reliven not:* "live not again, s.
[scilicet, 'that is to say'] not in their
earthly bodies; for in heaven they enjoy
their due reward" [E.K.].

91 *The branch:* "He meaneth Dido,
who being as it were the main branch
now withered, the buds, that is, beauty
(as he said afore) can no more flourish"
[E.K.].

96 *With cakes:* "fit for shepherds' ban-
quets" [E.K.].

98 *hame:* "for *home*, after the North-
ern pronouncing" [E.K.].

But now sik happy cheer is turned to heavy chance,°   *misfortune*
Such pleasance now displaced by dolor's dint.°   *grief's blow*
All music sleeps where death doth lead the dance,
And shepherds' wonted solace is extinct.
The blue in black, the green in gray is tinct,°   *dyed*
  The gaudy° garlands deck her grave,   *gay*
  The faded flowers her corse° embrace,°   *body, adorn*
110   O heavy hearse.
Mourn now, my muse, now mourn with tears besprint,°   *besprinkled*
  O careful verse.

O thou great shepherd, Lobbin, how great is thy grief!
Where been° the nosegays° that she dight° for thee,   *are, bouquets, made*
The colored chapelets° wrought with a chief,°   *wreaths for the head, crown*
The knotted rush-rings, and gilt rosemary?
For she deemèd nothing too dear° for thee.   *precious*
  Ah they been all y-clad° in clay;   *clothed*
  One bitter blast blew all away.
120   O heavy hearse,
Thereof nought remains but the memory.
  O careful verse.

Ay me, that dreary death should strike so mortal stroke,
That can undo Dame Nature's kindly° course: *natural*
The faded locks fall from the lofty oak;

105 *death doth lead the dance:* The Dance of Death (French *danse macabre*, German *Totentanz*) was a favorite subject in late medieval art. Its greatest English monument is John Lydgate's *Daunce of Machabree* (ed. F. Warren and B. White, Early English Text Society, OS 181 (1929), 1931), written about 1426 as the text for a series of murals in a cloister near St. Pauls in London. Both the poem and the now destroyed paintings were close imitations of originals in the cemetery of the Eglise des Innocents in Paris.
108 *The gaudy garlands . . . :* "The meaning is that the things which were the ornaments of her life are made the honor of her funeral, as is used [customary] in burials" [E.K.].
113 *Lobbin:* "the name of a shepherd which seemeth to have been the lover and dear friend of Dido" [E.K.]. Except for the name Lobbin, this line is a translation of Marot's "*O grand Pasteur, que tu as de soucy!*" (61). If E.K. is right, then this great shepherd cannot be the same as that of line 38, Dido's father. Many scholars have held that Lobbin (here and in *Colin Clout's Come Home Again*, 735–738) represents Robert Dudley, Earl of Leicester (1531–1588), the uncle of Sir Philip Sidney and a favorite of Queen Elizabeth's, whom Spenser had served

after he left Cambridge and to whom he always remained fiercely loyal. The name may thus be an anagram from R*obbin* Leicester.
115 *chapelets:* 1579 and later editions read *chaplets*.
116 *rush-rings:* "agreeable for such base gifts" [E.K.].
123–152 Of the many conventions of the pastoral elegy, "all nature mourns" is the most traditional. "Your sudden end, sweet Bion, was matter of weeping even unto Apollo; the Satyrs did lament you, and every Priapus made you his moan in sable garb. Not a Pan but cried woe for your music, not a Nymph o' the spring but made her complaint of it in the wood; and all the waters became as tears. . . . For sorrow that you are lost the trees have cast their fruit to the ground, and all the flowers are withered away. The flocks have given none of their good milk. . . . The nightingales and all the swallows, which once he delighted, which once he taught to speak, sat upon the branches and cried aloud . . ." (Moschus, Idyll III.26–47. *The Greek Bucolic Poets*, pp. 446–449).
125 *faded locks:* "dried leaves; as if Nature herself bewailed the death of the maid" [E.K.].

The floods° do gasp, for drièd is their source,   *lakes and streams*
And floods of tears flow in their stead perforce.°   *of necessity*
  The mantled meadows mourn,
  Their sundry colors turn.
130   O heavy hearse,
The heavens do melt in tears without remorse.
    O careful verse.

The feeble flocks in field refuse their former food,
And hang their heads as° they would lcarn to weep;   *as if*
The beasts in forest wail as they were wood,°   *mad*
Except the wolves, that chase the wandering sheep,
Now she is gone that safely did hem° keep.   *them*
  The turtle° on the barèd branch   *turtle dove*
  Laments the wound that death did launch,°   *cut*
140   O heavy hearse.
And Philomel her song with tears doth steep,
    O careful verse.

The water nymphs, that wont with her to sing and dance
And for her garland olive branches bear,
Now baleful boughs of cypress done advance.°   *do bring forward*
The muses, that were wont green bays° to wear,   *laurel leaves*
Now bringen bitter elder branches sere.
  The fatal sisters eke repent°   *grieve*
  Her vital thrend so soon was spent.
150   O heavy hearse,
Mourn now, my muse, now mourn with heavy cheer,°   *sorrowful mood*
    O careful verse.

---

126 *source:* "spring" [E.K.].

128 *mantled meadows:* "for the sundry flowers are like a mantle or coverlet wrought with many colors" [E.K.].

141 *Philomel:* "the nightingale; whom the poets feign once to have been a lady of great beauty, till being ravished by her sister's husband she desired to be turned into a bird of her name [Ovid, *Metamorphoses*, VI.424–674 (pp. 159–166)]; whose complaints be very well set forth of by Master George Cascoigne [spelled phonetically by E.K., "Gaskin"; 1535–1577; author of *Complaint of Philumene*], a witty gentleman and the very chief of our late rhymers, who and if some parts of learning wanted not [*i.e.*, who if he had not had an incomplete education] (albe it is well known he altogether wanted not learning) no doubt would have attained to the excellency of those famous poets, for gifts of wit and natural promptness appear in him abundantly" [E.K.].

145 *cypress:* "used of the old paynims in the furnishing of their funeral pomp, and properly the sign of all sorrow and heaviness" [E.K.].

147 *elder:* important in Northern European mythology and folk belief; a symbol of grief in renaissance England.

148 *The fatal sisters:* "Clotho, Lachesis, and Atropos, daughters of Herebus and the night, whom the poets feign to spin the life of man as it were a long thread which they draw out in length till his fatal hour and timely death be come; but if by other casualty his days be abridged, then one of them, that is, Atropos, is said to have cut the thread in twain. Hereof cometh a common verse: *Clotho colum bajulat, Lachesis trahit, Atropos occat* [Clotho wields the distaff, Lachesis draws out, Atropos cuts]" [E.K.].

O trustless state of earthly things, and slipper° hope   *slippery*
Of mortal men that swink° and sweat for nought,   *work*
And shooting wide, do miss the markèd scope,°   *target*
Now have I learned—a lesson dearly bought—
That n'is on earth assurance to be sought;
    For what° might be in earthly mold,°   *whatever, form*
    That did her buried body hold,
160   O heavy hearse,
Yet saw I on the bier when it was brought,
    O careful verse.

But maugre° death, and dreaded sisters' deadly spite,   *in spite of*
And gates of hell, and fiery Furies' force,
She hath the bonds broke of eternal night,
Her soul unbodied of the burdenous corse.°   *body*
Why then weeps Lobbin so without remorse?°   *moderation*
    O Lobb, thy loss no longer lament;
    Dido n'is dead, but into heaven hent,°   *taken*
170   O happy hearse.
Cease now, my muse, now cease thy sorrow's source,°   *flowing*
    O joyful verse.

Why wail we then? Why weary we the gods with plaints
As if some evil were to her betite?°   *happened*
She reigns a goddess now among the saints,
That whilom° was the saint of shepherds light,°   *once, simple*
And is installèd now in heaven's height.
    I see thee blessed soul, I see,
    Walk in Elysian fields so free.
180   O happy hearse,
Might I once come to thee—O that I might!—
    O joyful verse.

153–162 "A gallant exclamation mo-
ralized with great wisdom and passionate
with great affection" [E.K.]. The stanza
does not correspond to anything in
Marot and may for this reason have been
praised by E.K.
158–162 I.e., "that which her (now
buried) body held of whatever exists in
earthly form I still saw when it was
brought onto the bier."
161 *bier:* "a frame whereon they use
to lay the dead corse" [E.K.].
163–172 With this stanza begins the
traditional consolation and reversal of
feeling. Even the change of refrain had
been used by Theocritus and Moschus.
In Eclogue V.56–64 Virgil illustrates the
general convention: "Clothed in new
glory, Daphnis stands at Heaven's Gate,
where all is wonderful, watching the
clouds and stars below his feet. . . . For
very joy the shaggy mountains raise a
clamour to the stars; the rocks burst into
song, and the plantations speak. 'He is a
god' they say; 'Menalcas, he is a god!' "
(*The Pastoral Poems*, pp. 64–65).
164 *Furies:* "of poets be feigned to be
three: Persephone [Tisiphone]. Alecto,
and Megera, which are said to be the
authors of all evil and mischief" [E.K.].
165 *eternal night:* "death, or darkness
of hell" [E.K.].
178 *I see thee:* "a lively icon, or repre-
sentation, as if he saw her in heaven
present" [E.K.].
179 *Elysian fields:* "devised of poets
to be a place of pleasure like Paradise,
where the happy souls do rest in peace
and eternal happiness" [E.K.]. For the
classic description of the Elysian fields,
see *Aeneid*, VI.637–665 (pp. 166–167).
Spenser's other world is pagan in name
only; he clearly conceives of a Christian
heaven.

Unwise and wretched men to weet° what's good or ill,   *know*
We deem of death as doom° of ill desert.°   *judgment, guilt*
But knew we fools° what it us brings until,°   *if we fools knew,*
Die would we daily, once it to expert.°   *to*
    experience
No danger there the shepherd can astert;
Fair fields and pleasant leas there been,
The fields aye fresh, the grass aye green.
190   O happy hearse,
Make haste, ye shepherds, thither to revert,°   *return*
    O joyful verse.

Dido is gone afore°—whose turn shall be the next?   *has gone ahead*
There lives she with the blessed gods in bliss,
There drinks she nectar with ambrosia mixed,
And joys enjoys that mortal men do miss.
The honor now of highest gods she is
    That whilom° was poor shepherds' pride   *who once*
    While here on earth she did abide.
200   O happy hearse!
Cease now, my song, my woe now wasted° is.   *spent*
    O joyful verse!

Thenot

Aye, frank shepherd, how been thy verses meint°   *mixed*
With doleful pleasance, so as I ne wot°   *don't know*
Whether rejoice° or weep for great constraint!°   *to rejoice, distress*
Thine be the cosset,° well hast thou it got.   *lamb*
Up, Colin, up; enough thou mournèd hast.
Now gins° to mizzle,° hie we homeward fast.   *it begins, drizzle*

Colin's Emblem
La mort ny mord.

186 *Die would we daily:* "the very express saying of Plato in *Phaedon* [*Phaedo*]" [E.K.]. The exact words are not to be found; the sentiment, however, pervades the whole dialogue.
187 *astert:* "befall unwares" [E.K.]. The context demands some such gloss; Spenser seems, however, to be misusing an archaic intransitive verb meaning 'escape,' 'rise up,' 'occur to.'
195 *nectar . . . ambrosia:* "feigned to be the drink and food of the gods. Ambrosia they liken to manna in Scripture, and nectar to be white like cream, whereof is a proper tale of Hebe that spilled a cup of it and stained the heavens, as yet appeareth [i.e., in the Milky Way]. But I have already discoursed that at large in my commentary upon the *Dreams* of the same author" [E.K.]. Although Spenser's *Dreams* and E.K.'s commentary on them are now lost, the existence of both is attested to in a letter from Spenser to

Gabriel Harvey, printed in 1580 (*Variorum*, IX, 18).
Colin's Emblem: "Which is as much to say as 'Death biteth not.' For although by course of nature we be born to die, and being ripened with age as with a timely harvest, we must be gathered in time, or else of ourselves we fall like rotted ripe fruit fro the tree; yet death is not to be counted for evil, nor (as the poet said a little before) as doom of ill desert. For though the trespass of the first man brought death into the world as the guerdon [repayment] of sin, yet being overcome by the death of one that died for all, it is now made (as Chaucer saith) the green pathway to life. So that it agreeth well with that was said, that death biteth not, that is, hurteth not at all" [E.K.]. By adopting Marot's personal emblem Spenser acknowledges that his Colin is both Marot's Colin and Marot himself.

Amoretti

INTRODUCTION

The *Amoretti and Epithalamion* is a poetic account of a courtship and marriage. Because Spenser is thought to have married his second wife, Elizabeth Boyle, sometime before November 19, 1594, the date on which the *Amoretti and Epithalamion* was entered in the Stationers' Register for publication, the book has been interpreted as the description of actual events and of the poet's emotional response to them. If they are read by canons of nineteenth-century realism and poetic sincerity, Spenser's lyrics do seem to provide an intimate glimpse into the depths of the passionate heart, as well as a reliable chronology of the poet's most private affairs. And since there was an actual Elizabeth Boyle and courtship and marriage, the *Amoretti and Epithalamion* must, of course, have stood in some sort of relationship to those actualities, perhaps even, as Professor Louis Martz believes, a most delicious and sophisticated relationship indeed.[1] Of the actualities, however, we know nothing. We have only the fictional account; and it will do the least damage to Spenser's poetic meaning if we restrict our inquiries to the nature of that fiction alone.

The idea of constructing a sequence of sonnets telling the story of a lover's quest for the affection of a beautiful lady was far from original with Spenser. Important sonnet sequences in English—Sir Philip Sidney's *Astrophel and Stella*, Samuel Daniel's *Delia*, and Michael Drayton's *Idea's Mirror*—had appeared before Spenser's series of sonnets or, as he calls them, *amoretti* (literally, "little loves," "cupids"). The English sequences were heavily indebted to countless French and Italian models which, in their turn, looked back to one of the most important books in the history of Western literature, the *Canzoniere* of Francesco Petrarch. Adapting to Italian the conventions of the still earlier Provencal troubadours, Petrarch addressed nearly all of the odes and sonnets of the *Canzoniere* to the lady Laura. For nearly three hundred years, the tone and technique of Petrarch's "sweet new style" dominated Western love poetry. The history of the English sonnet is not an account of its debt to Petrarch, but rather of its gradual liberation from him. Such is the case of the *Amoretti*.

Spenser's metrical virtuosity, so brilliantly demonstrated in *The Shepherd's Calendar*, was from the very beginning of his career the product of his study of

---

[1] "The *Amoretti:* 'Most Goodly Temperature,'" *Form and Convention in the Poetry of Edmund Spenser* (Selected Papers from the English Institute), ed. William Nelson, Columbia University Press, 1961, pp. 146–168.

foreign models. The distinctive form of the "Spenserian" sonnet (used as early as 1580 for the dedicatory sonnet to *Virgil's Gnat*) was a synthesis of English, French, and Italian models. The English sonneteers had already declared metrical independence of Petrarch. They expanded the number of rhymes from five to seven; shifted from an octave-and-sestet to a three-quatrain-and-couplet structure; and alternated the rhymes. Petrarch's form had rhymed *abbaabba cdecde*, while the English form rhymed *abab cdcd efef gg*. It was apparently the French poet Clément Marot (1496–1544) who taught Spenser to link his quatrains (*abab bcbc*) as in the "November Eclogue," and thus return to the Italian scheme of five instead of seven rhymes while preserving the main features of the English sonnet structure.

That Spenser invented the form of his sonnet there can be little doubt. That he was not the only poet to invent it is equally clear, however. In a book entitled *The Essayes of a Prentise, in the Divine Art of Poesie*, which appeared in 1584—ten years prior to *Amoretti and Epithalamion* and four years after the composition of Spenser's earliest extant sonnet—King James VI of Scotland and five other Scottish poets published, among other poems by themselves and others, twenty sonnets in the "Spenserian" form. James wrote fifteen of them, and Thomas Hudson, Robert Hudson, "M. W.," William Fowler, and the great Scottish poet Alexander Montgomerie each composed one. The latest study of Spenser's sonnet form and the Scottish sonneteers supports the conclusion that Spenser and the Scottish poets developed the form independently.[2]

Taken as a whole, the *Amoretti* are, like *The Shepherd's Calendar*, more than the sum of the individual parts. Individually, the eighty-eight separate sonnets of the *Amoretti*[3] are among the most melodious and technically skillful compositions of the English Renaissance. But no one of them comes close to being the best short lyric of the time. They are perhaps too controlled, conventional, and "tame" for our modern taste. Collectively, however, they are rivalled only by Shakespeare's sequence for the complexity and interest of the story they tell. As in Spenser's collection of pastoral eclogues, the *Amoretti* are arranged against the cyclical scheme of the calendar. Sonnet 4 alludes to New Year's Day, Sonnet 12 to the first day of spring, Sonnet 22 (included here) to Lent, Sonnet 60 (included here) to the passage of the first year of love, Sonnet 62 to the second New Year's Day, and Sonnet 67 (included here) to the second Easter. In Sonnet 74 we are told that the lady's name is Elizabeth. This subtle narrative fiction amounts to more than a bare plot. In accordance with the ancient conventions stretching back in time through Petrarch to the troubadours, the speaker in the *Amoretti* is a poet. He is conscious of his double role of poet and lover (Sonnets 1, 28, 29, 40, 54, and 75) and on occasion even hints at the third role of religious devotee (Sonnets 22 and 68).

We need not confuse this fictional poet-lover-worshipper with the historical Edmund Spenser, for this is the rhetorical *ethos*, or character, that from time immemorial has characterized the lyric voice. Our culture has granted three

---

[2] Murray F. Markland, "A Note on Spenser and the Scottish Sonneteers," *Studies in Scottish Literature*, I, 136–140.
[3] The same sonnet appears as both Sonnet 35 and and Sonnet 83. The numbering of the *Amoretti*, therefore, goes from 1 to 89.

types of imagination—the artistic, the erotic, and the religious—a license to speak out in describing their vision of things inaccessible to the dull sublunary mind of ordinary man. Writers of lyric verse have assumed these masks and seized their license in order to create the illusion that their fictions are authentic. For thousands of years it has been conventional to write religious and erotic poetry *as if* it were the record of actual experience. Only since the Romantic Movement have we called in the historian to test the value of a poem by testing the biographical authenticity of the experience it records. Spenser's great contribution to the renaissance lyric does not rest upon the quality of his own personal experience as lover, poet, and religious worshipper; rather it rests upon his imaginative demonstration that in the highest civilization the three persons are really one.

The structure of ideas in the medieval and renaissance love poem can be considered separately from the outward syntactical and metrical structure which distinguishes, for example, the Petrarchan from the English sonnet. It was in the structure of ideas that Petrarch held the strongest sway over the renaissance imagination. By Spenser's time the English had not so successfully liberated themselves from Petrarch's ideas as they had from his meter. Many Elizabethan sonnets were little more than translations into English of Petrarch or his Italian and French followers. The central structure for controlling the thought of a Petrarchan sonnet is the *conceit*, or, as we might call it, the pattern of metaphor.

It is probably fair to say that conceits are mental ornaments or decorations analogous to the grammatical ornamentation of meter and rhyme. When in Sonnet 10 of the *Amoretti* the poet calls his mistress a tyranness and asks the lord of love to enroll her faults in his black book that she might be brought to justice, we recognize the idea as a highly figurative way of saying that the poet wishes that his mistress could feel how it is to be subject to a strong and humiliating passion. The main objection to this kind of "conceited writing" has been that it disguises good honest thought and emotion under a conventionalized crust of hackneyed clichés. It is commonly felt that the liberation of Western love poetry from the artificiality of Petrarchan conceits liberated emotion from the bonds of cliché. However, almost the opposite point can be—but rarely is—advanced in defense of conceited writing.

Even the elaborate or the far-fetched conceit was more than mere ornamentation. It permitted renaissance poets to explore with metaphorical imagery those areas of human emotion and thought which were otherwise inaccessible to them. The Renaissance had neither the vocabulary nor the philosophical and psychological orientation that might serve as the basis for any more straightforward analysis of the extremely sophisticated and civilized form of idealized eroticism that was coming to be known in Western culture as "love." The elaborately conceited Provençal, Italian, French, German, and English love lyric was not a cumbersome description of a well-known human emotion. Rather it was the very instrument by which our Western conception of love was invented and given form. As allegory in narrative fiction was a method of consciously controlling the meaning of mythical and romantic narrative and of making genuine discoveries about the ethical and spiritual nature of man, so the metaphorical conceit in lyric poetry was an instrument for disciplining and controlling the utterances of blind and unself-conscious emotion. Because in the twentieth century we seem to suffer from a deficiency of mystery and unrationalized myth, our naive reaction to allegory and conceit is one of boredom with its conventionality. The Middle Ages and the Renaissance faced an opposite problem: how to bring to the surface *for analysis and interpretation* the urgings of both our passionate human nature and the images of our most persistent dreams and visions. Contrary to the usual handbook definitions, allegory and the conceit do not hide or veil or conceal meaning. They are rationalizing and analyzing devices without which Western man could not have illuminated the dark secrets of his own deepest nature—a nature which, nostalgically perhaps, we now wish were once again hidden beneath the veil of unrationalized myth and emotion.

Like nearly all conceits in renaissance love poetry, Spenser's are largely conventional. Only the seasoned expert is willing to label a given image or phrase as "original." Striking verbal and intellectual originality was not a positive virtue in the Renaissance. If originality is to be sought in the *Amoretti* at all, it will be found in the details with which conventional elements are recombined to constitute a characteristically Spenserian synthesis of spirit, flesh, and imagination in the description of a civilized courtship. Spenser's conceits, like Petrarch's, are frequently based on what can be thought of as a set of traditional "parodies." These "parodies" provided the raw material and the rules for generating an almost endless flow of metaphorical images.

One such "parody" was the medieval literary convention of the Court of Love, which saw a quasi-judicial procedure as the pattern for all relationships between the sexes. Presiding over the court was the lord of love, he of the black book in Sonnet 10. The unfairly handled lover could have his mistress hailed before the court of love for judgment; she could be in contempt of court; the lover could serve a sentence in prison; the lover could call upon an advocate to plead his case; and so on. Another "parody" visualized love as an armed conflict, with siege engines, truces, captives, generals, and so forth.

By far the most important, and most difficult for the modern reader to understand, was the convention of love as a parody of the Christian religion. Because of the close similarity between the poetry of religious worship and the poetry of idealized sexual love, the two traditions are almost impossible to disentangle. Religious writing used parodies of legal procedure and of military combat—and had since St. Paul. It even parodied sexual love in the passionate poetry inspired by such biblical texts as the Song of Songs. If erotic poetry parodied religion, religious poetry parodied sexual love, and the two traditions continued their mutual dependence until long after Spenser's time.

"Parody" is perhaps too strong a word, especially if we grant that its resultant conceits were devices of discovery and analysis. When Spenser's poet asserts, as he does so often, the heavenly origin and divine nature of his mistress, he means it. And the nature of her divinity can best be explored by momentarily considering himself the priest who serves at her altar. It is disrespectful neither to Christ nor to his mistress for the poet to claim that his love for one increases his love for the other. The two kinds of love influence and illuminate each other. In Sonnet 13, for example, the poet is gently and intelligently paradoxical in praising the "goodly temperature" of pride and humility in the bearing of his mistress, hinting that through her humility in loving him she may ultimately be loftier yet. The pattern is that of Christ's exaltation, love, humility, and resurrection. In Sonnet 61 the second year of the courtship begins with a recapitulation of this theme of the lady's heavenly birth and reasonable pride; but it does so without the jarring note of the poet's misery and impatience that had characterized the first year. The tone is confident and idealistic, and the military and legal conceits have been left behind. We conclude that the mistress's "lowliness" has indeed succeeded in making her "lofty be," for the poet's conception of her is loftier.

Throughout the *Amoretti* the physical description of the poet's mistress is close to the description of Belphoebe in Book II of *The Faerie Queene* (iii.22–30). The pride and haughtiness of Belphoebe and the mistress imply a Trompart's-eye view of them. As the poet's vision matures, she loses her aristocratic and military aspect, becoming both more physical and more spiritual. In terms of *The Faerie Queene*, she changes from Belphoebe to Amoretta of Books III and IV. The source of the conceits changes from a parody of social institutions to a parody of nature. Remembering that the sequel to the *Amoretti* is the *Epithalamion*, we recall that the penultimate image is the fruitful marriage bed, presided over by Genius, while the final image is that of the generation of new souls to increase the count of saints in heaven. In Sonnet 63 the mistress's embrace becomes a "happy shore." Her kiss in Sonnet 64 brings perfumes sweeter than those of a garden. In Sonnet 67 the poet invokes the ancient religious and erotic conceit of the beloved as a tame deer. A similar idea is found in the spider and the bee conceit of Sonnet 71. The Spenserian conception of overcoming the wretched and destructive humiliation of erotic passion through the loving body and soul is neither strictly Petrarchan nor Neoplatonic. It is more profoundly spiritual than the former and more physical than the latter. Sonnet 76 well illustrates this harmony of idealism and sensuality in Spenser's love poetry.

The conclusion of the *Amoretti* is somewhat obscure. Petrarch's odes and sonnets fall into two groups, those addressed to Laura living and those addressed to her after her death. From this archetype, an elegiac note of sadness at physical separation and of hopefulness of eventual spiritual reunion came to be seen as the fitting conclusion for a sonnet sequence. The physical separation in the *Amoretti* ought probably to be understood as resulting from a happier cause than either the mistress's death or the alienation of her affection as the product of the "false-forgèd lies" of Sonnet 86. It is instead the unavoidable separation of the lovers between the time of the lady's acknowledgment of her love for the poet and the marriage to be celebrated in the *Epithalamion*.

Sonnet 1

Happy ye leaves, whenas those lily hands
Which hold my life in their dead-doing° might   *killing*
Shall handle you, and hold in love's soft bands,
Like captives trembling at the victor's sight.
And happy lines, on which with starry light
Those lamping° eyes will deign sometimes to look,   *flashing*
And read the sorrows of my dying sprite,°   *spirit*
Written with tears in heart's close° bleeding book.   *secretly*
And happy rhymes, bathed in the sacred brook
Of Helicon, whence she derivèd is,
When ye behold that angel's blessed look,
My soul's long lackèd food, my heaven's bliss.
Leaves, lines, and rhymes, seek her to please alone,
Whom if ye please, I care for other none.

Sonnet 10

Unrighteous lord of love, what law is this,
That me thou makest thus tormented be,
The whiles she lordeth in licentious bliss
Of her free will, scorning both thee and me?
See how the tyranness doth joy to see
The huge massacres which her eyes do make,
And humbled hearts brings captives unto thee,
That thou of them mayst mighty vengeance take.
But her proud heart do thou a little shake,
And that high look, with which she doth control
All this world's pride, bow to a baser make,°   *partner*
And all her faults in thy black book enroll;
That I may laugh at her in equal sort
As she doth laugh at me and makes my pain her sport.

1.9–10   *sacred brook / Of Helicon:* the stream Hippocrene, which flows from Helicon, the mountain in Boeotia sacred to the Muses. Helicon stands in Spenser's poetry generally both for heaven and for the exalted status within the natural order in which perfected human nature receives divine inspiration. See *The Faerie Queene,* I.x.53–54, where Helicon as a place of inspiration is likened to Mt. Sinai and the Mount of Olives. Spenser here combines, in typical medieval and renaissance fashion, the convention of the poet's divine inspiration with that of the heavenly origin of his beloved.
10   The parody of legal procedure (*what law is this,* 10.1) is combined with the parody of warfare (*huge massacres,* 10.6) in this imitation of Petrarch's Madrigale IV (*Or vedi, Amore, che giovinetta donna*):

Now, Love, at length behold a youthful fair,
Who spurns thy rule, and, mocking all my care,
'Mid two such foes, is safe and fancy free.

(Trans. MacGregor in *The Sonnets, Triumphs, and Other Poems Of Petrarch,* Bohn's Illustrated Library, G. Bell & Sons, 1916, p. 111. Subsequent citations of Petrarch's Sonnets refer to this edition).

Sonnet 13

In that proud port,° which her só goodly graceth	*carriage*
Whiles her fair face she rears up to the sky	
And to the ground her eyelids low embaseth,	
Most goodly temperature° ye may descry,	*proportion*
Mild humbless mixed with awful majesty.	
For looking on the earth whence she was born,	
Her mind remembreth her mortality;	
Whatso is fairest shall to earth return.	
But that same lofty countenance seems to scorn	
Base thing, and think how she to heaven may climb,	
Treading down earth as loathsome and forlorn,	
That hinders heavenly thought with drossy slime.	
Yet lowly still vouchsafe to look on me;	
Such lowliness shall make you lofty be.	

Sonnet 16

One day as I unwarily did gaze	
On those fair eyes, my love's immortal light,	
The whiles my stonished heart stood in amaze	
Through sweet illusion of her look's delight,	
I mote° perceive how in her glancing sight	*could*
Legions of loves° with little wings did fly,	*cupids (amoretti)*
Darting their deadly arrows fiery bright	
At every rash beholder passing by.	
One of those archers closely° I did spy,	*secretly*
Aiming his arrow at my very heart;	
When suddenly with twinkle° of her eye,	*blinking*
The damsel broke his misintended dart.	
Had she not so done, sure I had been slain;	
Yet as it was, I hardly° scaped with pain.	*barely*

13   The main idea is to be found (and may have originated) in Petrarch's Sonnet 179 (*In nobil sangue vita umile e queta*), "A noble birth and yet a humble life."

16.6   *Legions of loves:* Compare the *Hymn of Beauty*, 231–245, for an explanation of these agents, both of libido and compassion, traveling with their tiny arrows along the beams from one lover's eyes into the heart of the other. While the little cupids were part of a consciously conventional and artificial myth, a more sober theory of psychic communication held that beams were emitted from lovers' eyes that made their way from one heart to another. Typical is the speech of Mag- nifico Giuliano in Castiglione's *The Book of the Courtier*, III.66: "For those lively spirits that issue out at the eyes, because they are engendered nigh the heart, entering in like case into the eyes that they are levelled at, like a shaft to the prick, naturally pierce to the heart, as to their resting place and there are at rest with those other spirits: and with the most subtle and fine nature of blood which they carry with them, infect the blood about the heart, where they are come to, and warm it; and make it like unto themselves, and apt to receive the imprinting of the image, which they have carried away with them" (trans. Sir Thomas Hoby, Everyman, p. 247).

Sonnet 22

This holy season fit to fast and pray,
Men to devotion ought to be inclined;
Therefore I likewise on so holy day,
For my sweet saint some service fit will find.
Her temple fair is built within my mind,
In which her glorious image placèd is,
On which my thoughts do day and night attend,
Like sacred priests that never think amiss.
There I to her as th' author of my bliss
Will build an altar to appease her ire,
And on the same my heart will sacrifice,
Burning in flames of pure and chaste desire;
The which vouchsafe, O goddess, to accept,
Amongst thy dearest relics to be kept.

Sonnet 28

The laurel leaf which you this day do wear
Gives me great hope of your relenting mind,
For since it is the badge which I do bear,
Ye bearing it do seem to me inclined.
The power thereof, which oft in me I find,
Let it likewise your gentle breast inspire
With sweet infusion, and put you in mind
Of that proud maid whom now those leaves attire:
Proud Daphne, scorning Phoebus' lovely° fire,   amorous
On the Thessalian shore from him did flee;
For which the gods in their revengeful ire
Did her transform into a laurel tree.
Then fly no more, fair love, from Phoebus' chase,
But in your breast his leaf and love embrace.

Sonnet 29

See how the stubborn damsel doth deprave
My simple meaning with disdainful scorn,

22.1 *This holy season:* either some saint's day or (more likely) Lent.

28–29 The laurel leaf is appropriately the badge (28.3) of the poet, since it was sacred to Apollo, the god of science, divination, music, and hence, of poetic inspiration. Ovid in *Metamorphoses*, I.452–567 (pp. 44–47) tells the story of Cupid's wounding Apollo with a golden arrow, causing him to love, and Daphne with a leaden arrow, causing her to scorn the god. The nymph's desperate flight from Apollo's embrace ended in her transformation into a laurel tree, henceforth the sign of victory in military and athletic, as well as poetic, contests. Apollo tells her, "You will accompany the generals of Rome, when the Capitol beholds their long triumphal processions, when joyful voices raise the song of victory" (*Metamorphoses*, I.560–560, p. 47). Thus in Sonnet 28 the poet alludes to the laurel as his token, the sign of the ardent poet-lover, while in Sonnet 29 his mistress replies that the leaf is, on the contrary, her token, the sign of military conquest.

28.10 *flee:* (1617). 1595 reads *flie.*

And by the bay° which I unto her gave   *laurel leaf*
Accounts myself her captive quite forlorn.
'The bay,' quoth she, 'is of° the victors borne,   *by*
Yielded them by the vanquished as their meeds,°   *rewards*
And they therewith do poets' heads adorn
To sing the glory of their famous deeds.'
But sith she will° the conquest challenge needs,°   *must* (will needs)
Let her accept me as her faithful thrall,
That her great triumph, which my skill exceeds,
I may in trump of fame blaze over all.
Then would I deck her head with glorious bays,
And fill the world with her victorious praise.

Sonnet 37

What guile is this, that those her golden tresses
She doth attire under a net of gold,
And with sly skill so cunningly them dresses
That which is gold or hair may scarce be told?
Is it that men's frail eyes which gaze too bold
She may entangle in that golden snare,
And being caught, may craftily enfold
Their weaker° hearts, which are not well aware?   *too weak*
Take heed therefore, mine eyes, how ye do stare
Henceforth too rashly on that guileful net,
In which if ever ye entrappèd are,
Out of her bands ye by no means shall get.
Fondness° it were for any, being free,   *foolishness*
To covet fetters, though they golden be.

Sonnet 40

Mark when she smiles with amiable cheer,
And tell me whereto can ye liken it,
When on each eyelid sweetly do appear
An hundred Graces as in shade to sit.
Likest it seemeth, in my simple wit,
Unto the fair sunshine in summer's day,
That when a dreadful storm away is flit°   *passed*
Through the broad world doth spread his goodly ray;

37 The setting of the conceit is suggested by Petrarch's Sonnet 69 (*Erano i capei d' oro all' aura sparsi*), "Loose to the breeze her golden tresses flowed."
40.4 *An hundred Graces:* The Graces (Gr. *Charites*) are usually pictured in renaissance art as three beautiful women, associated with aspects of Venus. Like the nymphs and the Hours, however, the Graces were originally of indefinite number, presiding over all aspects of nature which evoke spontaneous joy and pleasure.

At sight whereof each bird that sits on spray,°   *branch*
And every beast that to his den was fled,
Comes forth afresh out of their late dismay,
And to the light lift up their drooping head.
So my storm-beaten heart likewise is cheered
With that sunshine when cloudy looks are cleared.

Sonnet 45

Leave, lady, in your glass of crystal clean
Your goodly self for evermore to view;
And in my self, my inward self I mean,
Most lively-like behold your semblant° true.   *image*
Within my heart, though hardly it can shew
Thing so divine to view of earthly eye,
The fair idea° of your celestial hue°   *mental image,*
And every part remains immortally;   *form*
And were it not that through your cruelty
With sorrow dimmèd and deformed it were,
The goodly image of your visnomy°   *face*
Clearer than crystal would therein appear.
But if yourself in me ye plain will see,
Remove the cause by which your fair beams darkened be.

Sonnet 50

Long languishing in double malady
Of my heart's wound and of my body's grief,
There came to me a leech° that would apply   *physician*
Fit medicines for my body's best relief.
'Vain man,' quod I, 'that hast but little prief°   *skill*
In deep discovery of the mind's disease,
Is not the heart of all the body chief,
And rules the members as itself doth please?
Then with some cordials seek first to appease
The inward languor of my wounded heart,
And then my body shall have shortly ease.'
But such sweet cordials pass° physician's art.   *surpass*

45.3   *And in my self:* Applied to the poet's *inward self*, the words *semblant, idea,* and *image* are metaphors based on the mirror (*glass of crystal clean*) mentioned in 45.1. The whole conceit, that a more faithful and spiritual "image" of his beloved is to be found in the lover's heart than in her mirror, is a commonplace of the French and Italian sonnet traditions. The argument of the conceit is based, in turn, on the vaguely Platonic notion that the divine "idea" of a beautiful form is "truer" than is the manifestation of form in mere physical matter. Beyond this basic notion, the further conceit of the sestet (45.9–14), that the "mirror" of the poet's heart is clouded by his sorrow and that the lady must treat him with greater kindness if she wants to see her true reflection, is not specifically Platonic in the least.

Then, my life's leech, do you your skill reveal,
And with one salve both heart and body heal.

Sonnet 54

Of this world's theater in which we stay,
My love like the spectator idly sits,
Beholding me that all the pageants° play,   *scenes*
Disguising diversely my troubled wits.
Sometimes I joy when glad occasion fits
And mask in mirth like to a comedy;
Soon after, when my joy to sorrow flits,
I wail and make my woes a tragedy.
Yet she beholding me with constant eye
Delights not in my mirth nor rues my smart;
But when I laugh she mocks, and when I cry
She laughs, and hardens evermore her heart.
What then can move her? If nor mirth nor moan,
She is no woman, but a senseless stone.

Sonnet 60

They that in course of heavenly spheres are skilled,
To every planet point° his° sundry year,   *appoint, its*
In which her° circle's voyage is fulfilled,   i.e. *the planet's*
As Mars in three score years doth run his sphere.
So since the wingèd god his planet clear
Began in me to move, one year is spent;
The which doth longer unto me appear

50.13 *my life's leech:* The comparison
of the lady to a physician was old when
Chaucer used it in *The Book of the
Duchess:* "For there is phisicien but oon /
That may me hele" (39–40). It may origi-
nally have been a courtly parody of God
as Physician: "He healeth those that are
broken in heart: and giveth medicine to
heal their sickness" (*Book of Common
Prayer,* Psalm 147).
54.1 *this world's theater:* For an his-
torical account of the metaphor of the
theatrum mundi (world's theater), from
Plato to Hofmannsthal, including Ron-
sard's "Le monde est un theatre, et les
hommes acteurs" and Shakespeare's
somewhat later "All the world's a stage,"
see Curtius, pp. 138–144. While the meta-
phor was a favorite of both classical and
medieval writers, it was not a stock
feature of the sonnet tradition.
60.2 *To every planet point his sundry*

year: Because of the movement of both
the earth and the other planets in orbits
about the sun, any given planet (Gr.
planētēs, 'wanderer') appears to move
irregularly with respect to both the sun
and the stars. The planetary "year" to
which Spenser refers is probably the time
required for a planet to move away from,
and to reappear in (approximately) a
given position in the sky with respect to
the sun.
60.6 *one year is spent:* This reference
to the passage of a year in the poet's
courtship of his mistress is a significant
element in the narrative plot of the
Amoretti. Such time references are com-
mon in the sonnet sequences. They do not
necessarily correspond to stages in an
actual courtship; but they are a useful
fictional device for creating the illusion of
actuality. See Introduction.

Than all those forty which my life outwent.
Then by that count which lovers' books invent,
The sphere of Cupid forty years contains;
Which I have wasted in long languishment,
That seemed the longer for my greater pains.
But let my love's fair planet short her ways
This year ensuing, or else short my days.

Sonnet 61

The glorious image of the Maker's beauty,
My sovereign saint, the idol of my thought,
Dare not henceforth above the bounds of duty
T' accuse of pride, or rashly blame for aught.
For being as she is divinely wrought,
And of the brood of angels heavenly born,
And with the crew of blessed saints upbrought,
Each of which did her with their gifts adorn—
The bud of joy, the blossom of the morn,
The beam of light, whom mortal eyes admire—
What reason is it then but she should scorn
Base things that to her love too bold aspire?
Such heavenly forms ought rather worshipped be
Than dare be loved by men of mean degree.

Sonnet 63

After long storms and tempests' sad assay,°   *painful ordeal*
Which hardly I endurèd heretofore,
In dread of death and dangerous dismay,
With which my silly° bark was tossèd sore,   *simple*
I do at length descry the happy shore
In which I hope ere long for to arrive.
Fair soil it seems from far, and fraught° with store   *loaded*
Of all that dear and dainty is alive.
Most happy he that can at last achieve

60.8   *all those forty:* Spenser probably was about forty-one years old when his relationship with Elizabeth Boyle had actually reached a point comparable to this stage in the fictional courtship. If the fictional marriage on June 11th in the *Epithalamion* corresponds exactly to the date of Spenser's own marriage, the year of the marriage may well have been 1594. This conjectural wedding date further suggests the date 1593 for the period in Spenser's actual life corresponding to this particular fictional moment in the *Amoretti.* We arrive by this process at the date 1552 for the year of Spenser's birth.

60.10–14   *The sphere of Cupid forty years contains:* The conceit is highly metaphorical. Its meaning is clear enough, however: one year of unrequited love *seems* as long as forty normal years.

63.1–8   The nautical metaphor is a commonplace of the sonnet tradition, as in Western literature generally. In Book I of *The Faerie Queene* Spenser used the metaphor (xii.42) of the poet's progress in his narrative as a sea journey. Here his progress in love is the journey. For examples of the metaphor in a dozen ancient and medieval poets, see Curtius, pp. 128–130.

The joyous safety of so sweet a rest,
Whose least delight sufficeth to deprive
Remembrance of all pains which him oppressed.
All pains are nothing in respect of this,
All sorrows short that gain eternal bliss.

Sonnet 64

Coming to kiss her lips—such grace I found—
Me seemed I smelled a garden of sweet flowers,
That dainty odors from them threw around,
For damsels fit to deck their lovers' bowers.
Her lips did smell like unto gillyflowers,
Her ruddy cheeks like unto roses red,
Her snowy brows like budded bellamours,
Her lovely eyes like pinks but newly spread;
Her goodly bosom like a strawberry bed,
Her neck like to a bunch of columbines,
Her breast like lilies ere their leaves be shed,
Her nipples like young blossomed jasamines.
Such fragrant flowers do give most odorous smell,
But her sweet odor did them all excel.

Sonnet 67

Like as a huntsman after weary chase,
Seeing the game from him escaped away,
Sits down to rest him in some shady place,
With panting hounds beguilèd of their prey;
So after long pursuit and vain assay,°   *attempt*
When I all weary had the chase forsook,
The gentle deer returned the selfsame way,
Thinking to quench her thirst at the next brook.
There she beholding me with milder look
Sought not to fly, but fearless still did bide,
Till I in hand her yet half trembling took,
And with her own good will her firmly tied.
Strange thing me seemed, to see a beast so wild
So goodly won, with her own will beguiled.

Sonnet 68

Most glorious Lord of Life, that on this day
Didst make thy triumph over death and sin,

64.2–14 Continuing the metaphor of the progress to a "happy shore" of "fair soil," Spenser draws upon the long tradition in erotic poetry of comparing his love to a garden. This metaphor received its classic statement in the Song of Songs 4:12–15 ("A garden inclosed is my sister, my spouse . . .").
67 The image of the deer may have been suggested by Petrarch's Sonnet 157 (*Una candida cerva sopra l' erba*), "A milk-white fawn upon the meadow green."
68.1 *this day:* Easter Sunday.

And having harrowed hell, didst bring away
Captivity thence captive, us to win,
This joyous day, dear Lord, with joy begin,
And grant that we for whom thou diddest die,
Being with thy dear blood clean washed from sin,
May live forever in felicity;
And that thy love we weighing worthily
May likewise love thee for the same again;
And for thy sake, that all like dear didst buy,
With love may one another entertain.
So let us love, dear love, like as we ought;
Love is the lesson which the Lord us taught.

Sonnet 71

I joy to see how in your drawen work
Yourself unto the bee ye do compare,
And me unto the spider that doth lurk
In close await° to catch her unaware.   *ambush*
Right so yourself were caught in cunning snare
Of a dear foe, and thrallèd to his love,
In whose strait bands ye now captivèd are
So firmly that ye never may remove.
But as your work is woven all about
With woodbind flowers and fragrant eglantine,
So sweet your prison you in time shall prove,°   *discover*
With many dear delights bedeckèd fine.
And all thenceforth eternal peace shall see
Between the spider and the gentle bee.

Sonnet 75

One day I wrote her name upon the strand,
But came the waves and washèd it away;
Again I wrote it with a second hand,
But came the tide and made my pains his prey.

68.3–4 "When he ascended up on high, he led captivity captive. . . . Now that he ascended, what is it but that he also descended first into the lower parts of the earth? He that descended is the same also that ascended up far above all heavens" (Ephesians 4:8–10).

68.7 "Unto him that loved us, and washed us from our sins in his own blood" (Revelation 1:5).

68.14 "This is my commandment, that ye love one another, as I have loved you" (John 15:12).

71 The enmity between the spider and the butterfly, with tragic conse-quences to the innocent intruder, is the subject of the mock-heroic *Muiopotmos*.

71.1 *drawen work:* drawn work; tapes-try.

75 For the *topos* of "poetry as per-petuation," of which this is a classic statement, see Curtius, pp. 476–477, where it is traced from Homer to Ariosto. In erotic poetry, it was old when Ovid wrote "Gowns will be rent to rags, and gems and gold be broke to fragments; the glory my songs shall give will last for ever" (*Amores,* I.X.61–62). Compare Shakespeare's Sonnet 55, "Not marble, nor the gilded monuments."

'Vain man,' said she, 'that dost in vain assay
A mortal thing so to immortalize,
For I myself shall like to this decay,
And eke° my name be wipèd out likewise.'   *also*
'Not so,' quod I, 'let baser things devise
To die in dust, but you shall live by fame;
My verse your virtues rare shall eternize,
And in the heavens write your glorious name.
Where whenas death shall all the world subdue,
Our love shall live, and later life renew.'

Sonnet 76

Fair bosom fraught with virtue's richest treasure—
The nest of love, the lodging of delight,
The bower of bliss, the paradise of pleasure,
The sacred harbor of that heavenly sprite—
How was I ravished with your lovely sight,
And my frail thoughts too rashly led astray!
Whiles diving deep through amorous insight,
On the sweet spoil of beauty they did prey;
And twixt her paps,° like early fruit in May   *breasts*
Whose harvest seemed to hasten now apace,
They loosely did their wanton wings display,
And there to rest themselves did boldly place.
Sweet thoughts, I envy your so happy rest,
Which oft I wished, yet never was so blessed.

Sonnet 79

Men call you fair, and you do credit° it,   *believe*
For that yourself ye daily such do see;
But the true fair,° that is the gentle wit   *beauty*
And virtuous mind, is much more praised of° me.   *by*
For all the rest, however fair it be,
Shall turn to nought and lose that glorious hue;
But only that is permanent and free
From frail corruption that doth flesh ensue.°   *outlast*
That is true beauty. That doth argue you
To be divine and born of heavenly seed,
Derived from that fair spirit from whom all true
And perfect beauty did at first proceed.
He only fair, and what he fair hath made;
All other fair like flowers untimely fade.

79.11 *that fair spirit:* the Holy Ghost;   Beauty is derived. See Spenser's *Hymn of*
or the Sapience from which Heavenly   *Heavenly Beauty.*

Sonnet 84

Let not one spark of filthy lustful fire
Break out that may her sacred peace molest,
Ne one light glance of sensual desire
Attempt to work her gentle mind's unrest.
But pure affections bred in spotless breast,
And modest thoughts breathed from well tempered sprites,°   *spirits*
Go visit her in her chaste bower of rest,
Accompanied with angelic delights.
There fill yourself with those most joyous sights,
The which myself could never yet attain;
But speak no word to her of these sad plights
Which her too constant stiffness doth constrain.
Only behold her rare perfection,
And bless your fortune's fair election.

Sonnet 86

Venomous tongue, tipped with vile adder's sting,
Of that self kind with which the Furies fell°   *horrible*
Their snaky heads do comb, from which a spring
Of poisoned words and spiteful speeches well!
Let all the plagues and horrid pains of hell
Upon thee fall for thine accursèd hire;°   *reward*
That with false forgèd lies which thou didst tell
In my true love did stir up coals of ire,
The sparks whereof let kindle thine own fire,
And catching hold on thine own wicked head
Consume thee quite, that didst with guile conspire
In my sweet peace such breaches to have bred.
Shame be thy meed, and mischief thy reward,
Due to thyself, that it for me prepared.

84.9 *yourself:* should perhaps read *yourselves,* referring to the *pure affections* and *modest thoughts* which may visit the mistress in her bedroom, though the poet himself is constrained from doing so.

84.14 *election:* suggests the theological concept of God's selection of a soul for salvation. The whole conceit is a less playful, more "Platonic" version of Sonnet 76.

86 The calumny of envious rivals is one of the traditional perils of the lover. Compare, for example, the poet's defense of himself against the slander of others in Petrarch's Canzone 19 (*S'i'l dissi mai, ch' i' venga in odio a quella*), "If I said so, may I be hated by her on whose love I live." Here, however, as elsewhere in his writings, Spenser goes beyond the conventions of love poetry in the bitterness of his complaint against the backbiters, liars, and envious defamers who threaten virtue, love, courtesy, and the whole fabric of civilized life. The spider Aragnoll in *Muiopotmos,* the false shepherd Menalcus in the June Eclogue, and the Blatant Beast in Book VI of *The Faerie Queene* are only three exemplars of this characteristically Spenserian conception of falseness in personal and social relationships. They are specific manifestations of the spiritual falseness of which Archimago in Book I of *The Faerie Queene* is the general symbol.

Sonnet 88

Since I have lacked the comfort of that light,
The which was wont to lead my thoughts astray,°   *my strayed thoughts*
I wander as in darkness of the night,
Afraid of every danger's least dismay.
Ne aught I see, though in the clearest day,
When others gaze upon their shadows vain,
But th' only image° of that heavenly ray,   *only the image*
Whereof some glance doth in mine eye remain.
Of which beholding the idea plain
Through contemplation of my purest part,
With light thereof I do myself sustain,
And thereon feed my love-affamished heart.
But with such brightness whilst I fill my mind,
I starve my body and mine eyes do blind.

Sonnet 89

Like as the culver° on the barèd bough   *dove*
Sits mourning for the absence of her mate,
And in her songs sends many a wishful vow
For his return that seems to linger late,
So I alone now left disconsolate
Mourn to myself the absence of my love,
And wandering here and there all desolate
Seek with my plaints to match that mournful dove.
Ne joy of aught that under heaven doth hove°   *spring*
Can comfort me, but her own joyous sight,
Whose sweet aspect both God and man can move
In her unspotted pleasance to delight.
Dark is my day whiles her fair light I miss,
And dead my life that wants° such lively bliss.   *lacks*

88–89 Compare Sonnets 76 and 84 for the comfort the poet had enjoyed when his "frail" (76.6) and "modest (84.6) thoughts" were led astray to the contemplation of his mistress's beauty. As in the two earlier sonnets, so here that beauty is both physical and spiritual. Its influence helps sustain both the poet's body and his mind. While one half of his being can find satisfaction in the spiritual image implanted in his mind, the separation from his mistress results in the poet's physical inability to function in the merely material world about him. In these last two sonnets of the *Amoretti*, the poet laments only the absence of his mistress's beauty. There is no suggestion that the separation was produced by the "venomous tongues" of Sonnet 86, or that her love has diminished—only that she is away.

Epithalamion

INTRODUCTION

The *Epithalamion* is Spenser's most conventional and, at the same time, his most original poem. It is also one of a few great lyric poems in English, to be compared in its variety and vitality with Keats' great odes and Wordsworth's *Tintern Abbey*. The form of Spenser's poem is that of the Italian *canzone*, a rare form in English poetry. The *canzone*, as practiced by Dante and Petrarch, consists of a few long stanzas of equal length followed by a short stanza called a *tornata*, which rhetorically is an address to the song just completed. Typically, in Dante and Petrarch, there are five or six long stanzas of thirteen lines in which the predominant five-foot line is varied by one or more three-foot lines. The *tornata* varies from five to seven lines and usually has one short line.[1] Although the *Epithalamion* depends in its form upon the *canzone*, its variations from the Italian models should be noted. Spenser's poem contains twenty-three long stanzas, varying in length from seventeen to nineteen lines; thus both the individual stanzas and the poem are longer than the Italian form, and the varying length of Spenser's stanza contrasts with the regular *canzone* stanza.

If the *Epithalamion* owes something to Dante and Petrarch, it owes still more to Latin poetry and to Catullus particularly. The great *Epithalamium 61* of Catullus is required reading for anyone who wants to understand Spenser's achievement. For the poets of the Renaissance the epithalamia of the Roman poet (61, 62, and 64) are both the beginning and the supreme models of the marriage song (*epithalamion* can be translated roughly as "on the marriage bed"). In the classical epithalamium two different developments took place. In the first of these, represented by Catullus 64, the development is rather epic than lyric, a song about the loves of gods and heroes, a marriage attended by all Olympus. The second type of epithalamium, represented by Catullus 61, does not lack mythological elements, but its subject is the marriage of real humans. Typically it sings of the dawning of the wedding day, of the festive celebrations, of the beauty of the bride, of the eagerness of the groom. It prays that the union may be fruitful so that the family line may be preserved. Renaissance poets generally chose to follow the first type of epithalamium, perhaps

[1] See examples of canzone in *The Penguin Book of Italian Verse*, ed. George Kay, pp. 85–88, 91–95, 116–119.

because of the concern of the age with mythology and because so many renaissance epithalamia were celebrations of marriages between the great aristocratic families of Europe. Spenser chose to follow the second type of epithalamium, partly because his poem was to be more personal and less public than the fully developed mythological type would have allowed, for his song celebrates his own marriage to Elizabeth Boyle in or near Kilcolman, Ireland, in the summer of 1594. No doubt Spenser felt that the epic epithalamium was inappropriate for the marriage of a middle-aged, widowed minor civil servant to the young daughter of an old but not great family. At any rate he chose the more private, more lyrical form and made it his own by mixing with the conventions of the epithalamium as practiced by Catullus and his French renaissance followers details of the Irish locale and folk customs of the English countryside. An even more important transformation of epithalamic convention was accomplished merely by the fact that Spenser decided to celebrate his marriage and praise his young bride by writing his own marriage song; Latin and most renaissance epithalamia had been rather official occasional pieces, written by poets not personally involved in the love they celebrated. If the greatness of the *Epithalamion* is to be explained at all, it may be due to a miraculous blending of the restraints imposed by long literary convention and the fervor of deep personal involvement.

Recently Professor Kent Hieatt has, we think, demonstrated a kind of originality in the *Epithalamion* never suspected before.[2] The basic facts are the following: 1) there are 365 long lines in the poem; 2) the poem is made up of 24 stanzas; 3) night falls, and the refrain changes in the 17th stanza; 4) there is an attempt, by similarities in diction, imagery, and thought, to establish a parallel between stanzas 1–12 and stanzas 13–24 (see our notes to stanzas 13–24); and 5) there are 359 long lines in the poem before the *tornata*. Some of these facts are perhaps not surprising. The *Epithalamion* begins at dawn and ends just before dawn the next day. Since it covers a twenty-four hour period, it is appropriate that the poem contain 24 stanzas. However, Spenser's concern to symbolize time and its passage is unusual and intricate. The hours of daylight at the summer solstice (when the wedding took place) in Southern Ireland (where the wedding occurred) were approximately 16¼. The refrain of the poem changes in stanza 17, which is divided into four sections by its short lines, and night is said to fall at the end of the first of these sections (16¼). Professor Hieatt argues, in fact, that *Epithalamion* is, in its structure, a symbol of time in all its aspects. The 365 long lines of the poem symbolize the year. The 24 stanzas represent not only the passage of time on Spenser's wedding day, but also the sidereal hours (see note on 98–102), which as Spenser says "allot the seasons." Indeed the various divisions of the 24 stanzas represent the seasons. The first 16 stanzas represent the summer solstice; the 8 following stanzas, the winter solstice, the shortest day; and the two parallel series of stanzas 1–12 and 13–24 represent the two equinoxes of spring and fall. Finally the 359 long lines before the *tornata* are symbolic of the fact that while the sphere of the fixed stars (and the sidereal hours) has completed its 360° east-west orbit, the sun, hanging back, has finished only 359° of its daily orbit. Spenser is saying that when his poem (the sphere of the fixed stars) is over, it

[2] A. Kent Hieatt, *Short Time's Endless Monument*, Columbia University Press, 1960.

is still not complete (359°). As explained in the note on 98–102, it is this hanging back of the sun that makes the seasons and the year. Professor Hieatt's discovery of the allegory of time in the *Epithalamion* is especially important because, for the first time, it provides a convincing interpretation of the *tornata*. The lines, "Which cutting off through hasty accidents, / Ye would not stay your due time to expect," always a problem before, now become clear. The song, which should have been a perfect ornament—a necklace perhaps—was "cut off" by being finished by the 359th line. Thus it was only an inadequate representation of the sun's orbit, the orbit of the sidereal hours, and the year. The "hasty accidents" are the poem's *accidence*, the sounds and rhythms which make up the poem. The poem would not "stay" its "due time to expect," again because it had come to an end before it has reached completion—360° and 365 days. It had been born before its time. But the *tornata* "recompenses" all of this. It makes a perfect ornament by making symbolically a full circle of the poem. Indeed the *Epithalamion*, celebrating the "short time" of a single day, is an endless monument, symbolizing the ceaseless circles of the sun, the hours, the seasons, and the years.

The modern reader is likely to have some reservations about the elaborate time symbolism of the *Epithalamion*. What has the intricate allegory of time to do with the subject of the poem? How is the marriage of the poet and his young bride related to this allegory? Spenser, in common with most men of his time and of earlier times, saw the life of man as a reflection in little of the operation of the whole of creation. There was the cosmos and then there was man, the *micro*cosm. For both, there was birth and youth (spring), maturity (summer), middle age (fall), and old age and death (winter). As the ceaseless revolutions of the stars and the planets usher in a continual round of change, making an eternity of endless mutability; so men and women, themselves creatures of change, create in marriage a kind of eternity by bringing children to life, children who, in their turn, will continue the life of the microcosm. Furthermore, human love and marriage create another kind of eternity of the merely temporary stuff of earthly life, for the children, who are the end of marriage and who guarantee the preservation of life within time, may inherit a true eternity outside of time. Their souls are immortal and they may die to live forever in heaven. The allegory of time, then, is a passionate exaltation of married love as the means by which imperfect, changeful mortals make eternity.

A modern reader, however, is likely to object in principle to this kind of symbolism as being external to the poem, or inorganic. What is organic in the literature of any time will depend partly upon what is organic in the life and thought of the time—what experiences, sensations, ideas are seen to be obviously or naturally or reasonably related in a coherent structure of belief and action. All that one can say is that the symbolism of time which informs the *Epithalamion* was part of such a coherent structure, in which marriage, sexual love, time, and eternity seemed obviously and naturally related. This answer may not modify anyone's reservations much, but perhaps an entirely satisfactory answer on this point is not necessary to an appreciation of the poem. Keats', Yeats', and Eliot's reasons for loving the *Epithalamion* are perfectly good ones. The marvelous variety of effects, in rhythm, in language, in tone, is satisfaction enough.

EPITHALAMION

Ye learned sisters, which have oftentimes
Been to me aiding, others to adorn
Whom ye thought worthy of your graceful rhymes,
That° even the greatest did not greatly scorn   *so that*
To hear their names sung in your simple lays,
But joyèd in their praise—
And when ye list your own mishaps to mourn,
Which death, or love, or fortune's wreck° did raise,   *destruction*
Your string could soon to sadder tenor° turn,   *song*
10 And teach the woods and waters to lament
Your doleful dreariment°—   *sorrow*
Now lay those sorrowful complaints aside,
And having all your heads with garland crowned,
Help me mine own love's praises to resound.°   *extol*
Ne let the same of° any be envied;   *by*
So Orpheus did for his own bride,
So I unto myself alone will sing.
The woods shall to me answer, and my echo ring.

Early, before the world's light-giving lamp
20 His golden beam upon the hills doth spread,
Having dispersed the night's uncheerful damp,
Do ye awake, and with fresh lustihead°   *vigor*
Go to the bower° of my beloved love,   *bedroom*
My truest turtledove.
Bid her awake, for Hymen is awake
And long since ready forth his masque° to move,   *pageant*

1 *learned sisters:* "the goddess alighted, and addressed the learned sisters" (Ovid, *Metamorphoses*, V, p. 133). The learned sisters are the nine muses.
2 Spenser refers to poems of his in praise of famous men and women of Elizabethan England: Queen Elizabeth (*The Faerie Queene*), Sir Walter Raleigh (*Colin Clout*), Sir Philip Sidney (*Astrophel*). Like most poets of the Renaissance, Spenser is largely an *epideictic* poet, concerned with praise of great men and great actions.
7–11 These lines refer especially to Spenser's poem "The Tears of the Muses," published with a number of other short poems in *Complaints*, 1591.
10–11 ". . . and you lie sprawling in the shade, teaching the woods to echo

back the charms of Amaryllis" (Virgil, *The Pastoral Poems*, I.4–5, trans. E. V. Rieu, Penguin Books, p. 21).
16 This line probably depends on the opening lines of Ovid's *Metamorphoses*, X, where Orpheus calls Hymen to attend his wedding and celebrate it in song.
18 "We are not singing to the deaf: the forest echoes every word" (Virgil, *The Pastoral Poems*, X.8, p. 113). A common refrain in Spenser's poetry.
24 The faithful love of the turtledove is mentioned in Ovid's *Amores*, II.6. "O my dove, that art in the clefts of the rock, in the secret places of the stairs, let me see thy countenance . . ." (Song of Solomon 2:14).
25 *Hymen:* the god of the marriage festival.

With his bright tead° that flames with many a flake,°   *torch, flash*
And many a bachelor to wait on him
In their fresh garments trim.
30 Bid her awake, therefore, and soon her dight;°   *dress*
For lo, the wishèd day is come at last
That shall for all the pains and sorrows past
Pay to her usury° of long delight.   *interest*
And whilst she doth her dight,
Do ye to her of joy and solace° sing,   *pleasure*
That all the woods may answer, and your echo ring.

Bring with you all the nymphs that you can hear,°   *can hear you*
Both of the rivers and the forests green
And of the sea that neighbors to her near,
40 All with gay garlands goodly well beseen.°   *beautifully adorned*
And let them also with them bring in hand
Another gay garland
For my fair love, of lilies and of roses,
Bound truelove-wise with a blue silk riband.
And let them make great store of bridal posies,°   *bouquets*
And let them eke° bring store of other flowers   *also*
To deck the bridal bowers.
And let the ground whereas her foot shall tread,
For fear the stones her tender foot should wrong,
50 Be strewed with fragrant flowers all along,
And diapered° like the discolored mead.°   *variegated, many colored meadow*
Which done, do at her chamber door await,
For she will waken straight.
The whiles do ye this song unto her sing;
The woods shall to you answer, and your echo ring.

Ye nymphs of Mulla, which with careful heed
The silver scaly trouts do tend full well,
And greedy pikes which use therein to feed—
Those trouts and pikes all others do excel—
60 And ye likewise which keep the rushy lake,

27 For the association of torches and Hymen and the marriage celebration see Catullus, *Odi et Amo* 61 (trans. Roy Arthur Swanson, Library of Liberal Arts, p. 52). "Hymen, choose thou the festal torches, and ye Graces gather flowers for the feast" (Claudian, "Epithalamium of Honorius and Maria," *Claudian*, trans. Maurice Platnauer, Loeb Classical Library, Vol. 1, p. 257).
37–51 For the convention which underlies these lines see Catullus, *Odi et Amo* 64, p. 74, and Claudian, "Epithalamium of Honorius and Maria," p. 259.
44 *blue silk riband:* a love knot, blue representing fidelity.
49 "They shall bear thee up in their hands, lest thou dash thy foot against a stone" (Psalms 91:12).
56 *Mulla:* Spenser's name for the river Awbeg, which lay on the eastern and southern borders of Spenser's Irish estate, Kilcolman. Kilcolman was a 3,000 acre grant about half way between Limerick in the north and Cork in the south.
60 *rushy lake:* A large lake lies immediately south of Kilcolman Castle. Even today fish are found only infrequently in this lake.

Where none do fishes take:°   *catch*
Bind up the·locks the which hang scattered light,
And in his waters, which your mirror make,
Behold your faces as the crystal bright,
That when you come whereas my love doth lie,
No blemish she may spy.
And eke ye lightfoot maids which keep the deer°   *animals*
That on the hoary mountain use to tower,°   *climb high*
And the wild wolves which seek them to devour
70 With your steel darts do chase from coming near,
Be also present here
To help to deck her and to help to sing,
That all the woods may answer, and your echo ring.

Wake now, my love, awake, for it is time.
The rosy morn long since left Tithon's bed,
All ready to her silver coach to climb,
And Phoebus gins to show his glorious head.
Hark how the cheerful birds do chant their lays
And carol of love's praise—
80 The merry lark her matins° sings aloft,   *morning prayer*
The thrush replies, the mavis° descant° plays,   *thrush, melody*
The ouzel° shrills, the ruddock° warbles soft—   *blackbird, robin*
So goodly all agree with sweet concent°   *harmony*
To this day's merriment.
Ah my dear love, why do ye sleep thus long,
When meeter° were that ye should now awake   *more fitting*
T' await the coming of your joyous make,°   *mate*
And hearken to the birds' love-learnèd song
The dewy leaves among.
90 For they of joy and pleasance to you sing,
That all the woods them answer, and their echo ring.

My love is now awake out of her dreams,
And her fair eyes like stars that dimmèd were
With darksome cloud now show their goodly beams,

67 *lightfoot maids:* Spenser's forest nymphs are followers of Diana, goddess of the hunt.
69 *wild wolves:* Wolves were plentiful in Ireland in Spenser's time.
74 "Rise up, my love, my fair one, and come away" (Song of Solomon 2:10). See Song of Solomon 2:11–13 for the full implications of Spenser's language here.
75 "By now Aurora, rising, had left the saffron bed of Tithonus and was sprinkling her fresh light on the world" (*Aeneid*, IV.584–585, p. 115).

78–79 Spenser's concert of birds is taken from the conventions of mĕdieval poetry: "The birds kept on performing all their rites; / Sweetly and pleasantly they sang of love / And chanted sonnets courteously and well" (Guillaume de Lorris, *The Romance of the Rose*, p. 15).
80 *matins:* morning prayer. "The bisy larke, messager of day" (Chaucer, *The Knight's Tale*, 1491). This too is conventional in medieval poetry, particularly in the French *aube*.

More bright than Hesperus's head doth rear.°   *sends forth*
Come now ye damsels, daughters of delight,
Help quickly her to dight;
But first come ye, fair Hours, which were begot
In Jove's sweet paradise of° Day and Night,   *by*
100   Which do the seasons of the year allot,
And all that ever in this world is fair
Do make and still° repair.   *continually*
And ye three handmaids of the Cyprian queen,
The which do still adorn her beauty's pride,
Help to adorn my beautifullest bride;
And as ye her array, still throw between°   *now and then*
Some graces to be seen,
And as ye use° to Venus, to her sing,   *do*
The whiles the woods shall answer, and your echo ring.

110   Now is my love all ready forth to come.
Let all the virgins therefore well await;
And ye fresh boys that tend upon her groom,
Prepare yourselves; for he is coming straight.°   *immediately*
Set all your things in seemly good array,°   *order*
Fit for so joyful day,
The joyful'st day that ever sun did see.
Fair sun, show forth thy favorable ray,
And let thy lifeful heat not fervent be,

95   *Hesperus:* the evening star. The reference here to Hesperus is a subtle reminder that the festivities which begin with dawn are to be consummated in the marriage bed with the coming of evening. The conventional association of Hesperus and the epithalamium begins with Catullus (*Odi et Amo* 62, pp. 60–62; and 64. 328–332, p. 76).

98–102   *fair Hours:* Spenser's Hours, unlike the Hours of classical myth, are the sidereal hours. In classical tradition they had represented only the seasons. In the astronomy of Spenser's time the Earth was the stationary center of the universe, and a "sphere" of fixed stars (stars which do not change their relationship to each other) stood at the outer limits of the universe. Between these two were the spheres of the sun and the planets. The sphere of the fixed stars rotated about the Earth once every 24 hours. The spheres of the sun and the planets rotated about the Earth in slightly more than 24 hours. The Hours can be considered as equal divisions (15°) of the sphere of fixed stars. When the sphere of fixed stars has completed its daily orbit (360°), the sun will have completed only about 359° of its orbit. Thus, although both the fixed stars and the sun move in an east-to-west circle about the Earth, the sun in relation to the fixed stars moves slightly less than one degree in a west-to-east direction. In 365 days it will have moved through each of the 24 sidereal hours on its west-to-east path.

In classical tradition, the Hours are daughters of Jove and Themis. Spenser makes them daughters of Jove (Day) and Night. The sidereal hours "allot" the seasons in the sense that they determine the length of day during the summer and winter solstices and the spring and fall equinoxes. They "make and repair" all things on earth because their continuous motion is the basis of all change on Earth —day to night, spring to winter, youth to old age, birth to death—and these changes are continually renewed by the passage of the Hours.

103   *three handmaids:* the three graces; *Cyprian queen:* Venus. The graces are the traditional attendants of Venus in classical tradition. Renaissance writers also make the Hours attendants of Venus. The Graces are conventional attendants in epithalamic poetry (Claudian, "Epithalamium of Honorius and Maria," 201–203, p. 257).

For fear of burning her sunshiny face,
120 Her beauty to disgrace.°   *mar*
O fairest Phoebus, father of the muse,
If ever I did honor thee aright,
Or sing the thing that mote° thy mind delight,   *could*
Do not thy servant's simple boon° refuse,   *request*
But let this day, let this one day be mine—
Let all the rest be thine.
Then I thy sovereign praises loud will sing,
That° all the woods shall answer, and their echo ring.   *so that*

Hark how the minstrels gin to shrill aloud
130 Their merry music that resounds from far,
The pipe, the tabor,° and the trembling crowd,°   *little drum, fiddle*
That well agree withouten breach or jar.°   *discord*
But most of all the damsels do delight
When they their timbrels° smite,   *tambourines*
And thereunto do dance and carol sweet,
That all the senses they do ravish quite,
The whiles the boys run up and down the street
Crying aloud with strong confusèd noise,
As if it were one voice.
140 *Hymen io Hymen, Hymen* they do shout,
That even to the heavens their shouting shrill
Doth reach, and all the firmament doth fill;
To which the people standing all about,
As in approvance do thereto applaud,
And loud advance her laud.
And evermore they *Hymen, Hymen* sing,
That all the woods them answer, and their echo ring.

Lo where she comes along with portly pace,
Like Phoebe from her chamber of the east
150 Arising forth to run her mighty race,
Clad all in white, that seems° a virgin best.   *suits*

121   In Hesiod and the classical tradition generally the muses are daughters of Jove. Spenser may be depending on a medieval tradition.
129–146   ". . . let the music of the flute resound and the crowd, set free from law's harsh restraints, with larger license indulge the permitted jest. Soldiers, make merry with your leaders, girls with boys. Be this the cry that re-echoes from pole to pole . . ." (Claudian, "Fescennine Verses," IV.30–36, *Claudian*, Vol. I, p. 239).
129–136   Details like these, though not entirely lacking in either Latin or French epithalamia, are one of the means by which Spenser Anglicizes the form.
137–142   "Boys, raise the torches: / I see the red veil. / Come, sing in rhythm, / 'Yo Hymen, Hymenaeus yo, / yo Hymen Hymenaeus' " (Catullus, *Odi et Amo* 61. 117–121, p. 56).
148–150   *Phoebe:* the moon. The comparison is appropriate because the bride is, like Phoebe (Diana), a virgin, and because the allusion to the moon looks forward to nightfall and the consummation of the marriage. The language of these lines is an obvious allusion to Psalms 19:4–5: "the sun, which is as a bridegroom coming out of his chamber, and rejoiceth as a strong man to run a race."

So well it her beseems that ye would ween°   *think*
Some angel she had been.
Her long loose yellow locks like golden wire,
Sprinkled with pearl, and purling° flowers atween,   *winding*
Do like a golden mantel her attire,
And being crownèd with a garland green,
Seem like some maiden queen.
Her modest eyes, abashèd to behold
160   So many gazers as on her do stare,
Upon the lowly ground affixèd are;
Ne dare lift up her countenance too bold,°   *boldly*
But blush to hear her praises sung so loud,
So far from being proud.
Nath'less° do ye still loud her praises sing,   *nevertheless*
That all the woods may answer, and your echo ring.

Tell me, ye merchants' daughters, did ye see
So fair a creature in your town before,
So sweet, so lovely, and so mild as she,
170   Adorned with beauty's grace and virtue's store?°   *wealth*
Her goodly eyes like sapphires shining bright,
Her forehead ivory white,
Her cheeks like apples which the sun hath rudded,°   *reddened*
Her lips like cherries, charming men to bite,
Her breast like to a bowl of cream uncrudded,°   *uncurdled*
Her paps like lilies budded,
Her snowy neck like to a marble tower,
And all her body like a palace fair,
Ascending up with many a stately stair
180   To honor's seat and chastity's sweet bower.°   *chamber*
Why stand ye still, ye virgins, in amaze°   *amazement*
Upon her so to gaze,
Whiles ye forget your former lay to sing,
To which the woods did answer, and your echo ring?

But if ye saw that which no eyes can see,
The inward beauty of her lively sprite,

154 *golden wire:* a common comparison in medieval and renaissance poetry. See *The Faerie Queene,* II.iii.30.1.
158 *maiden queen:* appropriate to Diana, but also an allusion to Queen Elizabeth, the virgin queen.
159–164 "Maiden shame now overcomes the anxious bride; her veil now shows traces of innocent tears" (Claudian, "Fescennine Verses," IV.3–4, p. 237). The blushing shame of the bride is a topic in most epithalamia.
167–180 This catalogue of the lady's physical beauties is a popular theme in classical, medieval, and renaissance poetry, and one which Spenser was especially drawn to. It occurs often both in *The Faerie Queene* and in the *Amoretti.* See Song of Solomon 4–8; Claudian, "Epithalamium of Honorius and Maria," 264–271, pp. 261–263; *Secular Lyrics of the XIVth and XVth Centuries,* ed. Rossell Hope Robbins, Oxford University Press, pp. 120–122.
177 "Thy neck is as a tower of ivory" (Song of Solomon 7:4).

Garnished with heavenly gifts of high degree,
Much more then would ye wonder at that sight
And stand astonished like to those which read°   *look at*
190 Medusa's mazeful° head.   *stupefying*
There dwells sweet love and constant chastity,
Unspotted faith and comely womanhead,°   *womanhood*
Regard of honor and mild modesty.
There virtue reigns as queen in royal throne
And giveth laws alone,
The which the base affections° do obey,   *passions*
And yield their services unto her will;
Ne° thought of thing uncomely° ever may   *nor, unbecoming*
Thereto approach to tempt her mind to ill.
200 Had ye once seen these her celestial treasures
And unrevealèd pleasures,
Then would ye wonder and her praises sing,
That all the woods should answer, and your echo ring.

Open the temple gates unto my love.
Open them wide that she may enter in,
And all the posts adorn as doth behoove,
And all the pillars deck with garlands trim,
For to receive this saint with honor due
That cometh in to you.
210 With trembling steps and humble reverence
She cometh in, before th' Almighty's view.
Of her ye virgins learn obedience—
When so ye come into those holy places,
To humble your proud faces.
Bring her up to th' high altar, that she may
The sacred ceremonies there partake,
The which do endless matrimony make;
And let the roaring organs loudly play
The praises of the Lord in lively notes,
220 The whiles with hollow throats
The choristers the joyous anthem sing,
That all the woods may answer, and their echo ring.

Behold whiles she before the altar stands,
Hearing the holy priest that to her speaks
And blesseth her with his two happy hands,

---

190 *Medusa:* The power of the horrible head of Medusa to turn men to stone is briefly alluded to in Ovid's *Metamorphoses,* IV (p. 121). An influential renaissance allegory of Medusa's power is that it represents the power of beauty to paralyze lustful desire.

206–207 "Let these haste to entwine the gleaming door-posts with my sacred myrtle" (Claudian, "Epithalamium of Honorius and Maria," 208–209, p. 257).
225 *happy hands:* In the blessing the priest's hands impart future happiness.

How the red roses flush up in her cheeks
And the pure snow with goodly vermeil stain
Like crimson dyed in grain;
That even th' angels, which continually
230 About the sacred altar do remain,
Forget their service and about her fly,
Oft peeping in her face, that seems more fair
The more they on it stare.
But her sad° eyes still fastened on the ground   *serious*
Are governèd with goodly modesty,
That suffers not one look to glance awry
Which may let in a little thought unsound.°   *unchaste*
Why blush ye, love, to give to me your hand,
The pledge of all our band?°   *marriage*
240 Sing ye sweet angels, *Alleluia* sing,
That all the woods may answer, and your echo ring.

Now all is done. Bring home the bride again,
Bring home the triumph of our victory,
Bring home with you the glory of her gain,
With joyance° bring her and with jollity.   *rejoicing*
Never had man more joyful day than this
Whom heaven would heap with bliss.
Make feast therefore now all this livelong day;
This day forever to me holy is.
250 Pour out the wine without restraint or stay,
Pour not by cups, but by the bellyfull,
Pour out to all that wull;°   *want it*
And sprinkle all the posts and walls with wine,
That they may sweat and drunken be withal.
Crown ye god Bacchus with a coronal,
And Hymen also crown with wreaths of vine,
And let the graces dance unto° the rest—   *for*
For they can do it best—
The whiles the maidens do their carol sing,
260 To which the woods shall answer, and their echo ring.

Ring ye the bells, ye young men of the town,
And leave your wonted° labors for this day.   *usual*

226–228 "And over his body's snow was a crimson flush, such as dyes the fair cheeks and blushing face of a maid when she is first escorted to her young husband's home . . ." (*Tibullus*, III.iv.30–32, trans. J. P. Postgate, Loeb Classical Library, p. 295).
240 The invocation of the angels here may be compared with the invocation of the muses in 14.
246–249 Compare the joyful day that will forever be holy to the groom with the "wished-for day" that will give to the bride "long delight" in 31–33.
253–254 "Do you sprinkle the palace with drops of nectar . . ." (Claudian, "Epithalamium of Honorius and Maria," 209–210, p. 257).
256 ". . . beflower your brows with sweet marjoram blossoms" (Catullus, *Odi et Amo* 61.6–7, p. 52). Note also the mention of Hymen in 25.
259 Compare the singing of the maidens and that of the muses in 35.

This day is holy; do ye write it down,
That ye forever it remember may.
This day the sun is in his chiefest height,
With Barnaby the bright,
From whence declining daily by degrees
He somewhat° loseth of his heat and light,   *something*
When once the Crab behind his back he sees.
270 But for this time° it ill ordainèd was   i.e. *wedding day*
To choose the longest day in all the year
And shortest night, when longest fitter were;
Yet never day so long but late° would pass.   *finally*
Ring ye the bells to make it wear away,
And bonfires make all day,
And dance about them, and about them sing,
That all the woods may answer, and your echo ring.

Ah when will this long weary day have end,
And lend me leave to come unto my love?
280 How slowly do the hours their numbers spend!
How slowly does sad time his feathers move!
Haste thee, O fairest planet, to thy home
Within the western foam;
Thy tirèd steeds long since have need of rest.
Long though it be, at last I see it gloom,
And the bright evening star with golden crest
Appear out of the east.
Fair child of beauty, glorious lamp of love,
That all the host of heaven in ranks dost lead
290 And guidest lovers through the night'ès dread,
How cheerfully thou lookest from above
And seemst to laugh atween thy twinkling light,
As joying in the sight
Of these glad many which for joy do sing,
That all the woods them answer, and their echo ring.

265–269 The wedding day was St. Barnabas' Day, June 11, also the day of the summer solstice. See the note on 98–102 for the sun's "declining daily by degrees." The sun is in the house of the Crab during the first half of June and then moves to the house of the Lion towards mid-June.

281 Time is not winged in classical literature, but he is in medieval and renaissance art and poetry. See Samuel Chew, *The Pilgrimage of Life*, Fig. 15–23.

282–284 ". . . if the crimson sun had not been already bathing his weary horses in the Spanish Sea" (*Aeneid*, XI.913–914, p. 307).

286–294 "Hesperus, golden lamp of the lovely daughter of the foam, dear Hesperus, sacred jewel of the deep blue night, dimmer as much than the moon as thou art among the stars pre-eminent, hail, friend, and as I lead the revel to the shepherd's hut, in place of moonlight lend me thine . . . a lover am I and 'tis well to favor lovers" (Bion, *Idylls*, IX, quoted from *Variorum*, VIII. 481). Spenser may have known Ronsard's version of Bion's Ninth Idyll.

286 Spenser's evening star is Venus, which he has, mistakenly, rising in the east.

Now cease, ye damsels, your delights forepast;°   *past*
Enough is it that all the day was yours.
Now day is done, and night is nighing fast;
Now bring the bride into the bridal bowers.
300 Now night is come, now soon her disarray,
And in her bed her lay.
Lay her in lilies and in violets,
And silken curtains over her display,°   *spread out*
And odored° sheets, and Arras coverlets.   *perfumed*
Behold how goodly my fair love does lie
In proud humility;
Like unto Maia whenas Jove her took
In Tempe, lying on the flowery grass
Twixt sleep and wake, after she weary was
310 With bathing in the Acidalian brook.
Now it is night, ye damsels may be gone
And leave my love alone,
And leave likewise your former lay to sing;
The woods no more shall answer, nor your echo ring.

Now welcome Night, thou night so long expected,
That long days' labor dost at last defray,°   *pay back*
And all my cares, which cruel love collected,
Hast summed in one and canceled for aye;°   *forever*
Spread thy broad wing over my love and me,
320 That no man may us see,
And in thy sable mantle us enwrap,
From fear of peril and foul horror free.
Let no false treason seek us to entrap,
Nor any dread disquiet once annoy
The safety of our joy;
But let the night be calm and quietsome,
Without tempestuous storms or sad affray;°   *dark fear*

296–297 "Close the doors, virgins: / we've played enough" (Catullus, *Odi et Amo* 61.227–228, p. 59).

300–301 Compare with 74–75 where the bride is asked to awaken and leave her bed, and with 77 where the dawn has just come.

302–304 "Let others unfold yellow-dyed silks from China and spread tapestries of Sidon on the ground. Do you employ all your arts in decorating the marriage bed" (Claudian, "Epithalamium of Honorius and Maria," 211–213, p. 257).

307–310 Spenser's allusion to the love of Jove for Maia may have been suggested by the tapestry of the love of Theseus and Ariadne on the wedding couch in Catullus' 64. According to the Homeric *Hymn to Hermes*, Maia, mother of Hermes,

daughter of Atlas, and one of the Pleiades, was a "shy goddess" who lived deep in a cave on Mount Cyllene in Arcadia. It is not known why Spenser assigns her to Tempe. The Acidalian brook is not associated with Maia in classical tradition; but it is appropriate here because it was sacred to Venus, and the Graces bathed themselves in it. The Homeric *Hymn* says that Jove came to Maia in the night, which might explain Spenser's "twixt sleep and wake."

319–321 "Night fell and embraced the earth in her dark wings" (*Aeneid*, VIII.369, p. 212).

321–323 Compare with 96–105 where the bride is to be dressed by the Hours and the Graces.

Like as when Jove with fair Alcmena lay,
When he begot the great Tirynthian groom,
330 Or like as when he with thyself did lie,
And begot Majesty.
And let the maids and young men cease to sing;
Ne let the woods them answer, nor their echo ring.

Let no lamenting cries nor doleful tears
Be heard all night within, nor yet without;
Ne let false whispers, breeding hidden fears,
Break gentle sleep with misconceivèd° doubt.   *unwarranted*
Let no deluding dreams nor dreadful sights
Make sudden sad affrights;
340 Ne let house fires nor lightning's helpless harms,
Ne let the Puck nor other evil sprites,
Ne let mischievous witches with their charms,
Ne let hobgoblins, names whose sense we see not,
Fray us with things that be not.
Let not the screech owl nor the stork be heard,
Nor the night raven that still° deadly yells,   *always*
Nor damnèd ghosts called up with mighty spells,
Nor grisly° vultures make us once afeared;   *horrible*
Ne let th' unpleasant choir of frogs still croaking
350 Make us to wish their choking.
Let none of these their dreary accents sing;
Ne let the woods them answer, nor their echo ring.

328–329 *Alcmena:* wife of Amphitryon, a Theban general. The story of Jove's seduction of Alcmena was available to Spenser from many sources. He would certainly have been familiar with Plautus' *Amphitryon.* The result of the union of Jove and Alcmena was the demi-god Hercules, called the Tirynthian groom because his birthplace was Tiryns.

330–331 Compare with 98–99 where Jove (Day) and Night are said to have begotten the Hours. The parentage of Majesty seems to be Spenser's invention.

334–335 George Puttenham, writing about the epithalamic tradition, says: ". . . the tunes of the songs were very loud and shrill, to the intent there might no noise be heard . . . by the shrieking and outcry of the young damsel feeling the first forces of her stiff and rigorous young man, she being, as all virgins, tender and weak. . . . This was . . . to diminish the noise of the laughing-lamenting spouse" (*The Arte of English Poesie,* I.xxvi, ed. Gladys D. Willcock and Alice Walker, Cambridge University, 1936, p. 51).

336–351 Imprecations against evil or disturbance are not uncommon in epithalamia. See Claudian's "Epithalamium of Honorius and Maria," 190–201 (p. 257) and Sir Philip Sidney's "Song of Dicus" in *The Countess of Pembroke's Arcadia* (*English Epithalamies,* ed. Robert H. Case, John Lane, 1896, pp. 1-3). Spenser's catalogue of evils appears to be original. It reads like a list of medieval charms (see "A Charm Against the Night Goblin," *Secular Lyrics of the XIVth and XVth Centuries,* p. 61).

341 *Puck:* In medieval tradition Puck was identified with Satan.

343 The goblins had such names as Pippin, Lusty Huff-Cap, Flibbertigibbet.

345 In classical tradition, the owl, like the night-raven, is a bird of ill-omen, presaging death: "And often on a rooftop a lonely owl would sound her deathly lamentations . . ." (*Aeneid,* IV.460, p. 111). In *The Parliament of Fowls,* Chaucer calls the stork an avenger of adultery. Perhaps Spenser means to protect the marriage from future unfaithfulness.

349–350 Spenser's humorous reference to the frogs which lived in the lake just south of Kilcolman Castle implies that the whole of this stanza is mock-serious.

But let still silence true night watches keep,
That sacred peace may in assurance reign,
And timely sleep, when it is time to sleep,
May pour his limbs forth on your° pleasant plain.   i.e. *Night's*
The whiles an hundred little wingèd loves,°   *cupids*
Like divers-feathered doves,
Shall fly and flutter round about your bed,
360 And in the secret dark that none reproves
Their pretty stealths shall work, and snares shall spread
To filch away sweet snatches of delight,
Concealed through covert night.
Ye sons of Venus, play your sports at will;
For greedy Pleasure, careless of your toys,
Thinks more upon her paradise of joys
Than what ye do, albe it good or ill.
All night therefore attend your merry play,
For it will soon be day;
370 Now none doth hinder you, that say or sing,
Ne will the woods now answer, nor your echo ring.

Who is the same which at my window peeps,
Or whose is that fair face that shines so bright?
Is it not Cynthia, she that never sleeps,
But walks about high heaven all the night?
O fairest goddess, do thou not envy
My love with me to spy;
For thou likewise didst love, though now unthought,°   *thought otherwise*
And for a fleece of wool, which privily
380 The Latmian shepherd once unto thee brought,
His pleasures with thee wrought.
Therefore to us be favorable now;
And sith of women's labors° thou hast charge,   i.e. *in childbirth*
And generation goodly dost enlarge,
Incline thy will t' effect our wishful vow,
And the chaste womb inform with timely seed,
That may our comfort breed.
Till which, we cease our hopeful hap to sing,
Ne let the woods us answer, nor our echo ring.

353   Contrast with the noise in 129–146.

357–359   "And around the Princess, the little Loves fluttered without cease, in thousands upon thousands of gyres" (Joachim Du Bellay, *Epithalame*, 307–310).

364   See Catullus 61.207, p. 59.

372–375   Compare with 148–150 where the bride appears like the moon "to run her nightly race."

374   *Cynthia:* the moon.

378–381   Spenser conflates two stories here. Virgil says, "With such snowy wool for dower . . . Pan the god of Arcady ensnared thee, O Moon, in his treachery, when he called thee into the depth of woodland and thou didst not scorn his call" (*Georgics*, III.391–393, pp. 332–333). Apollonius Rhodius in the *Argonautica*, IV.57–58, says that the Moon met her lover, Endymion, in the valley and caves of Latmos.

383   The goddess Diana (Cynthia) is, under the name Lucina, patroness of birth.

390 And thou, great Juno, which with awful might
 The laws of wedlock still dost patronize,
 And the religion of the faith first plight
 With sacred rites hast taught to solemnize,
 And eke for comfort often callèd art
 Of° women in their smart—   *by*
 Eternally bind thou this lovely° band,   *loving*
 And all thy blessings unto us impart.
 And thou, glad Genius, in whose gentle hand
 The bridal bower and genial bed remain
400 Without blemish or stain,
 And the sweet pleasures of their loves' delight
 With secret aid dost succor and supply,
 Till they bring forth the fruitful progeny—
 Send us the timely fruit of this same night.
 And thou, fair Hebe, and thou, Hymen free,
 Grant that it may so be.
 Till which, we cease your further praise to sing,
 Ne any woods shall answer, nor echo ring.

 And ye high heavens, the temple of the gods,
410 In which a thousand torches flaming bright
 Do burn, that to us wretched earthly clods
 In dreadful darkness lend desirèd light;
 And all ye powers which in the same° remain—   *i.e. heavens*
 More than we men can feign°—   *imagine*
 Pour out your blessing on us plenteously,
 And happy influence upon us rain,
 That we may raise a large posterity,
 Which from the earth—which they may° long possess   *may they*
 With lasting happiness—
420 Up to your haughty palaces may mount,
 And for the guerdon° of their glorious merit   *prize*
 May heavenly tabernacles there inherit,
 Of blessed saints for to increase the count.
 So let us rest, sweet love, in hope of this,

390–393 ". . . above all to Juno, for the tie of marriage lies in her care" (*Aeneid*, IV.59, p. 99).

394–395 "Women lost in labor pains / call you Lucina Juno" (Catullus, *Odi et Amo*, 34.13–14, p. 32).

398–404 *Genius:* Spenser's conception of Genius as patron of sex, pregnancy, and birth is fully developed in late medieval literature. For a good example of the tradition, see Genius' exortation to fecundity in Jean de Meun, *Romance of the Rose*, pp. 413–423.

405 *Hebe:* Juno's daughter, and wife of Hercules. Hebe could restore youth to men (*Metamorphoses*, IX, pp. 232–233).

409 *temple of the gods:* the planets, which are named after Roman gods and goddesses.

411 *earthly clods:* "All are of the dust, and all turn to dust again" (Ecclesiastes 4:20).

413–416 Spenser probably refers to the influence of the stars, as well as to ministering angels.

417–423 Compare these lines with 185–201 where the bride's spiritual perfection is praised.

And cease till then our timely joys to sing.
The woods no more us answer, nor our echo ring.

Song made in lieu of many ornaments,
With which my love should duly have been decked,
Which cutting off through hasty accidents,
430 Ye would not stay your due time to expect,
But promised both to recompense—
Be unto her a goodly ornament,
And for short time an endless monument.

427–433 For a full discussion of the last stanza, see the introductory note to this poem. Note the parallels in language between this stanza and 208 and 217.

427 *many ornaments:* "She spake and fitted to Maria's neck and shining limbs the rich gear which the happy Nereids had just given her" (Claudian, "Epithalamium of Honorius and Maria," 282–283, p. 263).

Four Hymns

INTRODUCTION

In his dedication of the *Four Hymns* to the Countesses of Cumberland and Warwick, Spenser writes

> Having in the greener times of my youth composed these former two hymns in the praise of love and beauty, and finding that the same too much pleased those of like age and disposition, which, being too vehemently carried with that kind of affection, do rather suck out poison to their strong passion than honey to their honest delight, I was moved by the one of you two most excellent ladies to call in the same. But being unable so to do, by reason that many copies thereof were formerly scattered abroad, I resolved at least to amend and, by way of retraction, to reform them, making, instead of those two hymns of earthly or natural love and beauty, two others of heavenly and celestial. The which I do dedicate jointly unto you two honorable sisters, as to the most excellent and rare ornaments of all true love and beauty, both in the one and the other kind. . . .

However this statement is read, either as a relatively accurate account of the facts behind the composition of the *Four Hymns* or as a largely fictional occasion for the poems, it does clearly announce the basic structure of the work as well as the poet's intention.

We learn first from the dedication that the last two hymns are meant as an amendment and a retraction of the first two. Opposed to the two earthly poems, hymns in praise of erotic love and feminine beauty, are two in honor of divine love and heavenly beauty. At the same time we are not encouraged to interpret this opposition as one simply between good and evil, for the two noble ladies are praised for their excellence in both kinds of love and beauty. Thus both the earthly and the heavenly hymns have subjects worthy of praise.

If the opposition between the earthly and the heavenly poems is not an absolute one, perhaps the dedication offers a clue to its nature. Spenser says that the earthly hymns were written "in the greener times of my youth." Whether or not we take this to be a true statement, it suggests that the earthly hymns embody the typical defects, as well as the typical virtues, of youth.

Writing about the characteristics of youth in the *Rhetoric*, Aristotle points out that the young man is hopeful, high-minded, and passionate, and that he is likely to be governed by a strong sexual desire (II.12). When Spenser called the earthly hymns a product of his youth, he meant to characterize them as typically youthful in their outlook. Combining some of Aristotle's terms, we might call that outlook hopefully, passionately, high-mindedly erotic. The opposition between the earthly and the heavenly poems is between youth and maturity, passion and wisdom.[1]

AN HYMN IN HONOR OF LOVE

The first of the *Four Hymns* can be divided into nine parts, actually nine related themes: 1) invocation of the great god Cupid (Eros) and his followers (1–42); 2) the cosmic function of love (43–102); 3) the object of human love (103–119); 4) the lover's suffering at the hands of a cruel god and a proud mistress (120–168); 5) the distinction between true love and lust (169–189); 6) love as a refining psychological force (190–217); 7) the relation of love to bravery (218–243); 8) the terrors of suspicion and jealousy occasioned by love (244–279); 9) the triumph of love in a paradise of sexual pleasure (280–307).

All of these themes are, as the notes suggest, common in medieval love poetry. Many of them are fully developed in the 11th century; others do not reach maturity until Dante (13th century) and Petrarch (14th century). The core of the poem, the long-suffering ordeal of the lover as he progresses from the first sight of his beloved through the pains of hopeless longing and cold indifference to the more intimate torture of jealousy and, finally, toward the triumph of erotic love, is a legacy from the Middle Ages which the poets of the Renaissance received with enthusiasm and developed with infinite variation.

AN HYMN IN HONOR OF BEAUTY

Like the first hymn, the second can be divided into themes: 1) invocation of Venus and the poet's mistress (1–28); 2) the cosmic function of beauty (29–56); 3) beauty as the cause of love (57–63); 4) the definition of beauty as an eternal spiritual light in all created beings, not a mere harmony between parts nor a mixture of colors (64–112); 5) spiritual beauty as the formal principle of physical beauty (113–147); 6) the corruption of the spiritual beauty in women by the lust of men (148–175); 7) the revelation and fruition of spiritual beauty through true love (176–189); 8) the process by which the lover idealizes the beauty of the beloved in true love (190–231); 9) the power of the physical beauties of the beloved over the lover (232–266); 10) praise of Venus, the queen of beauty, and the poet's plea for mercy from his mistress.

[1] The best study of the *Four Hymns* is Robert Ellrodt's *Neoplatonism in the Poetry of Spenser*, Librarie E. Droz, 1960. An interesting and more general study is in Alfred W. Satterthwaite's *Spenser, Ronsard, and Du Bellay*, Princeton University Press, 1960, especially pp. 138–168.

Although the essential theme of this poem is, like that of the first poem, the true love of the earthly lover for his lady, more especially it is the beauty of the beloved and the means by which her beauty works in the mind and heart of the lover. As the notes to this poem show, Spenser develops these themes largely in the language of the renaissance Neoplatonic philosophy of love. Yet he does not treat this Neoplatonic material at all as Ficino, the leading Neoplatonist of the age, would, nor even as such gentlemanly amateurs as Pietro Bembo or Baldassare Castiglione would. In the writings of renaissance Neoplatonists, the love of the lover for the beautiful woman is merely the first step of a process in which the soul of the lover divests itself of all that is earthly and rises to unite itself with eternal beauty in a mystical ecstasy. In Ficino's philosophy the love of physical beauty leads to the contemplation of eternity. For Spenser's lover the process of love begins and ends in the beauty of a particular woman. Though it is true that her beauty derives from the eternal source of all beauty, and is itself immortal, still it is the beauty of a lovely woman. And it is she who commands the lover's devotion and adoration. It is clear, and not only from this poem, that Spenser's imagination was not strongly engaged by the doctrines of Ficino. It was, on the other hand, deeply engaged by the themes of romantic love and feminine beauty. Like other great poets of the Renaissance, he appropriated to his own uses the Neoplatonic philosophy of love.

AN HYMN OF HEAVENLY LOVE

The third hymn begins with a retraction of the first two. It goes on to relate God's creation of the angelic orders through love, the revolt and fall of some of the angels, God's creation of man to fill the place of the fallen angels, and the disobedience and fall of man. But the heart of the poem is found in two accounts of the life of Christ, whose death on the cross for the sins of men is the ultimate expression of divine love. It is when Christ's love of mankind (*agape*) is measured against the earthly love of the lover for his lady (*eros*) that the latter is seen to be defective, narrow, superficial. What are the pains and frustrations of the earthly lover of the first hymn to the terrible self-sacrifice of Christ? What are the wounds of Cupid's arrow to the bleeding body of God? A realization of God's great love breeds in man the love of his neighbor, and the contemplation of Christ's life and death enflames him with a consuming love for his Saviour.

AN HYMN OF HEAVENLY BEAUTY

If the third hymn has as its subject the love of Christ the God-Man, the subject of the fourth is the beauty of Christ the second person of the Trinity. Beginning with the beauty of the world around him, the lover makes his way, by contemplation, through the beauties of the material universe and into the overwhelming glories of the spiritual world until, having left created beauty behind, he finds himself at the throne of God and face to face with Sapience (Wisdom), beauty itself, the Son of God.

To modern readers, the feminine Sapience must seem shockingly strange as a symbol of Christ the Son, but it was not strange to Spenser's age. Behind the symbol are the wisdom books of the Old Testament and the authority of church fathers and medieval biblical commentary. For Spenser the availability of this feminine symbol of the Son was most fortunate, for he needed to place her beside the earthly beauty of the second hymn, just as he had measured the earthly lover of the first hymn against Christ the divine lover. Again the same kind of questions are asked in making the comparison. What is the beauty of the most beautiful earthly woman, indeed of the most beautiful creature man is capable of imagining, to the beauty of Christ?

The *Four Hymns* make a single poem. They are symbols of a progress from the earthbound idealism of youth to the spiritual wisdom of age. They celebrate the truth which Yeats touched so beautifully in

> Bodily decrepitude is wisdom; young
> We loved each other and were ignorant.

AN HYMN IN HONOR
OF LOVE

Love, that long since hast to thy mighty power
Perforce° subdued my poor captivèd heart,   *forcibly*
And raging now therein with restless stour,°   *tumult*
Dost tyrannize in every weaker part—
Fain would I seek to ease my bitter smart
By any service I might do to thee,
Or aught that else might to thee pleasing be.

And now t' assuage the force of this new flame
And make thee more propitious in my need,
10 I mean to sing the praises of thy name,
And thy victorious conquests to aread;°   *proclaim*

1–4 The image of the lover as a captive to Cupid, the god of love, probably comes from Ovid's *Amores*, I.ii: "Lo, I confess, I am thy captive I, / And hold my conquered hands for thee to tie" (trans. Christopher Marlowe). It becomes a commonplace of medieval and renaissance love poetry. See especially Petrarch's "Triumph of Love" (*The Triumphs of Petrarch*, trans. Ernest Hatch Wilkins, University of Chicago Press, 1962).

11–14 Petrarch lists great numbers of Love's victims, including Julius Caesar, Theseus, Hercules, and David. Of Love's victims he says, "Some of them were but captives, some were slain, / And some were wounded by his pungent arrows" ("Triumph of Love," p. 6).

By which thou madest many hearts to bleed
Of mighty victors with wide wounds imbrued,°   *stained*
And by thy cruel darts to thee subdued.

Only I fear my wits, enfeebled late
Through the sharp sorrows which thou hast me bred,
Should faint, and words should fail me to relate
The wondrous triumphs of thy great godhead.
But if thou wouldst vouchsafe to overspread
20 Me with the shadow of thy gentle wing,
I should enabled be thy acts to sing.

Come then, O come, thou mighty god of love,
Out of thy silver bowers and secret bliss,
Where thou dost sit in Venus' lap above,
Bathing thy wings in her ambrosial kiss,
That sweeter far than any nectar is;
Come softly, and my feeble breast inspire
With gentle fury, kindled of thy fire.

And ye sweet muses, which have often proved°   *experienced*
30 The piercing points of his avengeful darts,
And ye fair nymphs, which oftentimes have loved
The cruel worker of your kindly smarts—
Prepare yourselves, and open wide your hearts
For to receive the triumph of your glory,
That made you merry oft when ye were sorry.

And ye fair blossoms of youth's wanton breed
Which in the conquests of your beauty boast,
Wherewith your lovers' feeble eyes you feed,
But starve their hearts, that needeth nurture most—
40 Prepare yourselves to march amongst his host,
And all the way this sacred hymn do sing,
Made in the honor of your sovereign king.

Great god of might, that reignest in the mind,
And all the body to thy hest° dost frame,°   *command, direct*

15–18 The inability of the lover, suffering the extremes of passion, to speak of his love is another commonplace of medieval and renaissance love poetry: "Hence 'tis, whene'er my lips would silence break, / Scarce can I hear the accents which I vent, / By passion render'd spiritless and weak" (Petrarch, *Piu volte già dal bel sembiante umano, Sonnets*, p. 160).
22–42 The triumphal pageant of Cupid which these lines suggest is based probably on Ovid's *Amores*, I.ii. However, Spenser was undoubtedly familiar with medieval and renaissance elaborations of the theme.
36–42 "Young men and women shalt thou lead as thrall, / So will thy triumph seem magnifical / . . . / Thee all shall fear, and worship as a king, / *Io Triumphe* shall thy people sing" (*Amores*, I.ii).
43–45 "Love was a great god, among men and gods a marvel" (Plato, *Symposium*, trans. W. R. M. Lamb, Loeb

Victor of gods, subduer of mankind,
That dost the lions and fell° tigers tame,   *savage*
Making their cruel rage thy scornful game,
And in their roaring taking great delight—
Who can express the glory of thy might?

50   Or who alive can perfectly declare
The wondrous cradle of thy infancy?
When thy great mother, Venus, first thee bare,
Begot of Plenty and of Penury,
Though elder than thine own nativity;
And yet a child, renewing still thy years,
And yet the eldest of the heavenly peers.°   *i.e. gods*

For ere this world's still° moving mighty mass   *continually*
Out of great Chaos' ugly prison crept,
In which his° goodly face long hidden was   *i.e. the world's*
60   From heaven's view and in deep darkness kept,
Love, that had now long time securely slept
In Venus' lap, unarmèd then and naked,
Gan rear his head, by Clotho being wakèd.

Classical Library, p. 101). "... the minds of mortals and immortals alike are ruled over by Love" (Marsilio Ficino, *Commentary on Plato's "Symposium,"* ed. and trans. Sears R. Jayne, University of Missouri, 1944, p. 125. This translation will be cited subsequently as *Commentary*). Marsilio Ficino of Florence (1433–1499) was the greatest Plato scholar of the Renaissance. His translations of Plato, Plotinus, and other Neoplatonic authors had a great influence on the Neoplatonism of the Renaissance, and his commentary on the *Symposium* was especially influential. It is the source, directly or indirectly, of most of the Neoplatoni ideas in *Four Hymns*. For an informative essay on Ficino's influence on renaissance Italian art, see Erwin Panofsky's *Studies in Iconology*, pp. 129–230.

45   "Thou [Love] with these soldiers conquerest gods and men" (*Amores*, I.ii). See also Ovid's *Metamorphoses*, p. 137. Petrarch's "Triumph of Love" lists the gods conquered by Love (p. 11).

46–48   The roaring of the wild beasts tamed by Love is the rage of sexual desire.

52–53   Spenser conflates the Platonic myth of the birth of Love from the union of Resource and Poverty (*Symposium*, pp. 179–181) with the more conventional idea of Love as the son of Venus.

54–56   Two different ideas from the *Symposium* are combined here. Agathon maintains that Love is the youngest of the gods (p. 153). On the other hand, Phaedrus claims, on the authority of Hesiod, that Love is the oldest of the gods (p. 51).

57–73   This account of the awakening of Love and his flight through chaos to heaven, though it would have scandalized a Neoplatonic philosopher, is probably derived from Ficino. The idea that Love issues from chaos comes ultimately from Hesiod's *Theogony* (trans. Norman O. Brown, Library of Liberal Arts, p. 56). Otherwise the account seems to depend on Ficino's *Commentary:* "It is that still formless substance which we mean by Chaos; that first turning toward God we call the birth of Love; the infusion of the divine light, the nourishing of love; the ensuing conflagration, the increment of love. . . . To beauty, Love, as soon as it was born, drew the Mind, and led the Mind formerly un-beautiful to the same Mind made beautiful" (p. 128). Spenser's originality is in the fact that he applied Ficino's exposition to the creation of the material universe. In the original it had described the formation of the "angelic mind," the seat of the "ideas" of all created things.

63   *Clotho:* One of the three Fates, she represents present time and has command over the planets in renaissance mythography.

And taking to him wings of his own heat,
Kindled at first from heaven's life-giving fire,
He gan to move out of his idle seat—
Weakly at first. But after with desire
Lifted aloft, he gan to mount up higher,
And like fresh eagle, make his hardy flight
70 Through all that great wide waste, yet wanting° light.   *lacking*

Yet wanting light to guide his wandering way,
His own fair mother, for all creatures' sake,
Did lend him light from her own goodly ray;
Then through the world his way he gan to take,
The world that was not till he did it make,
Whose sundry parts he from themselves did sever,
The which before had lain confusèd ever.

The earth, the air, the water, and the fire
Then gan to range° themselves in huge array,°   *organize, armies*
80 And with contrary forces to conspire
Each against other by all means they may,
Threatening their own confusion and decay;
Air hated earth, and water hated fire,
Till Love relented° their rebellious ire.   *made gentle*

He then them took, and tempering goodly well
Their contrary dislikes with lovèd means,
Did place them all in order and compel
To keep themselves within their sundry reigns,°   *places*
Together linked with adamantine chains;
90 Yet so as that in every living wight°   *creature*
They mix themselves, and show their kindly° might.   *natural*

So ever since, they firmly have remained,
And duly well observèd his behest;
Through which now all these things that are contained
Within this goodly cope,° both most and least,   *canopy*

64–73 Ficino's steps are handled rather loosely by Spenser. The heavenly heat from which Love forms his wings represents the "birth of Love." His increasing strength represents the "increment of love." The light lent to Love by his mother Venus seems to represent both the "nourishing of love" and Love's attraction to beauty.

76–84 "Nothing had any lasting shape, but everything got in the way of everything else; for . . . cold warred with hot, moist with dry, soft with hard, and light with heavy. This strife was finally resolved by a god . . . who separated earth from heaven, and the waters from the earth . . ." (Ovid, *Metamorphoses*, I.17–23, p. 31).

85–89 "God placed water and air in the mean between fire and earth, and made them to have the same proportion as far as possible . . . out of such elements, which are in number four, the body of the world was created, and it was harmonized by proportion and therefore has the spirit of friendship; and having been reconciled to itself, it was indissoluble by the hand of any other than the framer" (Plato, *Timaeus*, 32, Jowett translation).

Their being have and daily are increased
Through secret sparks of his infusèd fire,
Which in the barren cold he doth inspire.°　　　　　　　　　*breathe in*

Thereby they all do live, and movèd are
100　To multiply the likeness of their kind,
Whilst they seek only, without further care,
To quench the flame which they in burning find;
But man, that breathes a more immortal mind,
Not for lust's sake, but for eternity,
Seeks to enlarge his lasting progeny.

For having yet in his deducted° sprite　　　　　　　*weakened*
Some sparks remaining of that heavenly fire,
He is enlumined° with that goodly light　　　　　　*illumined*
Unto like goodly semblant° to aspire;　　　　　　　*likeness*
110　Therefore in choice of love he doth desire
That° seems on earth most heavenly to embrace.　　*what*
That same is beauty, born of heavenly race.

For sure of all that in this mortal frame°　　　　　*i.e. world*
Containèd is, nought more divine doth seem,
Or that resembleth more th' immortal flame
Of heavenly light, than beauty's glorious beam.
What wonder then if with such rage extreme
Frail men, whose eyes seek heavenly things to see,
At sight thereof so much enravished be?

120　Which well perceiving, that imperious boy
Doth therewith tip his sharp empoisoned darts,
Which glancing through the eyes with countenance coy,
Rest not till they have pierced the trembling hearts

99–119 "Hence has been born in everyone the instinct for generation. But since generation, by continuation, renders mortal things like divine, it is certainly a divine gift. Because divine things are beautiful, they . . . are similar to and consort with beautiful things. Therefore, generation, which is a divine function, is carried out exactly and easily in that which is beautiful. . . . Wherefore the impulse for generation seeks beautiful things and shuns the opposite. . . . The desire of generation in the beautiful so that ever-lasting life may be preserved in mortal things; this is the love of men living on earth and this is the goal of our love" (Ficino, *Commentary*, p. 203). The original passage in the *Symposium* (pp. 191–193) is also pertinent.

113–116 ". . . Love kindles souls with a desire for the supreme divine beauty . . . which being next to God, are bathed in the glow of God, and to that same glow lifts us" (*Commentary*, p. 194).

120–123 "And he [Love] drew sighs from your eyes then, which he shot so violently into my heart that I fled terrified" (Guido Cavalcanti (1255–1300), *Penguin Book of Italian Verse*, ed. George Kay, p. 59). Petrarch writes that Love tips his arrows in his Laura's eyes (Sonnet 118). The idea Spenser develops is a commonplace in medieval and renaissance love poetry. Spenser may have taken his cue from Sir Thomas Hoby's translation of Baldassare Castiglione's *The Book of the Courtier* (Everyman's Library, p. 247). Castiglione's work is one of the most important sources of Platonic and Neoplatonic ideas in Elizabethan love poetry.

And kindled flame in all their inner parts;
Which sucks the blood and drinketh up the life
Of careful° wretches with consuming grief.   *suffering*

Thenceforth they plain° and make full piteous moan   *complain*
Unto the author of their baleful bane.°   *deadly suffering*
The days they waste, the nights they grieve and groan,
130   Their lives they loathe, and heaven's light disdain;
No light but that whose lamp doth yet remain
Fresh burning in the image of their eye
They deign to see, and seeing it still die.

The whilst thou, tyrant Love, dost laugh and scorn
At their complaints, making their pain thy play.
Whilst they lie languishing like thralls forlorn,
The whiles thou dost triumph in their decay;°   *destruction*
And otherwhiles, their dying to delay,
Thou dost emmarble° the proud heart of her   *turn to marble*
140   Whose love before their life they do prefer.

So hast thou often done—aye me the more—
To me thy vassal, whose yet bleeding heart
With thousand wounds thou mangled hast so sore
That whole remains scarce any little part;
Yet to augment the anguish of my smart,
Thou hast enfrozen her disdainful breast,
That no one drop of pity there doth rest.

Why then do I this honor unto thee,
Thus to ennoble thy victorious name,
150   Since thou dost show no favor unto me,
Ne once move ruth° in that rebellious dame,   *pity*
Somewhat to slake the rigor of my flame?
Certes° small glory dost thou win hereby,   *certainly*
To let her live thus free, and me to die.

But if thou be indeed, as men thee call,
The world's great parent, the most kind preserver
Of living wights, the sovereign lord of all,

124–126 "The flames that ever on my bosom prey . . . so exhaust my veins and waste my core, almost insensibly I melt away" (Petrarch, *D' un bel, chiaro, polito e vivo ghiaccio, Sonnets*, p. 181).
127–133 Ficino explains how the lover, his attention "completely centered in the assiduous contemplation of the loved one," neglects every other concern and becomes sick and melancholy (*Com-* *mentary*, pp. 194–195). The idea is common in medieval poetry.
139 For the proud lady of the marble heart see Alain Chartier's (1385–1429) *La Belle Dame sans Merci* (*Penguin Book of French Verse*, Vol. I, ed. Brian Woledge, p. 269).
155–157 Ficino speaks of Love as the "author and preserver of everything" (*Commentary*, p. 149).

How falls it then that with thy furious fervor
Thou dost afflict as well the not-deserver
160 As him that doth thy lovely hests° despise,   *commands to love*
And on thy subjects most dost tyrannize?

Yet herein eke° thy glory seemeth more,   *also*
By so hard handling those which best thee serve,
That ere thou dost them unto grace restore
Thou mayst well try if they will ever swerve,
And mayst them make it better to deserve,
And having got it, may it more esteem.
For things hard gotten, men more dearly deem.

So hard those heavenly beauties be enfired°—   *set afire*
170 As things divine least passions do impress°—   *influence*
The more of steadfast minds to be admired
The more they stayèd° be on steadfastness.   *constant*
But baseborn minds such lamps regard the less
Which at first blowing take not hasty fire;
Such fancies feel no love, but loose° desire.   *lustful*

For Love is lord of truth and loyalty,
Lifting himself out of the lowly dust
On golden plumes up to the purest sky,
Above the reach of loathly sinful lust,
180 Whose base affect,° through cowardly distrust   *passion*
Of his weak wings, dare not to heaven fly,
But like a moldwarp° in the earth doth lie.   *mole*

His dunghill thoughts, which do themselves enure°   *accustom*
To dirty dross, no higher dare aspire;
Ne° can his feeble earthly eyes endure   *nor*
The flaming light of that celestial fire
Which kindleth love in generous desire,
And makes him mount above the native might
Of heavy earth, up to the heavens' height.

190 Such is the power of that sweet passion
That it all sordid baseness doth expel,

158–161 "Now the eleventh year comes around . . . since I was bent under the pitiless yoke which is crueller to the more submissive" (Petrarch, Sonnet 48 in *Penguin Book of Italian Verse*, p. 105). See also *Penguin Book of French Verse*, Vol. I, p. 100.

173–189 Spenser's condemnation of lust in these lines may be based on the discussion of "popular love," the love "we see in the meaner sort of men" in Plato's *Symposium* (pp. 109–110), or on Ficino's treatment of the same subject in the *Commentary* (pp. 143, 221–222). But the condemnation of lust and its opposition to "loyal love" are common themes in medieval poetry.

190–193 "No base desire lives in that heavenly light, / Honour alone and virtue!—fancy's dreams / Never saw passion rise refined by rays so bright" (Petrarch, *Le stelle e'l cielo, Sonnets*, pp. 149–150). "The gentle mind I have because of this young woman who has appeared makes me scorn silences and base dealings" (Lapo Gianni (1250–1330), *Penguin Book of Italian Verse*, p. 65). These ideas are frequent in medieval love poetry.

And the refinèd mind doth newly fashion
Unto a fairer form, which now doth dwell
In his high thought, that would itself excel;
Which he beholding still with constant sight,
Admires the mirror of so heavenly light.

Whose image printing in his deepest wit,
He thereon feeds his hungry fantasy,°   *imagination*
Still full, yet never satisfied with it,
200 Like Tantale, that in store° doth starvèd lie;   *plenty*
So doth he pine in most satiety,
For naught may quench his infinite desire,
Once kindled through that first conceivèd fire.

Thereon his mind affixèd wholly is,
Ne thinks on aught but how it to attain;
His care, his joy, his hope is all on this,
That seems in it all blisses to contain,
In sight whereof all other bliss seems vain.
Thrice happy man, might he the same possess,
210 He feigns° himself; and doth his fortune bless.   *imagines*

And though he do not win his wish to end,°   *completely*
Yet thus far happy he himself doth ween,
That heavens such happy grace did to him lend
As thing on earth so heavenly to have seen—
His heart's enshrinèd saint, his heaven's queen,
Fairer than fairest in his faining° eye,   *longing*
Whose sole aspect° he counts felicity.   *mere sight*

Then forth he casts in his unquiet thought
What he may do, her favor to obtain;
220 What brave exploit, what peril hardly wrought,°   *accomplished with*
What puissant conquest, what adventurous pain   *difficulty*
May please her best and grace unto him gain.
He dreads no danger, nor misfortune fears;
His faith, his fortune, in his breast he bears.

192–194 The lover's mind is transformed into the image of goodness and beauty which is the "fairer form" of his beloved.

195–196 ". . . a lover imprints a likeness of the loved one upon his soul, and so the soul of the lover becomes a mirror in which is reflected the image of the loved one" (Ficino, *Commentary*, p. 146).

204–208 See note to lines 127–133.

211–217 All of theee sentiments are usual in medieval and renaissance love poetry. For a good example see Adam de la Halle's (1250–1288) *chanson d'amour* in *Penguin Book of French Verse*, Vol. I, pp. 193–194.

218–224 "For he that loveth . . . passeth not to go a thousand times in a day to his death, to declare himself worthy of that love" (Castiglione, *The Courtier*, p. 234). See also Conon de Bethune's (1150–1220) *chanson de croisade* in *Penguin Book of French Verse*, Vol. I, p. 109; and Plato's *Symposium*, pp. 101–102.

Thou art his god, thou art his mighty guide;
Thou being blind, letst him not see his fears,
But carriest him to that which he hath eyed
Through seas, through flames, through thousand swords and
    spears.
Ne aught so strong that may his force withstand,
230 With which thou armest his resistless° hand.   *irresistible*

Witness Leander in the Euxine waves,
And stout Aeneas in the Trojan fire,
Achilles pressing through the Phrygian glaives,°   *swords*
And Orpheus daring to provoke the ire
Of damnèd fiends to get his love retire;°   *to return*
For both through heaven and hell thou makest way,
To win them worship which to thee obey.

And if by all these perils and these pains
He may but purchase° liking in her eye,   *win*
240 What heavens of joy then to himself he feigns;
Eftsoons he wipes quite out of memory
Whatever ill before he did aby.°   *suffer*
Had it been death, yet would he die again
To live thus° happy as her grace to gain.   *so*

Yet when he hath found favor to his will,
He nathemore° can so contented rest,   *in no way*
But forceth further on, and striveth still
T' approach more near, till in her inmost breast
He may embosomed be, and lovèd best.
250 And yet not best, but to be loved alone;
For love cannot endure a paragon.°   *equal*

The fear whereof, O how doth it torment
His troubled mind with more than hellish pain,
And to his feigning fancy represent
Sights never seen, and thousand shadows vain,
To break his sleep and waste° his idle brain.   *destroy*
Thou that hast never loved canst not believe
Least part of th' evils which poor lovers grieve.

231–237 The basis for this passage is probably a combination of Plato's *Symposium* (pp. 103–107) and Ficino's *Commentary* (p. 131). Spenser adds Leander (see Christopher Marlowe's *Hero and Leander*) and Aeneas to Plato's examples.

252–272 ". . . it is true love that makes lovers go in such grievous fear, for no true lover is confident, and false is the love that does not fear" (Gace Brule (1159–1212), *Penguin Book of French Verse*, Vol. I, p. 91). For a fuller treatment of the jealous suffering of the true lover see Eustache Deschamps' (1346–1407) *ballade* in *Penguin Book of French Verse*, Vol. I, pp. 235–236. See also Petrarch's Sonnet 149. The themes of envy and slander are treated in many medieval love poems (see *Penguin Book of French Verse*, Vol. I, pp. 127, 159; and Petrarch's Sonnets 100 and 139).

The gnawing envy, the heart-fretting fear,
260 The vain surmises, the distrustful shows,°   *appearances*
The false reports that flying tales do bear,
The doubts, the dangers, the delays, the woes,
The feignèd friends, the unassurèd° foes,   *unknown*
With thousands more than any tongue can tell
Do make a lover's life a wretch's hell.

Yet is there one more cursèd than they all,
That cankerworm, that monster jealousy,
Which eats the heart and feeds upon the gall,
Turning all love's delight to misery
270 Through fear of losing his felicity.
Ah gods, that ever ye that monster placed
In gentle love, that all his joys defaced.

By these, O Love, thou dost thy entrance make
Unto thy heaven, and dost the more endear
Thy pleasures unto those which them partake.
As after storms when clouds begin to clear,
The sun more bright and glorious doth appear,
So thou thy folk through pains of purgatory
Dost bear unto thy bliss, and heaven's glory.

280 There thou them placest in a paradise
Of all delight, and joyous happy rest,
Where they do feed on nectar heavenly-wise
With Hercules and Hebe and the rest
Of Venus' darlings, through her bounty blessed,
And lie like gods in ivory beds arrayed,
With rose and lilies over them displayed.°   *spread out*

There with thy daughter Pleasure they do play
Their hurtless sports without rebuke or blame,
And in her snowy bosom boldly lay
290 Their quiet heads, devoid of guilty shame,
After full joyance of their gentle game;
Then her they crown their goddess and their queen,
And deck with flowers thy altars well beseen.°   *beautiful*

Ay me, dear lord, that ever I might hope,
For all the pains and woes that I endure,
To come at length unto the wishèd scope°   *object*
Of my desire, or might myself assure
That happy port forever to recure.°   *recover*

283 *Hercules and Hebe:* After his   was married to Hebe, the beautiful
death and apotheosis the hero Hercules   daughter of Juno.

Then would I think these pains no pains at all,
300 And all my woes to be but penance small.

Then would I sing of thine immortal praise
An heavenly hymn, such as the angels sing,
And thy triumphant name then would I raise
'Bove all the gods, thee only honoring,
My guide, my god, my victor, and my king;
Till then, dread lord, vouchsafe to take of me
This simple song, thus framed° in praise of thee.   *made*

AN HYMN IN HONOR
OF BEAUTY

Ah whither, Love, wilt thou now carry me?
What wontless° fury dost thou now inspire°   *unaccustomed,*
Into my feeble breast, too full of thee?   *breathe*
Whilst seeking to aslake thy raging fire,
Thou in me kindlest much more great desire,
And up aloft above my strength dost raise,
The wondrous matter° of my fire to praise.   *i.e. beauty*

That as I erst° in praise of thine own name,   *before*
So now in honor of thy mother dear
10 An honorable hymn I eke° should frame,   *also*
And with the brightness of her beauty clear,
The ravished hearts of gazeful° men might rear   *admiring*
To admiration of that heavenly light,
From whence proceeds such soul-enchanting might.

Thereto do thou, great goddess, queen of beauty,
Mother of love and of all world's delight,
Without whose sovereign grace and kindly duty
Nothing on earth seems fair to fleshly sight—
Do thou vouchsafe with thy love-kindling light
20 T' illuminate my dim and dullèd eyne,°   *eyes*
And beautify this sacred hymn of thine.

That both to thee, to whom I mean it most,
And eke to her whose fair immortal beam
Hath darted fire into my feeble ghost,°   *spirit*
That now it wasted is with woes extreme,
It may so please that she at length will stream

1–7 For a discussion of "divine mad-   and poetry, see Ficino's *Commentary*, pp.
ness" or "fury" and its relation to love   230–233.

Some dew of grace into my withered heart,
After long sorrow and consuming smart.

What time° this world's great workmaster did cast°   *when, resolve*
30 To make all things, such as we now behold,
It seems that he before his eyes had placed
A goodly pattern, to whose perfect mold
He fashioned them as comely as he could,
That now so fair and seemly they appear,
As naught may be amended anywhere.

That wondrous pattern, wheresoe'er it be—
Whether in earth laid up in secret store,°   *storehouse*
Or else in heaven, that no man may it see
With sinful eyes, for fear it to deflore°—   *deflower*
40 Is perfect Beauty, which all men adore,
Whose face and feature doth so much excel
All mortal sense that none the same may tell.

Thereof as every earthly thing partakes,
Or more or less by influence divine,
So it more fair accordingly it makes,
And the gross matter of this earthly mine,°   *i.e. cave*
Which clotheth it, thereafter doth refine,
Doing away the dross which dims the light
Of that fair beam, which therein is empight.°   *implanted*

50 For through infusion of celestial power,
The duller earth it quickeneth with delight,
And lifeful spirits privily doth pour

29–35 "The work of the creator whenever he looks to the unchangeable and fashions the form and nature of his work after an unchangeable pattern, must necessarily be made fair and perfect. . . . If the world be indeed fair and the artificer good, it is manifest that he must have looked to that which is eternal . . . for the world is the fairest of creations and he is the best of causes" (Plato, *Timaeus*, 28, 29, Jowett translation).

36–42 Spenser appears here to mean the two kinds of beauty discussed by Ficino: "To sum it all up, Venus is twofold: one is clearly that intelligence which we said was in the Angelic Mind; the other is the power of generation with which the World-Soul is endowed" (*Commentary*, p. 142). The second Venus, earthly beauty, has its seat in nature and is the origin of material forms (p. 137). The first is divine beauty. Spenser's treatment of earthly beauty as the "wondrous pattern" of the created world would shock a strict Platonist, but not the Neoplatonists of the Middle Ages.

40 "In close order after these three splendors of the divine beauty . . . he [Plato] adds love of the soul for them . . ." (Ficino, *Commentary*, p. 139).

41–42 "Since human thought rises from the senses, we invariably judge the divine on the basis of what seems to us highest in physical bodies. . . . The soul as long as it judges divine things by mortal, speaks falsely of divinity . . ." (*Commentary*, pp. 139, 140).

43–54 For beauty as the result of the heavenly beauty's victory over "gross matter," see Castiglione's *The Courtier*, pp. 310–311. The principle Spenser alludes to here, that things are more beautiful as they partake more of divine beauty and less of gross matter, is developed in Ficino's *Commentary*, pp. 169–170.

Through all the parts, that to the looker's sight
They seem to please. That is thy sovereign might,
O Cyprian Queen, which flowing from the beam
Of thy bright star, thou into them dost stream.

That is the thing which giveth pleasant grace
To all things fair, that kindleth lively fire—
Light of thy lamp—which shining in the face,
60 Thence to the soul darts amorous desire
And robs the hearts of those which it admire;
Therewith thou pointest thy son's poisoned arrow,
That wounds the life and wastes the inmost marrow.

How vainly then do idle wits invent
That beauty is naught else but mixture made
Of colors fair, and goodly temperament°   *proportion*
Of pure complexions,° that shall quickly fade   *humors*
And pass away, like to a summer's shade;
Or that it is but comely composition°   *agreement*
70 Of parts well measured, with meet disposition.°   *arrangement*

Hath white and red in it such wondrous power
That it can pierce through th' eyes unto the heart,
And therein stir such rage and restless stour°   *tumult*
As naught but death can stint° his° dolor's smart?   *end, its*
Or can proportion of the outward part
Move such affection in the inward mind
That it can rob both sense and reason blind?

Why do not then the blossoms of the field,
Which are arrayed with much more orient hue,°   *bright color*
80 And to the sense most dainty odors yield,
Work like impression in the looker's view?
Or why do not fair pictures like power shew,
In which, ofttimes, we nature see of° art   *by*
Excelled in perfect limning° every part?   *painting*

55 *Cyprian queen:* Venus.
55–56 This reference to the influence
of the planet Venus is probably influenced
by Ficino, who accepts the old astrology
into his philosophy of love (*Commentary*,
pp. 176–177, 181, 186–188): "Hence it
happens that the souls of the planets
establish and strengthen in our souls, and
their bodies in our bodies, the powers of
those seven gifts . . . given us in the be-
ginning by God. . . . Venus inspires love
through Venerian daemons" (pp. 186–
187).
57–63 See "An Hymn in Honor of
Love," 120–127.
64–91 ". . . there are some who think
that beauty consists in a disposition of

parts or . . . size and proportion together
with a certain agreeableness of colors. We
do not agree . . . because this . . . disposi-
tion of parts would exist in composite
things only, there could be no such thing
as a beautiful simplicity. But we call
'beautiful' the pure colors . . . wisdom,
and the soul, all of which are simple. . . .
Then, too, we often see a more orderly
disposition and size of parts in one person
than in another, and yet the other person
. . . is nevertheless adjudged more beauti-
ful. . . . It sometimes happens among
those of equal age that one who surpasses
another in color is yet surpassed by the
other in charm and beauty" (Ficino,
Commentary, pp. 168–169).

But ah, believe me, there is more than so°
That works such wonders in the minds of men.
I that have often proved, too well it know.
And whoso list° the like assays° to ken°
Shall find by trial—and confess it then—
90 That beauty is not, as fond men misdeem,
An outward show of things that only seem.

For that same goodly hue of white and red
With which the cheeks are sprinkled shall decay;
And those sweet rosy leaves so fairly spread
Upon the lips shall fade and fall away
To that they were, e'en to corrupted clay.
That golden wire,° those sparkling stars° so bright,
Shall turn to dust, and lose their goodly light.

But that fair lamp, from whose celestial ray
100 That light proceeds which kindleth lovers' fire,
Shall never be extinguished nor decay,
But when the vital spirits do expire,
Unto her native planet shall retire;
For it is heavenly born and cannot die,
Being a parcel of the purest sky.

For when the soul, the which derivèd was
At first out of that great immortal Sprite°
By whom all live to love, whilom° did pass
Down from the top of purest heaven's height
110 To be embodied here, it then took light
And lively spirits from that fairest star,
Which lights the world forth from his fiery car.°

Which power retaining still, or° more or less,
When she in fleshly seed is eft° enraced,°
Through every part she doth the same impress
According as the heavens have her graced,
And frames° her house, in which she will be placed,

i.e. than red and white

desires, assaults, know

i.e. hair, eyes

spirit
formerly

chariot

either
again, implanted

makes

99   *that fair lamp:* the essential beauty of the beloved, which, Spenser argues, lies in the soul, not in the body.
102   *vital spirits;* see note on 110–119.
107   *great immortal Sprite:* God.
110–119   "There appear to be really three things in us: soul, spirit, and body. Soul and body, naturally very different from each other, are joined by the median, spirit, which is a certain very thin and clear vapor, created through the heat of the heart from the purest part of the blood; and thence diffused through all the parts. This spirit receives the powers of the soul and transfers them into the body" (Ficino, *Commentary,* p. 189). These ideas are commonplace in the Renaissance and the Middle Ages.
111   *that fairest star:* the sun. In deriving the vital spirits from the sun, Spenser differs from Ficino and most other renaissance writers.
117–119   The metaphor of the body as the soul's house is common in medieval and renaissance literature. See *The Faerie Queene,* Book II, Canto ix, and Ficino's treatment of the metaphor in *Commentary,* p. 172.

Fit for herself, adorning it with spoil
Of th' heavenly riches which she robbed erewhile.

120 Thereof it comes that these fair souls, which have
The most resemblance of that heavenly light,
Frame to themselves most beautiful and brave°   *splendid*
Their fleshly bower, most fit for their delight,
And the gross matter by a sovereign might
Tempers so trim° that it may well be seen   *neatly*
A palace fit for such a virgin queen.

So every spirit as it is most pure
And hath in it the more of heavenly light,
So it the fairer body doth procure
130 To habit° in, and it more fairly dight°   *live, adorn*
With cheerful grace and amiable sight.°   *appearance*
For of the soul the body form doth take;
For soul is form, and doth the body make.

Therefore wherever that thou dost behold
A comely corpse,° with beauty fair endued,°   *body, endowed*
Know this for certain: that the same doth hold
A beauteous soul, with fair conditions° thewed,°   *qualities, trained*
Fit to receive the seed of virtue strewed.°   *sowed*
For all that fair is, is by nature good;
140 That is a sign to know the gentle° blood.   *noble*

Yet oft it falls° that many a gentle mind   *happens*
Dwells in deformèd tabernacle drowned,
Either by chance, against the course of kind,°   *nature*
Or through unaptness° in the substance found,   *flaw*
Which it assumèd of some stubborn ground
That will not yield unto her form's direction,
But is performed° with some foul imperfection.   *shaped*

126 *virgin queen:* the soul. For another example of the soul as the virgin mistress of a castle see Langland's *Piers Plowman* (B. Passus IX). The metaphor is extremely common in medieval and renaissance literature.

132–133 For the soul as the form and maker of the body, see Ficino's *Commentary* (pp. 172–175): ". . . that perfect Form of man which the soul possesses will turn out more accurately in . . . quiet and compliant matter" (p. 174).

134–140 "Whereupon doth very seldom an ill soul dwell in a beautiful body. And therefore is the outward beauty a true sign of the inward goodness, and in bodies this comeliness is imprinted more

and less . . . for a mark of the soul, whereby she is outwardly known . . ." (Castiglione, *The Courtier*, p. 309). See also *The Courtier*, pp. 310–311.

141–147 "It frequently happens . . . that two souls may descend at different times. . . . One of them, finding a suitable seed on the earth, may have shaped out most accurately . . . a body according to those earlier ideas [the idea in the soul]. The other may likewise even have begun a work, but because of the unsuitability of its material, its body will not have been carried out with such great fidelity to its pattern. The first body, therefore, is more beautiful than the second" (Ficino, *Commentary*, p. 188).

And oft it falls—ay me the more to rue—
That goodly beauty, albe° heavenly born,   *although*
150 Is foul abused, and that celestial hue,°   *form*
Which doth the world with her delight adorn,
Made but the bait of sin, and sinners' scorn;
Whilst everyone doth seek and sue° to have it,   *plead*
But everyone doth seek but to deprave it.

Yet nathemore° is that fair beauty's blame,   *in no way*
But theirs that do abuse it unto ill.
Nothing so good but that through guilty shame
May be corrupt and wrested unto will.
Natheless° the soul is fair and beauteous still,   *nevertheless*
160 However flesh's fault it filthy make;
For things immortal no corruption take.

But ye fair dames, the world's dear ornaments
And lively images of heaven's light,
Let not your beams with such disparagements°   *disgraceful loves*
Be dimmed, and your bright glory darkened quite;
But mindful still of your first country's sight,
Do still preserve your first informèd° grace,   *formed*
Whose shadow yet shines in your beauteous face.

Loathe that foul blot, that hellish firebrand,
170 Disloyal lust, fair beauty's foulest blame,°   *fault*
That base affections, which your ears would bland,°   *flatter*
Commend to you by love's abusèd name,
But is indeed the bondslave of defame,°   *dishonor*
Which will the garland of your glory mar,
And quench the light of your bright shining star.

But gentle love, that loyal is and true,
Will more illumine your resplendent ray
And add more brightness to your goodly hue

148–161 "Neither yet ought beautiful women to bear the blame of that hatred, mortality, and destruction, which the unbridled appetites of men are the cause of. I will not now deny, but it is possible also to find in the world beautiful women unchaste, yet not because beauty inclineth them to unchaste living, for it rather . . . leadeth them into the way of virtuous conditions, through the affinity that beauty hath with goodness. But otherwhile ill bringing up, the continual provocation of lovers, tokens, poverty, hope, deceits, fear, and a thousand other matters overcome the steadfastness, yea of beautiful and good women . . ."

(Castiglione, *The Courtier*, p. 311).
176–182 "In the same way in which a mirror, struck in some way by the light of the sun, shines back and, by that reflection . . . sets on fire a piece of wool placed next to it, so . . . that part of the soul which they call dark fancy and the memory, like a mirror, is struck by an image of Beauty itself . . . as though by some beam taken in through the eyes, so that the soul makes for itself from that image another, the reflection as it were of the first. By this . . . the force of desire is kindled and the soul loves" (Ficino, *Commentary*, p. 216).

From light of his pure fire; which by like way
180 Kindled of yours, your likeness doth display,
Like as two mirrors by opposed reflection
Do both express the face's first impression.

Therefore to make your beauty more appear,
It you behooves to love, and forth to lay
That heavenly richess which in you ye bear,
That men the more admire their fountain may;
For else what booteth that celestial ray
If it in darkness be enshrinèd ever,
That it of loving eyes be viewèd never?

190 But in your choice of loves, this well advise:°   *consider*
That likest to yourselves ye them select,
The which your form's first source may sympathize,
And with like beauty's parts be inly° decked.   *inwardly*
For if you loosely° love without respect,   *carelessly*
It is no love, but a discordant war,
Whose unlike parts amongst themselves do jar.°   *fight*

For love is a celestial harmony
Of likely hearts composed of° stars' concent,°   *brought together*
Which join together in sweet sympathy   *by, harmony*
200 To work each other's joy and true content,
Which they have harbored since their first descent
Out of their heavenly bowers, where they did see
And know each other here beloved to be.

Then wrong it were that any other twain
Should in love's gentle band combinèd be
But those whom heaven did at first ordain
And make out of one mold, the more t' agree.
For all that like the beauty that they see
Straight do not love; for love is not so light°   *frivolous*
210 As straight to burn at first beholder's sight.

190–231 "Hence, it happens that a man loves . . . those who have a like birth. . . . In like manner, those who . . . are born under the same star, are so constituted, that the image of the more beautiful of the two flowing through the eyes into the soul of the other, corresponds to and agrees completely with a like image formed from its very generation both in the celestial body and in the inner part of the soul. The soul, thus struck, recognizes that image . . . as something its own. . . . It immediately compares that image with its own interior Idea and if anything is lacking to the image to be a perfect representation of the . . . body, the soul restores it by reforming, and then loves the reformed image . . . as its own work. Hence it happens that lovers . . . think a person is more beautiful than he is. For . . . they see him in an image already remade by the soul according to the likeness of . . . an image which is more beautiful than the body itself" (*Commentary*, p. 188).

199–200 See Ficino's discussion of mutual love in *Commentary*, pp. 144–145.

But they which love indeed look otherwise,
With pure regard and spotless true intent,
Drawing out of the object of their eyes
A more refinèd form, which they present
Unto their mind, void of all blemishment;
Which it reducing to her° first perfection,   *i.e. the form's*
Beholdeth free from flesh's frail infection.

      And then conforming° it unto the light,   *shaping*
Which in itself it hath remaining still,°   *always*
220 Of that first sun, yet sparkling in his sight,
Thereof he fashions in his higher skill
An heavenly beauty to his fancy's will,
And it embracing in his mind entire,°   *completely*
The mirror of his own thought doth admire.

      Which seeing now so inly fair to be
As outward it appeareth to the eye,
And with his spirit's proportion to agree,
He thereon fixeth all his fantasy
And fully setteth° his felicity,   *establishes*
230 Counting it fairer than it is indeed,
And yet indeed her fairness doth exceed.

      For lovers' eyes more sharply sighted be
Than other men's, and in dear love's delight
See more than any other eyes can see,
Through mutual receipt of beamès bright,
Which carry privy message to the sprite,
And to their eyes that inmost fair° display,   *beauty*
As plain as light discovers dawning day.

      Therein they see through amorous eye-glances
240 Armies of loves° still flying to and fro,   *cupids*
Which dart at them their little fiery lances,
Whom having wounded, back again they go,
Carrying compassion to their lovely foe;
Who seeing her fair eyes' so sharp effect,
Cures all their sorrows with one sweet aspect.°   *look*

      In which, how many wonders do they read
To their conceit° that others never see—   *conception*

    231–245 See Castiglione's *The Cour-*
tier, pp. 246–247.
    240 *Armies of loves*: cupids.
    246–252 "Let him lay aside . . . the
judgment of sense, and enjoy with his
eyes the brightness, the comeliness, the
loving sparkles, laughters, gestures, and
all the other pleasant furnitures of beauty:
especially with hearing the sweetness of
her voice, the tunableness of her words,
the melody of her singing . . ." (Castig-
lione, *The Courtier*, p. 313).

Now of her smiles, with which their souls they feed
Like gods with nectar in their banquets free,°   *abundant*
250 Now of her looks, which like to cordials be;
But when her words' embassade° forth she sends,   *embassy*
Lord, how sweet music that unto them lends!

Sometimes upon her forehead they behold
A thousand graces masking in delight;
Sometimes within her eyelids they unfold
Ten thousand sweet belgards,° which to their sight   *loving looks*
Do seem like twinkling stars in frosty night;
But on her lips like rosy buds in May,
So many millions of chaste pleasures play.

260 All those, O Cytheree, and thousands more
Thy handmaids be, which do on thee attend
To deck thy beauty with their dainties' store,
That may it more to mortal eyes commend,
And make it more admired of foe and friend,
That in men's hearts thou mayst thy throne install,
And spread thy lovely kingdom over all.

Then *Iŏ triumph*, O great beauty's queen!
Advance the banner of thy conquest high,
That all this world, the which thy vassals been,
270 May draw to thee, and with due fealty
Adore the power of thy great majesty,
Singing this hymn in honor of thy name,
Compiled by me, which thy poor liegeman° am.   *vassal*

In lieu whereof,° grant, O great sovereign,   *return for which*
That she whose conquering beauty doth captive
My trembling heart in her eternal chain,
One drop of grace at length will to me give,
That I her bounden thrall by her may live,
And this same life, which first fro me she reaved,°   *stole*
280 May owe to her, of whom I it received.

And you, fair Venus' darling, my dear dread,
Fresh flower of grace, great goddess of my life,
When your fair eyes these fearful lines shall read,
Deign to let fall one drop of due relief,
That may recure° my heart's long pining grief,   *cure*
And show what wondrous power your beauty hath,
That can restore a damnèd wight from death.

260 *Cytheree:* Venus.   note on "An Hymn in Honor of Love,"
267–273 See Ovid's *Amores* (I.ii) and   36–42.

AN HYMN
OF HEAVENLY LOVE

Love, lift me up upon thy golden wings
From this base world unto thy heaven's height,
Where I may see those admirable things
Which there thou workest by thy sovereign might,
Far above feeble reach of earthly sight,
That I thereof an heavenly hymn may sing
Unto the God of love, high heaven's king.

Many lewd lays—ah woe is me the more—
In praise of that mad fit which fools call love
10 I have in th' heat of youth made heretofore,
That in light wits did loose affection° move;   *passion*
But all those follies now I do reprove,
And turnèd have the tenor° of my string,   *pitch*
The heavenly praises of true love to sing.

And ye that wont with greedy vain desire
To read my fault, and wondering° at my flame   *marveling*
To warm yourselves at my wide sparkling fire,
Sith° now that heat is quenchèd, quench my blame,   *since*
And in her ashes shroud my dying shame;
20 For who my passèd follies now pursues
Begins his own, and my old fault renews.

Before this world's great frame, in which all things
Are now contained, found any being-place,
Ere flitting Time could wag his eyas° wings   i.e. *new-fledged*
About the mighty bound which doth embrace
The rolling spheres and parts their hours by space,
That high eternal power, which now doth move
In all these things, moved in itself by love.

1–5 See "An Hymn in Honor of
Love," 177–179.
  7 *high heaven's king:* Christ.
  8–14 Spenser here specifically rejects
the two earthly hymns. His retraction
may owe something to Petrarch's famous
retractions: "Love held me one and
twenty years enchain'd, / . . . / Now
weary grown, my life I had arraign'd /
That in its error check'd (to my belief) /
Blest virtue's seeds" (*Tennemi Amor,
Sonnets*, p. 314).
  19 *her:* my passion's.
  24–26 "Wherefore he resolved to have
a moving image of eternity, and when he
set in order the heaven, he made this
image . . . moving according to number . . .
and this image we call time. . . . Time,
then, and the heaven came into being at
the same instant . . ." (Plato, *Timaeus*,
Jowett translation, 37–38). Spenser sees
time as establishing the outer limits of
the physical universe in the sphere of the
fixed stars. The orbits (or spheres) of the
planets are contained within this sphere,
and their "hours" are measured in degrees
on the circle of the fixed stars.

It loved itself because itself was fair—
30 For fair is loved—and of itself begot
Like to itself, his eldest son and heir,
Eternal, pure, and void of sinful blot,
The firstling of his joy, in whom no jot
Of love's dislike or pride was to be found,
Whom he therefore with equal honor crowned.

With him he reigned, before all time prescribed,°   *ordained*
In endless glory and immortal might,
Together with that third from them derived,
Most wise, most holy, most almighty sprite,
40 Whose kingdom's throne no thought of earthly wight
Can comprehend. Much less my trembling verse
With equal° words can hope it to rehearse.   *appropriate*

Yet O most blessed spirit, pure lamp of light,
Eternal spring of grace and wisdom true,
Vouchsafe to shed into my barren sprite
Some little drop of thy celestial dew,
That may my rhymes with sweet infuse° imbrue;°   *tincture, drench*
And give me words equal unto my thought,
To tell the marvels by thy mercy wrought.

50 Yet being pregnant still with powerful grace,
And full of fruitful love, that loves to get°   *beget*
Things like himself, and to enlarge his race,
His second brood—though not in power so great,
Yet full of beauty—next he did beget,
An infinite increase° of angels bright,   *offspring*
All glistering glorious in their maker's light.

To them the heavens' illimitable height—
Not this round heaven which we from hence behold—

30 "must not Love be only love of beauty . . ." (Plato, *Symposium*, p. 171).

35 *with equal honor crowned:* Spenser expresses here the orthodox belief in the Son's equality (and unity) with the Father. "The Son . . . begotten from everlasting of the Father . . . and of one substance with the Father . . ." (Articles of Religion, Article II, *The Book of Common Prayer*).

38 *that third:* the Holy Ghost. "The Holy Ghost, proceeding from the Father and the Son, is of one substance, majesty, and glory, with the Father and the Son . . ." (Articles of Religion, Article V, *The Book of Common Prayer*).

43–49 Compare with the invocations in "An Hymn in Honor of Love," 22–28, and "An Hymn in Honor of Beauty," 15–21.

43–44 The equation of the Holy Ghost with light is ancient and conventional in Christian writings. The Holy Ghost is the "spring of grace" because, as Luther writes, "apart from the operation of the Holy Spirit, no one can come to God, nor receive any of the blessings effected through Christ . . ." (*A Short Exposition of the Apostles' Creed* in *Reformation Writings of Martin Luther*, trans. Bertram Lee Woolf, Vol. I, p. 87). It is the spring of "wisdom true" because Christ calls the third person "the Spirit of truth" (John 14:17).

58 *this round heaven:* the heavens under the sphere of the fixed stars.

Adorned with thousand lamps of burning light,
60 And with ten thousand gems of shining gold,
He gave as their inheritance to hold,
That they might serve him in eternal bliss,
And be partakers of those joys of his.

There they in their trinal triplicities
About him wait, and on his will depend,
Either with nimble wings to cut the skies,
When he them on his messages doth send,
Or on his own dread presence to attend,
Where they behold the glory of his light,
70 And carol hymns of love both day and night.

Both day and night is unto them all one,
For he his beams doth still° to them extend,   *always*
That darkness there appeareth never none;
Ne hath their day, ne hath their bliss an end,
But there their termless time in pleasure spend.
Ne ever should their happiness decay,
Had not they dared their lord to disobey.

But pride impatient of long-resting peace,
Did puff them up with greedy bold ambition,
80 That they gan cast° their state how to increase   *did plot*
Above the fortune of their first condition,
And sit in God's own seat without commission.
The brightest angel, even the child of light,
Drew millions more against their God to fight.

Th' Almighty seeing their so bold assay,°   *attempt*
Kindled the flame of his consuming ire,
And with his only breath° them blew away   *breath alone*
From heaven's height, to which they did aspire,
To deepest hell, and lake of damnèd fire,
90 Where they in darkness and dread horror dwell,
Hating the happy light from which they fell.

64 *trinal triplicities:* the three hierarchies of the nine orders of angels, each hierarchy containing three orders.
67 *on his messages:* Greek *angellos,* "messenger."
71–74 "And the city had no need of the sun, neither of the moon, to shine in it: for the glory of God did lighten it, and the Lamb is the light thereof" (Revelation 21:23).
77–82 ". . . others, being enamoured rather of their own power, as if they could be their own good, lapsed to this private good of their own . . . and barter-

ing the lofty dignity of eternity for the inflation of pride . . . they became proud, deceived, envious" (St. Augustine, *City of God,* XII.1).
83 *brightest angel:* Lucifer, who "drew the third part of the stars [angels] of heaven, and did cast them to the earth" (Revelation 12:4).
87–90 "God spared not the angels that sinned, but cast them down to hell and delivered them into chains of darkness, to be reserved unto judgment" (2 Peter 2:4). See also Jude 6.

So that next offspring of the Maker's love,
Next to himself in glorious degree,
Degendering° to hate, fell from above   *degenerating*
Through pride—for pride and love may ill agree—
And now of sin to all ensample° be.   *example*
How then can sinful flesh itself assure,
Sith purest angels fell to be impure?

But that eternal fount of love and grace,
100 Still flowing forth his goodness unto all,
Now seeing left a waste and empty place
In his wide palace through those angels' fall,
Cast to supply° the same, and to install   *fill*
A new unknowen colony therein,
Whose root from earth's base groundwork should begin.

Therefore of clay—base, vile, and next to nought,
Yet formed by wondrous skill, and by his might,
According to an heavenly pattern wrought,
Which he had fashioned in his wise foresight—
110 He man did make, and breathed a living sprite
Into his face most beautiful and fair,
Endued° with wisdom's riches, heavenly, rare.   *endowed*

Such he him made that he resemble might
Himself, as° mortal thing immortal could;   *as nearly as*
Him to be lord of every living wight
He made by love out of his own like mold,
In whom he might his mighty self behold.
For love doth love the thing beloved to see,
That like itself in lovely shape may be.

120 But man, forgetful of his maker's grace
No less than angels whom he did ensue,°   *follow in time*
Fell from the hope of promised heavenly place
Into the mouth of death, to sinners due;
And all his offspring into thralldom threw,

106–107 "And the Lord God formed man of the dust of the ground" (Genesis 2:7).
108–109 "So God created man in his own image" (Genesis 1:27). ". . . and man, whom He had not previously made, He made in time . . . by His unchangeable and eternal design" (*City of God*, XII.21).
· 110–111 ". . . and breathed into his nostrils the breath of life; and man became a living soul" (Genesis 2:7).
122 *heavenly place:* "Man . . . He created in such sort, that if he remained in subjection to his Creator as his rightful Lord, and piously kept the commandments, he should pass into the company of the angels" (*City of God*, XII.21).
123 "For the wages of sin is death" (Romans 6:23).
124–126 "For we all were in that one man, since we all were that one man who fell into sin. . . . thus, from the bad use of free will, there originated the whole train of evil, which . . . convoys the human race from its depraved state . . , on to the destruction of the second death, which has no end . . ." (*City of God*, XIII.14).

Where they forever should in bonds remain
Of never dead, yet ever dying pain.

    Till that great Lord of Love, which him at first
Made of mere love, and after likèd well,
Seeing him lie like creature long accursed
130 In that deep horror of despairèd° hell,   *hopeless*
Him wretch in dole° would let no lenger° dwell,   *misery, longer*
But cast out of that bondage to redeem,
And pay the price, all° were his debt extreme.   *although*

    Out of the bosom of eternal bliss,
In which he reignèd with his glorious sire,
He down descended, like a most demiss°   *servile*
And abject thrall, in flesh's frail attire,
That he for him might pay sin's deadly hire,°   *price*
And him restore unto that happy state
140 In which he stood before his hapless fate.

    In flesh at first the guilt committed was;
Therefore in flesh it must be satisfied.
Nor° spirit, nor angel, though they man surpass,   *neither*
Could make amends to God for man's misguide,°   *error*
But only man himself, who self did slide.
So taking flesh of sacred virgin's womb,
For man's dear sake he did a man become.

    And that most blessed body, which was born
Without all° blemish or reproachful blame,   *any*
150 He freely gave to be both rent and torn
Of° cruel hands; who with despiteful shame   *by*
Reviling him, that them most vile became,°   *became them most*
                          vilely
At length him nailèd on a gallow tree,
And slew the just by most unjust decree.

    O huge and most unspeakable impression
Of love's deep wound, that pierced the piteous heart
Of that dear Lord with so entire affection,

128 *and after likèd well:* "And God
saw every thing that he had made, and,
behold, it was very good" (Genesis 1:31).
    133 "For ye are bought with a price"
(1 Corinthians 6:20).
    136–137 "But made himself of no
reputation, and took upon him the form
of a servant, and was made in the likeness
of men" (Philippians 2:7).
    138–142 "For as by one man's dis-
obedience many were made sinners, so by
the obedience of one shall many be made
righteous" (Romans 5:19).
    141–147 This stanza states the most
influential of the various doctrines of the
Atonement. The argument is that since
Adam, a man, first sinned, only a man
could atone for the crime. But since no
man could atone, only God, taking the
flesh of man, could satisfy God and re-
deem man.
    148–154 See the account in Matthew
27:28–48.

And sharply launching° every inner part,   *piercing*
Dolors of death into his soul did dart,
160 Doing him die° that never it deserved,   *killing him*
To free his foes, that from his hest° had swerved. *commandment*

What heart can feel least touch of so sore launch,
Or thought can think the depth of so dear wound?
Whose bleeding source their streams yet never staunch,
But still do flow, and freshly still redound,°   *overflow*
To heal the sores of sinful souls unsound,
And cleanse the guilt of that infected crime,
Which was enrooted in all fleshly slime.

O blessed well of love, O flower of grace,
170 O glorious morning star, O lamp of light,
Most lively image of thy Father's face,
Eternal King of Glory, Lord of Might,
Meek Lamb of God before all worlds behight°— *ordained*
How can we thee requite for all this good?
Or what can prize° that thy most precious blood? *compare in value*
                   with

Yet nought thou askst in lieu of° all this love *return for*
But love of us° for guerdon of thy pain.   *our love*
Ay me, what can us less than that behoove?
Had he requirèd life of us again,°   *in payment*
180 Had it been wrong to ask his own with gain?° *interest*
He gave us life, he it restorèd lost;
Then life were least, that us so little cost.

But he our life hath left unto us free,
Free that was thrall, and blessèd that was band;° *bound*
Ne aught demands but that we loving be,
As he himself hath loved us aforehand,
And bound thereto with an eternal band
Him first to love that us so dearly bought,
And next, our brethren to his image wrought.

190 Him first to love, great right and reason is:
Who first to us our life and being gave;

164–168 These lines refer to the outpouring of grace with the crucifixion of Christ. Christ is "a pure river of water of life" (Revelation 22:1). They also refer to the sacrament of Holy Communion, established by Christ's words to the disciples at the Last Supper: "For this is my blood of the new testament, which is shed for many for the remission of sins" (Matthew 26:28).

170 *morning star:* "I am . . . the bright and morning star" (Revelation 22:16).
171 "Who being the brightness of his glory, and the express image of his person . . ." (Hebrews 1:3).
173 See John 1:29.
183–186 "For, brethren, ye have been called unto liberty; only use not liberty for an occasion to the flesh, but by love serve one another" (Galatians 5:13).

And after, when we farèd had amiss,
Us wretches from the second death did save;
And last, the food of life, which now we have,
Even himself in his dear sacrament,
To feed our hungry souls unto us lent.

Then next to love our brethren, that were made
Of that self mold and that self maker's hand
That° we, and to the same again shall fade,   *as*
200 Where they shall have like heritage of land,
However here on higher steps we stand;
Which also were with self same price redeemed
That we, however of us light esteemed.

And were they not, yet since that loving Lord
Commanded us to love them for his sake—
Even for his sake, and for his sacred word,
Which in his last bequest he to us spake—
We should them love, and with their needs partake,°   *share*
Knowing that whatso'er to them we give
210 We give to him, by whom we all do live.

Such mercy he by his most holy read°   *counsel*
Unto us taught, and to approve° it true   *prove*
Ensampled it by his most righteous deed,
Showing us mercy—miserable crew—
That we the like should to the wretches shew,
And love our brethren, thereby to approve
How much himself, that lovèd us, we love.

Then rouse thyself, O earth, out of thy soil,
In which thou wallowest like to filthy swine,
220 And dost thy mind in dirty pleasures moil,°   *besmirch*
Unmindful of that dearest Lord of thine.
Lift up to him thy heavy clouded eyne,°   *eyes*
That thou his sovereign bounty mayst behold,
And read through love his mercies manifold.

Begin from first, where he encradled was
In simple cratch,° wrapped in a wad of hay,   *crib*

193 *second death:* damnation. The first death is the fall of Adam.

194–196 "And Jesus said unto them, I am the bread of life: he that cometh to me shall never hunger" (John 6:35).

209–210 "Verily I say unto you, Inasmuch as ye have done it unto one of the least of these my brethren, ye have done it unto me" (Matthew 25:40).

211–212 "Be ye therefore merciful, as your Father also is merciful" (Luke 6:36).

218–221 See "An Hymn in Honor of Love," 176–179. Here probably an allusion to the parable of the prodigal son, who "would fain have filled his belly with the husks that the swine did eat" (Luke 15:16).

225–287 Spenser ends his poem with a traditional exhortation to meditate upon the life of Christ, and an explanation of how the Christian moves from meditation to intense remorse and repentance, then to an equally intense love of Christ, and finally to a mystical vision of the risen Christ and heaven. The

Between the toilful ox and humble ass;
And in what rags, and in how base array,
The glory of our heavenly riches lay,
230 When him the silly° shepherds came to see,   *humble*
Whom greatest princes sought on lowest knee.

From thence, read on the story of his life:
His humble carriage,° his unfaulty ways,   *behavior*
His cankered° foes, his fights, his toil, his strife,   *corrupt*
His pains, his poverty, his sharp assays,°   *trials*
Through which he passed his miserable days,
Offending none, and doing good to all,
Yet being maliced both of° great and small.   *by*

And look at last how of most wretched wights
240 He taken was, betrayed, and false accused;
How with most scornful taunts and fell despites
He was reviled, disgraced, and foul abused;
How scourged, how crowned, how buffeted, how bruised;
And lastly how twixt robbers crucified,
With bitter wounds through hands, through feet and side.

Then let thy flinty heart that feels no pain
Empiercèd be with pitiful remorse;
And let thy bowels bleed in every vein
At sight of his most sacred heavenly corse,°   *body*
250 So torn and mangled with malicious force;
And let thy soul, whose sins his sorrows wrought,
Melt into tears and groan in grievèd thought.

With sense whereof whilst so thy softened spirit
Is inly touched, and humbled with meek zeal,
Through meditation of his endless merit,
Lift up thy mind to th' author of thy weal,
And to his sovereign mercy do appeal;
Learn him to love that lovèd thee so dear,
And in thy breast his blessèd image bear.

260 With all thy heart, with all thy soul and mind,
Thou must him love, and his behests embrace.
All other loves, with which the world doth blind

---

spiritual exercises which Spenser describes
here were made extremely popular in the
late Middle Ages by the writings of St.
Bernard (1091–1153) and St. Bonaven-
ture (1221–1274). They were still very
widely practiced in the Renaissance in
both Roman Catholic and Protestant
communities. See Louis L. Martz, *The*
Poetry of Meditation, Yale University
Press, 1962, pp. 1–117, especially pp. 71–
117.
   260–261 "Thou shalt love the Lord
thy God with all thy heart, and with all
thy soul, and with all thy mind" (Mat-
thew 22:37).

Weak fancies and stir up affections base,
Thou must renounce and utterly displace,°   *put out*
And give thyself unto him full and free,
That full and freely gave himself to thee.

Then shalt thou feel thy spirit so possessed
And ravished with devouring great desire
Of his dear self, that shall thy feeble breast
270 Inflame with love and set thee all on fire
With burning zeal through every part entire,
That in no earthly thing thou shalt delight,
But in his sweet and amiable sight.

Thenceforth all world's desire will in thee die,
And all earth's glory on which men do gaze
Seem dirt and dross in thy pure-sighted eye,
Compared to that celestial beauty's blaze,
Whose glorious beams all fleshly sense doth daze
With admiration of their passing° light,   *supreme*
280 Blinding the eyes and lumining the sprite.

Then shall thy ravished soul inspirèd be
With heavenly thoughts, far above human skill,
And thy bright radiant eyes shall plainly see
Th' idea of his pure glory present still°   *always*
Before thy face, that all thy spirits shall fill
With sweet enragement° of celestial love,   *ecstasy*
Kindled through sight of those fair things above.

AN HYMN
OF HEAVENLY BEAUTY

Rapt with the rage° of mine own ravished thought,   *intensity*
Through contemplation of those goodly sights
And glorious images in heaven wrought,
Whose wondrous beauty breathing sweet delights   *high-minded*
Do kindle love in high-conceited sprites,°   *spirits*
I fain° to tell the things that I behold,   *want*
But feel my wits to fail and tongue to fold.

267–287 Compare "An Hymn in   Love," 204–210.
Honor of Love," 273–293.   1–5 Compare 281–287 of "An Hymn
274–280 See "An Hymn in Honor of   of Heavenly Love."

Vouchsafe then, O thou most almighty Sprite,
From whom all gifts of wit° and knowledge flow,   *intelligence*
10 To shed into my breast some sparkling light
Of thine eternal truth, that I may show
Some little beams to mortal eyes below
Of that immortal beauty there with thee,
Which in my weak distraughted mind I see.

That with the glory of so goodly sight
The hearts of men, which fondly° here admire   *foolishly*
Fair-seeming shows and feed on vain delight,
Transported with celestial desire
Of those fair forms, may lift themselves up higher,
20 And learn to love with zealous humble duty
Th' eternal fountain of that heavenly beauty.

Beginning then below, with th' easy view
Of this base world, subject to fleshly eye,
From thence to mount aloft by order due
To contemplation of th' immortal sky,
Of° the soar falcon so° I learn to fly,   *from, thus*
That flags awhile her fluttering wings beneath,
Till she herself for stronger flight can breathe.°   *rest*

Then look, who list° thy gazeful eyes to feed   *wants*
30 With sight of that is fair, look on the frame
Of this wide universe, and therein read
The endless kinds of creatures, which by name
Thou canst not count, much less their natures aim;°   *guess*
All which are made with wondrous wise respect,
And all with admirable beauty decked.

8 *almighty Sprite:* the Holy Spirit, the third person of the Trinity.
9 "But the Comforter, which is the Holy Ghost, whom the Father will send in my name, he shall teach you all things, and bring all things to your remembrance, whatsoever I have said unto you" (John 14:26).
11 ". . . he shall give you another Comforter. . . . Even the Spirit of truth . ." (John 14:16–17).
13 *immortal beauty:* compare "An Hymn of Heavenly Love," 277–280.
22–105 Here Spenser argues from the beauty of the creation to the infinite beauty of the creator. He moves from the least beautiful, the earthly, to the most, the angelic orders. His argument is traditional: "All these things, therefore, which have been made by the divine art, manifest a certain unity, form, and order in themselves. . . . When in our mind, therefore, we perceive the Creator through the things which have been made, we ought to recognize him as that Trinity of which a trace appears . . . in the creature. For in that Trinity is the highest origin of all things, their most perfect beauty . . ." (St. Augustine, *The Trinity*, VI.10, trans. Stephen McKenna, Catholic University of America, 1963, p. 214).
29–35 "On all sides appears the beauty of the work, revealing to you the Artificer. You admire the creation: love the Creator then! . . . Behold the innumerable host of stars . . . so many different species of animals . . . how great are all these things, how bright, how beautiful, how stupendous!" (St. Augustine, *Enarrationes in Psalmos*, CXLV.5, 12; quoted from Robert Ellrodt, *Neoplatonism in the Poetry of Spenser*, p. 180).

First th' earth, on adamantine° pillars founded,   *unbreakable*
Amid the sea engirt with brazen° bands;   *brass*
Then th' air, still flitting° but yet firmly bounded   *continually*
On every side with piles of flaming brands,   *moving*
40 Never consumed nor quenched with mortal hands;
And last, that mighty shining crystal wall
Wherewith he hath encompassèd this all.

By view whereof, it plainly may appear
That still as every thing doth upward tend,
And further is from earth, so still more clear
And fair it grows, till to his° perfect end   *its*
Of purest beauty it at last ascend—
Air more than water, fire much more than air,
And heaven than fire appears more pure and fair.

50 Look thou no further, but affix thine eye
On that bright-shiny, round, still-moving mass,
The house of blessed gods which men call *sky*,
All sowed with glistering stars more thick than grass,
Whereof each other doth in brightness pass,°   *surpass*
But those two most, which ruling night and day
As king and queen, the heavens' empire sway.°   *govern*

And tell me then, what hast thou ever seen
That to their beauty may comparèd be?
Or can the sight that is most sharp and keen
60 Endure their captain's° flaming head to see?   i.e. *God's*

36–63 These lines describe the beauty of the material creation. Spenser's universe was a series of concentric spheres, with the Earth at the center, a sphere called the *primum mobile* at the outer boundary, and spheres of the fixed stars and the various planets between. Below the sphere of the moon, the material world is divided into four regions: the earth at the center, the water covering the earth, air above, and a region of fire separating the region of air from the sphere of the moon.

36–37 "for the pillars of the earth are the Lord's, and he hath set the world upon them" (1 Samuel 2:8). "He hath compassed the waters with bounds, until the day and night come to an end" (Job 26:10).

41 *crystal wall:* the crystalline sphere, the outer boundary between the material world and the spiritual worlds beyond.

43–47 These lines are a succinct statement of one version of the idea of the "Great Chain of Being," one of the most important symbolic patterns in Western civilization. Briefly the idea is that all things in the universe are organized in a great hierarchy or chain of command according to superiority of substance or function. In Spenser's version purity, clarity, or simplicity of substance is the organizing principle of the hierarchy. Beauty, then, acts as a sort of law of gravity, holding everything in its proper place in the universe.

52 *blessed gods:* the planets, named after Roman deities.

56 *king* and *queen:* the sun and the moon.

59–60 *captain's flaming head:* the sun's light. Here and in other references to the sun in the poem there is probably an allusion to Plato's "myth of the cave" in *The Republic*, VII. In Plato's story, the last thing the prisoner is able to do is to look directly at the sun. Spenser, like Plato, treats the sun as a metaphor for God, and the material world as an analogy to the spiritual world.

How much less those, much higher in degree,
And so much fairer and much more than these
As these are fairer than the land and seas?

For far above these heavens, which here we see,
Be others far exceeding these in light,
Not bounded, nor corrupt, as these same be,
But infinite in largeness and in height,
Unmoving, uncorrupt, and spotless bright,
That need no sun t' illuminate their spheres
70   But their own native light, far passing theirs.

And as these heavens still by degrees arise,
Until they come to their first mover's bound,
That in his mighty compass doth comprise
And carry all the rest with him around,
So those likewise do by degrees redound
And rise more fair, till they at last arrive
To the most fair, whereto they all do strive.

Fair is the heaven where happy souls have place
In full enjoyment of felicity,
80   Whence they do still behold the glorious face
Of the divine eternal majesty;
More fair is that where those Ideas on high
Enrangèd be which Plato so admired,
And pure Intelligences from God inspired.

Yet fairer is that heaven in which do reign
The sovereign Powers and mighty Potentates,
Which in their high protections do contain
All mortal princes and imperial states;
And fairer yet, whereas the royal Seats
90   And heavenly Dominations are set,
From whom all earthly governance is fet.°   *derived*

61–63 I.e., "How much less can any-
one endure the brightness of those
heavens above the physical heavens. For
the spiritual heavens are as superior in
perfection to the physical heaven as the
heavenly bodies (planets) are to the
Earth."
69 "and they need no candle, neither
light of the sun; for the Lord God giveth
them light" (Revelation 22:5).
71 *these heavens:* the physical heavens.
72 *first mover's bound:* the sphere of
the *primum mobile.*
77 *most fair:* God.
82–84 Spenser's inclusion of the Pla-

tonic ideas in the spiritual heaven is
strange. Perhaps he means to show that
the highest reaches of pagan thought do
not approach in beauty and power the
perfection of the God of Christianity.
85–97 The various orders of angels,
which these lines are concerned with,
were first systematized by Dionysius the
Areopagite in *Of the Heavenly Hierarchy.*
The works of this Greek theologian be-
came influential in Western thought dur-
ing the 9th century, when they were
translated into Latin. Spenser's hierarchy
differs from the Dionysian order in many
cases.

Yet far more fair be those bright Cherubins,
Which all with golden wings are overdight,°   *covered over*
And those eternal burning Seraphins,
Which from their faces dart out fiery light;
Yet fairer than they both, and much more bright,
Be th' Angels and Archangels, which attend
On God's own person, without rest or end.

These thus in fair° each other far excelling   *beauty*
100 As to the Highest they approach more near,
Yet is that Highest far beyond all telling
Fairer than all the rest which there appear,
Though all their beauties joined together were.
How then can mortal tongue hope to express
The image of such endless perfectness?

Cease then, my tongue, and lend unto my mind
Leave to bethink how great that beauty is
Whose utmost parts so beautiful I find—
How much more those essential parts of his,
110 His truth, his love, his wisdom, and his bliss,
His grace, his doom,° his mercy, and his might,   *judgment*
By which he lends us of himself a sight!

Those unto all he daily doth display,
And show himself in th' image of his grace
As in a looking glass, through which he may
Be seen of all his creatures vile and base,
That are unable else to see his face—
His glorious face, which glistereth else so bright
That th' angels selves cannot endure his sight.

120 But we frail wights, whose sight cannot sustain
The sun's bright beams when he on us doth shine
But that their points, rebutted back again,
Are dulled—how can we see with feeble eyne°   *eyes*
The glory of that majesty divine,
In sight of whom both sun and moon are dark
Comparèd to his least resplendent spark?

96–98 "And all the angels stood round about the throne . . . and fell before the throne on their faces, and worshipped God" (Revelation 7:11).

108 *utmost parts:* parts most remote from the divine beauty—earthly beauty.

109 *essential parts:* the attributes of God.

109–119 John Calvin discusses at length God's revelation of his essential parts to men in *Institutes of the Christian Religion*, I.5.6–8, pp. 69–71.

115 *looking glass:* "For now we see through a glass, darkly; but then face to face" (1 Corinthians 13:12). ". . . the exact symmetry of the universe is a mirror, in which we may contemplate the otherwise invisible God" (Calvin, *Institutes*, I.5.1, p. 64).

120–124 "But, since the majority of men, immersed in their errors, are blind amidst the greatest opportunities of seeing, he [the Psalmist] accounts it a rare instance . . . of wisdom . . . to consider these works of God. . . . And, notwithstanding all the displays of the glory of God, scarcely one man in a hundred is really a spectator of it" (*Institutes*, I.5.8, p. 71).

The means, therefore, which unto us is lent
Him to behold, is on his works to look,
Which he hath made in beauty excellent,
130 And in the same, as in a brazen book,
To read enregistered in every nook
His goodness, which his beauty doth declare;
For all that's good is beautiful and fair.

Thence gathering plumes of perfect speculation
To imp° the wings of thy high-flying mind,   *refeather*
Mount up aloft through heavenly contemplation
From this dark world, whose damps the soul do blind,
And like the native brood of eagle's kind,°   i.e. *young eagles*
On that bright sun of glory fix thine eyes,
140 Cleared from gross mists of frail infirmities.

Humbled with fear and awful reverence,
Before the footstool of his majesty
Throw thyself down with trembling innocence;
Ne dare look up with corruptible eye
On the dread face of that great deity,
For fear lest, if he chance to look on thee,
Thou turn to nought and quite confounded be.

But lowly fall before his mercy seat,
Close covered with the Lamb's integrity
150 From the just wrath of his avengeful threat
That sits upon the righteous throne on high.
His throne is built upon eternity,
More firm and durable than steal or brass,
Or the hard diamond which them both doth pass.°   *surpass*

His scepter is the rod of righteousness,
With which he bruiseth all his foes to dust,
And the great dragon strongly doth repress
Under the rigor of his judgment just.
His seat is truth, to which the faithful trust,
160 From whence proceed her beams so pure and bright
That all about him sheddeth glorious light.

127–133 "For the invisible things of him from the creation of the world are clearly seen, being understood by the things that are made, even his eternal power and Godhead . . ." (Romans 1:20). See also Ecclesiasticus 43.
132 "But if we inquire the reason that induced him first to create all things and now to preserve them, we shall find the sole cause to be his own goodness" (Calvin, *Institutes*, I.5.6).
133 Compare "An Hymn in Honor of Beauty," 139.
139 *sun of glory:* God.
144–147 "And he said, Thou canst not see my face: for there shall no man see me, and live" (Exodus 33:20).
148–151 "And behold, a throne was set in heaven, and one sat on the throne" (Revelation 4:2). ". . . In the midst of the throne . . . stood a Lamb as it had been slain" (Revelation 5:6).
152–155 "Thy throne, O God is for ever and ever: the sceptre of thy kingdom is a right sceptre" (Psalms 45:6).
157–158 "And the great dragon was cast out, that old serpent, called the Devil, and Satan, which deceiveth the whole world" (Revelation 12:9).

Light far exceeding that bright blazing spark
Which darted is from Titan's° flaming head,   i.e. *the sun's*
That with his beams enlumineth the dark
And dampish air, whereby all things are read;°   *seen*
Whose nature yet so much is marvellèd°   *marvelled at*
Of° mortal wits, that it doth much amaze   *by*
The greatest wizards° which thereon do gaze.   *wise men*

But that immortal light which there doth shine
170 Is many thousand times more bright, more clear,
More excellent, more glorious, more divine;
Through which to God all mortal actions here,
And even the thoughts of men, do plain appear.
For from th' eternal truth it doth proceed,
Through heavenly virtue, which her° beams do breed.   i.e. *truth's*

With the great glory of that wondrous light
His throne is all encompassèd around,
And hid in his own brightness from the sight
Of all that look thereon with eyes unsound;
180 And underneath his feet are to be found
Thunder and lightning and tempestuous fire,
The instruments of his avenging ire.

There in his bosom Sapience doth sit,
The sovereign darling of the Deity,

162–171   ". . . leave one simple and clear light, the image of that light, which remains in the very globe of the sun and is not dispersed through the air; now you comprehend in a measure the beauty of God, which certainly excells the rest of the beauties as much as the true light of the sun in itself, pure, single, and inviolate, surpasses the splendor of the sun, which is split up, divided . . . obscured through the cloudy air" (Ficino, *Commentary*, p. 211).

172–173   "For the Lord searcheth all hearts, and understandeth all the imaginations of the thoughts" (1 Chronicles 28:9).

176–177   "And there was a rainbow round about the throne, in sight like unto an emerald" (Revelation 4:3).

180–182   "And out of the throne proceeded lightnings and thunderings" (Revelation 4:5).

183   *Sapience:* Wisdom. Spenser's Sapience comes primarily from the book of Proverbs and from the apocryphal books of Wisdom of the Old Testament. Early in Western Christianity the biblical Sapience becomes a symbol of the Son, the second person of the Trinity. St. Augustine writes, "Therefore, when anything concerning wisdom is said or recorded in the Scriptures, whether wisdom itself speaks or anything is said of it, then the Son is particularly meant" (*The Trinity*, VII.3, pp. 226–227). The 14th century English mystic, Julian of Norwich, makes the equation in a more startling manner: ". . . the high Might of the Trinity is our Father, and the deep Wisdom of the Trinity is our Mother. . . . Our high Father, God Almighty . . . willed that the second Person should become our Mother. . . . Our Kind Mother . . . He took the Ground of his Works full low and full mildly in the Maiden's womb" (*Revelations of Divine Love*, quoted from Ellrodt, *Neoplatonism in the Poetry of Spenser*, p. 167). To the modern mind, the equation of the Old Testament Sapience with Christ, the Word, the second person of the Trinity, seems strange and contradictory. However, the tradition was well established in Spenser's time. For an interesting account of the tradition in the Renaissance see *John Donne: The Anniversaries*, ed. Frank Manley, Johns Hopkins Press, 1963, pp. 20–40.

183–184   "Then I [Wisdom] was by him, as one brought up with him: and I was daily his delight, rejoicing always before him . . ." (Proverbs 8:30). ". . . the Lord of all things himself loved her [Wisdom]" (Wisdom 8:3). "And wisdom was with thee . . ." (Wisdom 9:4). Note that

Clad like a queen in royal robes, most fit
For so great power and peerless majesty;
And all with gems and jewels gorgeously
Adorned, that brighter than the stars appear,
And make her native brightness seem more clear.

190 And on her head a crown of purest gold
Is set, in sign of highest sovereignty;
And in her hand a scepter she doth hold,
With which she rules the house of God on high
And manageth the ever-moving sky,
And in the same,° these lower creatures all,   *in doing that*
Subjected to her power imperial.

Both heaven and earth obey unto her will
And all the creatures which they both contain,
For of her fullness, which the world doth fill,
200 They all partake and do in state remain—
As their great maker did at first ordain—
Through observation of her high behest,
By which they first were made and still increased.°   *continually repro-*
                                                           duced

The fairness of her face no tongue can tell,
For she the daughters of all women's race,
And angels eke, in beauty doth excell,
Sparkled on her from God's own glorious face,
And more increased by her own goodly grace,
That it doth far exceed all human thought,
210 Ne can on earth comparèd be to aught.

Ne could that painter, had he livèd yet,
Which pictured Venus with so curious° quill   *ingenious*

Spenser does not say that Sapience was "with" God, as the book of Wisdom does. His language makes it clear that Sapience is to be equated with the Son: "No man hath seen God at any time; the only begotten Son, which is in the bosom of the Father, he hath declared him" (John 1:18).

185–189 "For she is more beautiful than the sun, and above all the order of stars: being compared with the light, she is found before it" (Wisdom 7:29).

190–203 "Wisdom reacheth from one end to another mightily: and sweetly doth she order all things" (Wisdom 8:1). "For wisdom is a loving spirit. . . . For the Spirit of the Lord filleth the world . . ." (Wisdom 1:6–7). "And wisdom was with thee: which knoweth thy works, and was present when thou madest the world, and knew what was acceptable in thy sight . . ." (Wisdom 9:9). "When he prepared the heavens, I [Wisdom] was there: when

he set a compass upon the face of the depth: when he established the clouds above: when he strengthened the fountains of the deep . . . when he appointed the foundations of the earth . . ." (Proverbs 8:27–29). Compare these texts with St. John's opening lines on Christ the Word: "In the beginning was the Word, and the Word was with God. . . . All things were made by him: and without him was not anything made that was made. In him was life: and the life was the light of men" (John 1:1, 3–4).

211–224 In these two stanzas is stated directly the comparison upon which the structure of the *Four Hymns* is based. The highest pagan ideal of beauty is compared with divine beauty and found inferior. Venus, the idealized object of erotic love, is only a product of human imagination.

211 *that painter:* see note on 219 below.

That all posterity admirèd it,
Have portrayed this for all his mastering skill:
Ne she herself,° had she remainèd still   i.e. *Venus*
And were as fair as fabling wits do feign,°   *imagine*
Could once come near this beauty sovereign.

But had those wits, the wonders of their days,
Or that sweet Teian poet which did spend
220 His plenteous vein in setting forth her praise,
Seen but a glimpse of this which I pretend,°   *attempt*
How wondrously would he her face commend
Above that idol of his feigning thought,
That all the world should with his rhymes be fraught!°   *filled*

How then dare I, the novice of his art,
Presume to picture so divine a wight,
Or hope t' express her least perfection's part,
Whose beauty fills the heavens with her light
And darks the earth with shadow of her sight?
230 Ah, gentle muse, thou art too weak and faint,
The portrait of so heavenly hue° to paint.   *appearance*

Let angels, which her goodly face behold
And see at will, her sovereign praises sing,
And those most sacred mysteries unfold
Of that fair love of mighty heaven's king.
Enough is me t' admire so heavenly thing,
And being thus with her huge love possessed,
In th' only wonder° of herself to rest.   *only the wonder*

But whoso may, thrice happy man him hold
240 Of all on earth, whom God so much doth grace
And lets his own belovèd to behold;
For in the view of her celestial face
All joy, all bliss, all happiness have place;
Ne aught on earth can want unto the wight°   *person*
Who of herself can win the wishful sight.

For she out of her secret treasury
Plenty of riches forth on him will pour,

219   *Teian poet:* Anacreon, the Greek poet, born in Teos. His *Ode* 56 describes a painting showing Venus (Aphrodite) floating on the sea.
228   "For she [Wisdom] is the brightness of the everlasting light, the unspotted mirror of the power of God. . . ." (Wisdom 7:26).
246–247 "All good things together came to me with her [Wisdom], and innumerable riches in her hands" (Wisdom 7:11). ". . . who hath come into her treasures" (Baruch 3:15). "Unto me . . . is this grace given, that I should preach . . . the unsearchable riches of Christ" (Ephesians 3:8). "For she is a treasure unto men that never faileth" (Wisdom 7:14).

Even heavenly riches which there hidden lie
Within the closet of her chastest bower,
250 Th' eternal portion of her precious dower,°   *dowry*
Which mighty God hath given to her free,
And to all those which thereof worthy be.

None thereof worthy be but those whom she
Vouchsafeth to her presence to receive,
And letteth them her lovely face to see;
Whereof such wondrous pleasures they conceive,
And sweet contentment, that it doth bereave°   *rob*
Their soul of sense through infinite delight,
And them transport from flesh into the sprite.

260 In which they see such admirable things
As carries them into an ecstasy,
And hear such heavenly notes and carolings
Of God's high praise that fills the brazen sky,
And feel such joy and pleasure inwardly
That maketh them all worldly cares forget,
And only think on that before them set.

Ne from thenceforth doth any fleshly sense
Or idle thought of earthly things remain,
But all that erst° seemed sweet seems now offense,   *formerly*
270 And all that pleasèd erst now seems to pain.
Their joy, their comfort, their desire, their gain
Is fixèd all on that which now they see;
All other sights but feignèd° shadows be.   *imaginary*

And that fair lamp which useth to enflame
The hearts of men with self-consuming fire
Thenceforth seems foul and full of sinful blame,
And all that pomp to which proud minds aspire
By name of honor, and so much desire,
Seems to them baseness, and all riches dross,
280 And all mirth sadness, and all lucre loss.

252–254 "For she goeth about seeking such as are worthy of her, sheweth herself favorably unto them . . . and meeteth them in every thought" (Wisdom 6:16). "For by grace are ye saved through faith; and that not of yourselves; it is the gift of God" (Ephesians 2:8).

256 "To be allied unto wisdom is immortality; and great pleasure it is to have her friendship" (Wisdom 8:18).

267–280 See "An Hymn to Heavenly Love," 272–275.

277–280 "I preferred her [Wisdom] before scepters and thrones, and esteemed riches nothing in comparison of her. Neither compared I unto her any precious stone, because all gold in respect of her is as a little sand, and silver shall be counted as clay before her" (Wisdom 7:8–9). ". . . I count all things but loss for the excellency of the knowledge of Christ Jesus my Lord: for whom I have suffered the loss of all things, and do count them but dung, that I may win Christ" (Philippians 3:8).

So full their eyes are of that glorious sight,
And senses fraught with such satiety,
That in nought else on earth they can delight
But in th' aspect of that felicity
Which they have written in their inward eye;
On which they feed, and in their fastened° mind   *firmly fixed*
All happy joy and full contentment find.

Ah then, my hungry soul, which long hast fed
On idle fancies of thy foolish thought,
290   And with false beauty's flattering bait misled,
Hast after vain deceitful shadows sought,
Which all are fled, and now have left thee nought
But late repentance through thy folly's prief°—   *experience*
Ah cease to gaze on matter of thy grief.

And look at last up to that sovereign light
From whose pure beams all perfect beauty springs,
That kindleth love in every godly sprite,
Even the love of God, which loathing brings
Of this vile world and these gay-seeming things;
300   With whose sweet pleasures being so possessed,
Thy straying thoughts henceforth forever rest.

288–289 "Come eat of my [Wisdom's] bread, and drink of the wine which I have mingled" (Proverbs 9:5).

295–297 Compare "An Hymn of Heavenly Love," 283–287.

Muiopotmos or The Fate of the Butterfly

INTRODUCTION

Muiopotmos was published in a volume titled *Complaints* (1591), containing nine of Spenser's short poems. Most of these were early works (1570–1580), but *Muiopotmos*, which has a separate title page dated 1590, is a much more mature poem. It is the most interesting and sophisticated poem in the collection.

Since the 19th century two schools of criticism have developed around *Muiopotmos*. The first may be called the allegorical school, and the second, for lack of a more precise term, the Ovidian school. The first group of critics finds various moral, political, and theological arguments in Spenser's dazzling tale of the death of Clarion the butterfly. The second finds only wit, invention, and delightful artificiality. Opposing the interpretation of the second group, a recent critic has pointed out that such Ovidian myths as Spenser's tale of the metamorphosis of Arachne were commonly read, and written, as allegories. In fact Ovid's tale of the transformation of Arachne into a spider had been provided with a thorough moral and spiritual allegorical interpretation by the 13th century; and this interpretation was still common in the Renaissance. Finally, from earliest Christian times the spider was a symbol of hypocrisy, evil, and Satan himself. There is also a fairly long moralizing passage at lines 216–232 on the impermanence of human happiness and the helplessness of weak humans against heaven's decrees. These lines and other expressions, it is argued, require that the poem be interpreted morally and theologically.

On the other hand, the best of the Ovidian school of critics argues: "The tone of the poem, which most of the learned allegorical interpreters ignore, is the first and most important clue to the interpretation, and that tone would almost certainly rule out any heavy philosophical, military, or political allegory."[1] At least a part of the tone of *Muiopotmos* is mock heroic. The opening stanza, which introduces Clarion and Aragnoll the spider, is a parody of the opening lines of the *Iliad*, just as the arming of Clarion is a parody of the arming of Turnus in the *Aeneid*. And the abrupt ending of Spenser's poem is quite

[1] Hallett Smith, "The Use of Conventions in Spenser's Minor Poems," *Form and Convention in the Poetry of Edmund Spenser*, Columbia University Press, 1961, p. 131.

clearly an imitation of the close of the *Aeneid*.[2] If the mock heroic voice says anything, it tells us that the trivial incidents which are the poem's subject are not worth the high rhetoric in which it speaks. We are warned by it not to take its impressive statements too seriously.

But *Muiopotmos* is complicated by a mixture of tones, for the mock heroic voice speaks clearly only at the beginning and at the end of the poem. The middle of the poem is dominated first by two Ovidian metamorphoses, especially by Spenser's version of the Arachne legend, which is elaborated in nearly a hundred lines. Interspersed with these are descriptions of the real action of the poem, delicate and beautiful scenes of the first flight of Clarion, his flitting pleasures in the luxuries of an English garden, the garden itself. All of this is in harmony with the light touch of the Ovidian legends. At the same time, the delicate, artificial, and witty scenes are tempered by a sober moral and philosophical voice. Clarion is accused of having a "wavering wit." His "glutton sense" leads him to sample all the pleasures of the garden. His careless innocence leads to his destruction. There are solemn meditations on the impermanence of earthly life and the cruelty of fate. Finally, when Clarion's enemy Aragnoll is introduced, he is made sinister by a group of epithets which clearly relate him to Satan.

This brief survey of the tones of *Muiopotmos* is enough to account for the disagreement among critics about the meaning of the poem. Our own interpretation is a synthesis of views. Undoubtedly the moral voice in *Muiopotmos* suggests a serious allegorical interpretation. Conventional interpretations of the Arachne story, as well as the diabolical character of Aragnoll, suggest that the allegory is theological, that hidden beneath the surface of the tale is the story of fragile man's fall in the garden of Eden. Just as certainly, however, the mock heroic frame of the poem, as well as the delicate wit of the descriptions, demands that the moral voice—not to mention the Ovidian element—should not be interpreted in a serious allegorical way. Thus the various tones of the poem modify each other. *Muiopotmos* is an *exemplum* of the impermanence of all things beautiful and delicate, exquisitely tinged with the proper measure of pathos and melodrama.

---

[2] Professor Don Cameron Allen has argued that the tone of the poem is not mock heroic. His interpretation of the first two stanzas seems to us extremely complicated and based, in part, on a misreading of the syntax of the second stanza. His allegorical reading of the poem is, by all odds, the most closely argued and persuasive one yet offered. See his "Muiopotmos, or The Fate of the Butterflie," *Image and Meaning: Metaphoric Traditions in Renaissance Poetry*, The Johns Hopkins Press, 1960, pp. 20–41.

MUIOPOTMOS

I sing of deadly dolorous debate,
Stirred up through wrathful Nemesis' despite,
Betwixt two mighty ones of great estate,°   *rank*
Drawn into arms and proof° of mortal fight   *ordeal*
Through proud ambition and heart-swelling hate,
Whilst neither could the other's greater might
And 'sdainful° scorn endure; that from small jar°   *disdainful,*
Their wraths at length broke into open war.   *discord*

The root whereof and tragical effect,
10 Vouchsafe, O thou the mournfulest muse of nine,
That wontst° the tragic stage for to direct   *are accustomed*
In funeral complaints and wailful tine,°   *sorrow*
Reveal to me, and all the means detect
Through which sad Clarion did at last decline
To lowest wretchedness. And is there then
Such rancor in the hearts of mighty men?

Of all the race of silver-wingèd flies
Which do possess the empire of the air
Betwixt the centered earth and azure skies,
20 Was none more favorable° nor more fair,   *fortunate*
Whilst heaven did favor his felicities,
Than Clarion, the eldest son and heir
Of Muscaroll, and in his father's sight
Of all alive did seem the fairest wight.°   *creature*

With fruitful hope his aged breast he fed
Of future good, which his young toward° years,   *promising*
Full of brave courage and bold hardihead
Above th' ensample° of his equal peers,   *example*
Did largely promise, and to him foreread°   *prophesied*
30 (Whilst oft his heart did melt in tender tears)
That he in time would sure prove such an one
As should be worthy of his father's throne.

Title *Muiopotmos:* Greek, *muia,* "fly"; *potmos,* "fate."
 1–8 Spenser's opening stanza is modeled on the opening lines of the *Iliad.* His combatants, neither of whom "the other's greater might / And 'sdainful scorn" could endure, are like Achilles and Agamemnon in *Iliad,* I.
 10–15 *mournfulest muse:* Melpomene, the muse of tragedy. These lines show that Spenser's idea of tragedy was the conventional medieval idea—the fall to misery and death of a powerful person.
 15–16 *And is there . . . mighty men:* "It is hard to believe Gods in Heaven capable of such rancour" (Virgil, *Aeneid,* I.11, p. 27).
 23 *Muscaroll:* Latin, *musca,* "fly."

The fresh young fly, in whom the kindly° fire   *natural*
Of lustful youngth° began to kindle fast,   *youth*
Did much disdain to subject his desire
To loathsome sloth, or hours in ease to waste,
But joyed to range abroad in fresh attire
Through the wide compass of the airy coast,°   *region*
And with unwearied wings each part t' inquire°   *investigate*
40 Of the wide rule of his renowmèd sire.

For he so swift and nimble was of flight
That from this lower tract he dared to sty°   *mount*
Up to the clouds, and thence with pinions light
To mount aloft unto the crystal sky
To view the workmanship of heaven's height;
Whence down descending, he along would fly
Upon the streaming rivers, sport to find,
And oft would dare to tempt° the troublous wind.   *test*

So on a summer's day, when season mild
50 With gentle calm the world had quieted,
And high in heaven Hyperion's fiery child
Ascending did his beams abroad dispread,°   *spread out*
Whiles all the heavens on lower creatures smiled,
Young Clarion, with vauntful lustihead,°   *boastful vigor*
After his guise° did cast° abroad to fare,   *custom, resolve*
And thereto gan° his furnitures° prepare.   *did, equipment*

His breastplate first, that was of substance pure,
Before his noble heart he firmly bound,
That mought° his life from iron death assure,   *could*
60 And ward his gentle corpse° from cruel wound;   *body*
For it by art was framèd to endure
The bit° of baleful steel and bitter stound,°   *bite, conflict*
No less than that which Vulcan made to shield
Achilles' life from fate of Troyan field.

And then about his shoulders broad he threw
An hairy hide of some wild beast, whom he
In savage forest by adventure slew,
And reft° the spoil his ornament to be;   *took*
Which spreading all his back with dreadful view,°   *appearance*
70 Made all that him so horrible did see
Think him Alcides with the lion's skin,
When the Nemean conquest he did win.

51 *Hyperion's fiery child:* Apollo.
57–90 The arming of the hero is a conventional theme in epic poetry. Spenser's description imitates the arming of Agamemnon in the *Iliad*, XI (pp. 197–198) and the arming of Turnus in the *Aeneid*, XII.3 (pp. 11–312).

63–64 The description of Achilles' shield is found in the *Iliad*, XVIII, pp. 349–353.
71–72 For Hercules' victory over the Nemean lion see Robert Graves, *The Greek Myths*, Vol. 2, pp. 104–105.
71 *Alcides:* Hercules.

Upon his head his glistering burgonet,°   *helmet*
The which was wrought by wondèrous device
And curiously° engraven, he did set.   *elaborately*
The metal was of rare and passing price°—   *surpassing value*
Not Bilbo steel, nor brass from Corinth fet,°   *fetched*
Nor costly oricalche from strange Phoenice,
But such as could both Phoebus' arrows ward,
80   And th' hailing darts of heaven beating hard.

Therein two deadly weapons fixed he bore,
Strongly outlancèd° towards either side   *thrust out*
Like two sharp spears, his enemies to gore.
Like as a warlike brigandine, applied°   *made ready*
To fight, lays forth her threatful pikes afore,
The engines° which in them sad death do hide;   *weapons*
So did this fly outstretched his fearful horns,
Yet so as him their terror more adorns.

Lastly his shiny wings, as silver bright,
90   Painted with thousand colors, passing far
All painters' skill, he did about him dight.°   *put on*
Not half so many sundry colors are
In Iris' bow, ne° heaven doth shine so bright,   *nor*
Distinguishèd with many a twinkling star,
Nor Juno's bird in her eye-spotted train°   *tail*
So many goodly colors doth contain.

Ne (may it be withouten peril spoken)
The archer god, the son of Cytheree,
That joys on wretched lovers to be wroken,°   *avenged*
100   And heapèd spoils of bleeding hearts to see,
Bears in his wings so many a changeful token.°   *variegated mark-*
Ah my liege lord, forgive it unto me   *ing*
If aught against thine honor I have told;
Yet sure those wings were fairer manifold.

---

77   *Bilbo:* Bilboa, in northern Spain.
78   *oricalche:* Latin, *oricalcum,* a kind
of brass. Orichalcum is mentioned in the
previously cited passage from the *Aeneid*
(XII.87–88) describing the arming of
Turnus: "Ipse dehinc auro squalentem,
alboque orichalco / Circumdat loricam
humeris." The idea that orichalcum came
from Phoenicia seems to be Spenser's
invention.
79   *Phoebus:* the sun. Phoebus (Apollo)
attacks Agamemnon and his army with a
shower of deadly arrows in the *Iliad,* I.

84–85   *brigandine:* a small galley; the
"threatful pikes" are rams.
92–93   *Iris:* goddess of the rainbow.
Spenser probably remembers "So there-
fore Iris, saffron-winged, sparkling like
dew and trailing a thousand colours as
she caught the light of the sun . . ."
(*Aeneid,* IV.700–701, pp. 118).
95   *Juno's bird:* the peacock.
98   *archer god:* Cupid; *Cytheree:* Venus.
98–104   See *The Faerie Queene,* II.viii.
5–6, and notes.

Full many a lady fair, in court full oft
Beholding them, him secretly envied,
And wished that two such fans, so silken soft
And golden fair, her love would her provide;
Or that when them the gorgeous fly had doffed,°   *taken off*
110 Someone that would with grace° be gratified,   *i.e. the lady's*
From him would steal them privily away,   *favors*
And bring to her so precious a prey.°   *prize*

Report is that Dame Venus on a day
In spring, when flowers do clothe the fruitful ground,
Walking abroad with all her nymphs to play,
Bade her fair damsels, flocking her around,
To gather flowers, her forehead to array.
Amongst the rest a gentle nymph was found,°   *there was*
Hight° Astery, excelling all the crew   *named*
120 In courteous usage° and unstainèd hue.°   *behavior, appear-*
                                                ance

Who being nimbler jointed than the rest
And more industrious, gatherèd more store°   *a greater share*
Of the field's honor than the others' best;
Which they in secret hearts envying sore,°   *greatly*
Told Venus, when her as the worthiest
She praised, that Cupid (as they heard before)
Did lend her secret aid in gathering
Into her lap the children of the spring.

Whereof the goddess gathering jealous fear—
130 Not yet unmindful° how not long ago   *forgetful*
Her son to Psyche secret love did bear,
And long it close° concealed, till mickle° woe   *secretly, much*
Thereof arose, and many a rueful tear—
Reason with sudden rage did overgo,°   *overcome*
And giving hasty credit° to th' accuser,   *credence*
Was led away of° them that did abuse her.   *misled by*

Eftsoons° that damsel, by her heavenly might,   *immediately*
She turned into a wingèd butterfly,
In the wide air to make her wandering flight;
140 And all those flowers with which so plenteously

113–144 Spenser's story of the metamorphosis of Astery is an invention of his own, a brilliant imitation of the Ovidian metamorphosis.
119 *Astery:* The name comes from Ovid's description of Arachne's tapestry: "The tapestry showed Asterie too, held fast by the struggling eagle . . ." (*Metamorphoses,* VI.108, p. 149).
130–133 Spenser here refers, not very accurately, to the Cupid and Psyche story in Apuleius' *Metamorphoses.* See Edith Hamilton's *Mythology* (Mentor Books, pp. 92–100) for a summary of the story.
138 The metamorphosis of Astery is clearly related to the Cupid and Psyche myth. *Psyche* is Greek for soul. In ancient Greece the butterfly was a symbol of the soul, a fact which Spenser would have found in any Greek lexicon of his time.

Her lap she fillèd had, that bred her spite,
She placèd in her wings for memory
Of her pretended° crime, though crime none were.   *supposed*
Since which, that fly them in her wings doth bear.

Thus the fresh Clarion, being ready dight,°   *dressed*
Unto his journey did himself address,
And with good speed began to take his flight.
Over the fields, in his frank° lustiness,   *free*
And all the champion° he soarèd light;   *plain*
150   And all the country wide he did possess,
Feeding upon their pleasures bounteously,
That° none gainsaid, nor none did him envy.   *which*

The woods, the rivers, and the meadows green,
With his air-cutting wings he measured wide;
Ne did he leave the mountains bare unseen,
Nor the rank grassy fens' delights untried.
But none of these, however sweet they been,°   *are*
Mote° please his fancy, nor him cause t' abide;   *could*
His choiceful° sense with every change doth flit.   *finical*
160   No common things may please a wavering wit.°   *mind*

To the gay gardens his unstayed° desire   *vacillating*
Him wholly carried, to refresh his sprites.°   *spirits*
There lavish Nature, in her best attire,
Pours forth sweet odors and alluring sights;
And Art with her contending, doth aspire
T' excel the natural with made delights.
And all that fair or pleasant may be found,
In riotous excess doth there abound.

There he arriving, round about doth fly,
170   From bed to bed, from one to other border,
And takes survey, with curious busy eye,
Of every flower and herb there set in order;
Now this, now that, he tasteth tenderly,
Yet none of them he rudely doth disorder,
Ne with his feet their silken leaves deface,
But pastures on the pleasures of each place.

And evermore with most variety
And change of sweetness (for all change is sweet)
He casts his glutton sense to satisfy,
180   Now sucking of the sap of herb most meet,°   *proper*
Or of the dew, which yet on them does lie,
Now in the same bathing his tender feet.

And then he percheth on some branch thereby
To weather him, and his moist wings to dry.

And then again he turneth to his play,
To spoil the pleasures of that paradise:
The wholesome sage, and lavender still gray,
Rank-smelling rue, and cumin good for eyes,
The roses reigning in the pride of May,
190 Sharp hyssop, good for green wounds' remedies,
Fair marigolds, and bees-alluring thyme,
Sweet marjoram, and daisies decking prime,°   *spring*

Cool violets, and orpine growing still,°   *always*
Embathèd balm, and cheerful galingale,
Fresh costmary, and breathful camomill,°   *camomile*
Dull poppy, and drink-quickening setuale,
Vein-healing vervain, and head-purging dill,
Sound savory, and basil hearty-hale,
Fat coleworts, and comforting persiline,°   *parsley*
200 Cold lettuce, and refreshing rosemarine.°   *rosemary*

And whatsoelse of virtue° good or ill   *power*
Grew in this garden, fetched from far away,
Of every one he takes and tastes at will,
And on their pleasures greedily doth prey.
Then, when he hath both played and fed his fill,
In the warm sun he doth himself embay,°   *bathe*
And there him rests in riotous suffisance°   *abundance*
Of all his gladfulness and kingly joyance.

What more felicity can fall to creature
210 Than to enjoy delight with liberty,
And to be lord of all the works of nature,
To reign in th' air from earth to highest sky,

187–200 This catalogue of plants is a set piece in imitation of Ovid's catalogue of trees in *Metamorphoses*, X.90–104, pp. 247–248. See *The Faerie Queene*, I.i.8–9, and note.
188 In classical and medieval works on medical remedies *cumin* seed was considered a remedy against infected eyes.
190 *Hyssop* was a popular remedy for cuts and bruises.
191 "so long as bees eat thyme . . ." (Virgil, *The Pastoral Poems*, V.77, p. 67).
193 *orpine:* A popular name of this plant is "Livelong."
194 *galingale:* a variety of sedge. Its roots were used as a seasoning.

195 *costmary:* used as a seasoning; *camomill:* camomile, still used in laxatives.
196 *setuale:* valerian, an herb whose roots produce a drug; it was used as a spice in wine.
197 *vervain:* considered a medicine for wounds.
198 *hearty-hale:* Basil was used as a strengthener of the heart, as well as a remedy for melancholy.
199–200 *Coleworts, perseline* (purslane), and *lettuce* all served as remedies for fever because of their succulent leaves.
200 *rosmarine:* rosemary, a fragrant plant used in perfumes.

To feed on flowers and weeds of glorious feature,
To take whatever thing doth please the eye?
Who rests not pleasèd with such happiness,
Well worthy he to taste of wretchedness.

But what on earth can long abide in state,°   *secure*
Or who can him assure of happy day,
Sith morning fair may bring foul evening late,
220   And least mishap the most bliss alter may?
For thousand perils lie in close await°   *ambush*
About us daily to work our decay,
That° none except a god—or god him guide—   *so that*
May them avoid, or remedy provide.

And whatso heavens in their secret doom°   *judgment*
Ordainèd have, how can frail fleshly wight°   *creature*
Forecast, but it must needs to issue come?
The sea, the air, the fire, the day, the night,
And th' armies of their creatures, all and some,°   *one and all*
230   Do serve to them, and with importune° might   *vehement*
War against us, the vassals of their will.
Who then can save what they dispose to spill?

Not thou, O Clarion, though fairest thou
Of all thy kind, unhappy° happy fly,   *unfortunate*
Whose cruel fate is woven even now
Of° Jove's own hand, to work thy misery.   *by*
Ne may thee help the many hearty vow
Which thy old sire with sacred piety
Hath pourèd forth for thee, and th' altars sprent.°   *sprinkled*
240   Nought may thee save from heaven's avengèment.

It fortunèd, as heavens had behight,°   *ordained*
That in this garden where young Clarion
Was wont° to solace him,° a wicked wight,   *accustomed,*
                                                           himself
The foe of fair things, th' author of confusion,
The shame of nature, the bondslave of spite,
Had lately built his hateful mansion,
And lurking closely, in await now lay,
How he might any in his trap betray.

But when he spied the joyous butterfly
250   In this fair plot dispacing° to and fro,   *moving*
Fearless of foes and hidden jeopardy,
Lord, how he gan for to bestir him tho,°   *then*
And to his wicked work each part apply.

223   I.e., "No one unless he is a god or is guided by a god. . . ."

His heart did earn° against his hated foe,   *rage*
And bowels so with rankling poison swelled
That scarce the skin the strong contagion held.

The cause why he this fly so malicèd
Was (as in stories it is written found)
For that his mother, which him bore and bred,
260   The most fine-fingered workwoman on ground,°   *earth*
Arachne, by his means was vanquishèd
Of Pallas, and in her own skill confound,°   *defeated*
When she with her for excellence contended,
That° wrought her shame, and sorrow never-ended.   *which*

For the Tritonian goddess, having heard
Her blazèd° fame, which all the world had filled,   *acclaimed*
Came down to prove° the truth, and due reward   *test*
For her praiseworthy workmanship to yield;
But the presumptuous damsel rashly dared
270   The goddess self to challenge to the field,
And to compare° with her in curious° skill   *complete, expert*
Of works with loom, with needle, and with quill.°   *spindle*

Minerva did the challenge not refuse,
But deigned with her the paragon° to make;   *comparison*
So to their work they sit, and each doth choose
What story she will for her tapet° take.   *tapestry*
Arachne figured° how Jove did abuse   *pictured*
Europa like a bull, and on his back
Her through the sea did bear, so lively seen°   *appearing*
280   That it true sea and true bull ye would ween.°   *think*

She seemed still back unto the land to look,
And her playfellows' aid to call, and fear
The dashing of the waves, that° up she took   *so that*

257–352   Spenser's myth of Arachne is taken, with significant changes and additions, from Ovid's *Metamorphoses*, VI.1–145, pp. 146–150. The most significant change is in Spenser's treatment of the transformation of Arachne. In Ovid, Arachne is not defeated by Minerva's art. Her tapestry is so faultless that the goddess rips it to pieces in anger and begins beating Arachne with her shuttle. Arachne, partly out of defiance, tries to hang herself; and Minerva, pitying her rival, changes her into a spider. In Spenser's version, Arachne is decisively beaten by Minerva and turns into a spider as a natural result of extreme envy. Her metamorphosis is a revelation of her character. The most important addition

is Spenser's invention of the butterfly in Minerva's tapestry. It is this crowning detail that defeats Arachne, and thus motivates the hatred of the spider for the butterfly.
262   *Pallas:* Minerva (Athene).
265   *Tritonian goddess:* Minerva, who was brought up by the sea-god Triton.
277–296   Some of these details may be taken from Ovid's description of Arachne's tapestry; others are taken from his account of the Rape of Europa (*Metamorphoses*, II, p. 79). However, the Rape of Europa was an extremely popular subject in renaissance art, and Spenser's description may depend on one or more paintings and tapestries.

Her dainty feet, and garments gathered near.
But Lord, how she in every member shook
Whenas the land she saw no more appear,
But a wild wilderness of waters deep.
Then gan she greatly to lament and weep.

Before the bull she pictured wingèd Love,
290 With his young brother, Sport, light fluttering
Upon the waves, as each had been a dove.
The one his bow and shafts, the other spring°   *youth*
A burning tead° about his head did move,   *torch*
As in their sire's new love both triumphing;
And many nymphs about them flocking round,
And many Tritons, which their horns did sound.

And round about, her work she did impale°   *fence in*
With a fair border wrought of sundry flowers
Enwoven° with an ivy winding trail—   *interwoven*
300 A goodly work, full fit for kingly bowers;
Such as Dame Pallas—such as Envy pale,
That all good things with venomous tooth devours—
Could not accuse. Then gan the goddess bright
Herself likewise unto her work to dight.°   *prepare*

She made the story of the old debate
Which she with Neptune did for Athens try:°   *engage in*
Twelve gods do sit around in royal state,
And Jove in midst with awful majesty,
To judge the strife between them stirrèd late—
310 Each of the gods by his like visnomy°   i.e. *facial likeness*
Eath° to be known, but Jove above them all   *easy*
By his great looks and power imperial.

Before them stands the god of seas in place,°   *there*
Claiming that seacoast city as his right,
And strikes the rocks with his three-forkèd mace,
Whenceforth issues a warlike steed in sight—
The sign by which he challengeth the place—
That° all the gods which saw his wondrous might   *so that*
Did surely deem the victory his due.
320 But seldom seen,° forejudgment proveth true.   *seldom the case*

Then to herself she gives her aegid shield,
And steel-head spear, and morion° on her head,   *helmet*

290   *Sport:* sexual intercourse.
293   *burning tead:* The torch is an appropriate symbol for Sport because it is traditionally associated with sex and the marriage bed. See *Epithalamion,* 27, and note.
321   *aegid:* pertaining to the aegis, an ornament on the shield of Minerva.

Such as she oft is seen in warlike field.
Then sets she forth how with her weapon dread
She smote the ground, the which straight forth did yield
A fruitful olive tree with berries spread,
That all the gods admired. Then all the story
She compassed with a wreath of olives hoary.

    Amongst those leaves she made a butterfly,
330 With excellent device° and wondrous slight,°   *design, art*
Fluttering among the olives wantonly,
That seemed to live, so like° it was in sight: *real*
The velvet nap which on his wings doth lie,
The silken down with which his back is dight,
His broad outstretchèd horns, his hairy thighs,
His glorious colors, and his glistering eyes.

    Which when Arachne saw, as overlaid°   *overwhelmed*
And masterèd with workmanship so rare,
She stood astonied long, ne ought gainsaid,
340 And with fast-fixèd eyes on her did stare,
And by her silence, sign of one dismayed,
The victory did yield her as her share.
Yet did she inly fret and felly° burn,   *fiercely*
And all her blood to poisonous rancor turn;

    That shortly from the shape of womanhead,°   *womanhood*
Such as she was when Pallas she attempted,°   *challenged*
She grew to hideous shape of drearihead,°   *gloom*
Pinèd° with grief of folly late repented.   *wasted away*
Eftsoons her white straight legs were alterèd
350 To crooked crawling shanks, of marrow emptied,
And her fair face to foul and loathsome hue,
And her fine corpse to a bag of venom grew.

    This cursed creature, mindful of that old
Infestered grudge the which his mother felt,
So soon as Clarion he did behold,
His heart with vengeful malice inly swelt;
And weaving straight a net with many a fold
About the cave in which he lurking dwelt,
With fine small cords about it stretchèd wide,
360 So finely spun that scarce they could be spied.

    Not any damsel which her vaunteth most
In skillful knitting of soft silken twine,
Nor any weaver which his work doth boast
In diaper, in damask, or in line,°   *linen*

364   *diaper:* a fabric in which the same simple pattern is repeated over and over.

Nor any skilled in workmanship embossed,°   *raised ornamenta-*
Nor any skilled in loops of fingering fine,   *tion*
Might in their divers cunning° ever dare   *various skills*
With this so curious network to compare.

Ne do I think that that same subtle gin°   *net*
370 The which the Lemnian god framed craftily,
Mars sleeping with his wife to compass in,
That all the gods with common mockery
Might laugh at them and scorn their shameful sin,
Was like to this. This same he did apply
For to entrap the careless Clarion,
That ranged eachwhere without suspicion.

Suspicion of friend, nor fear of foe
That hazarded° his health, had he at all,   *threatened*
But walked at will, and wandered to and fro
380 In the pride of his freedom principal.°   *princely*
Little wist° he his fatal future woe,   *knew*
But was secure—the liker he to fall.
He likest is to fall into mischance
That is regardless of his governance.°   *conduct*

Yet still Aragnoll (so his foe was hight)
Lay lurking covertly him to surprise,
And all his gins,° that him entangle might,   *snares*
Dressed° in good order as he could devise.   *readied*
At length the foolish fly, without foresight,
390 As he that did all danger quite despise,
Toward those parts came flying carelessly
Where hidden was his hateful enemy.

Who seeing him, with secret joy therefore
Did tickle inwardly in every vein,
And his false heart, fraught with all treasons' store,
Was filled with hope his purpose to obtain.
Himself he close upgathered more and more
Into his den, that his deceitful train°   *plot*
By his there being might not be bewrayed,°   *revealed*
400 Ne any noise, ne any motion made.

Like as a wily fox, that having spied
Where on a sunny bank the lambs do play,
Full closely° creeping by the hinder side,   *secretly*

369–373 The story of Hephaestus'   in the *Odyssey*, VIII.266–369, pp. 129–
(Vulcan's) trapping Ares (Mars) and   132. It is found also in Ovid's *Metamor-*
Aphrodite (Venus) in bed together is told *phoses*, IV.176–189, p. 107.

Lies in ambushment of his hopèd prey,
Ne stirreth limb till, seeing ready tide,°   *the right time*
He rusheth forth, and snatcheth quite away
One of the little younglings unawares—
So to his work Aragnoll him prepares.

Who now shall give unto my heavy eyes
410   A well of tears that all may overflow?
Or where shall I find lamentable cries
And mournful tunes enough my grief to show?
Help, O thou tragic muse, me to devise
Notes sad enough t' express this bitter throe.°   *anguish*
For lo, the dreary stound° is now arrived,   *moment*
That of all happiness hath us deprived.

The luckless Clarion—whether cruel fate
Or wicked fortune faultless him misled,
Or some ungracious blast out of the gate
420   Of Aeol's reign° perforce him drove on head°—   *kingdom, ahead*
Was (O sad hap and hour unfortunate!)
With violent swift flight forth carrièd
Into the cursèd cobweb which his foe
Had framèd for his final overthrow.

There the fond° fly, entangled, struggled long   *foolish*
Himself to free thereout; but all in vain.
For striving more, the more in laces strong
Himself he tied, and wrapped his wingès twain
In limey snares the subtle loops among;
430   That in the end he breathless did remain,
And all his youthly forces idly spent,°   *exhausted in vain*
Him° to the mercy of th' avenger lent.°   *surrendered him-*
                                                            self

Which when the grisly° tyrant did espy,   *horrible*
Like a grim lion rushing with fierce might
Out of his den, he seizèd greedily
On the resistless prey, and with fell spite
Under the left wing stroke° his weapon sly   *struck*
Into his heart, that his deep groaning sprite
In bloody streams forth fled into the air,
440   His body left the spectacle of care.°   *image of suffering*

438–440   The death of Clarion is com-   ing, resentful, to the Shades" (*Aeneid*,
pared to that of Turnus: "His limbs re-   XII.951–952, p. 338).
laxed and chilled; and the life fled, moan-

Bibliography

Works Cited in the Introductions and Notes

Aguzzi, Danilo L. "Allegory in the Heroic Poetry of the Renaissance." Unpublished Ph.D. thesis, Columbia University, 1959.

Alanus de Insulis. *Anticlaudianus*, trans. William Hafner Cornung. Philadelphia: [n.p]., 1935.

————. *De Planctu Naturae*, trans. D. M. Moffat. Yale University Press, 1908.

Allen, Don Cameron. "Muiopotmos, or The Fate of the Butterflie," *Image and Meaning: Metaphoric Traditions in Renaissance Poetry*. The Johns Hopkins Press, 1960.

Aquinas, Thomas. *Summa Theologica*, trans. Fathers of the English Dominican Province, 21 vols. Burns, Oates, and Washburn, 1912–1925.

Ancrene Riwle, ed. Mabel Day. Early English Text Society, 1952.

Apollonius of Rhodes. *The Voyage of the Argo*, trans. E. V. Rieu. Penguin Books, 1959.

Ariosto, Ludovico. *Orlando Furioso*, trans. Allan Gilbert, 2 vols. S. F. Vanni, 1954.

Aristotle. *Ethics*, trans. J. A. K. Thompson. Penguin Books, 1953.

————. *Rhetoric*, trans. and ed. Lane Cooper. Appleton-Century-Crofts, 1932.

Augustine. *The City of God*, trans. Marcus Dods. Modern Library, Random House Inc., 1950.

Augustine. *The Trinity*, trans. Stephen McKenna, Catholic University of America, 1963.

Bale, John. *Select Works of John Bale, D.D.*, ed. Rev. Henry Christmas. Parker Society, 1848.

Berger, Harry, Jr. *The Allegorical Temper: Vision and Reality in Book II of Spenser's "Faerie Queene."* Yale University Press, 1957.

Bloomfield, Morton W. *The Seven Deadly Sins*. Michigan State University Press, 1952.

Boethius. *The Consolation of Philosophy*, trans. Richard Green. Library of Liberal Arts, Bobbs-Merrill, 1962.

Burton, Robert. *Anatomy of Melancholy*, ed. Floyd Dell and Paul Jordan Smith. Tudor Publishing Company, 1948.

Calvin, John. *The Institutes of the Christian Religion*, trans. John Allen. William B. Eerdmans, 1949.

Castiglione, Baldassare. *The Book of the Courtier*, trans. Sir Thomas Hoby. Everyman, 1928.

Catullus. *Odi et Amo*, trans. Roy Arthur Swanson. Library of Liberal Arts, 1959.

Chew, Samuel C. *The Pilgrimage of Life*. Yale University Press, 1962.

Cicero. *De Senectute*, trans. William A. Falconer. Loeb Classical Library, 1927.

Claudian. *Claudian,* trans. Maurice Platnauer, 2 vols. Loeb Classical Library, 1922.

Critical Approaches to Medieval Literature: Selected Papers from the English Institute, 1958–1959, ed. Dorothy Bethurum. Columbia University Press, 1960.

Curtius, Ernst R. *European Literature and the Latin Middle Ages,* trans. Willard R. Trask. Harper Torchbooks, 1963.

Daniélou, Jean. *From Shadows to Reality,* trans. Walston Hibberd. Burns and Oates, 1960.

Dante. *Inferno,* trans. Dorothy L. Sayers. Penguin Books, 1949.

————. *Purgatorio,* trans. Dorothy L. Sayers. Penguin Books, 1955.

Donne, John. *John Donne: The Anniversaries,* ed. Frank Manley. The Johns Hopkins Press, 1963.

Edwards, Calvin Roger. "Spenser and the Ovidian Tradition." Unpublished Ph.D. thesis, Yale University, 1957.

Ellrodt, Robert. *Neoplatonism in the Poetry of Spenser.* Librairie E. Droz, 1960.

English Epithalamies, ed. Robert H. Case. John Lane, 1896.

Ficino, Marsilio. *Commentary on Plato's "Symposium",* ed. and trans. Sears R. Jayne. University of Missouri Press, 1944.

First and Second Prayer Books of Edward VI. Everyman's Library, 1952.

Form and Convention in the Poetry of Edmund Spenser: Selected Papers from the English Institute, ed. William Nelson. Columbia University Press, 1961.

Fowler, A. D. S. "The Image of Mortality: *The Faerie Queene,* II.i-ii," *The Huntington Library Quarterly,* XXIV (1961), 91–110.

Frye, Northrop. *Anatomy of Criticism.* Princeton University Press, 1957.

Galen. *On the Natural Faculties,* trans. Arthur John Brock. Loeb Classical Library, 1916.

Geoffrey of Monmouth. *History of the Kings of Britain,* trans. Sebastian Evans. Everyman's Library, 1958.

Graves, Robert. *The Greek Myths,* 2 vols. Penguin Books, 1955.

The Greek Bucolic Poets, trans. J. M. Edmonds. Loeb Classical Library, 1912.

Hamilton, A. C. *The Structure of Allegory in "The Faerie Queene."* Oxford: Clarendon Press, 1961.

Hamilton, Edith. *Mythology.* Mentor Books, 1953.

Harper, Carrie A. *The Sources of the British Chronicle History in Spenser's "Faerie Queene."* Bryn Mawr, 1910.

Hesiod. *Theogony,* trans. Norman O. Brown. Liberal Arts Press, 1953.

Hieatt, A. Kent. *Short Time's Endless Monument.* Columbia University Press, 1960.

Hollander, John. *The Untuning of the Sky.* Princeton University Press, 1961.

Homer. *Iliad,* trans. E. V. Rieu. Penguin Books, 1963.

————. *Odyssey,* trans. E. V. Rieu. Penguin Books, 1960.

Hoopes, Robert. " 'God Guide Thee, Guyon': Nature and Grace Reconciled in *The Faerie Queene,* Book II," *Review of English Studies,* V (1954), 14–24.

Hough, Graham. *A Preface to "The Faerie Queene."* W. W. Norton, 1962.

Hughes, Merritt Y. "Spenser's Acrasia and the Circe of the Renaissance," *Journal of the History of Ideas,* IV (1943), 381–399.

Jewell, John. *An Apology of the Church of England,* ed. J. E. Booty. Cornell University Press, for the Folger Shakespeare Library, 1963.

Kermode, Frank. "The Cave of Mammon," *Elizabethan Poetry: Stratford-Upon-Avon Studies 2.* St. Martin's Press, 1960, pp. 151–173.

Kristeller, Paul Oskar. *Renaissance Thought.* Harper Torchbooks, 1961.

Later Medieval English Prose, ed. William Matthews. Appleton-Century-Crofts, 1963.

Lehmberg, Stanford E. *Sir Thomas Elyot: Tudor Humanist.* University of Texas Press, 1960.

Lewis, C. S. *The Allegory of Love.* Oxford University Press, 1936.

Lorris, Guillaume de and Jean de Meun. *The Romance of the Rose*, trans. Harry W. Robbins. Dutton, 1962.

Lotspeich, Henry G. *Classical Mythology in the Poetry of Edmund Spenser.* Princeton University Press, 1932.

Lucretius. *The Nature of the Universe*, trans. R. E. Latham. Penguin Books, 1951.

Luther, Martin. *Reformation Writings of Martin Luther*, Vol. I, trans. Bertram Lee Woolf. Philosophical Library, 1953.

Mâle, Emile. *The Gothic Image*, trans. Dora Nussey. Harper Torchbooks, 1958.

Martz, Louis. *The Poetry of Meditation.* Yale University Press, 1962.

———. "The *Amoretti:* 'Most Goodly Temperature,'" *Form and Convention in the Poetry of Edmund Spenser.* Columbia University Press, 1961, pp. 146–168.

Nelson, William. *The Poetry of Edmund Spenser.* Columbia University Press, 1963.

Ovid. *Amores*, trans. Christopher Marlowe, in *The Works of Christopher Marlowe*, ed. C. F. Tucker Brooke. Oxford: Clarendon Press, 1910.

———. *Metamorphoses*, trans. Mary M. Innes. Penguin Books, 1961.

Panofsky, Erwin. *Meaning in the Visual Arts.* Doubleday Anchor Books, 1955.

———. *Studies in Iconology.* Harper Torchbooks, 1962.

Pausanius. *Description of Greece*, trans. W. H. S. Jones, 5 vols. Loeb Classical Library, 1918.

Penguin Book of French Verse, Vol. I, ed. Brian Woledge. Penguin Books, 1961.

Penguin Book of Italian Verse, ed. George Kay. Penguin Books, 1958.

Petrarch, Francesco. *The Sonnets, Triumphs, and Other Poems of Petrarch.* Translated into English verse by various hands; with a life of the poet by Thomas Campbell. London: G. Bell & Sons, 1916.

———. *The Triumphs of Petrarch*, trans. Ernest Hatch Wilkins. University of Chicago Press, 1962.

Pindar. *The Odes of Pindar*, trans. Richmond Lattimore. University of Chicago Press, 1947.

Plato. *Republic*, trans. H. D. P. Lee. Penguin Books, 1958.

———. *Symposium*, trans. W. R. M. Lamb. Loeb Classical Library, 1932.

———. *Timaeus*, trans. B. Jowett in *The Dialogues of Plato*, 2 vols. Random House, 1937.

Puttenham, George. *The Arte of English Poesie*, ed. Gladys D. Willcock and Alice Walker. Cambridge University, 1936.

Robertson, D. W., Jr. *A Preface to Chaucer.* Princeton University Press, 1962.

Sarton, George. *The Appreciation of Ancient and Medieval Science During the Renaissance.* University of Pennsylvania Press, 1955.

Secular Lyrics of the XIVth and XVth Centuries, ed. Rossell Hope Robbins. Oxford: Clarendon Press, 1952.

Seneca. *The Stoic Philosophy of Seneca*, trans. Moses Hadas. Doubleday Anchor Books, 1958.

Seznec, Jean. *The Survival of the Pagan Gods*, trans. Barbara F. Sessions. Harper Torchbooks, 1961.

Simon, Marcel. *Hercule et le Christianisme.* L'Université de Strasbourg, 1955.

Sirluck, Ernest. "*The Faerie Queene*, Book II, and the *Nicomachean Ethics*," *Modern Philology*, XLIX (1951), 73–100.

Smith, Hallett. *Elizabethan Poetry: A Study in Conventions, Meaning, and Expression.* Harvard University Press, 1952.

Spenser, Edmund. *The Works of Edmund Spenser: A Variorum Edition*, ed. Edwin

Greenlaw, Charles Grosvenor Osgood, Frederick Morgan Padelford, Ray Heffner, 10 vols. The Johns Hopkins Press, 1932–1957.

Steadman, John M. "Una and the Clergy: the Ass Symbol in *The Faerie Queene*," *Journal of the Warburg and Courtauld Institute*, XXI (1958), 134–137.

Tasso, Torquato. *Jerusalem Delivered*, trans. Edward Fairfax. Capricorn Books, 1963.

Tibullus. *Tibullus*, trans. J. P. Postgate. Loeb Classical Library, 1950.

The Travels of Sir John Mandeville, ed. A. W. Pollard. Macmillan, 1900.

Virgil. *Aeneid*, trans. W. F. Jackson Knight. Penguin Books, 1958.

———. *Georgics*, trans. J. W. Mackail. Modern Library, 1950.

———. *The Pastoral Poems*, trans. E. V. Rieu. Penguin Books, 1954.

Williams, Ethel Carleton. "Mural Paintings of St. George in England," *Journal of the British Archaeological Association*, 3rd series XI (1948), 19–36.

Wind, Edgar. *Pagan Mysteries of the Renaissance*. Yale University Press, 1958.